McDougal, Littell Integrated Mathematics
Course 1

Brendan Kelly
Professor of Mathematics
University of Toronto
Toronto, Ontario

Bob Alexander
Assistant Co-ordinator
*   of Mathematics*
Toronto Board of Education
Toronto, Ontario

Paul Atkinson
Principal
Cameron Heights
Collegiate Institute
Kitchener, Ontario

Contributing Authors

Mr. Samuel Backer
New Hyde Park Memorial High School
New Hyde Park, New York

Mr. Irvin Barnett
New York City Board of Education
Brooklyn, New York

Ms. Becky Compton
North Junior High School
Boise, Idaho

Mr. Les Leibovitch
Mathematics Project
Los Angeles Unified School District
Los Angeles, California

Mr. Ed Wachtel
Mathematics Department Head
Orange High School
Pepper Pike, Ohio

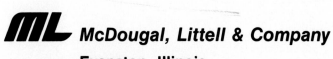 **McDougal, Littell & Company**

Evanston, Illinois

New York   Dallas   Sacramento   Columbia, SC

Reviewers
Mr. John Bailey
Kingston City Schools
Kingston, New York

Mr. Carl Goodman
Benjamin Cardoza High School
Bayside, New York

Mr. Roy Griggs
Capital High School
Boise, Idaho

Dr. Phil Reynolds
Niskayuna High School
Schenectady, New York

Mr. Kenneth Sohmer
Jamestown High School
Jamestown, New York

ISBN 0-8123-6884-3

Printed in the United States of America

91 92 93 94 95 - ROK - 10 9 8 7 6 5 4 3 2

Features of Integrated Mathematics Course 1

INTRODUCTION

A unique 14-page introductory unit entitled *The Nature of Mathematics* presents six men and women who have worked with mathematics. A quotation from each person is followed by discussion, examples, and exercises which introduce a feature of the text.

This material can be studied at any time as a unit, or the individual sections can be studied separately.

APPLICATIONS OF MATHEMATICS

Students can better understand mathematical principles when they are related to their applications. For this reason, applications are integrated throughout *Integrated Mathematics Course 1*.

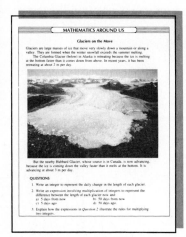

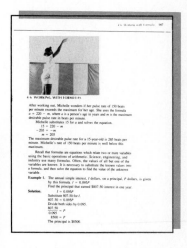

Each chapter begins with an illustrated application of the mathematics in the chapter.

Feature pages entitled *MATHEMATICS AROUND US* outline some applications of mathematics in the sciences, the arts, business, and industry.

Where appropriate, sections begin with an application which illustrates the necessity for the mathematics that follows. Applications are also included in most of the exercises.

CONCEPT DEVELOPMENT

This text is carefully sequenced to develop concepts in mathematics. Concepts are explained with several examples, each of which has a detailed solution.

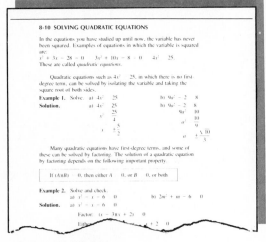

REINFORCEMENT

An abundance of exercises is provided to reinforce skills and concepts. These exercises are graded by difficulty with an appropriate balance of A, B, and C exercises. The A exercises may sometimes be completed mentally and the answers given orally or the questions may be used as additional examples when teaching the lesson. The B exercises are intended for the students to consolidate their learning of the concepts that were taught. The C exercises present a challenge and usually involve extensions of the concepts taught in that section.

Review Exercises and *Cumulative Reviews* provide additional practice. Answers to all odd-numbered questions are included in the text.

TECHNOLOGY

A contemporary mathematics program must reflect the impact of calculators and computers on society.

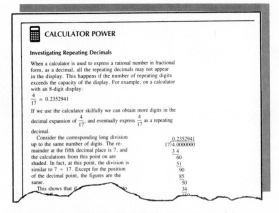

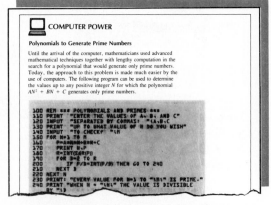

CALCULATOR POWER features provide opportunities for students to explore mathematical problems using a calculator. In addition, keying sequences are given for scientific calculators and 4-function calculators, where appropriate.

COMPUTER POWER features provide opportunities for students to explore mathematical problems using a computer. It is assumed that students know how to enter a program in BASIC, but it is not necessary for them to understand the program.

PROBLEM SOLVING

Problem solving is integrated throughout the program, with many of the exercises providing challenging problems for the students to solve. In addition, a variety of special features are included which promote the development of problem-solving skills.

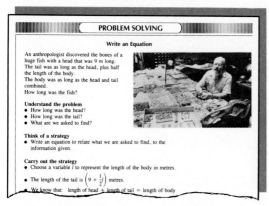

A two-page spread in every chapter focuses on the development of problem-solving strategies.

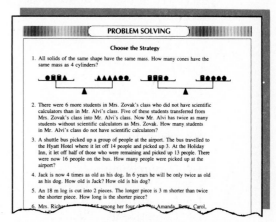

Choose the Strategy pages provide students with the opportunity to select and apply the learned strategies.

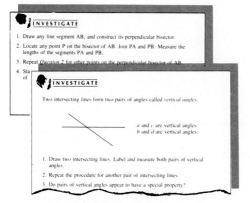

Frequent brief *INVESTIGATE* sections are starting points for mathematical investigations. They always relate to the concepts that are developed in the sections in which they occur.

Longer *INVESTIGATE* sections lead students to conclusions which they formulate. Students are more likely to retain knowledge that they discover for themselves.

THE MATHEMATICAL MIND highlights historical developments in mathematics, and includes anecdotes of human interest that are part of its history. In this context, interesting problems are presented for the students to solve.

Contents

The Nature of Mathematics

In previous years, your study of mathematics involved learning and practising the fundamental skills of arithmetic, measurement, and geometry. While all of these skills are an important part of this subject, they occupy only a small place in the broad spectrum of mathematics.

Throughout the ages and into the present, people have always appreciated the value of mathematics. Six men and women who have worked with mathematics are presented on the following pages, along with brief quotations which reflect their perceptions of the nature and use of mathematics.

"A mathematician, like a poet or a painter, is a maker of patterns."

Godfrey Harold Hardy
1877-1947

Hardy is famous for his discoveries in the theory of numbers — a branch of mathematics that still contains many unsolved problems.

THE SEARCH FOR PATTERN

Using patterns and relationships, scientists have been able to solve many of life's mysteries and expand their understanding of the world around us. Consider, for example, how remarkable it is that mathematics has enabled us:

- to predict the precise time that a comet, not seen in our lifetime, will reappear
- to estimate with surprising accuracy how long ago dinosaurs roamed the Earth, even though they have been extinct for millions of years
- to prove that the Earth approximates a sphere and to calculate its radius, without leaving the Earth.

These remarkable achievements provide only a glimpse of how far into space and back in time we have reached in our unrelenting search for patterns and relationships. In this book we will explore some patterns and relationships which take us in a natural way from the realm of arithmetic into the realms of algebra and geometry.

Example.   In 1682, Sir Edmund Halley saw the comet that now bears his name. He learned that a major comet had also been sighted in the years 1380, 1456, 1531, and 1607. Halley guessed that all these sightings were of the same comet, and he successfully predicted the year when it would return.
   a) In what year did Halley's prediction come true?
   b) Halley's comet last appeared in 1986. In what year might you next see Halley's comet?

Solution.   a) Write down the years when Halley's comet was sighted, and subtract the years which are next to each other.

$$1380 \quad 1456 \quad 1531 \quad 1607 \quad 1682 \ldots$$
$$76 \qquad 75 \qquad 76 \qquad 75$$

If this pattern were to continue, the next sighting would be 76 years after the 1682 sighting. Halley's prediction came true in 1758.
   b) Halley's comet should appear again 75 or 76 years after 1986. You might see it in 2061 or 2062.

Looking for a pattern is one of the fundamental problem solving strategies in mathematics. In each chapter of this book you will find a *PROBLEM SOLVING* feature which describes a particular strategy that you may find useful in solving problems.

EXERCISES

1. Check that each line is correct. Then predict the next three lines. Check that your prediction is correct.

a)
$$1 = 1 \times 1$$
$$1 + 3 = 2 \times 2$$
$$1 + 3 + 5 = 3 \times 3$$

b)
$$2 = 1 \times 2$$
$$2 + 4 = 2 \times 3$$
$$2 + 4 + 6 = 3 \times 4$$

2. Copy each pattern and predict its next three numbers.

a) 12, 23, 34, . . .

b) 1, 5, 10, 14, 19, . . .

c) 1, 3, 9, 27, . . .

d) 32, 16, 8, 4, . . .

e) 392, 400, 405, 413, 418, . . .

f) 1467, 1562, 1657, 1752, . . .

3. The diagram shows a pattern of whole numbers in three rows. Assume that the pattern continues.

a) Write the next five numbers in row 2.

b) In which row will the number 100 appear?

Row 1	1 4 7 10 13 . . .
Row 2	2 5 8 11 14 . . .
Row 3	3 6 9 12 15 . . .

4. These three patterns all start with the numbers 1, 2, 4. Predit the next three numbers in each pattern.

a) 1, 2, 4, 8, 16, . . .

b) 1, 2, 4, 7, 11, . . .

c) 1, 2, 4, 5, 7, 8, 10, . . .

5. Write three different patterns which start with the numbers 1, 2, 3.

6. The first three *triangular numbers* are shown. Write the next three triangular numbers.

7. The first three *square numbers* are shown. Write the next three square numbers.

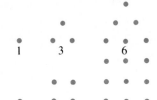

8. This table shows the first six powers of 3.

3^1	3^2	3^3	3^4	3^5	3^6
3	9	27	81	243	729

Look at the last digit in each power. Extend the pattern and predict the last digit of:

a) 3^7 b) 3^9 c) 3^{16} d) 3^{21}.

"Many who have never had an opportunity of knowing any more about mathematics confound it with arithmetic and consider it an arid science. In reality, however, it is a science which requires a great deal of imagination."

Sonya Kovalevskaya
1850-1891

Sonya Kovalevskaya was one of the prominent mathematicians of the nineteenth century. She studied the methods of mathematical research and made many brilliant discoveries.

THE VALUE OF MATHEMATICAL INVESTIGATION

Some people view mathematics as a set of rules for solving certain types of problems. They think mathematics is a static subject in which all the important problems have already been solved and only the step-by-step procedures for duplicating the solutions remain. No description of mathematics could be more misleading.

   To Sonya Kovalevskaya, mathematics was a dynamic and exciting field. She knew that interesting and challenging problems can be based on simple mathematical concepts. Posing and solving these problems gave her much pleasure and satisfaction.

Example.   A regular polyhedron with 12 faces is a *dodecahedron*. A dodecahedron has 20 vertices. How many edges has a dodecahedron?

Solution.   The solution can be found by investigating other polyhedrons with fewer vertices, for example, those illustrated below.

  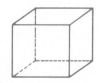 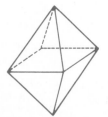

For each polyhedron, count the numbers of its faces, vertices, and edges. Record this information in a table.

	Square-based pyramid	Triangular prism	Cube	Octahedron
Faces	5	5	6	8
Vertices	5	6	8	6
Edges	8	9	12	12

If we study the numbers in each column of the table, we see that the number in the bottom row of each column is 2 less than the sum of the two numbers above it. That is, the number of edges of each polyhedron is 2 less than the total number of faces and vertices. If this relationship is true for the dodecahedron, then the number of edges of a dodecahedron would be: 12 + 20 − 2, or 30.

That is, we deduce that the dodecahedron has 30 edges.
We can verify that this is the correct answer by counting carefully the edges displayed in the diagram above.

After mathematicians have solved a problem, they usually try to extend the problem or think of related problems. In the above example, we might consider problems such as these.

- Is the number of edges 2 less than the total number of faces and vertices for all polyhedrons?
- Does the same relationship hold for solids with curved surfaces such as the cone or the cylinder?

In this book you will find special questions marked *INVESTIGATE*. Each of these is a mathematical investigation for you to explore. When you do this, you will be doing the kind of mathematics that Sonya Kovalevskaya is referring to in the quotation above.

EXERCISES

1. A truncated octahedron can be formed by cutting off each of the 6 corners of an octahedron. Determine, for a truncated octahedron, the number of:
   a) its faces   b) its vertices
   c) its edges.

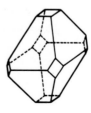

2. A truncated cube can be formed by cutting off each corner.
   a) Draw a diagram of a truncated cube.
   b) Determine, for a truncated cube, the number of:
      i) its faces   ii) its vertices   iii) its edges.

3. Draw a regular pentagon and all its diagonals. How many triangles can you find in the figure?

"How can it be that mathematics, being after all a product of human thought independent of experience, is so admirably adapted to the objects of reality?"

Albert Einstein
1879-1955

This question highlights the power of mathematical reasoning in helping us interpret and understand the world around us.

THE POWER OF MATHEMATICAL REASONING

In Konigsberg, a small town in Prussia, there were two islands in the river which passed through the village. The people wondered if they could walk around the town and cross each bridge exactly once. But whenever they tried it, they ended up either missing a bridge or crossing a bridge twice. They began to think that it was impossible to make the walk, but no one knew why.

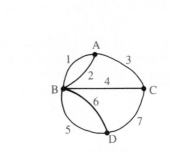

This is one of the most famous problems in mathematics. It was solved about two hundred years ago by the great Swiss mathematician, Leonhard Euler. He drew a simpler diagram by replacing the land by points and the bridges by lines joining them. The problem then is whether it is possible to draw this figure without lifting the pencil from the paper, and without retracing any line. Consider what happens each time a point is approached.

Each time the pencil passes through a point, it draws one line while approaching the point, and another line while leaving it.

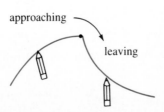

The same thing happens if that point is approached again; there must be one line for approaching and another one for leaving.

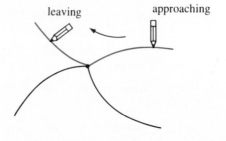

Therefore, the number of lines at each point must be an even number. Since all the points on the figure have an odd number of lines, it is impossible to draw the figure as described. This is the reason why the people in Konigsberg were unable to walk around the town and cross each bridge exactly once.

Example.   Is it possible to draw this figure and return to the starting point, without lifting your pencil from the paper or going over any line twice?

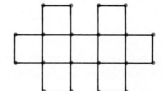

Solution.   Count the number of lines at each crossing point. Since they are all even numbers, it is possible to draw the figure as described.

In this book you will see feature pages called *THE MATHEMATICAL MIND*, which describe other famous problems in mathematics. These pages are designed to give you some insights into the history of mathematics and some of the people responsible for it.

EXERCISES

1. Determine if it is possible to draw each diagram without lifting your pencil from the paper, and without going over any line twice.

   a) 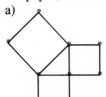   b)   c)   d)

2. Check your answers to *Exercise 1* by drawing those diagrams that can be drawn in the way described.

3. The adjacent diagram shows a floor plan of a house and the location of its doorways. The curve shows a path which passes through each doorway exactly once.

   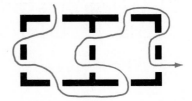

   For which of the floor plans below can you sketch a path which passes through each doorway exactly once?

   a)   b)   c)

   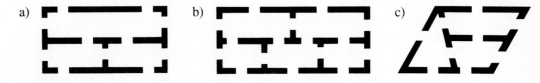

"Thus number may be said to rule the whole world of quantity, and the four rules of arithmetic may be regarded as the complete equipment of the mathematician."

James Clerk Maxwell
1831-1879

Maxwell was a nineteenth-century scientist who made important discoveries in electricity and magnetism.

THE POWER OF THE CALCULATOR

James Clerk Maxwell would have been surprised to learn that his work with electricity would eventually contribute to the invention of inexpensive electronic calculators. Today we take for granted that everyone can use a calculator to do the same kinds of computations that were done in Maxwell's time only by mathematicians.

Some of the ways in which calculators enhance mathematical investigations will be illustrated in the *CALCULATOR POWER* pages in this book. The following example is a problem for which a calculator is essential.

Example. Express as a decimal. $\frac{1}{1} + \frac{1}{2} + \frac{1}{3} + \ldots + \frac{1}{10}$

Solution. Using paper and pencil, this problem could be solved by expressing each fraction as a decimal and adding the results. The following strategy is used to solve the problem with a calculator.

clears memory

adds to memory

Key in: $\boxed{\text{CM}}$ $\boxed{1}$ $\boxed{\text{M+}}$ $\boxed{1}$ $\boxed{\div}$ $\boxed{2}$ $\boxed{=}$ $\boxed{\text{M+}}$ $\boxed{1}$ $\boxed{\div}$ $\boxed{3}$ $\boxed{=}$ $\boxed{\text{M+}}$ . . . $\boxed{1}$ $\boxed{\div}$ $\boxed{10}$ $\boxed{=}$ $\boxed{\text{M+}}$ $\boxed{\text{MR}}$ to display 2.9289683

recalls memory

Therefore, $\frac{1}{1} + \frac{1}{2} + \frac{1}{3} + \ldots + \frac{1}{10} \doteq 2.928\ 968\ 3$

The fractions in this example are called *unit fractions*. If you wanted to know the sum of more unit fractions, it would be necessary to continue the additions. But it would be impractical to use a calculator to find the sum of a very large number of unit fractions, say 100. To do this, a computer should be used.

EXERCISES
Use a calculator.

1. Express as a decimal.
   a) $\dfrac{1}{1} + \dfrac{1}{2} + \dfrac{1}{3} + \dfrac{1}{4} + \dfrac{1}{5}$

   b) $\dfrac{1}{1} + \dfrac{1}{2} + \dfrac{1}{3} + \ldots + \dfrac{1}{12}$

   c) $\dfrac{1}{2} + \dfrac{2}{3} + \dfrac{3}{4} + \ldots + \dfrac{9}{10}$

2. Simplify each product. Then predict what the next line should be. Check your prediction with your calculator.

   a) $9 \times 7 = $ ▩
        b) $6 \times 4 = $ ▩
        c) $9 \times 9 = $ ▩
          $99 \times 67 = $ ▩
           $66 \times 34 = $ ▩
          $99 \times 99 = $ ▩
        $999 \times 667 = $ ▩
         $666 \times 334 = $ ▩
        $999 \times 999 = $ ▩

   d) $5 \times 5 = $ ▩
        e) $101 \times 101 = $ ▩
        f) $1 \times 9 + 2 = $ ▩
          $65 \times 65 = $ ▩
         $202 \times 202 = $ ▩
        $12 \times 9 + 3 = $ ▩
        $665 \times 665 = $ ▩
       $303 \times 303 = $ ▩
      $123 \times 9 + 4 = $ ▩

3. Look for patterns in the numbers given in *Exercise 2* and try similar patterns with other numbers.

4. Choose any three consecutive whole numbers and multiply them together. Then divide the product by 6. Do this for other sets of three consecutive whole numbers. Is the product always divisible by 6? Can you explain why?

5. a) Use the $\boxed{y^x}$ key on your calculator to evaluate 2^{20}.
   b) What is the highest power of 2 which your calculator will display without rounding off?
   c) What is the largest power of 2 which is less than 10^9?

6. The product of the first n natural numbers is $1 \times 2 \times 3 \times 4 \times 5 \times \ldots \times n$. This product is called *factorial n* and is written $n!$.
   a) Calculate 8!
   b) If $n! = 39\ 916\ 800$, what is the value of n?
   c) For what value of n is $n!$ between 10^{10} and 10^{11}?

7. Use a scientific calculator. Enter as many 9s as your calculator will display then add 1. Assuming a display of 8 digits, it should show 1. 08. Explain this display.

8. For each calculator display, write the number as a decimal.
   a) 2.4   10   b) 3.7   12   c) 2.913   09

9. Write each number as it would appear on your calculator.
   a) 983 000 000   b) 10 300 000 000   c) 2 345 000 000
   Check by entering each number in your calculator.

"Perhaps the most astonishing achievement of our species has been the invention of a technology, namely the computer, that has the potential to be even more creative and powerful than our own brains."

David Suzuki

David Suzuki has brought science to millions of people through his many articles and television programs.

THE POWER OF THE COMPUTER

The computer has made it possible for us to solve certain problems which were previously considered unsolvable or too complex. For example, the program below can be used to find the sum of any number of consecutive unit fractions.

```
100 REM *** SUM OF UNIT FRACTIONS ***
110 INPUT "HOW MANY UNIT FRACTIONS? ";N
120 S=0
130 FOR K=1 TO N
140    S=S+1/K
150 NEXT K
160 PRINT:PRINT "THE SUM OF THE FIRST ";N
170 PRINT "UNIT FRACTIONS IS ";S
180 END
```

To enter a program such as this one, follow these steps.
- Type NEW and then press RETURN.
- Type each line exactly as it appears.
- After you have entered a line, check that the spacing and punctuation are exactly as shown.
- Make any necessary corrections.
- Press RETURN at the end of each line.
- To begin using the program, type RUN and press RETURN.

Example.   Express as a decimal.

a) $\dfrac{1}{1} + \dfrac{1}{2} + \dfrac{1}{3} + \ldots + \dfrac{1}{10}$

b) $\dfrac{1}{1} + \dfrac{1}{2} + \dfrac{1}{3} + \ldots + \dfrac{1}{100}$

Solution.   Use the program. Type RUN and then press ⟨RETURN⟩. The computer will ask for the number of unit fractions. Enter the number and press ⟨RETURN⟩. The computer will then calculate and print the sum in decimal form. Here are the results.

a) `HOW MANY UNIT FRACTIONS?`
   `10`
   `THE SUM OF THE FIRST 10 UNIT FRACTIONS IS 2.9289683`

b) `HOW MANY UNIT FRACTIONS?`
   `100`
   `THE SUM OF THE FIRST 100 UNIT FRACTIONS IS`
   `5.18737752`

Some of the ways in which the computer enhances mathematical investigations are illustrated in the *COMPUTER POWER* features of this book. These features contain programs in the BASIC computer language, such as the one above. You can use the programs to explore new problems using the power of this technology.

EXERCISES
Use the above program.

1. Express as a decimal.

   a) $\frac{1}{1} + \frac{1}{2} + \frac{1}{3} + \ldots + \frac{1}{17} + \frac{1}{18} + \frac{1}{19} + \frac{1}{20}$

   b) $\frac{1}{1} + \frac{1}{2} + \frac{1}{3} + \ldots + \frac{1}{47} + \frac{1}{48} + \frac{1}{49} + \frac{1}{50}$

   c) $\frac{1}{1} + \frac{1}{2} + \frac{1}{3} + \ldots + \frac{1}{197} + \frac{1}{198} + \frac{1}{199} + \frac{1}{200}$

   d) $\frac{1}{1} + \frac{1}{2} + \frac{1}{3} + \ldots + \frac{1}{497} + \frac{1}{498} + \frac{1}{499} + \frac{1}{500}$

   e) $\frac{1}{20} + \frac{1}{21} + \frac{1}{22} + \ldots + \frac{1}{27} + \frac{1}{28} + \frac{1}{29} + \frac{1}{30}$

   f) $\frac{1}{201} + \frac{1}{202} + \frac{1}{203} + \ldots + \frac{1}{497} + \frac{1}{498} + \frac{1}{499} + \frac{1}{500}$

2. Janet used the program to add some unit fractions, and she obtained the sum 7.380 165 88. Find out how many unit fractions she added.

3. Find how many unit fractions are needed to obtain a sum greater than each number.
   a) 4   b) 5   c) 6   d) 7   e) 8

4. Use a stopwatch to time how long it takes the computer to add different numbers of unit fractions using the program. Graph the results.

". . . tidal friction is gradually slowing down the rotation of the earth.
. . . the spinning of the globe has been so greatly slowed that a rotation now requires, as everyone knows, about 24 hours."

Rachel Carson
1907-1964

Rachel Carson was a biologist and author who was one of the first people to draw attention to environmental issues.

THE UTILITY OF MATHEMATICS

The quotation above is part of Rachel Carson's description of how we know that the Earth's rotation has been gradually slowing down for millions of years. This information has come to us through a knowledge of science and mathematics.

Although we are not aware of it, we are constantly moving in a circle, along with the Earth, making one complete rotation each day. If you were on the equator, you would complete a circle with a radius equal to the Earth's radius. We can use mathematics to find how far you would travel in any given length of time, such as one day or one hour.

Example. The circumference C of a circle is given by the formula $C = 2\pi r$, where $\pi \doteq 3.14$ and r is the radius. The radius of the Earth at the equator is 6378 km. If you were on the equator, find:
a) how far you would travel in one day
b) your speed in kilometres per hour.

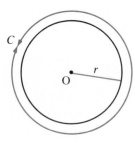

Solution. a) When $r = 6378$, $C \doteq 2(3.14)(6378)$
$$= 40\ 053.84$$
You would travel about 40 050 km in one day.
b) In 24 h you would travel 40 053.84 km.
In 1 h you would travel $\dfrac{40\ 053.84}{24}$ km or about 1668.91 km.
Your speed would be about 1669 km/h.

EXERCISES

1. How far does someone on the equator travel in:
   a) one minute b) one second?

2. People who are not on the equator move in smaller circles around the Earth, once every 24 h. The radius of the circle depends on the latitude of the location. Some values for American latitudes are given in the table below.
   a) Consult a map or an atlas to determine the approximate latitude of your location, to the nearest degree.
   b) Use the table to determine the radius of the circle you follow due to the Earth's rotation.
   c) What is the circumference of the circle for your location?
   d) What is your speed in kilometres per hour?

Radii of Circles Due to the Earth's Rotation

Latitude	Radius (km)	Latitude	Radius (km)	Latitude	Radius (km)
29°	5578	36°	5160	43°	4665
30°	5524	37°	5094	44°	4588
31°	5467	38°	5026	45°	4510
32°	5409	39°	4957	46°	4431
33°	5349	40°	4886	47°	4350
34°	5288	41°	4814	48°	4268
35°	5225	42°	4740	49°	4184

3. Use the result of *Exercise 2* to determine how far you travel in:
   a) one minute b) one second.

4. In one year the Earth travels once around the sun. It follows a circle with a radius of approximately 150 000 000 km.
   a) How far does the Earth travel in: i) one year ii) one day?
   b) What is the Earth's speed in kilometres per hour?

5. In *Exercise 4*, how far does the Earth travel in:
   a) one minute b) one second?

A FAMOUS UNSOLVED PROBLEM

Despite the best efforts of the world's greatest mathematicians, not all of the important problems in mathematics have been solved. In fact, there are far more unsolved problems than solved ones! One of the most baffling problems in mathematics involves prime numbers.

A *prime number* is one like 13 that has only two factors, the number itself, and 1. The ancient Greek mathematicians noticed that prime numbers frequently occur in pairs differing by 2. Some examples are: 11 and 13; 29 and 31; 347 and 349; 10 006 427 and 10 006 429. These are called *twin primes*, and the question of how many twin primes there are is known as the twin prime problem.

> **The Twin Prime Problem**
> How many pairs of twin primes are there?

Although some of the world's greatest mathematicians have tried to solve this problem, no one knows the answer. There may even be infinitely many twin primes. However, using computer techniques, we have been able to examine all the numbers up to 30 000 000. From this investigation we know that there are 152 892 pairs of twin primes less than 30 000 000. Even as you read this book, computers are finding twin primes far beyond 30 000 000, but it will require a mathematical proof to solve the problem for all possible numbers.

EXERCISES

1. How many pairs of twin primes can you find which are less than 50?

2. a) There are only two pairs of twin primes between 50 and 100. Can you find them?
   b) There are two pairs of twin primes between 100 and 110. Can you find them?

3. Twin primes differ by 2. Find examples of primes which differ by these numbers.
   a) 4   b) 6   c) 8   d) 10   e) 12   f) 14   g) 16

4. If we discovered by computer that there were no twin primes between 30 000 000 and 100 000 000, would that prove that we had found all the twin primes? Why?

5. There is only one pair of primes that differs by 3. Can you find it? Can you explain why there are no other pairs of primes that differ by 3?

6. Explain why the product of two prime numbers is never a multiple of 4.

7. Two prime numbers have a sum which is odd. Explain how you know that the product of those two prime numbers is even.

8. What prime number divides 2159 and 2176?

1 Logic

Suppose these two statements are both true:
    If Karen buys new skis, then Karen needs a new outfit.
    Karen needs a new outfit.
Can we conclude that Karen buys new skis?
(See Section 1-7.)

1-1 TRUE OR FALSE?

During the first mathematics class, Mrs. Santos asked her students to complete a survey. The survey contained 5 true-false questions.

True or False?

1. There are 12 months in a year.   _____
2. September has 31 days.   _____
3. Boston is the largest city in the United States.   _____
4. The product 143 × 21 is greater than 2000.   _____
5. 366 is not a multiple of 5.   _____

Each sentence in this survey is either true or false. A sentence which is either true or false (but not both) is called a *statement*. The truth or falsity of a statement is called its *truth value*.

The truth value of statements 1, 4, and 5 is T (true).
The truth value of statements 2 and 3 is F (false).

A sentence is a group of words that expresses a complete thought. According to the definition above, some sentences are not statements because they are neither true nor false.

Where is Mei going? ⎫
Open the window. ⎬ The first sentence is a question, the second is
Circles are friendly. ⎭ a command, and the third is meaningless.
It does not make sense to say that any one
of these sentences is true or false.

25 is a large number
This is neither true nor false because 25 is
large compared with some numbers and
small compared with other numbers.

Example 1. Which of the following sentences are statements? What is the truth value
of each statement?
a) 1993 is a leap year.
b) Is Tom a grade 9 student?
c) $25 \times 40 = 1000$

Solution. a) 1993 is a leap year.
This sentence is a statement because it is false.
b) Is Tom a grade 9 student?
This is a question. It is not a statement.
c) $25 \times 40 = 1000$
This sentence is a statement because it is true.

To tell if a sentence is a statement we do not need to know if the
sentence is true or if it is false. We only need to know that it must
be either true or false.

Example 2. Which of the following sentences are statements?
a) There are 23 states which touch salt water.
b) Today, the exact population of Buffalo is 329 475.
c) 23×43 is less than 1000.

Solution. All the sentences are statements, because they are either true or false.

In *Example 2a)*, we could consult an atlas to determine how many
states touch salt water, but we do not have to do this. If 23 states touch
salt water the sentence is true; if fewer than 23 or more than 23 states
touch salt water, it is false. In *part b)* there is no way of knowing the
exact population of Buffalo, but the given sentence is still either true or
false. In *part c)*, if the product is less than 1000 the sentence is true;
if not, it is false.

In logic we study what happens when we reason. That is, if we
know that some statements are true, how do we convince ourselves, just
by thinking, that other statements are true? We will see several examples
in this chapter.

EXERCISES 1-1

Ⓐ

1. Decide which of these statements are true and which are false.
   a) February 14 is Valentine's Day. b) Bicycles have three wheels.
   c) Today is Monday. d) All squares have 4 equal sides.
   e) $9 \times 6 = 64$ f) $8 \times 7 \neq 48$

2. Which of the following sentences are statements? What is the truth value of each statement?
   a) Monday comes after Sunday. b) Congratulations!
   c) September does not have 31 days. d) All money is green.
   e) Where is the cat? f) 8 is a bright number.

Ⓑ

3. Decide which of these statements are true and which are false.
   a) $50 \times 9 = 450$ b) $125 \times 8 = 1000$ c) $39 \times 58 = 2265$
   d) $65 \times 23 = 1497$ e) $43 \times 4 > 160$ f) $9 \times 24 > 240$
   g) $18 \times 28 < 600$ h) $19 \times 21 < 399$ i) $29 \times 31 > 899$

4. All but two of the following sentences are statements. Which ones are they?
   a) The Yankees are not in first place.
   b) The population of Houston is 1 735 924.
   c) Take me out to the ball game.
   d) Toronto is the capital of Canada.
   e) Toronto is not the capital of Canada.
   f) Washington is not the only city that has the same name as a state.
   g) There are no people who are over 10 feet tall.
   h) It is the most beautiful country in the world.
   i) 50% of the states in the United States have names with two words.
   j) During the 1989 major league baseball season, 687 391 pitches were thrown.
   k) When the numbers 56 897 455 and 35 307 738 are multiplied together, the third digit of the product is 2.

5. Determine the truth value of as many statements in *Exercise 4* as you can.

Ⓒ

6. Design a survey containing five true-false questions. Try out the survey on three people.

I N V E S T I G A T E

In everyday language, is there any difference in the meaning of the words "sentence" and "statement"? Consult a dictionary if you wish.

1-2 OPEN SENTENCES

In the last section we saw that any sentence which is either true or false is called a statement. Hence, a sentence such as the following is not a statement because we do not know who the word "he" represents.

He became President of the United States in 1989. . . . ①

When we replace the pronoun "he" with the name of a person, this sentence becomes a statement. If the person is George Bush, the statement is true. If the person is someone else, the statement is false.

Similarly, the equation below is not a statement because we do not know what number x represents.

$x + 3 = 10$ . . . ②

The letter x is called a *variable* because it represents a number that has not been specified. When we substitute a number for x, equation ② becomes a statement. If the number is 7, the statement is true. If the number is not 7, the statement is false.

Sentences ① and ② are examples of open sentences. An *open sentence* contains pronouns or variables, and becomes either true or false upon the replacement of those pronouns or variables.

Example 1. Which of the following sentences are open sentences?
a) In baseball, if you get 2 strikes you are out.
b) It is one of the winter months.
c) $n + 2 < 7$
d) Did he make the team?

Solution. The sentences in parts b) and c) are open sentences.
The sentence in part a) is false; hence, it is a statement and not an open sentence.
The sentence in part d) is a question. Although it contains the pronoun "he", it is not an open sentence because it does not become true or false when a substitution is made for the pronoun.

In sentence ① on page 5, when we replace the pronoun "he" with the name of a person we might be considering only the people shown in the photograph. We say that the "domain" is the set of people in the photograph. Similarly, in sentence ②, we might be considering only the numbers $\{1, 2, 3, \ldots\}$. We say that the "domain" is the set of natural numbers.

In any open sentence, the set from which replacements are made for a pronoun or a variable is called the *domain*. For open sentences involving numbers, the domain could be one of the following sets:

- Natural numbers $\{1, 2, 3, 4, \ldots\}$
- Even numbers $\{2, 4, 6, 8, \ldots\}$
- Odd numbers $\{1, 3, 5, 7, \ldots\}$
- Perfect squares $\{1, 4, 9, 16, \ldots\}$
- Prime numbers $\{2, 3, 5, 7, 11, 13, \ldots\}$

In *Example 1c)*, the domain could be the set of natural numbers. If we substitute 1, 2, 3, or 4 for n, this open sentence becomes a true statement. We say that the *solution set* of the open sentence is $\{1, 2, 3, 4\}$. Solution sets do not always contain numbers. In *Example 1b)*, the solution set is {December, January, February, March}.

Example 2. For the given domain, determine the solution set of each open sentence.
a) n is divisible by 5 Domain: odd numbers
b) $x + 1 < 7$ Domain: natural numbers
c) $9 - x = 5$ Domain: even numbers

Solution. a) Consider only odd numbers. The solution set is $\{5, 15, 25, \ldots\}$.
b) Consider only the natural numbers. When we add 1 to a natural number, the result must be less than 7. The solution set is $\{1, 2, 3, 4, 5\}$.
c) Consider only even numbers. When we subtract an even number from 9, the result is 5. The only even number for which this is true is 4. Hence, the solution set is $\{4\}$.

In *Example 2c)*, suppose the domain had been the set of odd numbers. Then the given open sentence would have no solution. We say that the solution set is empty, and indicate this by writing ϕ or $\{\ \}$.

In this chapter, if the domain is not stated, assume that it is the set of natural numbers.

EXERCISES 1-2

1. Which of the following sentences are open sentences? Which are statements?
   a) It is the capital of Brazil.   b) Albany is the capital of New York.
   c) $x + 3 > 10$ d) $2 \times 50 = 100$
   e) x is an even number.   f) The Mets have not won a game yet.
   g) Traffic laws must be obeyed.   h) They went to last night's concert.

2. Given the open sentence: n is divisible by 3,
   determine the solution set for each domain.
   a) natural numbers   b) even numbers   c) odd numbers   d) prime numbers

3. Given the open sentence: $x + 2 < 10$, where x is a natural number,
   determine the solution set for each domain.
   a) natural numbers   b) even numbers   c) perfect squares   d) prime numbers

4. For the given domain, determine the solution set of each open sentence.
   a) n is divisible by 9   Domain: natural numbers
   b) $n + 5 < 15$ Domain: even numbers
   c) $x + 3 = 25$ Domain: natural numbers
   d) $10 - x = 4$ Domain: even numbers

5. Determine the solution set of each open sentence. Use the domain
   $\{1, 2, 3, 4, \ldots\}$.
   a) $x + 8 = 12$ b) $n - 6 = 10$ c) $3 + x = 20$ d) $15 - x = 11$
   e) $y + 6 < 10$ f) $c + 5 \leqslant 8$ g) $1 + x > 9$ h) $2x = x$

6. Find the solution set of each open sentence. The domain is the set of states in the United States.
   a) It has more letters in its name than any other state.
   b) Four of the letters in its name are the same.
   c) Its name begins and ends with the same letter.
   d) Its name has two words.

7. Let n represent any natural number.
   a) Write an open sentence which is false for all values of n.
   b) Write an open sentence which is true for all values of n.

MATHEMATICS AROUND US

Symbols

We use symbols in many different ways.

1. Identify as many symbols in the illustrations above as you can.

2. Choose one of the illustrations above. Find another example of a symbol that is used in the same way.

3. Here are some symbols which can be found on a computer keyboard. What does each symbol mean?
   a) $ b) &   c) *   d) %   e) <   f) "

4. Find some other examples of symbols on a computer keyboard, and explain their meanings.

5. What do these symbols mean?
   a) $\therefore$ b) ?   c) $\sqrt{}$ d) π e) ♀   f) ♂

6. These symbols are often used in more than one way. Give as many different meanings for each symbol as you can.
   a) .   b) -   c) /   d) I   e) X   f) P

7. Look through the following pages of this chapter. Can you find three new symbols? What do they mean?

1-3 NEGATIONS

During another mathematics class, Mrs. Santos gave her students another survey. Like the first survey, this one also contained 5 true-false questions.

True or False?

1. It is not true that there are 12 months in a year.   _____
2. September does not have 31 days.   _____
3. Boston is not the largest city in the United States.   _____
4. The product 25 × 48 is less than or equal to 1000.   _____
5. 366 is a multiple of 5.   _____

Statements 1, 4, and 5 are false. Statements 2 and 3 are true. The students noticed that these statements are similar to those in the survey on page 2. Each statement above is called the *negation* of the corresponding statement on page 2.

We often use the word "not" to form the negation of a statement. For example, consider the following statement:

The Yankees won last night.

The negation of this statement can be expressed in different ways:

The Yankees did not win last night.
or   It is not true that the Yankees won last night.

Example 1.   Write the negation of each statement.
  a) The sun is shining.
  b) Luis does not know how to swim.
  c) $5 + 4 = 9$

Solution.   a) The sun is not shining.
  b) Luis knows how to swim.
  c) $5 + 4 \neq 9$

In *Example 1b)*, observe that the given statement already contains the word "not". The negation could also be written as "It is not true that Luis does not know how to swim", but it is simpler to write "Luis knows how to swim".

We can use letters to represent statements. For example, suppose we let p represent the following statement:

p: The Yankees won last night.

We use the symbol $\sim p$ to represent the negation of statement p:

$\sim p$: The Yankees did not win last night.

We can summarize the truth values for a statement and its negation in a table, called a *truth table*. This table shows that when p is true, $\sim p$ is false, and when p is false, $\sim p$ is true.

Negation Truth Table

p	$\sim p$
T	F
F	T

Example 2. Let p represent the statement: "The light is on."
Let q represent the statement: "John's car is red."
Write the statement represented by each symbol.
a) $\sim p$ b) $\sim(\sim p)$ c) $\sim q$ d) $\sim(\sim q)$

Solution. a) The light is off.   b) The light is on.
c) John's car is not red.   d) John's car is red.

Negations can often be expressed in different ways. In *Example 2a)*, we could write "The light is not on", and in *part b)* we could write "The light is not off". In *part d)* we could write "It is not true that John's car is not red".

Example 3. a) Write the negation of the open sentence: $x + 2 < 9$.
b) If the domain is the set of natural numbers, determine the solution set of the open sentence in part a).
c) Determine the solution set of the negation.

Solution. a) The negation of $x + 2 < 9$ is $x + 2 \not< 9$. This is usually written as $x + 2 \geqslant 9$.
b) Consider only natural numbers. When we add 2 to a natural number, the result must be less than 9. The only natural numbers for which this is true are 1, 2, 3, 4, 5, and 6. Hence, the solution set of the open sentence in part a) is {1, 2, 3, 4, 5, 6}.
c) When we add 2 to a natural number, the result must be greater than or equal to 9. The solution set is {7, 8, 9, 10, . . .}.

Example 3 shows that we can form negations of open sentences as well as negations of statements. When we form the negation of an open sentence, its solution set consists of the numbers in the domain which are not in the solution set of the original open sentence.

EXERCISES 1-3

1. What is the negation of each statement?
   a) Karen finished reading the book.
   b) The radio is on.
   c) The light is not green.
   d) The temperature is rising.
   e) Martha did not go shopping.
   f) The coin landed heads.

2. Write the negation of each statement. State the truth value of the statement and the truth value of its negation.
   a) July 4 is a national holiday.
   b) Christmas is not in December.
   c) Computers can't calculate.
   d) There are 8 days in a week.
   e) $7 \times 9 = 64$
   f) 7 and 9 are not consecutive numbers.

Ⓑ

3. Write the negation of each statement. What is the truth value of the statement and the truth value of its negation?
   a) Thanksgiving is in November.
   b) February is not the shortest month.
   c) The sun shines for 12 h each day.
   d) The Earth does not have two moons.
   e) $15 \times 8 = 120$
   f) $11 \times 29 > 500$

4. Write the negation of each open sentence. For the domain $\{1, 2, 3, 4, \ldots\}$, write the solution set of the open sentence and the solution set of the negation.
   a) $x + 3 = 7$ b) $2 + n = 4$ c) $10 - x = 5$ d) $y + 5 < 10$
   e) $n + 4 \leqslant 8$ f) $x + 3 > 9$ g) $7 + x \geqslant 4$ h) $x + x = (x)(x)$

5. If p is true and q is false, what is the truth value of each statement?
   a) $\sim p$ b) $\sim(\sim p)$ c) $\sim q$ d) $\sim(\sim q)$

Ⓒ

6. Use the survey you designed in *Exercise 6*, page 4. Replace each statement in your survey with its negation. Then try out the survey on three people. Compare the results of the two surveys.

7. Write the negation of each statement.
   a) Every state has a capital city.   b) Some calculators have a square-root key.
   c) All apples are green.   d) Some boys do not like sports.

 INVESTIGATE

The Word "and"

1. Write some examples of sentences containing the word "and".

2. What does the word "and" mean? Consult a dictionary if you wish.

1-4 CONJUNCTIONS

In Section 1-3 we formed negations of statements and open sentences. We can also combine two or more statements or open sentences. One way to do this is to use the word "and".

To promote sales, a chain of video stores gave out cards to its customers. Each card had two panels to be scratched off. If both panels show a VCR, the customer wins the VCR.

Consider the following statements:

p: The left panel shows a VCR. . . . ①
q: The right panel shows a VCR. . . . ②

Now combine ① and ② using the word "and".

The left panel shows a VCR and the right panel shows a VCR. . . . ③

If statements ① and ② are both true, then statement ③ is true. However, if ① is true and ② is false, or if ① is false and ② is true, or if ① and ② are both false, then statement ③ is false.

Statement ③ is called the *conjunction* of statements ① and ②. We write $p \land q$ for the conjunction of *p* and *q*. We can summarize the possible truth values for $p \land q$ in a truth table. It has four rows, since there are four possibilities for the truth values of *p* and *q*. These are shown in the first two columns of the table.

Conjunction Truth Table

When p and q are both
true, the conjunction
$p \wedge q$ is true. $\Bigg\} \rightarrow$

p	q	$p \wedge q$
T	T	T
T	F	F
F	T	F
F	F	F

$\leftarrow$ $\Big\{$ In all other cases,
$\leftarrow$ the conjunction is
$\leftarrow$ false.

Example 1. What is the truth value of each statement?
   a) February has 30 days and March has 31 days.
   b) Dogs bark and a square has 4 equal sides.

Solution. a) "February has 30 days" is false; "March has 31 days" is true. Hence, according to the 3rd line of the truth table, the given statement is false.
   b) "Dogs bark" is true; "a square has 4 equal sides" is true. According to the 1st line of the truth table, the given statement is true.

In *Example 1b)*, the given statements were not related. When we combine two or more statements to form other statements, the given statements do not have to be related.

Example 2. Let p represent the statement "Kari has blue eyes", and let q represent the statement "Kari has brown hair". Write each statement in words.
   a) $p \wedge q$ b) $p \wedge \sim q$ c) $\sim p \wedge \sim q$

Solution. a) Kari has blue eyes and brown hair.
   b) Kari has blue eyes but not brown hair.
   c) Kari has neither blue eyes nor brown hair.

   Conjunctions can be expressed in different ways. In *Example 2b)*, we could write "Kari has blue eyes and Kari does not have brown hair". When possible, we try to express statements in the simplest way. This was done in Example 2.

   We can form conjunctions of open sentences. For example, let p and q represent the following open sentences.

p: x is even
q: x is a perfect square

The conjunction of p and q is

$p \wedge q$: x is even and x is a perfect square

The truth value of $p \wedge q$ depends on the value of x, as indicated by the truth table.

p	q	$p \wedge q$
T	T	T
T	F	F
F	T	F
F	F	F

If $x = 16$, then both p and q are true.
If $x = 10$, then p is true and q is false.
If $x = 25$, then p is false and q is true.
If $x = 7$, then both p and q are false.

The solution set of $p \wedge q$ consists of all the numbers which make both p and q true. These are the even perfect squares: $\{4, 16, 36, 64, \ldots\}$.

Example 3. Let p represent the open sentence $x > 3$. Let q represent the open sentence $x < 9$. Determine the solution set of $p \wedge q$.

Solution. $p \wedge q$ represents the open sentence: $x > 3$ and $x < 9$. The natural numbers which are greater than 3 are 4, 5, 6, 7, . . . , . Those which are less than 9 are 1, 2, 3, . . . , 8. The natural numbers which are both greater than 3 and less than 9 are 4, 5, 6, 7, and 8. Hence, the solution set of $p \wedge q$ is $\{4, 5, 6, 7, 8\}$.

EXERCISES 1-4

1. What is the truth value of each statement?
   a) There are 25 cents in a quarter and 4 quarters in a dollar.
   b) There are 7 days in a week and 50 weeks in a year.
   c) Water freezes at 32°F and bears hibernate in winter.
   d) 4 is an odd number and a square has 4 right angles.
   e) $6 \times 70 = 420$ and $360 \div 9 = 4$
   f) All numbers ending in 2 are even and all even numbers end in 2.

2. Let p represent the statement "Donna likes mathematics", and let q represent the statement "Donna likes science". Write each statement in words.
   a) $p \wedge q$ b) $p \wedge {\sim}q$ c) ${\sim}p \wedge q$ d) ${\sim}p \wedge {\sim}q$

B

3. Let r and s represent the statements below, with the given truth values.
   r: Erik won a trip to Acapulco. (True)
   s: Mina won $10 000 cash. (False)
   Write each statement in words. What is the truth value of each statement?
   a) $r \wedge s$ b) $r \wedge {\sim}s$ c) ${\sim}r \wedge s$ d) ${\sim}r \wedge {\sim}s$

4. Let p and q represent these open sentences.
   p: x is divisible by 2
   q: x is divisible by 3
   a) Write the conjunction $p \wedge q$ in words.
   b) Find at least one value of x which makes:
       i) p and q both true   ii) p true and q false
       iii) p false and q true   iv) p and q both false.
   c) Write the solution set of $p \wedge q$.

5. Write the conjunction $p \wedge q$ in words, and determine the solution set.
   a) p: x is a perfect square   b) p: x is a multiple of 4
       q: x is less than 50 q: x is a multiple of 6

   c) p: $x > 5$ d) p: n is a prime number
       q: $x < 12$ q: n is even

6. Let p represent the statement "I like music", and let q represent the statement "I like sports". Write each statement using symbols.
   a) I like music and sports.   b) I like music but not sports.
   c) I like sports but not music.   d) I do not like music or sports.

7. Let p represent the statement "My calculator does not need batteries", and let q represent the statement "My calculator does square roots". Suppose these statements are both true. Write each statement below in words and determine its truth value.
   a) $p \wedge q$ b) $\sim p \wedge q$ c) $p \wedge \sim q$ d) $\sim p \wedge \sim q$

8. If p is true and q is false, determine the truth value of each statement.
   a) $p \wedge \sim q$ b) $\sim(p \wedge \sim q)$ c) $\sim p \wedge \sim q$ d) $\sim(\sim p \wedge \sim q)$

9. Write the negation of each statement.
   a) It is cold and windy today.   b) I have a nickel and a dime in my pocket.

INVESTIGATE

Words With More Than One Meaning

1. Some English words, such as "trip" and "reason" can have more than one meaning. Write three more examples of words like this.

2. Write some examples of sentences containing the word "or".

3. a) What does the word "or" mean? Consult a dictionary if you wish.
   b) The word "or" can have two different meanings. What are they?

1-5 DISJUNCTIONS

In Section 1-4 we combined two statements or open sentences using the word "and". The word "or" is another word we can use to combine statements or open sentences. Since this word has two different meanings, we must be sure which meaning is intended. It is used in two different ways here:

The first prize in a contest is a trip to London or $2000 cash. . . . ①

Tara said that she will buy tickets on Friday or Saturday. . . . ②

In sentence ①, the winner must choose between taking the trip to London or taking the money, and cannot take both. In sentence ②, Tara could buy tickets on Friday, or on Saturday, or on both days. To avoid confusion in this chapter, we will use the word "or" in the second way, unless stated otherwise.

Consider the following statements:
　Tara will buy tickets on Friday. . . . ③
　Tara will buy tickets on Saturday. . . . ④

Now combine statements ③ and ④ using the word "or":

　Tara will buy tickets on Friday or Tara will buy tickets on Saturday. . . . ⑤

If statements ③ and ④ are both true, then statement ⑤ is true. If ③ is true and ④ is false, or if ③ is false and ④ is true, then statement ⑤ is also true. But if ③ and ④ are both false, then statement ⑤ is false.

　　Statement ⑤ is called the *disjunction* of statements ③ and ④. We write $p \lor q$ for the disjunction of statements p and q.

Disjunction Truth Table

When p and q are both
true, or when only
one of them is true,
the disjunction $p \vee q$
is true.

$\left.\begin{array}{}\end{array}\right\} \begin{array}{l} \rightarrow \\ \rightarrow \\ \rightarrow \end{array}$

p	q	$p \vee q$
T	T	T
T	F	T
F	T	T
F	F	F

$\leftarrow \left\{ \begin{array}{l} \text{When } p \text{ and } q \text{ are both} \\ \text{false, the disjunction} \\ \text{is false.} \end{array} \right.$

Example 1. What is the truth value of each statement?
  a) May comes after April or there are 12 months in a year.
  b) 17 is an even number or a square has 4 right angles.

Solution. a) "May comes after April" is true; "there are 12 months in a year" is true. Hence, according to the 1st line of the truth table, the given statement is true.
  b) "17 is an even number" is false; "a square has 4 right angles" is true. The 3rd line of the truth table shows that the given statement is true.

Example 2. Let p represent the statement "I have a quarter", and let q represent the statement "I have a dime". Write each statement in words.
  a) $p \vee q$ b) $p \vee {\sim}q$ c) ${\sim}p \vee {\sim}q$

Solution. a) I have a quarter or a dime.
  b) I have a quarter or I do not have a dime.
  c) I do not have a quarter or I do not have a dime.

We can form disjunctions of open sentences. For example, let p and q represent the following open sentences:

p: x is divisible by 2
q: x is divisible by 5

The disjunction of p and q is

$p \vee q$: x is divisible by 2 or x is divisible by 5

The truth value of $p \vee q$ depends on the value of x, as indicated by the truth table.

p	q	$p \vee q$
T	T	T
T	F	T
F	T	T
F	F	F

If $x = 20$, then both p and q are true.
If $x = 12$, then p is true and q is false.
If $x = 15$, then p is false and q is true.
If $x = 9$, then both p and q are false.

The solution set of $p \vee q$ consists of all the numbers which make p and q both true, or only one of them true. These are the even numbers and the odd multiples of 5: {2, 4, 5, 6, 8, 10, 12, 14, 15, . . .}.

Example 3. Let p and q represent these open sentences.

p: x is a factor of 6
q: x is a factor of 10
Determine the solution set of $p \vee q$.

Solution. $p \vee q$ represents the open sentence "x is a factor of 6 or x is a factor of 10". The factors of 6 are 1, 2, 3, and 6. The factors of 10 are 1, 2, 5, and 10. Hence, the solution set of $p \vee q$ is {1, 2, 3, 5, 6, 10}. These are all the numbers which are factors of 6 or 10 or both.

EXERCISES 1-5

1. What is the truth value of each statement?
   a) There are 12 in. in a foot or 3 ft in a yard.
   b) There are 24 h in a day or 360 days in a year.
   c) Ice melts at 0°F or water boils at 100°F.
   d) New Jersey is larger than Massachusetts or smaller than New York.
   e) $50 \times 300 = 15\ 000$ or $480 \div 60 = 80$
   f) 8 is a prime number or $21 \times 31 < 600$.

2. Let p represent the statement "Joe gave me a dollar" and let q represent the statement "Sam gave me a dollar". Write each statement in words.
   a) $p \vee q$ b) $p \vee \sim q$ c) $\sim p \vee q$ d) $\sim p \vee \sim q$

B

3. Let r and s represent the statements below, with the given truth values.
   r: Sharon went to the game.   (True)
   s: Barb went to the movies.   (False)
   Write each statement in words. What is the truth value of the statement?
   a) $r \vee s$ b) $r \vee \sim s$ c) $\sim r \vee s$ d) $\sim r \vee \sim s$

4. Let p represent the statement "12 is a perfect square", and let q represent the statement "17 is a prime number". Write each statement using symbols. What is the truth value of the statement?
   a) 12 is a perfect square or 17 is a prime number.
   b) 12 is a perfect square or 17 is not a prime number.
   c) 12 is not a perfect square or 17 is a prime number.
   d) 12 is not a perfect square or 17 is not a prime number.

5. Let p and q represent these open sentences.

   p: x is between 3 and 10

   q: x is between 7 and 14

   a) Write the disjunction $p \vee q$ in words.

   b) Find at least one value of x which makes:

      i) p and q both true   ii) p true and q false

     iii) p false and q true   iv) p and q both false.

   c) Write the solution set of $p \vee q$.

6. Write the disjunction $p \vee q$ in words, and determine the solution set.

   a) p: x is a factor of 6

      q: x is a factor of 9

   b) p: x is a factor of 48

      q: x is less than 10

   c) p: y is a factor of 30

      q: y is between 5 and 10

   d) p: n is a factor of 32

      q: n is a perfect square

7. Suppose the statement "Martha has a dog or Lisa does not" is false. Determine the truth value of each statement.

   a) Martha has a dog.

   b) Lisa has a dog.

   c) Martha does not have a dog.

   d) Lisa does not have a dog.

8. The list of ingredients on a box of cereal contains the following: ". . . sugar and/or glucose-fructose. . ."

   a) Why are the words "and" and "or" combined as "and/or"?

   b) Reword the phrase without using "and/or".

Ⓒ

9. If p is true and q is false, determine the truth value of each statement.

   a) $p \vee \sim q$ b) $\sim(p \vee \sim q)$ c) $\sim p \vee \sim q$ d) $\sim(\sim p \vee \sim q)$

10. Determine the truth values of p and q if:

   a) $\sim p \vee q$ is false   b) $\sim p \vee \sim q$ is false   c) $\sim(p \vee q)$ is true.

11. Write the negation of each statement.

   a) John is wearing a jacket or a shirt.

   b) We will go swimming on Saturday or Sunday.

1-6 CONDITIONALS

After the practice, the coach announced:

If it rains tomorrow, then the game is cancelled. . . . ①

Observe that statement ① is formed by combining the statements "it rains tomorrow" and "the game is cancelled" with the words "if . . . then". Any statement or open sentence formed by combining two statements or open sentences with these words is called a *conditional*.

To determine the truth values of statement ①, consider the following possibilities.

Suppose it rains and the game is cancelled.   Statement ① is true.

Suppose it rains and the game is not cancelled.   Statement ① is false.

Suppose it does not rain. The coach did not say what would happen if it does not rain. The game might be played, but it might be cancelled for a different reason. Either way, we cannot say that the coach's statement is false. Hence, we will accept that it is true.

Therefore, the coach's statement is false when it rains and the game is not cancelled. Otherwise, it is true.

We write $p \rightarrow q$ for the conditional formed by p and q. This is read "If p then q". The truth table below gives the truth values of $p \rightarrow q$ corresponding to the four cases above.

Conditional Truth Table

When p and q are both true, the conditional $p \rightarrow q$ is true. $\rightarrow$

When p is false, the conditional is true. $\rightarrow$

p	q	$p \rightarrow q$
T	T	T
T	F	F
F	T	T
F	F	T

$\leftarrow$ When p is true and q is false, the conditional is false.

In the conditional $p \rightarrow q$, p is called the *hypothesis* and q is called the *conclusion*. Observe that the only time a conditional is false occurs when the hypothesis is true and the conclusion is false. In all other cases, a conditional is true.

Example 1. Identify the hypothesis and the conclusion of each statement. What is its truth value?
a) If $2 \times 3 = 6$, then $20 \times 3 = 60$.
b) If $2 \times 3 = 5$, then $20 \times 3 = 50$.
c) If $2 \times 3 = 6$, then $20 \times 3 = 50$.

Solution. a) Hypothesis: $2 \times 3 = 6$ (True)   Conclusion: $20 \times 3 = 60$ (True)
According to the 1st line of the truth table, the given statement is true.
b) Hypothesis: $2 \times 3 = 5$ (False)   Conclusion: $20 \times 3 = 50$ (False)
According to the 4th line of the truth table, the given statement is true.
c) Hypothesis: $2 \times 3 = 6$ (True)   Conclusion: $20 \times 3 = 50$ (False)
According to the 2nd line of the truth table, the given statement is false.

In *Example 1a)*, the fact that $2 \times 3 = 6$ is the reason why $20 \times 3 = 60$ because the factor 2 has been multiplied by 10. For the same reason, if it were true that $2 \times 3 = 5$, then 20×3 would have to be equal to 50 and not 60. Hence, it is reasonable that the conditional in *part b)* is true.

Conditionals can be expressed in different ways. For example, the statements below have the same meaning as statement ①. In each statement, the hypothesis is "it rains tomorrow" and the conclusion is "the game is cancelled".

If it rains tomorrow, the game is cancelled.   . . . ②
The game is cancelled if it rains tomorrow.   . . . ③
It rains tomorrow only if the game is cancelled.   . . . ④

In statement ② the word "then" is understood. In statement ③ the conclusion is stated before the hypothesis. Statement ④ is false when it rains and the game is not cancelled. Hence, it has the same meaning as ①.

We often form conditionals with open sentences. For example, let p and q represent the following open sentences.

p: x is divisible by 5 q: x is odd

The conditional $p \rightarrow q$ is: If x is divisible by 5, then x is odd.

The truth value of $p \rightarrow q$ depends on the value of x.

p	q	$p \rightarrow q$
T	T	T
T	F	F
F	T	T
F	F	T

If $x = 15$, then both p and q are true.
If $x = 20$, then p is true and q is false.
If $x = 17$, then p is false and q is true.
If $x = 24$, then both p and q are false.

The solution set of $p \rightarrow q$ consists of all natural numbers except those which make p true and q false. These are all natural numbers except 10, 20, 30, . . .

Example 2. Let p and q represent these open sentences, where x is a natural number.
p: x is a multiple of 10
q: x is a multiple of 2
If possible, find at least one value of x which makes:
a) p and q both true   b) p true and q false
c) p false and q true   d) p and q both false.

Solution.   a) Numbers which are multiples of both 10 and 2, such as 10, 20, 30, . . .
b) Numbers which are multiples of 10 but not multiples of 2. There are no such numbers.
c) Numbers which are not multiples of 10 but are multiples of 2, such as 6.
d) Numbers which are neither multiples of 10 nor multiples of 2, such as 15.

In *Example 2*, all natural numbers make the conditional $p \rightarrow q$ true. That is, the following open sentence is true for all natural numbers:

If x is a multiple of 10, then x is a multiple of 2.

Therefore, we can write this more simply as follows:

All multiples of 10 are multiples of 2.

EXERCISES 1-6

(A)

1. State the hypothesis and the conclusion of each conditional.
   a) If yesterday was Thursday, then today is Friday.
   b) If you get a good night's sleep, you will feel better in the morning.
   c) Your grades will improve if you do your homework regularly.
   d) We will stop for lunch only if it rains.

2. State the hypothesis and the conclusion of each conditional. What is its truth value?
   a) If this year is a leap year, then February has 29 days.
   b) If an animal has stripes, the animal is a tiger.
   c) The toaster will work only if it is plugged in.
   d) If there are 50 states, then Ronald Reagan was president.

(B)

3. State the hypothesis and the conclusion of each conditional. What is its truth value?
   a) If $7 \times 5 = 35$, then $7 \times 50 = 350$
   b) If $8 \times 3 = 26$, then $3 \times 8 = 26$
   c) If $9 + 5 = 14$, then $19 + 15 = 24$
   d) If $6 + 3 = 8$, then $6 + 4 = 10$

4. Let p and q represent these open sentences, where x is a natural number.
   p: x is a prime number
   q: x is an odd number
   a) If possible, find at least one value of x which makes:
      i) p and q both true   ii) p true and q false
      iii) p false and q true   iv) p and q both false.
   b) Is the conditional $p \rightarrow q$ true for all natural numbers?

5. Repeat *Exercise 4* for these open sentences.
   a) p: x is a multiple of 4   b) p: x is a multiple of 3
      q: x is a multiple of 2 q: x is a multiple of 6

   c) p: x is a factor of 12   d) p: x is a factor of 9
      q: x is a factor of 15 q: x is a factor of 27

   e) p: x is a perfect square   f) p: x is a 2-digit number
      q: x is an even number q: x is less than 100

6. For each conditional you found in *Exercises 4* and *5* which is true for all natural numbers, write the conditional in the form "All . . .".

7. Write each sentence in the form "If . . . then . . .". What is its truth value?
   a) A natural number is a multiple of 10 if it is a multiple of 5.
   b) Two rectangles have the same area if they have the same length and width.
   c) An even number is a prime number only if it is 2.
   d) A natural number is a perfect square only if it is not a prime number.
   e) All multiples of 4 are multiples of 2.

8. Let p and q represent these open sentences.
   p: Quadrilateral ABCD is a square
   q: Quadrilateral ABCD is a rectangle
   a) Is it possible to draw the figure in each case?
      i) p and q are both true   ii) p is true and q is false
      iii) p is false and q is true   iv) p and q are both false
   b) Is the conditional $p \rightarrow q$ true for all quadrilaterals ABCD?
   c) Write the conditional $p \rightarrow q$ in words in two different ways.

9. Repeat *Exercise 8* for these open sentences.
   a) p: Quadrilateral ABCD is a rectangle
      q: Quadrilateral ABCD is a parallelogram
   b) p: $\triangle$ABC is equilateral
      q: $\triangle$ABC is isosceles
   c) p: $\angle$DEF is a right angle
      q: $\angle$DEF $= 90°$
   d) p: Quadrilateral PQRS is a square
      q: Quadrilateral PQRS is a rhombus

ⓒ

10. Suppose that these two conditionals are both true.
    "If the Yankees win or the Jays lose, the Yankees will be in first place."
    "If the Yankees lose and the Jays win, the Jays will be in first place."
    Determine what happens if:
    a) the Yankees and the Jays both win   b) the Yankees and the Jays both lose
    c) the Yankees win and the Jays lose   d) the Jays win and the Yankees lose.

11. If p is false and q is true, determine the truth value of each statement.
    a) $p \rightarrow \sim q$ b) $\sim(p \rightarrow \sim q)$ c) $\sim p \rightarrow \sim q$ d) $\sim(\sim p \rightarrow \sim q)$

12. Write the following in the form "If . . . then . . .". Identify the hypothesis and the conclusion.
    a) Latecomers will not be admitted.   b) Goods satisfactory or money refunded.

 **INVESTIGATE**

Interchanging Hypothesis and Conclusion

Given the conditional $p \rightarrow q$, we can form a related conditional $q \rightarrow p$ by interchanging the hypothesis and conclusion.

1. Try this with some of the statements and open sentences in the examples and exercises of this section.

2. If the conditional $p \rightarrow q$ is true, does it follow that the conditional $q \rightarrow p$ is also true? Give examples to support your answer.

1-7 APPLICATIONS TO REASONING

In ordinary language we frequently encounter two or more statements, and draw conclusions based on them. We can use truth tables from the preceding sections to check if the conclusions we draw are correct. For example, suppose that these two statements are both true.

If Karen buys new skis, then Karen needs a new outfit. . . . ①
Karen buys new skis. . . . ②

Can we conclude that Karen needs a new outfit?

Let s and n represent these statements.
s: Karen buys new skis. n: Karen needs a new outfit.

Statements ① and ② can be represented by $s \rightarrow n$ and s. The truth table for $s \rightarrow n$ is shown. The only line of the truth table in which both $s \rightarrow n$ and s are true is the 1st line. On this line, n is true. Hence, we can conclude that Karen needs a new outfit.

s	n	$s \rightarrow n$
T	**T**	**T**
T	F	F
F	T	T
F	F	T

Now suppose that these two statements are both true.

If Karen buys new skis, then Karen needs a new outfit.
Karen needs a new outfit.

Can we conclude that Karen buys new skis?
From the truth table we see that the statements $s \rightarrow n$ and n are both true in the 1st and 3rd lines. Observe that s is true on one of these lines and false on the other. Therefore, we cannot conclude that Karen buys new skis. That is, she may need a new outfit even though she does not buy new skis.

s	n	$s \rightarrow n$
T	**T**	**T**
T	F	F
F	**T**	**T**
F	F	T

Example.   Suppose that these two statements are both true.

It is raining or the sun is shining.
The sun is not shining.

What can you conclude? Justify your conclusion.

Solution.   Let r and s represent these statements.
r: It is raining. s: The sun is shining.
The two given statements can be represented by $r \lor s$ and $\sim s$.

Construct a truth table for $r \lor s$. The statement $r \lor s$ is true in the 1st, 2nd, and 3rd lines. The only one of these lines in which $\sim s$ is true is the line in which s is false; that is, the 2nd line. On this line, r is true. Hence, we conclude that it is raining.

r	s	$r \lor s$
T	T	T
T	**F**	**T**
F	T	T
F	F	F

EXERCISES 1-7

Ⓐ

1. Suppose that the first two statements are both true. Can we conclude that the conclusion is also true?

a) If Joe sings, Yoko smiles.
Joe sings.
Conclusion: Yoko smiles.

b) If the dog wags its tail, it is happy.
The dog wags its tail.
Conclusion: The dog is happy.

c) The car is red or blue.
The car is not blue.
Conclusion: The car is red.

d) If you smoke, your health deteriorates.
Your health deteriorates.
Conclusion: You smoke.

2. Suppose that the first two statements are both true.
George read one or two books last weekend.
George did not read two books last weekend.
What can you conclude?

Ⓑ

3. Suppose that the first two statements are both true.
If Carlos likes math, then he knows his number facts.
Carlos likes math.
Can we conclude that Carlos knows his number facts? Use a truth table to justify your answer.

4. In *Exercise 3*, what can you conclude, if anything, if the second statement is replaced with each of these statements?
a) Carlos knows his number facts.   b) Carlos does not know his number facts.
c) Carlos does not like math.

5. Suppose that the first two statements are both true.
If you brush your teeth with CAVGONE, you will have fewer cavities.
You have fewer cavities.
Can we conclude that you brush your teeth with CAVGONE? Use a truth table to justify your answer.

6. Suppose that each pair of statements is true. What, if anything, can you conclude?
a) $x = 3$ or $x = 7$ b) $x < 5$ or $x = 5$ c) If $2x = 10$, then $x = 5$
   $x \neq 7$ $x \neq 5$ $2x = 10$
d) If n is divisible by 12, then n is divisible by 6.
   n is divisible by 12.
e) If ABCD is a square, then ABCD is a rectangle.
   ABCD is a rectangle.

Ⓒ

7. Suppose that the first two statements are both true. Can we conclude that the conclusion is also true? Justify your answer.
a) The cat purrs when it is eating.
The cat is purring.
Conclusion: The cat is eating.

b) We will rent a video unless it snows.
It did not snow.
Conclusion: We rented a video.

1-8 DETERMINING TRUTH VALUES OF STATEMENTS

In arithmetic the symbols $+$, $-$, $\times$, and $\div$ denote operations with numbers. We use these symbols to write arithmetical expressions such as $5 \times 3 - 6$ and $8 + 2 \times (7 - 3)$. The brackets serve as grouping symbols to indicate the operations which are to be done first.

Similarly, in logic, the symbols $\sim$, $\wedge$, $\vee$, and $\rightarrow$ are used to write statements. For example, we can write statements such as $\sim p \wedge q$ and $p \rightarrow (q \vee \sim p)$. We can determine their truth values by using the basic truth tables in the preceding sections.

Example 1. If p is true and q is false, determine the truth value of each statement.

a) $\sim p \wedge q$ b) $\sim (p \wedge q)$ c) $p \rightarrow (q \vee \sim p)$

Solution. a) $\sim p \wedge q$

This statement is a conjunction of $\sim p$ and q.

Since p is true, $\sim p$ is false. Also, q is false. According to the 4th line of the Conjunction Truth Table (page 13), the statement $\sim p \wedge q$ is false.

$$\begin{array}{cc} \text{False} & \text{False} \\ \sim p & \wedge & q \\ \underbrace{\hspace{3em}} \\ \text{False} \end{array}$$

b) $\sim (p \wedge q)$

This statement is the negation of $p \wedge q$. The brackets are grouping symbols to indicate that the conjunction $p \wedge q$ is considered first.

Since p is true and q is false, according to the 2nd line of the Conjunction Truth Table, $p \wedge q$ is false.

Therefore, the statement $\sim (p \wedge q)$ is true.

$$\begin{array}{cc} \text{True} & \text{False} \\ p & \wedge & q \\ \underbrace{\hspace{3em}} \\ \text{False} \\ \big\backslash \\ \sim (p \wedge q) \\ \underbrace{\hspace{3em}} \\ \text{True} \end{array}$$

c) $p \rightarrow (q \vee \sim p)$

This statement has the basic form of a conditional, but the brackets indicate that the disjunction $q \vee \sim p$ is considered first.

We know that q is false. Since p is true, $\sim p$ is false. According to the 4th line of the Disjunction Truth Table (page 17), the statement in the brackets is false.

p is true. $q \vee \sim p$ is false. According to the 2nd line of the Conditional Truth Table (page 21), the given statement is false.

$$\begin{array}{cc} \text{False} & \text{False} \\ q & \vee & \sim p \\ \underbrace{\hspace{3em}} \\ \text{False} \\ \text{True} \quad | \\ p \rightarrow (q \vee \sim p) \\ \underbrace{\hspace{3em}} \\ \text{False} \end{array}$$

Some statements contain more than one set of brackets.

Example 2. If p is false and q is true, determine the truth value of each statement.

a) $(p \land q) \to (p \lor q)$ 　　　　　　 b) $[\sim p \land (p \to \sim q)] \lor q$

Solution. a) $(p \land q) \to (p \lor q)$
This statement is a conditional.
Since p is false and q is true:
$p \land q$ is false
$p \lor q$ is true
According to the 3rd line of the
Conditional Truth Table, the given
statement is true.

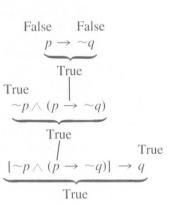

b) $[\sim p \land (p \to \sim q)] \lor q$
This statement is a disjunction, but
we must consider the statement inside
the square brackets first. Since the
round brackets are inside the square
brackets, we start with the conditional
$p \to \sim q$.
p is false and $\sim q$ is false.
According to the 4th line of the Conditional Truth Table, the statement
$p \to \sim q$ is true.
$\sim p$ is true and $p \to \sim q$ is true.
According to the 1st line of the Conjunction Truth Table, the statement
$\sim p \land (p \to \sim q)$ is true.
$\sim p \land (p \to \sim q)$ is true and q is true.
According to the 1st line of the Conditional Truth Table, the given statement is true.

EXERCISES 1-8

1. If p and q are both true, determine the truth value of each statement.
   a) $p \lor \sim q$ 　　　　 b) $\sim (p \lor q)$ 　　　　 c) $\sim p \lor \sim q$
   d) $(p \land q) \lor p$ 　　　 e) $p \land (p \lor q)$ 　　 f) $(p \lor q) \lor p$

2. If p and q are both false, determine the truth value of each statement.
   a) $p \to \sim q$ 　　　　 b) $\sim q \to p$ 　　　　 c) $\sim (p \to q)$
   d) $(p \lor q) \to p$ 　　 e) $p \to (p \land q)$ 　　 f) $\sim p \to \sim q$

Ⓑ

3. If p is true and q is false, determine the truth value of each statement.
   a) $\sim p \wedge q$
   b) $\sim(p \wedge q)$
   c) $\sim[p \vee (\sim q)]$
   d) $(p \vee q) \wedge (p \wedge q)$
   e) $[(p \rightarrow q) \rightarrow p] \rightarrow q$
   f) $(p \wedge q) \vee (\sim p \wedge q)$

4. If p is false and q is true, what is the truth value of each statement?
   a) $p \rightarrow \sim q$
   b) $(p \wedge q) \rightarrow p$
   c) $\sim(\sim p \vee q)$
   d) $\sim(p \rightarrow \sim q)$
   e) $(p \vee \sim q) \wedge (p \vee q)$
   f) $[p \vee (\sim q \wedge p)] \vee q$

5. Determine the truth value of the statement $\sim q \wedge (p \rightarrow q)$ if:
   a) p and q are both true
   b) p is true and q is false
   c) p is false and q is true
   d) p and q are both false.

6. Repeat *Exercise 5* for each statement.
   a) $q \wedge (p \rightarrow \sim q)$
   b) $(p \wedge \sim q) \vee p$
   c) $[(p \vee q) \rightarrow \sim p] \rightarrow q$
   d) $(\sim p \vee q) \rightarrow (p \wedge \sim q)$

7. If p is true, q is true, and r is false, what is the truth value of each statement?
   a) $p \vee (q \wedge r)$
   b) $(p \vee q) \wedge r$
   c) $(p \vee q) \rightarrow \sim r$
   d) $p \rightarrow (\sim q \vee r)$
   e) $[(p \rightarrow q) \rightarrow r] \rightarrow q$
   f) $(p \rightarrow q) \vee (q \rightarrow r)$

8. If p is false, q is true, and r is true, what is the truth value of each statement?
   a) $p \wedge (q \vee r)$
   b) $(p \wedge q) \vee r$
   c) $(\sim p \vee q) \rightarrow (p \vee \sim r)$
   d) $p \rightarrow (q \wedge r)$
   e) $[(p \vee q) \rightarrow \sim r] \rightarrow r$
   f) $(p \rightarrow \sim q) \vee (p \rightarrow \sim r)$

Ⓒ

9. If the given statement is false, what are the truth values of p and q?
   a) $\sim(p \wedge q)$
   b) $\sim p \vee \sim q$
   c) $\sim p \rightarrow q$
   d) $(p \rightarrow q) \rightarrow (q \rightarrow p)$

 INVESTIGATE

Negations

Suppose some statement containing p and q is given. Suppose a new statement is formed by replacing each p with $\sim p$ and each q with $\sim q$ throughout the given statement.

  Is the new statement the negation of the given statement? Give examples to support your conclusion.

PROBLEM SOLVING

Eliminate Possibilities

Inspector Columbo was investigating a crime. He interviewed the musician, the manager, and the server. Their statements are as follows:

Manager's statement:
The musician is guilty.

Musician's statement:
The manager or the server is guilty.

Server's statement:
If the musician is innocent, then the manager is guilty.

Two people were not telling the truth. Who committed the crime?

Understand the problem
Can we assume that one of these three people is guilty?

Think of a strategy
Try eliminating the possibilities. Suppose each person, in turn, is guilty. Then check to see who is telling the truth.

Carry out the strategy
Suppose the manager is guilty. Are any of the statements false?
Suppose the musician is guilty. Are any of the statements false?
Suppose the server is guilty. Are any of the statements false?
Who committed the crime?

Look back
Is it possible that two of the three people are guilty?
Is it possible for some other person to be guilty?

Solve each problem.

1. Ann says, "Barb is a liar". Barb says, "Chris is a liar". Chris says, "Ann and Barb are both liars". Who is telling the truth?

2. Andrea, Betty, and Carol have red, white, and blue caps, but not necessarily in that order. Only one of these statements is true:

   Andrea's cap is blue.
   Betty's cap is not blue.
   Carol's cap is not red.

   What color is each girl's cap?

3. Mrs. Santos showed Andy and Bill two white hats and one black hat. They closed their eyes while she put a hat on each of them. She hid the third hat so they could not see it. When they opened their eyes, Mrs. Santos asked Andy if he could tell the color of the hat on his head. Assume that you are Andy, and that you can see Bill's hat. Can you tell the color of your hat in each case shown below? If so, explain how you know. If not, explain why you cannot tell the color.

   a)    b)

4. In *Problem 3*, assume that you are Bill, and that you can see Andy's hat and hear his answer. Can you tell the color of your hat in each case shown below? If so, explain how you know. If not, explain why you cannot tell the color.

   a)    b)

1-9 CONSTRUCTING TRUTH TABLES

In Section 1-8, we determined the truth values of statements such as $\sim p \wedge q$ when the truth values of p and q are given. Suppose the truth values of p and q are not given. Then, we can construct a truth table. Truth tables help us to analyze statements in an organized way.

Example 1. Complete a truth table with this heading.

p	q	$\sim p$	$\sim p \wedge q$

Solution. In columns ① and ②, list all the possibilities for T and F.

When p is T, q can be T or F. →

When p is F, q can be T or F. →

①	②	③	④
p	q	$\sim p$	$\sim p \wedge q$
T	T		
T	F		
F	T		
F	F		

Use the Negation Truth Table (page 10) to complete column ③.

When p is T, $\sim p$ is F. →

When p is F, $\sim p$ is T. →

①	②	③	④
p	q	$\sim p$	$\sim p \wedge q$
T	T	**F**	
T	F	**F**	
F	T	**T**	
F	F	**T**	

Use the Conjunction Truth Table (page 13) to complete column ④. Use the entries in that table, not the headings. For example, in the first row below, the entries for $\sim p$ and q are F and T. Look for F and T *in the same order* in the Conjunction Truth Table. They occur in the 3rd row, where the result is F. Hence, enter F in the first row of column ④. Complete the other rows in the same way.

Entries used from the Conjunction Truth Table:

				①	②	③	④
				p	q	$\sim p$	$\sim p \wedge q$
Row 3:	F	T	F →	T	T	F	**F**
Row 4:	F	F	F →	T	F	F	**F**
Row 1:	T	T	T →	F	T	T	**T**
Row 2:	T	F	F →	F	F	T	**F**

In *Example 1*, the headings of the truth table were given. But when we construct a truth table for a particular statement, only the statement is given. Hence, the first step is to determine the statements which are to be written at the top of each column in the truth table.

Example 2.   Construct a truth table for each statement.

a) $\sim q \rightarrow p$ b) $q \wedge (p \rightarrow \sim q)$

Solution.   a) $\sim q \rightarrow p$

Start with columns for p and q. Since $\sim q$ occurs in the statement, include a column for $\sim q$. Also, include a column for the given statement $\sim q \rightarrow p$.

Columns ① and ② in the truth table show all the possibilities for T and F. Column ③ shows the negations of the entries in column ②. Use the Conditional Truth Table (page 21) to complete column ④. Again, use the entries in that table, not the headings. For example, in the first row, the entries for $\sim q$ and p are F and T. Look for F and T *in the same order* in the Conditional Truth Table. They occur in the 3rd row, where the result is T. Enter T in the first row of column ④. Complete the other rows in the same way.

Entries used from the
Conditional Truth Table:

	①	②	③	④
	p	q	$\sim q$	$\sim q \rightarrow p$
Row 3: F T T →	T	T	F	**T**
Row 1: T T T →	T	F	T	**T**
Row 4: F F T →	F	T	F	**T**
Row 2: T F F →	F	F	T	**F**

b) $q \wedge (p \rightarrow \sim q)$

Start with columns for p and q. Include a column for $\sim q$ and a column for $p \rightarrow \sim q$. Finally, include a column for the given statement, $q \wedge (p \rightarrow \sim q)$. Use the Conditional Truth Table to complete column ④ and the Conjunction Truth Table to complete column ⑤. As before, use the entries in these tables, not the headings.

①	②	③	④	⑤
p	q	$\sim q$	$p \rightarrow \sim q$	$q \wedge (p \rightarrow \sim q)$
T	T	F	F	F
T	F	T	T	F
F	T	F	T	T
F	F	T	T	F

EXERCISES 1-9

Ⓐ

1. Complete a truth table with each heading.

   a)

p	q	$p \vee q$	$(p \vee q) \wedge p$

   b)

p	q	$p \wedge q$	$(p \wedge q) \vee p$

   c)

p	q	$p \vee q$	$p \rightarrow (p \vee q)$

   d)

p	q	$p \rightarrow q$	$(p \rightarrow q) \wedge q$

   e)

p	q	$\sim q$	$p \vee \sim q$	$\sim(p \vee \sim q)$

   f)

p	q	$\sim p$	$p \wedge q$	$\sim p \vee (p \wedge q)$

Ⓑ

2. Construct a truth table for each statement.
   a) $(p \wedge q) \vee p$
   b) $\sim(p \rightarrow q)$
   c) $(p \rightarrow q) \wedge p$
   d) $(p \vee q) \rightarrow p$
   e) $(p \rightarrow q) \rightarrow p$
   f) $p \rightarrow (\sim p \wedge q)$

3. Complete a truth table with each heading.

   a)

p	q	$p \rightarrow q$	$(p \rightarrow q) \wedge p$	$[(p \rightarrow q) \wedge p] \rightarrow q$

   b)

p	q	$\sim p$	$\sim q$	$p \wedge q$	$\sim p \wedge \sim q$	$(p \wedge q) \vee (\sim p \wedge \sim q)$

4. Construct a truth table for each statement.
   a) $(p \rightarrow q) \wedge (q \rightarrow p)$
   b) $p \rightarrow \sim(\sim p \vee q)$
   c) $(\sim p \wedge q) \rightarrow (p \wedge \sim q)$
   d) $\sim(p \wedge q) \rightarrow (\sim p \wedge \sim q)$

Ⓒ

5. Write another statement which has the same truth values as the given statement.
   a) $\sim q \rightarrow \sim p$
   b) $q \wedge (\sim p \rightarrow q)$
   c) $(p \wedge q) \vee p$

 I N V E S T I G A T E

All Possible Truth Values

Each column in a truth table gives the truth values of the statement at its top. It also contains four entries, which are either T or F. For example, the truth table in *Example 1* of this section contains the four columns shown.

T	T	F	F
T	F	F	F
F	T	T	T
F	F	T	F

1. How many different ways can you find to write the letters T and F in columns like these? Use the truth tables in the examples and the exercises of this section to help you find them.

2. Write a statement corresponding to each result you found in *Question 1*.

1-10 RELATED CONDITIONALS

Herman is buying some food in the cafeteria. Let p and q represent the following statements:

p: He wants instant coffee.
q: He has to wait.

We form the conditional $p \rightarrow q$, with the truth table below.

If he wants instant coffee, then he has to wait.   . . . ①

p	q	$p \rightarrow q$
T	T	T
T	F	F
F	T	T
F	F	T

"If you want instant coffee, you'll have to wait!"

We can write three new conditionals which are related to ① as follows.

The Converse of a Conditional

A related conditional is $q \rightarrow p$.

If he has to wait, then he wants instant coffee.   . . . ②

Statement ② is called the *converse* of statement ①. It does not have the same meaning as ① because Herman might have to wait because he wants something else which is not ready either.

Conditional:
If . . . he wants
    instant coffee
then . . . he has to
    wait.

Converse:
If . . . he has to
    wait
then . . . he wants
    instant coffee.

$p \rightarrow q$

$q \rightarrow p$

To form the converse of a conditional, interchange the hypothesis and the conclusion.

Construct a truth table for the converse and compare with the truth table above.

The truth values in the 3rd column are not the same as in the truth table for $p \rightarrow q$. For example, the 3rd row shows that statement ② is false when Herman does not want instant coffee but has to wait. The 3rd row of the table for $p \rightarrow q$ shows that statement ① is true in this case.

p	q	$q \rightarrow p$
T	T	T
T	F	T
F	T	F
F	F	T

The Inverse of a Conditional

Another related conditional is $\sim p \to \sim q$.

If he does not want instant coffee, then he does not have to wait.   . . . ③

Statement ③ is called the *inverse* of statement ①. It also does not have the same meaning as statement ①.

Conditional:
If . . . he wants instant coffee then . . . he has to wait.

Inverse:
If . . . he does not want instant coffee then . . . he does not have to wait.

$$p \to q$$
$$\sim \bigm/ \quad \sim \bigm|$$
$$\sim p \to \sim q$$

To form the inverse of a conditional, replace both the hypothesis and the conclusion with their negations.

Construct a truth table for the inverse and compare with the truth table for $p \to q$. Observe that the truth values in the last column of the truth table for $\sim p \to \sim q$ are the same as those in the table for $q \to p$. Therefore, the inverse and the converse of a conditional have the same meaning.

p	q	$\sim p$	$\sim q$	$\sim p \to \sim q$
T	T	F	F	T
T	F	F	T	T
F	T	T	F	F
F	F	T	T	T

The Contrapositive of a Conditional

Another related conditional is $\sim q \to \sim p$.

If he does not have to wait, then he does not want instant coffee.   . . . ④

Statement ④ is called the *contrapositive* of statement ①.

Conditional:
If . . . he wants instant coffee then . . . he has to wait.

Contrapositive:
If . . . he does not have to wait then . . . he does not want instant coffee

$$p \to q$$
$$\sim \times \sim$$
$$\sim q \to \sim p$$

To form the contra-positive of a cond-itional, interchange the hypothesis and the conclusion *and* replace them with their negations.

Construct a truth table for the contrapositive
and compare with the truth table for $p \to q$.
The truth values in the last column of the
truth table for $\sim q \to \sim p$ are the same as
those in the table for $p \to q$. Therefore,
the contrapositive of a conditional has the
same meaning as the conditional itself.

p	q	$\sim q$	$\sim p$	$\sim q \to \sim p$
T	T	F	F	T
T	F	T	F	F
F	T	F	T	T
F	F	T	T	T

Example. Write the converse, the inverse, and the contrapositive of the following
conditional. What is the truth value of each?

If a quadrilateral has 4 equal sides, it is a square.

Solution. The given conditional is false, as the
diagram at the right indicates. This is a
quadrilateral with 4 equal sides, but it
is not a square.
Converse: If a quadrilateral is a square, it has 4 equal sides.   True
Inverse: If a quadrilateral does not have 4 equal sides, it is not a
square.   True
Contrapositive: If a quadrilateral is not a square, it does not
have 4 equal sides.   False

EXERCISES 1-10

1. State the converse of each conditional. What are the truth values of the conditional
and its converse?
a) If you live in Cleveland, then you live in Ohio.
b) If it rained, the ground is wet.
c) If you study, you will pass the test.
d) If the light is green, it is safe to cross the street.
e) If you don't buy a ticket, you won't win the lottery.

2. State the inverse of each conditional in *Exercise 1*. What are the truth values of
the conditional and its inverse?

3. State the contrapositive of each conditional in *Exercise 1*. What are the truth values
of the conditional and its contrapositive?

4. Write the converse, the inverse, and the contrapositive of each conditional. What
are their truth values?
a) If two circles have the same radius, they have the same area.
b) If two rectangles have the same area, they have the same length.
c) If $9 + 7 = 16$, then $19 + 7 = 26$
d) If two positive numbers have a product greater than 10, then both of the numbers
are greater than 10.

5. Write the converse, the inverse, and the contrapositive of each conditional. What are their truth values?
   a) If x is a multiple of 6, then x is a multiple of 3.
   b) If x is a prime number, then $2x$ is not a prime number.
   c) If a quadrilateral has 4 right angles, it is a square.
   d) A rectangle is a parallelogram.
   e) A multiple of 4 is a multiple of 2.

6. Write the converse, the inverse, and the contrapositive of each conditional.
   a) $r \rightarrow s$ b) $r \rightarrow \sim s$ c) $\sim r \rightarrow s$ d) $\sim r \rightarrow \sim s$

7. Make a truth table with this heading. Use your table to compare the truth values of a conditional and its converse, inverse, and contrapositive.

p	q	$\sim p$	$\sim q$	Statement $p \rightarrow q$	Converse $q \rightarrow p$	Inverse $\sim p \rightarrow \sim q$	Contrapositive $\sim q \rightarrow \sim p$

8. Identify the conditional below which has the same meaning as the conditional "If a quadrilateral is a square, then it is a rectangle."
   a) If a quadrilateral is not a square, then it is not a rectangle.
   b) If a quadrilateral is a rectangle, then it is a square.
   c) If a quadrilateral is not a rectangle, then it is not a square.

9. Find two statements below which have the same meaning.
   a) If the water is warm, we are going swimming.
   b) If the water is cold, we are not going swimming.
   c) If we are going swimming, the water is warm.
   d) If we are not going swimming, the water is cold.

10. Match each statement in Column 2 with that which has the same meaning in Column 1.

    Column 1
    a) If you are early, you are lucky.
    b) If you are early, you are unlucky.
    c) If you are late, you are unlucky.
    d) If you are late, you are lucky.

    Column 2
    1) If you are lucky, you are late.
    2) If you are lucky, you are early.
    3) If you are unlucky, you are late.
    4) If you are unlucky, you are early.

11. Write an example of
    a) a true statement which has: i) a true converse   ii) a false converse
    b) a false statement which has: i) a true converse   ii) a false converse.

12. Write an example of
    a) a true statement which has: i) a true inverse   ii) a false inverse
    b) a false statement which has: i) a true inverse   ii) a false inverse.

13. If possible, write an example of
    a) a true statement which has: i) a true contrapositive   ii) a false contrapositive
    b) a false statement which has: i) a true contrapositive   ii) a false contrapositive.

MATHEMATICS AROUND US

Logic in Cartoons

Cartoons frequently contain conditionals.

QUESTIONS

1. Identify a conditional in each cartoon on this page.

2. Write the converse, the inverse, and the contrapositive of each conditional you found.

"I can start work Monday if I don't win the lottery."

MATHEMATICS AROUND US

Logical Connectives in Sports Rules

Many of the situations and the rules in sports involve the logical connectives ''and'', ''or'', and ''if . . . then''. Here are some examples from four popular sports.

Football

- If a lineman moves before the ball is snapped, a penalty is called.

- If a team scores a touchdown, they receive 6 points and they can try for a conversion.

- The penalty for an offensive lineman down-field on a passing play is 10 yards and a loss of down.

- The winner of the coin toss may choose to kick off or to receive, or may choose which end of the field his team will defend in the first quarter.

Tennis

- If the first serve misses the correct service court, the server gets a second serve.

- If the ball hits the net on a serve and falls into the correct service court, a ''let'' is called.

- Players must hit the ball either before it bounces or after it has bounced only once.

- A set is won by the player who wins at least 6 games and has a lead of at least 2 games.

Baseball

- If there is a balk, the runners advance one base.

- If the home team is ahead after $8\frac{1}{2}$ innings, the game is over.

- A pitch is a strike if the batter swings and misses.

- A pitch is a ball if it does not enter the strike zone and the batter does not swing.

Basketball

- If there is a technical foul on a coach, two free throws are awarded.

- A college team must try for a basket within 45 s of gaining control of the ball.

- A team that has control of the ball in its back court must move the ball into its front court within 10 s.

- When a violation is called before a shot is attempted the ball becomes dead, and if a basket is made it is not counted.

QUESTIONS

Choose one or more of the sports above.

1. Write the given statements using letters and the logical connectives $\wedge$, $\vee$, $\rightarrow$. Be sure to explain what the letters you use represent.

2. Use your knowledge of that sport to write some additional statements containing the logical connectives ''and'', ''or'', and ''if . . . then'' involving the sport.

1-11 BICONDITIONALS

In Section 1-4 we formed the conjunction of two statements. A very useful conjunction is the one formed by a conditional and its converse. For example, consider the following statements.

Conditional: If you have a ticket, then you are
                  admitted to the theater.   . . . ①
Converse: If you are admitted to the theater, then
                  you have a ticket.   . . . ②

We form the conjunction of statements ① and ②:

If you have a ticket you are admitted to the theater, and if you are admitted to the theater you have a ticket.

We write this more simply as follows:

You are admitted to the theater if and only if you have a ticket.   . . . ③

The conjunction of a conditional and its converse is called a *biconditional*. Statement ③ is an example of a biconditional.

　　We write $p \leftrightarrow q$ for the biconditional formed by p and q. This is read "p if and only if q". To determine the truth values of $p \leftrightarrow q$, we construct a truth table for the conjunction of the conditionals $p \rightarrow q$ and $q \rightarrow p$.

p	q	$p \rightarrow q$	$q \rightarrow p$	$(p \rightarrow q) \wedge (q \rightarrow p)$
T	T	T	T	T
T	F	F	T	F
F	T	T	F	F
F	F	T	T	T

The last column gives the truth values for the biconditional $p \leftrightarrow q$.
Observe that $p \leftrightarrow q$ is true when p and q have the same truth value, and false when p and q have different truth values.

Biconditional Truth Table

When p and q have the same truth value, the biconditional $p \leftrightarrow q$ is true.

p	q	$p \leftrightarrow q$
T	T	T
T	F	F
F	T	F
F	F	T

When p and q have different truth values, the biconditional is false.

Example 1. What is the truth value of this biconditional?

$x + 3 = 7$ if and only if $x = 4$

Solution. When $x = 4$, both $x + 3 = 7$ and $x = 4$ are true.
When $x \neq 4$, both $x + 3 = 7$ and $x = 4$ are false.
Hence, $x + 3 = 7$ and $x = 4$ always have the same truth value.
Therefore, the biconditional is true.

Example 2. Write the biconditional formed by each statement and its converse. What is the truth value of the biconditional?
a) If a quadrilateral has 4 equal sides, it is a square.
b) If $x > 5$, then $x \neq 5$.

Solution. a) If a quadrilateral has 4 equal sides, it is a square.
    Converse: If a quadrilateral is a square, it has 4 equal sides.
    Biconditional: A quadrilateral is a square if and only if it has 4 equal sides.
    The given statement is false; the converse is true. Hence, the biconditional is false.
b) If $x > 5$, then $x \neq 5$.
    Converse: If $x \neq 5$, then $x > 5$.
    Biconditional: $x > 5$ if and only if $x \neq 5$.
    If $x = 3$, the first part of the given statement is false and the second part is true; hence, according to the 3rd line of the Conditional Truth Table, the given statement is true. If $x = 3$, the converse is false. Since the statement and its converse have different truth values, the biconditional is false.

EXERCISES 1-11

Ⓐ

1. What is the truth value of each biconditional?
   a) Tomorrow is Saturday if and only if today is Friday.
   b) Yesterday was Sunday if and only if tomorrow is Tuesday.
   c) Today is March 1 if and only if yesterday was February 28.

2. What is the truth value of each biconditional?
   a) $x - 5 = 2$ if and only if $x = 7$ b) $x + 9 = 15$ if and only if $x = 6$
   c) $2n = 16$ if and only if $n = 8$ d) $2 + y = 9$ if and only if $y = 6$
   e) $2x - 1 = 9$ if and only if $x = 5$ f) $z + 1 = 5$ if and only if $z - 1 = 3$

Ⓑ

3. Write the converse of each statement. Then write the biconditional which is the conjunction of the statement and its converse. What is the truth value of the biconditional?
   a) If a triangle has three equal sides, then it is an equilateral triangle.
   b) If a polygon has exactly five sides, then it is a pentagon.
   c) If two circles have different diameters, then they have different areas.
   d) If a quadrilateral is a square, then it is a rectangle.

4. Repeat *Exercise 3* for the following statements. In each case, the variable represents a natural number.
   a) If $x + 2 = 5$, then $x = 3$ b) If $2n = 32$, then $n = 16$
   c) If $n < 10$, then $n \neq 10$ d) If $x > 7$ or $x < 7$, then $x \neq 7$

5. Let p and q represent these open sentences, where x is a natural number.
   p: x is an even number
   q: x is a multiple of 2
   a) Write the biconditional $p \leftrightarrow q$.
   b) Is the biconditional true for all natural numbers?

6. Repeat *Exercise 5* for these open sentences.
   a) p: x is a multiple of 10   b) p: x is a multiple of 5
      q: The last digit of x is 0 q: The last digit of x is 5
   c) p: x is a factor of 24   d) p: x is an odd number
      q: 24 is a multiple of x q: x is not a multiple of 2

7. Let p and q represent these open sentences.
   p: $\triangle ABC$ is a right triangle
   q: $\triangle ABC$ contains a right angle
   a) Write the biconditional $p \leftrightarrow q$.
   b) Is the biconditional true for all triangles ABC?

8. Repeat *Exercise 7* for these open sentences.
   a) p: $\triangle ABC$ is a right triangle   b) p: $\triangle RST$ is an isosceles triangle
      q: $\angle B = 90°$ q: $\triangle RST$ has two equal sides

   c) *p*: ∠JKL is a right angle
     q: ∠K = 90°
   d) *p*: △PQR is an obtuse triangle
     q: △PQR has exactly two acute angles
   e) *p*: △ABC is an equilateral triangle
     q: The perimeter of △ABC is three times the length of one of its sides
   f) *p*: Quadrilateral PQRS is a square
     q: The area of quadrilateral PQRS is the square of the length of one of its sides

9. If p is true and q is false, determine the truth value of each statement.
   a) $p \leftrightarrow \sim q$ b) $\sim p \leftrightarrow q$ c) $\sim(\sim p \leftrightarrow q)$
   d) $(p \wedge q) \leftrightarrow (q \wedge p)$ e) $(p \vee q) \leftrightarrow (q \vee p)$ f) $(p \rightarrow q) \leftrightarrow (q \rightarrow p)$

10. Construct a truth table for each statement.
   a) $(p \rightarrow q) \leftrightarrow (q \rightarrow p)$ b) $(p \rightarrow q) \leftrightarrow (\sim p \rightarrow \sim q)$
   c) $(p \rightarrow q) \leftrightarrow (\sim q \rightarrow \sim p)$ d) $(q \rightarrow p) \leftrightarrow (\sim p \rightarrow \sim q)$
   e) $(q \rightarrow p) \leftrightarrow (\sim q \rightarrow \sim p)$ f) $(\sim p \rightarrow \sim q) \leftrightarrow (\sim q \rightarrow \sim p)$

Ⓒ

11. Write the converse of each statement. Then write the biconditional which is the conjunction of the statement and its converse. What is the truth value of the biconditional? In each case, the variables represent natural numbers.
   a) If $x < 10$ or $x > 10$, then $x \neq 10$.
   b) If $x < y$ and $y < z$, then $x < z$.
   c) If n is a prime number, then n is not a composite number.

12. The two biconditionals below are the same, except that the word "exactly" has been omitted from the second one:
   A polygon is a triangle if and only if it has exactly three sides.
   A polygon is a triangle if and only if it has three sides.
Decide if these biconditionals have the same meaning.

13. a) Can a biconditional have:
     i) a converse   ii) an inverse   iii) a contrapositive?
   b) Illustrate your answers in part a) with some examples.

INVESTIGATE

Investigate if it is possible to form the following conditionals.
- The converse of the converse of a statement
- The inverse of the inverse of a statement
- The contrapositive of the contrapositive of a statement
Illustrate your answer with some examples. How are these related to the original conditional?

1-12 TAUTOLOGIES

Suppose the weather forecaster said:

"Either it is raining or it is not raining." . . . ①

The weather forecaster is correct, of course, since it is either raining or it is not raining. That is, statement ① is always true.

We can use a truth table to show that ① is always true.
Let p represent "it is raining".
Then $\sim p$ represents "it is not raining".
Therefore, statement ① can be represented by $p \vee \sim p$.

p	$\sim p$	$p \vee \sim p$
T	F	T
F	T	T

Next, suppose the weather forecaster said:

"If it is raining and the sun is shining, then it is raining." . . . ②

Like statement ①, this statement is always true. We can also show this with a truth table. Let p and q represent these statements.
p: It is raining.
q: The sun is shining.

Statement ② can be represented by $(p \wedge q) \to p$. Notice that the last column in its truth table contains only Ts. Hence, the statement $(p \wedge q) \to p$ is always true, regardless of whether or not p and q are true.

p	q	$p \wedge q$	$(p \wedge q) \to p$
T	T	T	T
T	F	F	T
F	T	F	T
F	F	F	T

Any statement that is always true is called a *tautology*. The two statements on page 46 are examples of tautologies. To determine if a statement is a tautology, construct its truth table. If the last column contains only Ts, the statement is a tautology.

Example.   Determine which statement is a tautology.

a) $[(p \rightarrow q) \land p] \rightarrow q$ b) $[(p \rightarrow q) \land q] \rightarrow p$

Solution.   Construct a truth table for each statement.

a)

p	q	$p \rightarrow q$	$(p \rightarrow q) \land p$	$[(p \rightarrow q) \land p] \rightarrow q$
T	T	T	T	T
T	F	F	F	T
F	T	T	F	T
F	F	T	F	T

Since the last column contains only Ts, the statement $[(p \rightarrow q) \land p] \rightarrow q$ is a tautology.

b)

p	q	$p \rightarrow q$	$(p \rightarrow q) \land q$	$[(p \rightarrow q) \land q] \rightarrow p$
T	T	T	T	T
T	F	F	F	T
F	T	T	T	F
F	F	T	F	T

Since the last column does not contain only Ts, the statement $[(p \rightarrow q) \land q] \rightarrow p$ is not a tautology.

We can illustrate the results of the above example using statements from everyday language. Let p and q represent these statements.

p: The water is warm.
q: We are going swimming.

Suppose that the following two statements are both true. What can we conclude?

If the water is warm, then we are going swimming.
The water is warm.

We conclude: We are going swimming.

To justify this reasoning, observe that the conjunction $(p \rightarrow q) \wedge p$ represents the two given statements. Since $[(p \rightarrow q) \wedge p] \rightarrow q$ is a tautology, we conclude q: We are going swimming.

To illustrate why $[(p \rightarrow q) \wedge q] \rightarrow p$ is *not* a tautology, suppose that these two statements are both true.

If the water is warm, then we are going swimming.
We are going swimming.

Can we conclude that the water is warm?

Observe that the conjunction $(p \rightarrow q) \wedge q$ represents the two given statements. According to the 3rd line of the truth table in *Example 1b)*, the statement $[(p \rightarrow q) \wedge q] \rightarrow p$ can be false when $(p \rightarrow q) \wedge q$ is true. In this case, p is false and q is true. That is, the water is not warm, but we still went swimming. Hence, we cannot conclude that the water is warm.

EXERCISES 1-12

1. Which of these statements are tautologies?
   a) $p \rightarrow p$ b) $p \rightarrow \sim p$ c) $p \wedge p$
   d) $p \wedge \sim p$ e) $\sim(p \wedge \sim p)$ f) $\sim(p \vee \sim p)$

2. Illustrate your answers to *Exercise 1* using the statement p: It is raining.

3. Which of these statements are tautologies?
   a) $p \rightarrow (p \vee q)$ b) $p \rightarrow (p \wedge q)$ c) $(p \vee q) \rightarrow p$

4. Illustrate your answers to *Exercise 3* using these statements.
   p: It is raining. q: The sun is shining.

Ⓑ

5. Determine which statement is a tautology.
   a) $[(p \vee q) \wedge p] \rightarrow q$ b) $[(p \vee q) \wedge \sim p] \rightarrow q$

6. Suppose that these two statements are both true.
      Marlo likes broccoli or brussels sprouts.
      Marlo likes broccoli.
   Can we conclude that Marlo likes brussels sprouts? Use a tautology to justify your answer.

7. In *Exercise 6*, what can you conclude, if anything, if the second statement is replaced with each of these statements?
   a) Marlo does not like broccoli.
   b) Marlo likes brussels sprouts.
   c) Marlo does not like brussels sprouts.

8. Given each pair of statements, what, if anything, can you conclude? Justify your answer.
   a) Gina has long hair or Gina has red hair.
      Gina does not have long hair.
   b) n is divisible by 2 or by 3.
      n is not divisible by 3.
   c) n is a factor of 12 or 20.
      n is a factor of 20.

9. Given this statement: x is a multiple of 3 or x is less than 10
   what can you conclude, if anything, if each of these statements is also true?
   a) x is a multiple of 3
   b) x is less than 10
   c) x is not a multiple of 3
   d) x is not less than 10

10. Which of the following statements are tautologies? Justify your answer.
    a) $[(p \rightarrow q) \wedge p] \rightarrow q$
    b) $[(p \rightarrow q) \wedge q] \rightarrow p$
    c) $[(p \rightarrow q) \wedge \sim p] \rightarrow \sim q$
    d) $[(p \rightarrow q) \wedge \sim q] \rightarrow \sim p$

11. Suppose that the first two statements are both true.
       If Jason lives in Otego, then Jason lives in New York State.
       Jason lives in Otego.
    Can we conclude that Jason lives in New York State? Use a tautology to justify your answer.

12. In *Exercise 11*, what can you conclude, if anything, if the second statement is replaced with each of these statements?
    a) Jason lives in New York State.
    b) Jason does not live in New York State.
    c) Jason does not live in Otego.

13. What can you conclude if each pair of statements is true? Justify your answer.
    a) If x is divisible by 4, then x is divisible by 2.
       x is divisible by 4.
    b) If x is divisible by 10, then x is divisible by 5.
       x is divisible by 5.
    c) If x is a multiple of 6, then x is even.
       x is not even.
    d) If x is a factor of 6, then x is a factor of 12.
       x is not a factor of 12.

14. This statement is true: If $x > 5$, then $x > 3$.
    What can you conclude, if anything, if each of these statements is true?
    a) $x > 5$ b) $x > 3$ c) $x \leqslant 5$ d) $x \geqslant 3$

15. Which of these statements are tautologies?
    a) $p \rightarrow \sim(p \vee \sim q)$
    b) $(p \vee q) \rightarrow (q \vee p)$
    c) $(p \wedge q) \rightarrow (p \vee q)$
    d) $[(p \rightarrow q) \wedge \sim q] \rightarrow \sim p$
    e) $[(p \vee q) \wedge \sim p] \rightarrow q$
    f) $(p \leftrightarrow q) \leftrightarrow [(p \rightarrow q) \wedge (q \rightarrow p)]$

16. Show that each statement is a tautology.
    a) $(p \rightarrow q) \leftrightarrow (\sim q \vee \sim p)$
    b) $(p \rightarrow q) \leftrightarrow \sim(p \wedge \sim q)$
    c) $\sim(p \wedge q) \leftrightarrow (\sim p \vee \sim q)$
    d) $\sim(p \vee q) \leftrightarrow (\sim p \wedge \sim q)$

17. Which tautology in *Exercise 15* contains the definition of the biconditional statement $p \leftrightarrow q$? Explain how you know.

18. Let p and q represent these statements.
    p: Marie's car is red.
    q: Marie's car has 4 doors.
    Using these statements as meanings for p and q, write statements in everyday language to illustrate each tautology in *Exercises 15* and *16*.

INVESTIGATE

Statements Which Are Always False

When we work with truth tables, we occasionally encounter a statement which is always false. Such a statement is called a *contradiction*.
1. a) Find a contradiction in the exercises above.
   b) Give an example of this contradiction using everyday language.

2. a) Write another contradiction.
   b) Give an example of this contradiction using everyday language.

THE MATHEMATICAL MIND

The Search for Truth

1

About 2350 years ago, the ancient Greeks attempted to analyze the reasoning process.

Aristotle
384 BC – 322 BC

2

Aristotle and his followers studied patterns of reasoning in examples such as this:

All people are mortal.
Pat is a person.
Conclusion: Therefore, Pat is mortal.

This form of reasoning is called a *syllogism*. Aristotle hoped to reduce all kinds of thinking to a few basic forms of syllogisms like this one.

3

In the 17th century, Gottfried Leibniz renewed the dream of Aristotle. He used symbols to represent statements, and tried to build a special language of reasoning. His plan was to reduce all kinds of thinking to a mechanical procedure. This meant that errors in thinking would appear as mistakes in computation.

Gottfried Leibniz
1646 – 1716

QUESTIONS

1. What can you conclude in each syllogism?
   a) All students like to read.
      Sue is a student.
      Conclusion: Therefore, . . .
   b) All cats can purr.
      Some animals are cats.
      Conclusion: Therefore, . . .
   c) No dogs can talk.
      Dudley is a dog.
      Conclusion: Therefore, . . .
   d) All children like spinach.
      Some people do not like spinach.
      Conclusion: Therefore, . . .

2. Leibniz's plan to reduce all kinds of thinking to a mechanical procedure using symbols was not successful. Why do you think this happened?

Review Exercises

1. Which of these sentences are statements? What is the truth value of each statement?
   a) Alaska is the largest state.
   b) Why did you come back?
   c) A week has 8 days.
   d) There are 5 odd numbers less than 10.

2. Write the negation of each open sentence. For the domain $\{1, 2, 3, 4, \ldots\}$, write the solution set of each open sentence and the solution set of the negation.
   a) $x + 5 = 9$
   b) $5 - n = 3$
   c) $x - 1 > 4$
   d) $m + 2 \leqslant 6$

3. Write the conjunction $p \wedge q$ and determine the solution set.
   a) p: x is greater than 10.
      q: x is less than 15.
   b) p: x is a factor of 12.
      q: x is a factor of 20.

4. Write the disjunction $p \vee q$ and determine the solution set.
   a) p: y is between 7 and 14.
      q: y is between 5 and 10.
   b) p: z is a factor of 6.
      q: z is a factor of 8.

5. State the hypothesis and the conclusion of each conditional. What is its truth value?
   a) If $37 \times 23 = 852$, then $370 \times 230 = 85\,200$
   b) If quadrilateral ABCD is a rectangle, then quadrilateral ABCD is a parallelogram.

6. If p is true and q is false, what is the truth value of each statement?
   a) $\sim p \rightarrow q$
   b) $\sim(p \wedge \sim q)$
   c) $(p \vee \sim q) \leftrightarrow (\sim p \vee q)$

7. If the given statement is false, what are the truth values of p and q?
   a) $p \vee q$
   b) $p \rightarrow q$
   c) $p \leftrightarrow q$
   d) $\sim(p \wedge q)$

8. If each pair of statements is true, what can you conclude? Justify your answer.
   a) If Jan comes, we will be glad.
      Jan came.
   b) If it rains, we will go to the movies.
      We did not go to the movies.

9. Complete a truth table with this heading.

p	q	$\sim p$	$\sim q$	$p \wedge \sim q$	$\sim(p \wedge \sim q)$	$p \vee q$	$\sim(p \wedge \sim q) \rightarrow (p \vee q)$

10. Construct a truth table for each statement.
    a) $[(p \vee q) \wedge p] \rightarrow q$
    b) $[p \vee (\sim p \wedge q)] \rightarrow q$
    c) $(p \wedge \sim q) \leftrightarrow (\sim p \vee q)$

11. Write the converse, the inverse, and the contrapositive of each conditional. What are their truth values?
    a) If you work hard you will succeed.
    b) If n is an even prime number, then n is less than 10.

12. Which of these statements is a tautology?
    a) $(p \rightarrow q) \rightarrow q$
    b) $[(p \vee q) \wedge \sim p] \rightarrow q$

2 Revisiting Signed Numbers

Lake Tahoe   Altitude 6300 ft
Sacramento   Altitude   300 ft

It is 50°F in Sacramento.
The temperature decreases 10°F for every 3000 ft increase in altitude. If there is precipitation at Lake Tahoe, will it be rain or snow? (See Section 2-2, *Example 6.*)

2-1 INTEGERS: THE SIMPLEST SIGNED NUMBERS

Temperatures below zero are indicated on this thermometer by *negative integers*; temperatures above zero by *positive integers*.

Newspapers publish charts of the temperatures at different places in the country at a certain time of the day.

From the chart, it can be seen that Fargo, Chicago, Denver, and Minneapolis were below zero.

Which was the coldest place?

Temperatures at 2 p.m. EST yesterday:	
	°F
Washington D.C.	30
Detroit	12
Baltimore	33
San Francisco	50
Fargo	− 16
Chicago	− 3
New York	10
Denver	− 1
Minneapolis	− 12

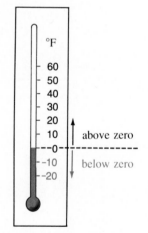

In land elevations, positive integers indicate heights *above* sea level and negative integers indicate heights *below* sea level.

The sectional drawing shows a high point of about + 220 or 220 ft above sea level The lowest point is about − 220 or 220 ft below sea level.

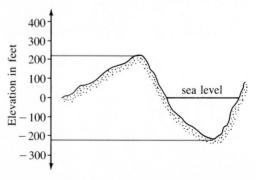

In general, numbers such as 1, 2, 3, . . . (sometimes written +1, +2, +3, . . .) are called positive integers; and numbers such as −1, −2, −3, . . . are called negative integers. The negative integers, zero, and the positive integers make up the set of integers, denoted by *I*.

$$I = \{\ldots, -3, -2, -1, 0, 1, 2, 3, \ldots\}$$

Integers such as 3 and −3 are called *opposite integers*. We say that 237 is the opposite of −237.

Integers can be represented on a number line.

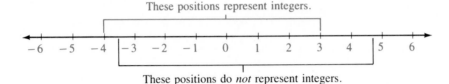

Any integer on the number line is *greater than* all the integers to its *left* and *less than* all the integers to its *right*.
For example, −2 is greater than −5. This is written −2 > −5.
Conversely, −5 is less than −2. This is written −5 < −2.

Example 1.   Compare.
a) −6 and 2   b) −5 and −1   c) 4 and −3   d) 0 and −5

Solution.   Draw a number line.

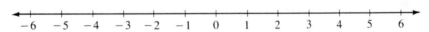

a) −6 is to the left of 2, so −6 is less than 2, or −6 < 2.
b) −5 is to the left of −1, so −5 is less than −1, or −5 < −1.
c) 4 is to the right of −3, so 4 > −3.
d) 0 is to the right of −5, so 0 > −5.

Example 2.   Arrange −5, 6, −3, −1, 0, 4, −2 in order from:
a) least to greatest   b) greatest to least.

Solution.   Draw a number line. Circle the given integers.

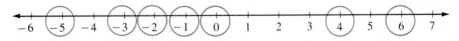

a) The integers are ordered from least to greatest when written in order
    from left to right. −5, −3, −2, −1, 0, 4, 6

b) The integers are ordered from greatest to least when written in the
    reverse order. 6, 4, 0, −1, −2, −3, −5

EXERCISES 2-1

Ⓐ

1. State which letters on this number line represent integers.

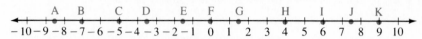

Write the integer represented by each letter.

2. Write using integers.
   a) a gain of $9
   b) a loss of $21
   c) 80°C above freezing
   d) 20°C below freezing
   e) a profit of $50
   f) a loss of $75
   g) a debt of $81
   h) a depth of 12 000 ft
   i) an altitude of 3000 ft

3. If + 100 represents a gain in altitude of 100 ft, state what these integers represent.
   a) − 300
   b) + 25
   c) − 100
   d) + 2

4. If − 5 represents a debt of $5, state what these integers represent.
   a) − 12
   b) + 7
   c) + 15
   d) − 53

5. State the opposite.
   a) a gain of $10
   b) an altitude loss of 500 ft
   c) a 3 lb loss of weight
   d) a temperature of − 14°C
   e) 18
   f) − 11
   g) the opposite of − 7
   h) the opposite of 5

Ⓑ

6. Compare.
   a) − 3 and 2
   b) 5 and − 6
   c) − 4 and − 1
   d) − 3 and 0
   e) 2 and − 5
   f) − 9 and − 1
   g) − 11 and 10
   h) − 8 and − 9

7. State the least integer.
   a) 1, − 2, 0
   b) − 6, − 3, 1
   c) − 1, 4, − 8
   d) 0, − 2, − 4
   e) 2, − 9, − 3
   f) − 5, 1, − 1
   g) − 4, 7, − 10, 1
   h) 3, − 2, 15, − 18, 7
   i) − 5, 3, 0, − 16, 17

8. Arrange in order from least to greatest.
   a) 3, − 1, 5, − 4
   b) − 2, 8, − 10, 5
   c) − 1, 4, − 8, − 2, 5, 0

9. Arrange in order from greatest to least.
   a) − 2, 7, 1, − 4
   b) − 3, 0, 2, − 1
   c) 5, − 8, − 2, 8, 0, 3

Ⓒ

10. State which integer is
    a) 3 less than 1.
    b) 2 more than − 1.
    c) 6 more than − 4.
    d) 8 less than 5.
    e) 7 more than the opposite of 3.
    f) 5 less than the opposite of − 1.

11. State which integer is
    a) 6 less than 2.
    b) 4 more than − 9.
    c) 3 more than 0.
    d) 5 less than − 2.
    e) 2 more than the opposite of − 3.
    f) 1 less than the opposite of − 1.

THE MATHEMATICAL MIND

Problems and their Solvers of Times Gone By

Some problems involving mathematics have required far more than correct arithmetic and the application of the right formulas. They have required the discovery of new principles, and the invention of special mathematical techniques. Here are three of the world's greatest mathematicians and the kinds of problems they solved.

Why does a small rock sink and a large block of wood float?

What holds up the moon?

Is there a way to send messages around the world instantly?

**Archimedes
287–212 B.C.**

**Sir Isaac Newton
1642–1727**

**Carl Friedrich Gauss
1777–1855**

Archimedes is regarded as the greatest problem solver of the ancient world. Apparently his powers of concentration were so deep that, when working on a problem, he became unaware of his surroundings. The story is told that he was in his bathtub when he discovered the principle of buoyancy. So great was his excitement that he leaped from his tub and ran through the streets naked shouting: ''Eureka! Eureka!'' (I have found it! I have found it!)

Before Isaac Newton, no one understood the idea of gravity. No one knew why the moon travels in an orbit instead of hurtling off into space or crashing to the Earth.

By the time Newton was 25 years old, he had formulated the law of gravitation and cracked the problem — a problem that had baffled scientists from the beginning of time.

Some consider Carl Friedrich Gauss to be the greatest mathematician of all time. In addition to his computer-like skill in performing mental calculations, he had an almost superhuman ability to solve problems. Though his achievements were mainly in pure mathematics, he is also known for his invention of the telegraph. This invention was a giant step forward in communications, and led the way to the development of the telephone and the radio.

2-2 ADDING AND SUBTRACTING INTEGERS

An elevator in an apartment block travels from the top floor (the 12th) to the first floor. Then it continues below ground level to the four parking levels beneath the building.

P3	P2	P1	P	1	2	3	4	5	6	7	8	9	10	11	12

Each floor can be considered as an integer on a number line.

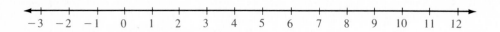

- The elevator is on the 8th floor. It goes up 2 floors. Each upward movement can be represented by a positive integer.
$$8 + (+2) = 10$$
  The elevator is then at the 10th floor.
- The elevator moves down 4 floors. Each downward movement can be represented by a negative integer.
$$10 + (-4) = 6$$
  The elevator is then at the 6th floor.

The addition of integers can be shown by moves on a number line. Start at the first integer. Move to the right for positive integers. Move to the left for negative integers

Example 1. Simplify. $(+5) + (-7) + (+3) + (-4)$

Solution. Start at $+5$.
Move 7 to the left to -2.
Move 3 to the right to 1.
Move 4 to the left to -3.

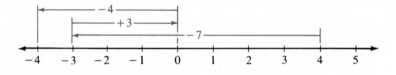

$$(+5) + (-7) + (+3) + (-4) = -3$$

To add several integers, it is easier to add the integers with the same sign first and then use the number line to obtain the final sum.

Example 2. Simplify. $(-25) + (+16) + (-11) + (-28) + (+34)$

Solution.
$$
\begin{aligned}
&(-25) + (+16) + (-11) + (-28) + (+34) \\
&= (-25) + (-11) + (-28) + (+16) + (+34) \\
&= (-64) + (+50) \\
&= -14
\end{aligned}
$$

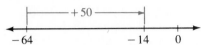

Positive integers are usually written without the positive sign. For example, the integer sum in *Example 2* could be written as $(-25) + 16 + (-11) + (-28) + 34$.

The number line is a useful device for showing addition of integers. However, after a little practice you should be able to add integers without its help.

Consider these examples of changes in height.

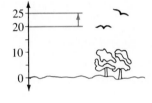

- A hawk at 20 m rises to a height of 25 m.
  Change in height = final height − initial height
  $$= 25 - 20$$
  $$= 5$$
  The hawk rose 5 m.

- A dolphin at a depth of 2 m leaps to a height of 1 m above the water surface.
  Change in height = final height − initial height
  $$= 1 - (-2)$$
  $$= 3$$
  The dolphin rose 3 m.

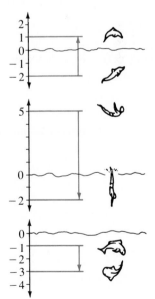

- A diver 5 m above a pool dives to a depth of 2 m.
  Change in height = final height − initial height
  $$= (-2) - (+5)$$
  $$= -7$$
  The diver dropped 7 m.

- A trout at a depth of 1 m swims to a depth of 3 m.
  Change in height = final height − initial height
  $$= (-3) - (-1)$$
  $$= -2$$
  The trout dropped 2 m.

Each example on the previous page illustrates the subtraction of one integer from another. The same results could have been obtained if each expression were written as the sum of integers.

We saw that $25 - 20 = 5$; we know that $25 + (-20) = 5$
Therefore, $25 - 20 = 25 + (-20)$

Similarly,

$1 - (-2) = 3$ but $1 + (+2) = 3$ so $1 - (-2) = 1 + (+2)$

$(-2) - (+5) = -7$ but $(-2) + (-5) = -7$ so
$(-2) - (+5) = (-2) + (-5)$

$(-3) - (-1) = -2$ but $(-3) + (+1) = -2$ so
$(-3) - (-1) = (-3) + (+1)$

This pattern suggests that adding the opposite of an integer gives the same result as subtracting the integer.

> To subtract an integer, add its opposite.

Example 3. Simplify.
   a) $(+6) - (-2)$ b) $(-7) - (+3)$ c) $7 - 9$

Solution. a) $(+6) - (-2) = (+6) + (+2)$
$$= 8$$
   b) $(-7) - (+3) = (-7) + (-3)$
$$= -10$$
   c) $7 - 9 = -2$

Frequently, expressions involving integers are written without the brackets.

Example 4. Simplify.
   a) $3 - 5 + 6 - 7$ b) $5 - 9 + 2 - 8 - 3 + 6$

Solution. a) $3 - 5 + 6 - 7$ can be written as $(+3) + (-5) + (+6) + (-7)$.
   Rearranging, $(+3) + (+6) + (-5) + (-7) = (+9) + (-12)$
$$= -3$$

   b) $5 - 9 + 2 - 8 - 3 + 6$ can be written as
   $(+5) + (-9) + (+2) + (-8) + (-3) + (+6)$
$= (+5) + (+2) + (+6) + (-9) + (-8) + (-3)$
$= (+13) + (-20)$
$= (-7)$

With practice, integer expressions can be simplified directly.

Example 5. Simplify. $-3 + 6 - 5 + 4 - 3 - 7$

Solution. $-3 + 6 - 5 + 4 - 3 - 7 = -3 - 5 - 3 - 7 + 6 + 4$
$$= -18 + 10$$
$$= -8$$

Example 6. It is 50°F in Sacramento (altitude 300 ft). The temperature decreases 10°F for every 3000 ft increase in altitude. If there is precipitation at Lake Tahoe (altitude 6300 ft), will it be rain or snow?

Solution. The difference in altitude is 6000 ft.

Therefore, the temperature at Lake Tahoe is 2(10°F), or 20°F lower than the temperature in Sacramento.

The temperature at Lake Tahoe is 50°F − 20°F = 30°F.
Any precipitation at Lake Tahoe will probably be snow.

EXERCISES 2-2

Ⓐ

1. Simplify.
   a) $(-6) + (+2)$ b) $(+8) + (-5)$ c) $(+5) + (-8)$ d) $(-3) + (+8)$
   e) $(+3) + (+2)$ f) $(-6) + (-4)$ g) $(+5) + (+3)$ h) $(+7) + (-5)$
   i) $(-4) + (+6)$ j) $(+12) + (-3)$ k) $(-5) + (+11)$ l) $(+9) + (-9)$

2. Simplify.
   a) $(-3) + (-4) + (+8)$ b) $(+2) + (-5) + (-7)$
   c) $(-2) + (-5) + (-9)$ d) $(+7) + (-8) + (+2)$
   e) $(-9) + (+3) + (+2)$ f) $(+4) + (-6) + (-2)$
   g) $(-8) + (-5) + (+7)$ h) $(-9) + (+7) + (-10)$

3. The temperature was −6°F. It is now 4°F. How much did the temperature change?

4. A balloon was 600 ft above the ground. It is now 250 ft above the ground. What is its change in altitude?

5. State the temperature change.
   a) from −12°F to 8°F   b) from −17°F to −5°F   c) from 27°F to −27°F
   d) from −6°F to 18°F   e) from 7°F to −1°F   f) from −1°F to −11°F

6. State the altitude change.
   a) from 3170 ft to 525 ft   b) from −265 ft to 425 ft
   c) from −350 ft to −580 ft   d) from −900 ft to −250 ft

7. Simplify.
   a) $(+4) - (+6)$ b) $(+7) - (+2)$ c) $(-8) - (+4)$
   d) $(+3) - (+1)$ e) $(+6) - (-1)$ f) $(-4) - (-3)$

Ⓑ

8. Simplify.
   a) $5 + (-3) + 7$ b) $(-5) + (-4) + 6$
   c) $2 + (-9) + 4$ d) $(-8) + 1 + (-2)$
   e) $(-13) + 27 + (-11)$ f) $37 + (-21) + (-52)$
   g) $18 + 39 + (-71)$ h) $(-87) + 78 + (-13)$
   i) $(-21) + (-29) + 50$ j) $91 + (-27) + 19 + (-72)$

9. a) Simplify.
     i) $(+4) + (-4)$ ii) $(-7) + (+7)$ iii) $(-36) + (+36)$
     iv) $(+81) + (-81)$ v) $(-23 + (+23)$ vi) $(-57) + (+57)$
   b) What can you conclude about the sum of an integer and its opposite?

10. Simplify.
    a) $(+45) - (-15)$ b) $(-23) - (-13)$ c) $(-14) - (+66)$
    d) $(-145) - (-35)$ e) $(+68) - (+98)$ f) $(-72) - (-42)$
    g) $(+75) - (-15)$ h) $(-187) - (-42)$ i) $(-27) - (+43)$
    j) $(+26) - (+31)$ k) $(-18) - (+42)$ l) $(+37) - (+34)$
    m) $(-29) - (-18)$ n) $(+54) - (-17)$ o) $(-99) - (+91)$

11. Simplify.
    a) $(-9) - (+2) + (-3) - (+5)$ b) $(+8) + (+4) - (+6) - (-3)$
    c) $(+8) - (+3) - (-4) - (-7)$ d) $(-6) - (-3) - (-7) + (-8)$
    e) $(-10) + (+6) - (+5) - (+7)$ f) $(+1) - (-6) - (+3) - (-4)$
    g) $(-7) + (-3) - (-5) - (+8)$ h) $(-2) - (+6) - (-4) - (+7)$

12. An elevator is at the 14th floor. It goes down 8 floors, then down 5 more floors, then up 4 floors, then down 1 floor. At which floor is the elevator now?

13. Simplify.
    a) $(-3) + (-8) - (+9) - (-7)$ b) $(+8) - (+13) + (-6) + (+3)$
    c) $(-7) - (-11) + (+3) - (+6)$ d) $(+15) - (-3) - (+11) + (-8)$
    e) $(+5) - (+10) - (+2) - (-12)$ f) $(+4) + (-5) + (-11) - (-1)$
    g) $(-9) + (+11) + (-14) - (+5)$ h) $(-16) - (+8) + (-4) - (-7)$

14. Simplify.
    a) $5 - 2 - 8 + 3 - 1$ b) $-4 + 6 + 2 - 7 - 3$
    c) $-1 - 5 + 9 - 2 + 3$ d) $7 - 2 - 6 + 4 - 8 + 2$
    e) $-3 - 9 + 1 - 5 + 7 - 4$ f) $17 - 14 - 2 + 13 - 9 - 10$
    g) $-7 - 2 + 3 - 6 + 8 - 4$ h) $14 - 11 - 8 + 12 - 2 - 14$
    i) $36 - 27 + 41 - 81 + 16$ j) $-40 - 22 + 31 + 17 - 54$

15. Simplify.
    a) $(-4 + 6) - (3 - 7)$ b) $(8 - 5) - (-4 + 6)$
    c) $(-8 + 3) + (-2 - 5)$ d) $(-9 + 4) + (-3 - 7)$
    e) $(7 - 4) + (8 - 3)$ f) $(-6 + 2) - (7 - 9)$
    g) $(8 - 6) + (9 - 4)$ h) $(-10 + 4) - (8 - 12)$
    i) $(10 - 9) + (8 - 10)$ j) $(-3 - 6) - (-1 - 8)$

16. Simplify.
    a) $(-3 + 7) + (6 - 4 + 10)$
    b) $(9 - 6 + 13) - (-4 + 5 - 11)$
    c) $(13 - 10 + 1) - (-2 - 8 + 1)$
    d) $(-15 + 18 + 4) + (12 - 3 - 13)$
    e) $(-2 - 16 + 10) + (17 + 9 - 27)$
    f) $(14 + 15 - 17) - (21 - 11 + 3)$
    g) $(18 + 21 - 32) + (-12 - 13 - 15)$

17. The lowest temperature ever recorded in Canada was −63°C in the Yukon in 1947. The highest temperature was 45°C in Saskatchewan in 1937. What is the difference between these temperatures?

18. The greatest temperature change in North America in a single day was from +7°C to −49°C in Montana. What is the difference between these temperatures?

 CALCULATOR POWER

Using the plus/minus key

If your calculator has a $\boxed{+/-}$ key, it can be used to simplify expressions involving integers.

Example 1. Simplify. $(-5) - (-20)$

Solution. Key in: $\boxed{5}$ $\boxed{+/-}$ $\boxed{-}$ $\boxed{2}$ $\boxed{0}$ $\boxed{+/-}$ $\boxed{=}$ to display 15
$(-5) - (-20) = 15$

If your calculator also has a memory, it can be used to simplify similar expressions.

Example 2. Simplify. $(-58) - (-39)$

Solution. Key in: $\boxed{CM}$ $\boxed{3}$ $\boxed{9}$ $\boxed{+/-}$ $\boxed{M+}$ $\boxed{5}$ $\boxed{8}$ $\boxed{+/-}$ $\boxed{-}$ $\boxed{RM}$ $\boxed{=}$

      ↑   ↑   ↑

    clears   adds −39   recalls −39
    memory   to memory   from memory

    to display −19
    $(-58) - (-39) = -19$

1. Use the methods of these examples to check the answers to *Exercises 7* and *10* on pages 61 and 62.

2. Modify the strategy of each example to check the answers to *Exercises 11* and *13* on page 62.

MATHEMATICS AROUND US

Times of the Day around the World

The time of day changes 1 h for every 15° difference in longitude. This means that when it is midday in London, England (0° longitude), it is midnight at the date line (180° longitude); a new day is just starting there. A place on the date line is 12 h ahead of London.

Find the date line and London, England on a globe.

Times are usually compared with the time in London.

London
England

Standard time difference in hours between London (England) and other cities					
Athens	+2	Halifax	−4	Peking	+8
Bangkok	+7	Jakarta	+7	Rome	+1
Bogota	−5	Jerusalem	+2	Santiago	−4
Brasilia	−3	Mexico City	−6	Washington	−5
Canberra	+10	Moscow	+3	Wellington	+12
Dublin	0	Ottawa	−5	Vancouver	−8

Halifax
Nova Scotia

Washington −5 means that Washington is 5 h behind London.
Moscow +3 means that Moscow is 3 h ahead of London.
Therefore, Moscow is 3 h − (−4 h) or 7 h ahead of Halifax.

QUESTIONS

1. It is 08:00 in London. State the time in each city.
   a) Ottawa   b) Mexico City   c) Jerusalem   d) Canberra

2. It is 22:00 in Jakarta. State the time in each city.
   a) Bangkok   b) Bogota   c) Wellington   d) Halifax

Moscow
U.S.S.R.

3. It is 21:00 in Ottawa. State the time in each city.
   a) Vancouver   b) Dublin   c) Washington   d) Peking

4. Team Canada is playing Moscow Selects and the game is being televised live via satellite.
   a) The game is in Moscow at 8 P.M. State the time that a viewer would be watching the game in each city.
      i) Halifax   ii) Vancouver   iii) Ottawa
   b) The game is in Toronto (the same time zone as Ottawa) at 8 P.M. State the time that a viewer in Moscow would be watching it.

5. The scenes of an earthquake in Chile are sent via television satellite from Santiago at 16:00. State the time that the transmission is received in these places.
   a) London   b) Ottawa   c) Bogota   d) Mexico City
   e) Moscow   f) Vancouver   g) Brasilia   h) Wellington

2-3 MULTIPLYING AND DIVIDING INTEGERS

To multiply integers, we must define these products.

$(+4)(+5)$ $(+4)(-5)$ $(-4)(+5)$ $(-4)(-5)$

To help us do this, we recall certain facts about multiplication of whole numbers, which is defined as repeated addition. For example, 4×5 means $5 + 5 + 5 + 5$.

The multiplication table contains patterns such as this.

The first numbers decrease by 1;		
$4 \times 5 = 20$		
$3 \times 5 = 15$		
$2 \times 5 = 10$		
$1 \times 5 = 5$	the products
$0 \times 5 = 0$	decrease by 5.

We would like integers to behave as much as possible like whole numbers. Therefore, we will extend these facts to apply to the multiplication of integers. For example, we can use repeated addition to define what we mean by $(+4)(+5)$ and $(+4)(-5)$.

$(+4)(+5)$ means $4(+5) = (+5) + (+5) + (+5) + (+5)$
$$= +20$$

$(+4)(-5)$ means $4(-5) = (-5) + (-5) + (-5) + (-5)$
$$= -20$$

To define what we mean by $(-4)(+5)$, we write the above number pattern using integers, and extend it to negative integers.

The first numbers decrease by 1;

$(+4) \times (+5) = +20$
$(+3) \times (+5) = +15$
$(+2) \times (+5) = +10$
$(+1) \times (+5) = +5$
$0 \times (+5) = 0$
$(-1) \times (+5) = -5$
$(-2) \times (+5) = -10$
$(-3) \times (+5) = -15$ the products
$(-4) \times (+5) = -20$ decrease by 5.

We see that we should define $(-4)(+5)$ to be equal to -20.
To define what we mean by $(-4)(-5)$, we use another number pattern.

The first numbers decrease by 1;

$(+4) \times (-5) = -20$
$(+3) \times (-5) = -15$
$(+2) \times (-5) = -10$
$(+1) \times (-5) = -5$
$0 \times (-5) = 0$
$(-1) \times (-5) = +5$
$(-2) \times (-5) = +10$
$(-3) \times (-5) = +15$ the products
$(-4) \times (-5) = +20$ increase by 5.

We see that we should define $(-4)(-5)$ to be equal to $+20$.

Summarizing the above results, we define the multiplication of two integers.

> The product of two integers with the same signs is positive.
> The product of two integers with different signs is negative.

These results can be illustrated in a multiplication table.

x	Positive	Negative
Positive	Positive	Negative
Negative	Negative	Positive

Example 1. Simplify.
a) $(-2)(+6)$ b) $(-7)(-8)$ c) $(+16)(-14)$

Solution. a) $(-2)(+6) = -12$
b) $(-7)(-8) = 56$
c) $(+16)(-14) = -224$

Example 2. Simplify. $(-3)(+2) - (-6)(-2)$

Solution.
$$(-3)(+2) - (-6)(-2) = (-6) - (+12)$$
$$= (-6) + (-12)$$
$$= -18$$

Division is the inverse of multiplication.
Since $7 \times 4 = 28$, then $28 \div 4 = 7$ and $28 \div 7 = 4$.
The same is true for integers.
Since $(+5)(-4) = -20$, then $(-20) \div (+5) = -4$ and $(-20) \div (-4) = +5$

Example 3. Simplify.
a) $(+6) \div (-3)$ b) $(-24) \div (-6)$

Solution. a) $(+6) \div (-3)$
Since $(-3)(-2) = 6$, then $(+6) \div (-3) = -2$
b) $(-24) \div (-6)$
Since $(-6)(+4) = -24$, then $(-24) \div (-6) = 4$

Example 4. Simplify.
a) $(+15) \div (+3)$ b) $(-20) \div (-2)$
c) $(+24) \div (-8)$ d) $(-33) \div (+3)$

Solution. a) $(+15) \div (+3) = 5$ b) $(-20) \div (-2) = 10$
c) $(+24) \div (-8) = -3$ d) $(-33) \div (+3) = -11$

The above examples suggest the following rules.

> The quotient of two integers with *like* signs is *positive*.
> The quotient of two integers with *unlike* signs is *negative*.

Example 5. Simplify.

a) $\dfrac{63}{-9}$ b) $\dfrac{-42}{-7}$ c) $\dfrac{(-8)(-9)}{3(-4)}$

Solution.

a) $\dfrac{63}{-9} = -7$ b) $\dfrac{-42}{-7} = 6$ c) $\dfrac{(-8)(-9)}{3(-4)} = \dfrac{+72}{-12}$

$$= -6$$

Example 6. Simplify. $\dfrac{(-24)}{4} - \dfrac{10}{(-2)}$

Solution. Perform the divisions before subtracting.

$$\dfrac{(-24)}{4} - \dfrac{10}{(-2)} = (-6) - (-5)$$
$$= -6 + 5$$
$$= -1$$

EXERCISES 2-3

(A)

1. Simplify.
   a) $(-5)(+6)$ b) $(+7)(-8)$ c) $(-7)(-9)$ d) $(+6)(+9)$
   e) $(-12)(+5)$ f) $(-3)(-13)$ g) $(+8)(+9)$ h) $(-5)(+5)$
   i) $(-5)(-5)$ j) $(+7)(-6)$ k) $(+3)(+4)$ l) $(-4)(-8)$
   m) $(+6)(-7)$ n) $(+4)(-7)$ o) $(+9)(+3)$ p) $(0)(-7)$

2. Simplify.
   a) $(-48) \div (+4)$ b) $(-36) \div (-4)$ c) $(+32) \div (-8)$
   d) $(-18) \div (+3)$ e) $(-60) \div (-12)$ f) $(-40) \div (-5)$

3. a) $\dfrac{-36}{4}$ b) $\dfrac{46}{-2}$ c) $\dfrac{-18}{-9}$ d) $\dfrac{-85}{5}$ e) $\dfrac{-49}{-7}$

   f) $\dfrac{81}{-9}$ g) $\dfrac{-76}{-19}$ h) $\dfrac{-121}{11}$ i) $\dfrac{132}{-12}$ j) $\dfrac{91}{13}$

4. Simplify.
   a) $\dfrac{(-4)(10)}{-8}$ b) $\dfrac{(6)(-15)}{-5}$ c) $\dfrac{(-10)(12)}{(5)(-3)}$ d) $\dfrac{(-15)(-20)}{(-10)(3)}$

   e) $\dfrac{(-50)(9)}{(15)(6)}$ f) $\dfrac{(14)(-16)}{(-8)(-7)}$ g) $\dfrac{(-5)(9)(-24)}{(-3)(4)}$ h) $\dfrac{(-6)(-8)}{(-2)(-1)(-3)}$

5. Simplify.
  a) $(-2)(+5)(-7)$
  b) $(-3)(-4)(-2)$
  c) $(+6)(-5)(+4)$
  d) $(-1)(+3)(-3)$
  e) $(+2)(-3)(-3)$
  f) $(-2)(-2)(-3)$
  g) $(+5)(-1)(-1)(-1)$
  h) $(-1)(-2)(-3)(-4)$
  i) $(-5)(+4)(+3)(-2)$

B

6. Simplify.
  a) $(-2)(+3) + (-6)(-2)$
  b) $(-4)(-3) + (-1)(-2)$
  c) $(-2)(-6) - (+5)(-2)$
  d) $(-3)(+7) - (+1)(+5)$
  e) $(-2)(+8) - (-3)(-3)$
  f) $(+4)(-7) + (-8)(+6)$
  g) $(-3)(+9) + (-2)(+7)$
  h) $(-7)(-9) - (-6)(-7)$
  i) $(-2)(-2)(+1) + (-3)(-3)(-2)$
  j) $(-5)(-2)(-2) - (+2)(-1)(-1)$

7. What must be true of two integers if their product is:
  a) positive
  b) negative
  c) zero?

8. By comparing the answers in *Exercise 5*, what appears to be true for:
  a) the product of an even number of negative numbers;
  b) the product of an odd number of negative numbers.

9. Simplify.
  a) $\dfrac{(-30)}{5} + \dfrac{15}{(-3)}$
  b) $\dfrac{(-20)}{10} + \dfrac{8}{(-2)}$
  c) $\dfrac{(-9)}{(-3)} - \dfrac{12}{4}$
  d) $\dfrac{14}{(-2)} - \dfrac{(-16)}{8}$
  e) $\dfrac{(-36)}{4} + \dfrac{(-56)}{(-8)}$
  f) $\dfrac{(-42)}{7} - \dfrac{54}{(-6)}$
  g) $\dfrac{(-63)}{(-7)} - \dfrac{(-56)}{(-8)}$
  h) $\dfrac{(-81)}{(-9)} + \dfrac{(-72)}{(-8)}$
  i) $\dfrac{35}{7} + \dfrac{48}{(-6)}$

 CALCULATOR POWER

Finding Quotient and Remainder

277 players join a football league.
16 players are needed for each team
How many teams can be formed?
How many players are left over?

Key in: 2 7 7 ÷ 1 6 = to display 17.3125
Hence, 17 teams can be formed. The remainder is 0.3125.
To display this remainder, subtract 17 from the number in the display.
Then, to display the remainder as a whole number, multiply by 16.
Key in: − 1 7 = x 1 6 = to display 5
Hence, 5 players are left over.

COMPUTER POWER

Finding Quotient and Remainder

The program below can be used to find the quotient and the remainder for any given division problem.

```
100 REM *** QUOTIENTS AND REMAINDERS ***
110 INPUT "WHAT IS THE DIVIDEND? ";A
120 INPUT "WHAT IS THE DIVISOR? ";B
130 Q=INT(A/B)
140 PRINT:PRINT "THE QUOTIENT IS ";Q
150 R=INT((A/B-Q)*B+0.1)
160 PRINT "THE REMAINDER IS ";R
170 END
```

To solve the problem on the facing page, enter the program in a computer. Type RUN and press RETURN. The computer will ask for the dividend. Enter the number 277 and press RETURN. Then the computer will ask for the divisor. Enter 16 and press RETURN. Then the computer will display this result.

```
THE QUOTIENT IS 17
THE REMAINDER IS 5
```

This indicates that 17 teams can be formed, and there will be 5 players left over.

QUESTIONS

1. Use a calculator or a computer to find each quotient and remainder.
   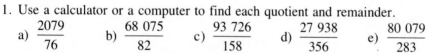
   a) $\dfrac{2079}{76}$ b) $\dfrac{68\ 075}{82}$ c) $\dfrac{93\ 726}{158}$ d) $\dfrac{27\ 938}{356}$ e) $\dfrac{80\ 079}{283}$

2. Marilyn works in a factory where she makes fruit tarts. On an 8 h shift, her team produced 136 240 tarts. These tarts are packaged in boxes of 12 tarts. The boxes are packed in cases of 24 boxes.
   a) How many cases of tarts were produced?
   b) How many boxes were left over?
   c) How many tarts were left over?

3. Use the computer program to investigate the results of using negative integers.
   a) Use a dividend of −31 and a divisor of 5.
   b) Use a dividend of 38 and a divisor of −6.
   c) Use a dividend of −33 and a divisor of −7.
   Explain the results.

PROBLEM SOLVING

Guess and Check

A theater charges for admission, as illustrated. A family of 10 paid a total of $58.00. How many children and senior citizens are in the family?

AJAX THEATER
TICKET PRICES
CHILDREN $4.00
ADULTS $10.00
SENIORS $6.00

Understand the problem
- What is the cost of a ticket for a child? an adult? a senior citizen?
- How many people are in the family?
- What was the total cost of admission?
- What are we asked to find?

Think of a strategy
- Try a guess and check strategy.

Carry out the strategy
- List a possible family of 10, for example, 4 children, 2 adults, 4 seniors.
- Calculate the admission for that family. The admission is $60, which is too high by $2.
- To decrease the admission price by $2, exchange 1 senior citizen for a child. There are 5 children, 3 senior citizens, and 2 adults in the family.

Children	Adults	Seniors	Total
4	2	4	$60

$$4(4) \ + \ 2(10) \ + \ 4(6) \ = \ 60$$

Children	Adults	Seniors	Total
5	2	3	$58

Look back
- Is there a total number of 10 people in the family?
- Is the total cost of admission $58.00?
- Is this the only possible solution?

Solve each problem

1. Ms. McCall cashed a check for $63.00. She received 6 bills, none of which was a $1 bill. What were the denominations of the bills she received?

2. An edition of the Daily Planet newspaper has its pages numbered starting at 1. The page numbers have a total of 121 digits. How many pages are in the newspaper?

3. Pietro had 20 problems for homework. His mother paid him 25¢ for each one he solved and deducted 35¢ for each one he couldn't solve. Pietro earned 80¢. How many problems was he able to solve?

4. Six darts were thrown into the dart board shown in the diagram. The total score was 211. Inside which rings did the six darts land? Is there more than one correct answer?

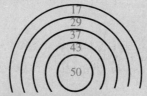

5. A gas station sells an average of 4000 L of gas per day when the price is 60¢ per litre. For each 1¢ increase in the price, the number of litres sold per day is reduced by 50 L. What price gives the greatest possible weekly revenue?

6. Erin collected $6.05 in nickels and dimes. She has 8 more dimes than nickels. How many coins does she have?

7. Minibuses seating 10, 12 or 15 passengers are used to transport hotel guests from the airport to the hotel. A hotel has 5 minibuses of each size available when a party of 120 people arrives. In how many different ways can these guests be transported using some of these minibuses if each bus used must be filled?

MATHEMATICS AROUND US

Glaciers on the Move

Glaciers are large masses of ice that move very slowly down a mountain or along a valley. They are formed when the winter snowfall exceeds the summer melting.

The Columbia Glacier (below) in Alaska is retreating because the ice is melting at the bottom faster than it comes down from above. In recent years, it has been retreating at about 2 m per day.

But the nearby Hubbard Glacier, whose source is in Canada, is now advancing, because the ice is coming down the valley faster than it melts at the bottom. It is advancing at about 3 m per day.

QUESTIONS

1. Write an integer to represent the daily change in the length of each glacier.

2. Write an expression involving multiplication of integers to represent the difference between the length of each glacier now and:
   a) 5 days from now
   b) 50 days from now
   c) 5 days ago
   d) 50 days ago.

3. Explain how the expressions in *Question 2* illustrate the rules for multiplying two integers.

2-4 WHAT ARE RATIONAL NUMBERS?

Just as integers are used to indicate change, so are positive and negative fractions.

Some newspapers publish the prices of stocks.

U.S. VALUE LEADERS				
INDUSTRIALS	Volume	Value	Last	Change
Ford M	909,900	40,263,075	$44\frac{1}{4}$	$+\frac{1}{2}$
McDnls	992,500	32,008,125	$32\frac{1}{4}$	$+\frac{7}{8}$
GenMills	296,500	20,199,062	$68\frac{1}{8}$	$+\frac{3}{4}$
KMart	457,600	15,901,600	$34\frac{3}{4}$	$+\frac{1}{4}$
Sears	521,400	9,356,975	$37\frac{1}{8}$	$+\frac{1}{4}$
Clorox	71,800	2,889,950	$34\frac{3}{4}$	
Dillard	29,900	2,051,887	$68\frac{5}{8}$	$-\frac{3}{8}$
Questar	11,100	419,025	$37\frac{1}{8}$	$-\frac{1}{4}$

On the stock market a change of $+\frac{3}{4}$ means that the price of the stock has *risen* by $\frac{3}{4}$ of a dollar, or $0.75, from the day before. A change of $-\frac{1}{4}$ means that the stock has *dropped* by $0.25 from the day before.

The stock market changes are examples of rational numbers. Rational numbers can be represented on a number line.

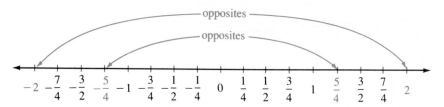

Each positive fraction has an opposite negative fraction, for example, $-\frac{1}{2}$ is the opposite of $\frac{1}{2}$. Similarly, each negative fraction has an opposite positive fraction, for example, $\frac{7}{8}$ is the opposite of $-\frac{7}{8}$.

A positive rational number like $\frac{1}{2}$ is usually written without the positive sign, but it could be written as $+\frac{1}{2}$ or as $\frac{+1}{+2}$. The rules for dividing integers suggest that it can also be written as $\dfrac{-1}{-2}$.

The rules for dividing integers also suggest that a negative rational number like $-\dfrac{1}{2}$ can be written as $\dfrac{-1}{+2}$ or as $\dfrac{+1}{-2}$. We can see why this is true by considering the product $(+2)\left(-\dfrac{1}{2}\right)$.

$$(+2)\left(-\frac{1}{2}\right) \text{ means } 2\left(-\frac{1}{2}\right) = \left(-\frac{1}{2}\right) + \left(-\frac{1}{2}\right)$$

$$= -1$$

With whole numbers, we can write, for example,

Since $(3)(4) = 12$, then $\dfrac{12}{3} = 4$

Similarly, with rational numbers,

Since $(+2)\left(-\dfrac{1}{2}\right) = -1$, then $\dfrac{-1}{+2} = -\dfrac{1}{2}$

In a similar manner, it can be shown that

$$\frac{+1}{-2} = -\frac{1}{2} \text{ and } \frac{-1}{-2} = +\frac{1}{2}.$$

Any number which can be written in the form $\dfrac{m}{n}$, where m and n are integers and $n \neq 0$, is called a *rational number*.

Example 1. State which of the following numbers are rational.

$$\frac{3}{2}, \frac{-8}{20}, 3\tfrac{1}{4}, 5, \frac{-6}{-7}, 0, 2.5, -11.27, \frac{-60}{-12}$$

Solution. Since $\dfrac{3}{2}, \dfrac{-8}{20}, \dfrac{-6}{-7}, \dfrac{-60}{-12}$ are in quotient form, we know that they are rational numbers.

Check to see if the other numbers can be written in quotient form.

$3\tfrac{1}{4} = \dfrac{13}{4}$;   5 can be written $\dfrac{5}{1}$;   0 can be written $\dfrac{0}{1}$.

Recall that 2.5 means 25 tenths or $\dfrac{25}{10}$.

-11.27 means -1127 hundredths or $-\dfrac{1127}{100}$.

All the given numbers are rational numbers.

A rational number can be reduced to lower terms by dividing the numerator and the denominator by a common factor. For example,

$$\frac{-8}{20} = -\frac{8}{20}$$
$$= -\frac{8 \div 4}{20 \div 4}$$
$$= -\frac{2}{5}$$

$$\frac{-60}{-12} = \frac{60}{12}$$
$$= \frac{60 \div 12}{12 \div 12}$$
$$= 5$$

When a rational number cannot be further simplified, it is said to be in *lowest terms* (or in *simplest form*).

The rational numbers $\frac{-8}{20}$ and $-\frac{2}{5}$ are said to be *equivalent* because they represent the same quantity. Similarly, $\frac{-60}{-12}$ and 5 are equivalent rational numbers.

Example 2. Find which of these rational numbers are equivalent.
$$\frac{18}{24}, \frac{-6}{8}, \frac{16}{-12}, \frac{-9}{-12}$$

Solution. Reduce each rational number to lowest terms.
$$\frac{18}{24} = \frac{3}{4}, \quad \frac{-6}{8} = -\frac{3}{4}, \quad \frac{16}{-12} = -\frac{4}{3}, \quad \frac{-9}{-12} = \frac{3}{4}$$

Since $\frac{18}{24}$ and $\frac{-9}{-12}$ both reduce to $\frac{3}{4}$, they are equivalent.

A rational number can be raised to higher terms by multiplying the numerator and the denominator by the same number.

Example 3. Arrange these numbers in order from least to greatest.
$$\frac{3}{4}, \frac{-2}{5}, \frac{-7}{-10}, -\frac{-9}{-20}$$

Solution. Express the rational numbers as fractions with a common denominator of 20.
$$\frac{3}{4} = \frac{3 \times 5}{4 \times 5}, \quad \frac{-2}{5} = \frac{-2 \times 4}{5 \times 4}, \quad \frac{-7}{-10} = \frac{-7 \times 2}{-10 \times 2}, \quad -\frac{-9}{-20} = \frac{-9}{20}$$
$$= \frac{15}{20} \qquad = \frac{-8}{20} \qquad = \frac{14}{20}$$

From least to greatest: $\frac{-9}{20}, \frac{-8}{20}, \frac{14}{20}, \frac{15}{20}$ or $-\frac{-9}{-20}, \frac{-2}{5}, \frac{-7}{-10}, \frac{3}{4}$

EXERCISES 2-4

Ⓐ

1. Write the rational numbers for the points indicated.

2. Compare each pair of rational numbers. Replace the comma with $>$ or $<$.

a) $\dfrac{1}{2}, \dfrac{3}{2}$ b) $-2.8, 3.1$ c) $\dfrac{7}{4}, \dfrac{-5}{4}$ d) $-1.25, 0.75$

e) $\dfrac{-13}{7}, \dfrac{5}{7}$ f) $0.01, -1.00$ g) $\dfrac{-10}{17}, \dfrac{-5}{17}$ h) $108.6, -116.8$

3. Reduce to lowest terms.

a) $\dfrac{5}{-10}$ b) $\dfrac{10}{-15}$ c) $\dfrac{-12}{-30}$ d) $-\dfrac{6}{15}$ e) $-\dfrac{-6}{11}$ f) $-\dfrac{-6}{18}$

g) $-\dfrac{4}{-14}$ h) $-\dfrac{-14}{-25}$ i) $-\dfrac{-15}{-35}$ j) $-\dfrac{-24}{-72}$ k) $-\dfrac{-42}{-28}$ l) $-\dfrac{54}{-81}$

4. Compare each pair of rational numbers. Replace the comma with $>$ or $<$.

a) $\dfrac{8}{6}, \dfrac{2}{3}$ b) $\dfrac{-7}{10}, \dfrac{-16}{20}$ c) $\dfrac{7}{5}, \dfrac{12}{5}$ d) $\dfrac{-8}{28}, \dfrac{-3}{7}$

e) $\dfrac{-110}{121}, \dfrac{9}{11}$ f) $\dfrac{-27}{24}, \dfrac{-10}{8}$ g) $\dfrac{52}{16}, \dfrac{-11}{4}$ h) $\dfrac{19}{6}, \dfrac{110}{30}$

Ⓑ

5. Round each rational number to the nearest integer.

a) -3.7 b) -5.2 c) -6.7 d) -0.4 e) 0.2 f) -0.6

g) -0.97 h) -0.35 i) -7.52 j) $-\dfrac{22}{5}$ k) $-\dfrac{67}{4}$ l) $-\dfrac{37}{5}$

6. The depths reached by divers wearing scuba gear are shown. Arrange the depths in order from greatest to least.

Diver	Depth in metres
Damont	-64.0
Giesler	-99.1
Hilton	-104.9
Trouth	-97.5

7. Write the rational number which is

a) 1 more than -3.   b) 1 less than -4.   c) 5 more than -6.

d) 7 more than -7.8.   e) 6 less than 3.5.   f) 10 less than 6.2.

g) $\dfrac{1}{2}$ more than $-\dfrac{17}{2}$.   h) $\dfrac{1}{2}$ less than $-\dfrac{3}{2}$.   i) $\dfrac{1}{2}$ less than $\dfrac{1}{4}$.

8. Compare each pair of rational numbers. Replace the comma with $>$ or $<$.

   a) $\dfrac{15}{6}, \dfrac{56}{16}$

   b) $\dfrac{-35}{15}, \dfrac{-30}{9}$

   c) $\dfrac{-72}{40}, \dfrac{72}{45}$

   d) $\dfrac{24}{44}, \dfrac{45}{55}$

   e) $\dfrac{-119}{70}, \dfrac{-57}{30}$

   f) $\dfrac{77}{28}, \dfrac{78}{32}$

   g) $\dfrac{126}{54}, \dfrac{-115}{45}$

   h) $\dfrac{-75}{35}, \dfrac{-64}{28}$

9. Reduce each set of rational numbers to lowest terms. Then list them from greatest to least.

   a) $\dfrac{28}{16}, \dfrac{30}{8}, \dfrac{33}{12}, \dfrac{15}{20}$

   b) $\dfrac{-65}{25}, \dfrac{36}{10}, \dfrac{-27}{15}, \dfrac{28}{20}$

   c) $\dfrac{34}{18}, \dfrac{-120}{54}, \dfrac{-91}{63}, \dfrac{-40}{36}$

   d) $\dfrac{-154}{49}, \dfrac{-100}{28}, \dfrac{-45}{21}, \dfrac{-22}{14}$

10. In each set, express the rational numbers with a common denominator. Then list them from least to greatest.

    a) $\dfrac{3}{2}, \dfrac{6}{5}, \dfrac{5}{4}, \dfrac{4}{3}$

    b) $\dfrac{-11}{4}, \dfrac{-8}{3}, \dfrac{-5}{2}, \dfrac{-23}{8}$

    c) $\dfrac{11}{8}, \dfrac{-3}{2}, \dfrac{-16}{10}, \dfrac{-7}{4}$

    d) $\dfrac{-29}{6}, \dfrac{21}{4}, \dfrac{-88}{18}, \dfrac{55}{12}$

11. List these rational numbers from least to greatest.

    $\dfrac{5}{-10}, \dfrac{-3}{2}, \dfrac{-7}{-28}, \dfrac{-5}{20}, -\dfrac{12}{16}, \dfrac{9}{-6}, \dfrac{10}{-8}, -\dfrac{18}{-9}$

12. List these rational numbers from greatest to least.

    $-\dfrac{3}{8}, \dfrac{-1}{3}, \dfrac{1}{-4}, -\dfrac{2}{9}, \dfrac{-7}{-18}, -\dfrac{13}{-36}$

13. List these rational numbers from least to greatest.

    $\dfrac{4}{-8}, \dfrac{-3}{-15}, \dfrac{-16}{40}, -\dfrac{19}{-60}, \dfrac{14}{30}, -\dfrac{13}{20}$

14. Find which five of these rational numbers are equivalent.

    $\dfrac{-2}{-3}, \dfrac{4}{-6}, \dfrac{-3}{4}, \dfrac{-12}{-20}, \dfrac{15}{-20}, \dfrac{12}{-16}, \dfrac{6}{-10}, \dfrac{-6}{-8}, \dfrac{-8}{-12}, \dfrac{9}{-12}$

15. If two numbers have a common factor, it is also a factor of their difference. Use this fact to determine which of these fractions are in lowest terms.

    $\dfrac{169}{182}, \dfrac{171}{188}, \dfrac{200}{201}, \dfrac{209}{247}$

16. a) Write a sentence to explain why the sum of two or more rational numbers is a rational number.

    b) Use the result in part a) to explain why any number that can be expressed as a decimal with a finite number of decimal digits is a rational number.

2-5 RATIONAL NUMBERS IN DECIMAL FORM

On the stock market, a change of $+\frac{1}{2}$ means an increase in price of $\frac{1}{2}$ a dollar or $0.50.

Consider a change of $-\frac{3}{8}$. To express this as a drop in price, $\frac{3}{8}$ of a dollar is expressed as a decimal. Divide 3 by 8.

$$
\begin{array}{r}
0.375 \\
8{\overline{\smash{\big)}\,3.000}} \\
\underline{2\,4} \\
60 \\
\underline{56} \\
40 \\
\underline{40} \\
0
\end{array}
$$

$\dfrac{3}{8} = 0.375$

The drop in price is $0.375.

The value $0.375 represents $37\frac{1}{2}$ cents. It is not possible to have $37\frac{1}{2}$ cents. However, shares are usually bought and sold in lots of 100, where a change of $37\frac{1}{2}$ cents per share would become $37.50 per 100 shares.

The decimal, 0.375, is a *terminating* decimal. After the third decimal place, the rest of the digits are zeros.
That is, $0.375 = 0.375\,000\,000\,\ldots$

This is not always the case. Consider the rational number $\frac{26}{11}$. To express this as a decimal, divide 26 by 11.

```
       2.3636
11) 26.0000
    22
    ──
    40
    33
    ──
    70
    66
    ──
    40
    33
    ──
    70
```

The remainders, after subtracting, alternate between 4 and 7. This produces a sequence of digits which repeats.

$$\frac{26}{11} = 2.3636 \ldots$$

The decimal, 2.3636 . . . , is a *repeating* decimal. It does not terminate. This decimal is written more simply as 2.3̄6̄ or 2.3̇6̇ with a line drawn over the repeating digits or periods placed over the first and last digits which repeat.

Example 1. Express $\frac{100}{7}$ as a decimal

        a) by dividing.   b) with a calculator.

Solution.   a)
```
        14.285 714
7) 100.000 000
   7
   ──
   30
   28
   ──
   20
   14
   ──
   60
   56
   ──
   40
   35
   ──
   50
   49
   ──
   10
    7
   ──
   30
```

When dividing, bring down zeros until the remainders repeat. This means that the digits in the decimal will repeat. Since there are only 7 possible remainders when dividing by 7 (namely 0, 1, 2, 3, 4, 5, 6) this decimal must repeat on or before the seventh digit.

$$\frac{100}{7} = 14.\overline{285\ 714}$$

b) $\frac{100}{7}$, with a calculator

Key in: $\boxed{1}$ $\boxed{0}$ $\boxed{0}$ $\boxed{\div}$ $\boxed{7}$ $\boxed{=}$ to display 14.285714

Since the calculator displays only 8 digits, it is not always possible to tell what the sequence of repeating digits is. See *CALCULATOR POWER*, page 84.

We can express a terminating decimal as a common fraction.

Example 2. Express these decimals as common fractions in lowest terms.

a) 3.5   b) 0.65   c) −7.4   ´d) −0.375

Solution. a) 3.5 means 35 tenths.

$$3.5 = \frac{35}{10}$$

$$= \frac{7}{2}$$

b) 0.65 means 65 hundredths.

$$0.65 = \frac{65}{100}$$

$$= \frac{13}{20}$$

c) −7.4 means −74 tenths.

$$-7.4 = \frac{-74}{10}$$

$$= -\frac{37}{5}$$

d) −0.375 means −375 thousandths.

$$-0.375 = \frac{-375}{1000}$$

$$= -\frac{15}{40}$$

$$= -\frac{3}{8}$$

Example 3. In football, the pass-completion average of a quarterback is found by dividing the number of passes completed by the number attempted.
a) Calculate the lifetime pass-completion average, to 3 decimal places, for the following quarterbacks.
b) List the averages in order from greatest to least.

	Name	Attempted Passes	Completed Passes
i)	Ken Anderson	4475	2654
ii)	Bert Jones	2551	1430
iii)	Bart Starr	3149	1808
iv)	Roger Staubach	2958	1685

Solution. a) i) Anderson's average $= \dfrac{2654}{4475}$

$$\doteq 0.593\,072\,626$$

$$= 0.593 \text{ to 3 decimal places}$$

ii) Jones' average is $\dfrac{1430}{2551}$, or 0.561 to 3 decimal places.

iii) Starr's average is $\dfrac{1808}{3149}$, or 0.574 to 3 decimal places.

iv) Staubach's average is $\dfrac{1685}{2958}$, or 0.570 to 3 decimal places.

b) From greatest to least: 0.593, 0.574, 0.570, 0.561

EXERCISES 2-5

Ⓐ

1. Write these numbers to 8 decimal places, rounding where necessary.
   a) $3.\overline{23}$ b) $42.\overline{307}$ c) $-81.4\dot{6}$ d) $690.04\overline{5}$
   e) $-2.65\dot{1}\dot{3}$ f) $2.6\dot{5}1\dot{3}$ g) $0.0\overline{69}$ h) $-0.00\dot{7}\dot{4}$

2. Write these repeating decimals, using a dot or a bar over the repeating digits.
   a) 6.3333 . . .   b) 0.17171717 . . .   c) 42.135135 . . .
   d) 0.0363636 . . .   e) -38.348348 . . .   f) -46.23333 . . .
   g) -0.717171 . . .   h) 813.813813 . . .   i) -0.0213232 . . .

3. State which of these numbers are: a) integers   b) rational numbers.
   $\dfrac{1}{12}$, -1.8, -0.611611611 . . .,   0, $2\frac{3}{4}$, $0.\overline{3}$,   7, $-13.85\overline{762}$,
   -17,   6.432432 . . .,   0.625

4. Write in decimal form.
   a) $\dfrac{3}{5}$ b) $\dfrac{2}{-3}$ c) $\dfrac{4}{9}$ d) $-\dfrac{3}{8}$ e) $\dfrac{7}{21}$ f) $\dfrac{-3}{22}$
   g) $\dfrac{15}{7}$ h) $-\dfrac{1}{6}$ i) $\dfrac{5}{16}$ j) $\dfrac{-17}{27}$ k) $\dfrac{11}{12}$ l) $\dfrac{13}{11}$

5. Express in fractional form.
   a) 0.75   b) 3.25   c) -0.625 d) 0.0625
   e) -2.75 f) -5.875 g) 16.4   h) -40.0625

Ⓑ

6. Compare each pair of rational numbers. Replace the comma with $>$ or $<$.
   a) $6.4, -\dfrac{25}{4}$ b) $-\dfrac{23}{7}, -3.5$ c) $\dfrac{3}{8}, -\dfrac{5}{11}$ d) $\dfrac{-57}{100}, -0.5$
   e) $-8.6, -\dfrac{75}{9}$ f) $-15.8, -\dfrac{76}{5}$ g) $\dfrac{51}{16}, 3.175$ h) $\dfrac{7}{11}, \dfrac{16}{25}$

7. In the hockey play-offs, a goalkeeper allowed 11 goals in 7 games. The goalkeeper for the opposing team allowed only 8 goals in the same number of games. Calculate ''the goals-against'' average, to 2 decimal places, for each goalkeeper.

8. A baseball player's batting average is found by dividing the number of hits by the number of times at bat, and rounding to 3 decimal places.
   a) Calculate the batting averages of these players.

	Batter	Year	Times at Bat	Number of Hits
i)	Hugh Duffy	1884	539	236
ii)	Ty Cobb	1911	591	248
iii)	Babe Ruth	1924	529	200
iv)	Lou Gehrig	1927	584	218
v)	Ted Williams	1941	456	185

   b) List the players in the order of their batting averages from greatest to least.

9. Arrange these fractions from greatest to least.

$$\frac{6}{7}, \quad \frac{5}{8}, \quad \frac{9}{11}, \quad \frac{10}{13}, \quad \frac{13}{15}$$

Ⓒ

10. a) Simplify $\frac{2}{3} + \frac{5}{6}$, and write the result in decimal form.

b) Write $\frac{2}{3}$ and $\frac{5}{6}$ in decimal form and find their sum. How does the result compare with that for part a)?

c) Repeat the procedure of parts a) and b) for these expressions.

   i) $\frac{3}{4} + \frac{2}{5}$

   ii) $\frac{5}{8} - \frac{1}{4}$

   iii) $\frac{1}{6} - \frac{5}{9}$

   iv) $\frac{2}{9} - \frac{5}{11}$

   v) $\frac{7}{16} + \frac{5}{12}$

   vi) $\frac{29}{37} - \frac{11}{37}$

11. Use a calculator to express these fractions in decimal form. What do you notice?

   a) $\frac{5}{173}$

   b) $\frac{50}{173}$

   c) $\frac{500}{173}$

   d) $\frac{5000}{173}$

12. Use the result of *Exercise 11* to express each fraction to as many decimal places as possible, with your calculator.

   a) $\frac{1}{810}$

   b) $\frac{6}{5293}$

   c) $\frac{6.9}{9572.6}$

   d) $\frac{2.3 \times 6.4}{168.7 \times 24.9}$

 **INVESTIGATE**

a) Use a calculator to express $\frac{1}{7}$ and $\frac{2}{7}$ as repeating decimals. The repeating decimals are the same for both fractions. They can be arranged in a circle.

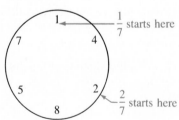

b) Find the decimal representations of $\frac{3}{7}, \frac{4}{7}, \frac{5}{7},$ and $\frac{6}{7}$. If they also fit the circle of digits, then the digits of the decimal representation of this set of fractions are said to form a *cyclic pattern*.

c) Investigate the cyclic pattern for each set of fractions.

   i) $\frac{1}{13}, \frac{2}{13}, \frac{3}{13}, \cdots$

   ii) $\frac{1}{14}, \frac{2}{14}, \frac{3}{14}, \cdots$

   iii) $\frac{1}{21}, \frac{2}{21}, \frac{3}{21}, \cdots$

COMPUTER POWER

Investigating Repeating Decimals

Since a computer is capable of repeating a sequence of steps very rapidly and accurately, it can be programmed to perform a division to any desired number of decimal places. Therefore, a computer is an ideal tool for investigating the patterns which occur when rational numbers are expressed as repeating decimals. The following program will cause the computer to print as many decimal digits as desired.

```
100 REM *** REPEATING DECIMALS ***
110 INPUT "WHAT IS THE NUMERATOR? ";N
120 INPUT "WHAT IS THE DENOMINATOR? ";D
130 INPUT "HOW MANY DECIMAL DIGITS? ";T
140 I=INT(N/D):PRINT
150 PRINT "THE DECIMAL EXPANSION TO ";T;" PLACES IS: "
160 PRINT:PRINT I;".";
170 R=N-I*D
180 FOR J=1 TO T
190    A=INT(R*10/D)
200    PRINT A;
210    R=R*10-D*A
220 NEXT J
230 END
```

To express $\dfrac{39}{17}$ as a repeating decimal, input the program. Type RUN and press RETURN . Answer each question that the computer asks and then press RETURN . Here is a sample of the output.

```
WHAT IS THE NUMERATOR? 39
WHAT IS THE DENOMINATOR? 17
HOW MANY DECIMAL DIGITS? 50
THE DECIMAL EXPANSION TO 50 PLACES IS:
2.29411764705882352941176470588235294117
647058823529
```

The result shows that $\dfrac{39}{17} = 2.\overline{2941176470588235}$

1. Express each fraction as a repeating decimal.

   a) $\dfrac{38}{23}$　　　b) $\dfrac{27}{31}$　　　c) $\dfrac{187}{84}$　　　d) $\dfrac{355}{113}$

2. Investigate the patterns in the repeating decimals for these fractions.

   a) $\dfrac{1}{19}, \dfrac{2}{19}, \dfrac{3}{19}, \ldots$ 　　　　b) $\dfrac{1}{43}, \dfrac{2}{43}, \dfrac{3}{43}, \ldots$

CALCULATOR POWER

Investigating Repeating Decimals

When a calculator is used to express a rational number in fractional form, as a decimal, all the repeating decimals may not appear in the display. This happens if the number of repeating digits exceeds the capacity of the display. For example, on a calculator with an 8-digit display:

$$\frac{4}{17} \doteq 0.2352941$$

If we use the calculator skilfully we can obtain more digits in the decimal expansion of $\frac{4}{17}$, and eventually express $\frac{4}{17}$ as a repeating decimal.

Consider the corresponding long division up to the same number of digits. The remainder at the fifth decimal place is 7, and the calculations from this point on are shaded. In fact, at this point, the division is similar to $7 \div 17$. Except for the position of the decimal point, the figures are the same.

This shows that if we use a calculator to express $\frac{7}{17}$ as a decimal, the first two decimals will be 0.41, and the rest will be the additional decimals for $\frac{4}{17}$.

```
        0.2352941
   17)4.0000000
       3 4
        60
        51
        90
        85
        50
        34
       160
       153
        70
        68
        20
        17
         3
```

```
      0.41
  17)7.00
     6 8
      20
      17
       3
```

$$\frac{7}{17} \doteq 0.4117647$$

Therefore, $\frac{4}{17} \doteq 0.235294117647$

We can obtain still more decimals if we can find a fraction having a denominator of 17 and a decimal expansion that starts with 0.47. Using a calculator, this can be found by systematic trial.

Key in: ☐1 ☐7 ☐× ☐· ☐4 ☐7 ☐= to display 7.99

This suggests that the fraction required is $\frac{8}{17}$.

Key in: ☐8 ☐÷ ☐1 ☐7 ☐= to display 0.4705882

Therefore, $\frac{4}{17} \doteq 0.235\ 294\ 117\ 647\ 058\ 82$

Now we want a fraction with a denominator of 17 and a decimal expansion that starts with 0.82.

Key in: ☐1 ☐7 ☐× ☐· ☐8 ☐2 ☐= to display 13.94

This suggests that the fraction required is $\frac{14}{17}$.

Key in: ☐1 ☐4 ☐÷ ☐1 ☐7 ☐= to display 0.82 352 94

Therefore, $\frac{4}{17} \doteq 0.235\ 294\ 117\ 647\ 058\ 823\ 529\ 4$

The final six digits are a repeat of the first six digits.
The repeating decimal is now evident.

$$\frac{4}{17} = 0.\overline{235\ 294\ 117\ 647\ 058\ 8}$$

1. Express each fraction as a repeating decimal.

   a) $\frac{4}{21}$ b) $\frac{87}{137}$ c) $\frac{23}{79}$

   d) $\frac{217}{82}$ e) $\frac{19}{84}$ f) $\frac{15}{23}$

2. Express each fraction as a repeating decimal.

   a) $\frac{100}{239}$ b) $\frac{328}{271}$ c) $\frac{55}{202}$

   d) $\frac{4762}{859}$ e) $\frac{424}{757}$ f) $\frac{155}{353}$

3. Investigate the patterns in the repeating decimals for each set of fractions.

   a) $\frac{1}{17}, \frac{2}{17}, \frac{3}{17}, \cdots$ b) $\frac{1}{41}, \frac{2}{41}, \frac{3}{41}, \cdots$

4. Investigate other repeating decimals using this method. Write a report of your findings.

2-6 MULTIPLYING AND DIVIDING RATIONAL NUMBERS

Submersibles like the Pisces III and the Aluminaut can perform numerous deep-water duties, such as search and rescue, repairing oil rigs, under-sea exploration, and scientific research. The maximum operational depth of Pisces III is −1.10 km while the Aluminaut can operate at a depth 4.5 times as great.

What is the maximum depth the Aluminaut can operate in?

Multiply to find the depth. $4.5 \times (-1.10)$

The rules for multiplying decimals and integers also apply when multiplying rational numbers.
$4.5 \times (-1.10) = -4.95$

The Aluminaut can operate to a maximum depth of −4.95 km.

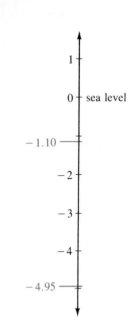

In 1 min, a diver with scuba gear can descend to a depth of −15.2 m. To secure the legs of an oil-drilling rig the diver must descend to a depth of −76 m. How long will it take to reach this depth?

Divide to find the length of time. $(-76) \div (-15.2)$

The rules for dividing decimals and integers apply when dividing rational numbers.
$(-76) \div (-15.2) = +5$

The diver will take 5 min to descend.

The rules for multiplying rational numbers in fractional form are the same as those for multiplying common fractions. The signs obey the same rules as those for multiplying integers.

Example 1. Simplify. $\left(-\dfrac{2}{3}\right)\left(-\dfrac{9}{11}\right)$

Solution. The product of an even number of negative numbers is a positive number.

$$\left(-\frac{2}{3}\right)\left(-\frac{9}{11}\right) = \frac{2}{3} \times \frac{9}{11}$$

$$= \frac{2}{\cancel{3}_{1}} \times \frac{\cancel{9}^{\,3}}{11}$$

$$= \frac{6}{11}$$

Two rational numbers with a product of 1 are called reciprocals. The reciprocal of a rational number is sometimes called its multiplicative inverse.

The *reciprocal* of any rational number $\dfrac{m}{n}$ (where $m, n \neq 0$) is

defined to be the rational number $\dfrac{n}{m}$.

Example 2. a) What is the reciprocal of $-\dfrac{2}{5}$?

b) What is the multiplicative inverse of 4?

Solution. a) Since $\left(-\dfrac{2}{5}\right)\left(-\dfrac{5}{2}\right) = +1$, the reciprocal of $-\dfrac{2}{5}$ is $-\dfrac{5}{2}$.

b) The multiplicative inverse of 4 is $\dfrac{1}{4}$.

The rule for dividing rational numbers in fractional form is the same as the rule for dividing common fractions — multiply by the reciprocal.

Example 3. Simplify. $\dfrac{25}{4} \div \left(-\dfrac{5}{8}\right)$

Solution. The reciprocal of $-\dfrac{5}{8}$ is $-\dfrac{8}{5}$.

$$\frac{25}{4} \div \left(-\frac{5}{8}\right) = \frac{25}{4} \times \left(-\frac{8}{5}\right)$$

$$= -10$$

Example 4. Simplify. a) $2.54 \times (-3.86)$ b) $(-9.0272) \div 0.52$

Solution.   a) $2.54 \times (-3.86)$

The product is negative. Use a calculator to multiply 2.54 by 3.86.

Key in: $\boxed{2}$ $\boxed{\cdot}$ $\boxed{5}$ $\boxed{4}$ $\boxed{\times}$ $\boxed{3}$ $\boxed{\cdot}$ $\boxed{8}$ $\boxed{6}$ $\boxed{=}$ to display 9.8044

Therefore, $2.54 \times (-3.86) = -9.8044$

b) $(-9.0272) \div 0.52$

The quotient is negative. Use a calculator to divide 9.0272 by 0.52.

Key in: $\boxed{9}$ $\boxed{\cdot}$ $\boxed{0}$ $\boxed{2}$ $\boxed{7}$ $\boxed{2}$ $\boxed{\div}$ $\boxed{\cdot}$ $\boxed{5}$ $\boxed{2}$ $\boxed{=}$ to display 17.36

Therefore, $(-9.0272) \div 0.52 = -17.36$

EXERCISES 2-6

(A)

1. Simplify.

a) $\dfrac{1}{2} \times \dfrac{8}{5}$ b) $\left(\dfrac{-2}{3}\right)\left(\dfrac{6}{-7}\right)$ c) $\left(\dfrac{-1}{4}\right)\left(\dfrac{-2}{-3}\right)$ d) $\left(\dfrac{-3}{-8}\right)\left(\dfrac{1}{-21}\right)$

e) $\left(\dfrac{15}{-2}\right)\left(\dfrac{-2}{45}\right)$ f) $-\left(\dfrac{-5}{12}\right)\left(\dfrac{36}{-5}\right)$ g) $\left(-\dfrac{7}{3}\right)\left(\dfrac{-6}{5}\right)$ h) $\dfrac{8}{3}\left(-\dfrac{9}{4}\right)$

2. Simplify.

a) $(7.2) \times 5$ b) $(-3) \times 6.4$ c) $(-4) \times (-0.8)$ d) $(-0.2) \times 0.6$
e) $1.3 \times (-0.5)$ f) 2.8×0.2 g) $(-1.5) \times 1.1$ h) $(-0.9) \times (-1.4)$

3. Write the multiplicative inverse for each rational number.

a) 9   b) -23 c) $\dfrac{16}{19}$ d) $-\dfrac{7}{13}$ e) -1.5 f) 0.8

g) 0.75   h) -2.5 i) $-\dfrac{1}{16}$ j) -0.6 k) -10 l) 0.01

4. Write the rational number represented by each square.

a) $\dfrac{3}{8} \times ▧ = 1$ b) $\dfrac{5}{9} \times ▧ = 1$ c) $\left(-\dfrac{4}{7}\right) \times ▧ = 1$

d) $2.5 \times ▧ = 1$ e) $\left(-\dfrac{2}{3}\right) \times ▧ = 1$ f) $\left(-\dfrac{7}{15}\right) \times ▧ = 1$

g) $\dfrac{3}{5} \times ▧ = -1$ h) $\left(-\dfrac{7}{8}\right) \times ▧ = -1$ i) $0.6 \times ▧ = -1$

5. Simplify.

a) $\dfrac{1}{8} \div \dfrac{1}{2}$ b) $\left(-\dfrac{7}{10}\right) \div \left(\dfrac{4}{-9}\right)$ c) $\left(\dfrac{5}{-8}\right) \div \left(\dfrac{-3}{-4}\right)$

d) $\left(\dfrac{-1}{5}\right) \div \left(\dfrac{8}{-15}\right)$ e) $\left(\dfrac{-8}{2}\right) \div \left(\dfrac{-4}{3}\right)$ f) $\left(-\dfrac{10}{3}\right) \div \dfrac{5}{4}$

g) $\dfrac{5}{4} \div \left(-\dfrac{5}{2}\right)$ h) $\left(-\dfrac{2}{3}\right) \div \dfrac{5}{7}$ i) $\dfrac{11}{6} \div \left(\dfrac{-7}{-12}\right)$

6. Simplify.
   a) $(-8.4) \div 2$ b) $(-3.6) \div (-4)$ c) $9.9 \div 0.3$
   d) $(-1.21) \div 1.1$ e) $16.8 \div (-0.8)$ f) $1.69 \div 0.13$
   g) $(-10.8) \div (-0.9)$ h) $0.288 \div (-0.12)$ i) $(-2.4) \div (-0.16)$

Ⓑ

7. In 1932 the record diving depth in a submersible was about 9 times as deep as the record depth of 1865. The record depth of 1865 was -74.7 m. What was the depth achieved in 1932?

8. The sperm whale is normally found at a depth of -252 m. The greatest depth that a sperm whale has reached is about 4.5 times as great as its normal depth. What depth did the whale reach?

9. Simplify.
   a) $\left(\dfrac{-18}{7}\right) \times \left(\dfrac{-21}{9}\right)$ b) $\left(\dfrac{-3}{28}\right) \div \dfrac{9}{7}$ c) $\left(\dfrac{36}{-5}\right) \times \left(\dfrac{-18}{-35}\right)$
   d) $\dfrac{4}{39} \div \left(\dfrac{-64}{13}\right)$ e) $\dfrac{9}{48} \times \left(\dfrac{-6}{16}\right)$ f) $\left(\dfrac{-15}{55}\right) \times \left(\dfrac{-2}{-11}\right)$
   g) $\left(-\dfrac{72}{7}\right) \div \left(-\dfrac{12}{49}\right)$ h) $\left(\dfrac{-75}{3}\right) \div \left(\dfrac{-15}{4}\right)$ i) $\left(-\dfrac{33}{4}\right) \times \left(\dfrac{7}{22}\right)$

10. Simplify.
    a) $(-2.38) \times 4.47$ b) $(-3.4336) \div (-9.28)$ c) $0.046 \times (-10.08)$
    d) $0.164\,15 \div (-24.5)$ e) $(-313.7) \times (-0.18)$ f) $(-106.2) \div 236$
    g) $0.000\,161\,2 \div 0.031$ h) $57.28 \times (-6.04)$ i) $6.4061 \div (-0.047)$

Ⓒ

11. Without using a calculator or simplifying the expression, replace each comma with $>$ or $<$.
    a) $\dfrac{13}{-14},\ \dfrac{-14}{13}$ b) $\dfrac{-6}{7},\ \dfrac{7}{-8}$ c) $\dfrac{-2387}{3592},\ \dfrac{-2388}{3593}$

12. Give an example of a rational number that can be expressed as a terminating decimal, and whose reciprocal can be expressed as a repeating decimal.

13. Write all the single digit numbers whose reciprocal is:
    a) a terminating decimal
    b) a repeating decimal
    c) neither a terminating decimal nor a repeating decimal.

14. Write these expressions in order from least to greatest.
    $$\left[(-25) \div \dfrac{2}{3}\right] \div \left(-\dfrac{1}{6}\right);\ -\left[(-5)^2 \div \dfrac{1}{9} \div \left(\dfrac{4}{-5}\right)\right];\ (-3)^2 \div \left[\dfrac{16}{5} \div \left(\dfrac{5}{-4}\right)^2\right]$$

2-7 ADDING AND SUBTRACTING RATIONAL NUMBERS

To swim underwater from the surface of a pool 6 m deep to the bottom
and back can be quite a challenge.

To an expert diver like Jacques Mayol, the challenge is to dive
deeper than anyone else. In 1973 he held the world's record for breath-
held diving at -85.95 m. In 1986 he still held the record but he had
reached a depth of -104.85 m.

What is the total depth descended on both dives?

Add to find the total depth. $(-85.95) + (-104.85)$

The rules for adding decimals and integers also apply when adding rational
numbers.

$(-85.95) + (-104.85) = -190.80$

Mayol descended 190.8 m on both dives.

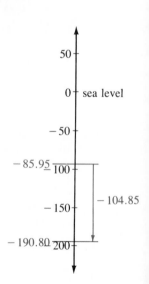

How much deeper is the 1986 record than the 1973 record?

Subtract to find the difference in depth. $(-104.85) - (-85.95)$

The rules for subtracting decimals and integers also apply when subtracting
rational numbers.

The opposite of -85.95 is $+85.95$.

Therefore, $(-104.85) - (-85.95)$ becomes

$$(-104.85) + (+85.95) = -18.90$$

The 1986 record is 18.9 m deeper than the 1973 record.

The rules for adding and subtracting rational numbers in fractional form are the same as those for adding and subtracting common fractions.

The operations are easier if rational numbers with negative denominators are first changed to their equivalents with positive denominators.

The signs obey the same rules as those for operating with integers.

Example 1. Simplify.

a) $\dfrac{3}{4} + \left(\dfrac{2}{-3}\right)$ b) $\left(\dfrac{-5}{6}\right) - \left(\dfrac{12}{-7}\right)$

Solution. a) $\dfrac{3}{4} + \left(\dfrac{2}{-3}\right) = \dfrac{3}{4} + \left(-\dfrac{2}{3}\right)$

$$= \dfrac{3}{4} - \dfrac{2}{3}$$

$$= \dfrac{9}{12} - \dfrac{8}{12}$$

$$= \dfrac{1}{12}$$

b) $\left(\dfrac{-5}{6}\right) - \left(\dfrac{12}{-7}\right) = -\dfrac{5}{6} - \left(-\dfrac{12}{7}\right)$

$$= -\dfrac{5}{6} + \dfrac{12}{7}$$

$$= -\dfrac{35}{42} + \dfrac{72}{42}$$

$$= \dfrac{37}{42}$$

Example 2. Simplify.

a) $(-0.928) + 37.089$ b) $1.37 - (-18.40)$

Solution. a) $(-0.928) + 37.089$
Rewrite the expression as $37.089 - 0.928$.
Use a calculator to subtract 0.928 from 37.089.
Key in:

| 3 | | 7 | | · | | 0 | | 8 | | 9 | | − | | · | | 9 | | 2 | | 8 | | = | to display 36.161

Therefore, $(-0.928) + 37.089 = 36.161$

b) $1.37 - (-18.40)$
Rewrite the expression as $1.37 + 18.40$.
Use a calculator to add 18.40 to 1.37.

Key in: | 1 | | · | | 3 | | 7 | | + | | 1 | | 8 | | · | | 4 | | = | to display 19.77

Therefore, $1.37 - (-18.40) = 19.77$

EXERCISES 2-7

Ⓐ

1. Simplify.

   a) $\dfrac{3}{4} + \dfrac{2}{3}$ b) $\dfrac{5}{7} - \dfrac{2}{5}$ c) $\dfrac{3}{8} - \dfrac{5}{6}$ d) $\dfrac{-5}{12} + \left(\dfrac{-3}{8}\right)$

   e) $\dfrac{2}{-9} + \dfrac{5}{6}$ f) $-\dfrac{4}{5} - \dfrac{2}{3}$ g) $\dfrac{3}{-4} - \left(\dfrac{-2}{5}\right)$ h) $-\left(\dfrac{-3}{8}\right) - \left(\dfrac{5}{-4}\right)$

2. Simplify.

   a) $(-1.7) + (-3.1)$ b) $2.8 - 5.9$ c) $(-3.6) - (-2.1)$
   d) $1.7 + (-8.9)$ e) $7.6 + 9.3$ f) $(-6.4) + 11.8$
   g) $(-8.7) - (-9.8)$ h) $(-15.6) + 23.9$ i) $36.3 - (+41.7)$

Ⓑ

3. Simplify.

   a) $-\dfrac{2}{3} + \left(\dfrac{1}{-4}\right)$ b) $-\left(\dfrac{-5}{6}\right) + \dfrac{3}{2}$ c) $\left(\dfrac{3}{-8}\right) - \dfrac{3}{4}$ d) $\dfrac{-5}{8} + \left(\dfrac{-1}{-6}\right)$

   e) $-\left(\dfrac{2}{-3}\right) - \dfrac{3}{10}$ f) $\dfrac{3}{4} - \left(\dfrac{-5}{8}\right)$ g) $\dfrac{9}{4} + \left(\dfrac{-7}{3}\right)$ h) $\dfrac{-20}{6} - \left(-\dfrac{13}{3}\right)$

4. Simplify.

   a) $\dfrac{7}{3} + \dfrac{21}{4}$ b) $\dfrac{47}{8} - \dfrac{8}{3}$ c) $\dfrac{13}{2} - \dfrac{49}{5}$ d) $\dfrac{17}{5} - \dfrac{35}{4}$

   e) $-\dfrac{14}{3} + \dfrac{12}{5}$ f) $\dfrac{9}{7} - \dfrac{9}{5}$ g) $-\dfrac{13}{5} + \dfrac{11}{6}$ h) $\dfrac{43}{3} - \dfrac{47}{7}$

5. Simplify.

   a) $-2.387 + 4.923$ b) $33.78 - (-64.35)$ c) $204.9 - 256.1$
   d) $-0.405 - 18.924$ e) $-12.37 + 8.88$ f) $-45.8 - (-327.6)$
   g) $4.29 + 563.08$ h) $84.91 - 37.08$ i) $-0.046 + (-0.104)$

6. Simplify.

   a) $\dfrac{-7}{10} - \left(\dfrac{-7}{3}\right)$ b) $\dfrac{-15}{4} - \dfrac{13}{6}$ c) $\dfrac{13}{8} + \left(\dfrac{-3}{7}\right)$

   d) $\dfrac{25}{2} - \left(-\dfrac{13}{4}\right)$ e) $\dfrac{-11}{4} + \left(\dfrac{-4}{3}\right)$ f) $\dfrac{20}{9} - \left(\dfrac{-22}{3}\right)$

   g) $-\left(-\dfrac{11}{6}\right) - \left(\dfrac{11}{-18}\right)$ h) $\dfrac{14}{-5} + \left(\dfrac{-3}{7}\right)$ i) $\dfrac{-3}{11} + \dfrac{16}{3}$

7. In 1988 the United States had a federal budget deficit of $-\$155.0$ billion. In 1989 the deficit increased by $-\$6.5$ billion over 1988.
   a) What was the total deficit at the end of 1989?
   b) In 1990 the deficit is projected to increase by $+\$69.0$ billion. What is the total deficit expected by the end of 1990?

8. The table shows the record depths achieved by a specially constructed submersible called a bathyscaphe.
   a) Calculate the difference in depth between consecutive records.
   b) Between which two dives was the difference in depth the largest?

Year	Record Depth in metres
1953	-3150.1
1954	-4049.9
1959	-5666.3
1960	-7315.2

9. Find the integer represented by each square.

a) $\dfrac{2}{5} + \dfrac{\blacksquare}{5} = \dfrac{6}{5}$

b) $\dfrac{2}{5} + \dfrac{\blacksquare}{5} = \dfrac{-6}{5}$

c) $\dfrac{3}{-7} - \dfrac{\blacksquare}{7} = \dfrac{5}{-7}$

d) $\dfrac{3}{-7} - \dfrac{\blacksquare}{7} = \dfrac{5}{7}$

e) $\dfrac{7}{8} - \dfrac{4}{\blacksquare} = \dfrac{11}{8}$

f) $\dfrac{5}{9} - \dfrac{8}{\blacksquare} = \dfrac{1}{9}$

▦ CALCULATOR POWER

Adding and Subtracting Rational Numbers in Fractional Form

Many scientific calculators will add and subtract fractions if the numbers are keyed in, in the order in which they appear.

For example, to simplify $\dfrac{2}{5} + \dfrac{3}{4}$,

key in: $\boxed{2}\ \boxed{\div}\ \boxed{5}\ \boxed{+}\ \boxed{3}\ \boxed{\div}\ \boxed{4}\ \boxed{=}$ to display 1.15
However, this is usually not the case when using a 4-function calculator. When the above sequence is keyed in, the result, 0.85, is incorrect. This is because the calculator adds 3 to the result of $2 \div 5$ before dividing by 4. However, by altering the sequence of operations, the correct result can be obtained.

Consider the sum $\dfrac{a}{b} + \dfrac{c}{d}$.

This can be written as $\dfrac{ad + bc}{bd} = \left(\dfrac{ad + bc}{b}\right)\dfrac{1}{d}$

$$= \left(\dfrac{ad}{b} + c\right)\dfrac{1}{d}$$

To simplify $\dfrac{2}{5} + \dfrac{3}{4}$,

key in: $\boxed{2}\ \boxed{\times}\ \boxed{4}\ \boxed{\div}\ \boxed{5}\ \boxed{+}\ \boxed{3}\ \boxed{\div}\ \boxed{4}\ \boxed{=}$
to display the correct result of 1.15

1. Use your calculator to simplify *Exercises 1* and *3* on page 92.

MATHEMATICS AROUND US

Niagara Falls is Moving!

The flow of water in the Niagara River is about 5700 m³/s. This great volume of water causes erosion at Niagara Falls and they moved upstream about 264 m, between the years 1700 and 1900.

Hydro-electric power plants, requiring the diversion of some of the water around the Falls, were opened in 1905, 1922, 1954, and 1960. Nowadays, as much as 75% of the water may go around, instead of over, the Falls. This has halved the rate of erosion.

QUESTIONS

1. About how far did Niagara Falls move upstream in 1800?

2. About how far does Niagara Falls move upstream each year now?

3. a) How far has Niagara Falls moved since you were born?
   b) How far will it move in your lifetime?

4. How long would it take Niagara Falls to move the length of your classroom?

5. Use the map to answer these questions.
   a) When will Niagara Falls reach the Three Sisters Islands?
   b) When was Niagara Falls at the location of the Rainbow Bridge?

6. What assumptions did you make when answering *Questions 1 to 5*?

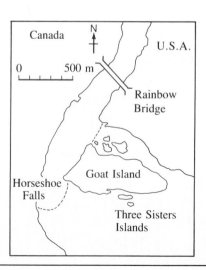

2-8 ORDER OF OPERATIONS WITH RATIONAL NUMBERS

CONTEST WINNERS
will be asked to answer correctly
the following skill-testing question.
What is the value of
$$\frac{3}{4} - \left(-\frac{1}{2}\right)\left(\frac{5}{8}\right) \div \left[\left(-\frac{1}{4}\right)\left(-\frac{1}{4}\right)\right]?$$

Merlin wrote:

$$\frac{3}{4} - \left(-\frac{1}{2}\right)\left(\frac{5}{8}\right) \div \left[\left(-\frac{1}{4}\right)\left(-\frac{1}{4}\right)\right]$$

$$= \frac{3}{4} - \left(\frac{-5}{16}\right) \div \frac{1}{16}$$

$$= \frac{3}{4} + \frac{5}{16} \div \frac{1}{16}$$

$$= \frac{17}{16} \div \frac{1}{16}$$

$$= 17$$

Jasmine wrote:

$$\frac{3}{4} - \left(-\frac{1}{2}\right)\left(\frac{5}{8}\right) \div \left[\left(-\frac{1}{4}\right)\left(-\frac{1}{4}\right)\right]$$

$$= \frac{3}{4} - \left(\frac{-5}{16}\right) \div \frac{1}{16}$$

$$= \frac{3}{4} - \left(\frac{-5}{16}\right) \times \frac{16}{1}$$

$$= \frac{3}{4} - (-5)$$

$$= \frac{3}{4} + 5$$

$$= \frac{23}{4}$$

Who is correct?
The order of operations with rational numbers is as follows:

- Operations within brackets are performed first.
- Multiplication and division are performed in order from left to right.
- Lastly, addition and subtraction are performed in order from left to right.

In the example above, Jasmine's solution is correct. Merlin made an error when he subtracted $\left(\frac{-5}{16}\right)$ from $\frac{3}{4}$ before he divided by $\frac{1}{16}$.

Example 1. Simplify. $\left(\dfrac{-9}{4}\right) \times \left(\dfrac{-10}{21}\right) \div \left(\dfrac{-45}{7}\right)$

Solution. Multiply and divide in order from left to right.

$$\left(\frac{-9}{4}\right) \times \left(\frac{-10}{21}\right) \div \left(\frac{-45}{7}\right) = \left(\frac{-9}{4}\right) \times \left(\frac{-10}{21}\right) \times \left(\frac{7}{45}\right)$$

$$= -\frac{1}{6}$$

Example 2. Simplify. $3\left(\dfrac{-5}{6}\right) + 5\left(\dfrac{-9}{8}\right) - 2\left(\dfrac{-3}{4}\right)$

Solution. Brackets imply multiplication, so perform these operations first.

$$3\left(\frac{-5}{6}\right) + 5\left(\frac{-9}{8}\right) - 2\left(\frac{-3}{4}\right) = 3\left(\frac{-5}{6}\right) + 5\left(\frac{-9}{8}\right) - 2\left(\frac{-3}{4}\right)$$

$$= \frac{-5}{2} - \frac{45}{8} + \frac{3}{2}$$

$$= -\frac{20}{8} - \frac{45}{8} + \frac{12}{8}$$

$$= -\frac{53}{8}$$

Example 3. Simplify. $3.78 - \dfrac{14.91}{4.26}(3.8 - 5.9)$

Solution. Use a calculator to do the arithmetic.
Evaluate the expression in the brackets first. Multiply and divide next.

$$3.78 - \frac{14.91}{4.26}(3.8 - 5.9) = 3.78 - \frac{14.91}{4.26}(-2.1)$$

$$= 3.78 - (-7.35)$$

$$= 3.78 + 7.35$$

$$= 11.13$$

Example 4. Simplify. $\left(-\dfrac{3}{5} + \dfrac{1}{2}\right) \times \left(-\dfrac{2}{3}\right)$

Solution. Simplify the expression in brackets first.

$$\left(-\frac{3}{5} + \frac{1}{2}\right) \times \left(-\frac{2}{3}\right) = \left(-\frac{6}{10} + \frac{5}{10}\right) \times \left(-\frac{2}{3}\right)$$

$$= \left(-\frac{1}{10}\right) \times \left(-\frac{2}{3}\right)$$

$$= \frac{1}{15}$$

EXERCISES 2-8

Ⓑ

1. Simplify.

a) $\dfrac{-2}{3} + \left(\dfrac{1}{-4}\right) - \left(\dfrac{-5}{6}\right)$

b) $\dfrac{3}{2} - \left(\dfrac{3}{-8}\right) - \dfrac{3}{4}$

c) $\dfrac{5}{-8} + \left(\dfrac{-1}{-6}\right) - \left(\dfrac{2}{-3}\right)$

d) $\dfrac{3}{-10} - \dfrac{3}{4} - \left(\dfrac{-5}{8}\right)$

e) $\dfrac{9}{4} + \dfrac{17}{3} - \dfrac{29}{6}$

f) $\dfrac{-3}{5} + \left(\dfrac{-7}{10}\right) - \dfrac{1}{2}$

g) $-\dfrac{7}{2} + \dfrac{4}{3} - \left(-\dfrac{5}{6}\right)$

h) $-\dfrac{5}{9} - \left(-\dfrac{2}{3}\right) + \left(-\dfrac{7}{6}\right)$

i) $\dfrac{13}{2} + \left(\dfrac{-2}{3}\right) - \dfrac{7}{4} + \left(\dfrac{4}{-3}\right)$

j) $\dfrac{4}{7} - \left(\dfrac{3}{-5}\right) + \left(\dfrac{-1}{2}\right) - \dfrac{3}{35}$

2. Simplify.

a) $\left(\dfrac{4}{-9}\right) \times \left(\dfrac{-21}{-32}\right) \times \left(\dfrac{-3}{14}\right)$

b) $\left(\dfrac{-10}{27}\right) \times \left(\dfrac{-8}{20}\right) \times \left(\dfrac{-45}{-28}\right)$

c) $\left(\dfrac{-6}{-25}\right) \div \left(\dfrac{-2}{-21}\right) \div \left(\dfrac{14}{-25}\right)$

d) $\left(\dfrac{12}{-39}\right) \div \left(\dfrac{-10}{-9}\right) \div \left(\dfrac{18}{-5}\right)$

e) $\left(\dfrac{15}{-32}\right) \times \left(\dfrac{-4}{5}\right) \div \left(-\dfrac{9}{16}\right)$

f) $\left(\dfrac{-12}{28}\right) \div \left(\dfrac{-8}{-15}\right) \times \left(\dfrac{-14}{-25}\right)$

g) $\dfrac{5}{2} \div \left(-\dfrac{10}{3}\right) \times \dfrac{8}{3}$

h) $\left(-\dfrac{15}{4}\right) \times \dfrac{8}{5} \div \left(-\dfrac{6}{5}\right)$

i) $\left(\dfrac{20}{-3}\right) \div \left(\dfrac{-35}{9}\right) \times \left(\dfrac{-14}{-6}\right) \div \dfrac{4}{3}$

j) $\dfrac{22}{3} \times \left(\dfrac{-6}{77}\right) \times \left(\dfrac{-3}{-2}\right) \div \left(\dfrac{2}{-7}\right)$

3. Simplify.

a) $3.7 + 0.4 - 17.6$

b) $-0.38 + 2.09 - 8.11$

c) $54.68 + (-18.07) - (+38.46)$

d) $-25.3 - (-27.9) + 60.0$

4. Simplify.

a) $(-14.6) \times (-23.7) \times 10.4$

b) $(-12.958) \div (-2.2) \div 1.9$

c) $(145.0) \times (-14.6) \div (-12.5)$

d) $(966.52) \div (-29.2) \times 0.9$

e) $(0.017\ 67) \div (-0.95) \div (-0.31)$

f) $0.08 \times (-1.03) \times 0.5$

5. Simplify.

a) $\dfrac{4}{5} \times \left[\dfrac{3}{8} + \left(\dfrac{-7}{4}\right)\right]$

b) $\left[\dfrac{-3}{7} - \left(\dfrac{-7}{2}\right)\right] \div \left(\dfrac{-7}{3}\right)$

c) $\left(\dfrac{-6}{7}\right) + \left[\dfrac{3}{4} \times \left(\dfrac{-16}{7}\right)\right]$

d) $\left[\left(\dfrac{-18}{5}\right) \div \dfrac{27}{5}\right] - \left(\dfrac{-6}{11}\right)$

e) $\left[\left(\dfrac{-5}{9}\right) - \dfrac{7}{6}\right] \times \dfrac{9}{5}$

f) $\left(\dfrac{-4}{9}\right) \div \left[\left(\dfrac{-3}{8}\right) + \left(\dfrac{-4}{3}\right)\right]$

2-9 PROPERTIES OF RATIONAL NUMBERS

Mathematics began over 6000 years ago when people attempted to use symbols to represent numbers. The first numbers grew out of attempts to count things. Today we use the symbols 1, 2, 3, . . ., to denote these counting numbers. We refer to the set of all counting numbers as the *natural numbers*. It wasn't until about A.D. 800 that the Hindus used negative integers to represent debt, and zero to represent no debt. The invention of zero and the negative integers extended the set of counting numbers to a larger set of numbers, the *integers*. The set of integers satisfies the following properties.

- Identity property for addition
  For any integer m, $m + 0 = m$
  We say that zero is the *identity element*.

- Inverse property for addition
  To every integer m, there corresponds an integer $-m$ called its *additive inverse* such that $m + (-m) = 0$
  For example, $5 + (-5) = 0$ and $-3 + 3 = 0$

- Closure property for addition
  For any pair of integers m and n, the sum $m + n$ is an integer.
  We say that the set of integers is *closed* under addition.

- Associative property for addition
  For any three integers l, m, and n, $l + (m + n) = (l + m) + n$
  That is, if we group three integers in different ways without changing their order, their sum is not changed.

Any set of numbers which satisfies the 4 properties above is said to be an *additive group*. In addition to the group properties above, the set of integers satisfies the following property:

- Commutative property for addition
  For any two integers m and n, $m + n = n + m$
  That is, the sum of two or more integers is independent of the order in which they are added.

Any set which satisfies the commutative property above is said to be *commutative under addition*.
Any set which satisfies all 5 properties above is said to be a *commutative group under addition*.

Example 1. What is the truth value of each statement?

    a) *p*: The set of natural numbers is closed under addition.

    b) *q*: The set of natural numbers has an identity element under addition.

    c) *r*: The set of natural numbers satisfies the inverse property under addition.

    d) *s*: The set of natural numbers satisfies the associative property for addition.

    e) $p \wedge q$

Solution. The set of natural numbers is the set of all positive integers $\{1, 2, 3, \ldots\}$.

    a) Since the sum of any pair of natural numbers is a natural number, then the natural numbers are closed under addition. Therefore, *p* is true.

    b) If $x + e = x$, then $e = 0$; but 0 is not a natural number. Therefore, the natural numbers have no identity element. Therefore, *q* is false.

    c) If *x* is a natural number, then $-x$ is a negative integer. But the set of natural numbers contains only positive integers. Therefore, *r* is false.

    d) For any three natural numbers *l*, *m*, and *n*,
$$l + (m + n) = (l + m) + n.$$
Therefore, the set of natural numbers satisfies the associative property. Therefore, *s* is true.

    e) Since *q* is false, the conjunction $p \wedge q$ is false.

It follows from *Example 1b)* and *c)* that the set of natural numbers is not an additive group.

Example 2. What is the truth value of each statement?

    a) *p*: For every rational number *x*, $(x)(1) = x$

    b) *q*: To every non-zero rational number *x*, there corresponds a rational number x^{-1} such that $(x)(x^{-1}) = 1$.

    c) *r*: The set of rational numbers is closed under multiplication.

    d) *s*: For any three rational numbers *x*, *y*, and *z*, $x(yz) = (xy)z$.

    e) $p \wedge q$

Solution. a) If $\dfrac{a}{b}$ is a rational number, then $\left(\dfrac{a}{b}\right)(1) = \dfrac{a \times 1}{b}$, or $\dfrac{a}{b}$

       Therefore, *p* is true.

    b) If $\dfrac{a}{b}$ is a non-zero rational number, then $\dfrac{b}{a}$ is a rational number such that $\left(\dfrac{a}{b}\right)\left(\dfrac{b}{a}\right) = 1$. That is, the reciprocal of a non-zero rational number is its multiplicative inverse.

       Hence, *q* is true.

    c) If $\dfrac{a}{b}$ and $\dfrac{c}{d}$ are rational numbers, then $\left(\dfrac{a}{b}\right)\left(\dfrac{c}{d}\right) = \dfrac{ac}{bd}$, which is a rational number. Therefore, *r* is true.

d) If $\dfrac{a}{b}, \dfrac{c}{d},$ and $\dfrac{e}{f}$ are rational numbers,

$$\text{then } \frac{a}{b}\left(\frac{c}{d} \times \frac{e}{f}\right) = \frac{ace}{bdf}$$

$$= \left(\frac{a}{b} \times \frac{c}{d}\right)\frac{e}{f}$$

Hence, s is true.

e) Since p and q are true, then $p \wedge q$ is true.

The properties in *Example 2a), b), c),* and *d)* are the group properties for multiplication. They are listed below for rational numbers.

- Identity property for multiplication
  For every rational number x, $(x)(1) = x$
  For example, $\left(\dfrac{-2}{3}\right)(1) = \dfrac{-2}{3}$

- Inverse property for multiplication
  To every non-zero rational number x, there corresponds a rational number x^{-1} such that $(x)(x^{-1}) = 1$
  For example, $\left(\dfrac{3}{5}\right)\left(\dfrac{5}{3}\right) = 1$

- Closure property for multiplication
  The set of rational numbers is closed under multiplication.

- Associative property for multiplication
  For any three rational numbers x, y, and z, $x(yz) = (xy)z$
  For example, $\dfrac{7}{10}\left(\dfrac{4}{5} \times \dfrac{3}{2}\right) = \left(\dfrac{7}{10} \times \dfrac{4}{5}\right) \times \dfrac{3}{2}$

The set of rational numbers satisfies the group properties for multiplication. We say that the set of rational numbers is a *multiplicative group*.

In addition to the group properties in *Example 2*, the set of rational numbers also satisfies the following commutative property for multiplication.

- Commutative property for multiplication
  For any two rational numbers $\dfrac{a}{b}$ and $\dfrac{c}{d}$, $\left(\dfrac{a}{b}\right)\left(\dfrac{c}{d}\right) = \left(\dfrac{c}{d}\right)\left(\dfrac{a}{b}\right)$

The operations of addition and multiplication on the rational numbers satisfy the following property.

- Distributive property
  For any rational numbers x, y, and z, $x(y + z) = xy + xz$

The distributive property indicates that to multiply the sum of y and z by x, we can multiply each of y and z by x and add the results.

Example 3. Use the distributive property to expand each expression.

  a) 24×103 b) $3(2x - 4)$

Solution.   a) $24 \times 103 = 24(100 + 3)$
  $= 24(100) + 24(3)$
  $= 2472$
  b) $3(2x - 4) = 3(2x) + 3(-4)$
  $= 6x - 12$

EXERCISES 2-9

1. What is the truth value of each statement?
   a) p: The set of integers satisfies the associative property for multiplication.
   b) q: The set of integers is closed under multiplication.
   c) r: The set of integers has an identity element for multiplication.
   d) $p \wedge q$
   e) s: The set of integers is a multiplicative group.

2. What is the truth value of each statement?
   a) p: $2.37 \times 8.59 = 8.59 \times 2.37$
   b) q: $7(13 - 5) = 7(13) - 7(5)$
   c) r: $4(3) - 4(5) = (5 - 3)4$
   d) $p \wedge q$
   e) $p \wedge r$
   f) $q \vee r$

B

3. W, the set of whole numbers, is the set of all non-negative integers. That is,
   $W = \{0, 1, 2, 3, \ldots\}$
   a) Is W closed under addition?
   b) Does W have an identity element for addition?
   c) Is W an additive group? Why?

4. E is the set of even integers; that is,
   $E = \{\ldots, -6, -4, -2, 0, 2, 4, 6, \ldots\}$.
   a) Is E closed under addition?
   b) Does E have an identity element for addition?
   c) Does E satisfy the inverse property for addition?
   d) Is E an additive group? Why?
   e) Is E commutative under addition?

5. Repeat *Exercise 4* for the set of rational numbers.

6. S is the set of perfect squares; that is, S = {0, 1, 4, 9, 16, 25, . . .}
   a) Is S closed under addition?
   b) Is S closed under multiplication?
   c) Does S have an identity element for multiplication?
   d) Is S a multiplicative group? Why?

7. P denotes the set of positive rational numbers. What is the truth value of each statement?
   a) p: P is closed under multiplication.
   b) q: P has an identity element for multiplication.
   c) r: P satisfies the inverse property for multiplication.
   d) $p \wedge q$
   e) s: P is a multiplicative group.   f) t: P is an additive group.

8. Use the distributive property to evaluate each expression.
   a) 36(50 + 5)   b) 48(91) − 48(90)
   c) 45(100 − 2)   d) 29(126) − 29(124)
   e) 147(389) − (399)147   f) 999 × 49

9. Use the distributive property to simplify each expression.
   a) 3 × 7π − 5 × 7π   b) 12(100π − π)
   c) 99π × 15   d) 8(9x − 6) − 7(9x − 6)

10. Use the diagram to verify the distributive property.
    a) Write an expression for the area of rectangle AEFD.
    b) Write an expression for the area of rectangle EBCF.
    c) Write an expression for the area of rectangle ABCD.
    d) Use your expressions to write an equation which states
       Area ABCD = Area AEFD + Area EBCF

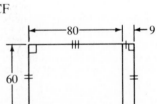

11. Apply the distributive property to multiply 60 × 89. That is, use the diagram to evaluate the areas of the smaller rectangles, then add them.

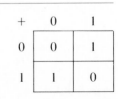

Ⓒ

12. Let Z_2 denote the set {0, 1} on which addition is defined by this table.
    a) Is Z_2 closed under addition?
    b) Is 0 an identity element for addition?
    c) Does Z_2 satisfy the inverse property for addition?
    d) Is Z_2 an additive group? Explain.

+	0	1
0	0	1
1	1	0

Review Exercises

1. Simplify.
   a) $(-4) + (+3) + (-5)$ b) $(+2) + (-7) + (-4)$
   c) $(-43) + (-17) + (+5)$ d) $(-39) + (+10) + (+31)$
   e) $(-91) + (+13) + (-26)$ f) $(-7) + (+104) + (-110)$

2. The greatest temperature variation in a single day in Alberta's chinook belt was from $17°$ C to $-28°C$. What was the change in temperature?

3. Simplify.
   a) $(+7) - (+4)$ b) $(-8) - (+2)$ c) $(-9) - (-2)$ d) $(+5) - (-2)$
   e) $(-7) - (-2)$ f) $(+8) - (-5)$ g) $(+6) - (-3)$ h) $(-5) - (+5)$

4. Simplify.
   a) $(-8) - (+3) + (-5) - (+7)$ b) $(-14) - (+12) - (+3)$
   c) $(-103) - (+27) - (-100)$ d) $(+283) - (-20) + (-60)$
   e) $(+70) - (+90) - (-100)$ f) $(-100) + (-70) - (+20)$
   g) $(-30) - (-72) + (-43)$ h) $(+981) - (-19) - (+891)$

5. Simplify.
   a) $(-8 + 5) - (17 - 9)$ b) $(-30 - 20) - (-20 - 30)$
   c) $(93 - 84) - (-67 + 89)$ d) $(-9 - 17) - (11 - 27)$

6. Simplify.
   a) $(-6)(+3)(-4)$ b) $(-8)(-2)(+7)$ c) $(+6)(+5)(+3)$ d) $(-8)(-2)(-3)$
   e) $(+5)(-3)(-4)$ f) $(-7)(-2)(-5)$ g) $(-9)(+9)(-9)$ h) $(+2)(-3)(+4)$

7. Simplify.
   a) $(-2)(-3)(-4)(-5)$ b) $(+8)(-2)(+6)(-3)$ c) $(-5)(+8)(-2)(-10)$
   d) $(+6)(+7)(-2)(0)$ e) $(-1)(+1)(+2)(+9)$ f) $(+5)(+5)(+4)(+4)$

8. Simplify.
   a) $(-16) \div (+4)$ b) $(-18) \div (-9)$ c) $(-48) \div (-16)$
   d) $(+81) \div (-3)$ e) $(-64) \div (-8)$ f) $(-54) \div (+18)$
   g) $(-108) \div (+36)$ h) $(+121) \div (-11)$ i) $(-144) \div (-9)$

9. Simplify.
   a) $\dfrac{(-8)(-12)}{(-24)(-4)}$ b) $\dfrac{(-5)(+39)}{(-13)(-3)}$ c) $\dfrac{(+121)(-7)}{(+77)(-11)}$ d) $\dfrac{(-42)(+6)}{(+14)(-9)}$
   e) $\dfrac{(+65)(-15)}{(+25)(+3)}$ f) $\dfrac{(+85)(+70)}{(-50)(-17)}$ g) $\dfrac{(-51)(-91)}{(-13)(-17)}$ h) $\dfrac{(+92)(+42)}{(+28)(-69)}$

10. Simplify.
    a) $\dfrac{(-40)}{5} + \dfrac{18}{(-6)}$ b) $\dfrac{(-42)}{6} - \dfrac{(-63)}{7}$ c) $\dfrac{42}{(-3)} + \dfrac{(-42)}{7}$
    d) $\dfrac{(-49)}{7} - \dfrac{26}{(-13)}$ e) $\dfrac{(-96)}{(-16)} - \dfrac{132}{12}$ f) $\dfrac{85}{17} + \dfrac{(-95)}{19}$

11. Express each rational number as a decimal.
    a) $\dfrac{3}{8}$
    b) $\dfrac{-4}{7}$
    c) $\dfrac{7}{-12}$
    d) $\dfrac{20}{9}$
    e) $-\dfrac{35}{16}$
    f) $\dfrac{2}{3}$

12. Express each decimal as a fraction in lowest terms.
    a) -1.5
    b) 20.25
    c) 2.007
    d) -41.6
    e) 10.75
    f) -3.875

13. Simplify.
    a) $-\dfrac{2}{3} \times \dfrac{7}{8}$
    b) $\left(\dfrac{5}{-8}\right)\left(\dfrac{-9}{12}\right)$
    c) $\left(\dfrac{3}{-5}\right)\left(\dfrac{-7}{-8}\right)$
    d) $\left(\dfrac{13}{15}\right)\left(\dfrac{30}{-39}\right)$
    e) $\left(-\dfrac{6}{5}\right)\left(\dfrac{12}{-15}\right)\left(\dfrac{-25}{36}\right)$
    f) $\left(\dfrac{8}{13}\right)\left(-\dfrac{6}{5}\right)\left(\dfrac{-4}{7}\right)$

14. Simplify.
    a) $\dfrac{3}{7} \div \left(\dfrac{-9}{14}\right)$
    b) $-\dfrac{13}{4} \div \left(\dfrac{2}{-3}\right)$
    c) $\dfrac{7}{-8} \div \left(-\dfrac{9}{4}\right)$
    d) $\dfrac{-24}{-35} \div \left(\dfrac{16}{-21}\right) \div \dfrac{9}{10}$

15. Simplify.
    a) $(-56.28) \times (0.09)$
    b) $(14.46) \div (-24.1)$
    c) $(143.7) \times (-206.8)$
    d) $(-1433.36) \div (43.7)$
    e) $(-7.9808) \div (-92.8)$
    f) $(-0.029) \times (-33.370)$

16. Simplify.
    a) $\dfrac{3}{5} + \dfrac{4}{7}$
    b) $\dfrac{5}{12} + \dfrac{3}{8}$
    c) $\dfrac{2}{9} + \dfrac{7}{12}$
    d) $\dfrac{3}{11} + \left(\dfrac{-5}{11}\right)$
    e) $\dfrac{17}{-20} - \left(\dfrac{-12}{20}\right)$
    f) $\dfrac{-7}{8} - \left(\dfrac{-1}{4}\right)$
    g) $\dfrac{9}{11} - \left(\dfrac{-3}{5}\right)$
    h) $-\dfrac{16}{5} - \left(-\dfrac{7}{4}\right)$

17. Simplify.
    a) $\left(\dfrac{3}{4}\right)\left(\dfrac{1}{-2}\right) + \left(\dfrac{5}{6}\right)\left(\dfrac{-1}{3}\right)$

    b) $\dfrac{3}{8} \times \dfrac{2}{3} - \left(\dfrac{1}{2}\right)\left(\dfrac{-5}{6}\right) + \left(\dfrac{3}{5}\right)\left(\dfrac{3}{-4}\right)$

    c) $\left[\dfrac{5}{2} \div \left(\dfrac{-4}{5}\right)\right] - \left(\dfrac{3}{-4}\right)\left(\dfrac{-8}{9}\right)$

18. O denotes the set of odd integers; that is, O = $\{..., -5, -3, -1, 1, 3, 5, ...\}$.
    What is the truth value of each statement?
    a) p: O is closed under addition.
    b) q: O is closed under multiplication.
    c) $p \wedge q$
    d) $p \vee q$
    e) $\sim p$
    f) $\sim q$
    g) $\sim q \wedge \sim p$

3 From Arithmetic to Algebra

A 4 m log is cut into 2 pieces. Suppose you knew the length of one piece. How could you find the length of the other piece? (See Section 3-5, *Example 1*.)

3-1 WHAT IS ALGEBRA?

A group of grade 9 students decided to participate in Junior Achievement. This involves setting up and running a business. The students decided to make trivets. After a few weeks, the students had a meeting to look at their sales figures. Here is a chart showing the sales for the first 3 weeks.

Trivets Sold	50	70	40
Profit	$300	$420	$240

How could the students calculate their profit if they knew how many trivets they sold?

We need to find a general rule relating the number of trivets sold and the profit. Notice that the profit in dollars is six times the number of trivets sold.

If we let t represent the number of trivets sold, then the profit is $6t$ dollars. This profit of $6t$ dollars represents many different amounts of money. Each amount depends on a value of t, which can vary. For this reason, t is called a *variable*.

The use of a letter to represent a number is the basis of *algebra*. Algebra is used to express patterns in arithmetic, in a general way.

Example 1. Suppose this pattern were continued.

a) How many toothpicks would be needed to make 10 triangles?
b) How could the number of toothpicks be found if the number of triangles were known?

Solution. a) Identify the pattern. The number of triangles in a figure coincides with its position in the pattern. For example, the third figure has 3 triangles. Every triangle has 3 sides but adjacent triangles have a common side. In any figure, there is 1 toothpick to begin the pattern and each triangle adds 2 toothpicks. Therefore, to make 10 triangles, we would need 1 + 2(10) or 21 toothpicks.

b) For any number of triangles, we need to *generalize* the pattern found in part a). That is, the number of toothpicks is 1 more than twice the number of triangles.

If the pattern were to continue, how many toothpicks would there be on the 150th figure?

Example 2. A rectangle has a length of 16 cm.
a) Calculate the perimeter of the rectangle if its width is:
i) 10 cm   ii) 8 cm   iii) 5 cm.
b) How could the perimeter of the rectangle be found if its width were known?
c) Write an expression for the perimeter of the rectangle in terms of a variable.

Solution. Draw a diagram.

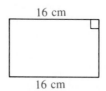

16 cm

16 cm

a) The perimeter is the distance around a rectangle.
i) The width is 10 cm so the perimeter is [2(10) + 2(16)] cm or 52 cm.
ii) The width is 8 cm so the perimeter is [2(8) + 32] cm or 48 cm.
iii) The width is 5 cm so the perimeter is [2(5) + 32] cm or 42 cm.
b) To find the perimeter for any width, look for a pattern in part a) of the solution.
The perimeter is the sum of twice the width, and 32.
c) Let *w* represent the width of the rectangle. Then, the perimeter is (2*w* + 32) centimetres.

EXERCISES 3-1

Ⓐ

1. Suppose this pattern were continued.

    a) How many regions would there be in the 14th circle?
    b) If the position of the circle in the pattern were known, how could the number of regions be found?

2. Suppose this pattern were continued.

    a) On the 8th figure, how many squares are: i) shaded ii) unshaded?
    b) How could the number of unshaded squares be found if the number of shaded squares were known?

3. Suppose this pattern were continued.

X	OX	OOX	OOOX
	XO	OXO	OOXO
		XOO	OXOO
			XOOO

    a) On the 20th diagram, how many:
      i) Xs are there   ii) Os are there?
    b) On any diagram, how could the number of Os be found if the number of Xs were known?
    c) Let *a* represent the number of Xs. Write an expression for the corresponding number of Os.

Ⓑ

4. A series of cubes are placed together as shown. The total number of faces that show are counted.

  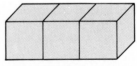

     5 faces   8 faces   11 faces

Suppose this pattern were to continue.
a) How many faces would show on the 12th diagram?
b) How many faces would show on the 30th diagram?
c) If the number of cubes were known, how could the number of faces be found?
d) Write an expression for the number of faces in terms of the number of cubes.

5. Suppose this pattern were continued.

a) How many shaded squares would there be on the 12th diagram?
b) How many unshaded squares would there be on the 12th diagram?
c) If the position of the diagram in the pattern were known, how could:
   i) the number of shaded squares be found
   ii) the number of unshaded squares be found?
d) Write an expression for the number of shaded squares in terms of the position of the diagram.

Ⓒ──

6. Suppose this pattern were continued.

```
                              O
              O              OO
O            OO             OOO
XX           XXX            XXXX
```

a) How many Xs would there be on the 10th diagram?
b) How many Os would there be on the 10th diagram?
c) If the number of Xs were known, how could the number of Os be found?
d) Write an expression for the number of Os in terms of the number of Xs.

7. Suppose this pattern were continued.

   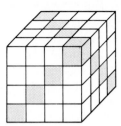

The cubes along one diagonal of each face of a cube are colored, as shown, including the diagonals of the faces that can't be seen.
a) How many cubes are colored on the 5th diagram?
b) How many cubes are plain on the 10th diagram?
c) If the position of the diagram in the pattern were known, how could:
   i) the number of colored cubes be found
   ii) the number of plain cubes be found?

3-2 SUBSTITUTING IN ALGEBRAIC EXPRESSIONS

In hockey standings, 2 points are given for a win and 1 point is given for a tie. Suppose you knew the numbers of wins and ties that a hockey team had in a season. How could you find the total points?

Let w represent the number of wins and t represent the number of ties. The total points scored can be expressed as $2w + t$. This is an example of an *algebraic expression*; $2w$ and t are called the *terms* of this expression.

A term usually has a variable (or variables). The term $2w$ has the variable w. A term always has a *coefficient*. For example, $2w$ has the coefficient 2 and t has the coefficient 1, that is, t represents $1t$. When a term has the coefficient 1, it is not usually written as part of the term.

In the first half of the 1986/87 season, the Maple Leafs had 17 wins and 5 ties. The team's total points can be calculated by *substituting* into the algebraic expression $2w + t$.

Substitute 17 for w and 5 for t.

$$2w + t$$
$$= 2(17) + 5$$
$$= 34 + 5$$
$$= 39$$

The Maple Leafs had a total of 39 points for the first half of the 1986/87 hockey season.

Example 1. Copy and complete.

Expression	Variables	Terms	Coefficients
$2m - 9n$			
$-35x + 17y$			
$5a - 4b + 6c$			

Solution.

Expression	Variables	Terms	Coefficients
$2m - 9n$	m, n	$2m, -9n$	$2, -9$
$-35x + 17y$	x, y	$-35x, 17y$	$-35, 17$
$5a - 4b + 6c$	a, b, c	$5a, -4b, 6c$	$5, -4, 6$

Example 2. Copy and complete.

a)

+	3	-1	x	w	$3d$
5	8	4	$x + 5$		
1			$w + 1$		
7					

b)

×	3	-1	x	w	$3d$
5	15	-5	$5x$		
1			w		
7					

Solution.

a)

+	3	-1	x	w	$3d$
5	8	4	$x + 5$	$w + 5$	$3d + 5$
1	4	0	$x + 1$	$w + 1$	$3d + 1$
7	10	6	$x + 7$	$w + 7$	$3d + 7$

b)

×	3	-1	x	w	$3d$
5	15	-5	$5x$	$5w$	$15d$
1	3	-1	x	w	$3d$
7	21	-7	$7x$	$7w$	$21d$

Example 3. Evaluate.
  a) $5x + 9$ for $x = 6$
  b) $3a - 7b$ for $a = -9$ and $b = 2$
  c) $2.6m$ for $m = 2.5$

Solution.   a) When $x = 6$, $5x + 9 = 5(6) + 9$
$$= 39$$

  b) When $a = -9$ and $b = 2$, $3a - 7b = 3(-9) - 7(2)$
$$= -41$$

  c) When $m = 2.5$, $2.6m = (2.6)(2.5)$
$$= 6.5$$

EXERCISES 3-2

1. Copy and complete.

	Expression	Variables	Terms	Coefficients
a)	$6p - 2q$			
b)	$a - 2b + 9c$			
c)	$1.8C + 32$			
d)	$2\pi r$			

2. Copy and complete.

a)
+	3	a	$2b$	ab
4				
9				
x				
y				
xy				

b)
×	3	a	$2b$	ab
4				
9				
x				
y				
xy				

3. The students at the John Cabot Secondary School write their examinations in the gymnasium. How many students can write at one time if:
   a) there are 11 rows and 32 desks in each row
   b) there are 11 rows and d desks in each row
   c) there are r rows and d desks in each row?

4. At a track and field meet, points are awarded as follows:
   first place — 5 points, second place — 3 points, third place — 1 point.
   How many points would be awarded for:
   a) 4 firsts, 2 seconds, and 6 thirds   b) x firsts
   c) y seconds   d) x firsts, y seconds, and z thirds?

5. Evaluate.
   a) $2x + 7$ for $x = 5$
   b) $28 - 5m$ for $m = -3.5$
   c) $9x - 4y$ for $x = -8$ and $y = 7$
   d) $8a + 19b$ for $a = 28$ and $b = -8$
   e) $8a - 4b - c$ for $a = 12$, $b = 18$, and $c = -3$

Ⓑ

6. Evaluate.
   a) $2.3x + 0.7y$ for $x = 4$ and $y = -8$
   b) $0.27j - 3k$ for $j = 2.3$ and $k = 0.09$
   c) $3.7a - 2.1b$ for $a = 4.8$ and $b = 3.7$
   d) $5m - 9.2n$ for $m = -2.8$ and $n = 0.6$
   e) $8.3r - 1.27s + 0.6t$ for $r = 0.8$, $s = -5$, and $t = -0.5$

7. Evaluate.
   a) $\frac{3}{4}c + \frac{5}{7}d$ for $c = 12$ and $d = -14$
   b) $\frac{5}{6}m - \frac{2}{9}n$ for $m = \frac{2}{5}$ and $n = \frac{3}{8}$
   c) $\frac{2}{5}x + \frac{1}{3}y$ for $x = \frac{3}{4}$ and $y = -\frac{4}{5}$
   d) $\frac{2}{5}p + \frac{2}{3}q$ for $p = \frac{1}{2}$ and $q = \frac{9}{22}$
   e) $\frac{3}{8}w + \frac{5}{6}y - \frac{3}{4}z$ for $w = \frac{1}{3}$, $y = -\frac{8}{15}$, and $z = \frac{2}{3}$

8. The cost, C dollars, of installing a steel-panel fence is given by this formula.
   $C = 7l + 15p + 80$
   l is the length of the fence in metres and p is the number of posts required. Find the total cost when:
   a) $l = 120$ and $p = 41$
   b) $l = 32$ and $p = 12$
   c) the fence is 65 m long and requires 25 posts
   d) 85 posts are required for a 250 m fence.

9. The formula for the curved surface area, A, of a cylinder is $A = 2\pi rh$ where r is its radius and h is its height. Find the curved surface area of a cylinder that has a radius 4 cm and a height 15 cm.

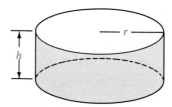

3-3 LIKE TERMS

Mrs. Zak wanted to fence her yard. She did not have a measuring tape
long enough, so she used a long piece of wood to measure each side.
Then, Mrs. Zak drew a plan of the yard. If she knew the length of
the wood, how could she find the length of fencing she needed?

On the plan, the letter s represents the length of the wood.

For side AB, the wood was placed 51 times.
For side BC, the wood was placed 29 times.
For side CD, the wood was placed 53 times.
For side DA, the wood was placed 22 times.

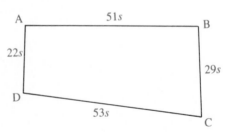

The total number of times the wood was placed is $51 + 29 + 53 + 22$ or 155.

Mrs. Zak measured the piece of wood and it was 83 cm long. She
calculated the length of fencing as $155(0.83)$ m or 128.65 m. She
ordered 130 m of fencing.

Algebraic terms that have the same variable (or variables) such as
$51s$, $29s$, $53s$, and $22s$ are called *like terms*.

The terms $3a$, $4b$, and $10c$ are *unlike terms* because they have different
variables. Similarly, $2p$, $7q$, and 9 are unlike terms.

Like terms can be combined into a single term by adding (or
subtracting) their coefficients. You will recall that the commutative and
associative properties hold for addition, but not for subtraction.

Commutative Property

$7 + 3 = 3 + 7$

but $7 - 3 \neq 3 - 7$

Associative Property

$(5 + 3) + 4 = 5 + (3 + 4)$

but $(5 - 3) - 4 \neq 5 - (3 - 4)$

Example 1. Simplify.

       a) $2x + 3x$ b) $5a - a$ c) $12y + 6 + 3y$

Solution.   a) Since $2x + 3x$ means $x + x + x + x + x$, or $5x$,

           then $2x + 3x = 5x$

       b) Since $5a - a$ means $a + a + a + a + a - a$, or $4a$,

           then $5a - a = 4a$

       c) $12y + 6 + 3y = 12y + 3y + 6$

                     $= 15y + 6$

          $15y$ and 6 are unlike terms and cannot be combined.

Example 2. Simplify. $26x - 11y - 12x + 3x - 5y$

Solution. $26x - 11y - 12x + 3x - 5y$ can be written as

          $(+26x) + (-11y) + (-12x) + (+3x) + (-5y)$

     $= (+26x) + (+3x) + (-12x) + (-11y) + (-5y)$

     $= (+29x) + (-12x) + (-16y)$

     $= (+17x) + (-16y)$

     $= 17x - 16y$

With practice, algebraic expressions can be simplified more directly.

Example 3. Simplify. $-6a + 14b - 13a + 7b + 10a - 11b$

Solution. $-6a + 14b - 13a + 7b + 10a - 11b$

     $= -6a - 13a + 10a + 14b + 7b - 11b$

     $= -19a + 10a + 21b - 11b$

     $= -9a + 10b$

At the beginning of this section, the lengths of the sides of a yard were represented by like terms.

     The perimeter of the yard can be found in two ways.

Method 1.

Perimeter $= 51s + 29s + 53s + 22s$

           $= 155s$

Substitute 0.83 for s.

Perimeter $= 155(0.83)$

           $= 128.65$

Method 2.

Perimeter $= 51s + 29s + 53s + 22s$

Substitute 0.83 for s.

Perimeter $= 51(0.83) + 29(0.83) + 53(0.83) + 22(0.83)$

           $= 42.33 + 24.07 + 43.99 + 18.26$

           $= 128.65$

These two methods illustrate that when substituting into an algebraic expression, it is more efficient to simplify by collecting like terms first.

Example 4. Simplify then evaluate.

a) $14p - 5p$ for $p = -5$ b) $16y - 29y - 15$ for $y = 3.7$

Solution.   a) $14p - 5p = 9p$ b) $16y - 29y - 15 = -13y - 15$
   When $p = -5$,   When $y = 3.7$,
   $9p = 9(-5)$ $-13y - 15 = -13(3.7) - 15$
   $= -45$ $= -48.1 - 15$
                                      $= -63.1$

EXERCISES 3-3

Ⓐ

1. Simplify.

a) $4a + 7a$ b) $19m - 6m$ c) $-42x + 29x$
d) $14p - 5p$ e) $-21g - 16g$ f) $12b + 37b$
g) $6r + 47r - r$ h) $13w + w - 9w$ i) $36p - 29p - 24p$

2. Simplify.

a) $-7x + 5x + 8y - 3y$ b) $-18m + 7m + 6p - 11p$
c) $9a - 23b - 4a - 11b$ d) $52x + 31y - 31x - 2y$
e) $44u + 17v - 4v + 41u$ f) $-7j + 13k + 5j - k$
g) $4s + 5t - 19t - 37s$ h) $28x + 15y - 19x - 11y$
i) $-6a + 9b - 7c + 5b - 3a - c$ j) $14x - 17y - 5x - 11z - 6y - 2z$

Ⓑ

3. Simplify where possible.

a) $4m + 5 - 3m$ b) $2c + d - 3c - d$ c) $5a + 3b + 5a$
d) $3x + 2y$ e) $8u + 3v - 11v - 7$ f) $5m + 4$
g) $-7x + y - 2x$ h) $15x - 3y - 9x + z$ i) $10p - 5 + 8q - 3p - 2$

4. Simplify.

a) $23a - 42b - 18b + 17a$ b) $12x - 10y - 6x - 6y + x$
c) $45m + 15n - 7 - 5m - 5n$ d) $-32c + 10 - 15c + 4d - 3$
e) $23a + 7a - 13 - 2a$ f) $16x - 17y + x - y$
g) $-2a - 3b - a + 4$ h) $48p - 16q - 3r - 18p - 3r$

5. Simplify.

a) $16a - 3b + 5a + b$ b) $-3 + 2m - 13n - 3n + 2$
c) $-2z + 12 + 10y - 15 + 4z - 15y$ d) $13s - 16r - 4s - 6 + 10 + 3r$
e) $4 + 7x - 3y - 7 - y + 18x$ f) $-4x + 7m - 11x - 10m + 8$
g) $-q + 8q - 11p - 7q + 11p$ h) $-13c - 15d - 18d - 3$

6. Simplify.

a) $-4p + 7s - 8r - 2s - 18s + 10r + 2p$
b) $-8z + 13p + 10x - 12z - x - 23p$
c) $5q - 7m + 6q - 11n + m - 8n + 7q$
d) $-10 + a - 13b + 8 - 15a + 2b - 17$
e) $0.3 + 1.5x - 7.0 + 2.4z - 1.0 - 1.3x + 8 - 1.4z$
f) $0.8 + 2.3m - 11.2n - 1.4 - 14.7n + 3.2m$

7. Simplify then evaluate.

    a) $4a + 7a$ for $a = 3$

    b) $19m - 6m$ for $m = -2.5$

    c) $42x - 29x$ for $x = -7$

    d) $-14p + 5p$ for $p = \dfrac{2}{3}$

    e) $23b + 17b$ for $b = 5$

    f) $-64k - 44k$ for $k = -\dfrac{3}{4}$

    g) $4x - 7x - 11x$ for $x = 4$

    h) $16y - 29y - 15y$ for $y = -\dfrac{1}{2}$

8. Write an expression for the perimeter of each figure.

    a)   b)   c)

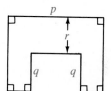

9. Simplify.

    a) $3x + 7y - 2z - 6y - 5x - 4z + 12x - 5y$
    b) $-10m + 3n - 4p - 7n - 5m - 8p + 17m$
    c) $7c - 2a - 5c - 3b + 8a + 6b - 10c$
    d) $4x - 6x + 5y - 7y + 3x - 4y - 12y - 7x$

Ⓒ

10. Simplify.

    a) $3x^2 + 2x - 5x - 4x^2$

    b) $6x - x^2 - 4x - 3x^2$

    c) $8a - 7b - 6a - 2b + 3ab$

    d) $-9p - q^2 + 3r^2 + 4q^2 - 7r$

    e) $4y^2 - 3y + 7 - 2y^2$

    f) $-6b - 3c + 4c^2 - 6 - 6b$

    g) $6x - 3x - 5x + x^2 - 5$

    h) $7x^2 - 9b + 5m^2 - 8b - 7x + 1$

    i) $-w^2 + 2v - 3w - 9v + 4w^2$

    j) $-3a^2 - 3ab + 3b - 4a - 7ab + 3$

11. Simplify.

    a) $3xy - 2yz + 5xz - 6yz + 4xy - 10xz$
    b) $-4ab - 5bc + 3ac + 8ab - 6bc - 9ac$
    c) $-3xyz + 4xyw - 5yzw + 8xyz + 5xyw - 6yzw$

12. Evaluate each expression for $x = 3$, $y = 2$, and $z = -1$.
    a) $-3xy + 5yz - 2xz + 6xy + yz - 5xz$
    b) $4x^2yz + 5xy^2z - 3xyz + 5xy^2z - 3x^2yz + 6xyz$

13. Write expressions for the perimeter and the area of each figure.

    a)   b)   c)

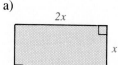
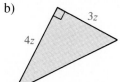
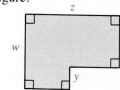

PROBLEM SOLVING

Use a Variable

How old is Janet?

Understand the problem
- How old is Janet's father?
- Is Janet's father more than 3 times Janet's age?
- How many years older than 3 times Janet's age is her father?
- What are we asked to find?

Think of a strategy
- Use a variable to represent Janet's age.
- Express Janet's father's age in terms of the variable.

Carry out the strategy
- Let n represent Janet's age.
- Then, 3 times Janet's age is $3n$.
- To obtain father's age, we add 6 to $3n$.
  $\boxed{3n} \rightarrow \boxed{+6} \rightarrow \boxed{42}$
- To calculate $3n$ we reverse the flow chart.
  $\boxed{36} \leftarrow \boxed{-6} \leftarrow \boxed{42}$
- From a comparison of the flow charts, $3n = 36$ so $n = 12$.
  Janet is 12 years old.

Look back
- What is three times Janet's age plus 6?
- Is that the same as her father's age?
- Is 12 the only solution to the problem?

Solve each problem

1. What is the mass of each colored cube?

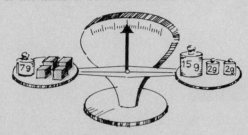

2. One-eighth of a number is 28.5 more than 76. What is the number?

3. The rental cost of a videocassette recorder is $25 plus a fixed daily amount. Ms. Singh was charged $64 for a 4-day rental period. What is the fixed daily rental fee?

4. Sung Choi saved his allowance for eight weeks. When he added to this the $15.50 he received for his birthday, he had a total of $61.50. How much allowance does he receive each week?

5. Margaret handed the cashier a $10 bill for the purchase of 3 tennis balls. After 54¢ tax was added, the clerk gave her $2.71 change. What was the cost of each tennis ball?

6. A rectangular table is twice as long as it is wide. How long is the table if its perimeter is 15.6 m?

7. A gold pen and pencil set cost $69.98. The pen costs $6.50 more than the pencil. What is the cost of the pencil?

8. The sum of two consecutive integers is 25. What are the two integers?

9. In an 18-game hockey tournament between Canada and the U.S.S.R., Canada won 4 more games than they lost. Since there was no tie, how many games did Canada win?

10. Find two integers with a sum of 8 and a difference of 42.

11. When 28 is added to seven times a number, the result is the same as if 16 were subtracted from eleven times that number. What is the number?

12. Find 3 consecutive integers with a sum of 375.

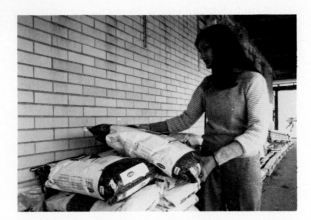

3-4 FROM PRODUCTS TO SUMS AND DIFFERENCES

Mr. Ying grows flowers and vegetables in a rectangular-shaped garden.
He needs to buy fertilizer for his garden. Each bag of fertilizer is
labelled with the area, in square metres, that the fertilizer should cover.
Mr. Ying can calculate the area of his garden in two ways.

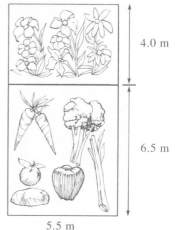

Method 1.
Total area = width × length
= 5.5(4.0 + 6.5)
= 5.5(10.5)
= 57.75

Method 2.
Total area = area with flowers + area with vegetables
= 5.5(4.0) + 5.5(6.5)
= 22.0 + 35.75
= 57.75

The area of Mr. Ying's garden is about 60 m².
Since both methods gave the same area, it follows that
5.5(4.0 + 6.5) = 5.5(4.0) + 5.5(6.5)
This is an example of the *distributive law*. It shows a product expanded
into a sum.

It can be shown that this law is true for a product expanded into a
difference.
For example, consider 5(9 − 4) = 5(9) − 5(4)
  5(9 − 4) = 5(5)   5(9) − 5(4) = 45 − 20
        = 25   = 25
This law can be written algebraically.

Distributive Law
$$a(b + c) = ab + ac$$
$$a(b - c) = ab - ac$$

Example 1. Use the distributive law to expand these products.

a) $6(x - 4)$ b) $3(4b + 8)$ c) $4(2x + y - 3)$

Solution. a) $6(x - 4) = 6(x) - 6(4)$
$$= 6x - 24$$

b) $3(4b + 8) = 3(4b) + 3(8)$
$$= 12b + 24$$

c) The distributive law can be extended to the sum or difference of more than two terms.
$$4(2x + y - 3) = 4(2x) + 4(y) - 4(3)$$
$$= 8x + 4y - 12$$

Some expressions must be expanded before they can be simplified.

Example 2. Simplify.

a) $12(3p + q) - 8(q + 2p)$
b) $1.5(2x - y) - 2.5(2y - x)$

Solution. a) Multiply both terms in the second bracket by -8.
$$12(3p + q) - 8(q + 2p) = 36p + 12q - 8q - 16p$$
$$= 20p + 4q$$

b) $1.5(2x - y) - 2.5(2y - x) = 3.0x - 1.5y - 5.0y + 2.5x$
$$= 5.5x - 6.5y$$

EXERCISES 3-4

(A)

1. Expand.
   a) $3(m - 8)$ b) $18(x + 5)$ c) $11(p + 7)$ d) $-23(a - 9)$
   e) $7(2p + 6)$ f) $4(a - b + 15)$ g) $-8(7a + b - 1)$ h) $6(2s + 11t - 5)$

2. Simplify.
   a) $5(m + 3) + 63$
   b) $18(2x + 4) - 27$
   c) $14 - 3(6x + 7)$
   d) $96 + 7(3a - 12)$
   e) $-17(3x + 5) - 2$
   f) $7a - 3(2a - 9 - b)$
   g) $15e + 5(12 + e - 4f)$
   h) $6t + 9(3t - 4) - 12t$
   i) $-2(5x - 7) - 3x - x$
   j) $8w - 6(3w + 5) - 19$
   k) $-3(c + 4) + 2(2c - 3)$
   l) $-12t + 3(5 - 2t) - 7$

3. Simplify.
   a) $5m - 2 + 3(4m + 1) - 2m$
   b) $-4(2c + 5d) - 2(3c - 7d)$
   c) $5(a + 3) + 2(a - 5) + (a - 1)$
   d) $4(2a + 5b + 3) - 3(6b - a - 1)$

(B)

4. Simplify.
   a) $3(2x + 5y) + 7(4x - 2y)$
   b) $5(7x + 2y) - 3(2y - x)$
   c) $-5(3m + 6n) - 8(9m - 2n)$
   d) $5(4a - 16b) + 2(17a - 29b)$
   e) $11(8k + 4l) + 3(13l - 2k)$
   f) $3(p + 2q) - 7(2p + q)$
   g) $-11(3r + 2s) + 7(2r + q)$
   h) $6(4u + 7v) - 9(u - w)$
   i) $10(3a + 2b + c) - 5(a - b - c)$
   j) $-8(12x + 5y + 4) + 3(2x - 4y + 2)$

5. Simplify.
   a) $0.5(4x + 6y) + 1.5(6x + 2y)$
   b) $-1.4(3x + 5y) - 2.8(5x + 2y)$
   c) $2.6(15x + 5y) - 5.2(5x - 3y)$
   d) $-3.8(5y + x) + 7.5(4x + y)$

6. Write the area of each shaded region as a sum or difference of terms.
   a)

   b)

   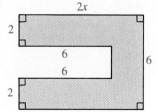

   c)

   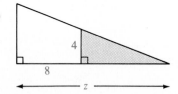

   d)

   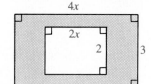

7. Simplify.
   a) $3a(x - y) - 5a(y - x)$
   b) $8c(b - 3a) - 2c(b - a)$
   c) $4x(x^2 - 2x + 3) - 5x^2(x^2 - x)$
   d) $2x(y - x) + (y - 2x^2)$
   e) $3x - 5y(x - y) + y^2$
   f) $4p(q - p) - (p^2 - q^2)$
   g) $x(x - y) - 3y(y - x)$
   h) $6a(a + b) + 3b(b - a)$

8. Write the area of each shaded region as a sum or difference of terms.
   a)

   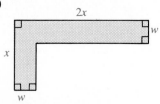

   b)

   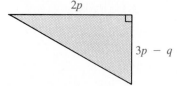

   c)

   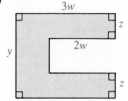

   d)

   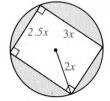

9. Evaluate for $x = -1.1$ and $y = 2.3$.
   a) $3(2x - y) + 2(x - 2y) - 2(x + y)$
   b) $4(x - 2y) - 3(3x - 4y) + 2(x + 2y)$
   c) $2(y - 3x) + 4(3x - 3y) - (3x + 2y)$
   d) $2x(y - x) - 3y(x - 2y) + x(3x - y)$

3-5 TRANSLATING WORDS INTO SYMBOLS

Five students in Mrs. Iverson's class each invested the same amount in stocks in September. They are now reviewing their gains and losses.

- Ian lost $16.
- Linda gained $7.
- Maria has two-and-a-half times her initial investment.
- Ravi gained $9.
- Susan has half of what she started with.

Suppose you knew how much the students started with. How could you find out whether, collectively, they now have more than or less than that?

This problem is most easily solved with algebra. Let x dollars represent each student's initial investment. Then, an algebraic expression can be written for the amount each student has now.

Student	Verbal Expression	Algebraic Expression
Ian	A loss of $16	$(x - 16)$ dollars
Linda	A gain of $7	$(x + 7)$ dollars
Maria	2.5 times the initial investment	$2.5x$ dollars
Ravi	A gain of $9	$(x + 9)$ dollars
Susan	Half of the initial investment	$0.5x$ dollars

The total amount the students have now is:

$$(x - 16) + (x + 7) + 2.5x + (x + 9) + 0.5x$$
$$= x - 16 + x + 7 + 2.5x + x + 9 + 0.5x$$
$$= x + x + 2.5x + x + 0.5x - 16 + 7 + 9$$
$$= 6x$$

The students started with x dollars each or $5x$ dollars together. Now they have $6x$ dollars. Collectively, the students have more than they started with.

By translating verbal expressions into algebraic expressions, the problem was solved without knowing the initial investment.

Study these verbal expressions and their algebraic equivalents.

Verbal Expression	Algebraic Expression
four more than a number	$n + 4$
a number increased by eight	$p + 8$
nine less than a number	$a - 9$
twice a number	$2d$
one-sixth of a number	$\frac{1}{6}s$ or $\frac{s}{6}$
five more than four times a number	$4f + 5$
the product of one more than a number, and seven	$7(n + 1)$
three less than five times a number	$5l - 3$

Sometimes, two numbers are related. Suppose one of these numbers is known. How can the other number be found? One number can be represented by a variable and the other number expressed in terms of this variable.

Example 1.   Choose a variable to represent one quantity. Express the other quantity in terms of this variable.
a) Two consecutive integers
b) Two numbers which differ by five
c) Mary's age now, and in six years
d) The lengths of the pieces if a 4 m log is cut in two

Solution.   a) Two consecutive integers
Let l represent the lesser integer.
Then, the greater integer is $(l + 1)$.
Alternatively, let j represent the greater integer.
Then, the lesser integer is $(j - 1)$.

b) Two numbers which differ by five
Let n represent the greater number.
Then, the lesser number is $(n - 5)$.
Can you think of an alternative way to describe the numbers?

c) Mary's age now, and in six years
Let a years represent Mary's age now.
Then in 6 years, Mary will be $(a + 6)$ years old.

d) The lengths of the pieces of a 4 m log cut into two
Let l metres represent the length of one piece.
Then, the length of the other piece is $(4 - l)$ metres.

Example 2. Express each quantity in terms of the variable.
  a) The value in cents of n quarters
  b) The value in dollars of x five-dollar bills
  c) The number of centimetres in k metres
  d) The number of minutes in t hours

Solution. a) The value in cents of n quarters
  1 quarter has a value of 25¢.
  n quarters have a value of $n(25¢)$ or $25n$ cents.

  b) The value in dollars of x five-dollar bills
  1 five-dollar bill has a value of $5.
  x five-dollar bills have a value of $x($5)$ or $5x$ dollars.

  c) The number of centimetres in k metres
  1 metre has a length of 100 cm.
  k metres have a length of $k(100$ cm$)$ or $100k$ centimetres.

  d) The number of minutes in t hours
  1 hour is 60 min.
  t hours are $t(60$ min$)$ or $60t$ minutes.

EXERCISES 3-5

1. Write an algebraic expression for each verbal expression.
  a) five more than a number
  b) six less than a number
  c) eight times a number
  d) one-fifth of a number
  e) the product of a number and eight
  f) four more than five times a number
  g) two less than eight times a number
  h) the product of two less than a number, and eight
  i) the sum of one-fourth of a number, and three
  j) one-fourth of the sum of a number and three

2. Express each quantity in terms of the variable.
  a) The number of seconds in m minutes
  b) The number of grams in k kilograms
  c) The value in cents of n nickels
  d) The value in dollars of x two-dollar bills
  e) The number of hours in m minutes
  f) The distance in metres of c centimetres

3. Write a verbal expression for each algebraic expression.
  a) $p + 6$ b) $q - 10$ c) $\frac{1}{4}r$ d) $10s$ e) $4 + \frac{3}{10}t$

  f) $3u + 2$ g) $4v - 5$ h) $2(w - 3)$ i) $\frac{1}{3}(x + 5)$ j) $x(x - 3)$

4. Choose a variable to complete the first statement. Using that variable, write an expression that completes the second statement.
   a) Clyde is 12 years older than Bonnie.
      Let Bonnie's age be represented by ※ years. Then, Clyde's age is ※ years.
   b) Ian's mass is 1.5 kg less than that of Sean.
      Let Sean's mass be represented by ※ kilograms. Then, Ian's mass is ※ kilograms.
   c) A 30 m log is cut into two pieces of unequal lengths.
      Let the length of the longer piece be represented by ※ metres.
      Then, the length of the shorter piece is ※ metres.

Ⓑ
5. Write an algebraic expression to complete each statement.
   a) The heights, in centimetres, of Lim and David are consecutive integers. Lim is the taller of the two.
      Let David's height be represented by ※ centimetres.
      Then, Lim's height is ※ centimetres.
   b) The ages of Alan, Becky, and Carmen are three consecutive numbers. Alan is the oldest and Carmen is the youngest.
      Let Carmen's age be represented by ※ years.
      Then, Becky's age is ※ years. Alan's age is ※ years.
   c) Two numbers have a product of 36.
      Let one number be represented by ※. Then, the other number is ※.
   d) Stefa's marks on two tests are consecutive even integers.
      Let one mark be represented by ※. Then, the other mark is ※.

6. Express each quantity in terms of the variable.
   a) The area in square centimetres of A square metres
   b) The area in square millimetres of B square centimetres
   c) The volume in cubic centimetres of V cubic metres
   d) The area in square centimetres of M square millimetres

7. Choose a variable to represent one quantity and express the other quantity (or quantities) in terms of the first.
   a) The ages of two brothers if one brother is twelve years older than the other
   b) Two numbers where one number is one-fifth of the other
   c) The ages of Angelo and Mary whose total age is 21 years
   d) The lengths of the jumps if Joan's jump was 15 cm longer than Enid's
   e) The speeds of the two cars if the Jaguar travelled 1.1 times as fast as the Mercedes
   f) Two numbers with a product of 76
   g) Three consecutive integers
   h) Three consecutive odd integers

Ⓒ
8. Choose a variable to represent one quantity and express the other quantity in terms of the first.
   a) Anita's age doubled is 4 years less than Ron's age tripled.
   b) Five times one number is 7 more than eight times a smaller number.
   c) Gloria is now twice as old as Chad was 9 years ago.

1. Suppose this pattern were continued.

   a) How many matchsticks would be needed to make 12 squares?

   b) How could the number of matchsticks be found if the number of squares were known?

   c) Let s represent the number of squares. Write an expression for the number of matchsticks needed to make s squares.

2. Suzy has a Saturday job where she works 8 h a day and is paid \$5/h.

   a) How much money does Suzy make in 1 week?

   b) How much money does Suzy make in 12 weeks?

   c) Suzy wants to buy a stereo system, which will cost \$160. How many weeks will she have to work to earn this money?

   d) If the amount of money earned is known, how could:

      i) the number of days worked be found

      ii) the number of hours worked be found?

3. For the expression $6x + 4y - 3z$, list:

   a) the terms   b) the variables   c) the coefficients.

4. Evaluate.

   a) $9 + 3y$ for $y = 16$

   b) $8s - 7$ for $s = 5.4$

   c) $5p + 8q$ for $p = 13$ and $q = -6$

   d) $6s - t$ for $s = -1.7$ and $t = 2.9$

   e) $14u + v - 9w$ for $u = -6$, $v = 29$, and $w = 12$

   f) $21s + 4t$ for $s = 0.4$ and $t = -1.2$

5. Simplify.

   a) $23x - 11x$ b) $4m + 13m$

   c) $15x - 9x + 3x$ d) $12a + 4b - 5a + 3b$

   e) $9x + 4y - x - 2y$ f) $14c + d - 3d + 11c$

   g) $6m - 5m - 5n + 5n$ h) $17w + 8x - 7x - 8w$

   i) $8.5e + 1.5e - 6.2f + 5.7f$ j) $-3.6d + 4.7c - 5.8c - 1.2d$

6. Evaluate.

   a) $\frac{9}{4}x - 3y$ for $x = \frac{2}{3}$ and $y = \frac{3}{8}$

   b) $7y + 9y - 4y$ for $y = \frac{9}{4}$

   c) $3.2x + 4.1y - z$ for $x = 0.3$, $y = -1.1$, and $z = 2.4$

   d) $\frac{3}{8}a - \frac{2}{5}b + \frac{5}{2}c$ for $a = \frac{5}{3}$, $b = \frac{3}{8}$, and $c = -\frac{4}{25}$

7. Simplify.
   a) $3x - 5x - 3$
   b) $-4a + 3b - 6a$
   c) $5p - 7q - 8p$
   d) $-11m - 9n - 2n + 6m$
   e) $16f - 3e + 10g - 6e$
   f) $-8d - 10b + 2c + 4d$

8. Simplify.
   a) $2(5a + 7) + 17$
   b) $2(3x + 5y) - 4x$
   c) $-7(3x - 2y) - 5(3y - 4x)$
   d) $5(2m + 7n) + 3(m - 4n)$
   e) $-3(2x + 4y) + 3(x - y)$
   f) $7(r + 3s) - 2(2r - 9s)$

9. Simplify.
   a) $4m - 3n - 15 + 14n - 2 + 6n$
   b) $-11 + 3b - 7a + 13 - 8b + 10a$
   c) $10x - 3z + 14 - 11y + 2z - 22$
   d) $14d - 23e + 11d - 16 + 5e$
   e) $4.8x - 3.2y + 2.4z + 1.7y - 3.9x$
   f) $-5.7b + 4.1a - 1.1b + 3.5b - 9.2a$

10. Write an expression for the area of each shaded region.
   a)

   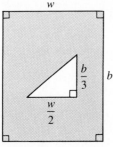

   b)

   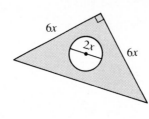

   c)

   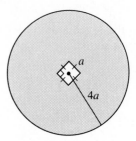

11. Write an algebraic expression for each verbal expression.
   a) one-tenth of a number
   b) eleven times a number
   c) twenty more than a number
   d) thirty-one less than a number
   e) fourteen more than five times a number
   f) the sum of one-seventh of a number, and nineteen

12. Choose a variable to represent one quantity and express the other quantity in terms of the first.
   a) The cost of two cars if one is $1300 more than the other
   b) Two consecutive odd numbers
   c) Three consecutive even numbers
   d) The heights of two trees if one is 2.6 m shorter than the other
   e) Two numbers with a sum of 37.8
   f) The lengths of the pieces of wood if a 15 m log is cut into two
   g) Two numbers which have a difference of 0.4
   h) The ages of two boys if Raj's age is four years less than twice Egino's age

1. a) State whether each sentence is a statement or an open sentence.
   i) She did really well on the last mathematics test.
   ii) Mountain ranges can be found in 13 states.
   iii) $2x + 3 > 10$ iv) $17 - x \leqslant 5$ v) $796.3 \times 52.7 > 42\ 000$
   b) Find the solution set for parts a) iii) and iv) if the domain is the set of even numbers.

2. a) Write the negation of each open sentence.
   b) For the domain $\{1, 3, 5, 7, \ldots \}$, write the solution set of the open sentence and the solution set of its negation.
   i) $x + 5 = 16$ ii) $x - 3 > 11$
   iii) $9 + x \geqslant 15$ iv) $12 - x < 8$

3. Given p: $x > 5$ q: x is a factor of 24; write:
   a) $p \wedge q$ and its solution set   b) $p \vee q$ and its solution set.

4. Let p and q represent these open sentences, where x is a natural number.
   p: x is a multiple of 5 q: x is an even number
   a) If possible, find at least one value of x which makes:
   i) p and q both true   ii) p true and q false
   iii) p false and q true   iv) p and q both false.
   b) Is $p \rightarrow q$ true for all natural numbers?

5. Construct a truth table for the statement $(\sim p \vee q) \rightarrow \sim (p \wedge q)$.

6. Is this statement a tautology? $[(p \wedge q) \vee \sim p] \rightarrow q$

7. Simplify.
   a) $(-14) + (-23)$ b) $(+9) - (-26)$ c) $(+31) + (-48)$
   d) $(-28) - (+17)$ e) $(-12) + (+35)$ f) $(-19) - (-11)$

8. Simplify.
   a) $(+7)(-9)$ b) $(-8)(-5)$ c) $(-60) \div (-12)$
   d) $(-21)(-7)$ e) $(-225) \div (+25)$ f) $(+240) \div (-30) \div (-2)$

9. Simplify.
   a) $\dfrac{(+5)(-8)}{(-4)} + \dfrac{(-4)(-6)}{(+3)}$ b) $15 - (+8)(-3)$
   c) $(+12)(-5 + 9) - (-3 - 7)$ d) $14 + (-5) - 3(2 - 9)$
   e) $\dfrac{6 + 15}{-7} - \dfrac{-4 + 19}{3}$ f) $\dfrac{19 - 28}{-3} - \dfrac{(-11) + 27}{4} + \dfrac{6 - 32}{-2}$

10. Simplify.
    a) $-\dfrac{7}{10} \div \dfrac{2}{-5}$ b) $\dfrac{-32}{15} \times \dfrac{-25}{-44}$ c) $-12.25 \div 3.5$
    d) $\dfrac{-21}{16} \div \dfrac{-7}{8} \times \dfrac{3}{-4}$ e) $(4.2)(-3.5) \div (-2.1)$ f) $\dfrac{18}{-5} \times \dfrac{10}{-27} \div \dfrac{-9}{2}$

11. Simplify.

    a) $-4.21 + 13.7$

    b) $\dfrac{-9}{4} - \dfrac{-3}{8}$

    c) $\dfrac{-16}{9} + \dfrac{5}{-6}$

    d) $\dfrac{-8}{-15} + \dfrac{3}{-10} - \dfrac{2}{3}$

    e) $3.17 - 5.04 - 1.317$

    f) $\dfrac{11}{6} - \dfrac{4}{3} - \dfrac{-15}{9}$

12. Simplify.

    a) $\dfrac{7}{8} + \left(-\dfrac{3}{4}\right)\left(\dfrac{5}{6}\right)$

    b) $2.17 - \dfrac{9.6}{3.2}(7.6 - 4.3)$

    c) $\left(-\dfrac{5}{8} - \dfrac{1}{2}\right) \times \left(\dfrac{7}{9} - \dfrac{2}{3}\right)$

    d) $\dfrac{17}{5} + \dfrac{-13}{10} - \dfrac{5}{8}\left(\dfrac{-4}{-15}\right)$

13. The volume of a cylinder is given by the formula $V = \pi r^2 h$, where r is the radius of the cylinder and h is its height. Find the volume of corn in a full silo, which has a radius of 3.4 m and a height of 8.9 m.

14. A series of tins are stacked as shown. Suppose the pattern were continued.

    a) How many tins would there be on the bottom row of:
       i) the 7th diagram   ii) the 11th diagram?
    b) How many tins would there be in:
       i) the 7th diagram   ii) the 11th diagram?
    c) Write an expression for the number of tins in terms of the position of the diagram.

15. Evaluate.

    a) $\dfrac{3}{4}x - 5$ for $x = -12$
    b) $3m + 7n - 11m - 5n$ for $m = -4$ and $n = 2$
    c) $1.7x - 4.3y$ for $x = -3$ and $y = 5$

16. Simplify.

    a) $-7p - 4q - 12p - 5q$
    b) $16x + 7y - 8z - 12x - 15y + 3z$
    c) $3.6a - 2.5b - 1.4a + 3.8b - 7.2a$

17. Simplify.

    a) $3a - 2(5a + 4b) - 3b$
    b) $5(4m - 3n) - 8m - 7n$
    c) $-2(7x + 4y) + 6(2x - 5y)$
    d) $8(-3p - 9q) - 3(4p - 12q)$

18. Write an algebraic expression for each verbal expression.

    a) the sum of a number and eleven
    b) six times a number, decreased by four
    c) the sum of two consecutive numbers

4 Solving Equations

If a car's rate of fuel consumption is known, how can the fraction of highway driving be determined? (See Section 4-5.)

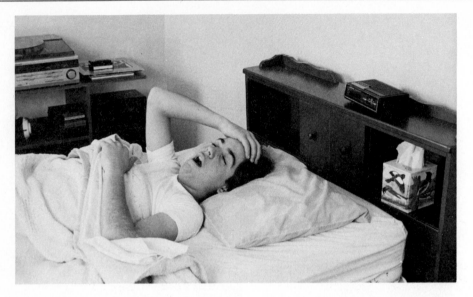

4-1 SOLVING SIMPLE EQUATIONS

The amount of sleep, n hours, that a 15-year-old person needs is given by this equation.

$$15 = 34 - 2n$$

To find how much sleep is needed at this age, a value must be found for n which *satisfies* this equation. There is exactly one value of n that will make both sides of the equation the same. Finding this value is called *solving* the equation.

The right side of the equation must equal the left side.
So, 34 minus twice a number must equal 15.
We know that 34 minus 19 equals 15.
Hence, twice the number must equal 19.

So, the number must be $\dfrac{19}{2}$ or 9.5.

A 15-year-old person needs 9.5 h sleep.
When an equation is solved in this way, it is called *solving by inspection.*

Example 1. Solve by inspection.

      a) $56 - n = 21$ b) $7d = 28$

Solution.   a) $56 - n = 21$
                This means, "56 less some number is 21."
                The number that is subtracted from 56 to give 21 is 35.
                Hence $n = 35$

         b) $7d = 28$
                This means, "7 times some number is 28."
                The number that is multiplied by 7 to give 28 is 4.
                Hence $d = 4$

Only very simple equations should be solved by inspection. Another method of solving equations is by *systematic trial*. Systematic trial means substituting values for the variable until the value which satisfies the equation is found.

Example 2. Solve by systematic trial. $54 - 7y = 26$

Solution. A value of y must be found such that $54 - 7y$ equals 26.

Suppose $y = 5$, $54 - 7y = 54 - 7(5)$
$$= 54 - 35$$
$$= 19$$

When $y = 5$, the value of $54 - 7y$ is less than 26.

Try $y = 3$. $\quad 54 - 7y = 54 - 7(3)$
$$= 54 - 21$$
$$= 33$$

When $y = 3$, the value of $54 - 7y$ is greater than 26.

Try $y = 4$. $\quad 54 - 7y = 54 - 7(4)$
$$= 54 - 28$$
$$= 26$$

The solution is $y = 4$.

The method of systematic trial can be a long one. It is the method used by computers to solve more complicated equations.

EXERCISES 4-1

Ⓐ

1. Solve by inspection.
   a) $x + 17 = 32$ b) $29 - x = 12$ c) $x - 7 = 27$ d) $x + 26 = 61$
   e) $43 + x = 79$ f) $11 - x = 11$ g) $15 - x = 0$ h) $20 + x = 15$

2. Solve by inspection.
   a) $4z = 24$ b) $7s = -63$ c) $12q = 132$ d) $\frac{1}{3}y = 12$

   e) $8v = 4$ f) $0.5w = 25$ g) $\frac{1}{4}x = \frac{1}{2}$ h) $0.7t = 3.5$

3. Solve by inspection.
   a) $m - 3.5 = 5$ b) $-8 + x = 12$ c) $t + 2.4 = 5.4$ d) $-9 + q = 7$
   e) $w - 3.6 = 5$ f) $1.3 + z = 3.3$ g) $2.5 - a = 1.5$ h) $1.1 - x = 0.6$

4. Solve by systematic trial.
   a) $3 + 2n = 11$ b) $7 + 3m = 13$ c) $7x - 5 = 30$ d) $4c - 1 = 23$
   e) $24 - 3y = 15$ f) $9k - 27 = 36$ g) $7m - 99 = 6$ h) $7 + 13d = 72$

Ⓑ

5. Solve.
   a) $2x + 7 = 17$ b) $28 - 5m = 18$ c) $6a - 4 = 20$
   d) $9 + 3y = 57$ e) $8s - 7 = 153$ f) $11t + 9 = 130$
   g) $40 - 13v = 1$ h) $110 - 9u = 2$ i) $15 = 3 - 2x$
   j) $-27 = 4a + 1$ k) $31 = -2 - 3y$ l) $-40 = -4 + 4z$

6. The number of hours of sleep that an 18-year-old person needs is given by the value of n in the equation $18 = 34 - 2n$. Solve the equation for n.

7. The rate, in chirps per minute, at which a cricket chirps at 30°C is given by the value of r in the equation $210 = r + 28$. Solve the equation for r.

8. The distance, in kilometres, that a taxi travels for a fare of $9.65 is given by the value of d in the equation $9.65 = 1.40 + 0.75d$. Solve the equation for d.

4-2 ISOLATING THE VARIABLE

An equation is a mathematical sentence that uses an equals sign to relate two expressions.

To solve an equation, it is helpful to think of a level balance. The masses in each pan can be changed but as long as the total masses on both sides are the same, the balance remains level. The same rule applies to equations.

> Whatever change is made to one side of an equation must also be made to the other side.

These changes are made to reduce an equation to its solution in the form $x = a$. In this form, the variable is said to be *isolated*.

Example 1. Solve. $x + 4 = 10$

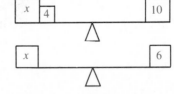

Solution. $x + 4 = 10$ means $x + 4$ balances 10.
Subtract 4 from both sides to isolate x.
$$x + 4 - 4 = 10 - 4$$
$$x = 6$$

Example 2. Solve. $y - 3 = 18$

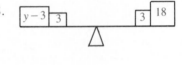

Solution. $y - 3 = 18$ means $y - 3$ balances 18.
Add 3 to both sides to isolate y.
$$y - 3 + 3 = 18 + 3$$
$$y = 21$$

> To solve an equation in the form $x + a = b$, where a and b are numbers, isolate x by subtracting a from both sides.
>
> To solve an equation in the form $x - a = b$, where a and b are numbers, isolate x by adding a to both sides.

Example 3. Solve.

    a) $\dfrac{z}{3} = 10$ b) $-2p = 12$

Solution.

    a) $\dfrac{z}{3} = 10$

         Multiply both sides by 3 to isolate z.

         $\dfrac{z}{3}(3) = 10(3)$

            $z = 30$

    b) $-2p = 12$

         Divide both sides by -2 to isolate z.

         $\dfrac{-2p}{-2} = \dfrac{12}{-2}$

           $p = -6$

To solve an equation in the form $\dfrac{x}{b} = c$, where b and c are numbers ($b \neq 0$), isolate x by multiplying both sides by b.

To solve an equation in the form $bx = c$, where b and c are numbers ($b \neq 0$), isolate x by dividing both sides by b.

EXERCISES 4-2

1. Solve.
     a) $x + 5 = 11$ b) $z - 3 = 10$ c) $y + 7 = 16$ d) $m - 4 = 9$
     e) $a - 11 = 25$ f) $x + 17 = 23$ g) $w - 23 = 61$ h) $p + 19 = 47$

2. Solve.
     a) $\dfrac{x}{5} = 2$ b) $3x = 21$ c) $\dfrac{z}{3} = -4$ d) $5w = 35$ e) $\dfrac{1}{9}m = 5$

     f) $6x = 54$ g) $11a = 88$ h) $\dfrac{y}{4} = -8$ i) $\dfrac{1}{3}p = 18$ j) $7b = 98$

     k) $8a = 128$ l) $-7a = 91$ m) $\dfrac{c}{10} = 80$ n) $\dfrac{x}{12} = 132$ o) $\dfrac{1}{8}x = -9$

3. Solve.
     a) $m + 13 = 9$ b) $x - 4 = -10$ c) $a - 8 = 2$ d) $p + 11 = 5$
     e) $s + 19 = 14$ f) $w - 7 = -18$ g) $y - 3 = 0$ h) $m - 14 = -37$

Ⓑ

4. Solve.

a) $\dfrac{w}{4} = 13$ b) $\dfrac{m}{7} = 4$ c) $5x = -35$ d) $7y = 91$ e) $\dfrac{1}{5}p = 3$

f) $\dfrac{1}{13}x = \dfrac{2}{13}$ g) $\dfrac{x}{7} = -9$ h) $-4s = -28$ i) $-56 = 8p$ j) $\dfrac{x}{-7} = -8$

5. Solve.
   a) $4 + y = -9$ b) $-8 = 2 + x$ c) $3 = y - 5$ d) $20 = 10 + z$
   e) $-11 = n + 21$ f) $-2 = x - 14$ g) $13 + x = 13$ h) $5.2 = 3.7 + p$

6. Solve.

a) $9.3 = a - 2.7$ b) $z - \dfrac{1}{4} = \dfrac{7}{4}$ c) $12 = m - 45$ d) $\dfrac{5}{2} = x + \dfrac{3}{4}$

e) $4.5 = -2.3 + x$ f) $-52 = 27 + y$ g) $q - \dfrac{9}{4} = \dfrac{43}{8}$ h) $\dfrac{2}{5} = a + \dfrac{3}{10}$

7. Solve.

a) $48 = -6y$ b) $-12 = \dfrac{x}{2}$ c) $13x = 169$ d) $5 = \dfrac{n}{15}$

e) $8.5 = 1.7m$ f) $2.5y = -10$ g) $72 = 18m$ h) $\dfrac{9}{4} = \dfrac{x}{12}$

8. A daytime, operator-assisted telephone call from Boston to Houston costs $7.50. The time, in minutes, for the call is given by the value of t in this equation.
$7.50 = 3.50 + 0.25t$
Find how long the call lasted.

9. A car is rented for one day and the charge at the end of the day is $172.95. The distance driven, in kilometres, is given by the value of d in this equation.
$172.95 = 28.50 + 0.15d$
Find how far the car was driven.

10. A loan company charges a flat rate of $50 to process a loan and charges interest at the rate of 27.5% per annum on the principal. After 1 year, the amount a person has to pay back is $2600.00. The principal, in dollars, is given by the value of p in this equation.
$2600.00 = 50.00 + 1.275p$
Find how much the person borrowed.

Ⓒ

11. Solve for x.
    a) $x + a = b$ b) $x - c = d$ c) $3x = m$

    d) $\dfrac{1}{4}x = w$ e) $a - b = x + 2b$ f) $\dfrac{x}{4} = c - d$

    g) $2y + x = z$ h) $b - 2a = c - x$ i) $-ax + b = c$

    j) $n = m - kx$ k) $-b - cx = d$ l) $-p - \dfrac{x}{q} = -r$

4-3 SOLUTIONS REQUIRING SEVERAL STEPS

Many equations require more than one step to isolate the variable. To solve these equations, isolate the term that contains the variable first.

Example 1.   Solve.

a) $-5w + 9 = 21$ b) $7.3 = 6.6y - 15.8$

Solution.   a) $-5w + 9 = 21$

Subtract 9 from both sides.

$$-5w + 9 - 9 = 21 - 9$$

$$-5w = 12$$

Divide both sides by -5.

$$\frac{-5w}{-5} = \frac{12}{-5}$$

$$w = -\frac{12}{5}$$

b) $7.3 = 6.6y - 15.8$

Add 15.8 to both sides.

$$7.3 + 15.8 = 6.6y - 15.8 + 15.8$$

$$23.1 = 6.6y$$

Divide both sides by 6.6.

$$\frac{23.1}{6.6} = \frac{6.6y}{6.6}$$

$$3.5 = y$$

It may be necessary to expand, using the distributive law, to solve an equation.

Example 2.   Solve. $23.98 = 11(1.10w + 2.07)$

Solution. $23.98 = 11(1.10w + 2.07)$

Expand the right side.

$$23.98 = 12.10w + 22.77$$

Subtract 22.77 from both sides.

$$23.98 - 22.77 = 12.10w + 22.77 - 22.77$$

$$1.21 = 12.10w$$

Divide both sides by 12.10.

$$\frac{1.21}{12.10} = \frac{12.10w}{12.10}$$

$$0.1 = w$$

Example 3.   The cost, C dollars, of taking n students on a weekend trip to Washington, D.C., is given by this formula.
$$C = 180 + 35n$$
The cost was $1685. How many students went on the trip?

Solution.
$$C = 180 + 35n$$
Substitute 1685 for C.
$$1685 = 180 + 35n$$
Solve for n. Subtract 180 from both sides.
$$1685 - 180 = 180 + 35n - 180$$
$$1505 = 35n$$
Divide both sides by 35.
$$\frac{1505}{35} = \frac{35n}{35}$$
$$43 = n$$
43 students went on the trip.

EXERCISES 4-3

Ⓐ

1. Solve.
   a) $2w - 5 = 11$
   b) $5n - 8 = 12$
   c) $8 - 2u = 12$
   d) $0 = 7p - 35$
   e) $-9p - 81 = 0$
   f) $10 = -3x - 5$
   g) $-11z - 2 = 20$
   h) $3 - 2y = -7$
   i) $-9 = 8b - 1$
   j) $17 = 5q + 2$
   k) $8 - 3z = -1$
   l) $-13 = 4p - 1$

2. Solve.
   a) $8t + 7 = -10$
   b) $9p - 2 = 6$
   c) $-5r + 6 = 8$
   d) $4x + \dfrac{3}{4} = \dfrac{7}{4}$
   e) $3x - \dfrac{1}{4} = 2$
   f) $-1 = 7x - \dfrac{5}{12}$
   g) $10t - \dfrac{2}{5} = \dfrac{3}{5}$
   h) $7x + \dfrac{5}{4} = -3$
   i) $11x - \dfrac{1}{2} = \dfrac{3}{2}$
   j) $9t - \dfrac{3}{5} = -\dfrac{6}{5}$
   k) $1 = 8s - \dfrac{1}{3}$
   l) $\dfrac{7}{6} + 8t = \dfrac{13}{6}$

Ⓑ

3. Solve.
   a) $\dfrac{1}{3}r - 3 = -6$
   b) $\dfrac{1}{4}x + 6 = 10$
   c) $\dfrac{1}{7}x - 1 = \dfrac{9}{7}$
   d) $1.5x - 3 = -12$
   e) $2.5y + 3 = -8$
   f) $1 = 3.8x - 0.9$
   g) $4.4y + 3 = 5.64$
   h) $1.3w + 65 = 26$
   i) $12.5z - 36 = 64$

4. Solve.
   a) $12 = 9 - 2t$
   b) $23 = 11 - 3r$
   c) $8 - 3z = -19$
   d) $5y + \dfrac{3}{5} = 3$
   e) $7x - \dfrac{5}{9} = 3$
   f) $\dfrac{5}{16} = \dfrac{11}{16} - \dfrac{1}{4}x$
   g) $0.2x + 4 = 7$
   h) $-1 = 5 - 0.3t$
   i) $0.25p + 0.25 = 0.5$

5. Solve.

a) $\dfrac{2}{5}t + 3 = 11$ b) $\dfrac{n}{3} + 4 = -6$ c) $-\dfrac{3}{4}z + 5 = -1$

d) $1.2(2x - 3) = 7.2$ e) $-3.5(1 + 3r) = 7$ f) $3\left(5.6 + \dfrac{x}{3}\right) = 0$

6. Solve.

a) $4(x - 2) = 9$ b) $-3 = 5(z + 7)$ c) $-\dfrac{2}{3}(x + 1) = 6$

d) $-3\left(y - \dfrac{1}{2}\right) = \dfrac{1}{2}$ e) $0.02 = 0.8(y + 0.1)$ f) $1.2(t + 2.3) = 3.96$

g) $0.6(5s - 6) = 2.4$ h) $1.21 = 11(0.51 + 0.4x)$ i) $2.4(6.7 + 1.2x) = 24.72$

7. If $3w = 6 - 9z$, find:
   a) the value of w for each given value of z
      i) 1   ii) -2 iii) 0.5   iv) -1.4 v) 0
   b) the value of z for each given value of w.
      i) 0   ii) -1 iii) 2.2   iv) -19 v) 110

8. To determine how far away the centre of a storm is, count the number of seconds, t, between a flash of lightning and the sound of thunder. Substitute this value for t in the formula $d = \dfrac{8t}{25}$ to find d, the distance in kilometres.
   a) Find how far away the storm is when the time lapse is:
      i) 5 s   ii) 10 s   iii) 3.5 s.
   b) Find the time lapse when the storm is:
      i) 8 km away   ii) 6 km away.

9. Typing speed, S, in words per minute, is calculated with the formula
   $S = \dfrac{w - 10e}{5}$, where w is the number of words typed in 5 min and e is the number
   of errors made in the same period.
   a) Find how many words must be typed in 5 min if, when 5 errors are made, the typing speed is 40 words/min.
   b) Find how many errors are made for the typing speed to be 30 words/min when 180 words are typed in 5 min.

10. Weekly mathematics tests have 15 questions. Each question has either one, two, or three parts.
    a) If, on one test, 9 questions have one part, 4 questions have two parts, and 2 questions have three parts, how many parts are there altogether?
    b) If a test has a total of 29 parts, 6 questions having one part and 5 questions having three parts, how many questions have two parts?
    c) One test has 8 questions, each with only one part and there is a total of 24 parts. How many questions have two parts and how many have three?

PROBLEM SOLVING

Write an Equation

An anthropologist discovered the bones of a
huge fish with a head that was 9 m long.
The tail was as long as the head, plus half
the length of the body.
The body was as long as the head and tail
combined.
How long was the fish?

Understand the problem
- How long was the head?
- How long was the tail?
- What are we asked to find?

Think of a strategy
- Write an equation to relate what we are asked to find, to the
  information given.

Carry out the strategy
- Choose a variable l to represent the length of the body in metres.

- The length of the tail is $\left(9 + \dfrac{1}{2}l\right)$ metres.

- We know that: length of head + length of tail = length of body

  that is,
  $$9 + \left(9 + \frac{1}{2}l\right) = l$$

- Solve the equation for l.
  $$18 + \frac{1}{2}l = l$$
  $$18 = \frac{1}{2}l$$
  $$l = 36$$

- The body is 36 m long.
  Length of fish = length of head + length of body + length of tail
  $$= 9 + 36 + 9 + \frac{1}{2}(36)$$
  $$= 72$$
  The fish was 72 m long.

Look back
- Calculate the length of the tail in two ways. Are the answers the
  same?

Solve each problem

1. The lengths of the sides of an isosceles triangle are shown in the diagram (below left). Find the value of x.

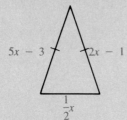

		19
51	50	
		82

2. All rows, columns, and diagonals of a magic square have the same sum. Complete the magic square (above right).

3. Kim lives at the bottom of a mountain. It took her 6 h to ride to the top of the mountain and back. Her average speed up the mountain was 6 km/h and her average speed down the mountain was 24 km/h. How long did it take Kim to ride down the mountain?

4. Peanuts worth $2.80/kg are mixed with pecans worth $4.20/kg. How many grams of each should be mixed to produce a 1 kg mixture worth $3.36?

5. A rectangular walk is a line of 9 identical square cement tiles. The perimeter of the walk is 20 m. What is the area of each cement tile?

6. The total mass of a can and the paint it contains is 5 kg when half full, and 4 kg when one-third full. What is the total mass when the can is:
   a) empty   b) full of paint?

7. A shopkeeper sets retail prices at $p\%$ above cost. On a special sale he reduces these prices by 20%. At these prices he makes no profit. What is the value of p?

8. If a block weighs 7 kg plus half a block, what is the mass of a block and a half?

9. Eric and Lois are trading hockey cards. If Eric gives one card to Lois, they will have the same number. If Lois gives one card to Eric, he will have twice as many as she. How many cards does each person have to start with?

10. The mass of a candy-bar wrapper is $\dfrac{1}{11}$ the mass of the wrapped bar. If the candy bar alone has a mass of 75 g, what is the mass of the wrapper?

11. The sum of the digits of a two-digit number is 9. When the digits are interchanged, the number is decreased by 45. What is the number?

4-4 COMBINING TERMS CONTAINING THE VARIABLE

To solve an equation, it is necessary to isolate the variable on one side of the equation. The numerical terms are combined on the other side of the equation. When several terms contain the variable they must be combined, too.

Example 1. Solve.

a) $6x - 5 = 2x + 7$ b) $2 - 3y = 7 + y$

Solution.   a) $6x - 5 = 2x + 7$

Subtract $2x$ from both sides.

$$6x - 5 - 2x = 2x + 7 - 2x$$
$$4x - 5 = 7$$

Add 5 to both sides.

$$4x - 5 + 5 = 7 + 5$$
$$4x = 12$$

Divide both sides by 4.

$$\frac{4x}{4} = \frac{12}{4}$$
$$x = 3$$

b) $2 - 3y = 7 + y$

Add $3y$ to both sides.

$$2 - 3y + 3y = 7 + y + 3y$$
$$2 = 7 + 4y$$

Subtract 7 from both sides.

$$2 - 7 = 7 + 4y - 7$$
$$-5 = 4y$$

Divide both sides by 4.

$$\frac{-5}{4} = \frac{4y}{4}$$
$$-\frac{5}{4} = y$$

These examples illustrate that it doesn't matter on which side of the equation the variable is isolated.

Sometimes it is necessary to expand before combining the terms and isolating the variable.

Example 2. Solve.

a) $5(y - 1) = 7(3 + y)$ b) $3(y - 1) - 5y = 2y - (y - 2)$

Solution.   a)

$$5(y - 1) = 7(3 + y)$$
$$5y - 5 = 21 + 7y$$
$$5y - 5 - 5y = 21 + 7y - 5y$$
$$-5 = 21 + 2y$$
$$-5 - 21 = 21 + 2y - 21$$
$$-26 = 2y$$
$$\frac{-26}{2} = \frac{2y}{2}$$
$$-13 = y$$

b)

$$3(y - 1) - 5y = 2y - (y - 2)$$
$$3y - 3 - 5y = 2y - y + 2$$
$$-2y - 3 = y + 2$$

Add 3 to, and subtract y from, both sides.

$$-2y - 3 + 3 - y = y + 2 + 3 - y$$
$$-3y = 5$$
$$\frac{-3y}{-3} = \frac{5}{-3}$$
$$y = -\frac{5}{3}$$

EXERCISES 4-4

(A)

1. Solve.

a) $7x - 3 = 4x + 3$ b) $5y + 9 = 2y - 3$
c) $-4m + 2 = 6m + 12$ d) $-8t - 5 = -9t - 7$
e) $3r - 2 = -5r + 14$ f) $6p - 7 = -6p - 7$
g) $5 - y = 3 - 2y$ h) $9 - 2x = 6 - x$
i) $3 - 2t = 5 - 5t$ j) $4 - p = 5 - 3p$
k) $7 - 5p = 6 + p$ l) $8 - 3r = -6 + r$
m) $-11 + 6v = -6v + 11$ n) $-8w = -4 - 6w$

(B)

2. Solve.

a) $3(x - 1) = 12$ b) $5(x + 2) = 10$
c) $-14 = x - 3$ d) $x - 2 = 2(x - 1)$
e) $3y - 2 = y + 4$ f) $4y = -2(9 - y)$
g) $y + 7 = 3y - 9$ h) $9y - 3 = 3(y - 4)$

3. Solve.

a) $2(t - 3) = -3(t - 1)$ b) $-3(r + 2) = -4(r - 1)$
c) $7(z + 3) = 5(z - 1)$ d) $4(2y - 1) = 5(3y + 1)$
e) $-3(4p + 2) = 4(2p - 2)$ f) $-2(1 - x) = -3(2 - x)$
g) $6(-2 - x) = -5(2x + 4)$ h) $2.5(2 - 3x) = 1.5(3x - 2)$

4. Solve.
   a) $6y - 2 = 5y + 4$ b) $3p + 2 = 5p - 7$
   c) $4 - r = 3 - 2r$ d) $9 - 2p = -8 - p$
   e) $5(x - 1) = 8(1 - x)$ f) $7(y - 2) = 13$
   g) $-2(x - 1) = 3(x + 2)$ h) $-3(y + 1) = -2(y - 1)$
   i) $r - 1 = 5r - 7$ j) $19t - 13 = 2t + 4$
   k) $17y + 3 = 15y - 3$ l) $z - 2 = 2z - 2$
   m) $x + 4 = 11x + 4$ n) $t - 8 = -12t + 18$

5. Solve.
   a) $4(x - 2) + 5 = 3 + 2(x - 3)$ b) $1 + 5(x - 1) = 4(x - 3) + 6$
   c) $-2(m + 4) = 3(5 - m) - 8$ d) $y + 3(y - 6) = 2(3 - y) + 3y$
   e) $3(n - 2) + 12 = 6n - 3(4 - n)$ f) $11 - 2(5 + 3x) = 2(x - 6) + 14$

4-5 EQUATIONS WITH FRACTIONAL COEFFICIENTS

Consider the problem posed at the beginning of the chapter. A car uses gasoline at an average rate of 23.4 miles per gallon. The fraction of driving that the car does on the highway is given by the value of f in this equation.

$$23.4 = \frac{84}{5}f + 15$$

To find the fraction of highway driving, solve the equation for f.

$$23.4 = \frac{84}{5}f + 15$$

Multiply both sides by the common denominator 5.

$$5(23.4) = 5\left(\frac{84}{5}f + 15\right)$$
$$117 = 5\left(\frac{84}{5}f\right) + 5(15)$$
$$117 = 84f + 75$$
$$117 - 75 = 84f + 75 - 75$$
$$42 = 84f$$
$$\frac{42}{84} = \frac{84f}{84}$$
$$\frac{1}{2} = f$$

Half the car's driving is done on the highway.

When an equation contains fractions, multiply both sides of the equation by a common denominator of the fractions to obtain an equivalent equation without fractions.

Example 1. Solve. $\dfrac{a}{3} - 3 = \dfrac{3}{4}a + \dfrac{1}{2}$

Solution.
$$\frac{a}{3} - 3 = \frac{3}{4}a + \frac{1}{2}$$

Multiply both sides by the common denominator 12.
$$12\left(\frac{a}{3} - 3\right) = 12\left(\frac{3a}{4} + \frac{1}{2}\right)$$
$$12\left(\frac{a}{3}\right) - 12(3) = 12\left(\frac{3a}{4}\right) + 12\left(\frac{1}{2}\right)$$
$$4a - 36 = 9a + 6$$
$$4a - 36 - 4a - 6 = 9a + 6 - 4a - 6$$
$$-42 = 5a$$
$$-\frac{42}{5} = \frac{5a}{5}$$
$$-\frac{42}{5} = a$$

Example 2. Solve. $\dfrac{3x + 2}{2} - \dfrac{x + 1}{3} = x$

Solution.
$$\frac{3x + 2}{2} - \frac{x + 1}{3} = x$$

Multiply both sides by 6.
$$6\left(\frac{3x + 2}{2} - \frac{x + 1}{3}\right) = 6(x)$$
$$\frac{6(3x + 2)}{2} - \frac{6(x + 1)}{3} = 6x$$
$$9x + 6 - 2x - 2 = 6x$$
$$7x + 4 = 6x$$
$$7x + 4 - 7x = 6x - 7x$$
$$4 = -x$$
$$\frac{4}{-1} = \frac{-x}{-1}$$
$$-4 = x$$

EXERCISES 4-5

Ⓐ

1. Solve.

a) $\dfrac{a}{4} = \dfrac{1}{2}$

b) $\dfrac{x}{5} = -\dfrac{2}{3}$

c) $\dfrac{1}{3} = \dfrac{-2x}{5}$

d) $\dfrac{1}{2}x + \dfrac{1}{3}x = 10$

e) $\dfrac{1}{4}y - \dfrac{1}{2}y = 4$

f) $\dfrac{y}{3} - \dfrac{2}{3} = 4$

g) $\dfrac{2}{5}a + \dfrac{a}{2} = a - 2$

h) $\dfrac{1}{2}n - \dfrac{2}{3}n + \dfrac{3}{4}n = -7$

i) $\dfrac{x}{3} + \dfrac{1}{2} = -2x$

2. Solve.

a) $-\dfrac{1}{3}x + \dfrac{3}{4}x = 10$

b) $\dfrac{3}{5}x - \dfrac{3}{2}x = 10$

c) $\dfrac{2a}{3} = \dfrac{3a}{5} + 4$

d) $\dfrac{2}{3}x + 9 = \dfrac{3}{4}x - 6$

e) $\dfrac{5x}{2} - 3 = 8 + \dfrac{2x}{3}$

f) $5 - \dfrac{4}{3}x = \dfrac{3}{4}x + \dfrac{5}{2}$

3. Nicole's car uses gasoline at a rate of 11.3 L/100 km. The fraction of driving that Nicole does on the highway is given by the value of f in this formula.

$$11.3 = -\dfrac{25}{4}f + \dfrac{69}{5}$$

Find the fraction of driving that Nicole does on the highway.

(B)

4. Solve.

a) $\dfrac{a}{5} - a = \dfrac{1}{2}$

b) $\dfrac{2x}{3} = \dfrac{x}{2} - \dfrac{1}{4}$

c) $\dfrac{m}{6} - 5 = \dfrac{1}{2}m$

d) $\dfrac{3k}{4} + \dfrac{1}{2} = \dfrac{k}{3}$

e) $\dfrac{1}{3}(x + 1) = \dfrac{1}{2}(x - 2)$

f) $\dfrac{1}{5}(2n + 1) = \dfrac{2}{3}(n - 1)$

g) $\dfrac{a + 5}{3} = \dfrac{3 - a}{7}$

h) $\dfrac{1}{5}\left(\dfrac{1}{2}x + 4\right) = \dfrac{1}{3}\left(\dfrac{1}{4}x + 3\right)$

i) $\dfrac{1}{4}(2 - x) + \dfrac{1}{2} = \dfrac{1}{2}\left(\dfrac{1}{3}x + 7\right)$

j) $-\dfrac{1}{2}(x - 2) + \dfrac{1}{4} = \dfrac{2}{5}(2 - x)$

5. Solve.

a) $\dfrac{4x}{5} - \dfrac{3}{2} = \dfrac{2}{3} + \dfrac{1}{3}x$

b) $\dfrac{1}{4}(x - 3) + \dfrac{1}{3}(3 + x) = 1$

c) $-\dfrac{x}{3} + \dfrac{x}{4} - \dfrac{x}{6} = \dfrac{1}{10}$

d) $-\dfrac{1}{6}(3 - 5x) = \dfrac{2}{3}(5x + 3)$

e) $-\dfrac{3}{4}x - \dfrac{4x}{5} + \dfrac{7x}{10} = \dfrac{-1}{20}$

f) $-\dfrac{3}{7} = \dfrac{5}{14}(4 - 6x) + \dfrac{2x}{7}$

g) $\dfrac{7}{8}(-x - 6) + \dfrac{3}{4}(2x + 3) = \dfrac{-3}{8}$

h) $\dfrac{3x}{10} - \dfrac{2x}{5} = \dfrac{3x}{2} + \dfrac{1}{2}$

i) $\dfrac{11}{2}(7x - 6) = -\dfrac{1}{4}x + \dfrac{9}{2}(3 - 2x)$

j) $-\dfrac{3}{2}(7 - 4x) = \dfrac{2}{7}x - \dfrac{1}{2}(-3x + 4)$

6. If $y = -\dfrac{3}{5}x - \dfrac{1}{4}$, find:

a) the value of y for each given value of x

i) 0 ii) $\dfrac{1}{3}$ iii) $-\dfrac{1}{3}$ iv) 2 v) -2

b) the value of x for each given value of y.

i) 0 ii) $\dfrac{1}{2}$ iii) $-\dfrac{1}{2}$ iv) 1.5 v) -1.5

4-6 WORKING WITH FORMULAS

After working out, Michelle wonders if her pulse rate of 150 beats per minute exceeds the maximum for her age. She uses the formula $a = 220 - m$, where a is a person's age in years and m is the maximum desirable pulse rate in beats per minute.

Michelle substitutes 15 for a and solves the equation.

$$15 = 220 - m$$
$$-205 = -m$$
$$m = 205$$

The maximum desirable pulse rate for a 15-year-old is 205 beats per minute. Michelle's rate of 150 beats per minute is well below this maximum.

Recall that formulas are equations which relate two or more variables using the basic operations of arithmetic. Science, engineering, and industry use many formulas. Often, the values of all but one of the variables are known. It is necessary to substitute the known values into a formula, and then solve the equation to find the value of the unknown variable.

Example 1. The annual simple interest, I dollars, on a principal, P dollars, is given by this formula. $I = 0.095P$
Find the principal that earned \$807.50 interest in one year.

Solution. $I = 0.095P$
Substitute 807.50 for I.
$807.50 = 0.095P$
Divide both sides by 0.095.
$$\frac{807.50}{0.095} = P$$
$8500 = P$
The principal is \$8500.

Example 2. A scientific experiment illustrates that a rubber band stretches according to this formula.

$$l = 9.2 + 0.17m$$

l is the length of the band in centimetres, and *m* is the mass in grams, suspended on one end of the band.

a) Calculate the length, to the nearest centimetre, of the rubber band when the mass on the end is 25 g.

b) Calculate the mass, to the nearest gram, that will stretch the band to 86 cm.

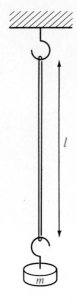

Solution.

a) $l = 9.2 + 0.17m$
Substitute 25 for *m*.
$l = 9.2 + 0.17(25)$
$\quad = 13.45$
The band is about 13 cm long.

b) $\quad l = 9.2 + 0.17m$
Substitute 86 for *l*.
$\quad 86 = 9.2 + 0.17m$
Solve for *m*.
$76.8 = 0.17m$
$\dfrac{76.8}{0.17} = m$

$\quad m \doteq 452$

A mass of 452 g will stretch the band to 86 cm.

To find the masses which correspond to several lengths of the rubber band, it is more efficient to solve the equation for *m* before substituting.

$$l = 9.2 + 0.17m$$
$$l - 9.2 = 0.17m$$
$$\frac{l - 9.2}{0.17} = m$$

For other types and thicknesses of rubber, the constant term and the coefficient in this formula would be different. Thus, the general formula for stretching any type of rubber band might be given by this formula.

$$l = a + bm$$

a and *b* are constants with values depending on the type of rubber band.

An equation of this type, in which the constants are represented by letters, is called a *literal* equation.

Example 3. a) Solve for F. $C = \frac{5}{9}(F - 32)$

b) Solve for x. $ax + 3c = d$

Solution. a)

$$C = \frac{5}{9}(F - 32)$$
$$9C = 5(F - 32)$$
$$9C = 5F - 160$$
$$9C + 160 = 5F$$
$$F = \frac{9C + 160}{5}$$

b)
$$ax + 3c = d$$
$$ax = d - 3c$$
$$x = \frac{d - 3c}{a}$$

EXERCISES 4-6

Ⓐ

1. The monthly interest, I dollars, on a loan is given by the formula $I = 0.0175P$, where P is the principal. Find the first month's interest on a principal of $1250.

2. The yearly interest, I dollars, is given by the formula $I = 0.11P$, where P is the principal.
   a) Find the interest for one year on each principal.
      i) $100   ii) $1000   iii) $2500   iv) $9000
   b) Find the principal which yields each interest, in one year.
      i) $22   ii) $55   iii) $132   iv) $159.50

3. Solve for x.
   a) $mx + n = p$ b) $\frac{1}{2}x - c = d$ c) $ax - b = d$

   d) $\frac{2}{3}x + 3 = k$ e) $wx + 1 = v$ f) $a - bx = d$

4. Solve for the variable indicated.
   a) $I = Prt$, for t b) $P = 2l + 2w$, for l c) $A = \frac{1}{2}bh$, for b
   d) $C = 2\pi r$, for r e) $l = a + bm$, for m f) $A = 50 + 1.275P$, for P

5. The area, A, of a parallelogram is given by the formula $A = bh$, where b is the length of the base and h is the height.
   a) Find the area of a parallelogram with base 10.3 cm and height 13.6 cm.

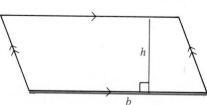

   b) Find the height of a parallelogram with area 25.2 cm² and base 5.6 cm.

(B)

6. When an object falls freely from rest, its approximate speed, v metres per second after t seconds, is given by the formula $v = 9.8t$.
   a) Solve the formula for t.
   b) Find the time, to the nearest tenth of a second, it will take the object to reach these speeds.
       i) 54 m/s   ii) 81 m/s   iii) 343 m/s   iv) 1 km/s

7. Solve for the variable indicated.
   a) $V = \pi r^2 h$, for h b) $F = \dfrac{Mm}{d}$, for m c) $I = \dfrac{100m}{P}$, for m

   d) $A = \dfrac{1}{2}h(a + b)$, for h e) $n = \dfrac{v}{4l}$, for l f) $\dfrac{1}{3}x + b = c$, for x

8. Solve for the variable indicated.
   a) $S = \dfrac{w - 10e}{5}$, for w b) $n = 17 - \dfrac{1}{2}a$, for a
   c) $L_2 = L_1(1 + at)$, for t d) $C = 3.7 + 0.99(n - 3)$, for n
   e) $S = \dfrac{n}{2}(a + l)$, for l f) $A = \dfrac{1}{2}h(a + b)$, for b

9. The length, l centimetres, of a rubber band suspending a mass of m grams is given by the formula $l = 14.3 + 0.27m$.
   a) Solve the formula for m.
   b) Find the mass, to the nearest gram, that stretches the band to each length.
       i) 98 cm   ii) 103 cm

10. When an object on the moon falls freely from rest, its approximate speed, v metres per second after t seconds, is given by the formula $v = 1.63t$.
    a) Find its speed, to one decimal place, after each time period.
        i) 1 s   ii) 5 s   iii) 8 s   iv) 10 s
    b) Find the time, to the nearest tenth of a second, the object takes to reach each speed.
        i) 5 m/s   ii) 32 m/s   iii) 57 m/s   iv) 0.6 km/s

11. The area, A, of a trapezoid is given by the formula, $A = \dfrac{1}{2}h(a + b)$, where a and b are the lengths of the parallel sides and h is the distance between them.

    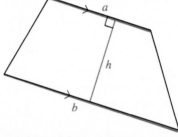

    a) Find the distance between the parallel sides if their lengths are 9 cm and 23 cm, and the area is 256 cm².
    b) Find the length of one parallel side if the other parallel side is 3.4 cm, the distance between them is 6.0 cm, and the area is 23.7 cm².

PROBLEM SOLVING

Choose the Strategy

1. All solids of the same shape have the same mass. How many cones have the same mass as 4 cylinders?

2. There were 6 more students in Mrs. Zovak's class who did not have scientific calculators than in Mr. Alvi's class. Five of these students transferred from Mrs. Zovak's class into Mr. Alvi's class. Now Mr. Alvi has twice as many students without scientific calculators as Mrs. Zovak. How many students in Mr. Alvi's class do not have scientific calculators?

3. A shuttle bus picked up a group of people at the airport. The bus travelled to the Hyatt Hotel where it let off 14 people and picked up 3. At the Holiday Inn, it let off half of those who were remaining and picked up 13 people. There were now 16 people on the bus. How many people were picked up at the airport?

4. Jack is now 4 times as old as his dog. In 6 years he will be only twice as old as his dog. How old is Jack? How old is his dog?

5. An 18 m log is cut into 2 pieces. The longer piece is 3 m shorter than twice the shorter piece. How long is the shorter piece?

6. Mrs. Richards divided $45 among her four children: Amanda, Betty, Carol, and Dan. When the children complained that the shares were not equal, she instructed Betty to give Amanda $2. Then she doubled Carol's share and cut Dan's share in half. Now all of the children have the same amount. How much money do they have in total?

7. a) Explain why every integer can be expressed in exactly one of the forms, $6n$, $6n + 1$, $6n + 2$, $6n + 3$, $6n + 4$, $6n + 5$ for some integer n.
   b) In which of these 5 forms can the prime numbers be expressed?
   c) Show that all prime numbers (except 2 and 3) when divided by 6 leave a remainder of either 1 or 5.

8. Raymond has a box of candy bars. He gave Monique half of what he had plus half a bar. Then he gave Claude half of what he had left plus half a bar. After which he gave Laura half of what he had left plus half a bar. And, finally, he gave Alfred half of what he had left plus half a bar. Then he had no bars left. How many candy bars did Raymond have to start?

4-7 WRITING EQUATIONS

When problems are solved with algebra, the first step is to translate the given facts into the language of algebra. The kinds of problems in this section give two facts. We use one fact to express each quantity in terms of the variable. The other fact enables us to write an equation.

Example 1. A number is 4 times another number. The sum of the numbers is 59. Write an equation with the smaller number as its solution.

Solution. The facts of the problem are
① A number is 4 times another number.
② The sum of the numbers is 59.
Method A. Use fact ① to express the larger number in terms of the smaller number.
Let the smaller number be represented by x.
Then, the larger number is $4x$.
Use fact ② to write the equation.
The sum of the numbers is 59.

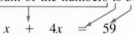

$$x + 4x = 59$$

Method B. Use fact ② to relate the two numbers.
Let the smaller number be represented by x.
Then, the larger number is $59 - x$.
Use fact ① to write the equation.
The larger number is 4 times the smaller number.

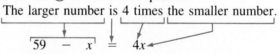

$$59 - x = 4x$$

In *Example 1*, the two methods produce two forms of the same equation. This illustrates that the equation is independent of the fact that was used to write it. However, when one fact is more complicated than the other, use the complicated fact to write the equation.

Example 2. The sum of two numbers is 117. Five times the smaller number is seven less than three times the larger. Write an equation with the larger number as its solution.

Solution. The simple fact is: The sum of two numbers is 117.
Let the larger number be represented by x.
Then, the smaller number is $117 - x$.
Use the complicated fact to write the equation.

Five times the smaller   is   three times the larger   less seven

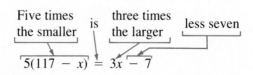

$$5(117 - x) = 3x - 7$$

Example 3. Find two consecutive odd numbers with a sum of 352.
Write an equation with the smaller number as its solution.

Solution. Let the smaller number be represented by x.
Then, the larger number is $x + 2$.
Write the equation.
The sum of
the numbers is 352

$$x + x + 2 = 352$$

EXERCISES 4-7

Ⓐ

In Exercises 1 to 4, write algebraic expressions to complete parts a) and b). Then write an equation for part c).

1. Ravi is 8 years older than Natasha.
   a) Let Natasha's age be represented by ▨ years.
   b) Then, Ravi's age is ▨ years.
   c) The sum of their ages is 42.

2. Gayle's mass is 2.5 kg less than Maria's.
   a) Let Maria's mass be represented by ▨ kilograms.
   b) Then, Gayle's mass is ▨ kilograms.
   c) The sum of their masses is 97.5 kg.

3. A 12 m tree trunk is cut into two pieces.
   a) Let the length of the shorter piece be represented by ▨ metres.
   b) Then, the length of the longer piece is ▨ metres.
   c) The shorter piece is one-third the length of the longer.

4. The ages of Paul and Judy total 27 years.
   a) Let Paul's age be represented by ▨ years.
   b) Then, Judy's age is ▨ years.
   c) Judy's age plus twice Paul's age is 43.

Ⓑ

Write an equation the solution of which will solve the problem for each of Exercises 5 to 15.

5. Brian ran 2 km less than Tom. They ran a total distance of 12 km. Find how far each boy ran.

6. Marie ran twice as far as Brenda. They ran a total distance of 12 km. Find how far each girl ran.

7. The length of a rectangle is 5 cm longer than the width. The perimeter is 68 cm. Find the dimensions of the rectangle.

8. Find two consecutive numbers with a sum of 263.

9. Find four consecutive numbers with a sum of 234.

10. Find two consecutive even numbers with a sum of 170.

11. One number is one-fifth of another number. The two numbers total 18. Find the numbers.

12. The combined mass of a dog and a cat is 24 kg. The dog is three times as heavy as the cat. Find the mass of each animal.

13. In a class of 33 students, there are 9 fewer boys than girls. Find how many girls there are.

14. Millie is four times as old as Marty. The sum of their ages is 65 years. Find how old the people are.

15. Find two numbers that
    a) are consecutive and have a sum of 83.
    b) differ by 17 and have a sum of 39.

In Exercises 16 to 18, write algebraic expressions to complete parts a) and b). Then write an equation for part c).

16. The sum of two numbers is 54.
    a) Let the smaller number be represented by ▨.
    b) Then, the larger number is ▨.
    c) Twice the smaller is 9 more than the larger.

17. The sum of Millie's and Marty's ages is 65.
    a) Let Millie's age be represented by ▨ years.
    b) Then, Marty's age is ▨ years.
    c) Three times Millie's age is 15 years less than twice Marty's age.

18. Adrienne is twice as old as René.
    a) Let René's age be represented by ▨ years.
    b) Then, Adrienne's age is ▨ years.
    c) The sum of their ages 3 years ago was 48.

Write an equation the solution of which will solve the problem for each of Exercises 19 to 24.

19. The sum of two numbers is 63. Three times the smaller number is 14 more than twice the larger number. Find the numbers.

20. The sum of Julio's and Ramona's ages is 35. Twice Ramona's age is 7 more than Julio's age. Find how old they are.

21. Susan is twice as old as Lana. The sum of their ages 4 years ago was 37. Find how old they are now.

Ⓒ

22. The sum of three numbers is 33. The second number is 7 less than the first, and the third number is 2 more than the second. Find the numbers.

23. The sum of three numbers is 75. The second number is 5 more than the first, and the third is three times the second. Find the numbers.

24. James has two-fifths the amount that Lorna has, and Muriel has seven-ninths the amount that James has. Together, they have $770. Find how much each person has.

4-8 SOLVING PROBLEMS USING EQUATIONS: PART ONE

Alexia sees a package deal for skis and boots costing $225. The salesman tells Alexia that the skis cost $60 more than the boots. Alexia wants to know what the skis cost.

She writes an equation, after listing the information in algebraic terms.

Let b dollars represent the cost of the skis.

Since the skis cost $60 more than the boots, the boots cost $(b - 60)$ dollars.

The total cost is $225, so the equation is

$$b + (b - 60) = 225$$
$$2b - 60 = 225$$
$$2b = 285$$
$$b = 142.5$$

The skis cost $142.50.

Solving a problem using an equation involves three steps.

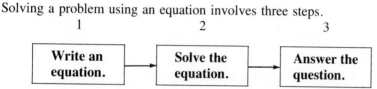

The previous sections prepared you for Step 1. Earlier sections in this chapter prepared you for Step 2. Step 3 is merely taking the solution of the equation and answering the question the problem asks.

When you check the solution, do *not* substitute in the equation, substitute in the problem. You could have made a mistake in writing the equation.

Example 1. When four times a number is increased by 25, the result is 77. Find the number.

Solution. Step 1.   Let the number be represented by x.
Then, 4 times the number, increased by 25 is $4x + 25$.
The equation is $4x + 25 = 77$.

Step 2. $4x + 25 = 77$
$$4x = 52$$
$$x = 13$$

Step 3.   The number is 13.

Check.   The number is 13.
Four times the number is 4(13) or 52.
52 increased by 25 is 77. The solution is correct.

Example 2. In a fishing derby, the mass of fish that Yvonne caught was four times the mass of Michael's catch. Their total catch was 59 kg. How much fish did each person catch?

Solution.   Step 1.   Let *m* kilograms represent the mass of Michael's fish.
Then, 4*m* kilograms is the mass of Yvonne's fish.
The equation is $m + 4m = 59$.

Step 2. $m + 4m = 59$
$$5m = 59$$
$$m = 11.8$$

Step 3.   Michael's catch was 11.8 kg.
Yvonne's catch was 4(11.8) kg or 47.2 kg.

Check.   The total catch was 11.8 kg + 47.2 kg or 59 kg.
The solution is correct.

In *Step 1* of this solution, the unit of mass was included with the variable
to represent the quantity of fish caught. It is important to state the unit
because a variable represents a number, not a quantity.

In reading the problem, look for the simple fact. Use it to express
each quantity in terms of a variable. Use the more complicated fact
to write the equation. Solve the equation, and answer the question the
problem asks. Check the answer by substituting in the problem.

EXERCISES 4-8

(A)

1. Six times a number increased by 7 is 103. Find the number.

2. When 19 is added to one-quarter of a number the result is 40. Find the number.

3. When 13 is subtracted from three-eighths of a number the result is 11. Find the number.

4. Find two numbers with a difference of 5 and a sum of 27.

5. Find two consecutive numbers with a sum of 45.

6. Mr. Zaluski is 4 years older than Mrs. Zaluski. Their total age is 76 years. How old is each person?

7. A ribbon 22 m long is cut into two pieces. One piece is 10 m longer than the other. How long is each piece?

8. Bruce is 10 years older than Cindy. The sum of their ages is 52. How old is each person?

(B)

9. Ian's mass is 2.5 kg less than that of Sean. The sum of their masses is 121.5 kg. What is the mass of each person?

10. The ages of John and Mary total 27 years. Mary's age plus twice John's age is 40. How old is each person?

11. Joan's jump was longer than Enid's jump by 15 cm. Joan's jump was 1.04 times as long as Enid's jump. How far did each person jump?

12. For two consecutive integers, the sum of the smaller and twice the larger is 38. What are the integers?

13. For two consecutive integers, the sum of twice the larger and three times the smaller is 242. Find the integers.

14. A Jaguar travelled 1.2 times as fast as a Mercedes. The difference in their speeds was 24 km/h. Find the speed of each car.

15. Marie ran twice as far as Brenda. They ran a total distance of 18 km. How far did each person run?

16. One number is five times another number. If the two numbers total 36, find the numbers.

17. The length of a rectangle is 5 cm longer than the width. The perimeter is 54 cm. Find the dimensions of the rectangle.

18. Find two consecutive numbers with a sum of 285.

19. Find three consecutive numbers with a sum of 159.

20. Find four consecutive numbers with a sum of 198.

21. Find two consecutive even numbers with a sum of 226.

22. In a cross-country marathon, Jack and Ted ran a total of 81 km. Ted ran 5 km farther than Jack. How far did each boy run?

23. In a class of 33 students, there are 7 more girls than boys. How many girls are there?

24. Maria is four times as old as Marty. The sum of their ages is 55 years. How old are they?

25. The difference between two numbers is 96. One number is nine times the other. What are the numbers?

26. One number is 0.25 less than another number. The sum of the numbers is 7.25. Find the numbers.

27. The sum of two numbers is 36. Four times the smaller is 1 less than the larger. What are the numbers?

Ⓒ

28. The sum of three numbers is 33. The second number is 7 less than the first, and the third is three times the second. What are the numbers?

29. The sum of three numbers is 75. The second number is 5 more than the first, and the third is three times the second. What are the numbers?

30. The least of three consecutive integers is divided by 10, the next is divided by 17, the greatest is divided by 26. What are the numbers if the sum of the quotients is 10?

4-9 SOLVING PROBLEMS USING EQUATIONS: PART TWO

In some problems where two facts are given, the statement of the second fact may seem quite complicated. It may not be immediately obvious how to write the equation in terms of the chosen variable. In such cases, it is often helpful to use a table to organize the information.

Example 1.   A parking meter contains $36.85 in dimes and quarters. If there is a total of 223 coins, how many quarters does the meter contain?

Solution.   Step 1.   Let x represent the number of quarters.
Then, the number of dimes is $(223 - x)$.
Before writing the equation, write the value of the quarters and the dimes.

	Number of Coins	**Value in Cents**
Quarters	x	$25x$
Dimes	$223 - x$	$10(223 - x)$

The total value of the coins is $36.85 or 3685 cents.
The equation is $25x + 10(223 - x) = 3685$.

Step 2. $25x + 10(223 - x) = 3685$
$25x + 2230 - 10x = 3685$
$15x = 1455$
$x = 97$

Step 3.   The parking meter contains 97 quarters.

Check.   Since there are 223 coins, the meter contains 126 dimes.
The value, in cents, of 97 quarters and 126 dimes is
$(25)(97) + (10)(126) = 2425 + 1260$
$= 3685$
This is $36.85. The solution is correct.

A table can be particularly useful in problems involving ages.

Example 2. A mother is three times as old as her daughter. Six years ago, she was five times as old. How old are the mother and the daughter now?

Solution. Step 1. Let x represent the daughter's age now in years. Then, the mother's age now is $3x$ years.

	Now	6 years ago
Daughter's age in years	x	$x - 6$
Mother's age in years	$3x$	$3x - 6$

The equation is $3x - 6 = 5(x - 6)$.

Step 2.
$$3x - 6 = 5(x - 6)$$
$$3x - 6 = 5x - 30$$
$$24 = 2x$$
$$12 = x$$

Step 3. The daughter is 12 years old and the mother is 36.

Check. Six years ago, the daughter's age was $12 - 6$, or 6. The mother's age was then $36 - 6$, or 30. Since $5(6) = 30$, the solution is correct.

EXERCISES 4-9

(A)

1. A vending machine contains nickels and dimes only. There is a total of 80 coins. Copy and complete the table to show the value of each kind of coin.

	Number of Coins	Value in Cents
Nickels	x	
Dimes	$80 - x$	

Write an algebraic expression for the total value of the coins.

2. A pay telephone contains twice as many dimes as nickels and four times as many quarters as nickels. Copy and complete the table.

	Number of Coins	Value in Cents
Nickels	x	$5x$
Dimes		
Quarters		

Write an algebraic expression for the total value of the coins.

3. Debbie is now twice as old as Sandra. Copy and complete the table to show algebraic expressions for their ages at different times.

	Now	Last Year	Next Year	4 Years Ago	3 Years From Now
Debbie's age in years	$2x$				
Sandra's age in years	x				

4. Tracey is 8 years older than Trevor. Copy and complete the table to show algebraic expressions for their ages at different times.

	Now	Last Year	Next Year	5 Years Ago	8 Years From Now
Trevor's age in years	x				
Tracey's age in years	$x + 8$				

5. Jeanne is twice as old as Michel. The sum of their ages three years ago was 45 years. What are their ages now?

6. Yvonne has equal numbers of nickels, dimes, and quarters. Their total value is $2.00. How many of each kind of coin does she have?

Ⓑ

7. Tanya is 12 years older than Leah. Three years ago, Tanya was five times as old as Leah. How old is Leah?

8. Find three consecutive odd numbers with a sum of 267.

9. The length of a rectangular pool is 12 m greater than its width. What is the length if the perimeter of the pool is 96 m?

10. Bill is twice as old as his brother Dan. In 7 years, Bill will be only one and one-half times as old as Dan. How old is Bill now?

11. A collection of nickels and dimes has a total value of $8.50. How many coins are there if there are 3 times as many nickels as dimes?

12. Roberta is three years younger than Rebecca. Eight years ago, Roberta was one-half of Rebecca's age. How old is each girl now?

13. A piggy bank contains 91 coins which are nickels, dimes, and quarters. There are twice as many quarters as dimes, and half as many nickels as dimes. How much is in the piggy bank?

©

14. Sophia's age is four years less than twice Beryl's age. In two years, Beryl's age will be three-quarters of Sophia's age. How old is each girl now?

15. A piece of string, 60 cm long, is cut into three pieces. The middle-sized piece is 2 cm longer than the shortest piece and 2 cm shorter than the longest piece. What is the length of each piece?

16. Girish had $2 more than three times the amount that Joseph had. He gave Joseph $5 who then had one-half as much as Girish. How much did each person have at first?

17. A 500 m track has semicircular ends. If the length of the track is three times its width, what is its width?

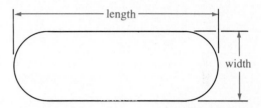

18. At Happy Snack, a milk shake costs twice as much as an order of french fries. If two milk shakes and three orders of french fries cost $4.20, what is the cost of a milk shake?

INVESTIGATE

An inequality is a mathematical sentence that uses the sign $>$ or the sign $<$.
   Investigate whether the rules for solving equations can be used to solve inequalities.

1. Write an inequality that is true, for example, $4 < 8$.

2. Apply each operation listed below. Each time, ask the question, "Is the inequality statement still true?"
   - Add the same integer to both sides.
   - Subtract the same integer from both sides.
   - Multiply both sides by the same positive integer.
   - Multiply both sides by the same negative integer.
   - Divide both sides by the same positive integer.
   - Divide both sides by the same negative integer.

3. What appears to be true?

4. Do the rules for solving equations apply to inequalities?

4-10 SOLVING INEQUALITIES

Boyd sees this sign on a rack of jackets for sale. He calculates that if a jacket has a ticket price of $100, then $\frac{1}{4}$ of $100 is $25. Since the saving is *more than* $\frac{1}{4}$, Boyd realizes that the saving would be more than $25.

If S represents the saving in dollars, then $S > 25$. Similarly, the sale price would be *less than* $75. If P represents the sale price in dollars, then $P < 75$. $S > 25$ and $P < 75$ are examples of *inequalities*.

Inequalities may also be written using these signs.
$\geqslant$, meaning "is greater than or equal to", and
$\leqslant$, meaning "is less than or equal to".
    In the previous investigation, you should have discovered that when both sides of an inequality are multiplied or divided by the same negative number, the statement is no longer true. To keep the statement true, the inequality sign must be reversed, For example,

$$4 < 8$$
$$\text{but } 4(-2) > 8(-2)$$
$$\text{since } -8 > -16$$
$$\text{Also } \frac{4}{-2} > \frac{8}{-2}$$
$$\text{since } -2 > -4$$

> When both sides of an inequality are multiplied or divided by a negative number, the inequality sign must be reversed.

Example 1. Solve. $3x < 5x + 12$

Solution.

$$3x < 5x + 12 \qquad \text{or} \qquad 3x < 5x + 12$$
$$-12 < 2x \qquad\qquad\qquad -2x < 12$$
$$-6 < x \qquad\qquad\qquad\qquad x > -6$$
$$x > -6$$

In the alternative solution, the inequality sign was reversed because of the division by -2.

The solution $x > -6$ means that any number greater than -6 satisfies the inequality. This solution can be illustrated on a number line.

An arrow is drawn in the direction "greater than -6". The open dot at -6 indicates that -6 is not part of the solution.

It is not possible to check the limitless number of solutions to an inequality. However, select one solution and substitute it into the inequality. If the resulting statement is correct, a reasonable conclusion is that the solution is correct.

Example 2. Solve, graph, and check. $3 - 2a \geq a + 9$

Solution.

$$3 - 2a \geq a + 9$$
$$3 \geq 3a + 9$$
$$-6 \geq 3a$$
$$-2 \geq a$$
$$a \leq -2$$

Graph the solution on a number line.

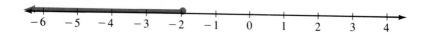

The solid dot at -2 indicates that it is part of the solution.

Check. Since the solution is less than or equal to -2, this includes -5. Substitute $a = -5$ in the inequality.

Left side $= 3 - 2a$	Right side $= a + 9$
$= 3 - 2(-5)$	$= -5 + 9$
$= 3 + 10$	$= 4$
$= 13$	

Since $13 > 4$, the left side *is* greater than the right side, and $a = -5$ satisfies the inequality. This suggests that $a \leq -2$ is the correct solution.

EXERCISES 4-10

1. Solve and graph.
   a) $x + 1 < 4$ b) $x - 1 \leqslant 3$ c) $x + 3 > 2$
   d) $4 > 9 - x$ e) $-13 \geqslant x - 11$ f) $9 \leqslant 15 - x$

2. Write the inequality represented by each graph.

   a)

   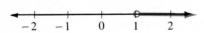

   b)

   c)

   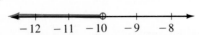

   d)

B

3. Solve and graph.
   a) $7x < 14$ b) $5x \geqslant 10$ c) $9 > -2x$
   d) $3y + 8 > 17$ e) $21 - 5z > 11$ f) $13.5 + 2y \leqslant 18.5$
   g) $13 \leqslant 1 - \dfrac{3}{4}x$ h) $61 < 13w - 4$ i) $18 \geqslant 4.5 - 1.5a$

4. Solve, graph, and check.
   a) $4x - 7 \geqslant 2x + 5$ b) $13 - 2y \leqslant 4y - 14$
   c) $-25 + 11z \leqslant 30 - 11z$ d) $39 + 4w \geqslant 13 - 6w$
   e) $3(x + 2) < 11$ f) $2(x + 8) \leqslant 4(3 + x)$
   g) $5(2 - x) \leqslant 2(x + 7)$ h) $\dfrac{2}{3}(15 - 3x) > \dfrac{1}{2}(2 + 5x)$

5. Solve and check.
   a) $-3y + 8 < 5 - 7y$ b) $18 + 10z \geqslant -12 - 2z$
   c) $14x - 9 \leqslant 17 + x$ d) $-35 - 8a > 6a - 7$
   e) $-4(7 + 2b) \geqslant 3b + 5$ f) $6(-2c - 11) < -5(3c + 8)$
   g) $3(-8 + 2x) > 4 - 2(3x + 5)$ h) $\dfrac{1}{4}(-3y + 7) \leqslant \dfrac{2}{5}(8 - 3y)$

 INVESTIGATE

Which of these statements is false?

- If $\dfrac{a}{b} = \dfrac{c}{d}$ and $a > c$, then $b > d$.
- If $x < y$, then $x < 2y$.

1. Solve.
   a) $5 + x = -11$ b) $y - 14 = 83$ c) $14 - z = -14$
   d) $8 - t = -2$ e) $w + 21 = -13$ f) $17 = 19 - t$

2. Solve.
   a) $5x = 45$ b) $-15 = -3n$ c) $\frac{1}{5}t = -3$ d) $\frac{n}{14} = -7$

3. Solve.
   a) $6p - 3 = 15$ b) $13 = 4 + 3x$ c) $-6 - 2r = 8$

   d) $5 - 5y = 1$ e) $8p - 3 = 7$ f) $3x - \frac{1}{5} = 4$

4. The cost, C cents, of making copies on a copying machine is given by the formula
   $C = 90 + 3n$, where n is the number of copies.
   a) What is the cost of making 200 copies?
   b) How many copies can be made for $6.00?

5. Solve.
   a) $5y - 2 = 3y + 4$ b) $-7x + 6 = 2x - 3$
   c) $r - 3 = 2r + 4$ d) $11 - 1.3x = 4.7x - 7$
   e) $4(x - 3) = -2$ f) $-5(y + 3) = 14$

6. Solve.
   a) $t + 17 - 2t = -3(t - 1) - 3$
   b) $9 - 3(1 - q) = 7 - 4(2 - q)$
   c) $-9(r + 3) - 9r = -3r - (3 - r) + 8$
   d) $3(7v + 8) - 9 = 14 - 2v + 6(3v - 4)$
   e) $5(6w - 3) - 7 = 17 + 3w - 5(2w + 1)$
   f) $-2(5x - 1) - 4 = 22 - 7x + 8(3x - 1)$

7. Solve and check.
   a) $4(t + 1) = 2t + (1 - t)$
   b) $6(w - 2) = 3w + 2(w + 1)$
   c) $7.2x - 7.5 - 1.7x = 4.6 + 4.4x$
   d) $15(0.3 - z) + 14.5z = 2(0.5z - 10)$

8. The sum of the angles of a triangle
   is 180°. For the triangle shown
   a) Find the value of a when b is:
      i) 30°   ii) 60°.
   b) Find the value of b when a is:
      i) 20°   ii) 50°.

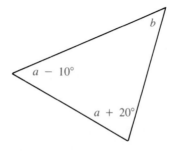

9. A ball, dropped from a height of d centimetres, bounces to a height of b centimetres where $b = \frac{3}{4}d$.
   a) Find the height from which the ball was dropped if the height of the bounce is:
      i) 90 cm   ii) 75 cm   iii) 60 cm   iv) 39 cm
   b) The ball is dropped from a height of 160 cm. Find the height of:
      i) its second bounce   ii) its third bounce.

10. Jeanne is twice as old as Michel. The sum of their ages 3 years ago was 45 years. Find their ages now.

11. Five times a number decreased by 8 is 17. Find the number.

12. Jason is three times as old as Mark. The sum of their ages is 20 years. How old is Mark?

13. Jackie ran 2 km farther than Pat. They ran a total distance of 14 km. How far did each person run?

14. The combined mass of a dog and a cat is 21 kg. The dog is two-and-one-half times as heavy as the cat. What are their masses?

15. Roger has some dimes and quarters with a total value of $2.50. If he has three more quarters than dimes, how many of each kind of coin does he have?

16. Mrs. Jenkins is three times as old as her son, Jerry. In 12 years, Mrs. Jenkins will only be twice as old. How old is Jerry now?

17. One number is seven times one-half of another number. The numbers differ by 35. What are the numbers?

18. Donna's average mark out of three tests was 84 out of 100. Her highest mark was one-and-one-quarter times her lowest mark. The middle mark was 81. What were Donna's marks on the three tests?

19. Write the inequality represented by each graph.
   a)

   b)

   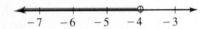

   c)

   d)

20. Solve and graph.
   a) $5x - 17 < 19 - 4x$
   b) $\frac{3}{4}y + \frac{1}{3} \geq \frac{1}{2}y + \frac{1}{4}$
   c) $7(3 - 2z) \leq -2(7 + 2z)$
   d) $-0.6(3a - 7) > -0.7(-4 + 2a)$

5 Geometry

Sami and Jane have a measuring tape and a compass.
How can they measure the width of a river they cannot
cross? (See Section 5-7, *Example 2*.)

5-1 WHAT IS GEOMETRY?

Geometry is all around us, as the photographs on these pages show.
Study each photograph and the question that accompanies it. The questions
and your answers involve some of the ideas and the language of
geometry.

Architecture
What shapes do you see?

Sports
Why do runners on an oval track start at
different places?

Nature
What is the shape of the horns?

Navigation
What measurements does a navigator make?

Art

How is the feeling of ''depth'' achieved?

Building and Decorating

What is the purpose of the weighted string?

The answers to these questions required knowledge of the following basic geometric concepts.

• A point A	B A line AB	B A line segment AB	 parallel lines
r O circle, center O, radius *r*	vertex A B side C triangle ABC	B ←—— vertex A C angle ABC	 perpendicular lines

The study of these concepts is the basis of geometry. The ancient Egyptians and Babylonians used geometric ideas to determine the areas of fields and the volumes of buildings such as temples and pyramids.

The word *geometry* comes from two Greek words *geos* and *metron* meaning earth measure. It was about 300 B.C. when the Greeks began to study geometry. Their contributions have influenced the study of the subject to the present time.

Example 1. Name all the line segments in this line.

Solution. The line segments are AB, BC, and AC.

Problems in geometry often involve investigations of relationships among the basic geometric concepts.

Example 2. Find in how many points a line and a circle can intersect.

Solution. Draw a diagram to show each case.

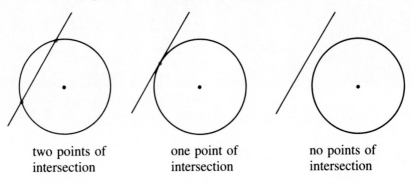

two points of   one point of   no points of
intersection   intersection   intersection

A line and a circle can intersect in 2 points, in 1 point, or not at all.

EXERCISES 5-1

Ⓐ

1. Collect some pictures that show geometry in the world around us.

2. Name all the line segments in this line.

3. Name all the angles in each figure.

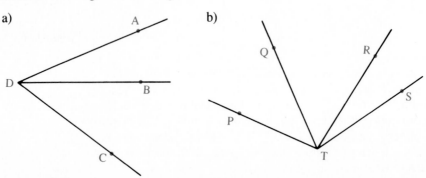

4. Name all the triangles in each figure.

a)

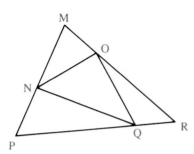

b)

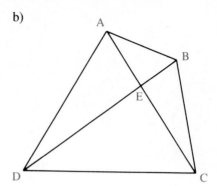

B

5. Find in how many points two circles can intersect if:
   a) the circles have equal radii   b) the circles have different radii.

6. Find in how many points two lines can intersect.

7. Find in how many points these figures can intersect.
   a) a line segment and a line   b) a line and a triangle

8. Find the greatest number of points in which each pair of figures can intersect.
   a) a triangle and a circle   b) two triangles   c) a square and a circle

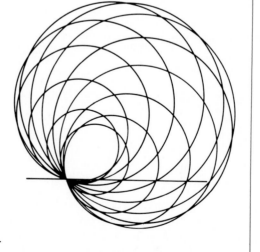

INVESTIGATE

Circle Patterns

Draw a circle and a point P, as shown. Use a protractor to mark several equally-spaced points on the circle. Using each point as a center, draw a circle through P. The result should look like the design shown.

Repeat the construction with P on the circle, then with P inside the circle.

5-2 GEOMETRIC CONSTRUCTIONS: PART ONE

Any great structure begins as an idea in a person's mind. As an architect translates these ideas into drawings, he or she must construct certain lengths, angles, and geometric figures. Many instruments and techniques are available for this purpose.

Ruler   Compasses   Protractor   Set squares

Transparent mirror   Paper folding   Tracing paper   Computer

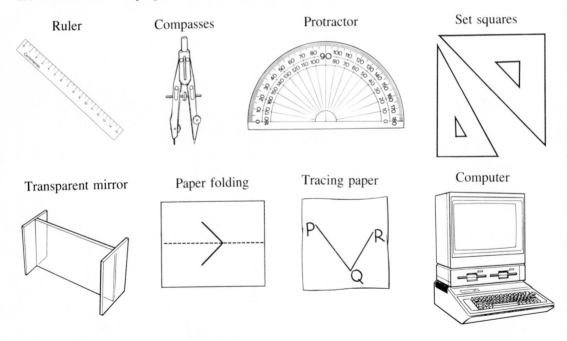

Today, most architectural drawings are prepared by a computer using a process called *computer assisted design*. The person who generates the drawing by computer is using a tool that is much more advanced than ruler and compasses. However, the mathematical principles of these constructions are unchanged.

Constructing the bisector of an angle

We can use geometrical instruments in a variety of ways to construct
the bisector of an angle.

Using two sides of a ruler

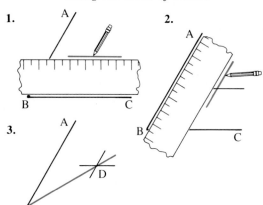

BD bisects ∠ABC.

Using a set square

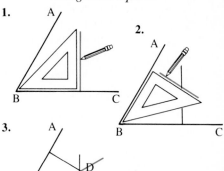

BD bisects ∠ABC.

Using ruler and compasses

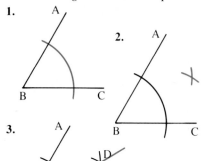

Using a protractor (without measuring)

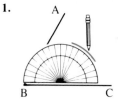

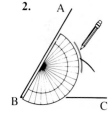

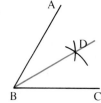

BD bisects ∠ABC.

In each construction, we do the same thing on each arm of the angle.
Hence, the constructions work because there is no reason for the line
BD to be closer to one arm than to the other.

I N V E S T I G A T E

Can you construct the bisector of an angle in other ways? How many different
ways can you find?

Example. Using ruler and compasses, construct a 60° angle.

Solution. Draw a line *l* and mark point A on *l*.

Place the compasses point on A and draw part of a circle to cross the line at B.

Without changing the setting of the compasses, place the compasses point on B and draw an arc intersecting the part circle at C.

Join AC. ∠CAB = 60°

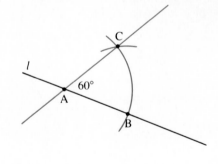

EXERCISES 5-2

Ⓐ

1. a) Draw any angle less than 90° and bisect it.
   b) Draw any angle greater than 90° and bisect it.

2. Construct a 60° angle and bisect it. Check by measuring.

Ⓑ

3. Draw any angle and divide it into four equal parts.

4. Construct each angle.
   a) 60°   b) 30°   c) 15°   d) 120°   e) 150°

5. Copy this diagram.
   a) Construct OD, the bisector of ∠COB.
   b) Construct OE, the bisector of ∠AOC.
   c) Measure ∠DOE.
   d) If the construction were repeated using a different position of line segment OC, would the answer to part c) be the same? Explain.

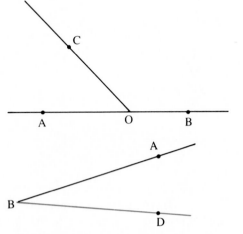

6. Copy this diagram. AB is one arm of ∠ABC, and BD is the bisector of ∠ABC. Construct the other arm of ∠ABC.

7. Draw any angle less than 90°. Construct an angle with double the measure of the angle you drew.

8. Explain the construction for the bisector of an angle which uses a protractor without measuring.

THE MATHEMATICAL MIND

A Problem that took Thousands of Years to Solve

1
The ancient Greeks established rules for constructing geometric figures. Since they considered the line and the circle to be the basic figures, only compasses and an unmarked straightedge could be used.

2
One of the constructions, which the Greek mathematicians attempted, was to *trisect* any given angle using compasses and a straightedge.

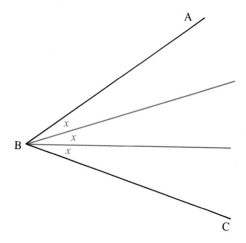

3
Since the 5th century B.C., mathematicians have tried to trisect any given angle using compasses and a straightedge. However, none has succeeded.

4
Finally, in 1837, P.L. Wantzel *proved* that such a construction is impossible! He did this by showing that a 20° angle cannot be constructed using compasses and a straightedge. This means that a 60° angle cannot be trisected.

Certain angles can be trisected using compasses and a straightedge, but there is no general method that works for all angles. If the restriction on compasses and a straightedge is removed, an angle can be trisected using a variety of other instruments.

QUESTIONS

For each of these angles
i) 180°   ii) 90°   iii) 30°   iv) 45°   v) 120°
a) Construct the angle using compasses and a straightedge.
b) Determine if it is possible to trisect it using compasses and a straightedge.
c) Trisect it if you can.

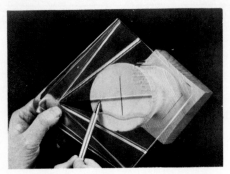

5-3 GEOMETRIC CONSTRUCTIONS: PART TWO

In the preceding section we illustrated four of many ways to construct the bisector of an angle. In this section we present methods of performing other constructions. Each construction can be done in many different ways.

Constructing the perpendicular bisector of a line segment

Infinitely many lines can be drawn perpendicular to a given line segment AB, but only one of them passes through the midpoint of AB. This line is called the *perpendicular bisector* of AB. Here are two methods of constructing the perpendicular bisector of AB.

Using two sides of a ruler

1.
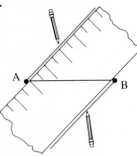

2.
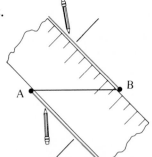

3.
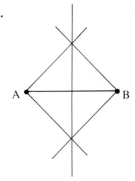

Using ruler and compasses

1.
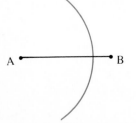

2.
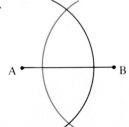

3.
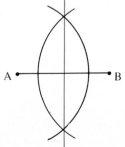

What other ways can you find to construct the perpendicular bisector of a line segment?

Constructing the perpendicular at a point on a line

Using a set square

1.

2.

Using ruler and compasses

1.

2.

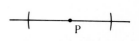

3.

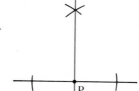

Constructing the perpendicular from a point to a line

Using a protractor

1.

2.

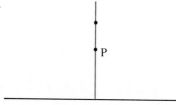

Using ruler and compasses

1.

2.

3.

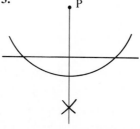

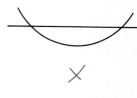

INVESTIGATE

What other ways can you find to construct perpendiculars at a point on a line or from a point to a line?

Example. Using a straightedge and compasses, construct a 45° angle.

Solution. Draw a line *l*.
Construct a perpendicular PB to
l at any point B on *l*.
Then, ∠PBC = 90°.
Bisect ∠PBC. Line BA is the
bisector of ∠PBC.
Hence, ∠PBA = ∠ABC = 45°

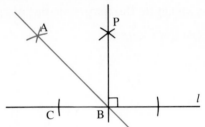

EXERCISES 5-3

Ⓐ

1. Draw a line *l*. Choose any point A on *l*. Construct the perpendicular to *l* at A.

2. Draw a line *l*. Choose any point B not on *l*. Construct the perpendicular from B to *l*.

3. Draw a line segment AB. Construct the perpendicular bisector of AB.

Ⓑ

4. Draw any line segment and divide it into four equal parts.

5. Construct each angle.
   a) 45°   b) 135°   c) 22.5°   d) 75°   e) 67.5°

6. Mark two points A and B on your paper. Construct a circle having AB as a diameter.

7. Draw a line *l*. Choose any point P not on *l*. Construct a line through P parallel to *l*.

8. Which of the constructions described in *Sections 5-2* and *5-3* can be done with ruler and compasses, with the compasses fixed at one setting?

Ⓒ

9. Mark two points A and B on your paper. Construct each square.
   a) A and B are the endpoints of one side.
   b) A and B are the endpoints of a diagonal.
   c) A and B are the midpoints of two opposite sides.
   d) A and B are the midpoints of two adjacent sides.

10. Construct a perpendicular at a point P on a line, using a plastic triangle. Can you do this without placing the right angle of the triangle at P?

11. Explain some of the constructions described on pages 176 and 177.

INVESTIGATE

1. Draw any line segment AB, and construct its perpendicular bisector.

2. Locate any point P on the bisector of AB. Join PA and PB. Measure the lengths of the segments PA and PB.

3. Repeat *Question 2* for other points on the perpendicular bisector of AB.

4. State a probable conclusion about any point on the perpendicular bisector of a line segment.

INVESTIGATE

1. Draw around a circular object such as a jar lid. Locate the center of the circle. Can you find more than one way to do this?

2. The photograph on page 176 shows a *center finder* used by carpenters to locate the center of round stock.
   a) How is the center finder used?
   b) Explain how it works.

INVESTIGATE

Two intersecting lines form two pairs of angles called *vertical angles.*

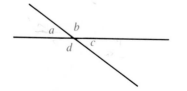

a and *c* are vertical angles.
b and *d* are vertical angles.

1. Draw two intersecting lines. Label and measure both pairs of vertical angles.

2. Repeat the procedure for another pair of intersecting lines.

3. Do pairs of vertical angles appear to have a special property?

4. Write a statement to describe a property of a pair of vertical angles formed when two lines intersect.

5-4 ANGLES AND INTERSECTING LINES

Angles are classified according to their measures in degrees.

One degree (1°) is $\frac{1}{360}$ of a complete rotation.

Measure	Angle	Example
Less than 90°	acute	
90°	right	
Between 90° and 180°	obtuse	
180°	straight	
Between 180° and 360°	reflex	

From the previous *INVESTIGATE* you may have discovered that, in this situation, $a = c$ and $b = d$.

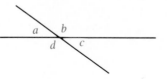

> When two lines intersect, the vertical angles are equal.

Two angles with a sum of 180° are
supplementary angles.
ABC is a straight line.
$\angle ABD + \angle DBC = 180°$
$\angle ABD$ and $\angle DBC$ are supplementary.

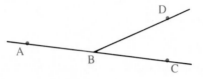

Two angles with a sum of 90° are
complementary angles.
$\angle PQR$ is a right angle.
$\angle PQS + \angle SQR = 90°$
$\angle PQS$ and $\angle SQR$ are complementary.

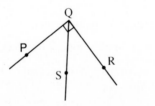

Example 1. ∠BOA and ∠AOC are supplementary
angles. ∠AOC = 65°
a) Find the measure of ∠BOA.
b) What is the complement of ∠AOC?

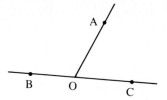

Solution.

a) Since ∠BOA and ∠AOC
are supplementary,
∠BOA + ∠AOC = 180°
∠BOA + 65° = 180°
∠BOA = 115°

b) Let the complement of
∠AOC be x.
∠AOC + x = 90°
65° + x = 90°
x = 25°

Example 2. Find the angle measure indicated by each letter.

a)
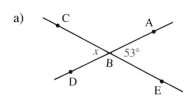

b)

Solution.

a) Since ∠CBD and ∠EBA
are vertical angles,
∠CBD = ∠EBA
x = 53°

b) Since ∠DGE and ∠AGB
are vertical angles,
∠DGE = ∠AGB
∠DGE = 105°
Since ∠CGF is a straight angle,
∠CGD + ∠DGE + ∠EGF = 180°
30° + 105° + y = 180°
135° + y = 180°
y = 45°

EXERCISES 5-4

Ⓐ

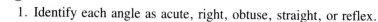

1. Identify each angle as acute, right, obtuse, straight, or reflex.

a)
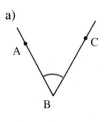

b)
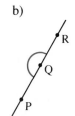

c)
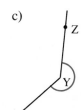

d)

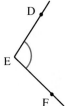

2. Name two pairs of vertical angles in each figure.

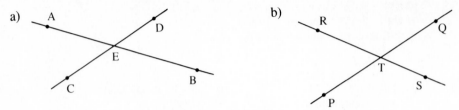

3. Find the angle measure indicated by each letter.

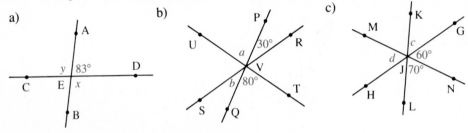

4. Draw, if possible, a triangle with:
   a) a right angle and an acute angle   b) an acute angle and an obtuse angle
   c) an obtuse angle and a right angle.

5. Two lines intersect to form four equal angles. What can be said about the lines?

6. Find in how many points a line and two parallel lines can intersect. Consider all possible cases.

7. Angle ABC has a measure of 74°. What is the measure of reflex angle ABC?

8. Find the value of each letter.

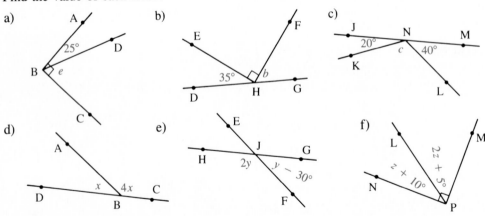

9. For the diagrams in *Exercise 8*, find pairs of:
   a) supplementary angles   b) complementary angles.

Ⓒ

10. Find in how many points these figures can intersect. Consider all possible cases.
   a) two parallel lines and a circle
   b) two parallel lines and a line segment

11. The adjacent numbers on the two scales of a double-scale protractor add up to 180°. Explain why.

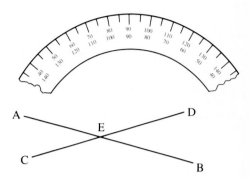

12. a) Two line segments AB and CD intersect at point E. Explain why each statement is true.
      i) ∠AED + ∠DEB = 180°
      ii) ∠AED + ∠AEC = 180°
   b) Use the equations in part a) to conclude that ∠DEB = ∠AEC.

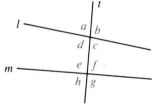

I N V E S T I G A T E

A line that intersects two or more lines is called a *transversal*. When a transversal intersects two other lines, the pairs of angles formed are described by their relative positions.

Transversal *t* intersects lines *l* and *m*.

There are two pairs of *alternate angles*: *d* and *f*; *c* and *e*.
There are four pairs of *corresponding angles*: *a* and *e*; *b* and *f*; *d* and *h*; *c* and *g*.
There are two pairs of *interior angles*: *d* and *e*; *c* and *f*.

When a transversal intersects two parallel lines, each pair of angles described above has a special property.

1. Draw two parallel lines and a transversal. Label and measure:
   a) each pair of alternate angles
   b) each pair of corresponding angles
   c) each pair of interior angles.

2. Repeat the procedure for another pair of parallel lines.

3. What property does each pair of angles appear to have?

4. Write a statement to describe for parallel lines a property of:
   a) a pair of alternate angles
   b) a pair of corresponding angles
   c) a pair of interior angles.
   Do these properties hold for non-parallel lines?

THE MATHEMATICAL MIND

Misleading Diagrams

Maurits Cornelis Escher was an artist, who was born in the Netherlands in 1898. He travelled extensively through Europe before his death in 1972.

Much of Escher's work is unique; one of his many talents was the ability to design and draw "impossible" pictures. What is impossible in the illustration of the waterfall?

When geometric figures are combined, the resulting diagrams can sometimes deceive the eye. This can happen in different ways.

© 1990 M.C. Escher Heirs/Cordon Art-Baarn-Holland

Reversing Diagrams
Some diagrams can be seen in different ways. What do *you* see?

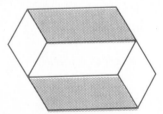

Optical Illusions
An optical illusion can lead to a false conclusion. Are the colored circles the same size?

Impossible Objects
A two-dimensional diagram can be drawn of a three-dimensional object that cannot exist. Do you think you could make this object?

Subjective Contours
Sometimes the outline of a figure is visible when it is not really there. Do you see a white triangle? Is it really there?

These examples show how careful we must be when drawing conclusions from a diagram.

QUESTIONS

1. Are the diagonal line segments parallel?

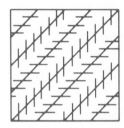

2. Can you make a physical model of this drawing?

3. Is there really a white square?

4. Do you see a white triangle? Are the line segments equal in length?

5. Can you make a model from this diagram?

6. Do you see two heads or a birdbath?

7. How many ways does this box open?

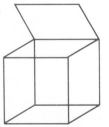

8. Are the horizontal lines ''bent''?

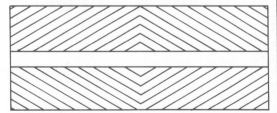

5-5 ANGLES AND PARALLEL LINES

Two lines, in the same plane, that never meet are called *parallel lines*.
    From the previous *INVESTIGATE*, you may have discovered the following properties of parallel lines.

When a transversal intersects two parallel lines, the alternate angles are equal.

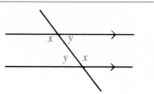

When a transversal intersects two parallel lines, the corresponding angles are equal.

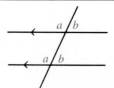 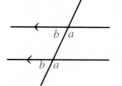

When a transversal intersects two parallel lines, the interior angles are supplementary.

$$a + b = 180°$$

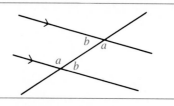

Example 1. Find the angle measure indicated by each letter.

a)

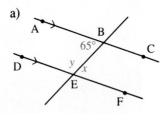

b)

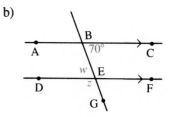

Solution.   a) Since $\angle FEB$ and $\angle ABE$ are alternate angles between parallel lines,

$\angle FEB = \angle ABE$

$x = 65°$

Since $\angle DEF$ is a straight angle,

$y + x = 180°$

$y + 65° = 180°$

$y = 115°$

b) Since $\angle DEB$ and $\angle CBE$ are alternate angles between parallel lines,

$\angle DEB = \angle CBE$

$w = 70°$

Since $\angle GEB$ is a straight angle,

$w + z = 180°$

$70° + z = 180°$

$z = 110°$

Example 2. Find the angle measure indicated by each letter.

a)

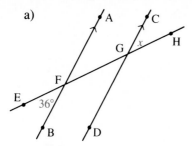

b)

Solution. a) Since ∠FGD and ∠EFB are corresponding angles between parallel lines,

∠FGD = ∠EFB
= 36°

Since ∠CGH and ∠FGD are vertical angles,

∠CGH = ∠FGD
$x = 36°$

b) Since ∠GFJ and ∠KJB are corresponding angles between parallel lines,

∠GFJ = ∠KJB
= 55°

∠GFI = ∠GFJ + ∠JFI
= 55° + 40°
= 95°

Since ∠GFI and ∠FIJ are interior angles between parallel lines,

∠GFI + ∠FIJ = 180°
95° + y = 180°
$y = 85°$

In this example, can you suggest other ways of finding the values of x and y?

EXERCISES 5-5

1. In this figure
   a) Name two pairs of alternate angles.
   b) Name four pairs of corresponding angles.
   c) Name two pairs of interior angles.

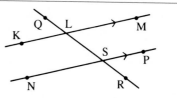

2. Find the angle measure indicated by each letter.

a)

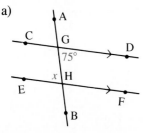

b)

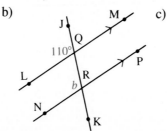

c)

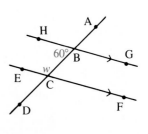

Ⓑ

3. Find the angle measure indicated by each letter.

a)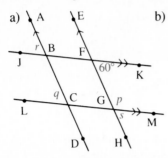

b)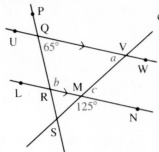

c)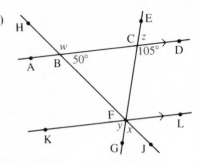

4. Can two intersecting lines both be parallel to a third line? Draw a diagram to support your answer.

5. Can two intersecting lines both be perpendicular to a third line in the same plane? Draw a diagram to support your answer.

6. In how many points can three lines intersect?

Ⓒ

7. a) Use the diagram to help you explain how you know that in parallelogram ABCD, ∠ABC = ∠ADC.
   b) Use part a) and a property of interior angles to explain why ∠A = ∠C.

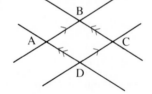

8. From the information given in the diagram, find the measures of the angles in △ABC. What is the sum of their measures?

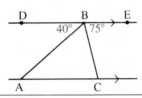

 INVESTIGATE

1. Draw a triangle with all of its angles less than 90°. Measure the angles. Add these measurements.

2. Draw a triangle with one angle of 90°. Measure the angles. Add these measurements.

3. Draw a triangle with one angle greater than 90°. Measure the angles. Add these measurements.

4. Do the angles of a triangle appear to have a special property?

5. Write a statement to describe a property of the angles of a triangle.

COMPUTER POWER

The Exterior Angles of a Triangle

If the sides of a triangle are extended in one direction, an *exterior angle* is formed at each vertex.

In Turtle Geometry, a small "turtle" which looks like this ▲ can be instructed to construct a triangle by a series of *Logo* commands such as these.

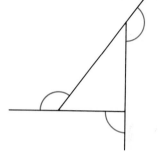

Verbal Command	Logo Command
Start at A.	HOME
Turn right 127°.	RT 127
Move forward 100 units (along AB).	FD 100
Turn right 143°.	RT 143
Move forward 80 units (along BC).	FD 80
Turn right 90°.	RT 90
Move forward 60 units (along CA).	FD 60

Graphics Display

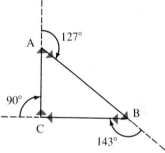

Observe that the turtle turns through the exterior angles as it traces the triangle.

1. What is the total number of degrees through which the turtle turned in drawing the triangle?

2. Write another set of Logo commands that cause the turtle to trace a triangle. (Ensure that the turtle starts and finishes facing upward.) What is the sum of the angles through which your turtle turned?

3. Write a statement about the sum of the three exterior angles of a triangle.

4. What is the sum of the exterior angle and the interior angle at any vertex of a triangle?

5. What is the sum of all three exterior and all three interior angles of a triangle?

6. Use your answers to *Questions 3* and *5* to make a statement about the sum of three interior angles of a triangle.

5-6 ANGLES AND TRIANGLES

Triangles may be classified by the measures of their angles.

Description	Triangle	Example
all angles are acute	acute triangle	
one angle is 90°	right triangle	
one angle is obtuse	obtuse triangle	

From the previous *INVESTIGATE*, you may have discovered that the sum of the measures of the angles of a triangle is 180°.

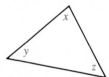

$$x + y + z = 180°$$

For convenience, we delete the phrase "of the measures" in the statement above.

> The sum of the angles in any triangle is 180°.

Example. Find the angle measure indicated by each letter.

a)

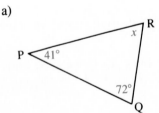

b)

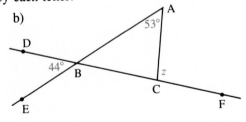

Solution. a) Since the sum of the angles in △PQR is 180°,
$$x + 41° + 72° = 180°$$
$$x + 113° = 180°$$
$$x = 67°$$

b) Since ∠ABC and ∠DBE are vertical angles,
$$∠ABC = ∠DBE$$
$$= 44°$$

Since the sum of the angles in △ABC is 180°,
$$∠ABC + ∠BCA + ∠CAB = 180°$$
$$44° + ∠BCA + 53° = 180°$$
$$∠BCA + 97° = 180°$$
$$∠BCA = 83°$$
Since ∠BCF is a straight angle,
$$∠BCA + ∠ACF = 180°$$
$$83° + z = 180°$$
$$z = 97°$$

EXERCISES 5-6

1. Identify each triangle as acute, right, or obtuse.

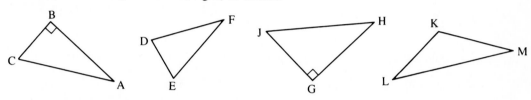

2. Each pair of angles represents the measures of two angles in a triangle. In each case, find the third angle and identify the triangle.
   a) 35°, 65°   b) 70°, 75°   c) 40°, 25°   d) 60°, 30°

3. Find the angle measure indicated by each letter.

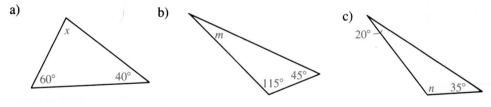

a)

b)

c)

4. Draw, if possible, a triangle with:
   a) a right angle and two equal sides
   b) an obtuse angle and two equal sides
   c) a right angle and three equal sides
   d) two right angles.

5. Cut any triangle from a piece of paper. Label the vertices A, B, and C.
   a) Tear off the corners at A and B and fit them at C, as shown in the diagram. Explain your findings.
   b) Can you fit the angles of a triangle in this way without cutting or tearing?

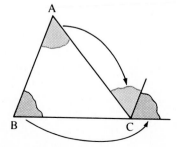

6. Find the angle measure indicated by each letter.

a)
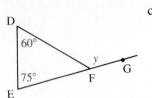

b)

c)
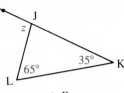

d)
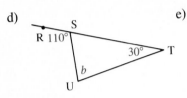

e)
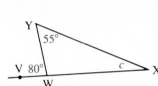

f)
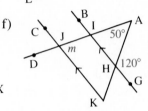

7. State whether a triangle can be drawn having these angles. Give reasons for your answers.
   a) 2 acute angles   b) 3 acute angles   c) 2 right angles
   d) 2 obtuse angles   e) a straight angle   f) 1 right angle, 1 obtuse angle

8. Explain why every triangle must have at least two acute angles.

9. a) State how many triangles there are in this figure.
   b) Name those that are:
      i)   acute triangles
      ii) right triangles
      iii) obtuse triangles.

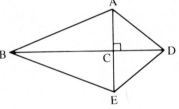

10. In this figure
    a) If the value of x is known, how can the value of y be found?
    b) Find the value of y for each value of x.
       i) $x = 30°$ ii) $x = 50°$ iii) $x = 87°$
    c) If the value of y is known, how can the value of x be found?
    d) Find the value of x for each value of y.
       i) $y = 110°$ ii) $y = 160°$ iii) $y = 175°$
    e) Find an equation relating x and y.

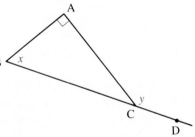

11. Find each value of x.

a)
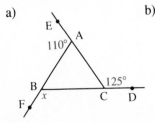

b)
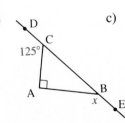

c)
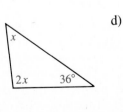

d)

Ⓒ

12. Find the sum of the shaded angles in each figure.

a)

b)

c)

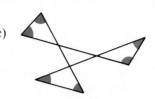

13. What is the sum of the measures of the interior angles of a quadrilateral?

INVESTIGATE

A triangle with at least two sides equal
is an isosceles triangle.

PR = QR

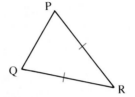

1. Draw an isosceles △PQR using ruler and compasses.
   ● Draw two equal line segments PR and QR, with the same end point R.
   ● Join PQ.
   ● Measure ∠RPQ and ∠PQR.

2. Repeat the procedure with an isosceles triangle of a different size.

3. Do the angles opposite the equal sides of an isosceles triangle appear to have a special property?

4. Write a statement to describe a property of the angles opposite the equal sides of an isosceles triangle.

A triangle with three sides equal is an
equilateral triangle.

LM = MN = NL

5. Draw an equilateral △LMN using ruler and compasses.
   ● Draw any line segment LM.
   ● With the distance between compasses point and pencil equal to the length of LM, put compasses point on L and draw an arc. Then put compasses point on M and draw an arc to intersect the first arc.
   ● Label the intersection of the arcs, N. Join LN and MN.
   ● Measure ∠LMN, ∠MNL, and ∠NLM.

6. Repeat the procedure with an equilateral triangle of a different size.

7. Do the angles of an equilateral triangle appear to have a special property?

8. Write a statement to describe a property of the angles of an equilateral triangle.

 **PROBLEM SOLVING**

Draw a Diagram

A 6.5 m ladder is placed against a wall with the foot of the ladder 2.5 m from the wall. If the top of the ladder slips 0.8 m, how far will the bottom of the ladder slip?

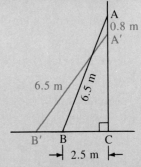

Understand the problem
- How long is the ladder?
- How far from the wall is the top of the ladder? the foot of the ladder?
- How far down the wall does the ladder slip?
- What are you asked to find?

Think of a strategy
- Try drawing a diagram to show the lengths and distances.

Carry out the strategy
- Draw a diagram showing the ladder before slipping (AB) and after slipping (A′B′).
- Mark the known lengths and distances on the diagram.
- We need to find the length BB′. We cannot find this directly. So, find AC, then A′C, then B′C.

- Use the Pythagorean theorem in △ABC.

$$AB^2 = BC^2 + AC^2$$
$$6.5^2 = 2.5^2 + AC^2$$
$$AC^2 = 6.5^2 - 2.5^2$$
$$AC = \sqrt{6.5^2 - 2.5^2}$$
$$= 6$$
$$A'C = AC - AA'$$
$$= 6 - 0.8$$
$$= 5.2$$

Use the Pythagorean theorem in △A′B′C.

$$A'B'^2 = B'C^2 + A'C^2$$
$$6.5^2 = B'C^2 + 5.2^2$$
$$B'C^2 = 6.5^2 - 5.2^2$$
$$B'C = \sqrt{6.5^2 - 5.2^2}$$
$$= 3.9$$
$$BB' = B'C - BC$$
$$= 3.9 - 2.5$$
$$= 1.4$$

The bottom of the ladder slips 1.4 m.

Look back
- Does a 1.4 m slip seem reasonable for a 0.8 m change in the height of the ladder?

Solve each problem

1. The Cougars lead a league of 5 teams and the Dolphins are last. The Bears are halfway between the Cougars and the Dolphins. If the Eagles are ahead of the Dolphins and the Stallions immediately behind the Bears, name the team that is second in the league.

2. During a game of blindfold bluff, Kevin walks 5 m north, 12 m east, 30 m south-west and 8 m north-west. How far is Kevin now from his starting position?

3. The surface area of a cube is 600 cm². The cube is cut into 64 smaller congruent cubes. What is the surface area of one of these cubes?

4. The 40 grade 9 students at Participation H.S. choose to play one or two of the three sports: football, basketball, and hockey. Nineteen play football, 16 play basketball, and 15 play hockey. Included in those numbers are the 6 students who play both football and hockey and 3 who play both football and basketball. How many students play both basketball and hockey?

5. A train leaves at 7:00 A.M. daily from Toronto bound for Vancouver. Simultaneously, another train leaves Vancouver for Toronto. The journey takes exactly 4 days in each direction. If a passenger boards a train in Vancouver, how many Vancouver bound trains will she pass en route to Toronto?

6. How many rectangles can be drawn on a grid of 9 equally spaced dots so that all the vertices are located on dots?

7. A rectangular park is 400 m long and 300 m wide. If it takes 14 min to walk around the perimeter once, how long would it take to walk across a diagonal of the park?

8. How can 10 chairs be arranged along the perimeter of a rectangular room so that there is an equal number of chairs along each wall?

9. The distances between a pine tree, an oak tree, and a maple tree were measured and recorded.

From	To	Distance
Pine	Maple	150 m
Pine	Oak	100 m
Maple	Oak	45 m

Were the measurements correct? Explain your answer.

10. A rectangular field is twice as long as its width. Its perimeter is less than 1.2 km. What does this tell you about the area of the field?

5-7 ISOSCELES AND EQUILATERAL TRIANGLES

In the previous section, triangles were classified according to the measures of their angles. Triangles are also classified according to the lengths of their sides.

Description	Triangle	Example
3 sides equal	equilateral triangle	
at least 2 sides equal	isosceles triangle	
no sides equal	scalene triangle	

From the previous *INVESTIGATE*, you may have discovered these properties of isosceles triangles and equilateral triangles.

In an isosceles triangle, the angles opposite the equal sides are equal.

In an equilateral triangle, the angles are equal and have a measure of 60°.

Example 1. Find the angle measure indicated by each letter.

a)

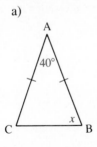

b)

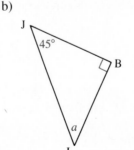

c)

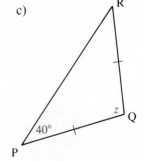

Solution. a) Since AB = AC, then ∠ACB = x
Since the sum of the angles in △ABC is 180°,
$$∠ABC + ∠BCA + ∠CAB = 180°$$
$$x + x + 40° = 180°$$
$$2x + 40° = 180°$$
$$2x = 140°$$
$$x = 70°$$

b) Since the sum of the angles in △BJI is 180°,
$$∠BJI + ∠JIB + ∠IBJ = 180°$$
$$45° + a + 90° = 180°$$
$$a + 135° = 180°$$
$$a = 45°$$

c) Since PQ = QR, ∠PRQ = 40°
Since the sum of the angles in △PQR is 180°,
$$∠PQR + ∠QRP + ∠RPQ = 180°$$
$$z + 40° + 40° = 180°$$
$$z + 80° = 180°$$
$$z = 100°$$

Example 2. Sami and Jane have only a measuring tape and a compass. How can they measure the width of a river that they cannot cross?

Solution. Sami and Jane draw a diagram to help them solve the problem.

On their side of the river, they mark a point S, opposite a large tree T on the far bank. ST represents the width of the river. After taking the compass bearing of T from S, Jane walks in a line perpendicular to ST. She walks until she reaches a point J, where the compass reading indicates that ∠SJT = 45°.

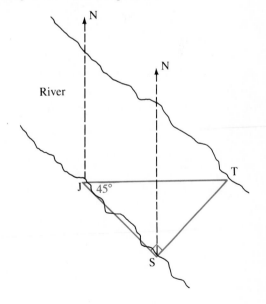

Since the sum of the angles in △SJT is 180°,
$$∠SJT + ∠JTS + ∠TSJ = 180°$$
$$45° + ∠JTS + 90° = 180°$$
$$∠JTS = 45°$$

Since ∠JTS = ∠SJT = 45°, △SJT is isosceles.
Hence, SJ = ST

Sami measures the distance SJ. This is the approximate width of the river.

EXERCISES 5-7

Ⓐ

1. Find the angle measure indicated by each letter.

a)

b)

c)

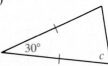

d)

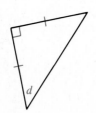

e)

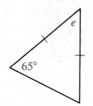

f)

g)

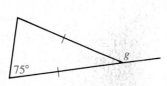

h)

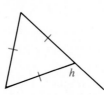

i)

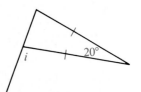

2. a) Are all equilateral triangles isosceles? b) Are all isosceles triangles equilateral?

Ⓑ

3. Find the angle measure indicated by each letter.

a)

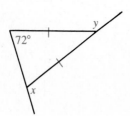

b)

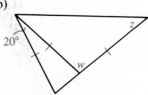

c)

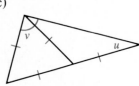

d)

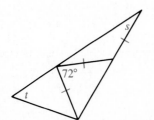

e)

f)

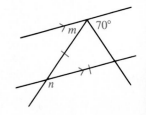

4. Draw an example of each triangle.
   a) an isosceles right triangle
   b) an isosceles obtuse triangle
   c) a scalene right triangle
   d) a scalene obtuse triangle
   e) an isosceles acute triangle
   f) a scalene acute triangle

5. In isosceles $\triangle ABC$

   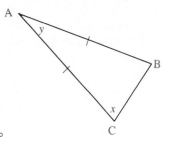

   a) If the value of x is known, how can the value of y be found?
   b) Find the value of y for each value of x.
      i) $x = 70°$ ii) $x = 25°$ iii) $x = 43°$
   c) If the value of y is known, how can the value of x be found?
   d) Find the value of x for each value of y.
      i) $y = 80°$ ii) $y = 110°$ iii) $y = 17°$
   e) Find an equation relating x and y.

6. In this figure

   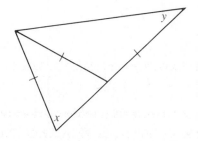

   a) If the value of x is known, how can the value of y be found?
   b) Find the value of y for each value of x.
      i) $x = 60°$ ii) $x = 40°$ iii) $x = 26°$
   c) If the value of y is known, how can the value of x be found?
   d) Find the value of x for each value of y.
      i) $y = 40°$ ii) $y = 25°$ iii) $y = 81°$
   e) Find an equation relating x and y.

7. Amanda wanted to find the height of a cliff. She drew a diagram in which BC represented this height.

   Amanda had a clinometer for measuring $\angle CAB$. She moved away from the base of the cliff to a point A, where the clinometer showed $\angle CAB$ as 45°. Amanda measured the distance AB as 30 m. How high was the cliff?

   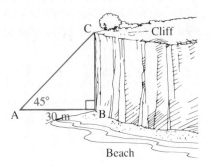

8. Michael and Julie are located at M and J respectively. A large tree is located at T on the opposite bank of the river. The distance MJ cannot be measured with the tape. Determine how Michael and Julie could find the approximate width MT of the river.

   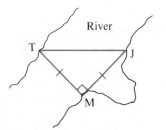

9. The measure of one angle of an isosceles triangle is given. Find the possible measures of the other angles.
   a) 30°   b) 40°   c) 80°   d) 90°   e) 110°

ⓒ ———

10. A number of equilateral triangles are joined together with whole sides touching. The diagram shows a figure formed with four equilateral triangles. Find how many different figures can be formed for each number of equilateral triangles used.
    a) 3   b) 4   c) 5

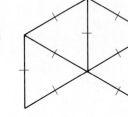

11. Explain how to find the height of a tree with a right, isosceles, plastic triangle and a measuring tape.

 **INVESTIGATE**

1. Draw △ABC with AB = 6 cm, BC = 8 cm, and CA = 12 cm.
    - Draw line segment AB 6 cm long.
    - With compasses point on B, and radius 8 cm, drawn an arc.
    - With compasses point on A, and radius 12 cm, draw an arc to intersect the first arc. Label the point of intersection C.
    - Draw BC and CA.
    Can you draw △PQR with PQ = 6 cm, QR = 8 cm, and RP = 12 cm such that its size and shape are different from △ABC?

2. Draw △ABC with ∠A = 65°, ∠B = 85°, and ∠C = 30°. Can you draw △PQR with ∠P = 65°, ∠Q = 85°, and ∠R = 30° such that its size and shape are different from △ABC?

3. Draw △ABC with AB = 8 cm, BC = 5 cm, and ∠B = 50°. Can you draw △PQR with PQ = 8 cm, QR = 5 cm, and ∠Q = 50° such that its size and shape are different from △ABC?

4. Draw △ABC with AB = 7 cm, AC = 4 cm, and ∠B = 30°. Can you draw △PQR with PQ = 7 cm, PR = 4 cm, and ∠Q = 30° such that its size and shape are different from △ABC?

5. Draw △ABC with ∠A = 62°, ∠B = 80°, and BC = 6 cm. Can you draw △PQR with ∠P = 62°, ∠Q = 80°, and QR = 6 cm such that its size and shape are different from △ABC?

    Which measurements of a triangle would you have to be given so that only one triangle could be drawn?

5-8 CONGRUENT TRIANGLES

If two geometric figures have the same size and shape, they are said to be *congruent*.

Two congruent triangles can be made to coincide because their corresponding sides and corresponding angles are equal.

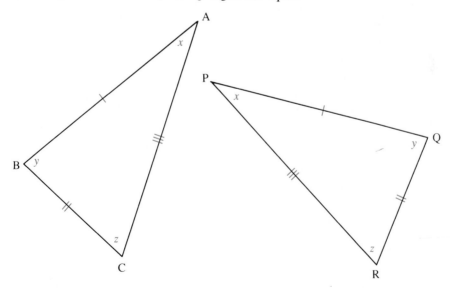

In △ABC and △PQR
   ∠A = ∠P, ∠B = ∠Q, ∠C = ∠R
   AB = PQ, BC = QR, CA = RP
   Therefore, △ABC ≅ △PQR
The sign ≅ is read "is congruent to".

The order in which the vertices are listed when pairs of triangles are congruent indicates which angles and sides correspond.

$$\triangle ABC \cong \triangle PQR$$

If the three sides and the three angles of two triangles are equal, then the triangles are congruent. However, it is not necessary to know this much information to show that two triangles are congruent.

From the previous *INVESTIGATE*, you may have discovered that given certain measurements of a triangle, there is only one possible triangle that can be drawn. This means that if two triangles are each described by this same set of measurements, those triangles must be equal in size and shape, and hence congruent.

The table shows three conditions. Any one of these conditions is sufficient to show that two triangles are congruent.

Conditions for Congruence	Illustration	Abbreviation
Three sides of one triangle are respectively equal to three sides of another triangle.		SSS (side, side, side)
Two sides and the contained angle of one triangle are respectively equal to two sides and the contained angle of another triangle.		SAS (side, angle, side)
Two angles and one side of one triangle are respectively equal to two corresponding angles and the corresponding side of another triangle.		AAS (angle, angle, side)

Example 1. For each pair of triangles, explain why they are congruent and state the condition for congruence. List the equal sides and the equal angles.

a)

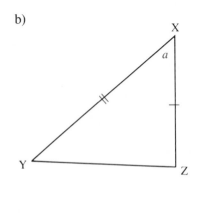
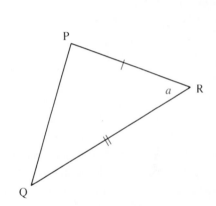

b)

Solution.   a) In △ABC and △DEF
      ∠A and ∠F are equal.
      Side AB and side FE are equal.
      ∠C and ∠D are equal.
      Therefore, △ABC ≅ △FED   AAS

      Since △ABC is congruent to △FED,
      BC = ED, AC = FD, and ∠B = ∠E

    b) In △XYZ and △PQR
      ∠X and ∠R are equal.
      Side XZ and side RP are equal.
      Side XY and side RQ are equal.
      Therefore, △XYZ ≅ △RQP   SAS

      Since △XYZ is congruent to △RQP,
      YZ = QP, ∠Y = ∠Q, and ∠Z = ∠P

Example 2.   △DEF is congruent to △GHK.
a) Find the length of HK.
b) Find the measures of the unmarked angles in the triangles.

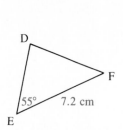

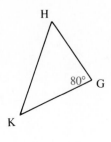

Solution.   a) Since △DEF is congruent to △GHK, EF = HK.
But EF = 7.2 cm, so HK = 7.2 cm

b) Since △DEF ≅ △GHK
∠E = ∠H, so ∠H = 55°
∠G = ∠D, so ∠D = 80°
∠F = ∠K
But ∠F = 180° − 80° − 55°
= 45°
So ∠K = 45°

The conclusions from showing that two triangles are congruent may be used to develop other geometric properties.

Example 3.   P is any point on the perpendicular bisector of line segment AB.
a) Explain why △PNA ≅ △PNB.
b) Explain why PA = PB.
c) State a conclusion about any point on the perpendicular bisector of a line segment.

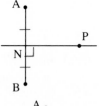

Solution.   a) Join PA and PB.
In △PAN and △PBN
AN and BN are equal.
∠PNA and ∠PNB are both equal to 90°.
PN is a common side to both triangles.
Therefore, △PNA ≅ △PNB   SAS

b) Since △PNA ≅ △PNB, corresponding sides are equal.
PA and PB are corresponding sides.
Hence, PA = PB

c) Any point on the perpendicular bisector of a line segment is equidistant from the ends of the line segment.

EXERCISES 5-8

1. Name the equal angles and the equal sides in each figure.

   a) $\triangle MRX \cong \triangle CLP$

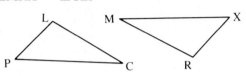

   b) $\triangle SQP \cong \triangle SQR$

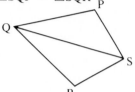

2. Name the equal sides and the equal angles.
   Figure PQRS $\cong$ figure XWZY

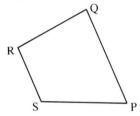

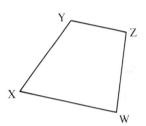

3. State which pairs of triangles are congruent. For those triangles that are congruent, state the condition for congruence.

   a)

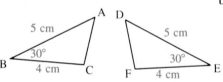

   b)

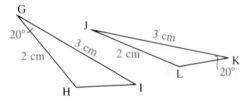

   c)

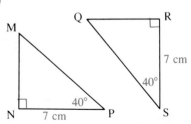

   d)

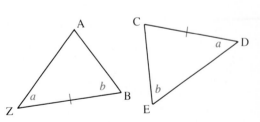

   e)

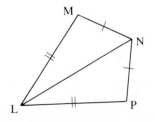

   f)

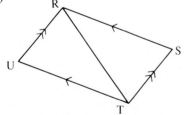

4. Find pairs of congruent triangles and state the condition for congruence.

a)

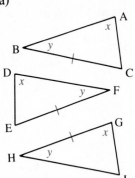

b)

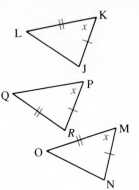

c)

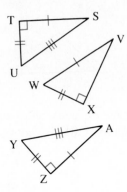

5. Find the value indicated by each letter.

a) $\triangle ABC \cong \triangle DEF$

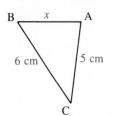

b) $\triangle PQR \cong \triangle STU$

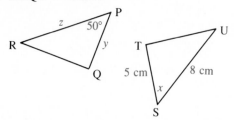

c) $\triangle JRC \cong \triangle MNP$

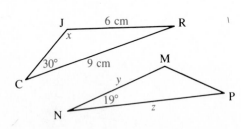

d) $\triangle FSN \cong \triangle TRC$

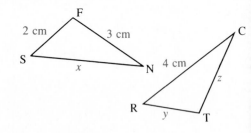

e) $\triangle BNA \cong \triangle AMB$

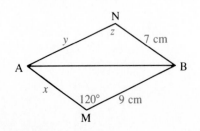

f) $\triangle PQB \cong \triangle RQA$

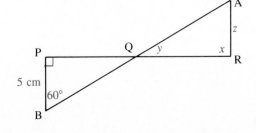

6. N is the midpoint of line segment AB.
   P is any point such that PA = PB.
   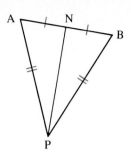
   a) Explain why △PNA ≅ △PNB.
   b) Explain why
      ∠PNA = ∠PNB = 90°.
   c) State a conclusion about any point
      that is equidistant from the
      endpoints of a line segment.

Ⓒ

7. Explain why any point on the bisector of an angle is equidistant from the sides of
   the angle.

INVESTIGATE

1. Draw a right triangle on squared
   paper, so that the arms of the
   right angle lie along the lines of
   the paper.

2. Draw a square on each side of
   the triangle.

3. Find the area of each square.
   To find the area of the square on
   the hypotenuse (the longest
   side), you can count the small
   squares and parts of squares.
   Alternatively, you can divide the
   square into right triangles and
   use the formula for the area
   of a triangle.

4. Repeat *Questions 1* to *3* for
   different right triangles. What
   do you notice about the areas
   of the squares?

5. Write a statement to describe a
   property of the areas of the
   squares drawn on the sides of a
   right triangle.

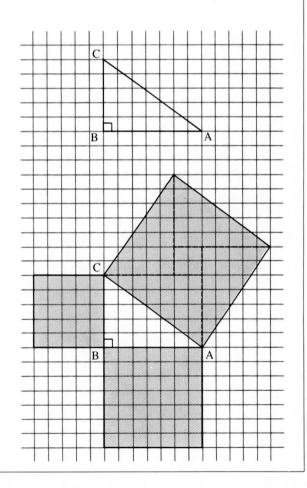

5-9 POLYGONS

Closed figures like those shown are called *polygons*. Their sides are line segments that do not cross.

These are polygons.   These are not polygons.

Polygons are named according to the number of sides they have. Some examples are shown in the table.

Name	Number of sides	Examples
Triangle	3	
Quadrilateral	4	
Pentagon	5	
Hexagon	6	
Octagon	8	
Decagon	10	

In the quadrilateral ABCD, AB and CD are *opposite* sides, AD and AB are *adjacent* sides, ∠A and ∠C are *opposite* angles, and DB is a *diagonal*.

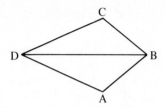

The classification of quadrilaterals involves relationships between sides, as shown in this diagram.

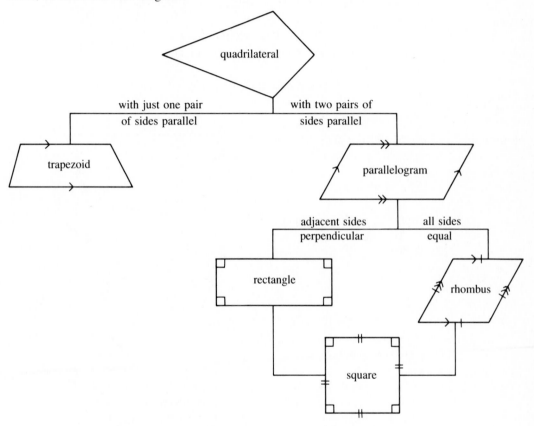

Any figure in the diagram has all the properties of any figure above it, but not below it.

Example 1. a) Is a square a parallelogram? Why?

b) Is a parallelogram a square? Why?

Solution. a) A square is a parallelogram because both pairs of opposite sides are parallel.

b) A parallelogram is not necessarily a square, because adjacent sides need not be perpendicular or equal.

Example 2. Show that the opposite sides and opposite angles of a parallelogram are equal.

Solution. In parallelogram ABCD, draw diagonal DB.
Since DC is parallel to AB,
∠CDB = ∠ABD   alternate angles
Since AD is parallel to BC,
∠ADB = ∠CBD   alternate angles
DB is a common side.
Therefore, △ADB ≅ △CBD   ASA
Since △ADB is congruent to △CBD,
∠A = ∠C, AB = CD and AD = CB
From the diagram where equal angles are indicated, it can be seen that
∠ADC = ∠ABC.
That is, the opposite sides and opposite angles of a parallelogram are equal.

Example 3. Find the values of x and y.

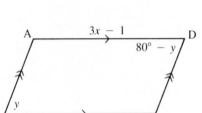

Solution. Since ABCD is a parallelogram, opposite sides are equal
$$3x - 1 = x + 5$$
$$2x = 6$$
$$x = 3$$
and opposite angles are equal.
$$y = 80° - y$$
$$2y = 80°$$
$$y = 40°$$

EXERCISES 5-9

Ⓐ

1. Give reasons for your answer to each question.
   a) i) Is a square a rectangle?   ii) Is a rectangle a square?
   b) i) Is a square a rhombus?   ii) Is a rhombus a square?
   c) i) Is a rectangle a parallelogram?   ii) Is a parallelogram a rectangle?
   d) i) Is a rhombus a parallelogram?   ii) Is a parallelogram a rhombus?
   e) i) Is a rectangle a trapezoid?   ii) Is a trapezoid a rectangle?
   f) i) Is a trapezoid a quadrilateral?   ii) Is a quadrilateral a trapezoid?

2. Find the values of w, x, y, and z.

   a)

   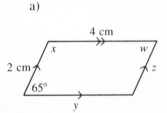

   b)

   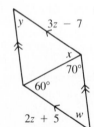

   c)

   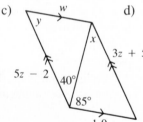

   d)

   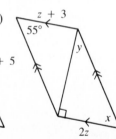

(B)

3. A *kite* is defined as a quadrilateral that has two distinct pairs of adjacent sides equal in length. Give reasons to support each statement.
   a) A kite has one pair of equal angles.
   b) The diagonals of a kite intersect at right angles.

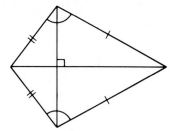

4. Find the values of *x* and *y*.
   a)

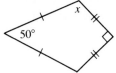

   b)

   c)

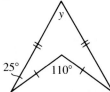

5. Draw any quadrilateral. Find the midpoint of each side. Join these midpoints to form another quadrilateral. What properties does this second quadrilateral appear to have?

(C)

6. Any polygon can be divided into triangles by joining vertices. The diagram shows a pentagon divided into three triangles.
   a) Copy and complete this table.

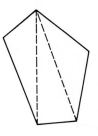

Polygon	Number of Sides	Number of Triangles	Sum of Angles
Triangle	3	1	180°
Quadrilateral	4		
Pentagon	5	3	
Hexagon			
Octagon			
Decagon			

   b) Write a simple formula for the sum of the angles in a polygon with *n* sides.

7. A *regular polygon* is one that has all sides the same length and all angles equal.
   a) Make an additional column to your table of *Exercise 6* giving the measure of each angle of a regular polygon.
   b) Write a simple formula for the measure of each angle in a regular polygon with *n* sides.

5-10 AREAS OF TRIANGLES AND QUADRILATERALS

The area A of a rectangle with length l and width w is $A = lw$.

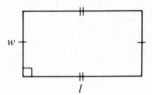

For a square with sides of length s, this formula becomes $A = s^2$, since $l = w = s$.

For a parallelogram with base b and height h, the area is $A = bh$.

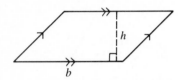

The diagonal of a parallelogram divides it into two equal triangles. The area A of a triangle is $A = \frac{1}{2}bh$.

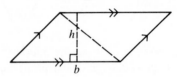

Example 1. Determine the area of each figure.

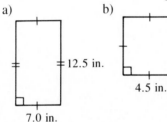

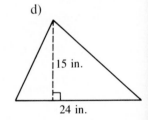

a)
b)
c)
12.5 in.
4.5 in.
15.0 in.
8.4 in.
7.0 in.
d)
15 in.
24 in.

Solution.
a) Area of a rectangle is $A = lw$.
$A = 12.5 \times 7.0$, or 87.5 in².

b) Area of a square is $A = s^2$.
$A = (4.5)^2$, or 20.25 in².

c) Area of a parallelogram is $A = bh$.
$A = 8.4 \times 15$, or 126 in².

d) Area of a triangle is $A = \frac{1}{2}bh$.
$A = \frac{1}{2} \times 24 \times 15$, or 180 in².

Example 2. Find the area of quadrilateral ABCD.

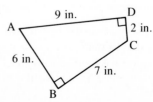

9 in.
A
D
2 in.
C
6 in.
7 in.
B

Solution. Join AC.

Area of $\triangle$ABC $= \dfrac{1}{2}bh$

$= \dfrac{1}{2} \times 6 \times 7$, or 21 in.²

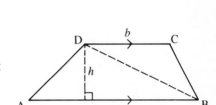

Area of $\triangle$ACD $= \dfrac{1}{2}bh$

$= \dfrac{1}{2} \times 9 \times 2$, or 9 in.²

Area of ABCD $= 21 + 9$, or 30 in.²

Example 3. The parallel sides in a trapezoid have lengths a and b. The perpendicular distance between these sides is h. Show that the formula for the area of a trapezoid is

$A = \dfrac{1}{2}h(a + b)$.

Solution. Area of $\triangle$ABD $= \dfrac{1}{2}ah$

Area of $\triangle$CDB $= \dfrac{1}{2}bh$

Area of ABCD $=$ area of $\triangle$ABD $+$ area of $\triangle$CDB

$= \dfrac{1}{2}ah + \dfrac{1}{2}bh$

$= \dfrac{1}{2}h(a + b)$

Example 4. The height of a trapezoid is represented by x inches. The length of one of the parallel sides is twice the height. The other parallel side is 8 in. longer than the first parallel side. Find the area of the trapezoid in terms of x.

Solution. Draw a diagram.
Since the height is x,
the first parallel side has length $2x$.
The second parallel side has length
$2x + 8$.

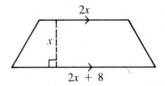

Area of the trapezoid $= \dfrac{1}{2}h(a + b)$

$= \dfrac{1}{2}x(2x + 2x + 8)$

$= \dfrac{1}{2}x(4x + 8)$

$= 2x^2 + 4x$

EXERCISES 5-10

Ⓐ

1. Identify each figure and determine its area.

a)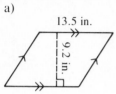
13.5 in.
9.2 in.

b)
65 cm

c)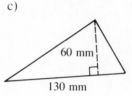
60 mm
130 mm

d)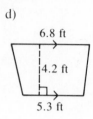
6.8 ft
4.2 ft
5.3 ft

2. Find the area of the shaded region of each figure.

a)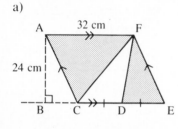
A   32 cm   F
24 cm
B   C   D   E

b)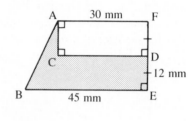
A   30 mm   F
C   D
12 mm
B   45 mm   E

c)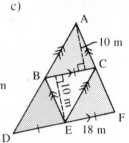
A
10 m
C
B
10 m
D   E   18 m   F

Ⓑ

3. The width of a rectangle is represented by *x* inches. The length is 5 in. longer than twice the width. Find the area of the rectangle in terms of *x*.

4. The height of a trapezoid is represented by *x* centimetres. One parallel side is 2 cm shorter than the height. The other parallel side is twice the height. Find the area of the trapezoid in terms of *x*.

5. Find an expression for the area of a rectangular skating rink if the length is 10 yd more than twice the width.

6. The base of a triangle is 4 in. less than three times the height. Find an expression for the area of the triangle.

7. A parallelogram of area 180 m² has a height of 9 m. What is the length of the base?

8. Find the height of a triangle whose base is 12 ft and whose area is 54 ft².

9. The parallel sides of a trapezoid are 12 cm and 15 cm. Find the height of the trapezoid if the area is 135 cm².

Ⓒ

10. The width of a rectangle is 2 in. shorter than its length. Find the dimensions if the area is 48 in².

11. The measure of one leg of a right triangle is 2 cm more than twice the measure of the other leg. The area of the triangle is 6 cm². Find the measure of each leg.

INVESTIGATE

Simple Closed Curves

These are simple closed curves:

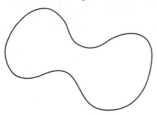  

These are not simple closed curves:

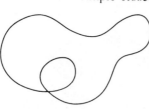 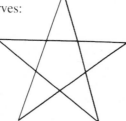 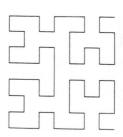

1. Which of these are simple closed curves?

   a)   b)   c)

  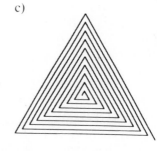

   d)   e)   f)

 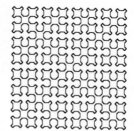

2. Explain what you think a simple closed curve is.

MATHEMATICS AROUND US

Geometry on the Earth's Surface

The geometry in this chapter is called plane geometry because the figures are all drawn on a plane. Geometry on the surface of the Earth is called *spherical geometry* because the figures are drawn on or visualized on a sphere. The shortest distance between two points can be represented by stretching a thread between them. On a plane, this is a straight line.

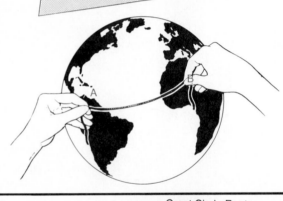

On a globe representing the Earth's surface, the shortest distance between two points is an arc of a *great circle* — the circle that is formed when a plane passes through the two points and the Earth's center.

The shortest distance between two cities is an arc of a great circle, but it does not look that way on most maps. On the adjacent map the straight line joining Winnipeg and Bombay crosses the Atlantic Provinces and North Africa. This route, however, is actually much longer than the great-circle route which passes near the North Pole. Similarly, the shortest route from Winnipeg to Hong Kong is the great-circle route along the north coast of Alaska.

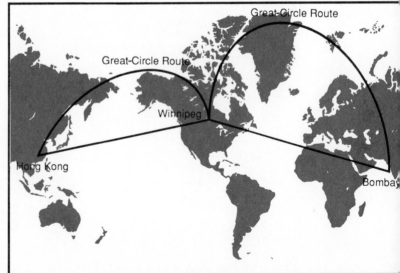

When a triangle is drawn on a plane, its three sides are line segments. The three sides of a *spherical triangle* are arcs of great circles.

On a globe representing the Earth, A is the North Pole, and B and C are points on the Equator. Spherical ∠ABC is 90° because AB is a north/south line and BC is an east/west line. Similarly, spherical ∠ACB is 90°. Spherical ∠BAC is 120° because AC is the 40° E longitude line and AB is the 45° W longitude line. The sum of the angles of spherical △ABC is:
90° + 90° + 120° = 300°

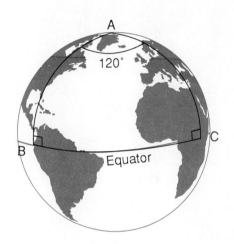

QUESTIONS

1. In the diagram above, if A and C are fixed and B moves along the Equator, how does the sum of the angles in spherical △ABC change?

2. On a globe, using tape and thread, show the great-circle routes from Winnipeg to Hong Kong and Bombay. Compare your routes with those shown on the maps.

3. Which routes do commercial aircraft fly? Why?

4. Which city on the globe is farthest from Winnipeg?

5. On a globe, with tape and thread, show the spherical triangles with vertices at the following cities. Measure their angles with a protractor. What is the sum of the angles in each spherical triangle?
   a) St. John's, Vancouver, Miami (Florida)
   b) Winnipeg, Cairo (Egypt), Rio de Janeiro (Brazil)
   c) Honolulu (Hawaii), Caracas (Venezuela), Nairobi (Kenya)

6. These statements are true for plane geometry. Are they true for spherical geometry? Explain.
   a) When two lines intersect, the opposite angles are equal.
   b) Parallel lines never meet.
   c) Each angle of an equilateral triangle measures 60°.
   d) The angles opposite the equal sides of an isosceles triangle are equal.

5-11 THE PYTHAGOREAN THEOREM

Anna and Lim are on a hike. They come to a field that is rectangular and measures 3.0 km by 1.6 km. Anna decides to take a short cut and walk diagonally across the field. Lim walks around two sides of the field. Who walks farther and by how much?

To find the distances walked, draw a diagram of the field.

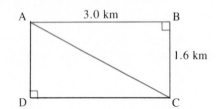

Lim walks (3.0 km + 1.6 km) or 4.6 km.

Anna walks along the path represented by AC. To find the length of the path, use the Pythagorean theorem. Recall that this theorem states that, for a right triangle, the area of the square on the hypotenuse is equal to the sum of the areas of the squares on the other two sides. You may have discovered this result in the previous *INVESTIGATE*.

Since the area of a square is equal to the square of the length of a side, the Pythagorean theorem is usually stated in terms of the lengths of the sides of a right triangle.

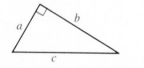

Pythagorean Theorem
For any right triangle with sides of lengths a, b, and c, where c is the hypotenuse, $c^2 = a^2 + b^2$

We can apply the Pythagorean Theorem in $\triangle ABC$, on the facing page.

$AC^2 = AB^2 + BC^2$
$\quad\quad = 3.0^2 + 1.6^2$
$\quad\quad = 11.56$
$AC = \sqrt{11.56}$
$\quad\quad = 3.4$

Anna walks 3.4 km.
The difference between the distances walked is (4.6 km $-$ 3.4 km) or 1.2 km.
Lim walks 1.2 km farther than Anna.

Example 1. Calculate each value of x.

a)

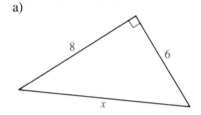

b)

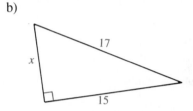

Solution.　　a) $x^2 = 6^2 + 8^2$
$\quad\quad\quad = 36 + 64$
$\quad\quad\quad = 100$
$\quad\quad x = \sqrt{100}$
$\quad\quad\quad = 10$

　　b) 　　$17^2 = x^2 + 15^2$
$\quad\quad\quad\quad 289 = x^2 + 225$
$\quad\quad 289 - 225 = x^2$
$\quad\quad\quad\quad 64 = x^2$
$\quad\quad\quad\quad x = \sqrt{64}$
$\quad\quad\quad\quad\quad = 8$

　　When taking the square root, ignore the negative root because length cannot be negative.

Example 2. Find the length, to one decimal place, indicated by each letter.

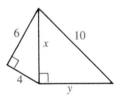

Solution.　　Label the diagram.
　　Use the Pythagorean theorem in each triangle.

In $\triangle ABC$
$x^2 = 6^2 + 4^2$
$\quad = 52$
$\quad x = \sqrt{52}$
$\quad\quad \doteq 7.2$

In $\triangle ACD$
$10^2 = x^2 + y^2$
$100 = 52 + y^2$
$\quad 48 = y^2$
$\quad\quad y = \sqrt{48}$
$\quad\quad\quad \doteq 6.9$

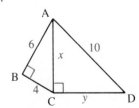

Example 3. The 12th hole at Sandy Dunes golf club is a right-angled "dog leg". What is the distance TG from the tee to the green?

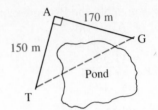

Solution. It follows from the Pythagorean theorem that

$$TG^2 = TA^2 + AG^2$$
$$= 150^2 + 170^2$$
$$= 51\ 400$$
$$TG = \sqrt{51\ 400}$$
$$\doteq 226.7$$

The distance from the tee to the green is approximately 227 m.

EXERCISES 5-11

1. Find the length indicated by each letter.

a)

b)

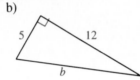

c)

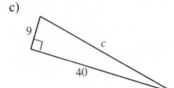

d)

e)

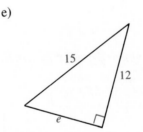

f)

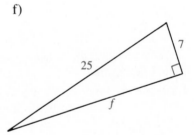

2. Find the length, to one decimal place, indicated by each letter.

a)

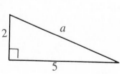

b)

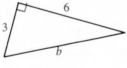

c)

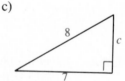

d)

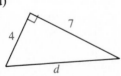

e)

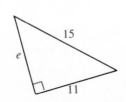

f)

(B)

3. Find the length, to one decimal place, indicated by each letter.

a)

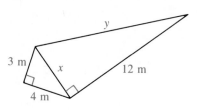

b)

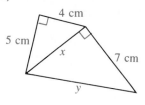

c)

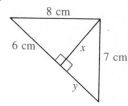

d)

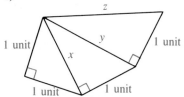

e)

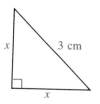

f)

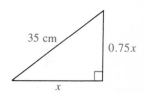

4. A guy wire is attached 50 m up a tower and 12 m from its base. Find the length of the guy wire to the nearest tenth of a metre.

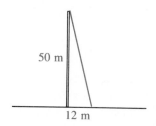

5. A ladder, 8.2 m long, is placed with its foot 1.8 m from a wall. How high up the wall will the ladder reach? Give the answer to the nearest tenth of a metre.

6. Find the length of the rafters for a building, which is 12 000 mm wide and has the peak of the roof 3000 mm above the ceiling. Give the answer to the nearest centimetre.

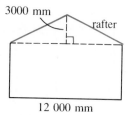

7. Can an umbrella 1.3 m long be packed flat in a box 1.1 m by 0.3 m? Give reasons for your answer.

8. A ramp is to be built from the top level of one parking garage to another. Calculate the length of the ramp to the nearest tenth of a metre.

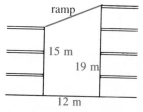

Ⓒ

9. Each colored square has sides 3 cm long.
   a) Find the lengths of the sides of the outer square, to the nearest millimetre.
   b) What percent of the outer square is covered by the five colored squares?

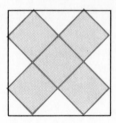

10. A TV set has a screen with a diagonal of length 66 cm. If the screen is 1.2 times as wide as it is high, find its width and height.

11. a) Show that the two isosceles triangles have the same area.
    b) Find another pair of isosceles triangles that have equal areas.

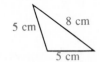

 CALCULATOR POWER

The Pythagorean Theorem

The evaluation of expressions such as $6^2 + 4^2$ (Example 2, page 219) is simplified with the use of a calculator.
For a scientific calculator, here is a possible keying sequence.

Key in: 6 x^2 + 4 x^2 = √‾ to display 7.2111026

If the calculator does not have a √‾ key, this symbol usually occurs above the x^2 key. Here is the keying sequence in this situation.

Key in: 6 x^2 + 4 x^2 = INV x^2

A 4-function calculator can be used to evaluate the expression. However, if the numbers are keyed in as they appear,

6 × 6 + 4 × 4 = √‾ , the result may be 12.649 111, which is wrong. If this happened, the calculator added the first 4 to the result of 6 times 6 before multiplying by the second 4.

This problem can be solved by rewriting the expression before keying it in.

$$6^2 + 4^2 = \left(\frac{6^2}{4} + 4\right)4$$

Key in: 6 × 6 ÷ 4 + 4 × 4 = √‾ ,
which gives the correct result.
The problem can also be solved by using the memory.

COMPUTER POWER

The Pythagorean Theorem

You can use the following program to find the length of any side
of a right triangle, given the lengths of the other two sides.

```
100 REM *** PYTHAGOREAN THEOREM ***
110 INPUT "DO YOU KNOW THE HYPOTENUSE (Y OR N)? ";Z$
120 IF Z$ = "Y" THEN 170
130 PRINT "ENTER THE LENGTHS OF THE SIDES"
140 INPUT "SEPARATED BY A COMMA: ";X,Y
150 Z = SQR (X * X + Y * Y)
160 PRINT "THE HYPOTENUSE IS: ";Z: GOTO 220
170 INPUT "ENTER THE HYPOTENUSE LENGTH: ";Z
180 INPUT "ENTER THE LENGTH OF THE OTHER SIDE: ";X
190 Y = SQR (Z * Z - X * X)
200 PRINT "THE LENGTH OF THE THIRD SIDE IS:"
210 PRINT Y
220 INPUT "PRESS S TO STOP, RETURN TO CONTINUE: ";Y$
230 IF Y$ < > "S" THEN 110
240 END
```

1. Use the program to find the length of the third side of each triangle.

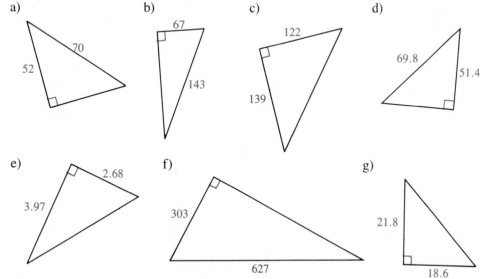

a) 70, 52

b) 67, 143

c) 122, 139

d) 69.8, 51.4

e) 2.68, 3.97

f) 303, 627

g) 21.8, 18.6

2. Find the third side of △ABC, where ∠ABC = 90°.
   a) AB = 2.37 cm, BC = 4.19 cm b) AB = 7.66 m, BC = 7.66 m
   c) BC = 44.9 cm, AC = 59.3 cm d) AB = 1.92 m, AC = 3.06 m

Review Exercises

1. Find the angle measure indicated by each letter.
   a)

   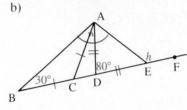

   b)

   c)

   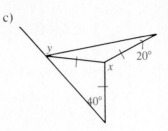

2. Find a pair of congruent triangles and state the condition for congruency.

   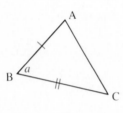

   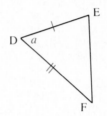

   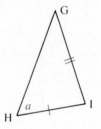

3. Find the length, to one decimal place, indicated by each letter.
   a)

   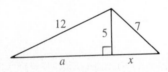

   b)

   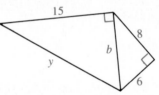

4. The size of a television screen is described by the length of its diagonal. Determine the size of a screen that is 34 cm by 40 cm.

5. Find each value of x.
   a)

   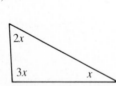

   b)

   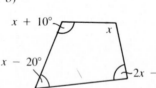

   c)

   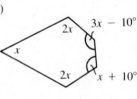

6. Find the area of each figure.
   a)   b)

   c)   d)

   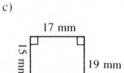

   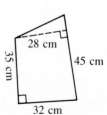

   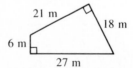

6 Powers, Roots, and Radicals

It has been estimated that if the average weight of an automobile were reduced from 3000 lb to 2000 lb, Canada would save about 8 000 000 gal of oil each day. How much oil would Canada save in one year? (See Section 6-5, *Example 3*.)

6-1 THE MEANING OF EXPONENTS

Scientists use bacteria in medical research. The bacteria are grown in dishes called petri dishes, named after Julius Petri, a noted bacteriologist. The bacteria 'garden' is called a culture. By counting the bacteria in the culture at regular intervals of time, scientists can study how bacteria grow under controlled conditions.

The table shows a typical bacteria count every hour, starting with a bacteria count of 1000 at midnight.

The number of bacteria doubles every hour.

Time	Number of Bacteria
midnight	1000
01:00	1000×2 or 2000
02:00	$1000 \times 2 \times 2$ or 4000
03:00	$1000 \times 2 \times 2 \times 2$ or 8000

If the pattern in the table is maintained, there would be at 08:00 a total of $1000 \times 2 \times 2 \times 2 \times 2 \times 2 \times 2 \times 2 \times 2$ bacteria. This is a large number which can be written more simply using *exponents*.

The value, $2 \times 2 \times 2 \times 2 \times 2 \times 2 \times 2 \times 2$, is written 2^8.

2^8 is a *power* with an exponent of 8 and a *base* of 2. We say that it is the eighth power of 2.

We say, "Two to the eighth."

power — 2^8 — exponent

base

The base is the number that is repeatedly multiplied. The exponent indicates how many of these numbers are multiplied.

The number of bacteria at 08:00 can be written as 1000×2^8 or 256 000 when expanded.

Example 1. Write each product as a power.

a) $(-9)(-9)(-9)(-9)$

b) $\left(\dfrac{7}{8}\right)\left(\dfrac{7}{8}\right)\left(\dfrac{7}{8}\right)\left(\dfrac{7}{8}\right)\left(\dfrac{7}{8}\right)$

c) $m \times m \times m$

d) $\left(\dfrac{2}{n}\right)\left(\dfrac{2}{n}\right)\left(\dfrac{2}{n}\right)\left(\dfrac{2}{n}\right)$

Solution.

a) $(-9)(-9)(-9)(-9) = (-9)^4$

b) $\left(\dfrac{7}{8}\right)\left(\dfrac{7}{8}\right)\left(\dfrac{7}{8}\right)\left(\dfrac{7}{8}\right)\left(\dfrac{7}{8}\right) = \left(\dfrac{7}{8}\right)^5$

c) $m \times m \times m = m^3$

d) $\left(\dfrac{2}{n}\right)\left(\dfrac{2}{n}\right)\left(\dfrac{2}{n}\right)\left(\dfrac{2}{n}\right) = \left(\dfrac{2}{n}\right)^4$

Example 2. If $n = 3$, evaluate: a) n^5 b) 5^n.

Solution.

a) If $n = 3$, $n^5 = 3^5$
$= (3)(3)(3)(3)(3)$
$= 243$

b) If $n = 3$, $5^n = 5^3$
$= (5)(5)(5)$
$= 125$

Example 3. Evaluate. a) $(-4)^3$ b) $(-4)^4$

Solution.

a) $(-4)^3 = (-4)(-4)(-4)$
$= -64$

b) $(-4)^4 = (-4)(-4)(-4)(-4)$
$= 256$

This example illustrates that
- a power with a negative base has a positive value when the exponent is even.
- a power with a negative base has a negative value when the exponent is odd.

The order of operations with exponents is the same as that for rational numbers. When evaluating expressions containing powers, evaluate the powers first unless brackets indicate otherwise.

Example 4. If $x = 5$ and $y = -2$ evaluate:

a) $x^2 - y^2$ b) $(x - y)^2$ c) $-3y^3$ d) $(-3y)^3$.

Solution. If $x = 5$ and $y = -2$

a) $x^2 - y^2 = 5^2 - (-2)^2$
$= 25 - 4$
$= 21$

b) $(x - y)^2 = [5 - (-2)]^2$
$= (7)^2$
$= 49$

c) $-3y^3 = -3(-2)^3$
$= -3(-8)$
$= 24$

d) $(-3y)^3 = [-3(-2)]^3$
$= (6)^3$
$= 216$

EXERCISES 6-1

Ⓐ

1. Write each product as a power.
   a) $y \times y \times y \times y$
   b) $(-3)(-3)(-3)(-3)(-3)(-3)$
   c) $\frac{2}{5} \times \frac{2}{5} \times \frac{2}{5} \times \frac{2}{5} \times \frac{2}{5}$
   d) $\left(-\frac{3}{8}\right)\left(-\frac{3}{8}\right)\left(-\frac{3}{8}\right)$
   e) $(4a)(4a)(4a)(4a)(4a)$
   f) $2.9 \times 2.9 \times 2.9 \times 2.9$
   g) $m \times m \times m \times m$
   h) $(-6x)(-6x)(-6x)(-6x)(-6x)$
   i) $\pi \times \pi \times \pi \times \pi \times \pi \times \pi$
   j) $a \times a \times a \times a \times a \times a \times a$

2. Write each phrase as a power.
   a) six cubed
   b) seven to the eighth power
   c) nine to the fourth power
   d) twenty squared
   e) eleven to the fifth power
   f) five to the eleventh power
   g) four to the nth power
   h) $2x$ to the tenth power

3. Evaluate.
   a) 4^3
   b) 3^4
   c) $(-2)^5$
   d) $(-5)^2$
   e) 10^4
   f) $\left(\frac{1}{4}\right)^2$
   g) $(0.2)^3$
   h) $(2.1)^2$
   i) $3(2^4)$
   j) $2^3\left(\frac{3}{4}\right)^2$
   k) $(3 \times 2)^4$
   l) $2(-3)^4$

4. Express each number as a power of 10.
   a) 1000
   b) 10 000
   c) 100
   d) 1 000 000
   e) 100 000
   f) 10
   g) 100 000 000
   h) 1 000 000 000 000

Ⓑ

5. Using the pattern in the table on page 226, write an expression involving powers of 2 for the number of bacteria in the culture at each time.
   a) 01:00
   b) 02:00
   c) 06:00
   d) 10:00

6. Evaluate.
   a) $2^3 + 3^2$
   b) $3^2 + 4^2$
   c) $(3 + 4)^2$
   d) $5(-4)^3$
   e) $3^2 - 5^2$
   f) $(-4)^2 - 7^2$
   g) $\left(-\frac{3}{2}\right)^3 - \left(\frac{1}{4}\right)^3$
   h) $(-5)^3 - (-2)^5$

7. Evaluate $2x^2 - 3x + 5$ for each value of x.
   a) 4
   b) -1
   c) -2
   d) 10
   e) -5
   f) $\frac{1}{2}$
   g) $-\frac{1}{3}$
   h) 1.5
   i) -0.4
   j) 100

8. If $x = -3$ and $y = \frac{2}{3}$, evaluate each expression.
   a) x^2
   b) y^3
   c) $-5x^3$
   d) $-x^4$
   e) $(-x)^4$
   f) $x^2 + y^2$
   g) $x^2 - y^2$
   h) $(x + y)^3$
   i) $x^3 + y^3$
   j) $x^3 - y^3$
   k) $(x + y)^9$
   l) $(3x - y)^2$
   m) $5(x^2 - 2y)$
   n) $(3x + y)^3$
   o) $4x^2 - 7y^2$
   p) $4x^2 + y^2$

9. Evaluate each expression for $n = -3$.
   a) n^3
   b) $n^2 - n^3$
   c) $4n^2$
   d) $(4n)^2$
   e) $-(n + 2)^3$
   f) $(-n - 2)^8$
   g) $(2 + n)^{15}$
   h) $-(3n - 7)^4$
   i) $(-4n - 2n^2)^4$
   j) $\left(\dfrac{n}{4}\right)^3$
   k) $\left(\dfrac{2}{n} - 1\right)^5$
   l) $(n - n^2)^3$

10. Arrange from greatest to least.
    a) 2^4, 3^2, 5^2, 2^3, 3^3
    b) $(-3)^4$, 4^3, 7^2, 2^5, 10^2
    c) $(1.2)^2$, $(1.1)^3$, $(1.05)^5$, $(1.15)^3$, $(1.3)^1$
    d) $(2.1)^4$, $(2.9)^3$, $(2.3)^2$, $(1.8)^7$, $(2.4)^5$
    e) $(0.3)^2$, $(0.2)^3$, $(0.2)^2$, $(0.3)^3$, $(0.4)^2$

Ⓒ

11. Use the information on page 226.
    a) If you knew how much time had elapsed since midnight, how could you find the number of bacteria in the culture?
    b) Write an expression for the number of bacteria in the culture n hours after midnight.
    c) At 01:30 there are about 2800 bacteria in the culture. Find approximately how many there would be:
       i) 1 h later
       ii) 2 h later
       iii) 1 h earlier.

    d) If a petri dish is half-covered by bacteria at midnight find when it will be completely covered.

12. Identify the greater number in each pair.
    a) 3^{22}, 3^{25}
    b) $3x^2$, $(3x)^2$
    c) $(-5n)^3$, $5n^3$
    d) $(-2)^{16}$, $(-2)^{19}$
    e) $(0.9)^{14}$, $(0.9)^{11}$
    f) $\left(-\dfrac{3}{4}\right)^{10}$, $(-3.4)^7$

13. a) For what values of y is $y^2 < y$?
    b) For what values of x is $x^3 < x^4$?

14. Solve for n.
    a) $2^n = 8$
    b) $3^n = 81$
    c) $10^n = 1\ 000\ 000$
    d) $3(2^n) = 48$
    e) $2(5^n) = 50$
    f) $10(3^n) = 810$

15. Identify the greater number in each pair.
    a) 2^5, 5^3
    b) 3^4, 4^3
    c) 10^4, 2^{10}
    d) 6^4, 11^{11}
    e) 6^3, 3^6
    f) 9^4, 3^8

16. Express the first number as a power of the second.
    a) 16, 4
    b) 27, 3
    c) 64, 2
    d) 625, 5
    e) 16, -2
    f) -243, -3
    g) 343, 7
    h) 256, -4
    i) 81, -3
    j) 6561, 9
    k) 7776, 6
    l) 1.4641, 1.1

CALCULATOR POWER

Using a Scientific Calculator to Evaluate Powers

To evaluate $9^2 + (-8)^2$ . . .

. . . Linda pressed these keys on her calculator   . . . Dan pressed these keys

| 9 | x^2 | + | 8 | $+/-$ | x^2 | = | | 9 | x^2 | + | $-$ | 8 | x^2 | = |

- What answers were obtained by Linda and Dan?
- What is the purpose of the $\boxed{+/-}$ key?
- Whose answer was correct?
- Explain where the error occurred in the incorrect keying sequence.

Evaluate each expression on your scientific calculator.

1. a) $6^2 + 12^2$ b) $5^2 - 9^2$ c) $(0.8^2) + (0.6^2)$ d) $(2.6^2) - (2.4^2)$
    e) $5^2 + (-7)^2$ f) $12^2 + (-5)^2$ g) $1.7(-9)^2$ h) $(2.3 - 12)^2$

   To evaluate, on a scientific calculator, powers with exponents greater than 2 we use the $\boxed{y^x}$ (or $\boxed{a^x}$) key.

To evaluate 3^7, key in: $\boxed{3}$ $\boxed{y^x}$ $\boxed{7}$ $\boxed{=}$ to display 2187

To evaluate $(-2)^9$, key in: $\boxed{2}$ $\boxed{+/-}$ $\boxed{y^x}$ $\boxed{9}$ $\boxed{=}$ to display -512

To evaluate $[5(-3)]^4$ . . .

. . . Linda pressed these keys on her calculator   . . . Dan pressed these keys

| 5 | $\times$ | 3 | $+/-$ | y^x | 4 | = | | 5 | $\times$ | 3 | $+/-$ | = | y^x | 4 | = |

- What answers did Linda and Dan obtain?
- Explain why their answers differ.
- Whose answer is correct?
- Explain where the error occurred in the incorrect sequence.

Evaluate each expression on your scientific calculator.

2. a) 17^3 b) 29^4 c) $(-3)^3$ d) $(-2)^7$

3. a) $0.3(5)^3$ b) $5.5(-4)^3$ c) $-7(3^4)$ d) $(8^3)(7^4)$
    e) $-6(-3)^7$ f) $(-9.1)^4(-2)^3$ g) $-(-2)^4(-3)^5$ h) $(-2)^3(3^2)(4^3)$

4. a) $2^9 - 3(5.7^4)$ b) $4(-3)^5 - 6(-2.8)^5$

6-2 EXPONENTS IN FORMULAS

In September 1979, an East German family crossed the heavily-guarded frontier into West Germany in a home-made hot air balloon. It was the first escape by this means. The balloon approximated the shape of a sphere with a diameter of about 22 m. What volume of air was in the balloon?

The volume of a sphere is given by the formula $V = \frac{4}{3}\pi r^3$, where r is the radius.

For the balloon, the radius is $\frac{1}{2}(22$ m) or 11 m.

$$V = \frac{4}{3}\pi r^3$$

$$= \frac{4}{3}\pi(11)^3 \quad \text{Use a calculator.}$$

Key in: $\boxed{4}$ $\boxed{\div}$ $\boxed{3}$ $\boxed{\times}$ $\boxed{\pi}$ $\boxed{\times}$ $\boxed{1}$ $\boxed{1}$ $\boxed{y^x}$ $\boxed{3}$ $\boxed{=}$ to display 5575.2798

The volume of the balloon was about 5600 m³.

The volume of air is usually expressed in kilolitres (kL).

Since 1 m³ = 1 kL, the volume of air in the balloon was about 5600 kL.

Other formulas which involve exponents are listed below.

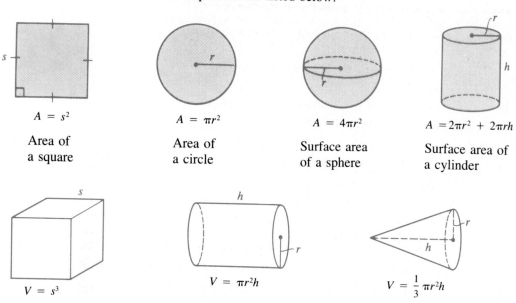

$A = s^2$	$A = \pi r^2$	$A = 4\pi r^2$	$A = 2\pi r^2 + 2\pi rh$
Area of a square	Area of a circle	Surface area of a sphere	Surface area of a cylinder

$V = s^3$	$V = \pi r^2 h$	$V = \frac{1}{3}\pi r^2 h$
Volume of a cube	Volume of a cylinder	Volume of a cone

Example 1. Find the area, to one decimal place, of the shaded region of each figure.

a)
3.6 m

b)
1.6 cm

Solution. a) Area of square, $A = s^2$

Shaded area of square, $\frac{1}{2}A = \frac{1}{2}s^2$

When $s = 3.6$, $\quad \frac{1}{2}A = \frac{1}{2}(3.6)^2$

$= 6.48$

The shaded region of the square has an area of about 6.5 m².

b) Area of circle, $A = \pi r^2$

Shaded area of circle, $\frac{1}{4}A = \frac{1}{4}\pi r^2$

When $r = 1.6$, $\quad \frac{1}{4}A = \frac{1}{4}\pi(1.6)^2$

$\doteq 2.01$

The shaded region of the circle has an area of about 2.0 cm².

Example 2. Find the volume of each solid, to the nearest unit.

a)

Cube of side
1.9 cm

b)

Sphere of diameter
9.4 cm

c)

Cylinder of height
11.0 cm, diameter 7.4 cm

Solution. a) Volume of cube, $V = s^3$
When $s = 1.9$, $\quad V = (1.9)^3$
$= 6.859$

The volume of the cube is about 7 cm³.

b) Volume of sphere, $V = \frac{4}{3}\pi r^3$

$r = \frac{1}{2}(9.4)$ or 4.7

$V = \frac{4}{3}\pi(4.7)^3$

$\doteq 434.89$

If your calculator does not have a $\boxed{\pi}$ key, use $\pi = 3.14$.

The volume of the sphere is about 435 cm³.

c) Volume of cylinder, $V = \pi r^2 h$

$r = \dfrac{1}{2}(7.4)$ or 3.7 and $h = 11.0$

$V = \pi(3.7)^2(11.0)$
$\doteq 473.09$

The volume of the cylinder is about 473 cm³.

Example 3. The distance d metres that an object falls from rest in t seconds is given by the formula $d \doteq 4.9t^2$. A pebble dropped from the top of a building takes 3.5 s to reach the ground. Find the height of the building.

Solution. Substitute $t = 3.5$ in the formula $d \doteq 4.9t^2$.
$d \doteq 4.9(3.5)^2$
$= 60.025$
The building is about 60 m high.

Example 4. A \$500 U.S. Savings Bond pays 7% interest annually. This interest compounds (earns more interest) each year. The value V dollars of the bond after n years is given by this formula.
$V = 500(1.07)^n$
Find the value of the bond after: a) 2 years   b) 5 years.

Solution. a) $V = 500(1.07)^n$
Substitute $n = 2$ into the formula.
$V = 500(1.07)^2$
$= 572.45$
After 2 years, the bond is worth \$572.45.
b) $V = 500(1.07)^n$
Substitute $n = 5$ into the formula.
$V = 500(1.07)^5$

$\doteq 701.28$
After 5 years, the bond is worth \$701.28.

EXERCISES 6-2

1. Express the area of each shaded region using exponents.

a)

2.5

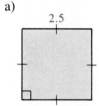

b)

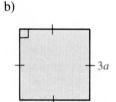

$3a$

c)

$\dfrac{2}{3}x$

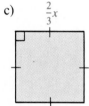

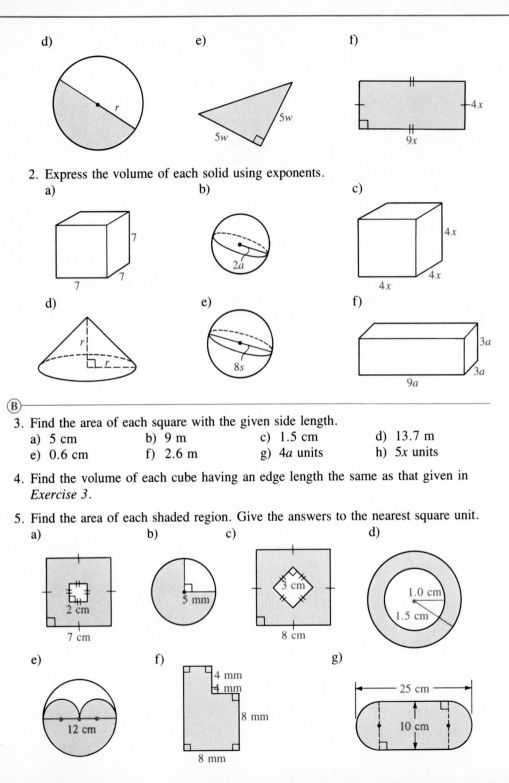

d)

e)

f)

2. Express the volume of each solid using exponents.

a)

b)

c)

d)

e)

f)

(B)

3. Find the area of each square with the given side length.
   a) 5 cm
   b) 9 m
   c) 1.5 cm
   d) 13.7 m
   e) 0.6 cm
   f) 2.6 m
   g) 4a units
   h) 5x units

4. Find the volume of each cube having an edge length the same as that given in *Exercise 3*.

5. Find the area of each shaded region. Give the answers to the nearest square unit.
   a)

   b)

   c)

   d)

   e)

   f)

   g)

6. A principal of $200 in a savings account that pays 8% interest annually grows to $200(1.08)^n in n years. What does the principal grow to in:
   a) 3 years   b) 6 years   c) 10 years?

7. A path 2 m wide is to enclose a circular lawn that has a 25 m radius. What will be the total cost of the material for the path if the cost per square metre is $3.00?

8. A label just covers the curved surface of a soup tin with height 10 cm and diameter 7 cm. What is the area of the label?

9. A punch bowl is hemispherical and 50 cm in diameter. How many litres of punch can it hold? Give the answer to the nearest tenth of a litre.

10. How many bouillon cubes with an edge length of 2 cm can be packed into a cubic box with an edge length of 0.5 m?

11. Find the volume of air contained in a spherical balloon with a radius of 12 cm. Give the answer to the nearest tenth of a litre.

12. A car brakes and decelerates uniformly. The distance d metres that it travels in t seconds is given by this formula.
    $$d = ut - 3.5t^2$$
    u is the speed, in metres per second, just as the brakes are applied.
    Find how far the car travels while braking for 5 s, when it was travelling 25 m/s just as the brakes were applied.

Ⓒ

13. A class found by measuring that the relationship of the area A of the maple leaf on the Canadian flag to the flag's length x is $A \doteq 0.072x^2$.
    a) Find the area of the maple leaf on a flag of each length.
         i)   20 cm   ii)   40 cm
         iii) 80 cm   iv) 1.6 m
    b) Find the length of the flag that has a maple leaf with each area.
         i)   583.2 cm²   ii)   1036.8 cm²
         iii) 0.45 m²   iv) 16.2 mm²

14. The balloon that made the first successful crossing of the Atlantic Ocean was filled with helium. It had the shape of a hemisphere on a cone.
    The balloon was 33.0 m high and 19.6 m in diameter.
    Find the volume, to the nearest kilolitre, of helium that the balloon contained.

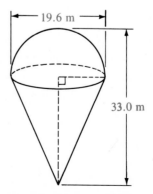

6-3 OPERATIONS WITH POWERS

Three operations involving powers are explained in this section.

- Multiplication of powers with the same base
- Division of powers with the same base
- Exponentiation of a power

All three operations are based on the definition of an exponent.

$x^n = x \times x \times x \times x \ldots$ to n factors

Example 1. Simplify.

   a) $5^3 \times 5^4$ b) $y^5 \times y^6$

Solution.   a) $5^3 \times 5^4 = 5 \times 5 \times 5 \times 5 \times 5 \times 5 \times 5$
                    $= 5^7$

   b) $y^5 \times y^6 = y \times y \times y \times y \times y \times y \times y \times y \times y \times y \times y$
                    $= y^{11}$

In each part of the example, the exponent of the simplified expression
is the sum of the exponents in the original expression. This example
illustrates the following rule for multiplying powers.

> To multiply powers with the same base, add the exponents.
> $x^m \times x^n = x^{m+n}, m > 0, n > 0$

Example 2. Simplify.

   a) $7^8 \div 7^3$ b) $z^9 \div z^2$

Solution.

   a) $7^8 \div 7^3 = \dfrac{7 \times 7 \times 7 \times 7 \times 7 \times 7 \times 7 \times 7}{7 \times 7 \times 7}$

   $= 7^5$

   b) $z^9 \div z^2 = \dfrac{z \times z \times z \times z \times z \times z \times z \times z \times z}{z \times z}$

   $= z^7$

In each part of the example, the exponent of the simplified expression
is the difference between the exponents in the original expression.

> To divide powers with the same base, subtract the exponents.
> $x^m \div x^n = x^{m-n}, m > n, m > 0, n > 0, x \neq 0$

Example 3. Simplify.

a) $(3^3)^4$ b) $(y^4)^5$

Solution. a) $(3^3)^4 = 3^3 \times 3^3 \times 3^3 \times 3^3$

$$= 3^{3+3+3+3}$$

$$= 3^{12}$$

b) $(y^4)^5 = y^4 \times y^4 \times y^4 \times y^4 \times y^4$

$$= y^{4+4+4+4+4}$$

$$= y^{20}$$

In each part of the example, the exponent of the simplified expression is the product of the exponents in the original expression.

> To raise a power to an exponent, multiply the exponents.
> $(x^m)^n = x^{mn}, \ m > 0, \ n > 0, \ x \neq 0$

Example 4. Simplify.

a) $3a^4 \times 2a^3$ b) $\dfrac{12n^5}{6n^2}$ c) $\dfrac{5(b^2)^3 \times (3b^4)^2}{2b^3}$

Solution. a) $3a^4 \times 2a^3 = 3 \times 2 \times a^{4+3}$

$$= 6a^7$$

b) $\dfrac{12n^5}{6n^2} = 2n^{5-2}$

$$= 2n^3$$

c) $\dfrac{5(b^2)^3 \times (3b^4)^2}{2b^3} = \dfrac{5 \times 3^2 \times b^{2\times3} \times b^{4\times2}}{2b^3}$

$$= \dfrac{45 \times b^6 \times b^8}{2b^3}$$

$$= \dfrac{45b^{6+8-3}}{2}$$

$$= \dfrac{45b^{11}}{2}$$

EXERCISES 6-3

(A)

1. Write each product as a power.

a) $3^4 \times 3^6$ b) $7^4 \times 7^7$ c) $(-5)^{16}(-5)^9$

d) $(2.1)^5(2.1)^{11}$ e) $(-8)^2(-8)^3(-8)$ f) $(-1.7)^4(-1.7)^2(-1.7)$

g) $\left(\dfrac{2}{5}\right)^8\left(\dfrac{2}{5}\right)^{14}$ h) $\left(\dfrac{3}{11}\right)^{21}\left(\dfrac{3}{11}\right)^{15}$ i) $\left(-\dfrac{5}{4}\right)\left(-\dfrac{5}{4}\right)^6\left(-\dfrac{5}{4}\right)^7$

2. Simplify.

a) x^7x^4 b) k^3k^9 c) n^6n^{17} d) $s^4s^5s^2$

e) $v^{12}v^5v$ f) y^7yy^2 g) $(-a)^4(-a)^6$ h) $(-c)^7(-c)$

3. Simplify.

a) $3^8 \div 3^3$

b) $2^{16} \div 2^7$

c) $m^{20} \div m^5$

d) $\dfrac{s^{18}}{s^6}$

e) $\dfrac{14z^{12}}{-2z^4}$

f) $\dfrac{24r^{24}}{8r^8}$

g) $\dfrac{6^8}{6^2}$

h) $\dfrac{(-2)^7}{(-2)^3}$

4. Simplify.

a) $\dfrac{2^3 \times 2^5}{2^6}$

b) $\dfrac{3 \times 3^7}{3^2 \times 3^2}$

c) $\dfrac{m^4 \times m^3}{m^2}$

d) $\dfrac{b^4 \times b}{b^2}$

e) $\dfrac{(-a)^5(-a)}{(-a)^2}$

f) $\dfrac{x^{12} \times x^6}{x^5 \times x^4}$

g) $\dfrac{c^8 \times c^6}{c^2 \times c^9}$

h) $\dfrac{(-5)^{41} \times (-5)^{19}}{(-5)^{50}}$

i) $\dfrac{7^{14}}{7^3 \times 7^4}$

5. Simplify.

a) $(m^4)^5$

b) $[(-t)^3]^5$

c) $(a^7)^7$

d) $(2^3)^4$

e) $(12^5)^7$

f) $(10^2)^6$

g) $[(-5)^4]^3$

h) $(z^9)^3$

Ⓑ

6. Simplify.

a) $3a^2 \times 5a^3$

b) $2m^3 \times 9m^5$

c) $4x^4 \times 9x^9$

d) $6y^5(-3y^7)$

e) $5(3)^8 \times 6(3)^4$

f) $8(-7)^4 \times 4(-7)^{11}$

g) $3x \times 19x^{10}$

h) $2p^5 \times 5p^2 \times 3p^3$

i) $4s^5 \times 7s^{10} \times 3s$

7. Simplify.

a) $\dfrac{20d^5}{4d^2}$

b) $\dfrac{36a^{12}}{-4a^3}$

c) $\dfrac{-42z^3}{-7z^2}$

d) $15m^9 \div 5m^3$

e) $-32x^{12} \div 8x^4$

f) $50a^{20} \div 20a^5$

g) $12(2)^7 \div 4(2)^3$

h) $-24(3)^{18} \div 4(3)^6$

i) $\dfrac{4n^{12} \times 5n^3}{10n^6}$

j) $\dfrac{3c^6 \times 2c}{4c^2}$

k) $\dfrac{18m^{14} \times 5m^7}{10m^3}$

l) $\dfrac{-9a^7 \times (-8)a^9}{-18a^8}$

8. Simplify.

a) $(6m^2)^3$

b) $(4x^5)^2$

c) $(13a^7)^4$

d) $(-3p^2)^8$

e) $(-6c^4)^6$

f) $(-3x^5)^2$

g) $\dfrac{(2k^2)^2}{k^3}$

h) $\dfrac{(3n^4)^3}{(2n)^2}$

i) $\dfrac{(4a^5)^3(4a^6)^2}{4a^4}$

j) $\dfrac{-(-2n^4)^2(-n^2)^4}{(3n)^3}$

k) $\dfrac{(0.5x^2)^3(-2x^3)^2}{(-0.5x)^2}$

l) $\dfrac{(10m^3)^4(0.1m^2)^4}{(100m^2)(0.01m^2)^2}$

9. Astronomers estimate that there are about 10^{11} galaxies in the universe, and that each galaxy contains about 10^{11} stars. About how many stars are there in the universe?

Ⓒ

10. Simplify.

a) $(a^2b^4)^3$

b) $(3x^2y^3z)^4$

c) $(-2mn^3p^4)^3$

d) $\dfrac{(-36m^2n^3)^2}{(12m^3n^2)^3}$

e) $\dfrac{(4ab^2c^3)^3}{(-3a^3b^2c)^4}$

6-4 THE EXPONENT LAWS

Consider the statement, $\dfrac{x^m}{x^n} = x^{m-n}$, $x \neq 0$.

We have shown that this is true if m and n are positive integers and $m > n$. What happens to this equation if the restriction $m > n$ does not hold? That is,

Suppose $m = n$

For example, if $m = 3$ and $n = 3$ and $x \neq 0$,

then $\dfrac{x^3}{x^3} = \dfrac{(x)(x)(x)}{(x)(x)(x)}$ also $\dfrac{x^3}{x^3} = x^{3-3}$

$\qquad = 1$ $\qquad\qquad\qquad = x^0$

Since x^m is defined only for positive values of m, the expression x^0 has not yet been defined.

However, if we define x^0 to be 1, then $\dfrac{x^3}{x^3} = 1 = x^{3-3}$, for $x \neq 0$.

That is, if we define x^0 to be 1 for $x \neq 0$, then the exponent law $\dfrac{x^m}{x^n} = x^{m-n}$, $x \neq 0$, is true for $m > n$ and $m = n$.

> For any number x, where $x \neq 0$, $x^0 = 1$

Suppose $m < n$

For example, if $m = 3$ and $n = 7$ and $x \neq 0$,

then $\dfrac{x^3}{x^7} = \dfrac{x \times x \times x}{x \times x \times x \times x \times x \times x \times x}$ also $\dfrac{x^3}{x^7} = x^{3-7}$

$\qquad = \dfrac{1}{x^4}$ $\qquad\qquad\qquad\qquad = x^{-4}$

Since x^m is defined only for non-negative values of m, the expression x^{-4} has not yet been defined.

However, if we define x^{-4} to mean $\dfrac{1}{x^4}$, then $\dfrac{x^3}{x^7} = x^{-4}$, for $x \neq 0$.

That is, if we define x^{-n} to mean $\dfrac{1}{x^n}$ for $x \neq 0$, then the exponent law, $\dfrac{x^m}{x^n} = x^{m-n}$, $x \neq 0$, is true for all integral values of m and n.

> For any number x and any integer n, x^{-n} is defined to be the reciprocal of x^n.
>
> $x^{-n} = \dfrac{1}{x^n}$, $x \neq 0$

These two statements, along with the 3 statements from the previous section, comprise the *exponent laws*.

> **Exponent Laws**
> For all integers *m* and *n*
> - $x^m \times x^n = x^{m+n}$
> - $x^m \div x^n = x^{m-n}, x \neq 0$
> - $(x^m)^n = x^{mn}$
> - $x^0 = 1, x \neq 0$
> - $x^{-m} = \dfrac{1}{x^m}, x \neq 0$

The pattern of this table is a further illustration of the relationship between positive and negative exponents.

$$2^4 = 2 \times 2 \times 2 \times 2 = 16$$

Reducing exponents by 1,

$$2^3 = 2 \times 2 \times 2 = 8$$
$$2^2 = 2 \times 2 = 4$$
$$2^1 = 2 = 2$$
$$2^0 = 1 = 1$$
$$2^{-1} = \frac{1}{2} = \frac{1}{2}$$
$$2^{-2} = \frac{1}{2} \times \frac{1}{2} = \frac{1}{4}$$
$$2^{-3} = \frac{1}{2} \times \frac{1}{2} \times \frac{1}{2} = \frac{1}{8} \quad \text{divides answers by 2.}$$
$$2^{-4} = \frac{1}{2} \times \frac{1}{2} \times \frac{1}{2} \times \frac{1}{2} = \frac{1}{16}$$

Example 1. Evaluate.

a) 5^{-2}

b) $\left(\dfrac{1}{4}\right)^{-3}$

c) $(3^0 - 3^{-1})^{-2}$

Solution.

a) $5^{-2} = \dfrac{1}{5^2}$

$= \dfrac{1}{25}$

b) $\left(\dfrac{1}{4}\right)^{-3} = \dfrac{1}{\left(\dfrac{1}{4}\right)^3}$

$= \dfrac{1}{\dfrac{1}{64}}$

$= 64$

c) $(3^0 - 3^{-1})^{-2} = \left(1 - \dfrac{1}{3}\right)^{-2}$ or $(3^0 - 3^{-1})^{-2} = \left(1 - \dfrac{1}{3}\right)^{-2}$

$$= \left(\dfrac{2}{3}\right)^{-2} \qquad\qquad\qquad = \left(\dfrac{2}{3}\right)^{-2}$$

$$= \dfrac{1}{\left(\dfrac{2}{3}\right)^2} \qquad\qquad\qquad = \left(\dfrac{3}{2}\right)^{2}$$

$$= \dfrac{1}{\dfrac{4}{9}} \qquad\qquad\qquad\quad = \dfrac{9}{4}$$

$$= \dfrac{9}{4}$$

Example 2. Evaluate.

      a) $4^{-3} \times 4^2 \times 4^{-1}$ b) $(-2)^{-4} \div (-2)^{-1}$ c) $(3^{-1})^{-2}$

Solution.   a) $4^{-3} \times 4^2 \times 4^{-1} = 4^{-3+2-1}$

$$= 4^{-2}$$

$$= \dfrac{1}{4^2}$$

$$= \dfrac{1}{16}$$

      b) $(-2)^{-4} \div (-2)^{-1} = (-2)^{-4-(-1)}$

$$= (-2)^{-3}$$

$$= \dfrac{1}{(-2)^3}$$

$$= -\dfrac{1}{8}$$

      c) $(3^{-1})^{-2} = 3^{(-1)(-2)}$

$$= 3^2$$

$$= 9$$

Example 3. Simplify.

      a) $(x^{-2})(x^5)(x^0)$ b) $x^3 \div x^{-5}$ c) $(x^2)^{-3}$

Solution.   a) $(x^{-2})(x^5)(x^0) = x^{-2+5+0}$

$$= x^3$$

      b) $x^3 \div x^{-5} = x^{3-(-5)}$

$$= x^8$$

      c) $(x^2)^{-3} = x^{2(-3)}$

$$= x^{-6}$$

Example 4. Evaluate each expression for $a = -2$ and $b = 3$.

a) $a^{-2} - b^{-1}$ b) $3a^{-1} + 2b^{-2}$

Solution. If $a = -2$ and $b = 3$

a) $a^{-2} - b^{-1} = (-2)^{-2} - (3)^{-1}$

$$= \frac{1}{(-2)^2} - \frac{1}{3}$$

$$= \frac{1}{4} - \frac{1}{3}$$

$$= \frac{3}{12} - \frac{4}{12}$$

$$= -\frac{1}{12}$$

b) $3a^{-1} + 2b^{-2} = 3(-2)^{-1} + 2(3)^{-2}$

$$= \frac{3}{-2} + \frac{2}{3^2}$$

$$= -\frac{3}{2} + \frac{2}{9}$$

$$= -\frac{27}{18} + \frac{4}{18}$$

$$= -\frac{23}{18}$$

EXERCISES 6-4

(A)

1. Evaluate.

a) 2^{-1} b) 5^{-1} c) 3^{-2} d) 2^{-3} e) 5^{-3} f) 10^{-2}

g) 12^{-3} h) 10^{-4} i) $\left(\frac{1}{2}\right)^0$ j) $\left(\frac{1}{4}\right)^{-2}$ k) 10^{-5} l) $\frac{1}{5^{-1}}$

m) $\frac{1}{2^{-5}}$ n) $\frac{3}{4^{-2}}$ o) $\left(\frac{3}{4}\right)^{-2}$ p) $\left(\frac{1}{10}\right)^{-1}$ q) $(0.1)^{-3}$ r) $(0.5)^{-2}$

2. Simplify.

a) $10^3 \times 10^{-5}$ b) $10^{-4} \div 10^{-3}$

c) $(10^{-4})^2 \times 10^{-1}$ d) $10^0 \times 10^8$

e) $10^4 \div 10^{-5} \times 10^6$ f) $10^4 \times 10^{-5} \div 10^6$

g) $(10^{-5})^3(10^5)^3$ h) $(10^4 \times 10^6)^0 \div 10^{-1}$

i) $(10^{-3})^4(10^{-4})^3 \div (10^{-2})^{-1}$ j) $10^{-5} \div 10^{-3} \times (10^4)^{-2}$

(B)

3. Write each expression as a power.

a) $5^4 \times 5^7$ b) $2^{-5} \times 2^{11}$ c) $3^4 \div 3^{-11}$

d) $7^{-8} \div 7^2$ e) $11^{-13} \times 11^{20}$ f) $(-5)^{-11} \div (-5)^{19}$

g) $6^{-8} \times 6^{-15}$ h) $(-9)^4 \div (-9)^4$ i) $19^{-7} \div 19^{12}$

4. Simplify.
   a) $x^{-9} \times x^{-4}$
   b) $p^{-7} \div p^2$
   c) $w^{-13} \times w^8$
   d) $y^5 \times y^{-9}$
   e) $x^{-5} \div x^{13}$
   f) $a^7 \div a^{-4}$
   g) $m^{-14} \div m^{-5}$
   h) $s^{-5} \times s^{17}$
   i) $t^{-9} \div t^{-17}$

5. Evaluate.
   a) $3^2 + 3^{-2}$
   b) $3^2 - 3^{-2}$
   c) $3^{-2} - 3^2$
   d) $3^2 \times 3^{-2}$
   e) $3^2 \div 3^{-2}$
   f) $3^{-2} \div 3^2$

6. Evaluate.
   a) $2^3 - 2^{-1}$
   b) $5^2 + 5^{-1}$
   c) $7^{-2} - 7$
   d) $(2 \times 3)^{-2}$
   e) $4^2 + 4^0$
   f) $3^{-1} + 3^{-2}$
   g) $6^2 + 6^0 + 6^{-2}$
   h) $(2^2 - 1)^{-2}$
   i) $3^{-2} - 2^{-4}$

7. Evaluate.
   a) $(-2)^3$
   b) $(-2)^{-3}$
   c) $-(-2)^{-3}$
   d) $(-5)^0$
   e) $-(5^0)$
   f) $(6 - 4)^{-3}$
   g) $(5 - 8)^{-1}$
   h) $\left(\dfrac{1}{4} - \dfrac{1}{4^2}\right)^{-2}$
   i) $[(-3)^{-2} + (-3)^{-1}]^{-1}$

8. Express as powers of 2, and then arrange in order from greatest to least.
   $\dfrac{1}{32}$, 16, 128, $\dfrac{1}{64}$, 1, $\dfrac{1}{2}$

9. Express as powers of 3, and then arrange in order from least to greatest.
   $\dfrac{1}{9}$, $\dfrac{1}{243}$, $\dfrac{1}{81}$, 27, $\dfrac{1}{729}$, 1

10. Express as powers with positive exponents.
    a) 49
    b) $\dfrac{1}{100}$
    c) $\dfrac{1}{343}$
    d) $\dfrac{1}{-32}$
    e) $\dfrac{1}{1\,000\,000}$
    f) 0.25
    g) 0.001
    h) 0.125

11. Express as powers with negative exponents other than -1.
    a) $\dfrac{1}{121}$
    b) $\dfrac{1}{169}$
    c) 0.01
    d) 0.1
    e) 0.000 01
    f) 0.008
    g) 0.0081
    h) $\dfrac{1}{1728}$

12. Simplify.
    a) $a^{-3} \div a^6 \div a^{-8}$
    b) $y^{-5} \div y^9 \times y^4$
    c) $(-3)^{-6} \times (-3)^4 \times (-3)^3$
    d) $2^3 \times 2^{-7} \div 2^{-5}$
    e) $m^{-6} \div m^{-2} \times m^{-9}$
    f) $x^{-4} \times x^{-8} \div x^{-7}$
    g) $p^{11} \div p^{15} \div p^{-9}$
    h) $(-7)^{12} \times (-7)^{-8} \div (-7)^{17}$
    i) $11^5 \div 11^{10} \div 11^{-3}$
    j) $(0.5)^2 \div (0.5)^{-2} \times (0.5)^{-5}$
    k) $(-0.1)^4 \times 10^6 \times (0.01)^2$
    l) $10^{-3} \div 100^{-2} \times (0.1)^{-1}$
    m) $(-2)^{-4} \times (-0.5)^{-5} \times 2^{-2}$
    n) $(0.25)^8 \div 4^{-7} \times 2^2$

13. Simplify.
   a) $(x^{-2})^3 \div (x^3)^2$
   b) $(y^4)^2 \times (y^{-2})^3$
   c) $(3^2)^5 \times (3^3)^2$
   d) $(2^{-4})^2 \div (2^2)^6$
   e) $(m^{-3})^4 \div (m^4)^{-3}$
   f) $(8^3)^{-3} \times (8^2)^{-2}$
   g) $(w^2)^{-7} \times (w^{-3})^{-4}$
   h) $(5^{-3})^4 \div (5^2)^3$
   i) $(x^2)^4 \times (x^{-4})^5$

14. Evaluate.
   a) $5^{-1} \div 3^{-2}$
   b) $(3^{-1} - 3^{-2})^{-1}$
   c) $\left(\dfrac{1}{4}\right)^{-1} - \left(\dfrac{1}{3}\right)^{-2}$
   d) $\left(\dfrac{1}{-2}\right)^{-3} + \left(\dfrac{1}{2}\right)^{-2}$
   e) $\left(\dfrac{2}{3^{-1}}\right)^{-3}$
   f) $(0.5)^{-3} + (0.5)^0$
   g) $\dfrac{4}{4^{-1} + 4^0}$
   h) $\dfrac{2^{-1}}{2^{-2} - 2^{-3}}$
   i) $[47(5)^{-2}]^0$

15. Simplify.
   a) $5n^{-4} \times 2n^{17}$
   b) $12t^4 \div 3t^{-3}$
   c) $60x^5 \div 12x^{-5}$
   d) $16w^{-8} \div 4w^{-2}$
   e) $7a^{-4} \times (-4a^{-2})$
   f) $-12y^{-9} \times 6y^{17}$
   g) $15s^{-15} \div 3s^5$
   h) $-4m^{-7} \times (-3m^{-2})$
   i) $18x^5 \div (-3x^8)$

16. Simplify.
   a) $2m^{-3} \times 5m^{-4} \times 3m^{11}$
   b) $6a^2 \div (-2)a^5 \times 4a^{-7}$
   c) $24y^6 \div 3y^2 \div 2y^{-2}$
   d) $45b^{-3} \div 5b^5 \times 3b^{-7}$
   e) $-9m^{-7} \times 8m^{-2} \div (-6m^{-3})$
   f) $-15y^{-4} \div 5y^8 \div 3y^{-12}$

17. Evaluate each expression for $a = -3$, $b = 2$, and $c = -1$.
   a) a^{-1}
   b) $-a^{-1}$
   c) $a^{-1} + b^{-1}$
   d) $(a + b + c)^{-1}$
   e) $a^{-1} + b^{-1} + c^{-1}$
   f) a^b
   g) $\left(\dfrac{a}{b - c}\right)^{-2}$
   h) $\left(\dfrac{2a}{b + 4c}\right)^{-3}$
   i) $\left(\dfrac{-3a}{-2b + c}\right)^{-2}$

18. Evaluate $3a^{-2} + b^c$ for these values of a, b, and c.
   a) $a = 4$, $b = 3$, $c = 0$
   b) $a = 3$, $b = 2$, $c = -1$
   c) $a = -\dfrac{1}{2}$, $b = -2$, $c = 3$
   d) $a = \dfrac{2}{3}$, $b = \dfrac{5}{4}$, $c = -1$

19. Evaluate each expression for: i) $x = 2$ ii) $x = -\dfrac{1}{2}$.
   a) x^3
   b) $(-x)^3$
   c) $-x^3$
   d) $-(-x)^3$
   e) x^{-3}
   f) $(-x)^{-3}$
   g) $-x^{-3}$
   h) $-(-x)^{-3}$

ⓒ

20. Solve.
   a) $5^x = 1$
   b) $2^x = \dfrac{1}{2}$
   c) $(-3)^x = \dfrac{1}{9}$
   d) $x^{-3} = \dfrac{1}{125}$
   e) $2^x = \dfrac{1}{32}$
   f) $x^2 = \dfrac{1}{25}$
   g) $4^{x-1} = \dfrac{1}{64}$
   h) $10^{2-x} = 0.001$
   i) $2^{-x-4} = \dfrac{1}{32}$
   j) $243 = \left(\dfrac{1}{3}\right)^{x+4}$
   k) $64 = (0.5)^{3-x}$
   l) $9^{1+x} = 27$

6-5 SCIENTIFIC NOTATION

Scientists tell us that there are about 120 000 000 000 stars in our galaxy, the Milky Way. Only the first two digits in this number are significant, the zeros are place holders to show the position of the decimal point.

Large numbers like this are awkward to write and difficult to read. To express very large numbers (and very small numbers) more simply, we use *scientific notation*.

When a number is expressed in scientific notation, it is written as the product of:
- a number greater than or equal to 1 but less than 10, and
- a power of 10.

To express 120 000 000 000 in scientific notation, write the decimal after the first non-zero digit and drop the trailing zeros, to get 1.2.

Since the true position of the decimal is 11 places to the right, we multiply the number 1.2 by 10^{11}.

That is, $120\ 000\ 000\ 000 = 1.2 \times 10^{11}$

The mass of a hydrogen atom is 0.000 000 000 000 000 000 000 001 67 g. To express this very small number in scientific notation, write the decimal after the first non-zero digit and drop the preceding zeros, to get 1.67.

Since the true position of the decimal is 24 places to the left, we multiply the number 1.67 by 10^{-24}.

That is, $0.000\ 000\ 000\ 000\ 000\ 000\ 000\ 001\ 67 = 1.67 \times 10^{-24}$

Example 1. Simplify. $\dfrac{24\ 000\ 000\ 000 \times 0.000\ 02}{3200}$

Solution. Rewrite the expression using scientific notation.

$$\frac{24\ 000\ 000\ 000 \times 0.000\ 02}{3200} = \frac{2.4 \times 10^{10} \times 2 \times 10^{-5}}{3.2 \times 10^{3}}$$

$$= \frac{2.4 \times 2}{3.2} \times \frac{10^{10} \times 10^{-5}}{10^{3}}$$

$$= 1.5 \times 10^{2}$$

$$= 150$$

Example 2. Write in scientific notation and estimate the answer to one significant digit.

$$\frac{389\ 527 \times 6\ 058\ 732}{4793.82}$$

Solution. Write each number in scientific notation to one significant digit.

$389\ 527 \doteq 4 \times 10^5; \quad 6\ 058\ 732 \doteq 6 \times 10^6; \quad 4793.82 \doteq 5 \times 10^3$

$$\frac{389\ 527 \times 6\ 058\ 732}{4793.82} \doteq \frac{4 \times 10^5 \times 6 \times 10^6}{5 \times 10^3}$$

$$\doteq 5 \times 10^8$$

Since the factors were rounded to one significant digit, the estimate should not exceed one significant digit.

Example 3. It has been estimated that if the average weight of an automobile were reduced from 3000 lb to 2000 lb, Canada would save about 8 000 000 gal of oil each day.
a) Find how much oil Canada would save in one year.
b) Three gallons of oil yield 2 gal of gasoline. Assume that there are 9 000 000 cars on Canadian roads and gasoline costs $2.33/gal. Find the annual saving per car.

Solution.
a) Oil saved per year $= 365 \times 8\ 000\ 000$
$= 3.65 \times 10^2 \times 8.0 \times 10^6$
$= 29.2 \times 10^8$
$= 2.92 \times 10^9$

The annual saving of oil would be about 3.0×10^9 gal.

b) 2.92×10^9 gal of oil are saved every year.

Hence, $\frac{2}{3}(2.92 \times 10^9)$ gal of gasoline are saved every year.

There are 9 000 000 cars on the road.

Hence, the gasoline saved per year per car is

$$\frac{1}{9\ 000\ 000} \times \frac{2}{3}(2.92 \times 10^9) \text{ gal.}$$

Gasoline costs $2.33/gal.

Hence, the annual saving per car in dollars is

$$\frac{1}{9\ 000\ 000} \times \frac{2}{3}(2.92 \times 10^9) \times 2.33$$

$$= \frac{2 \times 2.92 \times 10^9 \times 2.33}{9 \times 3 \times 10^6}$$

$$\doteq 0.5040 \times 10^3$$

$$\doteq 504$$

The annual saving per car could be about $500.

EXERCISES 6-5

Ⓐ

1. Write in scientific notation.
   a) 1000
   b) 100 000 000
   c) 100
   d) 750
   e) 1100
   f) 3 700 000
   g) 0.0001
   h) 0.000 000 1
   i) 0.000 001
   j) 0.000 85
   k) 0.000 092
   l) 0.000 000 008 2
   m) 85
   n) 0.038
   o) 9900
   p) 3 210 012

2. Write in scientific notation.
   a) Speed of light, 300 000 km/s
   b) World population in 1985, 4 843 000 000
   c) Mass of the Earth, 5 980 000 000 000 000 000 000 000 kg
   d) Time of fastest camera exposure, 0.000 000 1 s
   e) Mass of the ball in a ball-point pen, 0.004 g

3. What numbers complete this table?

	Physical Quantity	Decimal Notation	Scientific Notation
a)	Temperature of the sun's interior	1 300 000°C	
b)	Thickness of a plastic film	0.000 01 m	
c)	Mass of an electron		9.2×10^{-28} g
d)	Number of stars in our galaxy		1.2×10^{11}
e)	Estimated age of the Earth	4 500 000 000 years	
f)	Diameter of a hydrogen atom	0.000 000 011 3 cm	
g)	Land area of the Earth		1.5×10^{8} km^2
h)	Ocean area of the Earth		3.6×10^{8} km^2
i)	Mass of the Earth		5.9×10^{24} kg
j)	Cost of a Concorde aircraft	8 500 000 000 F	

Ⓑ

4. Write in scientific notation.
   a) 32×10^{4}
   b) 247×10^{8}
   c) 49.2×10^{7}
   d) 685×10^{10}
   e) 0.387×10^{4}
   f) 0.087×10^{3}
   g) 672×10^{-5}
   h) 43.7×10^{-6}
   i) 0.841×10^{-2}
   j) 0.49×10^{-7}
   k) 125×10^{0}
   l) $1.85 \div 10^{-2}$

5. Find each value for n.
   a) $1265 = 1.265 \times 10^{n}$
   b) $76.3 = 7.63 \times 10^{n}$
   c) $0.0041 = 4.1 \times 10^{n}$
   d) $0.860 = 8.60 \times 10^{n}$
   e) $0.005 = 5 \times 10^{n}$
   f) $0.000 056 3 = 5.63 \times 10^{n}$
   g) $1150 = 1.150 \times 10^{n}$
   h) $4 961 000 000 = 4.961 \times 10^{n}$
   i) $7 430 000 = 7.43 \times 10^{n}$
   j) $0.000 000 583 1 = 5.831 \times 10^{n}$

6. Write in scientific notation and estimate the answer.

a) $\dfrac{582\ 965 \times 7\ 123\ 085}{5034.8}$

b) $\dfrac{9\ 867\ 341 \times 403\ 928}{79\ 386.3}$

7. Simplify, and express the answer in scientific notation rounded to two significant digits.

a) $349\ 000 \times 2650 \times 120\ 000$

b) $8600 \times 1\ 500\ 000 \times 0.0003$

c) $\dfrac{480\ 000 \times 62\ 000\ 000}{300\ 000}$

d) $\dfrac{850\ 000 \times 400\ 000}{6\ 200\ 000}$

8. Write in scientific notation and estimate the answer.

a) $\dfrac{392\ 876 \times 48\ 731 \times 0.000\ 186}{0.000\ 007\ 7 \times 3\ 865\ 097}$

b) $\dfrac{0.000\ 000\ 28 \times 78\ 365\ 294}{1873.6 \times 29\ 586 \times 0.0038}$

9. Californium 252, one of the world's rarest metals, is used in treating cancer. If one-tenth of a microgram costs $100, what is its cost per gram?

10. The measured daily deposit of the pollutant sulphur dioxide on Metropolitan Toronto is approximately 4.8×10^{-6} g/cm². If Metropolitan Toronto has an area of about 620 km², and the pollutant is distributed evenly, calculate the amount of sulphur dioxide that falls on the city:

a) in 1 day b) in 1 year c) in your lifetime.

11. If it takes 1200 silkworm eggs to balance the mass of 1 g, what is the mass of one silkworm egg?

12. The volume of water in the oceans is estimated to be 1.35×10^{18} m³. If the density of sea water is 1025 kg/m³, what is the mass of the oceans?

13. A faucet is leaking at the rate of one drop of water per second. The volume of one drop is 0.1 cm³.
    a) Calculate the volume of water lost in a year.
    b) Calculate how long it would take to fill a rectangular basin 30 cm by 20 cm by 20 cm.

Ⓒ

14. In 1986, astronomers discovered a chain of galaxies, which stretches a billion light-years from one end to the other. It is the largest structure ever found in the universe. A light-year is the distance that light, with a speed of 300 000 km/s, travels in one year.
    a) Calculate the approximate number of kilometres in one light-year.
    b) Calculate the length, in kilometres, of the astronomers' discovery.

15. A drop of oil with a volume of 1 mm³ spreads out on the surface of water until it is a film one molecule thick. If the film has an area of 1 m², what is the thickness of an oil molecule?

MATHEMATICS AROUND US

How Bacteria Grow and Multiply

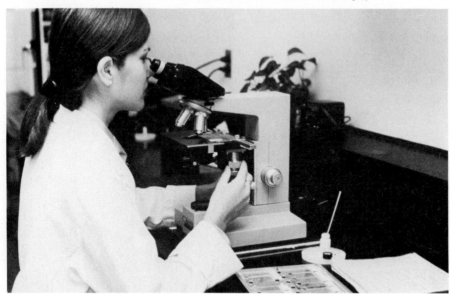

At midnight, there were 1000 bacteria in a culture. The number of bacteria doubles every hour so n hours later there would be $1000(2^n)$. Does this statement make sense if n is negative?

If n were -3, it would be like asking, "How many bacteria were there -3 h after midnight?"; -3 h after midnight is 3 h *before* midnight. To find the number of bacteria 3 h before midnight, multiply 1000 by 2^{-3}.

$$1000(2^{-3}) = 1000\left(\frac{1}{8}\right)$$
$$= 125$$

There were about 125 bacteria in the culture 3 h before midnight.

QUESTIONS

1. About how many bacteria were in the culture:
   a) 1 h before midnight
   b) 2 h before midnight?

2. At 00:30, there were about 1400 bacteria in the culture. About how many were there:
   a) 1 h earlier
   b) 2 h earlier
   c) 3 h earlier?

3. At 03:45, there were about 13 500 bacteria in the culture. About how many were there:
   a) 3 h earlier
   b) 4 h earlier
   c) 5 h earlier?

PROBLEM SOLVING

Solve a Simpler Problem

The city of Albany organized a hockey
league. However, the league organizer discovered that when the players were divided
into teams of 6, teams of 7 or teams of 8,
there was always one player left over. Finally
another player joined the league and now
the players could be divided into teams of 10,
without left overs.
How many teams were in the league?

Understand the problem
- What do we know about the number of players in the league?
- Was the number of players in the league a multiple of 6, 7 or 8
  before the last player joined?
- How is the number of players related to the number of teams?
- What are we asked to find?

Think of a strategy
- Try solving a simpler problem, for example, what number leaves
  a remainder of 0 when divided by 6, by 7, and by 8?

Carry out the strategy
- Any number which leaves a remainder of 0 when divided by 6, 7 or
  8 is a common multiple of 6, 7, and 8.
- To find the least common multiple of 6, 7, and 8, we write each
  number as a product of its prime factors.
  $6 = 2 \times 3; \quad 7 = 7; \quad 8 = 2^3$
- Then we form the product of all the prime factors to the highest power
  to which they occur. The least common multiple of 6, 7, and 8 is
  therefore $2^3 \times 3 \times 7$, or 168.
- All the common multiples of 6, 7, and 8 are of the form $168n$ where
  n is a integer.
- All numbers which leave a remainder of 1 when divided by 6, 7, or
  8 are of the form $168n + 1$.
- The smallest positive integers which leave a remainder of 1 when
  divided by 6, 7, or 8 are: $168(1) + 1$, or 169;
  $168(2) + 1$, or 337; $168(3) + 1$, or 505.
- Of these, only 169 is a multiple of 10 when 1 is added. There were
  170 players and hence 17 teams.

Look back

- List the smallest 6 numbers which leave a remainder of 1 when divided by 6, 7, or 8.
- Is 169 the only one of these which is a multiple of 10 when increased by 1?
- If there is another number which leaves a remainder of 1 when divided by 6, 7, or 8 and it is a multiple of 10 when increased by 1, why would it be rejected as an answer to the problem?

Solve each problem

1. What time will it be:
   a) 24 000 h from now
   b) 23 999 992 h from now?

2. Let $N = 1 \times 2 \times 3 \times 4 \times 5 \times \ldots \times 19 \times 20$
   a) What is the largest power of 5 of which N is a multiple?
   b) What is the largest power of 2 of which N is a multiple?
   c) How many zeros come at the end of the numeral for N?

3. a) What is the smallest multiple of 300 which has all its prime factors to an even power?
   b) What is the smallest multiple of 300 which is the square of a positive integer?
   c) What is the smallest multiple of 300 which is the cube of a positive integer?

4. What is the area of the shaded kite drawn on 1 cm paper (below left)?

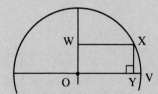

5. In rectangle WXYO, OY = 15 cm and YV = 2 cm. What is the length of WY if O is the center of the circle (above right)?

6. M and N are the midpoints of the sides of a rectangle. What fraction of the rectangle is shaded?

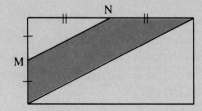

6-6 SQUARE ROOTS

When a skydiver leaves an airplane, the distance fallen during the first few seconds of free fall is related to the time that has elapsed by the formula $t^2 = \frac{1}{5}d$. d is the distance in metres and t is the time in seconds.

How long does it take the skydiver to fall a distance of 80 m?
To find the value of t, substitute $d = 80$ into the equation.

$$t^2 = \frac{1}{5}(80)$$
$$= 16$$

t^2 means $t \times t$. To solve the equation, we need to find the value of t that multiplied by itself gives 16.

We know that $4 \times 4 = 16$ and $(-4) \times (-4) = 16$.
Hence t must equal 4 or -4.

But a negative value for t has no meaning in this context.

Hence, the solution is $t = 4$.

The skydiver takes about 4 s to fall 80 m.

When a number (like 16) can be written as the product of two factors that are the same, each factor is a *square root* of that number.

That is, since $4 \times 4 = 16$ and $(-4) \times (-4) = 16$, then 4 and -4 are the square roots of 16.

Similarly, since $7 \times 7 = 49$ and $(-7) \times (-7) = 49$, then 7 and -7 are the square roots of 49.

Further, since $0.2 \times 0.2 = 0.04$ and $(-0.2) \times (-0.2) = 0.04$, then 0.2 and -0.2 are the square roots of 0.04.

Positive numbers always have two square roots — one positive, the other negative. The symbol, $\sqrt{}$, is the *radical sign* and it always denotes the positive square root.

Thus, $\sqrt{49} = 7$ and $\sqrt{0.04} = 0.2$

Example 1.   Evaluate.

      a) $\sqrt{121}$ b) $-\sqrt{1.21}$ c) $-\sqrt{12\ 100}$ d) $\sqrt{0.0121}$

Solution.   a)   Since $11 \times 11 = 121$, then $\sqrt{121} = 11$

      b)   Since $1.1 \times 1.1 = 1.21$, then $-\sqrt{1.21} = -1.1$

      c)   Since $110 \times 110 = 12\ 100$, then $-\sqrt{12\ 100} = -110$

      d)   Since $0.11 \times 0.11 = 0.0121$, then $\sqrt{0.0121} = 0.11$

Example 2.   Find the length of the side of each square.

      a)   b)

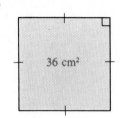
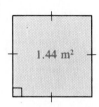

Solution.   The area A of a square is equal to the square of the length of the side s.

      That is, $A = s^2$

      a)   If $A = 36$, then $s = \sqrt{36}$
                            $= 6$

        The side of the square is 6 cm.

      b)   If $A = 1.44$, then $s = \sqrt{1.44}$
        We know that $\sqrt{144} = 12$, so $\sqrt{1.44} = 1.2$.

        The side of the square is 1.2 m.

    Radical signs are usually treated like brackets. Operations under radical signs are performed first.

Example 3.   Evaluate.

      a) $-3\sqrt{6.25}$ b) $\sqrt{9 + 16}$ c) $5\sqrt{4} - 3(\sqrt{121} - \sqrt{81})$

Solution.   a) $-3\sqrt{6.25} = -3(2.5)$
                               $= -7.5$

      b) $\sqrt{9 + 16} = \sqrt{25}$
                      $= 5$

      c) $5\sqrt{4} - 3(\sqrt{121} - \sqrt{81}) = 5(2) - 3(11 - 9)$
                                          $= 10 - 3(2)$
                                          $= 10 - 6$
                                          $= 4$

Example 4. Evaluate each expression for $x = -2$ and $y = 3$.

    a) $\sqrt{-x + y + 4}$ b) $-\sqrt{6x + 5y - xy}$

Solution. Substitute the given values for x and y.

$$a) \ \sqrt{-x + y + 4} = \sqrt{-(-2) + 3 + 4}$$
$$= \sqrt{2 + 3 + 4}$$
$$= \sqrt{9}$$
$$= 3$$

$$b) \ -\sqrt{6x + 5y - xy} = -\sqrt{6(-2) + 5(3) - (-2)(3)}$$
$$= -\sqrt{-12 + 15 + 6}$$
$$= -\sqrt{9}$$
$$= -3$$

EXERCISES 6-6

Ⓐ

1. Find the square roots of each number.

  a) 81   b) 10 000   c) 900   d) 0.16   e) 14 400
  f) 40 000   g) 0.64   h) 0.0001   i) 4900   j) 0.25

2. Evaluate.

  a) $\sqrt{49}$ b) $-\sqrt{0.04}$ c) $\sqrt{1600}$ d) $\sqrt{169}$ e) $-\sqrt{3600}$
  f) $\sqrt{1.44}$ g) $-\sqrt{225}$ h) $\sqrt{10^{12}}$ i) $\sqrt{625}$ j) $-\sqrt{2^4}$

3. Find the side length of each square with the given area.

  a) $16 \ m^2$ b) $10 \ 000 \ mm^2$ c) $6.25 \ cm^2$
  d) $2^6 \ m^2$ e) $10^4 \ m^2$ f) $4900 \ m^2$

Ⓑ

4. Simplify.

  a) $\sqrt{64 + 36}$ b) $\sqrt{16} + \sqrt{9}$ c) $2\sqrt{16} - 3\sqrt{4}$
  d) $3\sqrt{36} + 2\sqrt{25}$ e) $5\sqrt{100 - 36}$ f) $\sqrt{1 + 3 + 5 + 7 + 9}$
  g) $2\sqrt{81} - 7\sqrt{49}$ h) $4\sqrt{289 - 225}$ i) $2\sqrt{\sqrt{81}}$

5. Evaluate each expression for $a = 5$ and $b = -3$.

  a) $\sqrt{20a}$ b) $\sqrt{9a^2}$ c) $\sqrt{\dfrac{125}{a}}$

  d) $\sqrt{2a - 13b}$ e) $\sqrt{-12b}$ f) $-\sqrt{3a - 3b + 1}$
  g) $\sqrt{a^2 + 3b}$ h) $\sqrt{7a - 8b + 5}$ i) $-4\sqrt{11a - 3b}$
  j) $-3\sqrt{2a^2 - 4b^2 + 2}$ k) $0.5\sqrt{a^2 - 2ab + b^2}$ l) $2\sqrt{2a^2 - 3b^2 + 2}$

6. Evaluate each expression for $x = 3$, $y = -4$, and $z = -7$.

  a) $-\sqrt{12x}$ b) $\sqrt{z^2 + 6y}$ c) $4\sqrt{x^2 + y^2}$
  d) $\sqrt{6x - z}$ e) $5\sqrt{15x - y}$ f) $-\sqrt{7x - 4y - 1}$
  g) $2\sqrt{x - 2y - 2z}$ h) $-\sqrt{2z^2 + 5y + x}$ i) $6\sqrt{3y^2 + x^0}$
  j) $\sqrt{-(-2x + 4y + 2z)}$ k) $\sqrt{x^2 + 2x + z^2}$ l) $-\sqrt{3x^2 + y + 2z^2}$

7. From the area of each square, calculate:
   i)   the length of a side   ii)   the perimeter.

a)

289 mm²

b)

4.41 cm²

c)
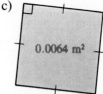
0.0064 m²

8. The distance d metres that an object falls from rest in t seconds is given by the formula $d \doteq 5t^2$. A pebble is dropped from a cliff 320 m high. Find how long the pebble takes to reach the ground.

©

9. For an equilateral triangle of side length x, the area A is given by $A \doteq 0.43x^2$. For each equilateral triangle with the given area, calculate:
   i) the length of a side
   ii) the perimeter.

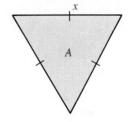

   a) 10.825 m²   b) 27.712 m²
   c) 0.350 73 m²   d) 389.7 cm²
   e) 0.004 33 km²   f) 97.425 km²

   Give the answers to 2 decimal places.

10. In a right triangle with side lengths as shown, the formula $z^2 = x^2 + y^2$ applies. Calculate z for each value of x and y.
    a) 6 mm, 8 mm
    b) 8 mm, 15 mm
    c) 0.5 m, 1.2 m
    d) 24 mm, 7 mm
    e) 0.03 km, 0.04 km
    f) 2.8 km, 9.6 km

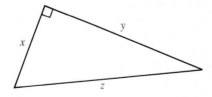

11. In winter, you should have noticed that the stronger the wind the colder it feels. Winter weather forecasts often give ''wind-chill'' temperatures.
    For wind speeds of 10 km/h and higher, the following formula gives an approximate value for the wind-chill temperature.
    $w = 33 - (0.23 \sqrt{v} + 0.45 - 0.01v)(33 - T)$
    w is the wind-chill temperature in degrees Celsius.
    v is the wind speed in kilometres per hour.
    T is the still-air temperature in degrees Celsius.
    For a still-air temperature of $-18°C$, calculate the wind-chill temperatures, to the nearest degree, at these wind speeds.
    a) 100 km/h   b) 80 km/h
    c) 30 km/h   d) 15 km/h

6-7 RADICALS

Gold leaf is so thin that one dollar's worth would cover a square with an area of 3600 cm². The length of a side of the square, in centimetres, is 60, since $60^2 = 3600$. We say that 60 is a square root of 3600, and write $\sqrt{3600} = 60$.

The gold produced in Canada in one day would almost fill a cube with a volume of 8000 cm³. The length of an edge of the cube, in centimetres, is 20, since $20^3 = 8000$. We say that 20 is a cube root of 8000, and write $\sqrt[3]{8000} = 20$.

Expressions such as $\sqrt{3600}$ and $\sqrt[3]{8000}$ are called *radicals*. Radicals occur when we work with square roots and cube roots of numbers.

Square Roots

A number, x, is the *square root* of a number, n, if $x^2 = n$. Positive numbers always have two square roots, one positive, the other negative. The *radical sign*, $\sqrt{}$, always denotes the positive, or *principal*, square root.

$\sqrt{n}$ means the principal square root of n.

Example 1. Find:

a) $\sqrt{1600}$ b) $\sqrt{2.25}$ c) $\sqrt{0.09}$

Solution. a) $\sqrt{1600} = 40$, since $40^2 = 1600$

b) $\sqrt{2.25} = 1.5$, since $1.5^2 = 2.25$

c) $\sqrt{0.09} = 0.3$, since $0.3^2 = 0.09$

In *Example 1*, the square roots were exact. Most numbers do not have exact square roots. The most efficient method of finding the square root of any number is to use a calculator with a $\boxed{\sqrt{}}$ key. Since the calculator can display only a fixed number of digits, the number displayed may not be the exact square root. It may only be an *approximation* of the square root.

Example 2. Use a calculator to find:

a) $\sqrt{33}$ correct to three decimal places.

b) $\sqrt{147}$ correct to four decimal places.

Solution.   a) $\sqrt{33} \doteq 5.745$

b) $\sqrt{147} \doteq 12.1244$

Cube Roots

A number, x, is the *cube root* of a number, n, if $x^3 = n$. The cube root of a positive number is positive and the cube root of a negative number is negative.

> $\sqrt[3]{n}$ means the cube root of n.

Example 3. Find:

a) $\sqrt[3]{125}$

b) $\sqrt[3]{-64}$

Solution.   a) $\sqrt[3]{125} = 5$, since $5^3 = 125$.

b) $\sqrt[3]{-64} = -4$, since $(-4)^3 = -64$.

Fourth and Fifth Roots

Similarly, the *fourth roots* of 16 are 2 and -2, since $2^4 = 16$, and $(-2)^4 = 16$. We write $\sqrt[4]{16} = 2$ to indicate the principal fourth root of 16.

And, the *fifth root* of -32 is -2, since $(-2)^5 = -32$. We write $\sqrt[5]{-32} = -2$.

> An expression of the form $\sqrt[n]{x}$ is called a *radical*. If n is even, the expression represents only the principal root.

EXERCISES 6-7

(A)

1. Find the square roots of these numbers.
   a) 49   b) 81   c) 121   d) 400   e) 529   f) 625

2. Simplify.
   a) $\sqrt{64}$ b) $\sqrt{100}$ c) $\sqrt{144}$ d) $\sqrt{900}$ e) $\sqrt{1600}$
   f) $\sqrt{0.25}$ g) $\sqrt{0.04}$ h) $\sqrt{0.01}$ i) $\sqrt{0.0016}$ j) $\sqrt{0.000\,025}$

3. Use a calculator to find, correct to three decimal places.
   a) $\sqrt{2}$ b) $\sqrt{3}$ c) $\sqrt{52.3}$ d) $\sqrt{128.5}$ e) $\sqrt{471}$
   f) $\sqrt{472}$ g) $\sqrt{473}$ h) $\sqrt{474}$ i) $\sqrt{1.48}$ j) $\sqrt{0.000\,25}$

4. Simplify.
   a) $\sqrt[3]{8}$ b) $\sqrt[3]{-27}$ c) $\sqrt[4]{81}$ d) $\sqrt[5]{32}$ e) $\sqrt[5]{243}$ f) $\sqrt[3]{0.001}$

Ⓑ

5. Find, correct to   i) two decimal places   ii) three decimal places.
    a) $\sqrt{6}$ b) $\sqrt{11}$ c) $\sqrt{13}$ d) $\sqrt{124}$ e) $\sqrt{139}$ f) $\sqrt{154}$

6. From the area of each square, calculate the length of a side and the perimeter.
    a)   b)

Area 9.61 m²

Area
6.4 m²

7. From the volume of each cube, find the length of an edge and the area of a face.
    a)   b)

Volume
1000 cm³

Volume
125 cm³

8. Simplify.
    a) $\sqrt[3]{64}$ b) $\sqrt[3]{125}$ c) $\sqrt[4]{16}$ d) $\sqrt[5]{-1}$ e) $\sqrt[3]{216}$
    f) $\sqrt[3]{-1000}$ g) $\sqrt[4]{256}$ h) $\sqrt[4]{10\,000}$ i) $\sqrt[3]{7^3}$ j) $\sqrt[5]{10^5}$

9. One litre of varnish will cover an area of 10 m².
    a) If a square area is covered, how long is its side?
    b) If 2 L of varnish are used to cover an area, how long is its side?

10. In one day a gold mine produces approximately 1600 cm³ of gold. If five days'
    gold production is cast into a cube, how long is its edge?

11. Simplify.
    a) $\sqrt{16+9}$ b) $\sqrt{4+9+36}$ c) $\sqrt[3]{27+64+125}$ d) $\sqrt{64}+\sqrt[3]{64}$
    e) $\sqrt[3]{\sqrt{64}}$ f) $\sqrt{6-\sqrt{4}}$ g) $\sqrt{25}+\sqrt[3]{27}-\sqrt[4]{16}$ h) $5\sqrt{9}-4\sqrt[3]{-8}$

Ⓒ

12. Without using the $\boxed{\sqrt{}}$ key, use a calculator to find, correct to two decimals:
    a) $\sqrt{6.5}$ b) $\sqrt{65}$ c) $\sqrt[3]{20}$ d) $\sqrt[3]{200}$

INVESTIGATE

Follow these steps on your calculator:

| Enter any positive number | → | Press $\sqrt{}$ | → | Multiply by 2 |

Continue doing this until you know you should stop. What do you notice?
Repeat with other starting numbers.

6-8 THE IRRATIONAL NUMBERS

Many numbers do not have terminating or repeating decimals. The most famous of these is the number π, which occurs in the formulas for the circumference and area of a circle. To twenty decimal places, the value of π is:

$$\pi \doteq 3.141\ 592\ 653\ 589\ 793\ 238\ 46\ldots$$

Mathematicians have always been interested in calculating π. In 1873 William Shanks reported that he had spent more than twenty years finding π to 707 decimal places. For decades this was considered the most impressive calculation ever performed. But in 1945 other mathematicians found that his 528th place, and all following places, were incorrect. π has now been calculated to more than 29 million decimal places using computers.

Mathematicians have proved that no matter how many decimal places are calculated for π, the representation will never terminate or repeat. Therefore, π cannot be expressed in the form $\frac{m}{n}$, where m and n are integers and $n \neq 0$. For this reason, π is called an irrational number.

Any number that cannot be expressed in the form $\frac{m}{n}$, where m and n are integers, and $n \neq 0$, is called an *irrational number*. The decimal representation of an irrational number neither terminates nor repeats.

Example 1. Does each number appear to be rational or irrational?
  a) $x = 0.123\ 456\ 789\ 101\ 112\ldots$
  b) $y = 2.131\ 131\ 131\ 131\ldots$
  c) $\sqrt{2} = 1.414\ 213\ 562\ 373\ldots$

Solution.　a) Although there is a pattern in the decimal representation of x, there is no sequence of digits that repeats. Therefore, x appears to be irrational.
  b) y appears to be rational since the sequence 131 repeats.
  c) There is no repeating sequence of digits. Therefore, $\sqrt{2}$ appears to be irrational.

In *Example 1c* we cannot be certain that $\sqrt{2}$ is irrational, since a sequence of digits that repeats could occur farther out in the decimal expansion. However, mathematicians have proved that $\sqrt{2}$ is irrational. This example suggests that certain square roots are irrational.

> Any number of the form $\sqrt{x}$, where $x > 0$, and x is not the square of a rational number, is irrational.

Example 2. Which of the following are irrational?

$$\sqrt{3} \qquad \sqrt{16} \qquad \sqrt{20} \qquad \sqrt{1.44} \qquad \sqrt{\frac{4}{9}} \qquad \sqrt{\frac{4}{5}}$$

Solution. $\sqrt{3}, \sqrt{20},$ and $\sqrt{\frac{4}{5}}$ are irrational since 3, 20, and $\frac{4}{5}$ are not perfect squares. The others are rational since the numbers are perfect squares:

$$\sqrt{16} = 4 \qquad \sqrt{1.44} = 1.2 \qquad \sqrt{\frac{4}{9}} = \frac{2}{3}$$

The numbers that can be expressed as decimals can be grouped into two sets:

Rational Numbers	*Irrational Numbers*
These numbers have decimal representations that terminate or repeat.	These numbers have decimal representations that neither terminate nor repeat.
$\frac{1}{2}$ 0.65 $-\frac{7}{3}$ $5.\overline{21}$	$\sqrt{2}$ $\sqrt{15} - 1$
Integers, I −8 Natural Numbers, N 0 5 144 −51	π $-\sqrt[3]{10}$ 1.71771777...

THE REAL NUMBERS

There are no other possibilities. All the numbers represented above are called *real numbers*. The set of real numbers consists of the rational and the irrational numbers. We say that it is the *union* of the set of rational numbers and the set of irrational numbers.

EXERCISES 6-8

Ⓐ

1. Does each number appear to be rational or irrational?
   a) 2.147 474 747 . . .   b) −6.132 133 . . .   c) 72.041 296 47 . . .
   d) 0.165 165 5 . . .   e) −2.236 067 . . .   f) −4.317 495

2. Which of the following are irrational?

   a) $\sqrt{21}$ b) $\sqrt{16}$ c) $\sqrt{2\frac{1}{4}}$ d) $\sqrt{200}$ e) $\sqrt{2.5}$

3. Which of the following are irrational?
   a) $5\sqrt{2}$ b) $5 + \sqrt{2}$ c) $5 - \sqrt{2}$ d) $2\sqrt{36}$ e) $7\sqrt{7}$
   f) $\sqrt{5} + \sqrt{2}$ g) $\sqrt{7 + 9}$ h) $\sqrt{7} + \sqrt{9}$ i) $6\sqrt{21}$ j) $\sqrt{17 + 12}$

Ⓑ

4. Give examples of two rational and two irrational numbers between the numbers in each pair.
   a) 3.65, 3.69   b) −1.476, −1.47
   c) $0.3\overline{97}$, 0.397 647 28....   d) $-5.3\overline{76}$, $-5.3\overline{7}$
   e) $\frac{8}{9}$, $\frac{9}{10}$ f) 2.236 067..., 2.236 071 23......

5. Classify each of the following as a natural number, an integer, a rational, or an irrational number.

   a) $\frac{3}{5}$ b) $0.2\overline{17}$ c) −6   d) 41 275

   e) 6.121 121 112...   f) $-2\frac{1}{4}$ g) $\sqrt{27}$ h) $\sqrt{225}$

Ⓒ

6. On a calculator with a $\boxed{\sqrt{}}$ key, $\sqrt{3}$ = 1.732 050 8.

   1.7320508 is rational, but $\sqrt{3}$ is irrational. Can a number be both rational and irrational? Explain.

7. On a calculator with a $\boxed{\sqrt{}}$ key, $\sqrt{0.111\ 111\ 1}$ = 0.333 333 3

   a) Write fractions in the form $\frac{m}{n}$ for 0.111 111 1 and 0.333 333 3. Use these fractions to explain why the above pattern appeared.
   b) Find another similar result.

8. a) Determine if it is possible for the square root of an irrational number to be rational; irrational.
   b) Give examples to support your conclusions in (a).

9. Mike wrote the formula for the circumference of a circle in the form $\pi = \frac{C}{d}$. He claimed that this proved that π is a rational number. Do you agree?

THE MATHEMATICAL MIND

A Short History of π

1
From ancient times, people have known that the circumference of a circle...

2
...is more than 3 times its diameter.

3
Through the centuries different civilizations have tried to find a fraction which would be exactly equal to the ratio:

$$\frac{\text{circumference}}{\text{diameter}}$$

About 1700 B.C., the Egyptians used the fraction $\frac{256}{81}$ to approximate this ratio.

4
About 220 B.C. the Greeks used the Greek letter π to represent this ratio. And they used the fraction $\frac{22}{7}$ as its approximate value

$$\frac{22}{7}$$

5
In their search for the elusive rational number equal to π, various other civilizations used these approximations.

Civilization	Date	Value for π
Chinese	470	$\frac{355}{113}$
Hindu	530	$\frac{3927}{1250}$
European	1220	$\frac{864}{275}$

6
Finally, in 1761, Johann Lambert proved that there is no rational number equal to π. That is, the decimal form of π does not repeat.

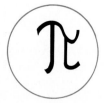

$\pi = 3.141\ 592\ 653\ 589\ldots$

In January, 1986, one mathematician computed π to 29 360 128 decimal places using a Cray 2 supercomputer. As expected, the decimal representation did not repeat.

Use your calculator to determine which civilization up to the year A.D. 1220 had the best approximation for π.

6-9 MULTIPLYING RADICALS

Consider the expressions: $\sqrt{4} \times \sqrt{9}$ and $\sqrt{4 \times 9}$.

$$\sqrt{4} \times \sqrt{9} = 2 \times 3 \qquad\qquad \sqrt{4 \times 9} = \sqrt{36}$$
$$= 6 \qquad\qquad\qquad\qquad = 6$$

Therefore, $\sqrt{4} \times \sqrt{9} = \sqrt{4 \times 9}$

The same is true for irrationals. Consider the expressions:
$\sqrt{3} \times \sqrt{5}$ and $\sqrt{3 \times 5}$. Square each expression.

$$(\sqrt{3} \times \sqrt{5})^2 = (\sqrt{3})(\sqrt{3}) \times (\sqrt{5})(\sqrt{5}) \qquad (\sqrt{3 \times 5})^2 = 3 \times 5$$
$$= 3 \times 5 \qquad\qquad\qquad\qquad = 15$$
$$= 15$$

Therefore, $\sqrt{3} \times \sqrt{5} = \sqrt{3 \times 5}$

The above results suggest the following property:

$$\sqrt{a} \times \sqrt{b} = \sqrt{ab}, \quad (a \geq 0, b \geq 0)$$

Example 1. Simplify.

      a) $3\sqrt{2} \times \sqrt{5}$ b) $5\sqrt{3} \times 4\sqrt{2}$ c) $4\sqrt{3} \times \sqrt{12}$

Solution. a) $3\sqrt{2} \times \sqrt{5}$ b) $5\sqrt{3} \times 4\sqrt{2}$ c) $4\sqrt{3} \times \sqrt{12}$

             $= 3\sqrt{2 \times 5}$ $= 20\sqrt{6}$ $= 4\sqrt{36}$

             $= 3\sqrt{10}$ $= 4 \times 6$

                                                    $= 24$

Example 2. Express as a product of radicals.

      a) $\sqrt{21}$ b) $\sqrt{30}$ c) $\sqrt{20}$

Solution. a) $\sqrt{21} = \sqrt{7 \times 3}$ b) $\sqrt{30} = \sqrt{2 \times 3 \times 5}$ c) $\sqrt{20} = \sqrt{2 \times 2 \times 5}$

                $= \sqrt{7} \times \sqrt{3}$ $= \sqrt{2} \times \sqrt{3} \times \sqrt{5}$ $= \sqrt{2} \times \sqrt{2} \times \sqrt{5}$

In *Example 2c*, since $\sqrt{2} \times \sqrt{2} = 2$, $\sqrt{20}$ may be written, $2\sqrt{5}$. An expression of the form $\sqrt{x}$, $(x > 0)$ is called an *entire radical*, and an expression of the form $a\sqrt{x}$, where a is any real number, is called a *mixed radical*.

$$\sqrt{20} = 2\sqrt{5}$$

                   entire radical   mixed radical

These are also entire radicals: $\sqrt{3.5}$, $\sqrt{\dfrac{3}{2}}$. These are also mixed radicals: $\dfrac{3}{2}\sqrt{6}$, $-2\sqrt{7}$.

    Any number of the form $\sqrt{x}$, where x has a perfect square as a factor, can be expressed as a mixed radical.

Example 3. Express as a mixed radical where possible.

      a) $\sqrt{18}$ b) $\sqrt{70}$ c) $\sqrt{48}$

Solution.

a) 18 has 9 as a perfect-square factor.
$$\sqrt{18} = \sqrt{9} \times \sqrt{2}$$
$$= 3\sqrt{2}$$

b) Since 70 does not have a perfect-square factor, $\sqrt{70}$ cannot be expressed as a mixed radical.

c) 48 has 16 as a perfect-square factor.
$$\sqrt{48} = \sqrt{16} \times \sqrt{3}$$
$$= 4\sqrt{3}$$

In *Example 3c*, both 4 and 16 are perfect-square factors of 48. We always choose the *greatest* perfect-square factor. This ensures that the result will be in simplest form.

EXERCISES 6-9

(A)

1. Simplify.
   a) $\sqrt{7} \times \sqrt{8}$ b) $\sqrt{11} \times \sqrt{14}$ c) $\sqrt{8} \times (-\sqrt{18})$
   d) $2\sqrt{5} \times 3\sqrt{2}$ e) $-4\sqrt{2} \times 3\sqrt{8}$ f) $(-7\sqrt{3})(-5\sqrt{8})$

2. Express as a product of radicals.
   a) $\sqrt{24}$ b) $\sqrt{18}$ c) $\sqrt{45}$ d) $\sqrt{28}$ e) $\sqrt{72}$ f) $\sqrt{60}$
   g) $\sqrt{39}$ h) $\sqrt{65}$ i) $\sqrt{96}$ j) $\sqrt{120}$ k) $\sqrt{126}$ l) $\sqrt{105}$

3. Express as a mixed radical.
   a) $\sqrt{32}$ b) $\sqrt{50}$ c) $\sqrt{27}$ d) $\sqrt{96}$ e) $\sqrt{8}$ f) $\sqrt{75}$

4. Express as a mixed radical in simplest form.
   a) $\sqrt{147}$ b) $\sqrt{54}$ c) $\sqrt{76}$ d) $\sqrt{180}$ e) $3\sqrt{20}$ f) $5\sqrt{18}$

(B)

5. Simplify.
   a) $2\sqrt{6} \times 3\sqrt{2}$ b) $3\sqrt{5} \times 7\sqrt{10}$ c) $-8\sqrt{6} \times 6\sqrt{8}$
   d) $5\sqrt{10} \times 4\sqrt{6}$ e) $(-7\sqrt{12})(-2\sqrt{6})$ f) $11\sqrt{3} \times 5\sqrt{6}$

6. Simplify.
   a) $\sqrt{24} \times \sqrt{18}$ b) $2\sqrt{24} \times 5\sqrt{6}$ c) $3\sqrt{20} \times 2\sqrt{5}$
   d) $2\sqrt{6} \times 7\sqrt{8} \times 5\sqrt{2}$ e) $3\sqrt{7} \times 2\sqrt{6} \times 5\sqrt{2}$ f) $4\sqrt{8} \times 3\sqrt{6} \times 7\sqrt{3}$

7. Simplify.
   a) $\sqrt{24} \times \sqrt{54} \times \sqrt{18}$ b) $\sqrt{20} \times \sqrt{32} \times \sqrt{18} \times \sqrt{125}$
   c) $\sqrt{27} \times \sqrt{12} \times \sqrt{45} \times \sqrt{80}$ d) $5\sqrt{18} \times 3\sqrt{8} \times 6\sqrt{32}$
   e) $3\sqrt{20} \times 5\sqrt{8} \times 4\sqrt{180} \times 6\sqrt{72}$ f) $0.8\sqrt{80} \times 0.125\sqrt{90} \times 0.5\sqrt{50}$

6-10 ADDING AND SUBTRACTING RADICALS

In the same way that $2x$ and $3x$ are called like terms, radicals such as $2\sqrt{3}$ and $3\sqrt{3}$ are called *like* radicals. Like radicals can be combined, that is, added or subtracted, using the distributive law. Radicals such as $2\sqrt{5}$ and $4\sqrt{7}$ are called *unlike* radicals; they cannot be combined.

Example 1. Simplify, if possible.

    a) $2\sqrt{3} + 3\sqrt{3}$ b) $6\sqrt{2} - 4\sqrt{2} + \sqrt{2}$ c) $4\sqrt{6} + 2\sqrt{10}$

Solution.   a) $2\sqrt{3} + 3\sqrt{3}$ b) $6\sqrt{2} - 4\sqrt{2} + \sqrt{2}$ c) $4\sqrt{6} + 2\sqrt{10}$ cannot be

                $= (2 + 3)\sqrt{3}$ $= (6 - 4 + 1)\sqrt{2}$ combined because they

                $= 5\sqrt{3}$ $= 3\sqrt{2}$ are unlike radicals.

Express radicals in simplest form before combining them.

Example 2. Simplify.

    a) $\sqrt{18} - \sqrt{2}$ b) $2\sqrt{98} + \sqrt{10} - 5\sqrt{8} - 3\sqrt{40}$

Solution.   a) $\sqrt{18} - \sqrt{2}$ b) $2\sqrt{98} + \sqrt{10} - 5\sqrt{8} - 3\sqrt{40}$

                $= 3\sqrt{2} - \sqrt{2}$ $= 2 \times 7\sqrt{2} + \sqrt{10} - 5 \times 2\sqrt{2} - 3 \times 2\sqrt{10}$

                $= 2\sqrt{2}$ $= 14\sqrt{2} + \sqrt{10} - 10\sqrt{2} - 6\sqrt{10}$

                                    $= 4\sqrt{2} - 5\sqrt{10}$

In *Example 2b*, $4\sqrt{2}$ and $5\sqrt{10}$ cannot be combined because they are unlike radicals. If required, the approximate numerical value can be found by using a calculator.

Although $\sqrt{a} \times \sqrt{b} = \sqrt{ab}$, it is not true that, in general, $\sqrt{a} + \sqrt{b} = \sqrt{a + b}$. Consider the expressions $\sqrt{4} + \sqrt{9}$ and $\sqrt{4 + 9}$.

          $\sqrt{4} + \sqrt{9} = 2 + 3$ $\sqrt{4 + 9} = \sqrt{13}$

                   $= 5$ $\doteq 3.6056$

Therefore, $\sqrt{4} + \sqrt{9} \neq \sqrt{4 + 9}$.   Similarly, in general, $\sqrt{a} - \sqrt{b} \neq \sqrt{a - b}$.

Example 3. Bay City is 8 km due west of Keyport and is linked to it by a straight stretch of railroad track. To travel from Bay City to Keyport by car one must go through Grenville, which is 1 km east and 1 km north of Bay City. How much farther is it by road than by train from Bay City to Keyport?

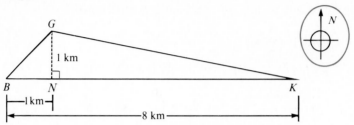

Solution. Let B, K, and G represent, respectively, the locations of Bay City, Keyport, and Grenville. N is the point on the track between B and K which is directly south of G.

Since $\triangle BNG$ is a right triangle, $BG = \sqrt{2}$.
Since $NK = 7$ and $\triangle GNK$ is a right triangle,

$$GK = \sqrt{1^2 + 7^2}$$
$$= \sqrt{50}$$

Total distance from B to G to K:

$$BG + GK = \sqrt{2} + \sqrt{50}$$
$$= \sqrt{2} + 5\sqrt{2}$$
$$= 6\sqrt{2}$$

That is, the distance from Bay City to Keyport by car is $6\sqrt{2}$ km. Since it is 8 km by train, it is $(6\sqrt{2} - 8)$ km, or 0.5 km farther by car.

EXERCISES 6-10

1. Simplify.
   a) $5\sqrt{7} - 3\sqrt{7}$
   b) $11\sqrt{6} + 5\sqrt{6}$
   c) $2\sqrt{13} - 8\sqrt{13}$
   d) $6\sqrt{19} - 31\sqrt{19}$
   e) $4\sqrt{3} + 29\sqrt{3}$
   f) $7\sqrt{15} - 2\sqrt{15}$

2. Simplify.
   a) $4\sqrt{5} - 11\sqrt{5} + 3\sqrt{5}$
   b) $2\sqrt{10} + 7\sqrt{10} - 6\sqrt{10}$
   c) $5\sqrt{2} - 16\sqrt{2} + 29\sqrt{2}$
   d) $2\sqrt{6} - 6\sqrt{2} + 11\sqrt{6}$
   e) $4\sqrt{10} - 10\sqrt{10} + 3\sqrt{5}$
   f) $3\sqrt{5} - 9\sqrt{2} + 5\sqrt{5} - 2\sqrt{2}$

3. Simplify.
   a) $\sqrt{40} + \sqrt{90}$
   b) $\sqrt{32} + \sqrt{8}$
   c) $\sqrt{12} - \sqrt{75}$
   d) $\sqrt{20} - \sqrt{45}$
   e) $\sqrt{50} - \sqrt{18}$
   f) $\sqrt{24} - \sqrt{96}$
   g) $3\sqrt{20} - 2\sqrt{80}$
   h) $\sqrt{54} + \sqrt{150}$

Ⓑ

4. Simplify.

   a) $\sqrt{54} + \sqrt{150} - \sqrt{6}$ b) $\sqrt{28} - \sqrt{63} + \sqrt{112}$ c) $\sqrt{80} + \sqrt{45} - \sqrt{125}$

   d) $\sqrt{12} + \sqrt{27} + \sqrt{48}$ e) $\sqrt{75} - \sqrt{3} + \sqrt{147}$ f) $\sqrt{98} - \sqrt{72} - \sqrt{50}$

   g) $\sqrt{20} - \sqrt{45} - \sqrt{125}$ h) $\sqrt{32} - \sqrt{8} - \sqrt{128}$ i) $\sqrt{75} - \sqrt{108} - \sqrt{147}$

5. Simplify.

   a) $2\sqrt{3} + 4\sqrt{12}$ b) $5\sqrt{48} - 7\sqrt{3}$ c) $3\sqrt{8} + 6\sqrt{18}$

   d) $4\sqrt{50} - 7\sqrt{32}$ e) $2\sqrt{24} + 3\sqrt{54}$ f) $6\sqrt{20} - 2\sqrt{45}$

   g) $3\sqrt{8} + 5\sqrt{18} - 6\sqrt{2}$ h) $5\sqrt{28} - 3\sqrt{63} + 2\sqrt{112}$ i) $8\sqrt{24} - 2\sqrt{54} - \sqrt{28}$

6. A straight stretch of railroad track connects Goshen to Humber, 16 km due west. The highway between the two towns passes through Ironton, 2 km east and 2 km north of Humber. How much farther is it to drive from Humber to Goshen than to take the train?

7. A rectangle has a 2 cm width and a 6 cm diagonal. Find the
   a) length   b) area   c) perimeter

8. Find the area and perimeter of a rectangle with diagonal 8 cm and one side 6 cm.

Ⓒ

9. In $\triangle XYZ$, $\angle Y = 90°$, $XY = \sqrt{12}$, and $YZ = \sqrt{8}$.

   a) Find the length of XZ.

   b) Is it true that $\sqrt{12} + \sqrt{8} = \sqrt{20}$?

   c) Explain your answer to (b).

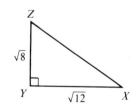

10. Each right triangle in the figure shown has a hypotenuse 4 cm and the shortest side 2 cm. Find the perimeter of the figure.

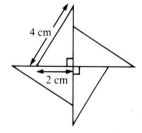

6-11 DIVIDING RADICALS

Division is the inverse of multiplication.

We know $56 \div 8 = 7$ because $7 \times 8 = 56$.

Similarly, $\sqrt{10} \div \sqrt{2} = \sqrt{5}$ because $\sqrt{5} \times \sqrt{2} = \sqrt{10}$

This suggests the following property for radicals:

$$\frac{\sqrt{a}}{\sqrt{b}} = \sqrt{\frac{a}{b}}, \quad (a \geq 0, b > 0)$$

Example. Simplify.

a) $\dfrac{2\sqrt{15}}{\sqrt{3}}$ b) $\dfrac{\sqrt{36}}{\sqrt{2}}$ c) $\dfrac{9\sqrt{24}}{2\sqrt{18}}$

Solution.

a) $\dfrac{2\sqrt{15}}{\sqrt{3}}$

$= 2\sqrt{\dfrac{15}{3}}$

$= 2\sqrt{5}$

b) $\dfrac{\sqrt{36}}{\sqrt{2}} = \sqrt{18}$

$= 3\sqrt{2}$

or $\dfrac{\sqrt{36}}{\sqrt{2}} = \dfrac{6}{\sqrt{2}}$

c) The radicals should be expressed in simplest form before dividing.

$$\frac{9\sqrt{24}}{2\sqrt{18}} = \frac{9 \times 2\sqrt{6}}{2 \times 3\sqrt{2}}$$

$$= \frac{3\sqrt{6}}{\sqrt{2}}$$

$$= 3\sqrt{3}$$

EXERCISES 6-11

(A)

1. Simplify.

a) $\dfrac{\sqrt{24}}{\sqrt{3}}$ b) $\dfrac{\sqrt{56}}{\sqrt{8}}$ c) $\dfrac{\sqrt{72}}{\sqrt{6}}$ d) $\dfrac{3\sqrt{35}}{\sqrt{7}}$ e) $\dfrac{6\sqrt{18}}{2\sqrt{6}}$

f) $\dfrac{5\sqrt{30}}{2\sqrt{15}}$ g) $\dfrac{4\sqrt{20}}{2\sqrt{5}}$ h) $\dfrac{3\sqrt{12}}{6\sqrt{3}}$ i) $\dfrac{\sqrt{24}}{7\sqrt{12}}$ j) $\dfrac{\sqrt{8}}{6\sqrt{18}}$

2. Simplify.

a) $\dfrac{3\sqrt{48}}{2\sqrt{27}}$ b) $\dfrac{6\sqrt{50}}{5\sqrt{18}}$ c) $\dfrac{4\sqrt{54}}{3\sqrt{12}}$ d) $\dfrac{3\sqrt{20}}{2\sqrt{10}}$ e) $\dfrac{5\sqrt{24}}{2\sqrt{18}}$

1. Evaluate.
   a) $3^2 + 2^3$
   b) $3^2 \times 2^3$
   c) $(1.6)^2$
   d) $3^2 + 4$
   e) $(-2)^3 + (-3)^2$
   f) $(2 + 3)^3$
   g) $(-4)^2 + (-2)^4$
   h) $\left(-\dfrac{3}{7}\right)^3$

2. If $x = -2$ and $y = 3$, evaluate each expression.
   a) $-5x^2$
   b) $(-5x)^2$
   c) $y^2 - x^2$
   d) $(x + y)^3$
   e) $4x^2 + 3y^2$
   f) $\dfrac{x^2 - y^2}{x - y}$
   g) $2(x + y)^2$
   h) $\dfrac{y^2 - x^3}{y - x}$

3. Find the area of the shaded region of each figure. Give the answers to 1 decimal place.
   a)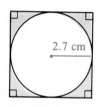
   b)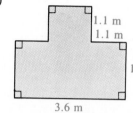
   c)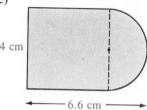

4. Find the volume of each solid. Give the answers to 1 decimal place.
   a)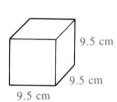
   b)
   c)

5. Simplify.
   a) $x^4 \times x^5$
   b) $x^{36} \div x^{12}$
   c) $x^{12} \times x^6$
   d) $(x)^7$
   e) $3x^2 \times 5x^4$
   f) $2^9 \div 2^4$
   g) $9m^4 \times 3m^2$
   h) $(-3)^{12} \div (-3)^4$
   i) $(5x)^2$
   j) $5(x^2)^3$
   k) $(3x^2)^3$
   l) $-42y^{12} \div 6y^8$

6. Simplify.
   a) $\dfrac{18x^4 \times 5x^2}{15x^3}$
   b) $\dfrac{120x^5}{-15x} \times \dfrac{15x^4}{5x^2}$

7. Evaluate each expression for $x = 4$.
   a) $x^2 \times x^4$
   b) $(2x^2)^2$
   c) $(2x^2)(3x^3)$

8. Evaluate.
   a) 5^{-3}
   b) $\left(\dfrac{1}{2}\right)^{-1}$
   c) $2^{-3} - 4^{-1}$
   d) $7^0 + 2^{-2}$
   e) $3^2 - 3^{-2}$
   f) $\left(\dfrac{2}{3}\right)^{-1} + \left(\dfrac{2}{3}\right)^0$
   g) $\left(\dfrac{1}{2}\right)^{-2} + 2^{-1}$
   h) $\left(\dfrac{1}{2}\right)^{-2} \div 2^{-1}$

9. Simplify.
   a) $w^8 \div w^{-4}$
   b) $w^{-9} \div w^{-12}$
   c) $15x^4 \div (-3x^{-4})$

10. Evaluate each expression for $a = -2$, $b = 2$, and $c = -1$.
    a) $a^{-1} + b^{-1}$
    b) $(a + b + c)^{-1}$
    c) a^b
    d) $a^{-1} + b^{-1} + c^2$

11. Write in scientific notation.
    a) 10 000
    b) 740 000
    c) 0.000 01
    d) 0.057

12. Simplify.
    a) $\sqrt{36}$
    b) $-\sqrt{0.25}$
    c) $\sqrt{14\ 400}$
    d) $\sqrt{0.0081}$

13. Find the side length of each square with the given area.
    a) 64 mm^2
    b) 0.81 m^2
    c) 49 cm^2
    d) 2.25 cm^2

14. The approximate velocity v metres per second of an orbiting satellite is given by the formula $v = \sqrt{9.8r}$, where r is the distance in metres of the satellite from the centre of the Earth. Find the velocity of the satellite if:
    a) $r = 2 \times 10^7$ m
    b) $r = 5 \times 10^8$ m.

15. When a ball is dropped from a height of 2 m, the height h metres to which it bounces is given by $h = 2(0.8)^n$, where n is the number of bounces. To what height does the ball bounce after:
    a) the first bounce
    b) the third bounce?

16. The width w of a rectangle with length l and diagonal length d is given by the formula $w = \sqrt{d^2 - l^2}$. Find the width of a rectangle with length 12.2 cm and a diagonal of length 15.8 cm.

17. Simplify.
    a) $\sqrt[3]{-8}$
    b) $\sqrt[3]{125}$
    c) $\sqrt[4]{81}$
    d) $\sqrt[3]{64}$
    e) $\sqrt[5]{-32}$
    f) $\sqrt[3]{0.001}$

18. Which of the following numbers are irrational?
    a) $\sqrt{48}$
    b) $\sqrt{49}$
    c) $\sqrt{1\frac{7}{9}}$
    d) $\sqrt{3.6}$
    e) $\sqrt{289}$
    f) $\sqrt{0.25}$

19. Express as a mixed radical in simplest form.
    a) $\sqrt{98}$
    b) $\sqrt{27}$
    c) $2\sqrt{45}$
    d) $-3\sqrt{360}$
    e) $2\sqrt{60}$
    f) $\sqrt{300}$

20. Simplify.
    a) $4\sqrt{6} \times 2\sqrt{3}$
    b) $(-4\sqrt{12})(-3\sqrt{3})$
    c) $-5\sqrt{20} \times 2\sqrt{5}$
    d) $-5\sqrt{6} \times 5\sqrt{12}$
    e) $(-3\sqrt{5})(-2\sqrt{15})$
    f) $-2\sqrt{8} \times 3\sqrt{6} \times \sqrt{12}$
    g) $(-3\sqrt{5})(2\sqrt{6})$
    h) $(-2\sqrt{13})(-\sqrt{52})$

21. Simplify.
    a) $\dfrac{\sqrt{24}}{\sqrt{2}}$
    b) $\dfrac{3\sqrt{32}}{\sqrt{2}}$
    c) $\dfrac{\sqrt{2}}{\frac{1}{2}}$
    d) $\dfrac{3\sqrt{12}}{4\sqrt{27}}$
    e) $\dfrac{2\sqrt{45}}{7\sqrt{80}}$

1. Solve.
   a) $7 + y = -6$
   b) $9 - t = -13$
   c) $-18 = -6p$
   d) $11 = 2.25w$
   e) $\frac{1}{7}x = -2$
   f) $\frac{r}{3} = \frac{1}{5}$
   g) $-2.75x = 16.5$
   h) $5x - 2 = 13$
   i) $3 - 3y = -3$

2. Solve.
   a) $5x - 3 = 2x + 6$
   b) $-3y + 5 = 2y - 10$
   c) $3(r - 1) = -2(r + 8)$
   d) $5(7x - 3) = 17x - (2 - 5x)$
   e) $\frac{4}{3} - \frac{1}{2}x = \frac{2}{3}x$
   f) $1.25 - 0.8x = 0.4x - 0.19$
   g) $2(3a - 5) = 7(2a + 3) - 3$
   h) $\frac{3}{2}p + \frac{1}{4} = \frac{3}{4}p - \frac{7}{8}$

3. Solve and check.
   a) $12 - 4a + 7 = 2a + 31$
   b) $-4(x - 3) = 2(x + 9)$
   c) $7(2s - 3) + 11 = 2(4s + 7)$
   d) $1.4x - 3.6 = 0.4(2x + 1.5)$

4. The cost C dollars of printing a school yearbook is given by this formula.
   $C = 2750 + 9.5n$, where n is the number of books printed
   a) Find the cost of printing:
      i)   600 copies
      ii)   940 copies
      iii)   1050 copies.
   b) How many copies can be printed for $13 010.00?

5. Express each statement as an equation and solve it.
   a) A number multiplied by seven equals fifty-six.
   b) A number divided by fifteen equals seventy-five.
   c) When twenty-nine is subtracted from a number, the result is negative two.

6. A father is three times as old as his daughter. In 12 years time, he will be only twice as old. What are their ages now?

7. Two numbers differ by 3. The sum of the larger and one-fourth the smaller is 13. Find the numbers.

8. Find the angle measure indicated by each letter.

   a)
   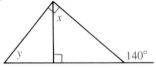

   b)
   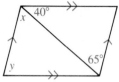

   c)
   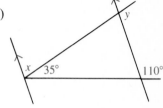

9. For each part, find a pair of congruent triangles and state the condition for their congruence.

a)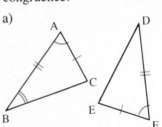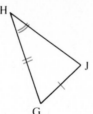

b)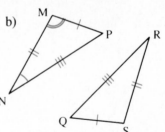

10. A conveyor belt 11.4 m in length is used to raise cartons of produce from one level to another, a distance of 3.7 m. How much floor space, measured in the direction of the conveyor, is required?

11. Simplify.
   a) $2^3 + 2^4$
   b) $2^3 \times 2^4$
   c) $(-3)^2 + (-3)^3$
   d) $(-2)^7 \div (-2)^4$
   e) $\left(\dfrac{3}{4}\right)^{-1} + \left(\dfrac{3}{4}\right)^0$
   f) $2^{-3} \div 2^{-4}$
   g) 3^{-2}
   h) $\left(-\dfrac{2}{3}\right)^{-2}$

12. If $m = 3$ and $n = -2$, find the value of each expression.
   a) $2m^2$
   b) $-4n^3$
   c) $8m^2 - 5n^2$
   d) $(m + n)^3$
   e) $(m - n)^3$
   f) $\dfrac{5m^2 - 3n^2}{m - n^3}$
   g) $\dfrac{3(m - n)^2}{m^2 + n}$
   h) $5n^3 - 2m^2$

13. Simplify.
   a) $x^3 \times x^7$
   b) $x^{14} \div x^8$
   c) $-3p^2 \times 7p^{-9}$
   d) $24m^{-3} \div (-8m^{11})$
   e) $(3x)^2 \times (2x)^3$
   f) $(4y^3)^2$
   g) $35a^3 \div 5a^{-7}$
   h) $3x^5 \times 12x^{-7} \div 4x^{-3}$
   i) $\dfrac{18s^4 \times 4s^{11}}{12s^7}$

14. Write in scientific notation.
   a) 15 000
   b) 2 700 000
   c) 21
   d) 0.000 016
   e) 0.000 37
   f) 0.19

15. Simplify.
   a) $\sqrt{2500}$
   b) $-\sqrt{1.96}$
   c) $\sqrt{2\,250\,000}$
   d) $2\sqrt{49} - 3\sqrt{16}$
   e) $9\sqrt{64} + 2\sqrt{9}$
   f) $7\sqrt{81} - 5\sqrt{100}$

16. Evaluate, to 2 decimal places, if $x = -3$ and $y = 2$.
   a) $\sqrt{-14x}$
   b) $\sqrt{2x^2 + 6y^3 - 2}$
   c) $-\sqrt{7x^2 - 4y^2 + 8}$

17. Simplify.
   a) $\sqrt{32}$
   b) $\sqrt{72}$
   c) $-3\sqrt{75}$
   d) $3\sqrt{5} \times 4\sqrt{10}$
   e) $(-2\sqrt{12})(3\sqrt{6})$
   f) $3\sqrt{8} \times 2\sqrt{6} \times 4\sqrt{12}$

18. Simplify.
   a) $\dfrac{1}{3}\sqrt{27} + \dfrac{1}{2}\sqrt{48} - 3\sqrt{3}$
   b) $2\sqrt{32} - 4\sqrt{50} + \sqrt{98}$

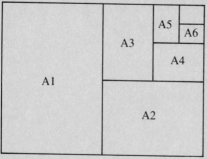

In a move to conserve the Earth's resources, an international standard of paper sizes was created. The largest, A0, has an area of 1 m². The ratio of the lengths of its sides are such that cutting it in half results in the next largest size, A1, with side lengths in the same ratio. The next size, A2, is obtained by cutting an A1 sheet in half, and so on. The length-to-width ratio is the same for all sizes.

There is only one length-to-width ratio that yields similar rectangles in this way. Can you find what it is? (See Section 7-3, *Example 3*.)

7-1 RATIOS

The newspaper headline indicates that 80 out of 100 Americans approve of recycling. Therefore, 20 out of 100 do not approve.

80 out of every 100 Americans approve of recycling

The comparison of the numbers of people who do not approve of recycling and those who do, can be written as a *ratio*, 20 : 80. This is read, "twenty to eighty".

A ratio is a comparison of quantities measured in the same units. The numbers 20 and 80 are the *terms* of the ratio. The order of the terms is important; they may not be interchanged.

When each term of a ratio is multiplied or divided by the same non-zero number, an equivalent ratio is produced. For example,
$20 : 80 = 200 : 800 = 2 : 8 = 1 : 4$

The ratio 1 : 4 is in *lowest terms* because the only factor that the terms have in common is 1.

A ratio can be written in fractional form; that is, 20 : 80 can be written as $\frac{20}{80}$.

Although a ratio can be written in fractional form, a ratio is *not* a fraction. A fraction is a comparison of part(s) of an amount (the numerator) to the whole amount (the denominator). A ratio is a comparison of two amounts, the second of which may not be the whole amount.

For example, the ratio above, $\frac{20}{80}$, can be written as $\frac{1}{4}$. But this does not mean that $\frac{1}{4}$ of the people do not approve of recycling. In fact, $\frac{1}{4}$ in this context has no meaning as a fraction because the denominator does not represent the whole group of people considered.

Example 1. Write each ratio in lowest terms.

    a) 9 : 6   b) 16 : 12   c) 25 : 20   d) $\frac{60}{15}$

Solution.   a) 9 : 6   b) 16 : 12
                     Divide by 3.   Divide by 4.
                     $9 : 6 = 3 : 2$ $16 : 12 = 4 : 3$

            c) 25 : 20   d) $\frac{60}{15}$
                     Divide by 5.
                     $25 : 20 = 5 : 4$ Divide by 15.
                                              $\frac{60}{15} = \frac{4}{1}$

Example 2.   The table shows the records of four tennis players in a Buffalo tennis club. Which two players have the same ratio of wins to games?

Name	Games	Wins
Anne James	28	7
Mike Sanchez	24	8
Tom Burgess	20	5
Tanya Stoffer	24	4

Solution.   The wins-to-games ratios are
James $7 : 28 = 1 : 4$ Sanchez $8 : 24 = 1 : 3$
Burgess $5 : 20 = 1 : 4$ Stoffer $4 : 24 = 1 : 6$
Anne James and Tom Burgess have the same wins-to-games ratio.

Example 3.   A parking lot contains domestic and foreign cars in the ratio $7 : 4$. If there are 77 cars in the lot, how many of them are foreign?

Solution.   The ratio of domestic cars to foreign cars is $7 : 4$.
Therefore, 7 out of 11 cars are domestic and 4 out of 11 cars are foreign.
The number of foreign cars is $\dfrac{4}{11}(77) = 28$
There are 28 foreign cars in the lot.

Example 4.   Fuel X is composed of ingredients A and B in the ratio $3 : 5$. Fuel Y is composed of ingredients A and B in the ratio $4 : 7$. Which fuel is richer in ingredient A?

Solution.   Ingredient A is $\dfrac{3}{8}$ of fuel X. Ingredient A is $\dfrac{4}{11}$ of fuel Y.

Raise these fractions to a common denominator.
$$\frac{3}{8} = \frac{33}{88} \quad \text{and} \quad \frac{4}{11} = \frac{32}{88}$$
Since $\dfrac{33}{88} > \dfrac{32}{88}$, then $\dfrac{3}{8} > \dfrac{4}{11}$
Fuel X is richer in ingredient A.

EXERCISES 7-1

(A)

1. Explain each statement without using the word "ratio".
   a) Mrs. Adams and Mr. Singh divided the profits in the ratio $3 : 2$.
   b) The ratio of girls to boys in the class is $7 : 5$.
   c) Mrs. Arbor's chain saw runs on a $25 : 1$ mixture of gasoline and oil.
   d) The scale of a map is $1 : 250\ 000$.
   e) Brass is an alloy of copper and zinc in the ratio $3 : 2$.

2. Write each ratio in lowest terms.
   a) 40 : 12
   b) 5 : 65
   c) 28 : 8
   d) 32 : 52
   e) 12 : 72
   f) 50 : 250
   g) $\dfrac{60}{12}$
   h) $\dfrac{144}{9}$

3. State which is the greater ratio.
   a) $\dfrac{5}{8}$ or $\dfrac{3}{5}$
   b) 6 : 7 or 7 : 8
   c) 6 : 5 or 12 : 11
   d) 8 : 3 or 13 : 5

Ⓑ

4. "Gran's" cookies have raisins and chocolate chips in the ratio 3 : 7. "Mum's" cookies have raisins and chocolate chips in the ratio 5 : 11. Which brand has the greater ratio of raisins to chocolate chips?

5. Air consists of oxygen and nitrogen in the approximate ratio 1 : 4, and negligible amounts of other gases.
   a) What fraction of air is oxygen?
   b) What fraction of air is nitrogen?

6. Sterling silver is an alloy of silver and copper in the ratio 37 : 3.
   a) What fraction of a sterling silver fork is silver?
   b) If the mass of a sterling silver ingot is 500 g, how much silver does it contain?

7. Write an equivalent ratio with a second term of 1.
   a) 5 : 2
   b) 2 : 0.5
   c) 3 : 10
   d) 4 : 0.8

8. Write an equivalent ratio with a second term of 24.
   a) 5 : 6
   b) 8 : 48
   c) 27 : 36
   d) 5 : 0.6

9. At a school dance, there are 15 teachers, 275 girls, and 225 boys. Express the following ratios in lowest terms.
   a) girls to boys
   b) teachers to girls
   c) students to teachers

10. A newspaper costs 25¢ each day from Monday to Friday and 75¢ on Saturday. What is the ratio of:
    a) the cost on Saturday to the cost for one week
    b) the cost on Monday to the cost for one week?

11. If the ratio of domestic cars to foreign cars in Metropolitan Cleveland is 9 : 5, how many domestic cars might you expect to find in a lot containing 247 cars?

12. The length and the width of a rectangle are in the ratio 9 : 7. If the perimeter is 256 cm, what are the dimensions of the rectangle?

Ⓒ

13. The front gear wheels of a ten-speed bicycle have 40 and 52 teeth. The back gear wheels have 14, 17, 20, 24, and 28 teeth.
    a) Write the ten different gear ratios (front:back).
    b) Arrange the ten gear ratios in order from lowest to highest.

14. The ratio of the mass of a hydrogen atom to the average mass of a person (70 kg) is about the same as the ratio of the average mass of a person to the mass of the sun. The mass of a hydrogen atom is about 1.7×10^{-29} kg. What is the approximate mass of the sun?

7-2 APPLICATIONS OF RATIOS

The amount of gold in jewellery and coins is measured in karats (K) with 24 K representing pure gold.

The mark 14 K on a ring means the ratio of the mass of gold in the ring to the mass of the ring is 14 : 24.

Since the second term of the ratio describing the purity of gold is always 24, it is omitted when describing the gold content.

In many ratios, only the first term is stated. The second term is omitted since it is always the same in each type of application of the ratio. Some further examples of ratios in which only the first terms are stated are Consumer Price Index, Mach numbers, and Intelligence Quotients.

Example 1. A gold bracelet is marked 18 K.
  a) Express the gold content of the bracelet as a fraction in lowest terms.
  b) The mass of the bracelet is 52 g and the value of pure gold is $25.50/g. Find the value of the gold in the bracelet.

Solution. a) Mass of gold : mass of bracelet $= 18 : 24$
$$= 3 : 4$$

  b) Mass of gold in the bracelet $= \dfrac{3}{4}(52 \text{ g})$
$$= 39 \text{ g}$$

Value of gold in the bracelet $= 39(\$25.50)$
$$= \$994.50$$

The gold in the bracelet is worth $994.50.

The *Consumer Price Index (CPI)* is a measure of the change in the cost of living. The ratio compares the price of 300 selected items at any time, to the price of the same items in 1981. The CPI is a ratio with its second term 100.

$$\frac{\text{CPI in year A}}{100} = \frac{\text{Cost of 300 items in year A}}{\text{Cost of 300 items in 1981}}$$

What is the Consumer Price Index today?

Example 2. In 1981 a family spent $14 000. If the CPI in 1990 were 187.4, how much would the family spend, to the nearest $100, in that year for the same items?

Solution.
$$\frac{\text{CPI in 1990}}{100} = \frac{\text{Cost of items in 1990}}{\text{Cost of items in 1981}}$$

Substitute the given information.

$$\frac{187.4}{100} = \frac{\text{Cost of items in 1990}}{\$14\ 000}$$

$$\text{Cost of items in 1990} = \$14\ 000 \left(\frac{187.4}{100}\right)$$

$$= \$26\ 236$$

In 1990, the family would spend about $26 200.

To compare more than two quantities, ratios with more than two terms are used. For example, the gravities of the Earth, Jupiter, and Mars are in the ratio 5 : 13 : 2. This means that a person on Jupiter would weigh $\frac{13}{5}$ of her or his weight on Earth, and $\frac{13}{2}$ of her or his weight on Mars.

Example 3. The profits in a business are to be shared by the three partners in the ratio 2 : 3 : 5. The profit for the year was $176 500. Calculate each partner's share.

Solution. Since the profit is shared in the ratio 2 : 3 : 5, we can think of the profit as consisting of a total of (2+3+5) or 10 shares.

The 1st partner's share is $\frac{2}{10}$($176 500) or $35 300.

The 2nd partner's share is $\frac{3}{10}$ ($176 500) or $52 950.

The 3rd partner's share is $\frac{5}{10}$ ($176 500) or $88 250.

EXERCISES 7-2

Ⓐ

1. Express the gold content as a ratio in lowest terms.
   a) a 22 K gold coin
   b) a 16 K gold pin
   c) a charm marked 9 K, the legal minimum for an article to be called gold

2. A 14 K gold ring has a mass of 24.7 g.
   a) Find the mass of the gold in the ring.
   b) At $25.50/g, find the value of the gold in the ring.

Ⓑ

3. In 1986, the Consumer Price Index rose to 131.1. How much did it cost a family in 1986 for goods that cost them $8700 in 1981?

4. Three people contributed to buy a lottery ticket, in the ratio 2 : 5 : 3. If the ticket wins $25 000, how should the prize be divided?

5. Four partners in a business agreed to share the profits in the ratio 4 : 2 : 3 : 6. The first year's profits were $84 000. Calculate each partner's share.

6. a) A 1-cent coin minted before 1860 had a mass of 4.50 g and contained copper, tin, and zinc in the ratio 95 : 4 : 1. What mass of tin did each coin contain?
   b) From 1876 to 1920, the mass of each 1-cent coin minted was 5.67 g, and the ratio of copper to tin to zinc was 95.5 : 3 : 1.5. What mass of copper did each coin contain?
   c) After 1942, each 1-cent coin minted had a mass of 3.24 g and contained copper, tin, and zinc in the ratio 98 : 0.5 : 1.5. What mass of zinc did each coin contain?

7. The *Intelligence Quotient (IQ)* is the first term of a ratio with a second term of 100. The IQ is always stated to the nearest whole number. It is calculated from this formula. The formula applies to physical ages up to 20 years.
   $$\frac{IQ}{100} = \frac{\text{mental age}}{\text{physical age}}$$
   a) Find the IQ of each child.
      i) a twelve-year old with a mental age of 12.5
      ii) a seven-year old with a mental age of 6.8
   b) Find the mental age of each child.
      i) a nine-year old with an IQ of 100
      ii) a six-year old with an IQ of 150 (genius level)

8. A *Mach number* is a ratio with second term 1. The Mach number of an airplane is the ratio of its speed to the speed of sound at the same altitude and temperature. Assume an altitude where the speed of sound is 1085 km/h.
   a) Calculate the Mach number of an airplane flying at each speed. Give the answers to one decimal place.
      i)   3255 km/h   ii)   1302 km/h   iii)   1000 km/h
   b) Find the speed of the North American Aviation X-15A-2 flying at Mach 6.72.

9. The frequencies of the notes in the musical scale of C major are related by an eight-term ratio.

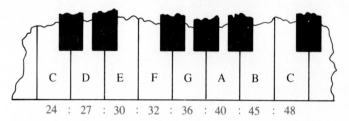

24 : 27 : 30 : 32 : 36 : 40 : 45 : 48

Musical instruments are usually tuned so that A in the scale has a frequency of 440 Hz (cycles per second). Find the frequencies of the other notes in the scale.

Ⓒ

10. Chemical fertilizers usually contain nitrogen, phosphorus, and potassium. The amount of each nutrient present is expressed as a percent of the total mass of the fertilizer in the three-term ratio, nitrogen : phosphorus : potassium.

A, B, and C are 10 kg bags of three kinds of fertilizer.

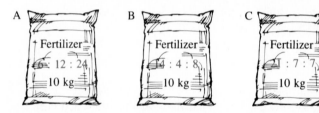

a) Which fertilizer contains the most nitrogen?
b) Which fertilizer has the greatest ratio of nitrogen to phosphorus?
c) Which fertilizer contains the most nutrients?
d) Why are the ratios not expressed in lowest terms?

11. The ratio of the approximate distances of the Earth and Uranus from the Sun is 4 : 77, and that of Mars and Uranus from the Sun is 2 : 25.
a) What is the ratio of the approximate distances of the Earth and Mars from the Sun?
b) How far is Mars from the Sun if the Earth's distance is 150 Gm?

12. The angles of a triangle are in the ratio 2 : 3 : 4. What are their measures?

13. The angles of a quadrilateral are in the ratio 2 : 3 : 3 : 4. What are their measures?

14. A sphere and a cone are each designed to fit snugly (at separate times) inside a cylinder of radius R and height $2R$.
a) Write the ratio of the volume of the sphere to the volume of the cone to the volume of the cylinder.
b) How many times is the volume of the cylinder as great as the volume of the largest sphere it will contain?

7-3 PROPORTIONS

One method of finding the height of a tall tree is to measure its shadow, and then compare that with the length of the shadow of an object whose height is known. If both shadows are measured at the same time of day, the ratio of their lengths will be equal to the ratio of the heights of the object and the tree.

$$\frac{\text{height of tree}}{\text{height of stick}} = \frac{\text{length of tree's shadow}}{\text{length of stick's shadow}}$$

Substitute the known measures.

$$\frac{\text{height of tree}}{1.0} = \frac{12.7}{0.7}$$

$$\text{height of tree} = \frac{12.7}{0.7}$$

$$\doteq 18.1$$

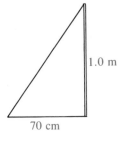

1.0 m

70 cm

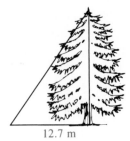

12.7 m

The tree is about 18 m high.

This solution used the fact that two ratios were equal.

A statement that two ratios are equal is called a *proportion*. For example, the statement $a : b = c : d$, is a proportion.

Since ratios can be written in fractional form, the statement $\dfrac{a}{b} = \dfrac{c}{d}$

is also a proportion.

To simplify an expression of this type, multiply both sides of the proportion by the lowest common denominator.

$$\frac{a}{b}(bd) = \frac{c}{d}(bd)$$

$$ad = cb$$

This equation can be used to find the unknown term in a proportion when the other three terms are known.

Example 1. Find each value of x.

    a) $\dfrac{7}{30} = \dfrac{14}{x}$
                        b) $\dfrac{3}{19} = \dfrac{x}{7}$

Solution.   a) $\dfrac{7}{30} = \dfrac{14}{x}$
                               b) $\dfrac{3}{19} = \dfrac{x}{7}$

               $7x = 14(30)$
                               Multiply both sides by 7.

               $x = \dfrac{14(30)}{7}$
                         $\dfrac{3(7)}{19} = x$

                $= 60$
                           $\dfrac{21}{19} = x$

Example 2. The scale, 1 : 300, of the floor plan indicates that 1 mm on the plan corresponds to 300 mm, or 0.3 m, in the actual building.
a) Find the dimensions, in metres, of the living room.
b) Find the total floor area to the nearest square metre.

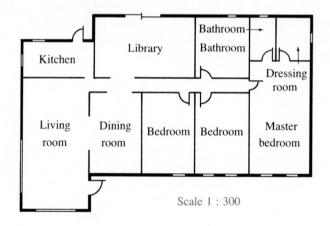

Scale 1 : 300

Solution.   a) By measurement of the floor plan, the living room is 35 mm by 20 mm. This corresponds to 35(0.3 m) by 20(0.3 m), or 10.5 m by 6.0 m.

           The living room is 10.5 m by 6.0 m.

     b) The floor plan can be divided into two rectangles. One rectangle comprises the living room and the kitchen. This measures 45 mm by 20 mm, or 45(0.3 m) by 20(0.3 m).

           The other rectangle comprises all the other rooms. It measures 60 mm by 42 mm, or 60(0.3 m) by 42(0.3 m).

           Total area $= [45(0.3) \times 20(0.3)] + [60(0.3) \times 42(0.3)]$
                                  $= 307.8$

           The floor area is approximately 308 m^2.

Example 3. A rectangular sheet of paper is 1 m wide. When cut in half, each half has the same length-to-width ratio as the original sheet. How long is the original sheet?

Solution. Draw a diagram.
The width 1 m of the original sheet is the length of the 2 cut sheets.

Let x metres represent the length of the original sheet.
Then $0.5x$ metres is the width of the cut sheet.

$$\frac{\text{original length}}{\text{original width}} = \frac{\text{cut length}}{\text{cut width}}$$

$$\frac{x}{1} = \frac{1}{0.5x}$$

$$0.5x^2 = 1$$

$$x^2 = \frac{1}{0.5}$$

$$= 2$$

$$x = \sqrt{2}$$

$$\doteq 1.4$$

When this equation was solved, the negative square root was ignored because a sheet of paper cannot have a negative length.

The original sheet of paper was about 1.4 m long.

This solution relates to the problem posed at the beginning of this chapter. If the paper with size A0 has a length-to-width ratio of $\sqrt{2}$ to 1, when it is cut in half the two sheets produced will have measurements in the same ratio. Subsequent cuts produce smaller sheets with the same ratio of length to width.

EXERCISES 7-3

1. Find the value of each variable.

a) $\frac{3}{8} = \frac{m}{24}$ b) $\frac{12}{16} = \frac{n}{8}$ c) $\frac{a}{12} = \frac{15}{36}$ d) $\frac{x}{18} = \frac{9}{54}$

e) $\frac{90}{b} = \frac{30}{11}$ f) $\frac{72}{x} = \frac{360}{15}$ g) $\frac{9}{8} = \frac{144}{d}$ h) $\frac{27}{5} = \frac{81}{x}$

2. Solve.

a) $\frac{11}{16} = \frac{n}{8}$ b) $\frac{x}{3} = \frac{2}{7}$ c) $\frac{5}{8} = \frac{9}{x}$ d) $\frac{7}{11} = \frac{9}{x}$

e) $\frac{t}{4} = \frac{5}{7}$ f) $\frac{9}{b} = \frac{5}{6}$ g) $\frac{3}{5} = \frac{w}{7}$ h) $\frac{5}{13} = \frac{10}{y}$

Ⓑ

3. In a photograph of a mother and her son standing together, the son measures 27 mm and the mother 63 mm. If the mother is actually 180 cm tall, how tall is her son?

4. At a given time of day, the ratio of the height of a tree to the length of its shadow is the same for all trees. A tree 12 m tall casts a shadow 5 m long. How tall is a tree that casts a shadow 3 m long?

5. The ratio of a person's height to her or his arm span is 24 : 32. How tall is a person whose arm span is 184 cm?

6. Assume that the headline statement is correct.
   a) How many out of 30 smokers want to quit?
   b) How many out of 600 smokers want to quit?
   c) How many smokers were polled if 200 want to quit?

   ### 5 out of 6 smokers want to quit

7. Find the actual dimensions and the area of the master bedroom shown in the floor plan of *Example 2*.

8. Find each distance from the map.
   a) Halifax to Sable Island
   b) Bathurst to Corner Brook
   c) The width of Cabot Strait
   d) The length of Prince Edward Island
   e) Bridgewater to Grand Bank
   f) Digby to Saint John

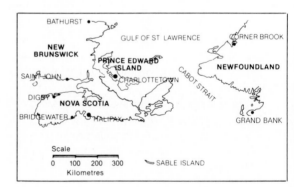

9. The distance between two towns is 180 km. How far apart will they be on a map drawn to a scale of 1 : 1 500 000?

10. Find the approximate length of each part of the mosquito.
    a) the abdomen
    b) the antennae
    c) the wings

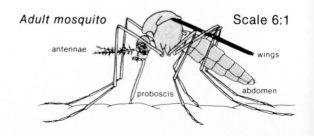

Adult mosquito   Scale 6:1

7-4 RATES

When a person buys a car, one of the considerations is usually how much gasoline the car uses. The distance the car travels, in miles, is compared to the fuel consumption, in gallons. Such a comparison is called a *rate* because the two quantities that are compared have different units.

Which of the cars above has the better fuel consumption?

Many familiar measurements are expressed as rates.
- speed in miles per hour
- pulse rate in heart beats per minute
- unit pricing on supermarket shelves in cents per oz
- wages in dollars per hour
- sports statistics in goals per game

Example 1. A car's fuel consumption is quoted as 25 miles per gallon.
      a) Find how much fuel is needed to travel 170 mi.
      b) Find how far the car will travel on 12 gal of gasoline.

Solution. A fuel consumption of 25 miles per gallon means that the car travels 25 miles on 1 gal of gasoline.

      a) The fuel for 1 mi would be $\frac{1}{25}$ gal.

          The fuel for 170 mi would be $170 \times \frac{1}{25}$ gal, or 6.8 gal.

          About 7 gal of fuel are needed to travel 170 mi.

      b) On 1 gal of fuel the car travels 25 mi.
          On 12 gal of fuel the car could travel 12(25) mi, or 300 mi.
          The car travels about 300 mi on 12 gal of fuel.

Example 2. In one season, Casey batted at the rate of 2 hits for every 5 official times at bat.

a) At this rate, how many hits should he get in 400 times at bat?

b) How many times should Casey have at bat to get 180 hits?

Solution. Casey's batting average is $\frac{2}{5}$ or 0.4.

a) In 400 times at bat, Casey should get 400(0.4) or 160 hits.
If the rate is constant, Casey should get 160 hits.

b) Casey bats 5 times to get 2 hits.

So he will bat $\frac{5}{2}$ times to get 1 hit.

To get 180 hits, Casey will bat $\frac{5}{2}(180)$ or 450 times.

If the rate is constant, Casey should bat about 450 times to get 180 hits.

EXERCISES 7-4

Ⓐ

1. Dale drives 45 km on 3 L of gasoline.
   a) Find how far would she drive on:
      i) 2 L of gasoline   ii) 5 L of gasoline.
   b) Find how much gasoline Dale needs to drive:
      i) 60 km   ii) 270 km.

2. Bob can type at the rate of 30 words per minute.
   a) Find how long it would take him to type:
      i) 20 words   ii) 100 words.
   b) Find how many words Bob can type in:
      i) 4 min   ii) 6.5 min.

3. A car uses fuel at the rate of 32 miles per gallon.
   a) Find how much fuel is needed to travel 220 mi.
   b) Find how far the car will travel on a full tank of 24 gal.

Ⓑ

4. An electronic typewriter can type 540 words per minute.
   a) Find how long it will take to type:
      i) 1000 words   ii) 1 000 000 words.
   b) How many words can it type in:
      i) 1 h   ii) 1 week.

5. In the first 20 games of the baseball season, Reggie Jackson hit 12 home runs. If he continued at this rate, how many home runs would he hit in 160 games?

6. A 350 g box of cornflakes costs $1.75. A 525 g box of the same cereal costs $2.29.
   a) Find the unit price, in cents per 100 g, for each box of cereal.
   b) Which box is the better buy?

7. Adrian works in a factory making pies. He is paid $9.55 per hour for a 7.5 h shift. He is paid "time and a half" for the first 4 h of overtime in a day. Then he is paid double time for any additional hours worked that day.

   In one week, Adrian worked these hours.

Monday	Tuesday	Wednesday	Thursday	Friday
15	7.5	7.5	11.5	7.5

   What are Adrian's gross wages for this week?

8. In the first 6 games of the football season, Dave Cutler scored 83 points. If he continued scoring at this rate, how many points would he score in 14 games?

9. If 18 houses are built in 45 days, find how long at this rate it would take to build:
   a) 63 houses
   b) 144 houses.

10. A brand of liquid detergent is sold in 2 sizes — $2.09 for 500 mL, and $3.55 for 1 L.
    a) Find the unit price for each size of detergent. Which is the better buy?
    b) The smaller size is "on special" for one week at a price of $1.79. For this week, which is the better buy?

11. Marilyn works in a car assembly plant. She is paid $14.50 per hour for an 8 h shift. She receives an additional 72.5¢ per hour for working the night shift.

    In one month, Marilyn works two 40 h day shifts and two 40 h night shifts. Find her gross wages for the month.

12. Milk is sold in 4 L bags and 2 L and 1 L cartons. The milk is priced at $3.49, $2.31, and $1.20, respectively. By how much would the cost of each carton have to be reduced so that its unit price was equal to that of the 4 L bags?

13. Two girls, 60 km apart, start cycling toward each other at the same time. One girl cycles at 18 km/h. How fast must the other girl cycle if they are to meet in 1.5 h?

14. Car A and car B leave Halifax on the same road 1 h apart. Car A leaves first and travels at a steady 80 km/h. How fast must car B travel to overtake car A in 4 h?

15. Machine X makes 200 boxes in 3 min and machine Y makes 200 boxes in 2 min. With both machines working, how long will it take to make 200 boxes?

16. A worker is paid $8.60/h for a 40 h week and time and a half for overtime. How many hours are worked to earn $414.95 in one week?

17. A study shows that an office staff of x people will consume y cups of coffee over a period of z days. At this rate, how long would it take a staff of $3x$ people to consume $\dfrac{y}{12}$ cups of coffee?

THE MATHEMATICAL MIND

The Golden Ratio

Twenty-three centuries ago Euclid posed the question, "What are the dimensions of a rectangle that has the property that when it is divided into a square and a rectangle, the smaller rectangle has the same shape as the original?"

The answer to Euclid's question can be found using this proportion.

$$\frac{\text{Length of original rectangle}}{\text{Width of original rectangle}} = \frac{\text{Length of smaller rectangle}}{\text{Width of smaller rectangle}}$$

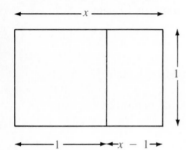

Let the length of the original rectangle be represented by x units and let its width be 1 unit.

The side of the square will then be 1 unit, and the proportion can be written.

$$\frac{x}{1} = \frac{1}{x - 1}$$

Multiply both sides of the proportion by $x - 1$.

$$x^2 - x = 1$$
$$x^2 - x - 1 = 0$$

The positive solution of the equation $x^2 - x - 1 = 0$ is called the *golden ratio*.

QUESTIONS

1. Use your calculator and the method of guess and check to solve the equation $x^2 - x - 1 = 0$.

2. Write down the value of the golden ratio to three decimal places.

3. Simplify this expression.

$$1 + \cfrac{1}{1 + \cfrac{1}{1 + \cfrac{1}{1 + \cfrac{1}{1 + 1}}}}$$

How close is this value to the value of the golden ratio?

A rectangle with a length-to-width ratio of the golden ratio is called a *golden rectangle*. Study the diagram. Then, using a pair of compasses and a straightedge, construct a golden rectangle.

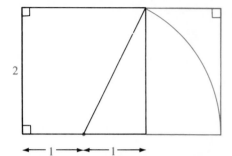

The rectangle obtained by dividing a golden rectangle into a square and a rectangle is itself a golden rectangle. Repeating this process with the small rectangle a number of times gives a set of successively smaller golden rectangles. The result of joining a set of corresponding vertices of these rectangles with a curve is a *spiral*. Such spirals can be found throughout nature, from the spiral galaxy in the heavens to the nautilus shells in the oceans.

Since Euclid's time, the golden ratio has been found in mathematics, architecture, art, and nature. In fact, the golden ratio is probably second only to π in its frequency of occurrence in the mathematical sciences.

MATHEMATICS AROUND US

Using Dimensional Analysis to Convert Units

Was the driver speeding?

To convert 25 metres per second to miles per hour we use the following relationships.
1 metre ≐ 6.213 × 10⁻⁴ mile
1 second ≐ 2.777 × 10⁻⁴ hour

Therefore, 25 metres per second $= \dfrac{25 \text{ m}}{1 \text{ s}}$

metres per second means
"metres divided by seconds"

$\doteq \dfrac{25(6.213 \times 10^{-4}) \text{ mile}}{2.777 \times 10^{-4} \text{ hour}}$

$\doteq \dfrac{25 \times 6.213 \text{ mile}}{2.777 \text{ hour}}$

$\doteq 55.9 \text{ mph}$

By his own admission, the driver was exceeding the 55 mph speed limit.

In the example above, we observe that we can replace any measurement in a given unit by an equivalent measurement in a different unit. Such replacements can occur within a particular measurement system; for example, converting centimetres to metres or between different measurement systems; for example, converting metres per second to miles per hour. The process of converting units in the numerator and denominator of a fraction to express it in different units is called *dimensional analysis*.

QUESTIONS

1. a) How many seconds in one hour?
   b) How many hours in one second?

2. a) If 1 cm $\doteq$ 0.0328 ft, express 1 ft in centimetres.
   b) Express 100 ft in centimetres.
   c) How tall is a 6-ft person in centimetres?

3. a) How many metres in one mile?
   b) Express a speed of 65 mph in metres per second.

4. Gravity causes an object to accelerate toward the Earth at 9.8 m/s². Express this acceleration in feet per second squared.

5. Use the fact that 100 cm = 1 m to express 1 m³ in cubic centimetres.

6. The density of a solid is defined to be its mass divided by its volume. The density of a lump of gold is 19.3 g/cm³. What is the density of that gold expressed in kilograms per cubic metre?

7. A particular property of a pendulum is given by the formula $2\pi\sqrt{\dfrac{L}{g}}$ where L is the length of the pendulum and g is the acceleration due to gravity. Perform a dimensional analysis to find the simplest units in which $\sqrt{\dfrac{L}{g}}$ can be expressed. What property does the expression represent?

8. In the M.K.S. system of measurement, all units can be expressed as a product of powers of metres, kilograms, and seconds. For example, density D is equal to mass m divided by volume V. That is, $D = \dfrac{m}{V}$

   The unit for mass is kilograms (kg) and the unit for volume is cubic metres (m³). Therefore, the unit for density in the M.K.S. system is kilograms per cubic metre (kg m⁻³).

   Express the units in the M.K.S. system for each of the quantities given below.

   a) Velocity v, where $v = \dfrac{d}{t}$; that is, distance per unit time

   b) Acceleration a, where $a = \dfrac{v}{t}$; that is, velocity per unit time

   c) Force F, where $F = ma$; and m represents mass, a represents acceleration
   d) Energy E, where $E = mc^2$; and m represents mass, c represents the speed of light

7-5 PERCENT

The weather forecast says that there is a 40% chance of rain today.

A store is closing down and offers everything for sale at 50% off.

A car manufacturer offers 6.9% financing to a customer who is buying a car.

A newspaper quotes a cost of living increase of 2.4% last month because of price rises in fuel and fresh produce.

A *percent* is a fraction with a denominator 100. For example,

40% is $\dfrac{40}{100}$ and 6.9% is $\dfrac{6.9}{100}$.

The word ''percent'' means ''per hundred''.

Example 1. Write each ratio as a percent.

a) $\dfrac{27}{100}$ b) 6:100 c) 7:25

Solution. a) $\dfrac{27}{100} = 27\%$

b) 6 : 100 written in fractional form is $\dfrac{6}{100}$, which is 6%.

c) 7 : 25 written in fractional form is $\dfrac{7}{25}$.

Multiply numerator and denominator by a factor that produces a denominator of 100.

$$\dfrac{7}{25} = \dfrac{7}{25} \times \dfrac{4}{4}$$
$$= \dfrac{28}{100}$$
$$= 28\%$$

Each solution could have been obtained by writing the ratio in fractional form and then multiplying by 100%.

For example, 7 : 25 can be written as $\left(\dfrac{7}{25}\right)100\%$ which is 28%

Here is a general rule for expressing ratios as percents.

> To change a ratio to a percent, write the ratio in fractional form and multiply by 100%.

Example 2. Write each ratio as a percent.

a) 2 : 5 b) 0.1 : 4 c) 19 : 6

Solution. Write each ratio in fractional form.

a) $\dfrac{2}{5} = \left(\dfrac{2}{5}\right)100\%$ b) $\dfrac{0.1}{4} = \left(\dfrac{0.1}{4}\right)100\%$ c) $\dfrac{19}{6} = \left(\dfrac{19}{6}\right)100\%$

$= 40\%$ $= 2.5\%$ $= \dfrac{950}{3}\%$

$\doteq 317\%$

Similarly, decimals can be written as percents by multiplying by 100%.

> To change a decimal to a percent, multiply the decimal by 100%.

Example 3. Express each decimal as a percent.

      a) 0.64   b) 0.018   c) 0.0073   d) 2.15

Solution.   a) $0.64 = (0.64)100\%$
                    $= 64\%$

         b) $0.018 = (0.018)100\%$
                     $= 1.8\%$

         c) $0.0073 = (0.0073)100\%$
                      $= 0.73\%$

         d) $2.15 = (2.15)100\%$
                    $= 215\%$

Conversely, to express a percent as a decimal, divide by 100%.

> To change a percent to a decimal, divide the percent by 100%.

Example 4. Express each percent as a decimal.

      a) 27%   b) 7.5%   c) 156%   d) 0.9%

Solution.   a) $27\% = \dfrac{27\%}{100\%}$ b) $7.5\% = \dfrac{7.5\%}{100\%}$

                $= 0.27$ $= 0.075$

         c) $156\% = \dfrac{156\%}{100\%}$ d) $0.9\% = \dfrac{0.9\%}{100\%}$

                $= 1.56$ $= 0.009$

Example 5. Express each percent as a fraction in lowest terms.

      a) 18%   b) 175%   c) 12.5%   d) 0.4%

Solution.   a) $18\% = \dfrac{18}{100}$ b) $175\% = \dfrac{175}{100}$

                  $= \dfrac{9}{50}$ $= \dfrac{7}{4}$

         c) $12.5\% = \dfrac{12.5}{100}$ d) $0.4\% = \dfrac{0.4}{100}$

                  $= \dfrac{125}{1000}$ $= \dfrac{4}{1000}$

                  $= \dfrac{1}{8}$ $= \dfrac{1}{250}$

EXERCISES 7-5

Ⓐ

1. Write each ratio as a percent.
   a) 7 : 100   b) 18.5 : 100   c) 57 : 100   d) 0.8 : 100
   e) 365 : 100   f) 36.5 : 100   g) 540 : 100   h) 1875 : 100

2. Express each decimal as a percent.
   a) 0.38   b) 0.57   c) 0.81   d) 0.06   e) 0.035
   f) 0.072   g) 0.091   h) 0.007   i) 0.0086   j) 0.0051
   k) 0.0007   l) 3.6   m) 3.06   n) 3.006   o) 30.6

3. Express each percent as a decimal.
   a) 24%   b) 39%   c) 57.4%   d) 3%   e) 5.8%
   f) 11.5%   g) 1.6%   h) 0.9%   i) 137%   j) 264%
   k) 375%   l) 375.8%   m) 0.1%   n) 2.03%   o) 0.25%

Ⓑ

4. Write each ratio as a percent.
   a) 1 : 4   b) 5 : 8   c) 7 : 10   d) 11 : 20   e) 5 : 6
   f) 3 : 5   g) 8 : 5   h) 2 : 3   i) 13 : 10   j) 31 : 40
   k) 20 : 3   l) 19 : 50   m) 1 : 25   n) 7 : 40   o) 11 : 200

5. Estimate what percent of each figure is colored.
   a)   b)   c)   d)

    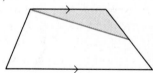

6. Write as a percent.
   a) one-half   b) three-quarters   c) seven-eighths
   d) one-hundredth   e) one-thousandth   f) two-thirds

7. Express each percent as a fraction in lowest terms.
   a) 26%   b) 35%   c) 64%   d) 75%
   e) 62.5%   f) 125%   g) $81\frac{1}{3}\%$ h) $16\frac{2}{3}\%$
   i) 185%   j) 360%   k) 0.8%   l) 0.125%

8. What percent of the mass of a 16 K gold ring is gold?

9. The weights of a person on Mars and on the Earth are in the ratio 2 : 5. What percent of the weight on Mars is a person's weight on Earth?

Ⓒ

10. A fertilizer contains nitrogen, phosphorus, and potassium in the ratio 1 : 2 : 4 by mass. If 58% of the mass consists of materials other than these nutrients, what percent of the total mass of the fertilizer is phosphorus?

Construct a Table

An aircraft flies from city A to city B against the wind at an average speed of 600 km/h. On the return trip, the average speed is 1000 km/h. What is the average speed for the round trip?

Understand the problem
- What does average speed mean?
- How can it be calculated?
- Is the average speed for the return trip, the average of 600 km/h and 1000 km/h?

Think of a strategy
- Construct a table showing the time, the distance, and the average speed for each journey.

Carry out the strategy
- Write the given information in the table.

	Distance	Time	Speed
A → B			600 km/h
B → A			1000 km/h

- To complete the table, we let d represent the distance between A and B in kilometres.
- Then we use the equation:
  time = distance ÷ speed
  to calculate the times for the trips A to B and B to A. These expressions are entered in the table.

	Distance	Time	Speed
A → B	d km	$\dfrac{d}{600}$ h	600 km/h
B → A	d km	$\dfrac{d}{1000}$ h	1000 km/h

- To calculate the average speed we use the equation:
  Average speed = total distance ÷ total time

$$= \frac{2d}{\dfrac{d}{600} + \dfrac{d}{1000}}$$

Multiply numerator and denominator by 3000.
Then divide numerator and denominator by d.

$$= \frac{6000}{5 + 3}$$

$$= 750$$

- The average speed for the round trip is 750 km/h.

Look back

- Is the average speed for the round trip somewhere between 600 km/h and 1000 km/h?
- Should the average speed for the round trip be closer to 600 km/h or to 1000 km/h?
- Does 750 km/h seem to be a reasonable answer?

Solve each problem

1. A boat has an average speed of 50 km/h on the first lap of a two-lap race. On the second lap it averages only 30 km/h. What is its average speed for the whole race?

2. If Mr. Swan drives at an average speed of 100 km/h he arrives at work at 09:00. If he leaves home at the same time but averages 80 km/h, he arrives at 09:06. How far does he live from work?

3. A car's cooling system contains a 25% solution of antifreeze. Half the system is drained and then topped up with pure antifreeze. What is the strength of the antifreeze in the system now?

4. Dianne rode her dirt bike up a hill and down the same distance on the other side. She rode down the hill at 4 times the speed she rode up the hill. If the entire trip took 20 min, how many minutes did it take her to ride down the hill?

5. Marie drove her 18 wheeler 762 mi from Bangor to Philadelphia in 15.2 h. Part of the trip she drove in a snow storm at an average speed of 35 mph. The rest of the time she drove at 60 mph. How far did she drive in the storm?

6. Two people, 60 km apart, start cycling towards each other at the same time. One person cycles at 18 km/h. How fast must the other person cycle if the people meet in 1.5 h?

7. Car A and car B leave Syracuse on the same road, 1 h apart. Car A leaves first and travels at a steady 50 mph. How fast must car B travel to overtake car A in 4 h?

MATHEMATICS AROUND US

Election to the Baseball Hall of Fame

To be elected to the Baseball Hall of Fame a player must receive at least 75% of the votes cast by sportswriters who have had 10 or more years of experience. Each sportswriter can vote for up to 10 players.

QUESTIONS

1. In 1982 Henry Aaron was elected to the Hall of Fame with the highest percent of votes since 1936, the year the Hall of Fame started. He received 406 votes out of a total of 415 ballots.
   a) What percent of the votes did Henry Aaron receive?
   b) Frank Robinson, with 370 votes, was also elected in 1982. What percent of the votes did Frank Robinson receive?
   c) What was the minimum number of votes needed for election in 1982?

2. In 1986 there were 425 ballots. Willie McCovey received 81.4% of the votes. Billy Williams just missed being elected, with 74.1% of the votes.
   a) How many votes did each player receive?
   b) How many more votes did Billy Williams need to be elected?

3. Three players were elected to the Hall of Fame in 1936: Ty Cobb with 98.2%; and Babe Ruth and Honus Wagner, each with 95.1%. Ty Cobb received 222 votes.
   a) How many ballots were cast that year?
   b) How many votes did Babe Ruth and Honus Wagner receive?

7-6 APPLICATIONS OF PERCENT

Sita wants to buy a car. On the windshield of a car she sees a price of $8750 with an additional sign, "15% off sticker price". Sita calculates what the car will cost.

The reduction in price is 15%.

The sale price is 100% − 15%, or 85% of the sticker price of $8750.

$$85\% \text{ of } \$8750 = \frac{85}{100}(\$8750)$$
$$= \$7437.50$$

Sita knows that she will have to pay state sales tax which is currently 7%. The cost will be $7437.50 plus 7% of $7437.50.

$$\text{Total cost} = 107\% \text{ of } \$7437.50$$
$$= 1.07(\$7437.50)$$
$$= \$7958.13$$

Sita will have to pay $7958.13 for the car.

Example 1. a) Calculate 16% of 85.
        b) 18% of a number is 54. What is the number?
        c) What percent of 65 is 0.13?

Solution. a) $16\% \text{ of } 85 = \dfrac{16}{100}(85)$
                              $= 13.6$

       b) 18% of a number is 54.

          1% of the number is $\dfrac{54}{18}$.

          100% of the number is $\dfrac{54}{18}(100)$ or 300.

       c) To find what percent of 65 is 0.13, express 0.13 as a fraction of 65, that is, $\dfrac{0.13}{65}$.

          Multiply the fraction by 100%.

          $\left(\dfrac{0.13}{65}\right)100\% = 0.2\%$

          0.13 is 0.2% of 65.

Example 2. Assume that the gas company gets the increase that it wants. A family's natural-gas bill last year was approximately $860. Calculate the gas bill for this year if the same amount of gas is used.

Gas company wants 6% increase in rates

Solution This year's gas bill will be 106% of last year's bill.

106% of 860 = 1.06(860)
= 911.60

This year's gas bill will be about $910.

Example 3. Which game has the greater percent reduction?

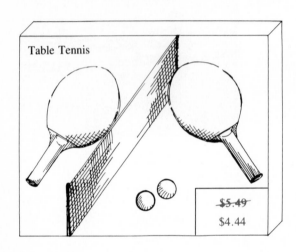

Table Tennis

~~$5.49~~

$4.44

Darts

~~$4.89~~

$3.98

Solution. To find the percent reduction, express the reduction as a percent of the original price.

Reduction in price of table-tennis set = $5.49 − $4.44
= $1.05

$$\text{Percent reduction of table-tennis set} = \left(\frac{1.05}{5.49}\right)100\%$$

$$\doteq 19.1\%$$

Reduction in price of dart game = $4.89 − $3.98
= $0.91

$$\text{Percent reduction of dart game} = \left(\frac{0.91}{4.89}\right)100\%$$

$$\doteq 18.6\%$$

The table-tennis set has the greater percent reduction.

Example 4. What was the original price of this radio?

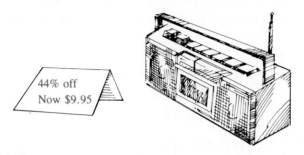

44% off
Now $9.95

Solution.   The reduction in price is 44%.
So, $9.95 must represent 100% − 44%, or 56% of the original price.

1% of the original price is $\dfrac{\$9.95}{56}$.

100%, the original price, is $\dfrac{\$9.95}{56}(100)$ or about $17.77.

The radio was originally $17.77.

Interest is the money paid for the use of money. If you have a savings account, the bank pays you interest for the use of your savings. If you borrow money from the bank, it charges you interest for the use of its money. The interest rate is always expressed as a percent.

Tara received $150 from her grandparents as a birthday present. She deposited it into her daily-interest savings account, which pays interest at a rate of 8% per annum.
The interest is calculated daily and is added to the account at the end of each month. How much interest has the money earned in 30 days?
The yearly interest is 8% of $150, or 0.08(150).

The daily interest is $\dfrac{1}{365}$ of this amount, or $\dfrac{1}{365}(0.08)(150)$.

After 30 days, the interest is $\dfrac{30}{365}(0.08)(150)$ or approximately 0.99.

After 30 days, $150 has earned $0.99 interest.

When interest is calculated in this way, it is called *simple interest*. Simple interest can be calculated using this formula.

$I = Prt$

I is the interest in dollars.
P is the principal, the money saved or borrowed.
r is the annual interest rate expressed as a decimal.
t is the time in years for which the money is saved or borrowed.

Example 5. Find the simple interest.
      a) On a $324 credit-card bill for 28 days at 21% per annum
      b) $6500 in a daily-interest savings account for 25 days at $11\frac{1}{2}$% per annum

Solution.   a) Use the formula.
The rate is 21% or 0.21. The time is 28 days or $\dfrac{28}{365}$ years.

$$I = Prt$$

$$= 324(0.21)\left(\frac{28}{365}\right) \qquad \text{Use a calculator.}$$

Key in: ③ ② ④ ✕ · ② ① ✕ ② ⑧ ÷ ③ ⑥ ⑤
to display 5.2195068
The interest is $5.22.

b) The rate is $11\frac{1}{2}$% or 0.115. The time is 25 days or $\dfrac{25}{365}$ years.

$$I = Prt$$

$$= 6500(0.115)\left(\frac{25}{365}\right)$$

$$\doteq 51.20$$

The interest is $51.20.

EXERCISES 7-6

Ⓐ

1. Find.
  a) 25% of 40   b) 20% of 40   c) 0.6% of 150   d) 5% of 35
  e) 109% of 75   f) 4% of 150   g) 0.7% of 95   h) 65% of 18

2. Determine the number in each statement.
  a) 50% of a number is 10.   b) 20% of a number is 3.
  c) 40% of a number is 10.   d) 75% of a number is 30.
  e) 60% of a number is 42.   f) 15% of a number is 15.
  g) $66\frac{2}{3}$% of a number is 18.   h) 10% of a number is 8.
  i) 104% of a number is 26.   j) 130% of a number is 91.

3. a) What percent of 80 is 16?   b) What percent of 135 is 15?
  c) What percent of 75 is 125?   d) What percent of 50 is 45?
  e) What percent of 144 is 18?   f) What percent of 81 is 270?
  g) What percent of 1900 is 1.9?   h) What percent of 6000 is 3?

Ⓑ

4. Find the simple interest.
  a) On $1200 at 16% per annum for 3 months
  b) On $8500 at 18% per annum for 6 months
  c) On $3000 at 15% per annum for 30 days

5. A ten-speed bicycle regularly sells for $227.50. What will it cost during a ''15% off'' sale?

6. Skis are being sold at a discount of 45%. What will be the cost of a pair of skis that regularly sells for $180?

7. Food costs for the coming year are estimated to rise by 11.7%. What will be the coming year's food costs for a family who spent $8400 last year?

8. This year, AKA Ltd. hopes that its sales income will be 160% of last year's sales of $2 500 000. If the company succeeds, what will its sales income be?

9. In April, the unemployment figure was 800 000 people. In May, there was a modest 0.16% decrease. How many people apparently found work in May?

10. In all of William Shakespeare's works, he used 31 534 different words. Of these, 14 356 were used only once. What percent of the words did he use only once?

11. During a ''20% off'' sale, a clock radio is priced at $29.95. What is its regular price?

12. A calculator is priced at $9.98 during a ''25% off'' sale. What is its regular price?

13. Express each reduction as a percent, to 1 decimal place, of the original price.
   a) A TV set regularly priced at $540 is selling for $499
   b) An overcoat regularly priced at $195 is selling for $156

14. Sterling silver is an alloy of silver and copper in the ratio 37 : 3.
   a) What percent of a sterling silver bracelet is pure silver?
   b) If the bracelet has a mass of 30 g, how much silver does it contain?

15. Long distance telephone rates are reduced by 35% between 6 P.M. and 11 P.M., and by 60% between 11 P.M. and 8 A.M.
   a) A 5 min call from San Antonio to Seattle at 10 A.M. cost $1.30. Calculate the cost of a 5 min call at: i) 8 P.M.   ii) 7 A.M.
   b) A 5 min call from Detroit to Los Angeles at 9 P.M. costs $0.85. Calculate the cost of a 5 min call at: i) noon   ii) 2 A.M.

16. a) In the news item, what percent, to 1 decimal place, of the cars stopped yesterday had defective equipment?
   b) Estimate the number of cars found with defective equipment since the campaign began. What assumption are you making?

Police checks nab 187
Police spot-check crews stopped 860 vehicles yesterday and found 187 with defective equipment, in the holiday safety traffic blitz across the city.

A total of 28 759 cars and trucks have been stopped for safety checks since the campaign began.

17. A pair of skis is priced at $185. Find the cost:
   a) when a 7% sales tax is added   b) with a 15% discount and a 7% sales tax.

Review Exercises

1. In a bracelet of 18 K gold, the ratio of gold to copper is 18 : 6.
   a) Write this ratio in lowest terms.
   b) Find the mass of gold in a bracelet with a mass of 72 g.

2. State which is the greater ratio.
   a) $\dfrac{7}{9}$ or $\dfrac{10}{13}$ b) 5 : 6 or 29 : 34   c) 8 : 17 or 11 : 25   d) 21 : 8 or 24 : 9

3. Find the value of each letter.
   a) $\dfrac{7}{10} = \dfrac{m}{15}$ b) $\dfrac{n}{4} = \dfrac{13}{8}$ c) $\dfrac{39}{a} = \dfrac{13}{3}$ d) $\dfrac{17}{21} = \dfrac{51}{b}$

4. Bill contributes $3.50 and Laura $6.50 for the purchase of a $10 lottery ticket. It is drawn for a prize of $125 000. How should the money be divided?

5. The partners in a business agree to share the profits in the ratio 3 : 8 : 4. How much does each partner receive from a total profit of $45 000?

6. The shadow of a tree is 26.5 m long when that of a vertical metre rule is 58 cm long. How high is the tree?

7. On a map, two towns are 85 mm apart. If the scale of the map is 1 : 1 500 000, what is the actual distance between the towns?

8. The length of Lake Tahoe at the California/Nevada border is 20 mi. What will this distance be on a map drawn to a scale of 1 : 200 000?

9. A person's heart beats 13 times in 10 s.
   a) How many times does it beat in 1 h?
   b) How long does it take to beat: i) 1000 times   ii) 1 000 000 times?

10. A car's rate of fuel consumption is 27 miles per gallon.
    a) How much fuel is needed to travel 350 mi?
    b) If the car's tank holds a maximum of 15 gal of fuel, will one tankful be enough to travel 430 mi from Corner Brook to St. John's in Newfoundland?

11. A person's rate of pay increases from $5.00/h to $7.00/h. What is the percent increase?

12. What is the sale price of a $165 bicycle selling at a 15% discount?

13. The price of oil is $150/m³ and the price is raised 10% every year. What will be its price at the end of three years?

14. Find the simple interest on each amount.
    a) A $215 credit-card bill for 1 month at 18% per annum
    b) $150 in a daily-interest savings account for 20 days at $12\frac{1}{4}$% per annum

8 Polynomials and Rational Expressions

How many tennis rackets must be produced to make a given profit from their sale? (See Section 8-2, *Example 6.*)

8-1 SIMPLIFYING POLYNOMIALS

The simplest algebraic expression is a term. Recall that a term is either a number, called a constant term, or the product of a number (called a coefficient) and one or more variables.

A *polynomial* is the general name for one term or the sum or difference of two or more terms. The variables in the terms have positive integral exponents.

A polynomial with one term is called a *monomial*.

For example, 2, $-3y^2$, $\frac{3}{4}x^2y^3$ are monomials.

A polynomial with two terms is called a *binomial*.

For example, $3x + 7$, $2y^2 - y$, $\frac{1}{2}z^3 - 4zy$ are binomials.

A polynomial with three terms is called a *trinomial*.

For example, $4y^5 - \frac{3}{5}x^2y + y$, $-2 - 6x + 5y$ are trinomials.

These expressions are *not* polynomials.

$$5 + \frac{2}{x}, \sqrt{x} + 3, 3a^{-3} + 2a^2 - 1$$

Can you explain why?

In a polynomial, terms that have the same variable raised to the same exponent are like terms. For example, x, $-x$, and $7x$ are like terms but $7x$ and $7x^2$ are unlike terms. Also, $3x^2y$ and $-9x^2y$ are like terms but the terms xy, x^2y, and xy^2 are unlike terms.

The following example shows how a polynomial can be simplified by combining like terms.

Example 1. Simplify. $5x + 3y - 4x + 9y$

Solution.   Combine like terms.
$$5x + 3y - 4x + 9y = 5x - 4x + 3y + 9y$$
$$= x + 12y$$

When the terms of a polynomial are arranged in order from the highest to the lowest powers of the variable, the polynomial is in *descending powers* of the variable. These polynomials are in descending powers.

$x^3 - 3x^2 + 4x - 5$; $4x^2 - 9$; $5x^4 - 2x^2 + 11$

When the terms of a polynomial are arranged from the lowest to the highest powers of the variable, the polynomial is in *ascending powers* of the variable.

Example 2. Simplify and write in descending powers of y.
$$3y - 2y^3 + 5y - 7 + y^2 + y^3$$

Solution.   Combine like terms.

$$3y - 2y^3 + 5y - 7 + y^2 + y^3 = 3y + 5y - 2y^3 + y^3 - 7 + y^2$$
$$= 8y - y^3 - 7 + y^2$$
$$= -y^3 + y^2 + 8y - 7$$

The term with the greatest exponent, or exponent sum, determines the *degree* of the polynomial.

$x + y - 3$ is a first-degree polynomial.

$xy + 4x$ is a second-degree polynomial, since the term xy has the greatest exponent sum, 2.

$x^2 + 3x^3 + 2x - 7$ is a third-degree polynomial.

$x^4 + 2y^3x^2 - 5$ is a fifth-degree polynomial, since the term $2y^3x^2$ has the greatest exponent sum, 5.

The following example shows how we arrange the terms of a polynomial in descending powers before we identify its degree.

Example 3.   Simplify each polynomial and state its degree.
a) $-3x^2 + x^3 - 2x + 7 + 5x^2 + 2x^3 - 8x + 3$
b) $7x^4 + 2y^2 - 5x^4 + 3xy^4 + 5x^3y - 6y^2 + 8$

Solution.   a) $-3x^2 + x^3 - 2x + 7 + 5x^2 + 2x^3 - 8x + 3$
$$= -3x^2 + 5x^2 + x^3 + 2x^3 - 2x - 8x + 7 + 3$$
$$= 2x^2 + 3x^3 - 10x + 10$$
$$= 3x^3 + 2x^2 - 10x + 10$$
It is a third-degree polynomial.

b) $7x^4 + 2y^2 - 5x^4 + 3xy^4 + 5x^3y - 6y^2 + 8$
$$= 7x^4 - 5x^4 + 2y^2 - 6y^2 + 3xy^4 + 5x^3y + 8$$
$$= 2x^4 - 4y^2 + 3xy^4 + 5x^3y + 8$$
$$= 3xy^4 + 5x^3y + 2x^4 - 4y^2 + 8$$
It is a fifth-degree polynomial.

EXERCISES 8-1

Ⓐ

1. State the coefficient in each term.
   a) $14x$ b) $7y^2$ c) a d) $-b^2$ e) $-4c^3$

2. State the variable in each term.
   a) $5t$ b) $3x^2$ c) $2w^2$ d) $6z^5$ e) 6

3. State whether the terms are like or unlike.
   a) $2a, 3a$ b) $5x, x$ c) $4m, n$ d) $9c, -6c$
   e) $7x^2, 3x^2, -x^2$ f) $8a^2, 8a$ g) $-2a^2, -4b^2$ h) $4t^3, 2t^3, 3t$
   i) $2.3b, 6.9b$ j) $5, \pi, \sqrt{2}$ k) $\dfrac{3}{4}x, -\dfrac{2}{3}x, \dfrac{1}{2}x$ l) $\sqrt{2}n, \dfrac{3}{2}n$

4. State the like terms.
   a) $5a$, $3b$, $5c$, a^2, $-a$, $3d$, $3e$
   b) $4x$, $3y^2$, $4z$, $2y$, y^2, $4w$
   c) $9g$, $6h$, $9g^2$, $\frac{1}{9}g$, $\frac{1}{6}h^2$, g^2
   d) 16, d^2, d, f, -8, $0.5d$, $7d^3$
   e) $3q^3$, $17q^2$, $-3t^3$, $6q$, $3t^2$, $-15q^2$

5. Simplify.
   a) $3m + 11m$
   b) $-5k + 3k$
   c) $-2x + 7x$
   d) $2n - 6n + n$
   e) $-3a + 4a - 5a$
   f) $-2x^2 + 9x^2 - x^2$
   g) $-y^3 - 5y^3 + 2y^3$
   h) $-3c - 5c$
   i) $2.7m - 6.9m - 5.2m$
   j) $\frac{1}{2}t^2 - t^2 + \frac{1}{2}t^2$
   k) $\frac{3}{4}x + \frac{2}{3}x + \frac{1}{2}x$
   l) $-\frac{1}{3}a + \frac{5}{6}a + \frac{2}{9}a$

6. Simplify.
   a) $3x - 10y + 4y - 7x$
   b) $-2a - 7b + 5a + 11b$
   c) $-4p + 13q - 9q + 8p$
   d) $-5d - 6c - c + 10d$
   e) $m + 11n - 12n - 7m$
   f) $-7h + 12g - 13h + 2g$
   g) $-3e - 7f + 14e - 3f$
   h) $-y - 15x + 13x - 18y$

7. Simplify.
   a) $3t + 5t$
   b) $4a - 3a + 2ab$
   c) $-14m + 5mn - m$
   d) $-5s^2 + s^3 + 9s^2$
   e) $12k^3 - 15k^3 + 2k^3$
   f) $-5c^4 - 3c^2 + 7c^4$
   g) $\frac{1}{2}x + \frac{1}{3}x$
   h) $0.5r + 0.7r$
   i) $\frac{3}{4}a^2 - \frac{2}{5}a^2$
   j) $8.2h - 11.2h$
   k) $\frac{3}{2}c^2 - \frac{11}{3}c^2$
   l) $1.3n - 1.7n + 0.8n$

(B)

8. Simplify.
   a) $(+6x) - (+2x)$
   b) $(+3a) - (+7a)$
   c) $(+5p) - (-3p)$
   d) $(-n^2) - (+5n^2)$
   e) $(-7x^3) - (-2x^3)$
   f) $(-y) - (-8y)$
   g) $(+4.5c) - (+5.3c)$
   h) $(+2.9x) - (+9.7x)$
   i) $(+2.5b^2) - (-3.5b^2)$
   j) $\left(+\frac{1}{3}a\right) - \left(-\frac{1}{2}a\right)$
   k) $\left(\frac{1}{4}m\right) - \left(+\frac{3}{4}m\right)$
   l) $\left(+\frac{2}{5}y^2\right) - \left(+\frac{2}{5}y^2\right)$

9. Simplify.
   a) $0.5a + 0.7a - 0.2a$
   b) $-0.6m - 0.9m + m$
   c) $\frac{2}{3}x - \frac{1}{6}x + \frac{1}{4}x$
   d) $\frac{5}{3}y + \frac{1}{4}y - \frac{3}{2}y$
   e) $12c^2 - c^2 - 9c^2$
   f) $24b^2 - 14b^2 + 3b^2$
   g) $-7x^3 - 5x^3 - 4x^3$
   h) $3x^2y - 5x^2y + 7x^2y$
   i) $-3abc + 5bca + bac$
   j) $3mnp - 7mpn + 4npm - 11pmn$
   k) $5xyz + 6yzx - zyx + 2zxy$
   l) $-9fgh + 4gfh - 3fhg - 8hfg$

10. Simplify.
    a) $3x - 5y + 2x - 7x - 6y + 3z$
    b) $-2b - 5a + 3b - 7c + 8a - c$
    c) $8g + 7f + 4g - 3e - 11f - 7e$
    d) $-5m - 6x + 10p + x - 12p + 11m$
    e) $11e - d - 8e + 7f - 4d - 9f$
    f) $4 - 7y + 8 - 3x - 9 + 10y - 11x$
    g) $-1 + 3a - 12b + 8 - 3b + 12a$
    h) $13x + 10 - 2y - 4x + 8y - 15$

11. Simplify.
    a) $8x + 2x - 3x$ b) $-5a - a - 2a$ c) $-3p^2 + p^2 + 5p^2$
    d) $-2y^2 - 3y + y$ e) $5m^2 - 2m - 3m$ f) $7x^3 + 5x^3 - 4x^2$
    g) $-3a^2 + 8a^2 + a^2$ h) $-x^2 - 2x - 3x^2$ i) $2.5c - 3.2c^2 + 1.7c$

12. Simplify.
    a) $32m^2 - 15m - 7m$ b) $-65x^2 + 37x - 27x$
    c) $38c^2 + 45c - 20c$ d) $-18n - 24n + 20n^2$
    e) $6.3x^2 - 9.7x^2 + 2.5x^2$ f) $-4.7x^3 - 3.9x^3 + 11.7x^2$
    g) $-\frac{1}{4}c + \frac{1}{3}c - \frac{1}{2}c$ h) $\frac{1}{5}a^2 - \frac{1}{2}a - \frac{1}{3}a$

13. Simplify.
    a) $14n^2 + 7n - 8n^2$ b) $3x^3 - 5x^2 + 8x^2$ c) $5.4y^2 - 1.8y + 1.9y^2$
    d) $-6a^2 + 5a^2 - 3a$ e) $-\frac{3}{4}c^2 + \frac{2}{3}c + \frac{3}{2}c^2$ f) $\frac{3}{8}m^3 - \frac{3}{4}m^2 + \frac{3}{2}m^3$
    g) $0.7x^2 - 0.8x + 0.5x$ h) $-3y + 7y^2 - 2y^2$ i) $5a^3 - 2a - a^3 + 3a$

14. Simplify each expression and write it in descending powers of the variable. State the degree of each expression.
    a) $3a + 2 + 5a + 7$ b) $2x - 6 + 8x + 4$
    c) $5n + 1 - 9n + 2$ d) $-6c + 3 - c - 5$
    e) $7x - 2 - 3x - 1$ f) $3x^2 - 5x + x^2 - 2x$
    g) $-4a^2 - 3a - a^2 + 2a$ h) $-m - 2 + 3m - 1$

15. Simplify.
    a) $2xy - 3x^2y + 2xy^2 - 3yx + 5xy^2 - 2yx^2$
    b) $4xy^2 - 3xy + 2yx^2 - 4y^2x^2 + 2yx - 4y^2x + 3$
    c) $9y^2a - 2a^2 + a^2y - 7ay + 3a^2y - 8ay^2$
    d) $9w + 4z - 3wz + 2w^2z - 8zw^2 + 2w - 3z$
    e) $5ab - 6a^2b - 3ab + 8a^2b - 4a + 7ab$

16. Simplify.
    a) $3x + 4y - 5xy + 3y + 5yx - 4x$
    b) $9xy^2 + 6xy - 8xy^2 - 8x^2y + 6x^2y^2 - 6xy$
    c) $5a^2b + 10ab^2 + 12a^2b^2 + 6ab^2 - 12a^2b - 8a^2b^2 + 7a^2b$
    d) $8x^2y - 6xy^2 - 7yx^2 + 6y^2x - x^2y^2$
    e) $4abc - 5a^2bc + 6abc^2 - 8abc + 7a^2bc + 3abc^2 - 2abc$

THE MATHEMATICAL MIND

The Search for a Polynomial to Generate Prime Numbers

A prime number is any whole number, greater than 1, which is divisible by only itself and 1. Since the discovery of prime numbers, mathematicians have attempted to find a polynomial for generating them.

Leonhard Euler 1707-1783

In 1772, the great Swiss mathematician, Leonhard Euler, devised the polynomial $n^2 - n + 41$ for the generation of primes.

This polynomial does, in fact, produce primes for $n = 1, 2, 3, 4, \ldots, 40$.

If $n = 1$, $n^2 - n + 41 = 1^2 - 1 + 41$, or 41
If $n = 2$, $n^2 - n + 41 = 2^2 - 2 + 41$, or 43
If $n = 3$, $n^2 - n + 41 = 3^2 - 3 + 41$, or 47
If $n = 4$, $n^2 - n + 41 = 4^2 - 4 + 41$, or 53
However, if $n = 41$, $n^2 - n + 41 = 41^2 - 41 + 41$, or 1681. This number is divisible by 41 and therefore is not a prime number.

In 1879, E.B. Escott devised the polynomial $n^2 - 79n + 1601$.

1. Test this polynomial for several values of n to see if the results are prime numbers.

2. a) Substitute 80 for n, and show that the result is *not* a prime number.
   b) Find another value of n which gives a result that is not a prime number.

3. Find a value for n for which the following polynomials do *not* produce a prime number.
   a) $n^2 + n - 1$ b) $n^2 - n + 17$ c) $n^2 - n + 41, n \neq 41$

At the present time, there is no known polynomial that produces *only* prime numbers. There is also no known polynomial that will produce all the prime numbers.

 **COMPUTER POWER**

Polynomials to Generate Prime Numbers

Until the arrival of the computer, mathematicians used advanced mathematical techniques together with lengthy computation in the search for a polynomial that would generate only prime numbers. Today, the approach to this problem is made much easier by the use of computers. The following program can be used to determine the values up to any positive integer N for which the polynomial $AN^2 + BN + C$ generates only prime numbers.

```
100 REM *** POLYNOMIALS AND PRIMES ***
110 PRINT  "ENTER THE VALUES OF A, B, AND C"
120 INPUT  "SEPARATED BY COMMAS:  ";A,B,C
130 PRINT  "UP TO WHAT VALUE OF N DO YOU WISH"
140 INPUT  "TO CHECK?  ";M
150 FOR N=1 TO M
160     P=A*N*N+B*N+C
170     PRINT N,P
180     R=INT(SQR(P))
190     FOR D=2 TO R
200         IF P/D=INT(P/D) THEN GO TO 240
210     NEXT D
220 NEXT N
230 PRINT: "EVERY VALUE FOR N=1 TO ";M;" IS PRIME."
240 PRINT "WHEN N = ";N;" THE VALUE IS DIVISIBLE
    BY ";D
260 END
```

1. Use the program to test whether the polynomial $n^2 + n + 17$ generates prime numbers for all positive integers up to 100.

2. Find a value of n for which each of the following polynomials does *not* produce a prime number.
   a) $n^2 + n + 1$
   b) $n^2 - n + 17$
   c) $n^2 - n + 41$
   d) $n^2 - 79n + 1601$

3. Find the smallest possible integer n for which the polynomial $\dfrac{n^2 + 2n + 653}{16}$ yields a composite integer.

4. Prove that 2 is the greatest integral value of n for which $n^2 - 1$ is a prime number.

8-2 ADDING AND SUBTRACTING POLYNOMIALS

In one factory, the cost of making a model of tennis racket is given by this formula.

$C = 6n + 2000$

C represents the cost in dollars.

n represents the number of rackets made.

The income from the sale of these rackets is given by this formula.

$I = 15n$

The profit from selling these rackets can be found by subtracting the cost from the income.

Profit = Income − Cost

Example 1. Find the profit from the production and sale of 500 rackets.

Solution. The income from the sale of 500 rackets is obtained by substituting $n = 500$ into this formula.

$I = 15n$
$ = 15(500)$
$ = 7500$

The income is $7500.

The cost of making 500 rackets is obtained by substituting $n = 500$ into this formula.

$C = 6n + 2000$
$ = 6(500) + 2000$
$ = 3000 + 2000$
$ = 5000$

The cost is $5000.

Hence, the profit is $7500 − $5000, or $2500.

If we want to know the profit from the sale of different numbers of rackets, it is easier to subtract the polynomials first and then substitute. To do this, we need to learn how to subtract polynomials.

The addition of polynomials resembles the addition of numbers.

Arithmetic	Algebra
$\begin{array}{r} 7258 \\ +2431 \\ \hline 9689 \end{array}$ $\begin{array}{l} 7(10^3) + 2(10^2) + 5(10) + 8 \\ 2(10^3) + 4(10^2) + 3(10) + 1 \\ \hline 9(10^3) + 6(10^2) + 8(10) + 9 \end{array}$	$\begin{array}{l} 7x^3 + 2x^2 + 5x + 8 \\ +2x^3 + 4x^2 + 3x + 1 \\ \hline 9x^3 + 6x^2 + 8x + 9 \end{array}$

Polynomials, like numbers, can also be added horizontally. We use the commutative, associative, and distributive properties to combine like terms.

Example 2. Simplify.
 a) $(3n + 5) + (2n + 3)$ b) $(-2x^2 + 6x - 7) + (3x^2 - x - 2)$

Solution. a) $(3n + 5) + (2n + 3) = 3n + 5 + 2n + 3$
$$= 3n + 2n + 5 + 3 \quad \text{grouping like terms}$$
$$= 5n + 8$$
 b) $(-2x^2 + 6x - 7) + (3x^2 - x - 2)$
$$= -2x^2 + 6x - 7 + 3x^2 - x - 2$$
$$= -2x^2 + 3x^2 + 6x - x - 7 - 2 \quad \text{grouping like terms}$$
$$= x^2 + 5x - 9$$

Recall that to subtract an integer, we add its opposite (sometimes called its *additive inverse*). The same rule applies to polynomials. To subtract a polynomial, add its *additive inverse*.

To find the additive inverse of a polynomial, multiply it by -1.

Example 3. Find the additive inverse of each polynomial.
 a) $7x - 4$ b) $-x^2 + 2x - 6$

Solution. a) $(-1)(7x - 4) = -7x + 4$
 The additive inverse of $7x - 4$ is $-7x + 4$.
 b) $(-1)(-x^2 + 2x - 6) = x^2 - 2x + 6$
 The additive inverse of $-x^2 + 2x - 6$ is $x^2 - 2x + 6$.

Example 4. Simplify.
 a) $(2x + 7) - (6x - 2)$ b) $(8 - n + n^2) - (-2 + 3n - n^2)$

Solution. Add the additive inverse.
 a) $(2x + 7) - (6x - 2) = 2x + 7 + (-1)(6x - 2)$
$$= 2x + 7 - 6x + 2$$
$$= 2x - 6x + 7 + 2$$
$$= -4x + 9$$
 b) $(8 - n + n^2) - (-2 + 3n - n^2)$
$$= 8 - n + n^2 + (-1)(-2 + 3n - n^2)$$
$$= 8 - n + n^2 + 2 - 3n + n^2$$
$$= 8 + 2 - n - 3n + n^2 + n^2$$
$$= 10 - 4n + 2n^2$$

Example 5. Simplify.
 a) $(2a - 3) - (a^2 - 5a) + (4 - a)$
 b) $3a^2b - (a - b^2) + (a + 8) - (a - 2b^2 + a^2)$

Solution. a) $(2a - 3) - (a^2 - 5a) + (4 - a)$
$= 2a - 3 - a^2 + 5a + 4 - a$
$= -a^2 + 2a + 5a - a - 3 + 4$
$= -a^2 + 6a + 1$

b) $3a^2b - (a - b^2) + (a + 8) - (a - 2b^2 + a^2)$
$= 3a^2b - a + b^2 + a + 8 - a + 2b^2 - a^2$
$= 3a^2b - a + 3b^2 - a^2 + 8$

Consider the problem posed at the beginning of the chapter.

Example 6. a) Find a formula for the profit P dollars on the sale of n tennis rackets. Use the information on page 312.
b) Use the formula to calculate the profit from the production and sale of:
   i)   500 rackets   ii)   1500 rackets.
c) If all the rackets that are produced are sold, how many rackets must be sold to earn a profit of $34 000?
d) How many rackets must be produced and sold for the company to "break even"?

Solution. a) The cost C of making n tennis rackets is given by $C = 6n + 2000$. The income I from the sale of n tennis rackets is given by $I = 15n$. The profit P is the difference between the income I and the cost C. That is, $P = I - C$
$$= 15n - (6n + 2000)$$
$$= 15n - 6n - 2000$$
$$= 9n - 2000$$
The formula $P = 9n - 2000$ gives the profit in dollars on the production and sale of n tennis rackets.

b) i) If 500 rackets are sold, then the profit $P = 9(500) - 2000$
$$= 2500$$
The profit is $2500.

ii) If 1500 rackets are sold, then the profit $P = 9(1500) - 2000$
$$= 11\ 500$$
The profit is $11 500.

c) If $P = 34\ 000$, then $34\ 000 = 9n - 2000$
$$36\ 000 = 9n$$
$$4000 = n$$
4000 rackets must be sold.

d) To break even, we must have a zero profit.
$$0 = 9n - 2000$$
$$2000 = 9n$$
$$n = \frac{2000}{9}$$
$$\doteq 222$$
Since n is greater than 222, the company must sell 223 rackets.

Example 6, part b) illustrates that it is easier to find the profit by substituting into the formula, than using the method of *Example 1*.

EXERCISES 8-2

Ⓐ

1. Simplify.
   a) $(6x + 2) + (3x + 4)$ b) $(5a - 3) + (2a + 7)$
   c) $(8 - 4m) + (-3 - 2m)$ d) $(-x + 4) + (7x - 2)$
   e) $(-1 - 3t) + (4 - 5t)$ f) $(9c - 2) + (-5c - 3)$
   g) $(4n^2 - 3n - 1) + (2n^2 - 5n - 3)$ h) $(3x^2 + 6x - 8) + (-5x^2 - x + 4)$
   i) $(2 - 3c + c^2) + (5 - 4c - 4c^2)$ j) $(8 - 2n - n^2) + (-3 - n + 4n^2)$

2. Write the additive inverse of each polynomial.

   a) $2 - 3x$ b) $5a + 4$ c) $\frac{1}{2}x - 5$

   d) $4n^2 - 3n + 1$ e) $-3 - 2t + t^2$ f) $0.2a^2 + 0.4a - 0.6$

3. Simplify.
   a) $(-2x + 3) - (3x + 2)$
   b) $(4 - 5n) - (-6n + 2)$
   c) $(3a - 5) - (6 - 7a)$
   d) $(1 - 3t) - (-2 - 5t)$
   e) $(n + 13) - (7n + 16)$
   f) $(7x - 25) - (17 + 5x)$
   g) $(-2x - 7) - (-14x - 6)$
   h) $(8a^2 + 2a - 3) - (-6a^2 + 4a + 7)$
   i) $(-6x + 5x^2 + 1) - (4x^2 + 5 - 2x)$

   j) $\left(-\frac{1}{2}k - 3 + k^2\right) - \left(-\frac{3}{2}k + 4\right)$

Ⓑ

4. Simplify.
   a) $(3x - 2) - (x - 1) + (4x - 3)$
   b) $(2a + 3) + (6a - 1) - (a - 5)$
   c) $(7c - 5) - (-c + 3) - (2c - 1)$
   d) $(4x^2 - 3x) - (x^2 + 2x) + (3x^2 - x)$
   e) $(2m^2 - 5) + (3m - 2) - (m^2 + 1)$
   f) $(5t - 4) + (3t^2 - t) - (-2t + t^2)$
   g) $(2 - 3n) - (1 - n) + (5 - 2n)$
   h) $(5 - 2s) - (3 - s) + (7s - 2)$
   i) $(3 - 4x + x^2) - (2x - x^2) + (4 - x + 5x^2)$
   j) $(3n^2 - 6n + 5) - (3n^2 - 2n - 1) + (n^2 + 4n - 3)$

5. Simplify.
   a) $(17x - 25) + (34x + 19) - (23x - 11)$
   b) $(45 - 10x) - (-15 - 25x) - (35x + 10)$
   c) $(25n^2 - 6) - (30n^2 - 2n) + (5n^2 + 3n)$
   d) $(37 - 42t) - (61 + 23t) + (21 - 17t)$
   e) $(16n^2 - 10n - 4) + (3n^2 + 25n - 21) - (n^2 - 15n + 19)$
   f) $(2.5x - 3.7) - (1.4x + 4.2) + (-0.8x - 1.3)$

6. The cost in dollars of producing n records is $1.9n + 20\ 000$. The income in dollars from selling them is $4.4n$.
   a) Write a formula for the profit earned from producing and selling n records.
   b) Calculate the profit from the production and sale of:
      i)   10 000 records   ii)   20 000 records.
   c) If all the records made are sold, how many must be made and sold:
      i) to earn a profit of \$10 000
      ii) to earn a profit of \$20 000
      iii) to break even?

7. Simplify.
   a) $(5x^2 - 3y^2) + (x^2 + 4y^2)$
   b) $(3x^2 + 5xy + 7y^2) - (2x^2 - 4xy + 9y^2)$
   c) $(x^2 + 5x^2y - 7) - (3x^2 - 5x^2y + y^2) - (x^2 - 7y^2)$
   d) $(5x^2 - 5x + 7) + (2y^2 - 3x + 7) - (2x^2 - 2x + 7y)$
   e) $(3x^2 - 5x + 7) - [4 - (2x^2 + 3x) - 2]$
   f) $(7y^2 - 3y + 6) - [(2y^2 + 3) - (y^2 + 6y - 8)]$
   g) $(8x^2y^2 + 3xy - 12) - x^2y^2 - (5xy - 6 - 2x^2y^2)$

8. Simplify.
   a) $(4x^2y - 4xy^2 + 2x) - (x^2y - 4y^2x + y)$
   b) $(a^2 - ba) - (b^2 - ab) + (a^2 + b^2 + 2ab)$
   c) $-(3 - x^2y) - (2 - yx^2) - (-3 + x^2y^2)$
   d) $3z - x^2 - [(2x^2y - z) - (3yx^2 + 4z)]$
   e) $b^2a - a^2b - (ab^2 - ba^2) - (2ab^2 + 2a^2b)$
   f) $-3p^2q + 3pq + [p + q^2 - 3qp - (q^2 - 3qp^2)]$

9. The profit P millions of dollars earned from constructing an office building having x stories is given by this polynomial. $P = 3.5x - (0.5x + 0.1x^2) - 1$
   a) Express P as a polynomial in descending powers of x.
   b) Find the profit earned from constructing an office building with:
      i)   5 stories   ii)   15 stories.

© ——————————————————————————

10. For $y = (8x - 5) - (x - 4) + (3x + 1)$
   a) Find the value of y for each value of x.
      i)   4   ii) -2 iii) 1   iv) 10
   b) Find the value of x when $y = 30$.

11. Arrange each expression in descending powers of x, then evaluate it for $x = -2$.
   a) $7 - (3x^2 + 2x) - (5x + x^2 - 6) - (3x + 3x^2 - 12)$
   b) $(x^2 + x - 6) - 5x - [(6x - 2x^2 + 3) - (4 - x^2)]$

12. Simplify.
   a) $4a^2b - 5(a - b^2) + a(a + 5)$
   b) $x(x + 4) - 4(x - y^2) + 3x^2y$
   c) $m(n^2 - 3) - 3(n^2 - m) + 6m$
   d) $a(a + b^2) - 2(a^2 - b^2) + ab^2$
   e) $2x^2y^2 - 3(x^2 - 2) + y^2(x^2 - 3) + 7$

8-3 MULTIPLYING POLYNOMIALS BY MONOMIALS

On a farm, in one year, the value of an acre of wheat is given by this formula.

$V = 0.05x(140 - x)$, for $x \leq 70$

V represents the value of the crop in dollars.

x represents the number of days after planting the wheat.

To express V as a polynomial, we expand the right side of the equation using the distributive law.

$$V = 0.05x(140 - x)$$
$$= 0.05x(140) - 0.05x(x)$$
$$= 7x - 0.05x^2$$

To find the value of the crop, for example, 60 days after planting, substitute $x = 60$ into the polynomial.

$$V = 7(60) - 0.05(60)^2$$
$$= 240$$

The crop is worth \$240/acre 60 days after planting.

In earlier work, the product of two monomials was evaluated as follows.

Multiply the coefficients.

$$(3x^5)(4x^2) = 12x^7$$

Add the exponents.

Example 1. Simplify.

      a) $(-6b^3)(3b^2)$ b) $(-4x^2)(-5x)(3x^3)$

Solution.   a) $(-6b^3)(3b^2) = (-6)(3)(b^3)(b^2)$
$$= -18b^5$$

           b) $(-4x^2)(-5x)(3x^3) = (-4)(-5)(3)(x^2)(x)(x^3)$
$$= 60x^6$$

To multiply monomials in more than one variable, first multiply the coefficients. Then combine like variables using the exponent laws for multiplication.

Example 2. Simplify.

a) $(x^2y^3)(x^3y^4)$ 　　　　b) $(3p^2q)(2pq^3)$ 　　　　c) $(5w^2y)(4y^2z)$

Solution. 　a) $(x^2y^3)(x^3y^4) = (x^2)(x^3)(y^3)(y^4)$
$$= x^5y^7$$

b) $(3p^2q)(2pq^3) = (3)(2)(p^2)(p)(q)(q^3)$
$$= 6p^3q^4$$

c) $(5w^2y)(4y^2z) = (5)(4)(w^2)(y)(y^2)(z)$
$$= 20w^2y^3z$$

When a polynomial is multiplied by a monomial, the distributive law is used.

Example 3. Expand.

a) $3x(5x - 4)$ 　　　　　　b) $-6x^2(-3 + x + 2x^2)$

Solution. 　a) $3x(5x - 4) = 3x(5x) - 3x(4)$
$$= 15x^2 - 12x$$

b) $-6x^2(-3 + x + 2x^2) = -6x^2(-3) + (-6x^2)(x) + (-6x^2)(2x^2)$
$$= 18x^2 - 6x^3 - 12x^4$$

To multiply a polynomial in more than one variable by a monomial, multiply each term in the polynomial by the monomial.

Example 4. Expand.

a) $3m^2(mn - n^2)$ 　　　　　　b) $-4xy^3(x^2 + xy - y^2)$

Solution. 　a) $3m^2(mn - n^2) = (3m^2)(mn) - (3m^2)(n^2)$
$$= 3m^3n - 3m^2n^2$$

b) $-4xy^3(x^2 + xy - y^2) = (-4xy^3)(x^2) + (-4xy^3)(xy) - (-4xy^3)(y^2)$
$$= -4x^3y^3 - 4x^2y^4 + 4xy^5$$

EXERCISES 8-3

Ⓐ

1. Simplify.

a) $(6n)(5n)$ 　　　　b) $(-2a)(3a)$ 　　　c) $(-5x)^2$ 　　　　d) $(3n)(-6n)$
e) $(-5x^2)(-2x^2)$ 　f) $(3a)(2a)$ 　　　g) $(5x^4)(2x)$ 　　h) $(8y)(-7y)$
i) $(-x)(-5x^3)$ 　　j) $\left(\dfrac{1}{2}n\right)\left(\dfrac{1}{4}n\right)$ 　k) $(2.5m)(1.2m^2)$ 　l) $(0.5x^3)(3x^2)$

2. Simplify.

a) $(12x)^2$ 　　　　　　　b) $(-10a)(17a^2)$ 　　　c) $(-25n^2)(8n^2)$
d) $(-35c^3)(-4c^2)$ 　　e) $(17x^2)(5x^3)$ 　　　　f) $(-28n)(5n^3)$
g) $(3x)(5x)(2x)$ 　　　　h) $(-4n)(-2n)(-3n)$ 　i) $(3a)^2$
j) $(-2x^2)^2$ 　　　　　k) $(-2x^2)(6x^2)(-3x)$ 　l) $(-10m)(-8m)(-5m^2)$

3. Simplify.

a) $(xy^3)(x^2y)$
b) $(m^2n^3)(mn)$
c) $(a^2b^2)(ab^2)$
d) $(c^3d)(c^2d^2)$
e) $(pq^2)(p^2q^2)$
f) $(x^4y)(y^4x)$
g) $(2x^2y)(3xy^2)$
h) $(-3x^2y)(4y^2x)$
i) $(-3a^2b^2)(-2ab^3)$
j) $(2ab^2c)(5a^2bc^2)$
k) $(4m^2n^2p)(-3mp^2)$
l) $(-2x^2yz^2)(-5xy^2)$

4. Expand.

a) $5(x - 3)$
b) $7(a + 1)$
c) $-3(2 + n)$
d) $-4(x - 2)$
e) $-1(2x - 5)$
f) $3(6x - 4)$
g) $-6(5 + 2t)$
h) $5(x^2 - 6x + 3)$
i) $-2(-3 + 5n - 3n^2)$

j) $7(x^2 - 3x + 9)$
k) $0.4(1.5x - 2.5)$
l) $\dfrac{1}{2}\left(\dfrac{1}{3} - \dfrac{1}{2}a\right)$

5. Expand.

a) $x(3x + 2)$
b) $a(5a - 1)$
c) $n(3 - 7n)$
d) $-x(x - 2)$
e) $-c(3c + 5)$
f) $x^2(3x - 1)$
g) $y^3(y - 5)$
h) $r^2(2 - 7r)$
i) $n^2(3n^2 - 5n + 1)$
j) $-x^3(5x^2 - x)$
k) $a^2(3a^2 - 2a + 1)$
l) $-s(7 - 2s + s^2)$

Ⓑ───────────────────────────────────

6. Expand.

a) $5x(2x + 3)$
b) $2a(3a - 4)$
c) $3c(5 - 2c)$
d) $-4n(2n - 1)$
e) $-7y(2y^2 - 5)$
f) $6k(3 - k + 2k^2)$
g) $2x^2(3x - 5)$
h) $-4a^2(3a^2 - 2a)$
i) $5s(3s^2 - 2s - 7)$
j) $3p^2(2 - 3p - p^2)$
k) $-7a^2(3a^2 - 2a - 4)$
l) $-1.5x^2(4 - 1.5x - 12x^2)$

7. Expand.

a) $3x^2(xy - y^2)$
b) $-2a^2(ab^2 - b)$
c) $4m(mn - n^2)$
d) $-3p(pq^2 - pq)$
e) $5a^2(b^2 - a)$
f) $-4xy(x^2 - y^2)$
g) $-2m^2n(mn - 3n^2)$
h) $7ab(2a^2b - 3ab^2)$
i) $-3pqr(2pq - 4qr)$
j) $0.25mn^2(5mn - 10m^2)$

8. Expand.

a) $3x(x^2y + y^2x + xy)$
b) $-2a(ab^2 - b + a^2b)$
c) $-3m(mn - m^2n - m)$
d) $4w(-3zw + w^2z - wz^2)$
e) $2xy^2(y - 2x^2y + 3xy)$
f) $-6xyz(-3xz^2 + 2xy^2 - yz^2 + 2xyz)$

9. The number N of baskets of apples that can be produced by x trees in a small orchard ($x \leqslant 125$) is given by this formula.
$$N = x(25 - 0.1x)$$
Find how many baskets of apples can be produced by:

a) 60 trees
b) 80 trees
c) 125 trees.

10. A field is x metres wide and $(2x + 3)$ metres long.
    a) Write expressions for the area and the perimeter of the field.
    b) Find the area and the perimeter if $x = 250$.

11. Find the area of each figure in two ways.
    a)
    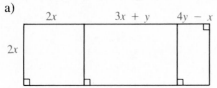
    b)
    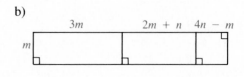

12. A person of mass x kilograms standing on the end of a diving board causes it to dip d centimetres. The relation between d and x is $d = 0.000\,01x^2(x + 50)$. Find how much the board dips under a person of each mass.
    a) 50 kg   b) 100 kg

ⓒ ──

13. The surface area S and the volume V of a right circular cylinder of radius r and height h are given by these formulas.
    $S = 2\pi r^2 + 2\pi rh$ and $V = \pi r^2 h$
    Find the surface area of a can of height 10 cm and volume 160π cm³.
    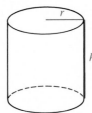

14. The dimensions, in centimetres, of a cereal box are $(5x - 1)$ by $3x$ by x.
    a) Find an expression for:
        i) the volume V of the box
        ii) the surface area S of the box.
    b) Find the volume and the surface area when $x = 7$.

15. The dimensions, in metres, of a room are $4x$ by $3x$ by $(x + 2)$.
    a) Find an expression for:
        i) the volume V of the room
        ii) the surface area S of the walls and the ceiling
        iii) the area A of the floor.
    b) If $x = 2$, find the cost of:
        i) carpeting the floor if underlay costs $3.00/m² and carpeting costs $16.99/m²
        ii) painting the walls and the ceiling if 1 L of paint covers 8 m², the walls and the ceiling require 3 coats of paint, and the paint costs $24.99 for a 4 L can.
    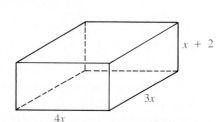

8-4 MULTIPLYING TWO BINOMIALS: PART ONE

A binomial is a polynomial with two terms. The product of two binomials can be illustrated geometrically.

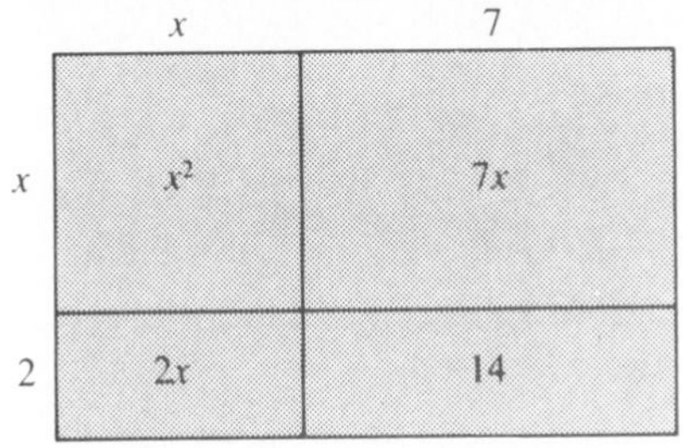

The length of the large rectangle is $(x + 7)$ units and its width is $(x + 2)$ units.

The area of the rectangle is $(x + 7)(x + 2)$.

The area is also the sum of the areas of the four small rectangles, $x^2 + 7x + 2x + 14$.

Therefore, $(x + 7)(x + 2) = x^2 + 7x + 2x + 14$

If we expand the product on the left, using the distributive law, then we obtain the expression on the right.

$$(x + 7)(x + 2) = x(x + 2) + 7(x + 2)$$
$$= x^2 + 2x + 7x + 14$$
$$= x^2 + 9x + 14$$

Example 1. Find the product. $(3a - 2)(a + 4)$

Solution.

$$(3a - 2)(a + 4)$$
$$= 3a(a + 4) - 2(a + 4)$$
$$= 3a^2 + 12a - 2a - 8$$
$$= 3a^2 + 10a - 8$$

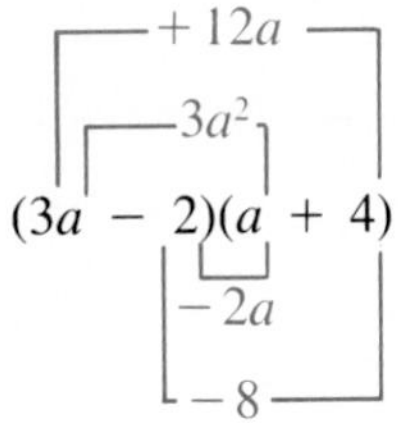

The diagram shows that, to find the product of two binomials, we multiply each term of one binomial by each term of the other binomial.

Example 2. Find each product.

a) $(2x + 1)(7x - 3)$ b) $(n - 3)^2$ c) $5(3 + x)(2 - x^2)$

Solution. a) $(2x + 1)(7x - 3) = (2x + 1)(7x - 3)$

$$= 14x^2 - 6x + 7x - 3$$
$$= 14x^2 + x - 3$$

b) $(n - 3)^2 = (n - 3)(n - 3)$

$$= n^2 - 3n - 3n + 9$$
$$= n^2 - 6n + 9$$

c) First find the product of the two binomials.

$$5(3 + x)(2 - x^2) = 5(6 - 3x^2 + 2x - x^3)$$
$$= 30 - 15x^2 + 10x - 5x^3$$
$$= 30 + 10x - 15x^2 - 5x^3$$

Example 3. Find an expression for the area of the rectangle. Write it as a polynomial in descending powers of x.

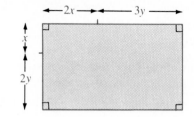

Solution. Area = length × width
The length is $2x + 3y$.
The width is $x + 2y$.
Area $= (2x + 3y)(x + 2y)$
$$= 2x^2 + 4xy + 3xy + 6y^2$$
$$= 2x^2 + 7xy + 6y^2$$

The area of the rectangle can be expressed as $2x^2 + 7xy + 6y^2$.

EXERCISES 8-4

Ⓐ

1. Use the diagram to find the product.

a) $(x + 3)(x + 5)$ b) $(a + 2)(a + 4)$ c) $(n + 7)(n + 1)$

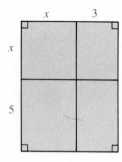
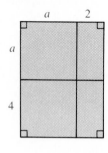
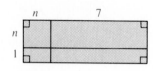

2. Find each product.

a) $(x + 3)(x + 4)$ b) $(n + 2)(n + 6)$ c) $(a - 5)(a - 3)$
d) $(t - 1)(t - 4)$ e) $(x - 2)(x + 5)$ f) $(n + 3)(n - 4)$
g) $(a + 6)(a - 8)$ h) $(x + 9)(x - 7)$ i) $(x + 12)(x - 5)$

j) $(s - 11)(s - 3)$ k) $\left(n + \dfrac{1}{2}\right)\left(n + \dfrac{1}{2}\right)$ l) $\left(a - \dfrac{2}{3}\right)\left(a + \dfrac{1}{2}\right)$

3. Find each product.
   a) $(a + 1)(a - 2)$
   b) $(n - 3)(n - 2)$
   c) $(y - 4)(y + 5)$
   d) $(b - 6)(b + 3)$
   e) $(a - 10)(a - 6)$
   f) $(n + 10)(n + 12)$

Ⓑ

4. Find each product.
   a) $(x - 3)(5x + 2)$
   b) $(2a + 1)(2a + 3)$
   c) $(8n - 3)(2n - 1)$
   d) $(4a + 3)(4a + 3)$
   e) $(3x - 2)(4x - 3)$
   f) $(5x + 1)(6x - 4)$
   g) $(6x - 3)(2x - 5)$
   h) $(3b + 2)(3b - 2)$
   i) $(5a + 1)(4a - 7)$
   j) $(a + 8)(8a + 1)$
   k) $(2a - 3)^2$
   l) $(3a + 4)^2$

5. Find each product.
   a) $(a - 3)(1 - a)$
   b) $(x - 1)(1 - x)$
   c) $(2y - 1)(5 + y)$
   d) $(2z - 4)(1 + z)$
   e) $\left(\frac{1}{2}x + 3\right)\left(3 - \frac{1}{4}x\right)$
   f) $(3x - 2)(2 + 5x)$

6. Find each product.
   a) $5(4 - a)(3 + a)$
   b) $-(6 - 3n)(2 + n)$
   c) $3(x + 3)(4 - x)$
   d) $10(x - 4)(2 + x)$
   e) $6(2a - 5)(3 + a)$
   f) $-7(c + 3)(5 - 2c)$

7. Find each product.
   a) $(x + 2y)(x + 5y)$
   b) $(a - 3b)(a + 2b)$
   c) $(3m - n)(2m - n)$
   d) $(5x + 3y)(4x - y)$
   e) $(6r + s)(r - 3s)$
   f) $(8a + 7b)(7a + 8b)$

8. Find each product.
   a) $(x - y)(y - x)$
   b) $(a - 2b)(b - a)$
   c) $(2q - p)(-3p + 4q)$
   d) $(x - 2y^2)(y^2 - 3x)$

9. a) Find an expression for the area of each rectangle.
   b) Find an expression for the perimeter of each rectangle.
   c) Evaluate each area and perimeter for $x = 10$.
   i)

   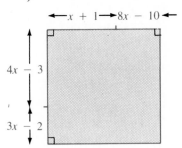

   ii)

   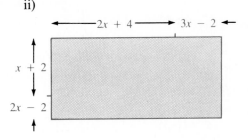

Ⓒ

10. Find each product.
   a) $(x + 5)(x^2 + 2x + 1)$
   b) $(a + 3)(a^2 - 4a + 2)$
   c) $(t - 4)(t^2 + 3t - 5)$
   d) $(2x - 3)(x^2 - 6x + 4)$
   e) $(x + 1)(x + 2)(x + 3)$
   f) $(2x - 1)(3x - 1)(x + 1)$
   g) $3(x - 4)(x^2 - 7x + 5)$
   h) $2x(x + 1)(x - 1)(3x + 2)$

8-5 MULTIPLYING TWO BINOMIALS: PART TWO

Two special cases of the products of two binomials will be considered in this section.

Squaring a Binomial

When we multiply a binomial by itself, we *square* the binomial.

Consider the product $(x + 3)^2$.

$$\begin{aligned}(x + 3)^2 &= (x + 3)(x + 3) \\ &= x^2 + 3x + 3x + 9 \\ &= x^2 + 6x + 9\end{aligned}$$

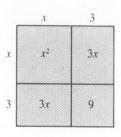

The diagram shows how the square of the binomial is represented geometrically.

Because the product involves two equal binomials, there is a pattern in the terms of the expansion. This pattern is illustrated below.

$$(x + 3)^2 = x^2 + 6x + 9$$

$\left[\text{the square of the first term } (x) \text{ of the binomial}\right.$

$\left[\text{twice the product of the terms } (3 \text{ and } x) \text{ of the binomial}\right.$

$\left[\text{the square of the second term } (3) \text{ of the binomial}\right.$

This pattern can be used to square a binomial directly.

Example 1. Expand.

    a) $(x - 4)^2$ b) $(3x - 2)^2$ c) $(5 + 6n)^2$

Solution.   a) $\begin{aligned}[t](x - 4)^2 &= (x)^2 + 2(x)(-4) + (-4)^2 \\ &= x^2 - 8x + 16\end{aligned}$

        b) $\begin{aligned}[t](3x - 2)^2 &= (3x)^2 + 2(3x)(-2) + (-2)^2 \\ &= 9x^2 - 12x + 4\end{aligned}$

        c) $(5 + 6n)^2 = 25 + 60n + 36n^2$

The pattern resulting from squaring a binomial can be used to square numbers.

Example 2. Calculate.

    a) 41^2 b) 58^2

Solution.   a) $\begin{aligned}[t]41^2 &= (40 + 1)^2 \\ &= 40^2 + 2(40)(1) + 1^2 \\ &= 1600 + 80 + 1 \\ &= 1681\end{aligned}$

        b) $\begin{aligned}[t]58^2 &= (60 - 2)^2 \\ &= 60^2 + 2(60)(-2) + (-2)^2 \\ &= 3600 - 240 + 4 \\ &= 3364\end{aligned}$

The pattern for squaring a binomial can be expressed in general terms.

$$(a + b)^2 = a^2 + 2ab + b^2$$
$$(a - b)^2 = a^2 - 2ab + b^2$$

Product of a Sum and a Difference

An interesting case of the product of two binomials occurs when one binomial is the sum of two terms and the other binomial is the difference of the *same* two terms.

Consider the product $(x + 6)(x - 6)$.

$$(x + 6)(x - 6) = x^2 - 6x + 6x - 36$$
$$= x^2 - 36$$

The product $x^2 - 36$ is the difference between the squares of the two terms in the binomials. This pattern can be used to find the product of two binomials of this form directly.

Example 3. Expand.

      a) $(a - 4)(a + 4)$ b) $(2x - 7)(2x + 7)$ c) $(6 + y)(6 - y)$

Solution.   a) $(a - 4)(a + 4) = (a)^2 - (4)^2$
                             $= a^2 - 16$

      b) $(2x - 7)(2x + 7) = (2x)^2 - (7)^2$
                                 $= 4x^2 - 49$

      c) $(6 + y)(6 - y) = 36 - y^2$

The pattern resulting from the product of two binomials of this form can be used to find certain numerical products.

Example 4. Evaluate.

      a) 41×39 b) 18×22

Solution.   a) $41 \times 39 = (40 + 1)(40 - 1)$
                         $= 40^2 - 1^2$
                         $= 1600 - 1$
                         $= 1599$

      b) $18 \times 22 = (20 - 2)(20 + 2)$
                         $= 20^2 - 2^2$
                         $= 400 - 4$
                         $= 396$

How must the two numbers be related to enable us to calculate their product in this way?

The pattern for the product of two binomials, when one binomial is the sum of two terms and the other binomial is the difference of the same terms, can be expressed in general terms.

$$(a - b)(a + b) = a^2 - b^2$$

EXERCISES 8-5

Ⓐ

1. Expand.
   a) $(x + 5)^2$ b) $(x + 1)^2$ c) $(a - 3)^2$ d) $(n - 7)^2$
   e) $(c + 4)^2$ f) $(x - 1)^2$ g) $(a + 2)^2$ h) $(a - 6)^2$
   i) $(2 + a)^2$ j) $(5 - x)^2$ k) $(t + 9)^2$ l) $(10 - m)^2$

2. Expand.
   a) $(x + 2)(x - 2)$ b) $(a - 3)(a + 3)$ c) $(x - 4)(x + 4)$
   d) $(x + 8)(x - 8)$ e) $(y + 1)(y - 1)$ f) $(d + 12)(d - 12)$
   g) $(s + 25)(s - 25)$ h) $(m + 40)(m - 40)$ i) $(x - 11)(x + 11)$
   j) $(8 - x)(8 + x)$ k) $(6 - a)(6 + a)$ l) $(9 - y)(9 + y)$

Ⓑ

3. Expand.
   a) $(3a - 1)^2$ b) $(2a + 3)^2$ c) $(7x - 5)^2$ d) $(6a + 4)^2$
   e) $(3n - 8)^2$ f) $(5 - 9x)^2$ g) $(10 - 3c)^2$ h) $(12x + 5)^2$

4. Expand.
   a) $(3x + 2)(3x - 2)$ b) $(4x - 3)(4x + 3)$
   c) $(3 - 5x)(3 + 5x)$ d) $(6s - 5)(6s + 5)$
   e) $(12x - 7)(12x + 7)$ f) $(5y + 13)(5y - 13)$

5. Square each binomial.
   a) $x + 7$ b) $a - 2$ c) $n + 4$ d) $2x - 1$
   e) $5c + 3$ f) $2 - 3m$ g) $4 + 5x$ h) $8 - 3x$

6. Expand.
   a) $(n + 0.2)^2$ b) $(x + 1.5)(x - 1.5)$

   c) $\left(c + \dfrac{1}{2}\right)\left(c - \dfrac{1}{2}\right)$ d) $\left(x + \dfrac{1}{4}\right)^2$

   e) $\left(k + \dfrac{2}{3}\right)\left(k - \dfrac{2}{3}\right)$ f) $\left(\dfrac{2}{3}a - 1\right)\left(\dfrac{2}{3}a + 1\right)$

7. Expand. What do you notice?
   a) $(x - 3)^2$ b) $(-x + 3)^2$ c) $(3 - x)^2$ d) $(-3 + x)^2$

8. Expand.
   a) $3(x - 2)^2$ b) $4(x + 5)(x - 5)$ c) $5(a + 1)(a - 1)$
   d) $-4(2x - 3)^2$ e) $-3(5 - n)^2$ f) $2(3x - 4)(3x + 4)$

9. Use the pattern for squaring a binomial to calculate each product.
   a) 31^2 b) 13^2 c) 29^2 d) 103^2 e) 61^2 f) 92^2

10. Calculate each product.
    a) 31×29 b) 32×28 c) 59×61 d) 57×63

Ⓒ

11. Calculate mentally.
    a) $(1\,000\,000)^2 - (999\,999)^2$ b) 501×499

8-6 COMMON FACTORS

To factor a number means to write it as a product, for example,
$15 = 3 \times 5$.

If two or more numbers have the same factor, it is called a *common factor*.

To find the common factors of three numbers, for example, 24, 42, and 60, we express each number as a product.
$24 = 2 \times 2 \times 2 \times 3$
$42 = 2 \times 3 \times 7$
$60 = 2 \times 2 \times 3 \times 5$
2, 3, and 2×3 or 6, are the common factors of 24, 42, and 60.
6 is the *greatest common factor* of 24, 42, and 60.

When the greatest common factor is known, the sum of two or more numbers can be written as a product.
For example,
$$24 + 42 + 60 = 6(4) + 6(7) + 6(10)$$
$$= 6(4 + 7 + 10)$$
$$= 6(21)$$

To factor a polynomial also means to write it as a product. In an earlier section, a product such as $3(2x + 1)$ was written as the sum, $6x + 3$, using the distributive law. Factoring is the reverse process. A sum like $6x + 3$ is written as the product $3(2x + 1)$.

Example 1. a) Find the common factors of $2x^3$, $4x^2$, and $-6x$.
  b) Find the greatest common factor of $2x^3$, $4x^2$, and $-6x$.
  c) Express $2x^3 + 4x^2 - 6x$ as a product.

Solution. a) Express each monomial as a product.
  $$2x^3 = 2(x)(x)(x)$$
  $$4x^2 = 2(2)(x)(x)$$
  $$-6x = -(2)(3)(x)$$
  2, x, and $2x$ are the common factors of $2x^3$, $4x^2$, and $-6x$.
  b) The greatest common factor of $2x^3$, $4x^2$, and $-6x$ is $2x$.
  c) Use the greatest common factor found in part b).
  $$2x^3 + 4x^2 - 6x = 2x(x^2) + 2x(2x) + 2x(-3)$$
  $$= 2x(x^2 + 2x - 3)$$

Example 2. Factor then check.
  a) $6x - 15$ \qquad\qquad b) $a^3 - 4a^2 + 2a$

Solution. a) $6x - 15 = 3(2x) - 3(5)$
  $$= 3(2x - 5)$$
  Check by expanding. $3(2x - 5) = 6x - 15$
  b) $a^3 - 4a^2 + 2a = a(a^2) - a(4a) + a(2)$
  $$= a(a^2 - 4a + 2)$$
  Check. $a(a^2 - 4a + 2) = a^3 - 4a^2 + 2a$

When factoring, always look for the *greatest* common factor.

Example 3. Factor.

a) $18n^2 - 12n$ b) $36x^3 - 27x^2 + 54x$

c) $-20x^4y + 10x^2y$ d) $24a^3b - 3a^2b^2 + 12ab^2$

Solution. a) $18n^2 - 12n = 6n(3n - 2)$

b) $36x^3 - 27x^2 + 54x = 9x(4x^2 - 3x + 6)$

c) $-20x^4y + 10x^2y = -10x^2y(2x^2 - 1)$

d) $24a^3b - 3a^2b^2 + 12ab^2 = 3ab(8a^2 - ab + 4b)$

In *Example 3* part c), the solution could have been written as $10x^2y(1 - 2x^2)$.

EXERCISES 8-6

Ⓐ

1. Find the greatest common factor.

a) 9, 6, 12 b) 16, 28, −44 c) $2x, 4x^2, 6x^3$

d) $-14x, 21x^2, 28x^3$ e) $8y^4, 2y^3, -3y^2$ f) $16z^2, 12z^3, 32z^5$

2. Express as products.

a) $5y - 10$ b) $12a + 18$ c) $-3x^2 + 6x - 12$

d) $2a^2 - 10a + 2$ e) $4w + 3w^2 - 7w^3$ f) $8y^3 - 4y^2 + 2y$

g) $-6s + 2s^2 + 4s^3$ h) $-7k^3 - 35k^4 + 49k^5$ i) $6m^2 - 36m^3 - 54m^4$

3. Factor then check.

a) $14x^2 + 35x - 7$ b) $-10 - 25a + 30a^2$ c) $20n^2 - 30n + 80$

d) $5x + 10x^2 + 15x^3$ e) $9c^3 + 15c$ f) $-x^3 + x^2$

g) $4x - 8x^2 + 12x^3$ h) $-6y^2 - 3y^3 - 12y^4$ i) $12m + 16m^2 - 4m^3$

4. Factor.

a) $16x + 40$ b) $15n - 24$ c) $-2a^2 - 6a$

d) $a^3 - 9a^2 + 3a$ e) $-27x^2 - 9x + 3$ f) $5x^3 + 3x^2 - x$

g) $9a^3 + 7a^2 + 18a$ h) $-8d - 24d^2 - 8d^3$ i) $17k - 85k^2 - 51k^3$

Ⓑ

5. Find the greatest common factor.

a) xy, x^2y b) $3x^2y^2, 6xy$ c) $ab, -a^2b^2$ d) $-4xy, 16$

e) $-5xy, -10x^2y^2$ f) $6p^2q, -12pq^2$ g) $2m^2n, -4mn^2$ h) $3x^2y, 9x^2y^2$

6. Factor.

a) $xy + x^2y$ b) $-3x^2y^2 + 6xy$ c) $ab - a^2b^2$

d) $-4xy - 16$ e) $5xy + 10x^2y^2$ f) $6p^2q - 12pq^2$

g) $2m^2n - 4mn^2$ h) $3x^2y + 9x^2y^2$ i) $-5x^6y - xy^6$

7. Factor.

a) $b^4 - 3b^3$ b) $3b^4 - 6b^5$

c) $-a^4 + 3a^3 - 2a^2$ d) $21x + 42x^2 + 63x^3$

e) $-d^4 + 5d^5$ f) $24m^3 + 6m^2 - 12m$

g) $-12x - 9x^2 - 3x^3 - 6x^4$ h) $2x^3 + 3x^4 - 4x^5 + 5x^6$

8. The surface area S of a right circular cylinder of radius r and height h is given by this formula.
$$S = 2\pi rh + 2\pi r^2$$
Express S as a product.

9. Factor.
a) $18a - 6ab^2$
b) $12x^2y + 16xy$
c) $-8ab^2c - 12a^2bc^2$
d) $5m^2 + 15mn + 25n^2$
e) $4x^2y^2z - 16xy^2z^2$
f) $3x^2 + 6y^2x - 12x^2y^2$
g) $-5xy + 6y + 3xy^2$
h) $9a^3b^2 + 7a^2b^2 + 18a^2b^3$
i) $-7a^3b^2 + 14a^2b^3 - 21a^2b^2$
j) $-12p^2q^3 - 20p^3q^3 + 8p^2q^4$

10. Factor.
a) $3xy^2 + 6x^2y - 9xy$
b) $-2a^2b + 6ab^2 - 4ab$
c) $5m^2n^2 - 10m^3n^2 + 25m^2n$
d) $-28x^2y^2 + 14x^3y^3 - 7x^2y^3$

11. Factor.
a) $2a^3b - 16a^2b^3 + 4a^3b^2 + 6a^2b^2 - 8a^3b^3 + 12a^2b$
b) $15x^4y^3 - 25x^3y^4 + 10x^2y^3 - 5x^3y^2 + 30x^4y^4 - 35x^2y^2$

12. Express as products.
a) $a(a + 6) + 7(a + 6)$
b) $x(x - 9) - 2(x - 9)$
c) $-8(1 + y) - 3y(1 + y)$
d) $5(2 - x) + x(2 - x)$
e) $2x(x + 3) + 4(x + 3)$
f) $-3a(2a - 1) + 6(2a - 1)$

13. Factor.
a) $6t(3t - 1) + 9(3t - 1)$
b) $a^2(a + 2) - a(a + 2)$
c) $5x^2(x + 7) - 10x(x + 7)$
d) $-(2n + 3)n - (2n + 3)4$
e) $(r - 3)2r + (r - 3)8$
f) $-(x + 4)x^2 + (x + 4)x^3$
g) $3a^3(a - 1) - 6a^2(a - 1)$
h) $12a^2(2a - 5) + 16a(2a - 5)$

14. Factor.
a) $a^2 + 2a + ab + 2b$
b) $3x - xy + 3y - y^2$
c) $3a + 3b + ab + b^2$
d) $4x - 4 + ax - a$
e) $2p - 2q - p^2 + pq$
f) $-4x - 4y + xy + y^2$
g) $-3m + 3n - mn + n^2$
h) $-5c - 5d - cd - d^2$

INVESTIGATE

Choose any positive number.
- Add 2.
- Multiply by the original number.
- Add 1.
- Take the positive square root.

How is the result related to the original number?
Show that this pattern applies for any number chosen.

PROBLEM SOLVING

Look For a Pattern

What is the last digit of 7^{134}?

Understand the problem
- What does 7^{134} mean?
- How could this number be calculated?
- What are we asked to find?
- Do we need to know all the digits in the number to answer the question?

Think of a strategy
- Expand 7^2, 7^3, 7^4, 7^5, . . . and look for a pattern in the last digits.

Carry out the strategy
- The table shows the expansions for 7^1, 7^2, 7^3, . . . 7^8, with their last digits in color.
- The last digits of successive powers of 7 appear to run through the sequence 7, 9, 3, 1 and then repeat.
- When the power of 7 is a multiple of 4, the last digit is 1, so 7^{132} has a last digit 1.
- Therefore, 7^{133} has a last digit 7.
- And so 7^{134} has a last digit 9.

Powers of 7	
$7^1 = 7$	$7^5 = 16\ 807$
$7^2 = 49$	$7^6 = 117\ 649$
$7^3 = 343$	$7^7 = 823\ 543$
$7^4 = 2401$	$7^8 = 5\ 764\ 801$

Look back
- There are other ways to consider the pattern, for example,
$7^{132} = (7^4)^{33}$
Since 7^4 has a last digit of 1, when this power is raised to a power, the result will always have a last digit of 1.
Hence 7^{132} has a last digit of 1.
But $7^{134} = 7^{132} \times 7^2$
Since 7^{132} has a last digit of 1, and 7^2 has a last digit of 9, the product $7^{132} \times 7^2$ will have a last digit of 9.

Solve each problem

1. Find the next two numbers in each sequence.

   a) $\dfrac{3}{8}, \dfrac{1}{2}, \dfrac{5}{8}, \ldots$

   b) $x + y,\ 2x + 3y,\ 3x + 5y, \ldots$

   c) 1, 2, 4, 7, . . .

   d) 5, 11, 17, 23, . . .

2. What is the missing number? 1, 5, 13, __, 41, 61, . . .

3. Sketch the figures missing from spaces A, B, C, and D (below left).

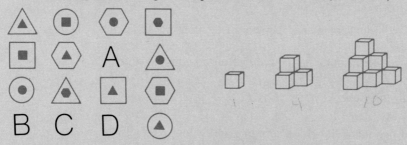

4. How many cubes are in the next figure in this sequence (above right)?

5. Study the pattern in the table. Can you find a formula for the sum of the whole numbers from 1 to n?

n	1	2	3	4	5	6	7
Sum to n	1	3	6	10	15	21	28
$\dfrac{\text{Sum to } n}{n}$	$\dfrac{1}{1}$	$\dfrac{3}{2}$	$\dfrac{6}{3}$	$\dfrac{10}{4}$	$\dfrac{15}{5}$	$\dfrac{21}{6}$	$\dfrac{28}{7}$

6. Copy and complete the table. Use the table in *Question 5* to complete the last row.

n	1	2	3	4	5	6	7
n^3	1	8					343
Sum of cubes to n^3	1	9					784
$\dfrac{\text{Sum of cubes to } n^3}{\text{Sum to } n}$	1	3					28

   Study the pattern in the table. Can you find a formula for the sum of the cubes of the whole numbers from 1 to n?

8-7 FACTORING TRINOMIALS OF THE FORM $x^2 + bx + c$

A polynomial with three terms is a trinomial. The product of two binomials is often a trinomial.

For example, $(x + 3)(x + 4) = x^2 + 7x + 12$

Factoring is the reverse process. A sum like $x^2 + 7x + 12$ is written as the product $(x + 3)(x + 4)$.

Consider this expansion.

7 is the sum of 3 and 4

$$x^2 + 7x + 12 = (x + 3)(x + 4)$$

12 is the product of 3 and 4

The coefficient of x in the trinomial is the sum of the constant terms in the binomials.

The constant term in the trinomial is the product of the constant terms in the binomials.

Example 1. Factor then check. $x^2 + 5x + 6$

Solution. $x^2 + 5x + 6$

Find two numbers whose sum is 5 and whose product is 6.
List pairs of factors of 6: 1, 6; -1, -6; 2, 3; -2, -3.
The pair of factors whose sum is 5 is 2, 3.
$x^2 + 5x + 6 = (x + 2)(x + 3)$

Check. $(x + 2)(x + 3) = x^2 + 3x + 2x + 6$
$$= x^2 + 5x + 6$$

Example 2. Factor then check. $a^2 - 8a + 12$

Solution. $a^2 - 8a + 12$

Find two numbers whose sum is -8 and whose product is 12.
List pairs of factors of 12: 12, 1; -12, -1; 6, 2; -6, -2; 4, 3; -4, -3.
The pair of factors whose sum is -8 is -6, -2.
$a^2 - 8a + 12 = (a - 6)(a - 2)$

Check. $(a - 6)(a - 2) = a^2 - 2a - 6a + 12$
$$= a^2 - 8a + 12$$

Example 3. Factor then check. $m^2 - 5m - 14$

Solution. $m^2 - 5m - 14$

Find two numbers whose sum is -5 and whose product is -14.
List pairs of factors of -14: -14, 1; 14, -1; -7, 2; 7, -2.
The pair of factors whose sum is -5 is -7, 2.
$m^2 - 5m - 14 = (m - 7)(m + 2)$

Check. $(m - 7)(m + 2) = m^2 + 2m - 7m - 14$
$$= m^2 - 5m - 14$$

Example 4. Factor.
        a) $n^2 - 14n + 49$ b) $k^2 + 12k + 36$

Solution.   a) $n^2 - 14n + 49$
           Find two numbers whose sum is -14 and whose product is 49.
           The numbers are $-7, -7$.
$$n^2 - 14n + 49 = (n - 7)(n - 7)$$
$$= (n - 7)^2$$

        b) $k^2 + 12k + 36$
           Find two numbers whose sum is 12 and whose product is 36.
           The numbers are 6, 6.
$$k^2 + 12k + 36 = (k + 6)(k + 6)$$
$$= (k + 6)^2$$

In *Example 4*, the first and last terms of each trinomial are perfect squares; that is, in $n^2 - 14n + 49$, $n^2 = n \times n$ and $49 = (-7) \times (-7)$. Also, the middle term is $2(-7)n$.

If you recognize this pattern in a trinomial, you know that it is a perfect square, with two equal factors.

Not all trinomials can be factored using rational numbers.

Example 5. Factor if possible.
        a) $x^2 + 6x - 7$ b) $x^2 + 9x + 12$

Solution.   a) $x^2 + 6x - 7$
           List pairs of factors of -7: $-7, 1; 7, -1$.
           Select the pair of factors whose sum is 6; that is, $7, -1$.
$$x^2 + 6x - 7 = (x + 7)(x - 1)$$

        b) $x^2 + 9x + 12$
           List pairs of factors of 12: $12, 1; -12, -1; 6, 2; -6, -2; 3, 4;$
           $-3, -4$.
           None of the pairs of factors has a sum of $+9$.
           $x^2 + 9x + 12$ is not factorable.

If the terms of the trinomial have a common factor, it should be removed before the other factors are found.

Example 6. Factor completely.
        a) $3x^2 - 18x + 24$ b) $x^4 + 4x^3 - 5x^2$

Solution.   a) $3x^2 - 18x + 24 = 3(x^2 - 6x + 8)$
$$= 3(x - 4)(x - 2)$$

        b) $x^4 + 4x^3 - 5x^2 = x^2(x^2 + 4x - 5)$
$$= x^2(x + 5)(x - 1)$$

When factoring, always look for a common factor first.

EXERCISES 8-7

Ⓐ

1. Factor.
   a) $x^2 + 7x + 10$
   b) $a^2 + 5a + 6$
   c) $m^2 + 10m + 24$
   d) $a^2 + 8a + 7$
   e) $x^2 + 6x + 9$
   f) $n^2 + 14n + 49$
   g) $t^2 + 13t + 40$
   h) $x^2 - 12x + 36$
   i) $x^2 + 9x + 20$

2. Factor.
   a) $x^2 - 8x + 15$
   b) $c^2 - 12c + 32$
   c) $a^2 - 8a + 16$
   d) $x^2 - 6x + 5$
   e) $x^2 + 2x + 1$
   f) $n^2 - 9n + 14$
   g) $y^2 - 15y + 54$
   h) $s^2 - 18s + 81$
   i) $k^2 - 11k + 30$

3. Factor.
   a) $x^2 - 8x + 16$
   b) $x^2 + 12x + 36$
   c) $a^2 + 4a + 4$
   d) $p^2 - 2p + 1$
   e) $x^2 - 6x + 9$
   f) $t^2 - 10t + 25$
   g) $x^2 + 14x + 49$
   h) $b^2 - 16b + 64$
   i) $x^2 + 20x + 100$

Ⓑ

4. Factor.
   a) $x^2 + 6x - 16$
   b) $a^2 + 4a - 12$
   c) $x^2 + 6x - 27$
   d) $c^2 + 2c - 35$
   e) $x^2 + x - 12$
   f) $a^2 + a - 30$
   g) $y^2 + y - 56$
   h) $t^2 - 2t - 24$
   i) $x^2 - 2x - 15$

5. Factor and check.
   a) $x^2 - 6x + 8$
   b) $x^2 + 9x + 18$
   c) $a^2 - 11a + 18$
   d) $m^2 + 11m + 28$
   e) $n^2 - 10n + 25$
   f) $30 - 13n + n^2$
   g) $p^2 + 16p + 64$
   h) $y^2 - 13y + 42$
   i) $x^2 + 15x + 56$

6. Factor.
   a) $r^2 - 5r - 36$
   b) $a^2 - 4a - 45$
   c) $n^2 - 3n - 54$
   d) $m^2 - 2m - 48$
   e) $k^2 - 2k - 63$
   f) $x^2 - 7x - 30$
   g) $81 - 18a + a^2$
   h) $m^2 + 22m + 121$
   i) $n^2 - 4n + 4$

7. Factor and check.
   a) $x^2 - 5x - 24$
   b) $x^2 + 5x - 50$
   c) $a^2 + a - 72$
   d) $n^2 - 3n - 40$
   e) $m^2 + m - 42$
   f) $8 - 7x - x^2$
   g) $y^2 + 3y - 4$
   h) $s^2 - 7s - 18$
   i) $2 + t - t^2$

8. Factor.
   a) $x^2 + 7x - 8$
   b) $a^2 + 5a - 14$
   c) $t^2 - 2t - 3$
   d) $n^2 + 13n + 42$
   e) $x^2 - 17x + 72$
   f) $c^2 - 11c + 30$
   g) $m^2 + 6m - 55$
   h) $a^2 + 10a + 9$
   i) $s^2 + s - 20$
   j) $c^2 + 9c - 36$
   k) $12 + 4m - m^2$
   l) $15 - 8y + y^2$

9. Consider the trinomial $x^2 - 2x - 15$.
   a) Find its value when $x = 17$.
   b) Factor the trinomial.
   c) Evaluate the factored expression when $x = 17$.

10. Consider the trinomial $x^2 - 13x + 36$.
   a) Find its value when $x = 59$.
   b) Factor the trinomial.
   c) Evaluate the factored expression when $x = 59$.

11. Factor if possible.
   a) $x^2 + 16x + 63$
   b) $a^2 + 12a + 30$
   c) $x^2 - 4x + 32$
   d) $t^2 + 11t + 24$
   e) $n^2 - 12n + 35$
   f) $k^2 - 5k - 21$
   g) $x^2 + 7x - 60$
   h) $n^2 + 7n - 7$
   i) $x^2 - 6x + 24$
   j) $a^2 - a - 45$
   k) $56 + t - t^2$
   l) $6 - x + x^2$

12. Factor completely.
   a) $2x^2 + 12x + 10$
   b) $5a^2 - 10a - 40$
   c) $10n^2 + 10n - 20$
   d) $4a^2 - 16a - 20$
   e) $3x^2 + 15x + 6$
   f) $7a^2 - 35a + 42$
   g) $x^3 - 2x^2 - 3x$
   h) $a^3 - 2a^2 - 9a$
   i) $2y^3 + 14y^2 + 24y$
   j) $3x^3 + 6x^2 - 24x$
   k) $60n + 50n^2 + 10n^3$
   l) $14s + 7s^2 - 7s^3$

13. If a hockey arena increases its ticket prices by x dollars, the predicted revenue R thousands of dollars from all ticket sales is given by this formula.
   $R = 35 + 2x - x^2$, where $x < 7$
   a) Factor the trinomial.
   b) Find the predicted revenue if ticket prices are increased by each amount.
   i) $1
   ii) $2
   iii) $3

14. If a transit company increases its fares by x cents, the total daily revenue R thousands of dollars is given by this formula.
   $R = 55 + 6x - x^2$, where $x < 11$
   a) Factor the trinomial.
   b) Find the total daily revenue for each fare increase.
   i)   1¢
   ii)   2¢
   iii)   3¢
   iv)   5¢
   v)   6¢

Ⓒ

15. Factor.
   a) $x^2 + 8xy + 15y^2$
   b) $x^2 - 9xy + 14y^2$
   c) $x^2 - 4xy - 5y^2$
   d) $x^2 + 7xy - 18y^2$
   e) $c^2 - 4cd - 21d^2$
   f) $m^2 + 14mn + 45n^2$
   g) $6x^2 + xy - y^2$
   h) $8a^2 - 2ab - b^2$
   i) $28a^2 + 3ab - b^2$
   j) $12x^2 + 8xy + y^2$
   k) $25x^2 - 10x + 1$
   l) $20a^2 - 9ab + b^2$

16. Find an integer to replace each square so that each trinomial can be factored.
   a) $x^2 + \blacksquare x + 12$
   b) $x^2 - \blacksquare x + 20$
   c) $x^2 + \blacksquare x - 18$
   d) $x^2 + 5x + \blacksquare$
   e) $x^2 + 4x + \blacksquare$
   f) $x^2 - 2x + \blacksquare$

17. Consider the equation $y = x^2 + 12x + 11$.
   a) Factor the trinomial.
   b) Evaluate y for $x = 1, 2, 3, \ldots, 10$.
   c) For which values of x is y a perfect square?

18. Find values of x which make these trinomials perfect squares.
   a) $x^2 + 7x + 6$
   b) $x^2 + 8x - 9$
   c) $x^2 - 11x + 24$

8-8 FACTORING TRINOMIALS OF THE FORM $ax^2 + bx + c$

A method for factoring a trinomial of the form $ax^2 + bx + c$ is suggested by a study of how one is formed from the product of two binomials. Consider this example.

$$
\begin{aligned}
(2x + 3)(x + 6) &= 2x(x + 6) + 3(x + 6) \\
&= 2x^2 + 12x + 3x + 18 \\
&= 2x^2 + 15x + 18
\end{aligned}
$$

The integers 12 and 3 have a sum of 15 and a product of 36. This is the same as the product of 2 and 18.

A trinomial of the form $ax^2 + bx + c$ can be factored if two integers can be found with a sum of b and a product of ac.

Example 1. Factor. $2y^2 - 11y + 12$

Solution.

$2y^2 - 11y + 12$

What two integers have a sum of -11 and a product of 24?

The integers needed are -3 and -8. The trinomial can be factored after writing the second term as $-3y - 8y$.

$$
\begin{aligned}
2y^2 - 11y + 12 &= 2y^2 - 3y - 8y + 12 \\
&= y(2y - 3) - 4(2y - 3) \\
&= (2y - 3)(y - 4)
\end{aligned}
$$

The order in which the decomposition of the second term is written is unimportant. The solution for *Example 1* could have been written:

$$
\begin{aligned}
2y^2 - 11y + 12 &= 2y^2 - 8y - 3y + 12 \\
&= 2y(y - 4) - 3(y - 4) \\
&= (y - 4)(2y - 3)
\end{aligned}
$$

Example 2. Factor. $4a^2 + 12a + 9$

Solution.

$4a^2 + 12a + 9$

What two integers have a sum of 12 and a product of 36?

The integers needed are 6 and 6.

$$
\begin{aligned}
4a^2 + 12a + 9 &= 4a^2 + 6a + 6a + 9 \\
&= 2a(2a + 3) + 3(2a + 3) \\
&= (2a + 3)(2a + 3) \\
&= (2a + 3)^2
\end{aligned}
$$

In *Example 2*, the trinomial $4a^2 + 12a + 9$ is a perfect square.

As always, look for a common monomial factor before factoring any trinomial.

Example 3.   Factor.

a) $5a^2 + a - 4$ b) $18y^2 - 48y + 32$

Solution.   a) $5a^2 + a - 4 = 5a^2 + 5a - 4a - 4$

$$= 5a(a + 1) - 4(a + 1)$$
$$= (a + 1)(5a - 4)$$

b) $18y^2 - 48y + 32 = 2(9y^2 - 24y + 16)$

$$= 2(9y^2 - 12y - 12y + 16)$$
$$= 2[3y(3y - 4) - 4(3y - 4)]$$
$$= 2(3y - 4)(3y - 4)$$
$$= 2(3y - 4)^2$$

EXERCISES 8-8

(A)

1. Find two integers with the given properties.

	Product	Sum			Product	Sum
a)	5	6	d)		-12	-4
b)	-9	8	e)		15	-8
c)	-5	6	f)		-8	2

2. Factor.
   a) $2b^2 + 5b + 2$ b) $2x^2 - 3x - 2$ c) $2z^2 + 3z - 2$
   d) $2x^2 - 5x + 2$ e) $3c^2 + 5c - 2$ f) $3x^2 - 7x + 2$

3. Factor.
   a) $5x^2 - 9x - 2$ b) $2d^2 - 7d + 3$ c) $3x^2 + x - 4$
   d) $2f^2 - 3f - 5$ e) $4x^2 + 4x + 1$ f) $3h^2 - 8h + 4$

4. Factor.
   a) $3x^2 + 14x - 5$ b) $5e^2 - 16e + 3$ c) $2x^2 + 6x + 4$
   d) $5z^2 - 19z - 4$ e) $9x^2 - 12x + 4$ f) $4m^2 - 4m + 1$

(B)

5. Factor.
   a) $2n^2 + 7n + 6$ b) $5x^2 - 13x + 6$ c) $3x^2 - 2x - 8$
   d) $9k^2 + 12k + 4$ e) $2x^2 + x - 6$ f) $5m^2 - 14m + 8$

6. Factor.
   a) $25a^2 - 20a + 4$ b) $5p^2 - 27p + 10$ c) $2x^2 - 9x + 9$
   d) $3g^2 - 14g + 8$ e) $2b^2 + 11b + 12$ f) $16x^2 + 24x + 9$

7. Factor.
   a) $5u^2 - 39u - 8$
   b) $12q^2 - 20q + 7$
   c) $6x^2 - 7x - 3$
   d) $12m^2 + 19m + 4$
   e) $14x^2 - 37x + 5$
   f) $10x^2 + 7x - 6$

8. Factor.
   a) $10p^2 + p - 21$
   b) $14m^2 + 19m - 40$
   c) $9x^2 - 30x + 25$
   d) $8n^2 + 24n + 18$
   e) $12y^2 - 4y - 56$
   f) $12m^2 - 38m + 30$

9. Factor.
   a) $6y^2 + 17y + 12$
   b) $24q^2 + 10q - 6$
   c) $18z^2 + 35z + 12$
   d) $40b^2 + 66b + 14$
   e) $21a^2 + 13a - 20$
   f) $8a^2 - 14a + 3$

10. Factor.
   a) $6c^2 + 2c - 20$
   b) $12r^2 - r - 35$
   c) $12s^2 - 53s + 56$
   d) $12n^2 + 10n - 12$
   e) $15a^2 - 2a - 24$
   f) $35c^2 + 31c + 6$

Ⓒ

11. Factor.
   a) $4c^2 + 20c + 25$
   b) $28x^2 - 47x + 15$
   c) $12d^2 - 30d + 12$
   d) $35z^2 - 66z + 16$
   e) $24e^2 + 38e + 15$
   f) $8y^2 - 26y + 15$

12. Factor.
   a) $18n^2 + 30n - 12$
   b) $15x^2 - 4x - 4$
   c) $10m^2 - 17m - 6$
   d) $21a^2 + 52a + 32$
   e) $35b^2 + 41b + 12$
   f) $56x^2 - 19x - 10$

13. Find two integers with the given properties.

	Product	Sum		Product	Sum
a)	-250	-15	d)	112	-22
b)	160	-37	e)	-216	6
c)	112	23	f)	-117	-4

14. Factor.
   a) $8x^2 - 30xy + 27y^2$
   b) $21a^2 - 44ab - 32b^2$
   c) $15m^2 - 31mn + 14n^2$
   d) $8p^2 + 22pq + 15q^2$
   e) $6a^2 - 19ab - 36b^2$
   f) $14c^2 - 29cd - 15d^2$

15. Factor.
   a) $18ac^2 - 24ac + 8a$
   b) $36xy^2 - 6x^2y - 6x^3$
   c) $56pq^2 + 62p^2q - 10p^3$
   d) $35m^2n - 43mn + 12n$
   e) $18c^2d^2 + 42c^2d + 20c^2$
   f) $21x^2y - xy - 10y$

CALCULATOR POWER
Evaluating Polynomials by Factoring

A steep cliff is the boundary of one side of
a piece of land which is to be fenced as a
rectangular-shaped corral. The rancher has
840 m of fencing. This fencing is to form
3 sides of the corral, so that it has the greatest
possible area. What are the dimensions of
the corral with the largest area?

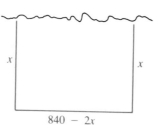
$840 - 2x$

Let x metres represent the length of the two equal sides which are to be
fenced. Then, the third side is $(840 - 2x)$ metres.
The area, in square metres, is $x(840 - 2x)$ or $840x - 2x^2$. This can be
factored as $2x(420 - x)$.

The total length of the two equal sides, $2x$ metres, must be less than
the total length of the fence, 840 m.
Therefore, $2x < 840$
$$x < 420$$

To find the maximum area, the rancher substituted values of x up to
400 into the polynomial. The results are shown below.

x	100	150	200	250	300	350	400
$840x - 2x^2$	64 000	81 000	88 000	85 000	72 000	49 000	16 000

This table suggests that $840x - 2x^2$ is largest when x is between 150 and 250.
The rancher made another table for values of x from 150 to 240.

x	160	170	180	190	200	210	220	230	240
$840x - 2x^2$									

1. Copy the table above.
   a) Use your calculator to evaluate the polynomial $840x - 2x^2$ for $x = 160, 170,$
      180, 190, and 200.
   b) Use your calculator and the product $2x(420 - x)$ to evaluate the polynomial
      $840x - 2x^2$ for $x = 200, 210, 220, 230,$ and 240.
   c) In which form is it easier to evaluate the polynomial: $840x - 2x^2$ or
      $2x(420 - x)$? Explain your answer.

2. Use your completed table to estimate the dimensions of the corral of largest area.

3. a) Use your calculator to evaluate the trinomial $x^2 - 24x + 140$ for all integral values
      of x from 5 to 15. Record your answers in a table.
   b) Use your table to estimate the value of x for which the trinomial
      $x^2 - 24x + 140$ has its minimum value.

8-9 FACTORING A DIFFERENCE OF SQUARES

Recall the product of two binomials that differ only by one sign.
For example, $(x + 5)(x - 5) = (x)^2 - (5)^2$
$$= x^2 - 25$$
The product is written as a difference of squares.

The "difference of squares" can be
illustrated geometrically.

The larger square has area x^2.

The smaller square has area 25.

The area of the shaded region, which is
the difference in areas of the two squares,
is $x^2 - 25$.

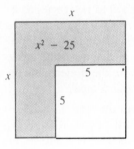

Consider the shaded region cut along the dotted line and the two
pieces repositioned.

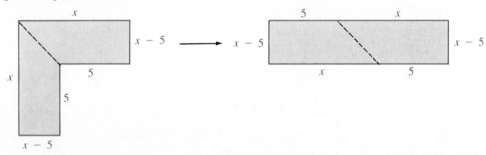

The resulting rectangle has area $(x - 5)(x + 5)$. This is equal to the
area of the original figure, $x^2 - 25$.

If a binomial is expressed as a difference of squares, it can be
factored easily.

Example 1. Factor.

      a) $x^2 - 9$ b) $a^2 - 0.16$ c) $49x^2 - 64$

Solution.   a) $x^2 - 9$ can be written as $(x)^2 - (3)^2$.
$$x^2 - 9 = (x + 3)(x - 3)$$

          b) $a^2 - 0.16$ can be written as $(a)^2 - (0.4)^2$.
$$a^2 - 0.16 = (a + 0.4)(a - 0.4)$$

          c) $49x^2 - 64$ can be written as $(7x)^2 - (8)^2$.
$$49x^2 - 64 = (7x + 8)(7x - 8)$$

A difference of squares may occur after a common factor is removed.

Example 2. Factor.

a) $5x^2 - 45$ b) $8x^3 - 2x$

Solution.   a) $5x^2 - 45$

The terms have a common factor of 5.

$5x^2 - 45 = 5(x^2 - 9)$

Factor the difference of squares.

$= 5(x + 3)(x - 3)$

b) $8x^3 - 2x = 2x(4x^2 - 1)$

$= 2x(2x + 1)(2x - 1)$

Example 3. Factor.

a) $x^2 - y^2$ b) $36x^2 - 9y^2$

Solution.   a) $x^2 - y^2 = (x - y)(x + y)$ b) $36x^2 - 9y^2 = 9(4x^2 - y^2)$

$= 9[(2x)^2 - (y)^2]$

$= 9(2x - y)(2x + y)$

EXERCISES 8-9

Ⓐ

1. Factor.

a) $x^2 - 25$ b) $a^2 - 49$ c) $x^2 - 36$ d) $y^2 - 100$

e) $x^2 - 1$ f) $x^2 - 4$ g) $m^2 - 64$ h) $n^2 - 144$

Ⓑ

2. Draw two diagrams to illustrate the factoring of each difference of squares.

a) $x^2 - 1$ b) $x^2 - 16$ c) $x^2 - 36$ d) $x^2 - 4$

3. Factor.

a) $9a^2 - 4$ b) $25x^2 - 9$ c) $16s^2 - 1$ d) $36 - 100n^2$

e) $100x^2 - 121$ f) $144p^2 - 49$ g) $\frac{1}{4}x^2 - \frac{4}{9}$ h) $6.25 - n^2$

4. Factor.

a) $49a^2 - 1$ b) $4 - 36x^2$ c) $9 - 64m^2$ d) $81y^2 - 49$

e) $1.44x^2 - 1$ f) $1600a^2 - 81$ g) $0.64x^2 - 1.21$ h) $\frac{1}{9} - \frac{1}{16}x^2$

5. Factor completely.

a) $2x^2 - 18$ b) $5x^2 - 5$ c) $3a^2 - 48$ d) $3n^2 + 30$

e) $7 - 28y^2$ f) $2a^2 + 12$ g) $x^3 - 25x$ h) $a^3 - 49a$

6. Factor.

a) $a^2 - b^2$ b) $x^2 - 4y^2$ c) $9m^2 - 16n^2$ d) $36x^2 - 49y^2$

e) $a^2b^2 - c^2$ f) $4a^2b^2 - 9c^2d^2$ g) $4c^4 - 81c^2d^2$ h) $25x^2y^2 - 9y^4$

Ⓒ

7. Factor completely.

a) $x^4 - 1$ b) $a^4 - 16$ c) $16c^4 - 1$ d) $2 - 2x^4$

8-10 SOLVING QUADRATIC EQUATIONS

In the equations you have studied up until now, the variable has never been squared. Examples of equations in which the variable is squared are:

$$x^2 + 3x - 28 = 0 \qquad 3x^2 + 10x - 8 = 0 \qquad 4x^2 = 25.$$

These are called *quadratic equations*.

Quadratic equations such as $4x^2 = 25$, in which there is no first-degree term, can be solved by isolating the variable and taking the square root of both sides.

Example 1. Solve. a) $4x^2 = 25$ b) $9a^2 - 2 = 8$

Solution. a) $4x^2 = 25$ b) $9a^2 - 2 = 8$

$$x^2 = \frac{25}{4} \qquad\qquad 9a^2 = 10$$

$$x = \pm\frac{5}{2} \qquad\qquad a^2 = \frac{10}{9}$$

$$a = \pm\frac{\sqrt{10}}{3}$$

Many quadratic equations have first-degree terms, and some of these can be solved by factoring. The solution of a quadratic equation by factoring depends on the following important property.

> If $(A)(B) = 0$, then either $A = 0$, or $B = 0$, or both

Example 2. Solve and check.

a) $x^2 - x - 6 = 0$ b) $2m^2 + m - 6 = 0$

Solution. a) $x^2 - x - 6 = 0$

Factor: $(x - 3)(x + 2) = 0$

Either $x - 3 = 0$ or $x + 2 = 0$

$x = 3 \qquad\qquad x = -2$

Check. a) If $x = 3$,

$$x^2 - x - 6 = (3)^2 - (3) - 6$$
$$= 9 - 3 - 6$$
$$= 0$$

If $x = -2$,

$$x^2 - x - 6 = (-2)^2 - (-2) - 6$$
$$= 4 + 2 - 6$$
$$= 0$$

Solution.   b) $2m^2 + m - 6 = 0$

Factor: $(2m - 3)(m + 2) = 0$

Either $2m - 3 = 0$ or $m + 2 = 0$

$\qquad\qquad\quad 2m = 3 \qquad\qquad\qquad\qquad m = -2$

$\qquad\qquad\quad m = \dfrac{3}{2}$

Check.   b) If $m = \dfrac{3}{2}$,

$$2m^2 + m - 6 = 2\left(\dfrac{3}{2}\right)^2 + \dfrac{3}{2} - 6$$

$$= \dfrac{9}{2} + \dfrac{3}{2} - 6$$

$$= 0$$

If $m = -2$,

$$2m^2 + m - 6 = 2(-2)^2 + (-2) - 6$$

$$= 8 - 2 - 6$$

$$= 0$$

The solutions are correct.

When an object is projected into the air, its speed changes. The speed decreases as the object goes up, then increases as the object falls back to the ground. Problems involving this situation often involve quadratic equations. The actual equation depends on the initial speed.

Example 3.   If a football is kicked with a vertical speed of 20 m/s, its height h metres after t seconds is given by the formula $h = 20t - 5t^2$. How long after the kick is the football at a height of 15 m?

Solution.   Substitute 15 for h in the formula.

$$15 = 20t - 5t^2$$

$$5t^2 - 20t + 15 = 0$$

$$t^2 - 4t + 3 = 0$$

$$(t - 1)(t - 3) = 0$$

Either $t - 1 = 0$ or $t - 3 = 0$

$\qquad\qquad t = 1 \qquad\qquad\qquad\qquad t = 3$

The football is at a height of 15 m on the way up, 1 s after the kick, and on the way down 3 s after the kick.

EXERCISES 8-10

1. Solve.

a) $x^2 - 2 = 7$ b) $3x^2 = 75$ c) $2x^2 - 3 = 5$

d) $4p^2 - 5 = 11$ e) $3t^2 + 7 = 10$ f) $2a^2 = 12$

g) $2n^2 - 49 = n^2$ h) $8b^2 = 49 + b^2$

2. Solve and check.
   a) $x^2 + 8x + 15 = 0$ b) $x^2 - 7x + 12 = 0$ c) $x^2 - x - 20 = 0$
   d) $x^2 + 5x - 24 = 0$ e) $x^2 + 8x + 12 = 0$ f) $x^2 - 5x - 36 = 0$
   g) $x^2 - 10x + 24 = 0$ h) $x^2 + 15x + 56 = 0$ i) $x^2 - x - 42 = 0$

3. Solve.
   a) $3x^2 - 27 = 0$ b) $3x^2 - 7x + 2 = 0$ c) $2x^2 + 3x - 2 = 0$
   d) $6x^2 + 5x + 1 = 0$ e) $5x^2 - 20 = 0$ f) $3x^2 + x - 2 = 0$
   g) $4x^2 - 3x - 1 = 0$ h) $2x^2 - 128 = 0$ i) $4x^2 + 12x + 9 = 0$

(B)

4. Solve.
   a) $x^2 - 9x + 25 = 5$ b) $x^2 - 16x + 50 = -13$
   c) $x^2 - 6x - 20 = -4$ d) $x^2 + 10x + 25 = 4$
   e) $x^2 - 5x - 20 = -6$ f) $x^2 + 6x - 15 = 4x$
   g) $x^2 - 5x + 16 = 3x$ h) $x^2 - 10x + 16 = 4 - 2x$
   i) $x^2 - 8x - 40 = 4 - x$

5. The height h metres of an infield fly ball t seconds after being hit is given by the formula $h = 30t - 5t^2$. How long after being hit is the ball at a height of 25 m?

6. Solve.
   a) $3x^2 + 15x + 18 = 0$ b) $2x^2 - 24x + 54 = 0$
   c) $4x^2 - 12x - 40 = 0$ d) $2x^2 - 26x + 60 = 0$
   e) $3x^2 + 6x - 72 = 0$ f) $5x^2 - 20x + 20 = 0$

7. The area A of a rectangular picture is given by the formula $A = 28x - x^2$. Calculate the dimensions of a picture that has an area of:
   a) 192 cm²   b) 196 cm²   c) 160 cm².

8. The lengths of the sides of a right triangle are $(x - 1)$ feet, x feet, and $(x + 1)$ feet. Find the lengths of the sides.

9. If the sides of a right triangle are x centimetres, $(x + 7)$ centimetres, and $(x + 9)$ centimetres, what is the actual length of the hypotenuse?

10. The sum S of the first n terms of the number pattern $2 + 4 + 6 + 8 + \ldots$ is given by the formula $S = n(n + 1)$.
    a) Find the sum of the first 20 terms.
    b) If the sum of the first n terms is 110, find n.

11. The sum S of the first n terms of the number pattern $10 + 8 + 6 + 4 + \ldots$ is given by the formula $S = n(11 - n)$.
    a) Find the sum of the first 20 terms.
    b) If the sum of the first n terms is 28, find n.
    c) Why are two values of n possible in part b)?

12. Solve for the variable indicated. Assume all variables represent positive real numbers.

    a) $A = \pi r^2$, r b) $E = \frac{1}{2}mv^2$, v c) $V = \frac{1}{3}\pi r^2 h$, h d) $F = \frac{mn}{d^2}$, d

13. An object falls d metres in t seconds when dropped from rest. The relation between d and t is given by the formula $d = 4.9t^2$. How long would it take an object to hit the ground when dropped from a height of:

    a) 10 m   b) 20 m   c) 40 m?

14. The area A of an equilateral triangle is given approximately by the formula $A = 0.433x^2$, where x is the length of its sides. What is the side length of an equilateral triangle with area:

    a) 10 cm²   b) 20 cm²   c) 40 cm²?

15. From a height of 2500 m, a parachutist lands on a circular target with an area of 20 m². What is the radius of the target?

16. A rectangular ice surface has area 5500 yd². The length is 10 yd more than twice the width. Find the dimensions of the ice.

17. The area of a trapezoid is 180 in². The length of one parallel side is twice the height of the trapezoid. The other parallel side is 4 in. longer than the first parallel side. Find the height of the trapezoid.

18. Two numbers differ by 6. The sum of their squares is 90. Find the numbers.

19. Two numbers have a sum of 12. The square of one number is double the other number. Find the numbers.

20. The ones digit of a two-digit number is 1 less than the tens digit. The sum of the squares of the digits is 85. Find the number.

21. A rectangular lawn measures 40 m by 30 m. If it is being cut from the outside in, how wide a strip has been cut when the job is half finished?

22. Write a quadratic equation with these roots.

    a) 9, −2   b) 4, 10   c) $-5, -\frac{1}{3}$ d) $\frac{7}{8}, -\frac{1}{4}$

INVESTIGATE

Is it possible for a quadratic equation to have no solution in the set of real numbers?

8-11 DIVIDING POLYNOMIALS BY MONOMIALS

To divide a monomial by a monomial, recall this exponent law.

$$\frac{x^m}{x^n} = x^{m-n}, \, x \neq 0$$

Example 1. Simplify.

a) $\dfrac{x^5}{x^3}$ 　　　　　b) $\dfrac{21y^6}{3y^2}$ 　　　　　c) $12x^3y^2 \div 8x^2y$

Solution. 　a) $\dfrac{x^5}{x^3} = x^{5-3}$ 　　b) $\dfrac{21y^6}{3y^2} = 7y^{6-2}$ 　　c) $12x^3y^2 \div 8x^2y$

$= x^2$ 　　　　　　　　　$= 7y^4$ 　　　　　　　　$= \dfrac{12x^3y^2}{8x^2y}$

$= \dfrac{3}{2}xy$

In arithmetic, you will recall that we cannot divide by zero. Such an operation is undefined. This principle also applies in algebra. In *Example 1*, and the following examples, we assume that no denominator is equal to zero.

To divide a polynomial by a monomial, perform the division with each term.

Example 2. Simplify.

a) $\dfrac{9a + 15}{3}$ 　　　b) $\dfrac{24x^2 - 9x}{-3x}$ 　　　c) $\dfrac{20x^4 - 15x^3 + 5x^2}{5x^2}$

Solution. 　a) $\dfrac{9a + 15}{3} = \dfrac{9a}{3} + \dfrac{15}{3}$ 　　　b) $\dfrac{24x^2 - 9x}{-3x} = \dfrac{24x^2}{-3x} - \dfrac{9x}{-3x}$

$= 3a + 5$ 　　　　　　　　　　　$= -8x + 3$

c) $\dfrac{20x^4 - 15x^3 + 5x^2}{5x^2} = \dfrac{20x^4}{5x^2} - \dfrac{15x^3}{5x^2} + \dfrac{5x^2}{5x^2}$

$= 4x^2 - 3x + 1$

Here is an alternative method of dividing a polynomial by a monomial.

Example 3. Simplify. $\dfrac{x^3y^2 - 3x^2y^4 + 2x^4y^2}{4x^2y}$

Solution. 　Factor the polynomial. Then, divide the polynomial and the monomial by their greatest common factor.

$$\frac{x^3y^2 - 3x^2y^4 + 2x^4y^2}{4x^2y} = \frac{x^2y^2(x - 3y^2 + 2x^2)}{4x^2y}$$

$$= \frac{y(x - 3y^2 + 2x^2)}{4}$$

The solution to *Example 3* could be written as the sum of terms.

$$\frac{y(x - 3y^2 + 2x^2)}{4} = \frac{xy}{4} - \frac{3y^3}{4} + \frac{2x^2y}{4} \text{ , or } \frac{xy}{4} - \frac{3y^3}{4} + \frac{x^2y}{2}$$

EXERCISES 8-11

In each exercise, assume that no variable in the denominator is equal to zero.

Ⓐ

1. Simplify.

a) $\dfrac{12x^3}{3}$ b) $\dfrac{32y^4}{16}$ c) $\dfrac{18y^4}{2y}$ d) $\dfrac{27m^3}{-9m}$

e) $\dfrac{-45y^6}{-5y^4}$ f) $\dfrac{3n^6}{5n^4}$ g) $\dfrac{25x^4}{-5x^4}$ h) $\dfrac{36c^5}{24c^2}$

i) $18x^4 \div 3x$ j) $-52y^6 \div 13y^5$ k) $-45a^5 \div 20a^3$ l) $\dfrac{3}{4}x^3 \div \dfrac{1}{2}x^2$

2. Simplify.

a) $\dfrac{8a + 4}{4}$ b) $\dfrac{12y - 3}{3}$ c) $\dfrac{18x^2 - 6}{6}$ d) $\dfrac{6a + 15}{3}$

e) $\dfrac{24x - 4}{4}$ f) $\dfrac{-10 + 4m}{-2}$ g) $\dfrac{15 - 5n}{-5}$ h) $\dfrac{-21 + 7x}{-7}$

Ⓑ

3. Simplify.

a) $\dfrac{36x^4y^2}{9xy}$ b) $\dfrac{54a^5b^2}{-9a^3b^2}$ c) $\dfrac{-28m^2n^2}{-4m^2n^2}$

d) $\dfrac{-18a^2b^5}{6a^2b^3}$ e) $\dfrac{42x^5y^5}{-14x^3y^3}$ f) $\dfrac{-25a^2b^3c^4}{-5ab^2c^3}$

4. Simplify.

a) $\dfrac{3x^2 - 6x}{3x}$ b) $\dfrac{5x^2 - 10x}{5x}$ c) $\dfrac{18a - 21a^2}{3a}$

d) $\dfrac{-28n^2 - 7n}{7n}$ e) $\dfrac{36y^3 - 9y^2}{-9y}$ f) $\dfrac{32b^4 + 8b^3}{-4b^2}$

g) $\dfrac{-3m^5 + 18m^2}{-3m^2}$ h) $\dfrac{-4x^5 - 12x^3}{-4x^2}$ i) $\dfrac{-7c^2 + 6c^3}{-6c^2}$

5. Simplify.

a) $\dfrac{18x^2 - 6x + 30}{6}$ b) $\dfrac{-5 - 15c + 10c^2}{-5}$ c) $\dfrac{4x^3 - 12x^2 + 8x}{4x}$

d) $\dfrac{8a + 2a^2 - 2a^3}{2a}$ e) $\dfrac{15x^4 - 30x^3 + 5x^2}{5x^2}$ f) $\dfrac{18a^4 + 6a^3 - 12a^2}{-6a^2}$

6. Simplify.

a) $\dfrac{3x^2 - 9x^3 + 27x^5}{3x^2}$ b) $\dfrac{28m^5 - 14m^3 + 7m^2}{-7m^2}$ c) $\dfrac{36a^6 + 18a^4 - 12a^3}{6a^3}$

d) $\dfrac{-10y^6 - 15y^4 + 25y^2}{-5y^2}$ e) $\dfrac{12n^4 - 18n^3 + 24n^2}{9n^2}$ f) $\dfrac{60x^7 - 36x^5 + 12x^3}{-12x^2}$

7. Simplify.

a) $\dfrac{3x^2y^2 - 9x^4y^4 + 18x^3y^5}{3x^2y^2}$

b) $\dfrac{24a^4b^5 - 18a^3b^4 + 12a^2b^3}{6a^2b^2}$

c) $\dfrac{16m^2n^6 - 32m^3n^5 + 48m^4n^4}{-16m^2n^3}$

d) $\dfrac{12x^6y^4 - 8x^5y^3 + 4x^2y^2}{4x^4y^2}$

e) $\dfrac{-27a^5b + 18a^4b^2 - 9a^3b^3}{-9a^3b}$

f) $\dfrac{54x^2y^3z^4 - 36x^3y^4z^5 + 18x^4y^5z^6}{18x^2y^2z^2}$

8. The volume V of a sphere of radius R is given by the formula $V = \dfrac{4}{3}\pi R^3$. The surface area S is given by the formula $S = 4\pi R^2$. Write an expression for the quotient $\dfrac{V}{S}$ for a sphere of radius R.

9. The surface area S of a cylinder of radius R and height h is given by $S = 2\pi Rh + 2\pi R^2$. The volume V is given by $V = \pi R^2 h$. Write an expression for the quotient $\dfrac{V}{S}$ for a cylinder with $h = 2R$.

8-12 RATIONAL EXPRESSIONS

The set of numbers obtained by adding, subtracting, multiplying, or dividing integers is called the set of rational numbers.

Just as integers are the "building blocks" for rational numbers, so polynomials are the building blocks for rational expressions.

> The sum, difference, product or quotient of any two polynomials is called a *rational expression*.

These are rational expressions.

$$3, \quad 4x + 2, \quad 5xy, \quad 3x^2y - 2y, \quad \frac{5x}{7y}, \quad \frac{3x^2 - y}{z}$$

Each expression can be written as the sum, difference, product or quotient of two polynomials. In addition, 3, $4x + 2$, $5xy$, and $3x^2y - 2y$ are polynomials.

These are not rational expressions.

$$\sqrt{x^2 + x + 3}, \quad \frac{1 + \sqrt{x}}{3}, \quad \frac{\sqrt{x} - 1}{3x}$$

These expressions cannot be written as the sums, differences, products, or quotients of polynomials.

Operations with rational expressions are performed in the same way as operations with rational numbers.

It is important to realize that rational expressions are not defined for values of the variables which would make the denominator equal to zero. This is because division by zero is not defined.

Example 1. Simplify.

a) $\dfrac{3m^2n}{4m^2} \times \dfrac{2m^3n}{5n}$

b) $\dfrac{3a^2b}{4} \div \dfrac{2b}{5a}$

c) $\dfrac{x - 2}{3} \times \dfrac{2}{x}$

d) $\dfrac{x - 1}{2x} \div \dfrac{3}{x}$

Solution.

a) $\dfrac{3m^2n}{4m^2} \times \dfrac{2m^3n}{5n} = \dfrac{6m^5n^2}{20m^2n}$

$= \dfrac{3m^3n}{10}$

b) To divide by a rational expression, multiply by its reciprocal.

$\dfrac{3a^2b}{4} \div \dfrac{2b}{5a} = \dfrac{3a^2b}{4} \times \dfrac{5a}{2b}$

$= \dfrac{15a^3b}{8b}$

$= \dfrac{15a^3}{8}$

c) $\dfrac{x - 2}{3} \times \dfrac{2}{x} = \dfrac{2(x - 2)}{3x}$

$= \dfrac{2x - 4}{3x}$

d) $\dfrac{x - 1}{2x} \div \dfrac{3}{x} = \dfrac{x - 1}{2x} \times \dfrac{x}{3}$

$= \dfrac{x(x - 1)}{6x}$

$= \dfrac{x - 1}{6}$

Rational expressions are added and subtracted in the same way as rational numbers.

Example 2. Simplify.

a) $\dfrac{m - 4}{3} + \dfrac{m + 5}{3}$

b) $\dfrac{x + 2}{3x^2} + \dfrac{2(x - 3)}{3x^2}$

c) $\dfrac{3}{2y^2} - \dfrac{5 - y}{2y^2}$

d) $\dfrac{a - 2}{3} - \dfrac{3(a - 1)}{4}$

Solution.

a) $\dfrac{m - 4}{3} + \dfrac{m + 5}{3} = \dfrac{m - 4 + m + 5}{3}$

$= \dfrac{2m + 1}{3}$

b) $\dfrac{x + 2}{3x^2} + \dfrac{2(x - 3)}{3x^2} = \dfrac{x + 2 + 2(x - 3)}{3x^2}$

$= \dfrac{x + 2 + 2x - 6}{3x^2}$

$= \dfrac{3x - 4}{3x^2}$

c) $\dfrac{3}{2y^2} - \dfrac{5-y}{2y^2} = \dfrac{3-(5-y)}{2y^2}$

$\qquad\qquad\qquad = \dfrac{3-5+y}{2y^2}$

$\qquad\qquad\qquad = \dfrac{y-2}{2y^2}$

d) Write the rational expressions with a common denominator of 12.

$\dfrac{a-2}{3} - \dfrac{3(a-1)}{4} = \dfrac{a-2}{3} \times \dfrac{4}{4} - \dfrac{3(a-1)}{4} \times \dfrac{3}{3}$

$\qquad\qquad\qquad = \dfrac{4(a-2) - 9(a-1)}{12}$

$\qquad\qquad\qquad = \dfrac{4a - 8 - 9a + 9}{12}$

$\qquad\qquad\qquad = \dfrac{-5a + 1}{12}$

EXERCISES 8-12

Ⓐ

1. Which of these expressions are rational expressions?

a) $\dfrac{3a^2b}{2}$ b) $\dfrac{4m^2n^2}{3mn}$ c) $\dfrac{3}{5}$ d) $\dfrac{1}{2\sqrt{a}}$ e) $\dfrac{3\sqrt{a}}{4}$ f) $\dfrac{x-6}{5}$

g) $\dfrac{3-4y}{2y}$ h) $\dfrac{3x}{1+\sqrt{x}}$ i) $-\dfrac{4}{3}$ j) $3x^2 + 1$ k) $\dfrac{4+3m^2}{2m^3}$ l) $\dfrac{x^2+\sqrt{x}}{3}$

2. Simplify.

a) $\dfrac{2x^2}{y} \times \dfrac{3x}{2y^3}$ b) $\dfrac{-4m^2n^2}{m} \times \dfrac{3mn}{n^2}$ c) $\dfrac{8xy^3}{3} \times \dfrac{x^2y}{4x^2y^2}$

d) $\dfrac{-5n}{3mn} \times \dfrac{-2m^2n^2}{n^2}$ e) $\dfrac{3a}{2b} \times \dfrac{2a^2b}{3ab^2}$ f) $\dfrac{2c^2d^3}{3c^3} \times \dfrac{-4c^2d^2}{d^3}$

g) $\dfrac{6x^2y^5}{x^2y^2} \times \dfrac{2x^2y}{3xy^2}$ h) $\dfrac{m^2n^3}{3m} \times \dfrac{-4m^2n}{5n}$ i) $\dfrac{2x^5}{3y^2} \times \dfrac{5x^2y^3}{-4x^3}$

3. Simplify.

a) $\dfrac{x^3y}{2} \div \dfrac{y^2}{4x}$ b) $\dfrac{2x^2y^3}{3} \div \dfrac{6xy^2}{5x^2}$ c) $\dfrac{4m^2n^3}{3mn} \div \dfrac{8mn^2}{m}$

d) $\dfrac{a^2b^3}{2a} \div \dfrac{ab^2}{3ab}$ e) $\dfrac{-x^4y^3}{2xy} \div \dfrac{xy^2}{4x}$ f) $\dfrac{6c^2d^3}{5cd} \div \dfrac{12cd^2}{25c^2d}$

g) $\dfrac{3x^2y^4}{2xy^2} \div \dfrac{-4x^2y^2}{3xy}$ h) $\dfrac{-2a^2b^3}{5ab^2} \div \dfrac{-8ab}{15a}$ i) $\dfrac{7x^2y^5}{-3xy} \div \dfrac{-14x^2y^2}{x^2y}$

j) $\dfrac{3p^2q}{5pq^2} \div \dfrac{-15pq}{20p^3q^4}$ k) $\dfrac{28a^3b^4}{-9ab^7} \div \dfrac{7a^5}{27b^6}$ l) $\dfrac{-6m^3n^4}{55m^4n} \div \dfrac{21mn}{-22mn^4}$

4. Simplify.

a) $\dfrac{a + 3}{2} + \dfrac{2a - 1}{2}$

b) $\dfrac{3x - 1}{5} - \dfrac{x + 1}{5}$

c) $\dfrac{3 + y}{7} + \dfrac{2y - 1}{7}$

d) $\dfrac{3m - 2}{4} + \dfrac{m + 1}{4}$

e) $\dfrac{4 - 3n}{3} - \dfrac{n + 5}{3}$

f) $\dfrac{5x - 2}{6} - \dfrac{3x - 4}{6}$

g) $\dfrac{4y - 5}{5} - \dfrac{2(y + 1)}{5}$

h) $\dfrac{2(x + 4)}{3} + \dfrac{3(x - 2)}{3}$

i) $\dfrac{3(m + 2)}{4} - \dfrac{(4 - m)}{4}$

(B)

5. Simplify.

a) $\dfrac{3x + 1}{2x^2} + \dfrac{x - 1}{2x^2}$

b) $\dfrac{2a - 5}{3a^2} - \dfrac{6 + a}{3a^2}$

c) $\dfrac{4 - 3m}{2m} - \dfrac{2 + m}{2m}$

d) $\dfrac{2y - 3}{3y^3} + \dfrac{4 + 3y}{3y^3}$

e) $\dfrac{x - 2}{x^4} - \dfrac{5 - 2x}{x^4}$

f) $\dfrac{7 - 2n}{4n^2} + \dfrac{4n - 3}{4n^2}$

g) $\dfrac{2(x - 1)}{3x^2} + \dfrac{4(x + 1)}{3x^2}$

h) $\dfrac{y - 5}{2y^3} - \dfrac{3(y - 1)}{2y^3}$

i) $\dfrac{8a + 3}{5a} - \dfrac{2(3 + a)}{5a}$

6. Simplify.

a) $\dfrac{-3x^2y^2}{2y^3} \times \dfrac{5xy}{3x^2}$

b) $\dfrac{14ab^4}{3ab} \div \dfrac{-7ab^2}{6a^2b}$

c) $\dfrac{3m^2n^4}{2mn} \div \dfrac{6m^4n^2}{m^2n^2}$

d) $\dfrac{2x^2yz^2}{3xy} \times \dfrac{xy^2z}{2yz}$

e) $\dfrac{3a^2bc}{-a^2bc^2} \div \dfrac{6ab^2c}{ab^2c^3}$

f) $\dfrac{-3xyz^2}{2x^2y^2z} \times \dfrac{5x^2y^2z}{-4xyz^3}$

7. Simplify.

a) $\dfrac{3(x + 1)}{2x^2} - \dfrac{2(x - 1)}{2x^2}$

b) $\dfrac{4(1 - y)}{3y^3} + \dfrac{2(y + 3)}{3y^3}$

c) $\dfrac{1 - m}{2m} - \dfrac{3 - 2m}{2m}$

d) $\dfrac{5(2 - a)}{a^3} + \dfrac{3(2a + 1)}{a^3}$

e) $\dfrac{-2(x + 5)}{3x^2} - \dfrac{4(1 - x)}{3x^2}$

f) $\dfrac{3(a + 2)}{4a^3} + \dfrac{5(1 - a)}{4a^3}$

8. Simplify.

a) $\dfrac{x - 1}{3} + \dfrac{2x + 1}{4}$

b) $\dfrac{2a + 3}{3} - \dfrac{a + 4}{2}$

c) $\dfrac{4 - 3m}{2} - \dfrac{5 + m}{5}$

d) $\dfrac{3(y + 1)}{4} + \dfrac{y - 1}{3}$

e) $\dfrac{n - 1}{2} + \dfrac{3(4 - n)}{7}$

f) $\dfrac{2(x + 6)}{5} - \dfrac{x - 3}{4}$

(C)

9. It takes x hours to fill a swimming pool when only hose #1 is used. It takes y hours to fill the pool if only hose #2 is used. Write a rational expression to show how long it takes to fill the pool if both hoses are used.

10. An aircraft has an air speed of v miles per hour. When there is a tail wind of w miles per hour, the resultant speed of the aircraft is $(v + w)$ miles per hour. When there is a head wind of w miles per hour, the resultant speed of the aircraft is $(v - w)$ miles per hour.

   A and B are two towns D miles apart. The aircraft travels from A to B and back to A.

   a) Write a rational expression for the total time taken for the round trip.

   b) Write a rational expression for the average speed of the round trip.

Review Exercises

1. Simplify each expression. Arrange each polynomial in descending powers, and state its degree.
   a) $5x - 2x + 7 - 4x$ b) $15y^2 - 3y + 6y^3 - 2y^2 + 7y$
   c) $2a - 5a^4 + 6a^2 - 4a^2 + 7a + 8a^4 - a^3$

2. Simplify.
   a) $(5y - 3) + (2y + 4)$ b) $(7x - 2) - (5x + 3)$
   c) $(8r - 5) - (-3r + 2)$ d) $(5y^2 - 3y) + (6y - 2y^2)$
   e) $(4x - 3) - (2x + 1) - (-3x + 4)$

3. Simplify.
   a) $(7a)(5a)$ b) $(-3b)(5b)$ c) $(-4y)^2$ d) $(-9x^3)(7x^2)$ e) $(-2y)^3$

4. Expand.
   a) $4(y - 2)$ b) $-4(x + 2)$ c) $3x(5 - x)$ d) $-5x(3 - x)$

5. Factor and check.
   a) $6y + 18y^2$ b) $-3a + 12a^4$ c) $5a^2 - 25a^3$
   d) $3a^3 + 4a^2 + 7a$ e) $6x^2y - 3xy + 9xy^2$ f) $8ab - 4a^2b^2 + 6ab^2$

6. Find each product.
   a) $(x - 3)(x - 4)$ b) $(y + 7)(y + 3)$ c) $(a - 2)(a + 5)$
   d) $4(x - 5)(x - 6)$ e) $y(y - 2)(y + 9)$ f) $-3y(1 - y)(7 + y)$

7. Expand.
   a) $(x + 3)^2$ b) $(y - 5)^2$ c) $(5 - q)^2$ d) $(6 - 5y)^2$

8. Factor.
   a) $x^2 - 7x + 10$ b) $x^2 - 6x + 9$ c) $x^2 + 6x + 5$
   d) $a^2 - 4a - 12$ e) $x^2 - x + 12$ f) $15 + 2x - x^2$
   g) $2y^2 + 3y - 27$ h) $3n^2 + 19n - 40$ i) $2x^2 + 7x + 5$

9. Find each product.
   a) $(a - 4)(a + 4)$ b) $(x + 8)(x - 8)$ c) $(2 - y)(2 + y)$

10. Factor.

   a) $b^2 - 25$ b) $x^2 - 81$ c) $y^2 - 121$ d) $m^2 - \dfrac{1}{4}$

11. Solve.
    a) $x^2 - 4x - 21 = 0$ b) $x^2 + x - 56 = 0$ c) $4x^2 - 12x + 9 = 0$

12. Simplify.
    a) $\dfrac{15x - 20}{5}$ b) $\dfrac{-12 + 2x}{-2}$ c) $\dfrac{12x^2 + 4x}{4x}$

13. Simplify.
    a) $\dfrac{a^2b^2}{10bc} \times \dfrac{-25b^2c}{4a^2c}$ b) $\dfrac{3}{2}x^3 \div \dfrac{1}{4}x^2$ c) $\dfrac{3m^2n^3}{-5mn^2} \div \dfrac{9m^4n^2}{30mn}$
    d) $\dfrac{x + 3}{2} + \dfrac{2x + 5}{2}$ e) $\dfrac{2m - 7}{3} - \dfrac{3m + 4}{3}$

9 Analytic Geometry

The height to which a ball bounces varies directly as the distance from which it was dropped. If it is dropped from a height of 2.4 m, it bounces to a height of 1.6 m. If it is dropped from a height of 3.0 m, how high will it bounce? (See Section 9-7, *Example 2*.)

9-1 THE CARTESIAN COORDINATE SYSTEM

There is a story that the great 17th century French mathematician, René Descartes, in bed because of illness, was watching a spider on the ceiling. As he watched, he thought of how he might describe the position of the spider at any instant. The technique he devised is called the *Cartesian coordinate system*. Although the system is named after Descartes, another French mathematician, Pierre de Fermat, is equally deserving of acclaim. For, quite independently, he developed the same technique at about the same time.

In coordinate geometry, we represent points, lines, circles, and other curves by numbers and equations. Geometric problems can be solved using arithmetic and algebra. Descartes, de Fermat, and others were able to apply these methods to practical problems in astronomy, optics, ballistics, and navigation.

The plane is divided into four regions by the *x*- and *y*-axes, which are perpendicular. These regions are called *quadrants*.

Point A has *coordinates* (3,4). The *x*-coordinate is always written first, hence, (3,4) is an *ordered pair of numbers*. The coordinates of B appear to be $(-4.5, -2.5)$.

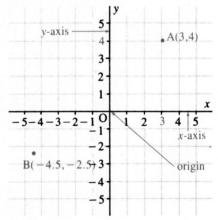

Example 1.
a) State the coordinates of the points P, Q, R, and S.
b) Plot these points.
   A$(-3, -1)$, B$(4, -4)$, C$(-2,4)$, D$(4,4)$
c) Where are the points with:
   i) -3 as their *x*-coordinate
   ii) 2 as their *y*-coordinate
   iii) 0 as their *y*-coordinate?

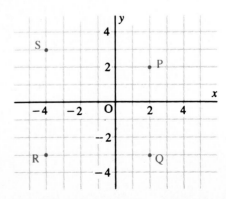

Solution.   a) The coordinates are P(2,2), Q(2, − 3), R(− 4, − 3), S(− 4,3).

b)

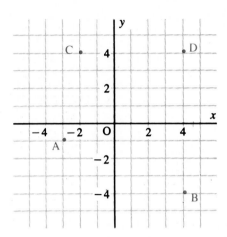

c)   i) The points with − 3 as their *x*-coordinate lie on a line 3 units to the left of the *y*-axis and parallel to it.
ii) The points with 2 as their *y*-coordinate lie on a line 2 units above the *x*-axis and parallel to it.
iii) The points with 0 as their *y*-coordinate lie on the *x*-axis.

Example 2. Plot these points. P(− 2.5,2.5), Q(2.5,2.5), R(4, − 1), S(− 1, − 1)
a) Draw PQ, QR, RS, and SP.
b) What polygon have you drawn?

Solution.   a)

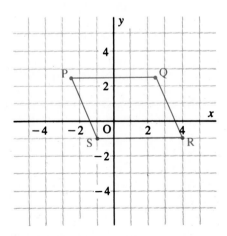

b) The polygon appears to be a parallelogram.

EXERCISES 9-1

Ⓐ

1. State the coordinates of the points A to J.

2. Plot these points. M(3,4), N(−2,−6), P(−4,5), Q(0,4), R(−4,0), S(−5,−2), T(0,−5), U(3,−4)

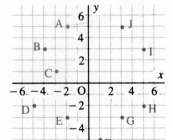

3. Where are the points with:
   a) *x*-coordinate 0
   b) *y*-coordinate −4
   c) *x*-coordinate negative
   d) *x*-coordinate negative, *y*-coordinate positive
   e) *x*-coordinate and *y*-coordinate equal?

Ⓑ

4. Plot these points on the same axes and draw the line segments named.
   a) A(−4,3), B(−3,−2), C(−2,1), D(−1,−2), E(0,3); AB, BC, CD, DE
   b) F(2,3), G(2,−2), H(4,3), J(4,−2), K(2,0), L(4,0); FG, HJ, KL
   c) M(6,3), N(8,3), P(7,0), R(7,−2); MP, NP, RP
   d) What word is formed?

5. a) Plot these points. T(−4,1), C(−3,−3), E(5,−1), R(4,3)
   b) Draw these line segments. TC, CE, ER, RT
   c) What polygon have you drawn?

6. Plot each set of points and determine which sets of points do *not* form triangles.
   a) A(−3,1), B(1,−1), C(3,−4)   b) O(0,0), E(6,2), F(9,3)
   c) G(2,−3), H(5,−1), I(8,1)   d) K(4,−6), L(2,−2), M(−4,10)
   e) O(0,0), P(8,3), Q(13,4)   f) R(−1,1), S(2,3), T(5,5)

7. The coordinates of three vertices of a square are given. Find the coordinates of the fourth vertex.
   a) A(3,5), B(−4,5), C(−4,−2)   b) D(1,2), E(5,−2), F(1,−6)
   c) G(−3,−1), H(4,2), J(2,−3)   d) K(−3,−1), L(4,0), M(1,−4)

8. Plot each set of points and join them by line segments to form a quadrilateral. State whether the quadrilateral is a parallelogram, trapezoid, rhombus, rectangle, square, or none of these.
   a) A(1,1), B(−4,1), C(−4,−4), D(1,−4)
   b) E(−2,5), F(−5,−3), G(−5,−5), H(−2,−3)
   c) J(3,0), K(0,3), L(−3,0), M(0,−3)
   d) N(0,4), P(1,0), Q(−1,0), R(0,−4)

Ⓒ

9. The coordinates of three vertices of a parallelogram are given. Find the coordinates of a fourth possible vertex.
   a) B(3,0), C(6,3), D(0,3)   b) E(2,1), F(5,3), G(2,7)
   c) H(1,6), J(−5,1), K(3,1)   d) L(0,−3), M(0,3), N(2,0)

10. Which polygon has these vertices? P(*a*,0), Q(*b*,0), R(*a*,*b* − *a*), S(*b*,*b* − *a*)?

9-2 AREAS OF POLYGONS IN A COORDINATE SYSTEM

When you fly over rural areas, you will notice that the farms appear to be a patchwork quilt of polygons of different colors.

You can estimate the area of any farm by superimposing a Cartesian grid on an aerial photo.

If the grid lines are sufficiently close together, the perimeters of most of the farms will appear to lie along grid lines.

To calculate the area of a polygon on a grid, we need to recall the formulas for the areas of some familiar polygons.

Area of a triangle

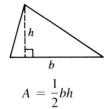

$$A = \frac{1}{2}bh$$

Area of a rectangle

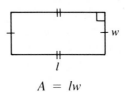

$$A = lw$$

Area of a parallelogram

$$A = bh$$

Area of a trapezoid

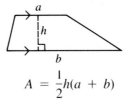

$$A = \frac{1}{2}h(a + b)$$

To find the area of a polygon drawn on a grid
- Write the coordinates of each vertex.
- Subtract the coordinates of pairs of adjacent vertices to find dimensions such as length, width, and height.
- Substitute the appropriate dimensions into the formula to calculate the area.

Example 1. Find the area of each polygon on the grid.

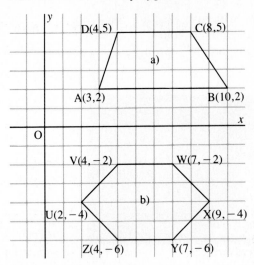

Solution.

a) ABCD is a trapezoid with coordinates A(3,2), B(10,2), C(8,5), and D(4,5).
DC = 8 − 4, or 4
AB = 10 − 3, or 7
The height of DC above AB is the vertical distance between them, 3.
Use $A = \frac{1}{2}h(a + b)$

$$A = \frac{1}{2}(3)(4 + 7)$$

$$= \frac{33}{2}$$

The area of the trapezoid is 16.5 square units.

b) Join U and X to divide the hexagon into 2 congruent trapezoids. For trapezoid UVWX, the coordinates of the vertices are U(2, −4), V(4, −2), W(7, −2), and X(9, −4).
VW = 7 − 4, or 3
UX = 9 − 2, or 7
The height of VW above UX is 2.
Use $A = \frac{1}{2}h(a + b)$

$$A = \frac{1}{2}(2)(3 + 7)$$

$$= 10$$

The area of hexagon UVWXYZ is double the area of trapezoid UVWX. So, area UVWXYZ is 20 square units.

Example 2. Find the area of square ABCD with coordinates A(7,6), B(10,13), C(17,10), and D(14,3).

Solution. Plot A, B, C, and D on a grid and join them to form a square.

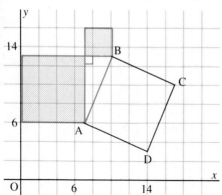

Draw the triangle which has one side, AB, of the square as its hypotenuse. From the Pythagorean Theorem, the area of ABCD is the sum of the areas of the two shaded squares.

Area ABCD $= 7^2 + 3^2$
$= 49 + 9$
$= 58$

The area of ABCD is 58 square units.

If a polygon is drawn on a grid without axes, draw the *y*-axis along a vertical grid line and the *x*-axis along a horizontal grid line. Label the axes so each vertex of the polygon can be described by its coordinates.

EXERCISES 9-2

Ⓐ

1. Find the area of each triangle.

a)

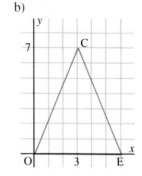

b)

c)

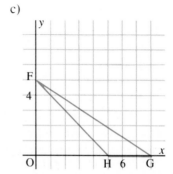

2. Find the area of each trapezoid.

a)

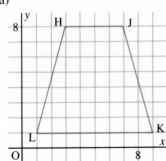

b)

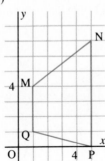

c)

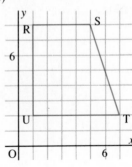

Ⓑ

3. a) Name the polygon with vertices O(0,0), G(0,2), H(3,3), and J(3,5).
   b) Find the area of the polygon.

4. a) Name the triangle with vertices O(0,0), L(7,8), and M(14,0).
   b) Find the area of the triangle.

5. Find the area and side length of each square.

a)   b)   c)

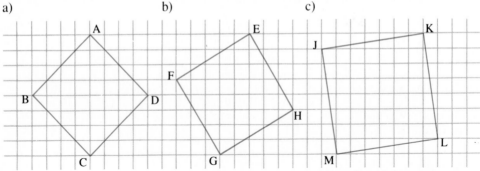

6. Find the area of the quadrilateral with vertices A(3, −1), B(3,2), C(−4,2), and D(−4, −1).

7. a) Find the area of each square on the grid.
   b) What fraction of the area of the larger square is the area of the smaller square?

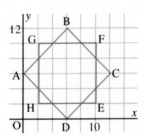

8. Find the area of the triangle with vertices D(−1,2), E(−1,7), and F(11,2).

9. Find the area of the polygon with vertices O(0,0), K(2,9), L(9,8), M(12,5), N(12,0).

9-3 DISPLAYING RELATIONS

Tickets to a theatre cost $6.00 each. The cost of a number of tickets (less than seven for convenience) can be displayed in a table and in a graph.

Number of Tickets	Total Cost ($)
0	0
1	6
2	12
3	18
4	24
5	30
6	36

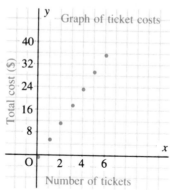

Both the table and the graph relate numbers in pairs. A more concise way of doing this is as a set of ordered pairs.

{(0,0), (1,6), (2,12), (3,18), (4,24), (5,30), (6,36)}

This set of ordered pairs is an example of a *relation*. The first number in each pair is the number of tickets. The second number is the total cost of the tickets. Thus, the ordered pair (3,18) indicates that 3 tickets cost $18.

Example 1. The graph shows the relation between the service charge on a checking account and the number of checks written.
a) From the graph, determine:
 i) the service charge on 4 checks
 ii) the number of checks handled for a charge of $1.25.
b) Write the relation as a set of ordered pairs.

Graph of service charges

Solution. a) i) The ordered pair, (4,1.00) indicates that the service charge on 4 checks is $1.00.
 ii) The ordered pair (5,1.25) indicates that $1.25 is the service charge on 5 checks.
b) The relation defined by the graph is:
 {(0,0), (1,0.25), (2,0.50), (3,0.75), (4,1.00), (5,1.25)}

Example 2. When Jessica arrived for the first day of her summer job, she saw this chart on the bulletin board.
 Draw a graph to show the wages earned for working up to 10 h.

Hours worked	Wages earned
3	$20.82
5	$34.70
8	$55.52
10	$69.40

Solution. To draw a graph, follow these steps.
Step 1. *Count the number of squares available in the horizontal direction.*

On the graph paper shown, there are 18 squares in this direction. Some of these will be needed to write the scale along the vertical axis. Therefore, approximately 15 squares are available for the graph.

Step 2. *Compare the number of squares available with the greatest value to be plotted in the horizontal direction. Choose an appropriate value to be represented by each square.*

We plot the number of hours in the horizontal direction. The greatest value to be plotted is 10 h. We can let one square represent 1 h, and the graph will occupy 10 squares horizontally.

Step 3. *Count the number of squares available in the vertical direction.*

There are 20 squares in this direction. Some of these will be needed to write the scale along the horizontal axis. Therefore, approximately 17 squares are available for the graph.

Step 4.   *Compare the number of squares available with the greatest value to be plotted in the vertical direction. Choose an appropriate value to be represented by each square.*

We plot wages in the vertical direction. The greatest value to be plotted is $69.40. We can let 2 squares represent $10, and the graph will occupy 14 squares vertically.

Step 5.   *Draw a set of axes scaled as in Steps 2 and 4.*

The scale we chose does not enable us to show the cents on the values of the wages earned. Hence, round the values to the nearest dollar before plotting the points. Then draw a straight line through them.

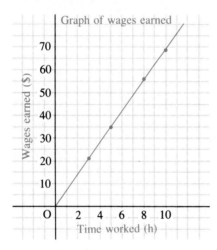

Sometimes there is no simple arithmetical relationship between the numbers in the ordered pairs of a relation.

Example 3.   Write the relation as a set of ordered pairs.

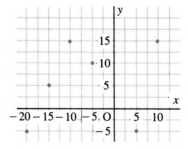

Solution.   The relation defined by the graph is this set of ordered pairs.

$$\{(-20, -5), (-15, 5), (-10, 15), (-5, 10), (5, -5), (10, 15)\}$$

It does not matter in what order the ordered pairs are listed.

EXERCISES 9-3

Ⓐ

1. Write each relation as a set of ordered pairs.

a)

Number	Cost ($)
1	0.50
2	0.95
3	1.35
4	1.70
5	2.00

b)

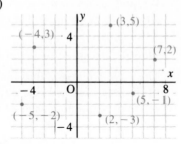

2. Write each relation as a set of ordered pairs.

a)

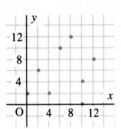

b)

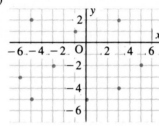

c)

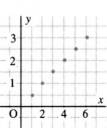

d)

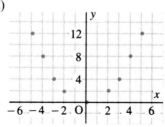

Ⓑ

3. Draw the graph for each relation.

a)

Rectangles with same Perimeter	
Length (cm)	Width (cm)
11	1
10	2
9	3
8	4
7	5
6	6

b)

Average Statistics for Women	
Height (cm)	Mass (kg)
152	47
160	52
167	56
175	63
181	70

c)

Pizza Toppings	
Number of Toppings	Cost ($)
1	5.90
2	6.60
3	7.30
4	8.00
5	8.70
6	9.40

4. The graph represents the sums of the natural numbers from 1 to 6.
   a) From the graph, determine:
      i) the sum of the first five numbers
      ii) how many numbers are required for a sum of 10.
   b) Write the relation as a set of ordered pairs.

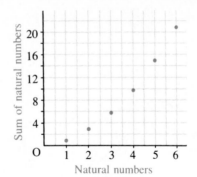

5. For the graph shown
   a) State the value(s) of y that correspond(s) to each value of x.
      i) 2   ii) 6   iii) 10   iv) 13
   b) State the value(s) of x that correspond(s) to each value of y.
      i)   15   ii)   25   iii)   30   iv)   40
   c) Write the relation as a set of ordered pairs.

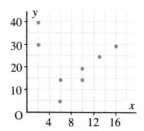

ⓒ

6. A copy shop displays this advertisement.

FOR EACH ORIGINAL		
first 5 copies	**second 5 copies**	**all additional copies**
15¢ each	11¢ each	8¢ each

   a) Make a table of values for up to 15 copies of one original.
   b) Graph the relation between the total cost and the number of copies.

7. A bank allows 3 free checks per months but makes a service charge of 32¢ for each check after that. Graph the relation between the service charge and the number of checks for up to 8 checks.

8. The local drama group is selling tickets for its latest production. The tickets cost $5 for adults and $2 for students.
   a) Graph the relation between the number of each kind of ticket that can be bought for each total expenditure.
      i)   exactly $20   ii) $20 or less
   b) Write the relation for each part of a) as a set of ordered pairs.

9. Some parents decide that their children should receive a weekly allowance from age 4 to age 16. The amount is 75¢ the first year and increases by 75¢ each year.
   a) Make a table of values for the relation.
   b) Graph the relation.
   c) Find a formula relating the allowance to the child's age.

PROBLEM SOLVING

Use a Graph

What will be the correct time when the slow watch reads 15:00?

Understand the problem
- How many minutes per hour does the slow watch lose?
- What will the slow watch read when the correct time is 15:00?
- What are we asked to find?

Think of a strategy
- Try drawing a graph of the time shown by the slow watch against the correct time. Use the graph to determine the correct time corresponding to the slow watch time of 15:00.

Carry out the strategy
- Since the slow watch loses 10 min every hour, we know the times on the slow watch at 13:00, 14:00, and 15:00. These are shown on the chart below.

Correct time	Time on slow watch
12:00	12:00
13:00	12:50
14:00	13:40
15:00	14:30

- Plot these points and join them with a straight line. From the graph, we see that when the slow watch reads 15:00, the correct time is 15:36.

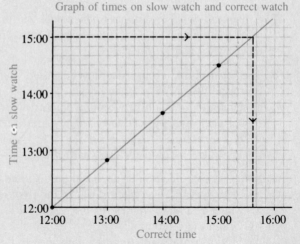

Graph of times on slow watch and correct watch

Look back

● Our answer indicates that it takes 3 h and 36 min for the slow watch to show a time elapse of 3 h. The slow watch moves at $\frac{5}{6}$ of the correct rate. Is $\frac{5}{6}$ of 3 h and 36 min equal to 3 h?

Solve each problem

1. Mr. Jenkins left for work at 9:00 and drove at an average speed of 50 km/h. After he left, Mrs. Jenkins discovered that he had forgotten his briefcase. She set out at 9:15 at an average speed of 70 km/h. Approximately what time did she reach her husband?

2. A graph of temperature in degrees Fahrenheit against temperature in degrees Celsius is a straight line. When the temperature is $-40°C$ it is also $-40°F$. A temperature of 50°F corresponds to 10°C. Use these facts to determine $-13°F$ in degrees Celsius.

3. The table shows the total distance which an object falls during the first few seconds after it is dropped. Estimate the total distance fallen in the first 5.5 s.

Falling time (s)	Distance fallen (m)
1	4.8
2	19.2
3	43.2
4	76.8
5	120.0
6	172.8

4. Anita wired her electrical digital clock so that it would run backwards. If she set the clock to the correct time at 16:00, when will the clock next show the correct time?

5. One side of a field is bounded by a river. A farmer wants to fence a rectangular pasture with the river as one side. She has 192 m of fencing for the three sides. What are the dimensions of the largest pasture that can be enclosed?

9-4 LINEAR RELATIONS

The weekly cost of operating a car is $40 for the fixed costs (insurance, maintenance and repairs, depreciation, etc.) and $0.05/km for gasoline and oil. The relation between the weekly cost C dollars and the distance traveled x kilometres is given by this equation.

C = 40 + 0.05x

The graph of this relation is a straight line.

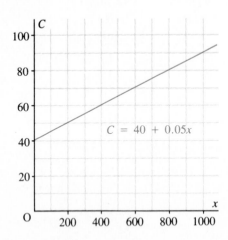

Any relation whose graph is a straight line is called a *linear relation*. Every linear relation is defined by a linear equation; that is, an equation in which each variable term has an exponent sum of 1.

For example, $3x + 5y = 15$
$4x - 7y = -3$
$h = 17 - \frac{1}{2}a$

These are linear equations. Each linear equation defines a linear relation.

To graph a linear relation, we require the coordinates of only two points. The coordinates of a third point should be determined, as a check.

Example 1. Graph the relation defined by $2x - 5y = 10$.

Solution. Two of the easiest points to find are the ones where the graph intersects the axes.

Substitute $x = 0$ into the equation $2x - 5y = 10$.
$$2(0) - 5y = 10$$
$$- 5y = 10$$
$$y = -2$$
One point on the graph is $(0, -2)$.
Substitute $y = 0$ into the equation $2x - 5y = 10$.
$$2x - 5(0) = 10$$
$$2x = 10$$
$$x = 5$$
Another point on the graph is $(5, 0)$.
For the third point, choose any value of x, for example, $x = 10$.
Substitute $x = 10$ into the equation $2x - 5y = 10$.
$$2(10) - 5y = 10$$
$$- 5y = -10$$
$$y = 2$$
A third point on the graph is $(10, 2)$.
For convenience, we record the results in a table of values.

x	y
0	-2
5	0
10	2

Plot these points on a grid. Join them with a straight line. Then label the line with its equation.

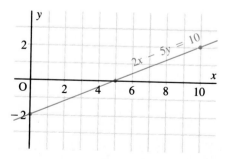

Example 2. The number h of hours of sleep needed by people up to the age of 18 is given by this equation.

$h = 17 - \dfrac{1}{2}a$, where a is the person's age in years

a) Graph the relation defined by this equation.
b) From the graph, find how many hours of sleep a 5-year-old child needs.

Solution. a) The relation is linear because its defining equation is linear.
Select the vertical axis for the values of h and the horizontal axis for the values of a.
Find 3 points which lie on the graph.
Substitute $a = 0$ into $h = 17 - \dfrac{1}{2}a$ to obtain

$h = 17 - \dfrac{1}{2}(0)$

$\quad = 17$

It is not reasonable to substitute $h = 0$ into the equation because everyone needs some sleep. Choose other values for a.

Substitute $a = 10$.   Substitute $a = 18$.

$h = 17 - \dfrac{1}{2}(10)$ $h = 17 - \dfrac{1}{2}(18)$

$\quad = 12$ $\quad = 8$

Record the results in a table of values. Plot the points on a grid. Join the points with a straight line. The graph is restricted to values of a between, and including, 0 and 18 years.

a	h
0	17
10	12
18	8

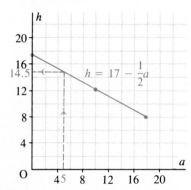

b) From the graph, a 5-year-old child needs 14.5 h sleep.

When graphing relations, care should be taken that only reasonable values of the variable are included.

EXERCISES 9-4

Ⓐ

1. State which graphs represent linear relations.
   a) 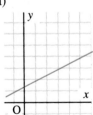 b) 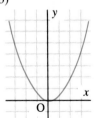 c) 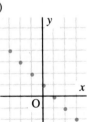 d)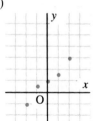

2. State which of these equations define linear relations.
   a) $3x - y = 7$ b) $7x - 5 = 2y$ c) $8x + 2xy = 11$

   d) $3x^2 + 16y^2 = 48$ e) $y = x^2 - 3$ f) $\dfrac{1}{x} + \dfrac{1}{y} = 1$

3. State the coordinates of the points where each line intersects the axes.
   a) b) 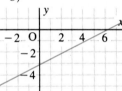 c)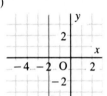

   d) e) f)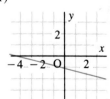

4. Find the coordinates of the points where each line intersects the axes.
   a) $2x + 3y = 18$ b) $4x - 3y = 12$ c) $7x - 4y = -28$
   d) $x + 5y = 10$ e) $y = 2x - 6$ f) $3x + 6y = 9$

Ⓑ

5. The graph shows the relation between the time required to cook a turkey and the mass of the turkey. Find the cooking time for a turkey of each mass.
   a) 8 kg b) 5 kg c) 11 kg

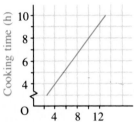

6. The graph shows the distance traveled by a car over a 6 h period.
   a) How far had the car traveled in 4 h?
   b) How long did it take to travel the first 125 km?
   c) How much farther did the car travel in the first 3 h than in the last 3 h?
   d) Does the graph represent a linear relation?

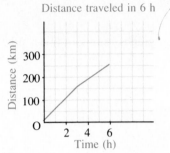

Distance traveled in 6 h

7. Make a table of values then graph the relation defined by each equation.
   a) $4x + 5y = 10$
   b) $6x - 8y = 12$
   c) $3y = 2x - 8$
   d) $5x - 7y = 0$
   e) $y = x - 7$
   f) $y = 3$

8. A car travels at a constant speed from Chicago to St. Louis. The relation between the distance traveled d miles and the time taken t hours is given by this equation. $d = 300 - 60t$
   a) Graph the relation defined by this equation, after making a table of values.
   b) From the graph, how far is it from Chicago to St. Louis?
   c) What was the total traveling time?
   d) After 2 h
      i) How far was the car from St. Louis?
      ii) How far was the car from Chicago?

9. The thermometer of an oven is calibrated in Fahrenheit degrees. The relation between the Fahrenheit temperature F and the Celsius temperature C is given by this equation.

$$C = \frac{5}{9}(F - 32)$$

   a) Graph the relation defined by this equation.
   b) Find the Fahrenheit setting for each Celsius temperature.
      i) 90°C
      ii) 120°C
      iii) 200°C
   c) Find the Celsius temperature equivalent to each Fahrenheit temperature.
      i) 90°F
      ii) 120°F
      iii) 200°F
   d) Extend the graph to find the Celsius temperature equivalent to each Fahrenheit temperature.
      i) 20°F
      ii) 0°F
      iii) −10°F
      iv) −20°F

10. The relation between Len's height and his age was linear between the ages of 8 and 15 years. He was 132 cm tall when he was 8 and 156 cm tall when he was 12.
    a) Graph the relation between Len's height and age.
    b) Estimate Len's height at each age.
       i) 10 years
       ii) 13 years
       iii) 14 years
    c) Estimate Len's age for each height.
       i) 140 cm
       ii) 145 cm
       iii) 150 cm

9-5 SLOPE

The *slant* of a ladder against a wall, the *gradient* of a road up a hill, and the *pitch* of a roof are all examples of a mathematical concept called *slope*.

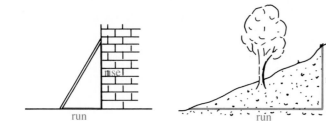 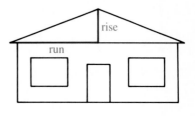

In each case, it is the ratio of the difference in the vertical position of two points (rise) to the difference in horizontal position (run).

$$\text{Slope} = \frac{\text{rise}}{\text{run}}$$

In a coordinate system, we can find the slope of a line or line segment if we know the coordinates of any two points on the line or segment.

$$\text{Slope} = \frac{\text{difference in } y\text{-coordinates}}{\text{difference in } x\text{-coordinates}}$$

Example 1. Find the slope of:
a) line JK
b) line segment PQ.

Solution.
a) The coordinates are J($-2, -4$) and K($4, 5$).
$$\text{Slope of JK} = \frac{5 - (-4)}{4 - (-2)}$$
$$= \frac{9}{6}$$
$$= \frac{3}{2}$$

b) The coordinates are P($-5, 7$) and Q($-2, 1$).
$$\text{Slope of PQ} = \frac{1 - (7)}{-2 - (-5)}$$
$$= \frac{-6}{3}$$
$$= -2$$

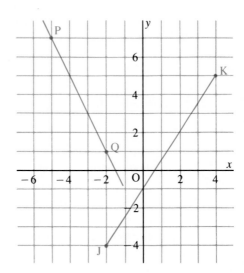

In *Example 1a)*, for every run to the right of 2, there is a rise of 3.
In *Example 1b)*, for every run to the right of 1, there is a rise of -2.
● Lines rising to the right have positive slope.
● Lines falling to the right have negative slope.

Example 2.   Draw the line passing through:

   a) the point (0,0) with slope $\dfrac{2}{3}$ b) the point (4,1) with slope $-\dfrac{3}{2}$.

Solution.   a) Slope $\dfrac{2}{3}$ means that for every difference
of $+2$ in y there is a corresponding
difference of $+3$ in x. The line rises
to the right.
      Begin at (0,0). Move 3 to the
right and 2 *up*. This is point J on the
line. Any number of points can be
obtained in this way.

   Since $\dfrac{2}{3} = \dfrac{-2}{-3}$, we can also

move 3 to the *left* and 2 *down* to get
another point K.
Line JK is the required line.

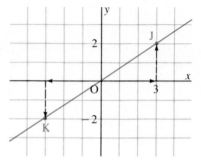

   b) Since $-\dfrac{3}{2} = \dfrac{-3}{2}$, for every difference
of -3 in y there is a corresponding
difference of $+2$ in x. The line falls to
the right.
      Begin at (4,1). Move 2 to the
right and 3 *down*. This is point Q on
the line. Other points can be obtained
in this way.

   Since $-\dfrac{3}{2} = \dfrac{3}{-2}$, we can also

move 2 to the *left* and 3 *up* to get
another point P.
      Line PQ is the required line.

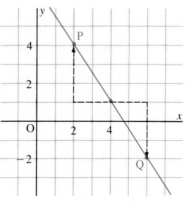

Example 3.   Drilling has revealed that a layer of limestone has a uniform slope away
from a ridge that the layer has formed. Point A is 500 m below a point
800 m from the base of the ridge.
a) Find the slope of the layer.
b) What is the depth of the layer 4 km from the ridge?

Solution. a) Slope of the layer $= \dfrac{-500 - 0}{800 - 0}$

$= -\dfrac{5}{8}$

b) The layer falls 500 m every 800 m. In 4000 m, the layer will fall

$\dfrac{4000}{800} \times 500$ m, or 2500 m.

The depth of the layer 4 km from the ridge is 2.5 km.

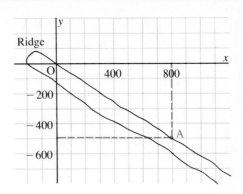

EXERCISES 9-5

Ⓐ

1. What is the slope of the ramp (below left)?

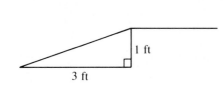
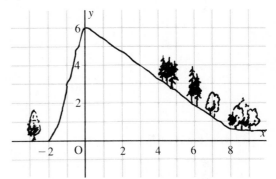

2. The diagram (above right) represents a ridge. Find the slope of each side of the ridge.

3. Find the slope of the line passing through each pair of points.
   a) A($-4,1$), B($3,5$)   b) C($-3,-2$), D($5,-1$)
   c) E($2,3$), F($-3,3$)   d) G($7,3$), H($-2,-4$)
   e) J($-3,6$), K($8,-4$)   f) L($-1,5$), M($6,-3$)
   g) N($2,7$), P($-5,-5$)   h) Q($-1.5,6.5$), R($8.5,-3.5$)

4. Find the slope of each line.

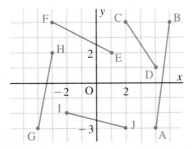

5. On a grid, draw the line through:

    a) point A(0,0) with slope 2   b) point B(1,4) with slope $\frac{3}{2}$

    c) point C($-1,2$) with slope $-\frac{1}{2}$ d) point D($-4,3$) with slope $-\frac{2}{3}$

6. The diagram is the side view of a ski tow. Each section of the tow approximates a straight line.

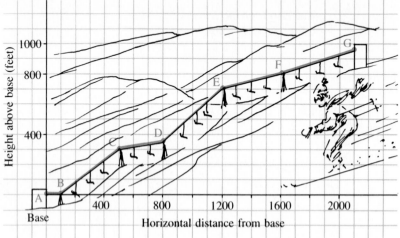

    a) List the coordinates of points A, B, C, D, E, F, and G.
    b) Find the slopes of the segments AB, BC, CD, DE, EF, and FG.
    c) Which segment is the steepest?

7. Find the slope of a road that rises 25 m in every kilometre.

8. What can be said about the slope of a line parallel to:
    a) the *x*-axis   b) the *y*-axis?

9. On the same grid, draw the line through point (1,1) with slope $\frac{2}{3}$, and the line through point ($-2,4$) with slope $\frac{4}{6}$. What seems to be the relationship between the two lines?

10. On the same grid, draw the line through point (2,3) with slope $\frac{3}{2}$, and the line through point (0,7) with slope $-\frac{2}{3}$. What seems to be the relationship between the two lines?

11. a) Locate the vertices and draw the sides of the quadrilateral with these vertices:
        A(4,-5.5), B(2,4), C($-6,9.5$), D($-4,0$).
    b) Compare the slopes of: i)   AB and CD   ii)   BC and AD.
    c) What kind of quadrilateral is this?

9-6 USING SLOPE TO GRAPH A LINEAR EQUATION

One method of graphing a linear equation is to construct a table of values.
Consider the equation $y = 3x - 2$.

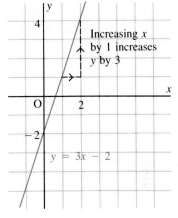

	x	y	
	-1	-5	
Increasing	0	-2	... increases
x by 1 ...	1	1	y by 3.
	2	4	

The table and the graph suggest another way
of graphing a linear equation.
This method is based on two numbers.
- The y-intercept; that is, the value of y
  when $x = 0$
- The slope

$y = 3x - 2 \leftarrow y$-intercept
   $\uparrow$
   slope

> In general, the graph of a linear equation in the form
> $y = mx + b$
> has a slope m and a y-intercept b.

The equation $y = mx + b$ is called the *slope y-intercept form* of a
linear equation.

Example 1. Graph each equation.

a) $y = \dfrac{3}{4}x - 1$ b) $y = -3x + 2$

Solution. a) $y = \dfrac{3}{4}x - 1$

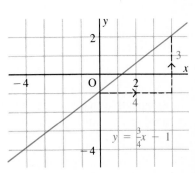

The slope is $\dfrac{3}{4}$ and the y-intercept
is -1.
Begin at $(0, -1)$. Move 4 to the right
and 3 up. This is a point on the line.
Other points on the line are obtained
by continuing in this way, or by
moving 4 to the left and 3 down.

b) $y = -3x + 2$

The slope is -3 and the y-intercept is 2. Begin at $(0,2)$. Move 1 to the right and 3 down. This is a point on the line. Other points on the line are obtained by continuing in this way, or by moving 1 to the left and 3 up.

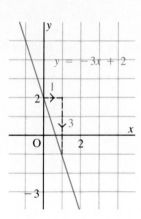

Example 2. Find the equation of each line shown on the grid.

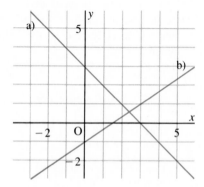

Solution. The slope and the y-intercept of each line can be read from its graph.

a) This line has a slope of -1 and a y-intercept of 3.

Its equation is $y = -1x + 3$

or $y = -x + 3$

b) This line has a slope of $\frac{2}{3}$ and a y-intercept of -1.

Its equation is $y = \frac{2}{3}x - 1$

or $3y = 2x - 3$

Rearrange. $2x - 3y = 3$

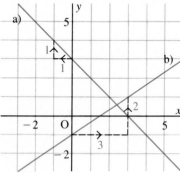

An equation that is not in the slope y-intercept form can be put into that form by solving for y.

Example 3. Graph this equation. $\qquad 3x + 4y - 12 = 0$

Solution. $\qquad 3x + 4y - 12 = 0$

Solve for y.

$$4y = -3x + 12$$

$$y = -\frac{3}{4}x + 3$$

The slope is $-\frac{3}{4}$ and the y-intercept is 3.

The graph is drawn using this information.

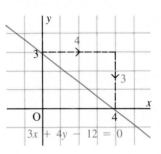

EXERCISES 9-6

Ⓐ

1. Graph each equation.

   a) $y = \frac{5}{2}x - 3$ b) $y = \frac{4}{3}x + 2$ c) $y = -2x - 1$

   d) $y = -\frac{2}{3}x + 1$ e) $y = -3$ f) $x = 2$

2. For each line, state the slope, the y-intercept, and the equation.

   a)   b)   c)

   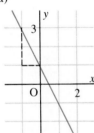   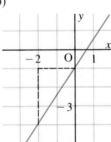   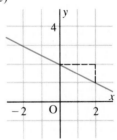

3. Find the equation of each line.

   a)   b)   c)

   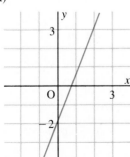   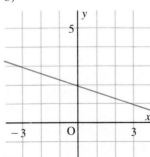   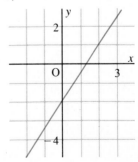

4. State the slope and the y-intercept for each line.

   a) $y = 2x + 4$

   b) $y = -3x + 5$

   c) $y = \dfrac{5}{2}x - 3$

   d) $y = -\dfrac{1}{3}x + 2$

   e) $y = -5x - 8$

   f) $y = \dfrac{8}{3}x - \dfrac{2}{5}$

   g) $y = \dfrac{3}{4}x - 1$

   h) $y = 3$

   i) $y = -4$

(B)

5. a) Graph these equations on the same grid.

   i) $y = 3x$

   ii) $y = 2x$

   iii) $y = 1x$

   iv) $y = \dfrac{1}{2}x$

   v) $y = 0x$

   vi) $y = -3x$

   vii) $y = -2x$

   viii) $y = -\dfrac{1}{2}x$

   b) Describe how the graph of $y = mx$ changes as m changes.

6. a) Graph these equations on the same grid.

   i) $y = x + 4$

   ii) $y = x + 2$

   iii) $y = x$

   iv) $y = x - 4$

   v) $y = x - 2$

   b) Describe how the graph of $y = mx + b$ changes as b changes.

7. Write the equation of the line that has:

   a) slope 2, y-intercept 3

   b) slope -1, y-intercept 4

   c) slope $\dfrac{2}{3}$, y-intercept -1

   d) slope $-\dfrac{4}{5}$, y-intercept 8.

8. State the slope and the y-intercept of each line.

   a) $3x - 4y - 12 = 0$ b) $5x - 2y + 10 = 0$ c) $2x + y - 3 = 0$

   d) $3x + 5y + 20 = 0$ e) $x + 2y - 5 = 0$ f) $4x - 7y + 15 = 0$

9. Graph each equation.

   a) $3x - 2y = 6$ b) $2x + y = 4$ c) $5x - 2y = 10$

(C)

10. The three equations represent lines containing the sides of a triangle. Determine if the triangle is a right triangle.

    a) $y = 2x + 3$, $x + 2y - 2 = 0$, $3x + 2y + 7 = 0$

    b) $3x - 5y = 10$, $4x + 2y - 9 = 0$, $5x - 3y + 8 = 0$

11. Find expressions for the slope and y-intercept of the line with equation $Ax + By + C = 0$.

12. Draw a line through each pair of points and find its equation.

    a) A(2,2), B(4,3)

    b) C(3,4), D(-3,0)

    c) E(-1,5), F(2,-1)

    d) G(3,-3), H(-6,0)

13. The equations of the lines containing three sides of a square are as follows:

    $$y = -\dfrac{1}{2}x + 8, \qquad y = -\dfrac{1}{2}x - 2, \qquad y = 2x - 12$$

    Find the equation of the line containing the fourth side.

9-7 DIRECT VARIATION

Marcie earns $6/h working as a lifeguard. Her total pay is related to the number of hours she works. Since the graph is a straight line, we say that it is linear.

Hours worked, h	Pay in dollars, p
0	0
2	12
4	24
6	36
8	48
10	60

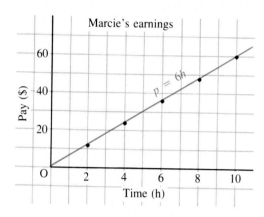

The table and graph show that when h is doubled, p is doubled; when h is tripled, p is tripled, and so on.
We say that *p varies directly as h.*
The pattern of numbers in the table suggests that the relation between h and p can be expressed by a formula. In each case, the pay earned is 6 times the number of hours worked. That is, the numbers in the table satisfy the formula:
$p = 6h$, where 6 is the pay in dollars per hour.

Direct Variation
If y varies directly as x, then y can be expressed in terms of x.
- The equation of this relationship has the form $y = mx$
  where m is the constant of proportionality.
- The graph of this relationship is a straight line with slope m through $(0,0)$.

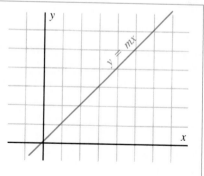

Example 1. y varies directly as x and when $x = 12$, $y = 16$.

a) Write y in terms of x.

b) Find y when $x = 5$.

c) Find x when $y = 30$.

Solution.

a) Since y varies directly as x, $y = kx$, where k is the constant of proportionality. Substitute 12 for x and 16 for y in the equation.

$$y = kx$$
$$16 = k(12)$$
$$k = \frac{4}{3}$$

Hence, the equation expressing y in terms of x is $y = \frac{4}{3}x$.

b) When $x = 5$:
$$y = \frac{4}{3}(5)$$
$$= \frac{20}{3}$$

c) When $y = 30$:
$$30 = \frac{4}{3}x$$
$$4x = 90$$
$$x = 22.5$$

Example 2. The height to which a ball bounces varies directly as the distance from which it was dropped. If it is dropped from a height of 2.4 m, it bounces to a height of 1.6 m.

a) Express the height b that the ball bounces in terms of the height d from which it was dropped.

b) If it is dropped from a height of 3.0 m, how high will it bounce?

c) If it bounces 80 cm, from what height was it dropped?

d) Sketch a graph of the equation relating b to d.

Solution.

a) Let b metres represent the height the ball bounces from a height of d metres. Since b varies directly as d:

$b = kd$, where k is the constant of proportionality.

Substitute 2.4 for d and 1.6 for b.

$$b = kd$$
$$1.6 = k(2.4)$$
$$k = \frac{1.6}{2.4}$$
$$= \frac{2}{3}$$

The equation relating b and d is $b = \frac{2}{3}d$.

b) Substitute 3.0 for d.

$$b = \frac{2}{3}(3.0)$$

$$= 2.0$$

From a height of 3.0 m, the ball will bounce 2.0 m.

c) Substitute 0.8 for b.

$$0.8 = \frac{2}{3}d$$

$$2d = 2.4$$

$$d = 1.2$$

For an 80 cm bounce, the ball was dropped from 120 cm.

d) The graph is a straight line with slope $\frac{2}{3}$ through $(0, 0)$.

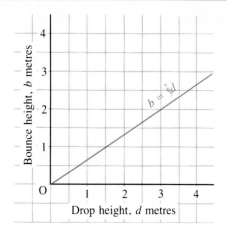

EXERCISES 9-7

(A)

1. In each table, y varies directly as x.
   a) State the missing numbers.   b) Express y in terms of x.

i)

x	y
0	■
1	■
2	■
3	21
4	■

ii)

x	y
1	■
2	−6
3	■
4	■
5	■

iii)

x	y
4	■
8	■
12	■
16	■
20	5

iv)

x	y
3	■
6	■
9	6
12	■
15	■

2. If y varies directly as x, what happens to y if:
   a) x is doubled   b) x is halved?

(B)

3. y varies directly as x and when $x = 12$, $y = 8$.
   a) Write y in terms of x.   b) Find y when $x = 21$.
   c) Find x when $y = 15$.

4. *y* varies directly as *x*. Find the missing numbers.

a)

x	■	3	5	7	13
y	−4	■	−10	■	■

b)

x	2	■	15	45	■
y	■	8	■	18	22

5. It is estimated that the volume of blood in the human body varies directly as the body weight. A 176 lb person has a blood volume of about 6 L.
   a) Express the blood volume *V* in terms of the body weight *W*.
   b) Find the blood volume of a 132 lb person.
   c) Sketch a graph of the equation relating *V* and *W*.

6. A supertanker traveling at 15 mph needs 3 mi to come to a complete stop.
   a) If the stopping distance varies directly as the speed, express the stopping distance in terms of the speed.
   b) What distance will the supertanker need to stop from a speed of 10 mph?
   c) Sketch a graph of the equation relating speed and stopping distance.

Ⓒ

7. In chemistry, Charles' Law states that if the pressure is kept constant, the volume of a gas varies directly as the absolute temperature in degrees Kelvin (°K). The relation between *k* degrees Kelvin and *c* degrees Celsius is $k = c + 273°$. A balloon contains 2 L of helium at 10°C.
   a) What is its volume when the temperature is: i) 30°C   ii) 0°C?
   b) What is its temperature if its volume is: i) 4 L   ii) 1 L?

8. If the pressure of a gas is kept constant, what happens to its volume if the absolute temperature is:
   a) doubled   b) tripled   c) divided by 2?

9. For any planet, its year is the time that it takes to circle the sun once. Kepler's Third Law in astronomy states that, for any planet, the square of the number of earth-days in its year varies directly as the cube of its mean distance from the sun. Find the number of earth-days in the year for each planet.

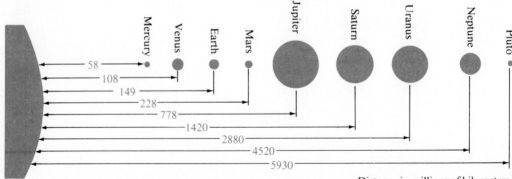

Distance in millions of kilometres

PROBLEM SOLVING

Choose the Strategy

1. Consider this expression. $1 - 2 + 3 - 4 + \ldots n$
   a) For what values of n is the value of the expression positive?
   b) For what values of n is the value of the expression negative?
   c) Write a formula for the value of the expression:
      i) when n is even   ii) when n is odd.

2. The squares ABCD and BEFC (below left) are congruent. Which has the greater perimeter, the colored region or the black region?

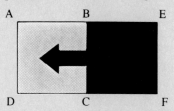

3. a) Use the pattern suggested by the diagram (above right) to evaluate this sum. $1 + 3 + 5 + 7 + \ldots + 15$
   b) Find a formula for this sum.
      $1 + 3 + 5 + 7 + \ldots + (2n - 1)$

4. a) If $x\%$ of x is 16, what is x?   b) If $y\%$ of $y\%$ is 36%, what is y?

5. The pieces of this puzzle fit together to form a square. What is the length of each side of the square that they form?

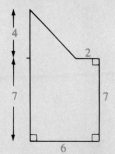 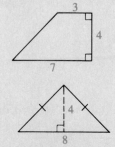 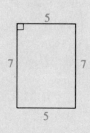

6. At winter ski-camp all the students were required to register for cross-country skiing or alpine skiing or both. If 68% of the students registered for cross-country skiing and 52% signed up for alpine skiing, what percent registered for both?

7. Mrs. McLeod was offered three successive discounts of 10%, 20%, and 25% on a videocassette recorder. The salesperson said that the discounts could be taken in any order she chose. Which would be best for her?

MATHEMATICS AROUND US

The Line of Best Fit

In *Section 9-3*, we graphed linear relations from given data. In each example, the plotted points appeared to lie on a straight line. One reason for this is the fact that in each case there is an underlying physical law relating the variables.

We often encounter situations in which the plotted points only approximate a straight line. In these cases there may not be a physical law relating the variables, but nevertheless a noticeable trend may still be evident.

The Mile Record

Although the mile is not a metric distance the one-mile race has always been an important track event. The four-minute mile, once considered impossible to achieve, was accomplished in 1954 by two runners in the same race. Since then, the record for the mile has dropped steadily.

The Mile Record

Record holder	Year	Record time minutes:seconds	Record time seconds
Jules Ladoumègue	1931	4:09.2	249.2
Glenn Cunningham	1934	4:06.8	246.8
Gunder Hagg	1945	4:01.3	241.3
Roger Bannister	1954	3:59.4	239.4
John Landy	1954	3:57.9	237.9
Jim Ryun	1967	3:51.1	231.1
Sebastian Coe	1981	3:47.3	227.3
Steve Cram	1985	3:46.3	226.3

To graph the data, we converted the times to seconds by multiplying the number of minutes by 60 and adding the number of seconds.

The graph shows that the record has fallen at a fairly constant rate. An approximate relationship, between the time t seconds and y the number of years since 1930, can be found by drawing a *line of best fit* which passes near the plotted points.

When we use the graph to find other values, it must be done with caution. For example, we might attempt to predict the mile record for some year in the distant future by extending the line far to the right. But we cannot be certain that the trend will continue indefinitely. It has been suggested that, for physiological reasons, the record may never become much lower than 3:30.

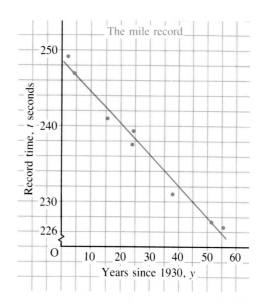

QUESTIONS

1. a) Plot the points from the table, and draw the line of best fit.
   b) Use your line of best fit to estimate what the record might be in the year 2000.
   c) Estimate when the record might be as low as 3:30.

2. Use the vertical intercept and one other point on the line to obtain an approximate equation of the line of best fit. Then use the equation to check your predictions in *Question 1*.

3. Your calculator may have the capability of determining the slope and the vertical intercept of the line of best fit when you enter the known data. For the above data, such a calculator gives the slope as -0.4397 and the vertical intercept as 248.8. Hence, the equation of the line of best fit is $t = -0.4397y + 248.8$.
   a) Use this equation to check the predictions in *Question 1*.
   b) If your calculator has this capability, use it to determine the slope and the vertical intercept for the data. Consult your manual.

The Irish Elk

A magnificent animal known as the Irish elk was once the world's largest deer. It inhabited the open tundra in northern Europe. But during the last Ice Age, about 12 000 years ago, it became extinct.

The Irish elk was noted for its extremely large antlers, which seemed out of proportion with the size of the animal. Skeletal remains show that its antlers spread as wide as 4 m. Stephen Gould, of Harvard University, wondered if the antlers grew at the same rate as the rest of the animal. He compared measures of antler size and skull length of dozens of specimens. Some results are shown in the table.

From data like this, Stephen Gould concluded that the animal's antlers grew about 2.5 times as fast as the rest of its body. Investigations of other species of deer, including those living today, have yielded similar results.

The Irish Elk					
Skull length (cm)	46.0	47.1	48.1	49.0	50.1
Antler size (cm)	31.5	34.1	36.2	39.1	41.4

QUESTIONS

1. Graph the data, and then determine the equation of the line of best fit.

2. Use the equation to find:
   a) the approximate antler size for a skull length of 47.5 cm
   b) the skull length for an antler size of 40 cm.

3. How did Stephen Gould reach his conclusion about the comparative rates of growth of the antlers and the rest of the animal from the equation of the line of best fit?

4. Suggest why the Irish elk may have become extinct.

Continental Drift

Geographers have studied sediments found near islands in the Atlantic Ocean and related the age of the sediment to the distance from the Mid-Atlantic Ridge. The table shows the results for a few islands.

Islands	Age of sediment (millions of years)	Distance to Mid-Atlantic Ridge (km)
Azores	25	350
Bahamas	135	2800
Bermuda	95	1900
Faroes	20	250
St. Helena	35	700

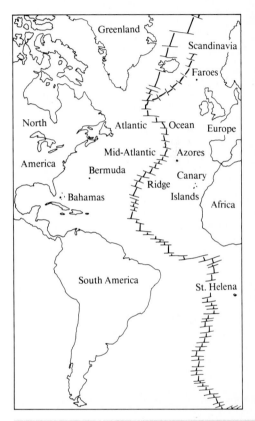

In 1961, a Canadian, J. Tuzo Wilson, theorized that this data provides evidence for the *continental drift*. He reasoned that volcanic activity at the Mid-Atlantic Ridge forms new parts of the Earth's crust. These tend to push aside the older crust. Over millions of years, this spreading of the sea floor has caused the continents to move to their present positions.

QUESTIONS

1. Find the equation of the line of best fit. What does the slope represent?

2. Use the equation of the line of best fit:
   a) to predict the age of sediment near the Canary Islands, which are about 1500 km from the Mid-Atlantic Ridge
   b) to find the approximate yearly increase in distance between Europe and North America.

Review Exercises

1. a) Plot these points   K($-4,-1$), L($-1,-4$), M($5,2$), N($2,5$)
   b) Draw these line segments   KL, LM, MN, NK
   c) What polygon have you drawn?

2. Find the area of:
   a) a triangle with vertices O($0,0$), A($0,1$), and B($1,0$)
   b) a square with vertices O($0,0$), C($0,5$), D($5,5$), and E($5,0$).

3. Write each relation as a set of ordered pairs.

   a) 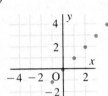   b)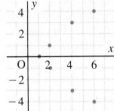

4. Graph the relation defined by each equation.
   a) $3x + y = 9$ b) $5x - 3y = 15$
   c) $y = 5x$ d) $y = 7 - 2x$

5. On a grid, draw the line through:

   a) point E($6,1$) with slope 2   b) point F($-3,0$) with slope $\dfrac{4}{3}$.

6. Find the slope of the line passing through each pair of points.
   a) A($6,-1$), B($2,7$)   b) C($-5,-1$), D($7,-2$)
   c) E($2,7$), F($-4,4$)   d) G($6,3$), H($-5,-2$)

7. Draw each line on a grid.
   a) the line through A($-1,-1$) with slope 3
   b) the line through A($-1,-1$) with slope -3
   c) the line through C($-2,-4$) with slope $\dfrac{1}{3}$
   d) the line through D($2,1$) with slope $-\dfrac{3}{4}$

8. State the slope and the y-intercept of the graph of each equation.

   a) $y = 4x - 3$ b) $y = -\dfrac{5}{3}x + 7$ c) $y = -\dfrac{9}{4}x - 3$

   d) $2x + 5y = 15$ e) $3x - 4y = 16$ f) $5x - 3y - 18 = 0$

9. Write the equation of the line that has:

   a) slope $-\dfrac{1}{2}$ and y-intercept -4 b) slope $\dfrac{4}{3}$ and y-intercept -6.

10. y varies directly as x and when $x = 15$, $y = 24$.
    a) Write the equation relating x and y.
    b) Find y when $x = 4$.   c) Find x when $y = 18$.

1. Solve each proportion.

   a) $\dfrac{r}{3} = \dfrac{8}{15}$ b) $\dfrac{16}{25} = \dfrac{48}{x}$ c) $\dfrac{12}{39} = \dfrac{s}{13}$ d) $\dfrac{19}{t} = \dfrac{57}{42}$

2. Jacques contributes \$4.00 and Jeanne \$6.00 for the purchase of a lottery ticket. It is drawn for a prize of \$25 000. How should the money be divided?

3. On a map, two cities are 120 mm apart. The scale of the map is 1 : 1 250 000. What is the actual distance between the cities?

4. In an orienteering exercise, Sharon's location is 3.2 cm from town A on the map. If the actual distance is 24 km, what is the scale of the map?

5. a) 24% of a number is 18. What is the number?
   b) What percent of 1210 is 484?

6. A calculator regularly priced at \$15.75 is on sale for \$12.60. What is the percent of discount?

7. A television that lists for \$480 is on sale at a 15% discount. What is the sale price?

8. Find the simple interest on:
   a) a loan of \$650 for 3 months at 14% per annum
   b) a deposit of \$125 for 90 days at 6.5% per annum.

9. Simplify.
   a) $14m - 9n - 5m - 3n$
   b) $5a + 7b - 11a - 4b$
   c) $7x - 3 + 2x - 8 - 12x$
   d) $(3y^2 - 7y + 2) - (5y - y^2 + 9)$

10. Simplify.

    a) $(3m)(-5m)$ b) $\left(-\dfrac{1}{2}x\right)^3$

    c) $(-8a^3)(-6a^2)$ d) $4x(2x^2 - 5x + 3)$
    e) $(2xy^2)(-7x^2y^5)$ f) $-2m^2(5m^3 - 2m + 4n)$

11. Find each product.
    a) $(x - 4)(x + 11)$ b) $(2x - 7)(x - 3)$
    c) $(4 + 3a)(5 + 9a)$ d) $(3m - 5)(3m + 5)$
    e) $x(2x + 3)(4x - 1)$ f) $-4a(7a + 2)(3a - 8)$

12. Factor.
    a) $6m^2 - 15m$
    b) $2y^3 - 6y^2 + 8y$
    c) $4x^2 - 49$
    d) $x^2 + 3x - 28$
    e) $m^2 - 9m + 18$
    f) $20 + a - a^2$
    g) $y^2 + 16y + 39$
    h) $2x^2 - 10x - 12$
    i) $4a^3 - 100a$
    j) $-3x^3 + 15x^2 - 6x$
    k) $3m^2 - \dfrac{3}{4}$
    l) $y^3 - 15y^2 + 56y$

13. Simplify.
    a) $\dfrac{-10x + 35}{-5}$
    b) $\dfrac{8x^3 - 12x^2 + 20x}{4x}$
    c) $\dfrac{4x^2y}{9xy^2} \times \dfrac{15xy}{16y^3}$
    d) $\dfrac{-17m^2n}{24mn} \times \dfrac{40m^4n^3}{51m^3n}$
    e) $\dfrac{9x^5y^2}{16} \div \dfrac{3x^2y}{8}$
    f) $\dfrac{-28a^2bc}{33ab^2} \div \dfrac{-21abc^3}{-44b^2c}$

14. Simplify.
    a) $\dfrac{3x - 4}{3} + \dfrac{x + 5}{3}$
    b) $\dfrac{2m + 7}{5} - \dfrac{3m + 1}{5}$

15. Plot these points: A($-3,1$), B($3,3$), C($5,-3$), and D($-4,-6$). Join the points in order and name the figure drawn.

16. Draw a graph of each relation.
    a) $y = 2x + 1$
    b) $x + 4y = 12$
    c) $3x - 2y = 6$

17. Find the slope of the line passing through each pair of points.
    a) A($5,-3$), B($-4,6$)
    b) C($-4,3$), D($6,-8$)

18. State the slope and y-intercept of the graph of each equation.
    a) $y = -2x + 7$
    b) $3x - 4y = 12$
    c) $5x + 2y = -6$
    d) $-4x - 2y + 5 = 0$

19. Write the equation of the line that has:
    a) slope $-\dfrac{2}{3}$ and y-intercept 4
    b) slope $\dfrac{6}{5}$ and y-intercept 3.

A sports club charges an initiation fee and a monthly fee. At the end of 1 month a member had paid a total of $260, and at the end of 6 months she had paid a total of $435. What is the initiation fee? (See Section 10-6, *Example 2*.)

10-1 SOLVING SYSTEMS OF LINEAR EQUATIONS BY GRAPHING

Sales personnel at a sporting goods store are given a choice of two methods of remuneration:

Plan A
A monthly salary of $200 plus a 2% commission on all sales.

Plan B
No monthly salary, but a 5% commission on all sales.

Which is the better plan for the employee? This question can be answered using graphs. Let x represent the total monthly sales.

Plan *A*
The monthly remuneration is:
  $y = 200 + 0.02x$

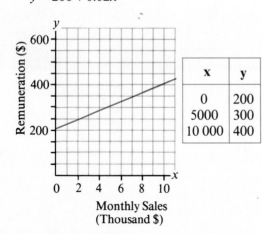

x	y
0	200
5000	300
10 000	400

Monthly Sales
(Thousand $)

Plan *B*
The monthly remuneration is:
  $y = 0.05x$

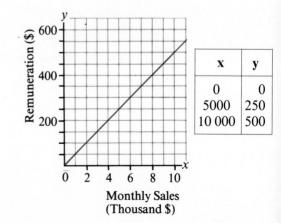

x	y
0	0
5000	250
10 000	500

Monthly Sales
(Thousand $)

When the two plans are graphed on the same grid, the two lines intersect. The point of intersection indicates that Plan *A* is the better plan if sales are less than about $7000. If sales are greater than $7000, then Plan *B* is better.

A pair of linear equations, considered together, is called a *linear system*. To solve a linear system means to find all the ordered pairs (x, y) which satisfy *both* equations. These may be found by graphing both equations on the same grid. If the lines intersect, the coordinates of the point of intersection satisfy both equations. This gives the solution of the linear system.

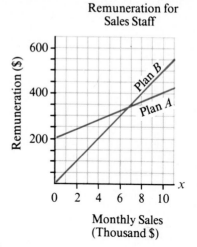

Remuneration for Sales Staff

Example. Solve the following linear system graphically.

$$x - 2y = 6 \quad \dots \text{①}$$
$$3x + y = 11 \quad \dots \text{②}$$

Solution. Make a table of values for each equation.

For $x - 2y = 6$

x	y
6	0
2	-2
0	-3

For $3x + y = 11$

x	y
0	11
1	8
2	5

Graph each equation on the same grid. The only point common to both lines is the point of intersection, $(4, -1)$. The solution of the linear system is $(4, -1)$.

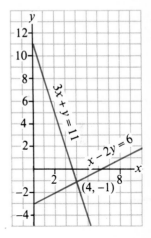

Check. Substitute $x = 4$ and $y = -1$ in *both* equations ① and ②.

L.S. $= x - 2y$ R.S. $= 6$ L.S. $= 3x + y$ R.S. $= 11$
$= 4 - 2(-1)$
$= 4 + 2$
$= 6$

$= 3(4) + (-1)$
$= 12 - 1$
$= 11$

The solution $(4, -1)$ is correct.

It is not always possible to obtain the exact solution of a linear system by graphing. If the lines do not intersect on the grid lines, it is necessary to estimate the solution. The exact solution can only be found algebraically.

EXERCISES 10-1

Ⓐ

1. Solve by graphing, and check.
   a) $x + y = 5$
      $3x - y = 3$
   b) $x - y = -2$
      $4x + 2y = 16$
   c) $x + y = 7$
      $3x + 4y = 24$
   d) $x - y = 2$
      $3x + y = -14$

   e) $x - y = 4$
      $2x + y = -4$
   f) $5x + 4y = 40$
      $5x + 6y = 50$
   g) $6x - 2y = -20$
      $4x + 2y = -10$
   h) $2x + 8y = 8$
      $-2x + y = 10$

2. Solve by graphing.
   a) $x - 2y = 10$
      $3x - y = 0$
   b) $4x - 6y = 4$
      $3x + 2y = -12$
   c) $10x + 2y = -5$
      $4x + 6y = 2$
   d) $5x - 2y = 8$
      $3x + y = -14$

Ⓑ

3. Solve by graphing.
   a) $2x - y = 80$
      $x + 3y = -30$
   b) $3x + 2y = 60$
      $3x - 5y = -150$
   c) $x + y = -5$
      $2x + y = 20$
   d) $x + 2y = -6$
      $3x + 2y = -34$

4. Solve by graphing.
   a) $x + y = 4$
      $x - y = 1$
   b) $x + 2y = 5$
      $x - 2y = 2$
   c) $2x - y = 8$
      $3x + 6y = 2$
   d) $2x - 3y = 0$
      $4x + 6y = 6$

   e) $3x - 6y = 180$
      $2x + 3y = 30$
   f) $2x + 3y = 2$
      $4x - 3y = 1$
   g) $5x + 4y = 2$
      $2x - 3y = -15$
   h) $2x + 3y = 3$
      $3x - 5y = 25$

Ⓒ

5. a) Solve the following system by graphing.
      $$x + 2y = 8$$
      $$3x - y = 3$$

   b) Form a new equation by *adding* the two equations in (a). Graph this equation on the same grid. What do you notice?

   c) Form another equation by *subtracting* the two equations in (b). Graph this equation on the same grid. What do you notice?

6. Solve by inspection.
   a) $x + y = 6$
      $2x + y = 8$
   b) $x - y = 1$
      $5x + 2y = 5$
   c) $x + y = -8$
      $2x + y = -11$
   d) $2x + y = 13$
      $x + 2y = 7$

 INVESTIGATE

If two lines are drawn on the same grid, do they always intersect at only one point? What other possibilities are there for two lines?

10-2 PROPERTIES OF LINEAR SYSTEMS

Linear systems have two basic properties which will be used later to
develop algebraic methods to solve them.

Multiplying an Equation by a Constant

When we solve the following system graphically, the
solution is found to be (4, 1).

$$3x - y = 11 \quad \dots \text{①}$$
$$x + 2y = 6 \quad \dots \text{②}$$

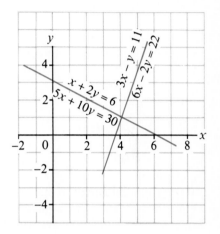

$3x - y = 11$

x	y
0	−11
5	4
3	−2

$x + 2y = 6$

x	y
0	3
6	0
2	2

Consider what happens if we multiply both sides of equation ① by 2
and both sides of equation ② by 5.

$$\text{①} \times 2: \quad 6x - 2y = 22 \quad \dots \text{③}$$
$$\text{②} \times 5: \quad 5x + 10y = 30 \quad \dots \text{④}$$

$6x - 2y = 22$

x	y
0	−11
5	4
3	−2

$5x + 10y = 30$

x	y
0	3
6	0
2	2

If we make tables of values for these equations, we see that they are the
same as for equations ① and ②. The graphs of the new equations are
the same lines as before. This illustrates a basic property of linear
systems:

> Multiplying both sides of either equation of a linear system by
> a constant does not change the solution.

Adding or Subtracting the Equations

When we solved this system, the solution was found to be (4, 1):

$$3x - y = 11 \quad \ldots ①$$
$$x + 2y = 6 \quad \ldots ②$$

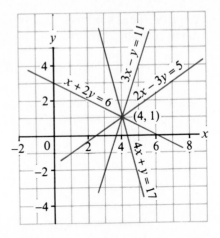

Consider what happens if we *add* equations ① and ②.

$$
\begin{array}{r}
3x - y = 11 \\
x + 2y = 6 \\
\hline
4x + y = 17
\end{array}
$$

If we graph this equation on the same grid as equations ① and ②, we see that the line passes through the same point (4, 1).

$4x + y = 17$

x	y
3	5
4	1
5	−3

Consider what happens if we *subtract* equations ① and ②.

$$
\begin{array}{r}
3x - y = 11 \\
x + 2y = 6 \\
\hline
2x - 3y = 5
\end{array}
$$

If we graph this equation on the same grid as equations ① and ②, we see that the line also passes through (4, 1).

$2x - 3y = 5$

x	y
1	−1
4	1
7	3

This example illustrates another basic property of linear systems:

> Adding or subtracting the equations of a linear system does not change the solution.

The properties of linear systems allow us to combine the equations of a linear system without changing the solution.

Example. Given the following linear system:
a) Solve the system graphically.
b) Give examples of two other linear systems which have the same solution.

$$3x + 2y = 18 \quad \ldots ①$$
$$x - y = 1 \quad \ldots ②$$

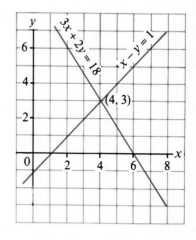

Solution. a) For $3x + 2y = 18$

x	y
6	0
0	9
2	6

For $x - y = 1$

x	y
1	0
0	-1
6	5

From the graph, the solution is (4, 3).

b) Add equations ① and ②:

$$3x + 2y = 18$$
$$\underline{x - y = \ 1}$$
$$4x + \ y = 19$$

Subtract equations ① and ②:

$$3x + 2y = 18$$
$$\underline{x - y = \ 1}$$
$$2x + 3y = 17$$

This system has the same solution as the system in (a). We can check this by substituting 4 for x and 3 for y.

$$4x + \ y = 19$$
$$2x + 3y = 17$$

To obtain another linear system which has the same solution, we may multiply equations ① and ② by any constant before combining them. For example:

Multiply ① by 2: $6x + 4y = 36$
Multiply ② by 3: $\underline{3x - 3y = \ 3}$
Add: $9x + \ y = 39 \quad \ldots ③$

The system formed by equation ③ and equation ② has the same solution as the system in (a).

$$9x + y = 39$$
$$x - y = \ 1$$

EXERCISES 10-2

Ⓐ

1. State the equations formed by adding the equations; subtracting the equations.
   a) $5x + 2y = 10$

      $x + y = 4$
   b) $2x - 3y = 12$

      $3x + 5y = 15$
   c) $x + 5y = 9$

      $3x - 2y = -7$
   d) $7x - 4y = -8$

      $-9x + 2y = -12$

2. a) Write the equations formed by adding and by subtracting the equations of the linear system shown in each graph below.
   b) Check that the solution of the system is a solution of the equations found in (a).
      i)   ii)

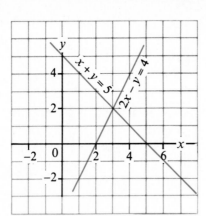
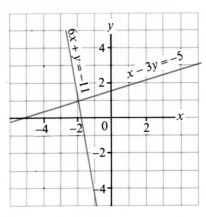

3. Given the linear system:
$$2x + y = 5$$
$$x - 3y = -8$$

   a) Solve the system graphically.
   b) Give an example of another linear system which has the same solution.
   c) Check that the solution found for the system in (a) is also the solution of the system in (b).

Ⓑ

4. Give an example of another linear system which has the same solution as each of the following systems.
   a) $2x + 7y = 9$

      $6x - y = 5$
   b) $5x - y = 17$

      $x + 4y = -5$
   c) $x - 3y = -11$

      $4x + 9y = 2$
   d) $3x - 2y = 12$

      $6x + 6y = 30$

5. a) Multiply by the numbers indicated and write the equations formed.
      i) $3x - y = -7$ ①

         $x + 4y = 2$ ②

         Multiply ① by 2 and ② by 3.
      ii) $x + 2y = 8$ ①

          $5x - 3y = 1$ ②

          Multiply ① by 3 and ② by 2.

   b) Write the equations formed by adding the equations found in (a).

   c) Write the equations formed by subtracting the equations found in (a).

10-3 SOLVING LINEAR SYSTEMS BY ADDITION OR SUBTRACTION

Solving linear systems by graphing is time-consuming and does not always give exact solutions. It is therefore important to develop algebraic methods to solve them. One method depends on the properties of linear systems illustrated in the previous section.

Example 1. Solve: $3x - 5y = -9$ ...①
$4x + 5y = 23$ ...②

Solution. Since $-5y$ and $5y$ occur in both equations, we can *eliminate* y by adding the equations. According to the properties of linear systems, this will not change the solution.

$$3x - 5y = -9$$
$$4x + 5y = 23$$
Add: $7x\quad\ \ = 14$
$$x = 2$$

Since the value of x is 2, we can find the value of y by *substituting* 2 for x in either ① or ②. Using ②:

$$4(2) + 5y = 23$$
$$5y = 23 - 8$$
$$5y = 15$$
$$y = 3$$

The solution of this linear system is (2, 3).

Check. Substitute $x = 2$ and $y = 3$ in both equations ① and ②.

L.S. = $3x - 5y$ R.S. = -9 L.S. = $4x + 5y$ R.S. = 23
  = $3(2) - 5(3)$ = $4(2) + 5(3)$
  = $6 - 15$ = $8 + 15$
  = -9 = 23

The solution (2, 3) is correct.

Sometimes it is necessary to multiply one, or both, of the equations by a constant before one of the variables can be eliminated by addition or subtraction. According to the properties of linear systems, this will not change the solution.

Example 2. Solve: $\quad x - 2y = 7 \quad \ldots ①$
$\qquad\qquad\qquad 3x + 4y = 1 \quad \ldots ②$

Solution. If we multiply ① by 3, the coefficients of x will be the same in both equations.

$$
\begin{array}{ll}
\text{Multiply ① by 3:} & 3x - 6y = 21 \\
\text{Subtract ②:} & \underline{3x + 4y = 1} \\
& -10y = 20 \\
& y = -2
\end{array}
$$

Substitute -2 for y in equation ①:

$$
\begin{aligned}
x - 2(-2) &= 7 \\
x + 4 &= 7 \\
x &= 3
\end{aligned}
$$

The solution of this linear system is $(3, -2)$.

If the value of the first variable found is not an integer, it may be easier to find the value of the other variable by elimination rather than by substitution.

Example 3. Solve: $\quad 2x + 3y = 8 \quad \ldots ①$
$\qquad\qquad\qquad 5x - 4y = -6 \quad \ldots ②$

Solution.
$$
\begin{array}{ll}
\text{Multiply ① by 5:} & 10x + 15y = 40 \\
\text{Multiply ② by 2:} & \underline{10x - 8y = -12} \\
\text{Subtract:} & 23y = 52 \\
& y = \dfrac{52}{23}
\end{array}
$$

$$
\begin{array}{ll}
\text{Multiply ① by 4:} & 8x + 12y = 32 \\
\text{Multiply ② by 3:} & \underline{15x - 12y = -18} \\
\text{Add:} & 23x = 14 \\
& x = \dfrac{14}{23}
\end{array}
$$

The solution is $\left(\dfrac{14}{23}, \dfrac{52}{23}\right)$.

EXERCISES 10-3

1. For which linear systems is $(-1, 1)$ a solution?
   a) $5x + 6y = 1$
      $6x + 2y = -3$
   b) $3x + 4y = 1$
      $5x - 3y = -8$
   c) $3x - 4y = -6$
      $3x + 3y = 1$
   d) $7x - 3y = 10$
      $6x + 5y = -1$

2. Solve and check.
   a) $2x + 3y = 18$
      $2x - 3y = -6$
   b) $3x + 5y = 12$
      $7x + 5y = 8$
   c) $7x - 4y = 26$
      $3x + 4y = -6$
   d) $3x - 4y = 0$
      $5x - 4y = 8$
   e) $2x - 5y = -18$
      $8x - 13y = -58$
   f) $4x + y = -11$
      $3x - 5y = 9$
   g) $6x - 5y = -2$
      $2x + 3y = 18$
   h) $3x - 10y = 16$
      $4x + 2y = 6$

(B)

3. Solve.
   a) $8x - 3y = 38$
      $4x - 5y = 26$
   b) $3x + 4y = 29$
      $2x - 5y = -19$
   c) $6a - 5b = \frac{4}{3}$
      $10a + 3b = 6$
   d) $3s + 4t = 18$
      $2s - 3t = -5$

   e) $3x - y = 5$
      $2x + 3y = 10$
   f) $4x + 3y = 3$
      $3x - 2y = -19$
   g) $\frac{x}{3} + \frac{y}{2} = \frac{1}{6}$
      $x - 6y = 8$
   h) $\frac{1}{2}x - \frac{2}{3}y = 6$
      $\frac{1}{4}x + \frac{1}{3}y = -1$

4. Solve.
   a) $\frac{1}{3}x + \frac{1}{4}y = 0$
      $x + y = -1$
   b) $\frac{1}{2}x - \frac{1}{3}y = 1$
      $x + \frac{1}{4}y = 2$
   c) $\frac{2}{3}x + \frac{1}{5}y = -2$
      $\frac{1}{3}x - \frac{1}{2}y = -7$

   d) $\frac{x}{4} + \frac{y}{2} = 0$
      $x + y = 2$
   e) $\frac{1}{3}x + \frac{1}{2}y = -\frac{1}{2}$
      $\frac{1}{5}x - \frac{1}{3}y = \frac{27}{5}$
   f) $\frac{3}{4}x + \frac{y}{3} = \frac{11}{2}$
      $\frac{2x}{5} - \frac{3y}{2} = -\frac{21}{10}$

5. Solve.
   a) $x + 2y = 8$
      $y + x = 5$
   b) $2x - y = 19$
      $3y - 5x = -46$
   c) $2x + 3y = 12$
      $4y - 3x = -1$
   d) $2x + 3y = 32$
      $2y + 22 = 3x$
   e) $3y - 7x = x$
      $3x - 1 = y$
   f) $3x - 10 = 4y$
      $6y + 2x = 11$
   g) $y + 2x = 10 + 4y$
      $4(x + y) = 42 - y$
   h) $2(x - 2y) = 26 - 5y$
      $3(y - x) = -2(y - 7)$

(C)

6. a) Solve this linear system by graphing.
      $$7x - 11y = -22$$
      $$2x + 3y = 18$$

   b) Solve the system in (a) by addition or subtraction, and give the solution correct to two decimal places.

   c) Compare the results of (a) and (b). What do you notice?

10-4 SOLVING LINEAR SYSTEMS BY SUBSTITUTION

In the preceding section, a linear system was solved by adding or subtracting equations to eliminate one of the variables. Another way to eliminate a variable is to use substitution.

Example 1. Solve: $\begin{aligned} 2x - y &= 13 \quad \ldots① \\ 4x + 3y &= 1 \quad \ldots② \end{aligned}$

Solution. Choose equation ① and express y in terms of x.
$$2x - y = 13$$
$$y = 2x - 13 \quad \ldots③$$
Substitute this expression for y in equation ② and solve for x:
$$4x + 3(2x - 13) = 1$$
$$4x + 6x - 39 = 1$$
$$10x = 40$$
$$x = 4$$
Substitute 4 for x in ③ and solve for y:
$$y = 2(4) - 13$$
$$= -5$$
The solution of the linear system is $(4, -5)$.

It makes no difference which variable is chosen for elimination. However, if one has a coefficient of 1 or -1, its choice makes for easier work since fractions are avoided. In the next example, x is eliminated because it has a coefficient of 1 in one of the equations.

Example 2. Solve: $\begin{aligned} x + 6y &= 9 \quad \ldots① \\ 3x - 2y &= -23 \quad \ldots② \end{aligned}$

Solution. Choose equation ① and express x in terms of y.
$$x + 6y = 9$$
$$x = 9 - 6y \quad \ldots③$$
Substitute $9 - 6y$ for x in ② and solve for y:
$$3(9 - 6y) - 2y = -23$$
$$27 - 18y - 2y = -23$$
$$-20y = -50$$
$$y = \frac{5}{2}$$

Substitute $\frac{5}{2}$ for y in ③ to find the value of x:
$$x = 9 - 6\left(\frac{5}{2}\right)$$
$$= 9 - 15$$
$$= -6$$
The solution is $\left(-6, \frac{5}{2}\right)$.

Check. Substitute $x = -6$ and $y = \dfrac{5}{2}$ in both equations ① and ②.

L.S. $= x + 6y$ R.S. $= 9$ L.S. $= 3x - 2y$ R.S. $= -23$

$= -6 + 6\left(\dfrac{5}{2}\right)$ $= 3(-6) - 2\left(\dfrac{5}{2}\right)$

$= -6 + 15$ $= -18 - 5$

$= 9$ $= -23$

The solution is correct.

EXERCISES 10-4

Ⓐ

1. For which of the given linear systems is $(-2, 5)$ a solution?

a) $3x + y = 1$
   $2x + 3y = 11$

b) $5x - 3y = -5$
   $3x + 2y = 4$

c) $-5x - 3y = -5$
   $3x + 2y = 4$

d) $\dfrac{3}{2}x + \dfrac{2}{5}y = -1$
   $\dfrac{5}{4}x - \dfrac{3}{10}y = -4$

2. Solve by substitution.

a) $x + y = 9$
   $2x + y = 11$

b) $x + y = 1$
   $3x - y = 11$

c) $x - y = 7$
   $2x + y = -10$

d) $3x + y = 7$
   $5x + 2y = 13$

e) $2x + 3y = 11$
   $5x - y = -15$

f) $4x + y = -5$
   $2x + 3y = 5$

g) $3x + 2y = 19$
   $2x - 3y = -9$

h) $5y + 2x = -2$
   $5x - 2y = 24$

Ⓑ

3. Solve by substitution and check.

a) $3x - 4y = -15$
   $5x + y = -2$

b) $2x + y = 2$
   $3x - 2y = 10$

c) $3m - n = 5$
   $5m - 2n = 8$

d) $4s - 3t = 9$
   $2s - t = 5$

e) $5v + u = -17$
   $3u - 4v = 6$

f) $x + 5y = -11$
   $4x - 3y = 25$

g) $\dfrac{x}{2} + \dfrac{y}{2} = 7$
   $3x + 2y = 48$

h) $\dfrac{a}{2} + \dfrac{b}{3} = 1$
   $\dfrac{a}{4} + \dfrac{2b}{3} = -1$

4. Solve.

a) $3x + 6y = 4$
   $x - 2y = 1$

b) $7x + y = 13$
   $3x - 2y = 8$

c) $4x + 6y = 1$
   $x + y = 4$

d) $5x + 3y = 5$
   $2x + y = 8$

e) $9x + 2y = 2$
   $1 - y = 4x$

f) $8x + 4y = 1$
   $7x = -2y$

g) $9x + 6y = 4$
   $8x + 3y = 9$

h) $2x + 8y = 1$
   $x = 2y$

Ⓒ

5. For what values of m and n is $(-1, 2)$ the solution of each linear system?

a) $mx + 3y = 1$
   $2x + ny = -4$

b) $mx + ny = 3$
   $4x + ny = -2$

c) $mx + ny = 1$
   $mx + 5y = 7$

d) $2mx + ny = 6$
   $3mx - 2ny = 2$

INVESTIGATE

Pairs of Linear Equations

1. Graph on the same axes the relations defined by these equations.
   i) $y = 3x + 2$
   ii) $y = -2x + 7$
   What do you notice?

2. Graph on the same axes the relations defined by these equations.
   i) $y = 4x - 6$
   ii) $y = 4x + 3$
   What do you notice?

3. Graph on the same axes the relations defined by these equations.
   i) $4x - 2y = -10$
   ii) $y = 2x + 5$
   What do you notice?

● The graphs of two linear relations may intersect at one point.
● The graphs of two linear relations may be parallel.
● The graphs of two linear relations may coincide.

4. Graph each pair of linear equations. For each pair state whether:
   i) the graphs intersect, if so, state the coordinates of their points of intersection
   ii) the graphs are parallel
   iii) the graphs coincide.

   a) $y = 2x - 2$
      $3x + y = 13$

   b) $y = 5x + 6$
      $y = 5x - 3$

   c) $x + 2y = 3$
      $2x + 4y = 6$

   d) $2x + 5y = -3$
      $2x + 5y = 4$

   e) $5x + 2y = 0$
      $y = x + 7$

   f) $3x + y = -2$
      $9x + 3y = -6$

   g) $4x + 3y = 1$
      $-4x - 3y = -1$

   h) $y = \frac{5}{2}x - \frac{7}{2}$
      $-5x + 2y = -7$

   i) $x = -6$
      $y = 3x + 17$

5. By inspecting the equations of a pair of linear relations, describe how to tell:
   i) if the graphs will be parallel   ii) if the graphs will coincide.

10-5 SOLVING PROBLEMS USING LINEAR SYSTEMS: PART ONE

To solve a problem using linear systems, the facts of the problem must be translated into algebraic symbols. If two different variables are used, then *two* different equations must be found. When the system of equations is solved, the problem can be answered.

Example 1. The sum of two numbers is 176, and their difference is 48. Find the numbers.

Solution. Let x represent the larger number. Let y represent the smaller number.

The equations are:
$$x + y = 176 \quad \ldots ①$$
$$x - y = 48 \quad \ldots ②$$
Add:
$$2x = 224$$
$$x = 112$$
Substitute 112 for x in ①:
$$112 + y = 176$$
$$y = 176 - 112$$
$$= 64$$
The numbers are 112 and 64.

Check. The sum of the numbers is $112 + 64 = 176$.
The difference is $112 - 64 = 48$.
The solution is correct.

Example 2. The coin box of a vending machine contains $4.55 in dimes and quarters. If there are 23 coins altogether, how many of each kind are there?

Solution. Let x be the number of dimes, and y the number of quarters. Then the value of the dimes, in cents, is $10x$. The value of the quarters is $25y$.
Since there are 23 coins: $\qquad x + y = 23 \quad \ldots ①$
Since the total value of the
coins is $4.55, or 455 cents: $\quad 10x + 25y = 455 \quad \ldots ②$
Multiply ① by 10: $\qquad\qquad 10x + 10y = 230$
Subtract: $\qquad\qquad\qquad\qquad 15y = 225$
$$y = 15$$
Substitute 15 for y in ①: $\qquad x + 15 = 23$
$$x = 8$$
There are 8 dimes and 15 quarters in the coin box.

Check. Value of the dimes, in cents: $\qquad 8 \times 10 = 80$
Value of the quarters, in cents: $\quad 15 \times 25 = 375$
Total value: $ 455$ cents, or $4.55
The solution is correct.

Example 3.   Four chocolate bars and three ice-cream cones cost $5.30. Two chocolate bars and one ice-cream cost $2.20. Find the cost of a chocolate bar and the cost of an ice-cream cone.

Solution.   Let the cost of a chocolate bar be x cents. Let the cost of an ice-cream cone be y cents.

The equations are: $4x + 3y = 530$ ...①
$\qquad\qquad\qquad\quad 2x + y = 220$ ...②

Multiply ② by 3: $6x + 3y = 660$
Subtract ①: $\underline{4x + 3y = 530}$
$\qquad\qquad\qquad\qquad 2x = 130$
$\qquad\qquad\qquad\qquad\ x = 65$

Substitute 65 for x in ②: $2(65) + y = 220$
$\qquad\qquad\qquad\qquad\qquad\qquad y = 220 - 130$
$\qquad\qquad\qquad\qquad\qquad\qquad\ \ = 90$

A chocolate bar costs 65 cents and an ice-cream cone costs 90 cents.

Check.   Chocolate bars: $4 \times \$0.65 = \$2.60$ $2 \times \$0.65 = \$1.30$
Ice-cream cones: $3 \times \$0.90 = \underline{\$2.70}$ $1 \times \$0.90 = \underline{\$0.90}$
$\qquad\qquad\qquad\qquad\qquad$ Total: $\$5.30$ Total: $\$2.20$

The solution is correct.

EXERCISES 10-5

1. The sum of two numbers is 25, and their difference is 7. Find the numbers.

2. Find two numbers which have a sum of 53 and a difference of 21.

3. When two numbers are added, the result is 182. When they are subtracted, the result is 48. What are the numbers?

4. Two numbers have a sum of 10. The first number plus three times the second number is 24. Find the numbers.

5. Corina has $31 in $2 and $5 bills. There are 11 bills in all. How many of each does she have?

6. Lucian has $1.15 in dimes and quarters. There are 7 coins altogether. How many of each does he have?

7. The coin box of a vending machine contains $6.20 in dimes and quarters. There are 32 coins in all. How many of each kind are there?

8. For a school play, Janis sold 6 adult tickets and 15 student tickets, and collected $48. Parviz sold 8 adult tickets and 7 student tickets, and collected $38. Find the cost of adult and student tickets.

9. Lorraine buys 6 cheap golf balls and 4 expensive ones for $12.50. Bob buys 4 cheap and 3 expensive balls for $9.00. What are the prices of the two kinds of balls?

Ⓑ

10. The sum of two numbers is 7. Three times one of the numbers is 15 more than the other number. Find the numbers.

11. Two numbers differ by 5. Four times the smaller number is 5 less than three times the larger. Find the numbers.

12. Mirella has $4.80 in nickels and quarters. She has 6 more nickels than quarters. How many of each does she have?

13. The cost of 4 qt of oil and 15 gal of gasoline is $24.30. The cost of 3 qt of oil and 10 gal of gasoline is $16.90. Find the cost of 1 qt of oil and 1 gal of gasoline.

14. When Chana rented a car for 3 days and drove 100 mi, the charge was $124. When she rented the same car for 5 days and drove 250 mi, the charge was $240. What was the charge per day and the charge per mile?

15. The perimeter of a rectangle is 64 cm. Twice the width is 4 cm more than the length. Find the dimensions of the rectangle.

16. Divide 10 into two parts such that when the larger is doubled and the smaller is tripled, the sum is 22.

17. Divide 15 into two parts such that when the larger is divided by 3 and the smaller is divided by 2, the quotients are equal.

18. When three times one number is added to four times another, the result is 44. When five times the first number is added to two times the second, the result is 50. What are the numbers?

Ⓒ

19. The sum of two numbers is five times their difference. What is the quotient when the larger number is divided by the smaller?

20. If 1 is added to the numerator of a fraction, the result is equivalent to $\frac{3}{4}$. If 1 is added to the denominator of the same fraction, the result is equivalent to $\frac{2}{3}$. Find the fraction.

10-6 SOLVING PROBLEMS USING LINEAR SYSTEMS: PART TWO

When solving problems using linear systems, remember that one variable
requires one equation, and two variables require two equations.

Example 1. The sum of the digits of a two-digit number is 12. The number formed by
reversing the digits is 54 more than the original number. What is the original number?

Solution. Let the tens digit be x and the ones digit be y.
Original number: $\qquad$ $10x + y$
Number with digits reversed: $\quad$ $10y + x$
Since their difference is 54:

$$(10y + x) - (10x + y) = 54$$
$$9y - 9x = 54$$
$$y - x = 6$$
$$-x + y = 6 \quad \ldots \text{①}$$

Since sum of digits is 12: $\qquad \underline{x + y = 12 \quad \ldots \text{②}}$
Add ① and ②: $\qquad\qquad\qquad 2y = 18$
$$y = 9$$

Substitute 9 for y in either ① or ②: $x = 3$
The original number is 39.

Check. $93 - 39 = 54$. The solution is correct.

Although a problem may ask for only one unknown to be found, it is often best to
use two unknowns and two equations.

Example 2. A sports club charges an initiation fee and a monthly fee. At the end of 1 month a member had paid a total of $260, and at the end of 6 months she had paid a total of $435. What is the initiation fee?

Solution. Let x represent the initiation fee and y the monthly fee.

Amount paid after 1 month is $260: $\quad x + 1y = 260 \quad \ldots ①$
Amount paid after 6 months is $435: $\quad x + 6y = 435 \quad \ldots ②$

$$\text{Subtract } ①: \quad \begin{array}{r} x + y = 260 \\ \hline 5y = 175 \\ y = 35 \end{array}$$

$$\text{Substitute 35 for } y \text{ in } ①: \quad x + 35 = 260 \\ x = 225$$

The initiation fee is $225.

Check. The monthly fee is $35.

Amount paid after 1 month: $\qquad \$225 + \$35 = \$260$
Amount paid after 6 months: $\quad \$225 + 6 \times \$35 = \$225 + \$210$
$$= \$435$$

The solution is correct.

Example 3. Barry invested $2000, part at 8% per annum and the rest at 10% per annum. After one year the total interest earned was $190. How much did he invest at each rate?

Solution. Let x represent the amount invested at 8%. The interest on this amount in one year, in dollars, is $0.08x$. Let y represent the amount invested at 10%. The interest on this amount in one year, in dollars, is $0.10y$.

Total money invested: $\qquad x + y = 2000 \quad \ldots ①$
Total interest earned: $\qquad 0.08x + 0.10y = 190 \quad \ldots ②$

$$\begin{array}{ll} \text{Multiply } ② \text{ by 100:} & 8x + 10y = 19\,000 \\ \text{Multiply } ① \text{ by 8:} & 8x + 8y = 16\,000 \\ \hline \text{Subtract:} & 2y = 3000 \\ & y = 1500 \end{array}$$

$$\text{Substitute 1500 for } y \text{ in } ①: \qquad x = 500$$

Barry invested $500 at 8% and $1500 at 10%.

Check. Interest on $500 at 8%: $\quad 0.08 \times 500 = \$ 40$
Interest on $1500 at 10%: $\quad 0.10 \times 1500 = \$150$
Total interest earned: $\qquad\qquad\qquad\qquad\quad \$190$

The solution is correct.

EXERCISES 10-6

Ⓐ

1. The sum of the digits of a two-digit number is 14. The number formed by reversing the digits is 36 more than the original number. What is the original number?

2. The sum of the digits of a two-digit number is 13. The number formed by reversing the digits is 27 more than the original number. Find the original number.

3. The sum of the digits of a two-digit number is 7. The number formed by reversing the digits is 45 less than the original number. What is the original number?

Ⓑ

4. A sports club charges an initiation fee and monthly fee. At the end of 5 months a member had paid a total of $170, and at the end of 10 months she had paid a total of $295. What is the initiation fee?

5. A tennis club charges an annual fee and an hourly fee for court time. One year, Tony played for 39 h and paid $384. Sandra played for 51 h and paid $456. Find the annual fee and the hourly fee.

6. Jennifer invested $500, part at 7% per annum and the rest at 10% per annum. After one year the total interest earned was $44. How much did she invest at each rate?

7. The tens digit of a two-digit number is 6 more than the ones digit. The sum of the number, and the number formed by reversing the digits, is 88. Find the number.

8. The sum of the digits of a two-digit number is 7. The number formed by reversing the digits is two more than double the original number. Find the original number.

9. When 20 bolts are placed in a box the total mass is 340 g. When there are 48 bolts in the box the total mass is 760 g. Find the mass of the box and the mass of each bolt.

10. A crate of 36 grapefruit has a total mass of 4 kg. When 12 grapefruit are removed the total mass becomes 3 kg. Find the mass of the crate and the mass of a grapefruit.

11. Vien invested $800, part at 9% per annum and the rest at 12% per annum. After one year the total interest earned was $79.50. How much did he invest at each rate?

12. Mee Ha invested $2500, part at 8% per annum, and the rest at 12% per annum. In one year, the two parts earned equal amounts of interest. How much did she invest at each rate?

13. Naomi invested $1000, part at 8% per annum and the rest at 10% per annum. In one year, the two parts earned equal amounts of interest. How much did she invest at each rate?

14. The sum of two numbers is 56. The larger exceeds twice the smaller by 2. What are the numbers?

15. The difference of two numbers is 22. Twice the smaller exceeds the larger by 17. Find the numbers.

16. The coin box of a vending machine contains half as many quarters as dimes. If the total value of the coins is $22.50, how many dimes are there?

17. A collection of dimes and quarters has a value of $5.20. If the number of quarters is 4 more than twice the number of dimes, how many dimes are there?

18. The ones digit of a two-digit number is 5 more than the tens digit. The number formed by reversing the digits is eight times the sum of the digits. Find the number.

19. The sum of the digits of a two-digit number is 6. The number formed by reversing the digits is equal to three times the ones digit. Find the original number.

20. Three footballs and one soccer ball cost $155. Two footballs and three soccer balls cost $220. Find the cost of a football and the cost of a soccer ball.

21. For the school play, adult tickets cost $5.00 and student tickets cost $3.00. Twice as many student tickets as adult tickets were sold. If the total receipts were $1650, how many of each kind of ticket were sold?

22. For the athletic banquet, adult tickets cost $15.00 and student tickets cost $10.00. If 140 tickets were sold, and the total receipts were $1600, how many student tickets were sold?

23. The cost of renting a car depends on the number of days it is rented and the distance it is driven. The cost for one day and 240 km is $39, and the cost for three days and 800 km is $125. What is the cost per day and the cost per kilometre?

24. Denise invested $2000, part at 7% per annum and the rest at 8% per annum. After one year, the interest earned on the 7% investment was $50 more than the interest on the 8% investment. How much did she invest at each rate?

25. Vito invested $500, part at 9% per annum and the rest at 11% per annum. After one year, the interest earned on the 9% investment was $20 less than the interest on the 11% investment. How much did he invest at each rate?

© ───

26. A lifeguard earns an hourly rate for 20 h work in one week and an increased rate for overtime. One week Theresa worked 24 h and received $166.40. The next week she worked 27.5 h and received $200.00. Find her hourly rate and her overtime rate of pay.

27. In a three-digit number, the hundreds digit is equal to the tens digit, and is 2 more than the ones digit. The number formed by reversing the digits is 19 times the sum of the digits. Find the original number.

28. A two-digit number is equal to seven times the sum of its digits.
    a) Show that the tens digit must be double the ones digit.
    b) Show that the number formed by reversing the digits must be equal to four times the sum of the digits.

Use A Table

A power boat has two separate motors. When motor A is used, the boat will run for 3 h on a tank of fuel. When motor B is used, the boat will run for 4 h on the same amount of fuel. How long would a tank of fuel last if both motors were using it?

Understand the problem

- Is the capacity of the tank known?
- What should be assumed about the speed of the boat?
- How can all the information be organized?

Think of a strategy

- Summarize the given information in a table.

Carry out the strategy

- Introduce variables to represent the things we want to know. Let t represent the time the tank of fuel would last if both motors used it. Let V represent the capacity of the tank.

- Make a table with appropriate headings. For this problem, the columns are labelled amount of fuel consumed, rate of consumption, and time. The rows are labelled motor A and motor B.

	Fuel Consumed (gal)	Rate of Consumption (gal/h)	Time (h)
Motor A		$\dfrac{V}{3}$	t
Motor B		$\dfrac{V}{4}$	t

• Insert the given information and the variables. Complete the table. Note that this formula can be used.

$$\text{Amount of Fuel Consumed} = \text{Rate of Consumption} \times \text{Time}$$

Use this formula to complete the table.

	Fuel Consumed (gal)	Rate of Consumption (gal/h)	Time (h)
Motor *A*	$\dfrac{Vt}{3}$	$\dfrac{V}{3}$	t
Motor *B*	$\dfrac{Vt}{4}$	$\dfrac{V}{4}$	t

• Write equation(s) to relate the variables. The total amount of fuel used is equal to the capacity of the tank.

$$\frac{Vt}{3} + \frac{Vt}{4} = V$$

Can you divide both sides of this equation by V?

• Solve the equation and answer the question. How long will the tank of fuel last if both motors are using it?

Look back

• Is it necessary to know the capacity of the tank?
• Is it possible to find the capacity of the tank from the given information?
• How much fuel does motor *A* use? How much does motor *B* use?
• Can you solve the problem using a system of two equations in two variables?

The Andersons traveled 550 mi from Chicago to Memphis via Cairo, Illinois. Part of the trip was by car at 50 mph, and the rest by riverboat at 10 mph. If the total traveling time for the entire trip was 27 h, how many hours were spent by car, and how many by riverboat?

Understand the problem

- What does the travelling time depend on?
- How can all the information be organized?

Think of a strategy

- Summarize the given information in a table.

Carry out the strategy

- Introduce variables to represent the things we want to know. Let x represent the time in hours by car. Let y represent the time in hours by boat.
- Make a table with appropriate headings. For this problem, the columns are labelled distance, speed, and time. The rows are labeled car and boat.

	Distance (mi)	Speed (mph)	Time (h)
Car		50	x
Boat		10	y

- Insert the given information and the variables. Complete the table. Recall that distance, speed, and time are related by this formula:

	Distance (mi)	Speed (mph)	Time (h)
Car	$50x$	50	x
Boat	$10y$	10	y

Distance = Speed × Time

- Write two equations to relate the variables. Use the columns containing the variables.

The total distance is 550 mi. $\qquad 50x + 10y = 550 \ldots ①$
The total traveling time is 27 h. $\qquad x + y = 27 \ldots ②$

- Solve the equations and answer the question. How many hours did the Andersons spend traveling by car and by boat?

Look back

- How far did the Andersons travel by car and by boat?
- Is this total distance 550 mi?

Solve each problem

1. From Memphis, the Andersons traveled 840 mi to St. Petersburg, Florida via New Orleans. Part of the trip was by car at 50 mph, and the rest by boat at 30 mph. If the total traveling time for the entire trip was 22 h, how many hours were spent by car and how many by boat?

2. It is a 230 km journey to the Jacksons' cottage. Part of the trip is on gravel roads at 50 km/h and part is on paved roads at 80 km/h. If the total trip takes 4 h, how much time is spent on gravel roads, and how much is spent on paved roads?

3. As part of her physical fitness training, Brenda cycled at 30 km/h and then jogged at 8 km/h. The total time spent was 2 h, and she covered a total distance of 49 km. How much time did she spend jogging?

4. The school hockey team travelled 150 km to a tournament by bus. The bus drove at 90 km/h most of the way, but was delayed by a storm, when its speed was only 30 km/h. If the trip took 3 h, how far did the bus travel in the storm?

5. A farmer set out to travel on a 170 km stretch of lonely prairie highway at an average speed of 105 km/h. He was more than halfway across when his car broke down and he had to complete the journey on foot. He walked at 6 km/h, and the whole trip took 7 h. How long did he walk? How far did he walk?

6. A boat at constant power travels 60 km upriver in 3 h and returns in 2 h. What is the speed of the
   a) boat relative to the water?   b) current?

7. An aircraft travels 1100 mi from Minneapolis to Boston in 3.2 h and returns in 4 h. If the wind speed is constant, find the wind speed and the speed of the aircraft in still air.

8. A boat has two motors, one large and one small. If only the large motor is running, a tank of fuel lasts 2 h. If only the small motor is running, the tank of fuel lasts 4 h. How long will the fuel last if both motors are running?

9. A tank has two taps. If tap A is open, the tank drains empty in 10 min. If tap B is open, the tank drains empty in 6 min. How long would it take to drain the tank if both taps are open?

10. Machine A makes 50 records in 2 min, and machine B makes 50 records in 3 min. With both machines working, how long would it take to make 1000 records?

11. A butcher has supplies of lean beef containing 15% fat, and fat trim containing 100% fat. How many kilograms of lean beef and fat trim does she need to make 50 kg of hamburger, which is 25% fat?

MATHEMATICS AROUND US

How Fast Do Glaciers Move?

The Columbia Icefield in Jasper National Park is the largest accumulation of ice in the Rocky Mountains. It is estimated that 6–10 m of snow falls in this region each year. Not all of this snow melts in the summer and, over the centuries, the accumulated snow has been pressed into ice.

The Athabasca Glacier flows from the rim of the Columbia Icefield, and can be seen by travellers from the Banff-Jasper highway. This glacier is about 5.3 km long, 1.2 km wide, and has a maximum thickness of approximately 300 m. However, the glacier is presently receding, because the ice is melting at the end at a faster rate than it can be resupplied from above.

There are two rates associated with the Athabasca Glacier which have been measured:
- The rate of flow of the ice down the mountain—about 10 cm per day;
- The rate of recession of the end of the glacier—about 12 m per year.

These rates depend on the season or on the location on the glacier where the measurements are made.

QUESTIONS

1. a) About how many years might it take ice at the top of the glacier to flow to the end?
   b) About how long would it take to flow the length of your classroom?
   c) About how far has it flowed since you were born?

2. a) About how far has the end of the glacier receded since you were born?
   b) About how long would it take to recede the length of your classroom?
   c) About how long might it take for the glacier to disappear?

3. If the ice stopped flowing down the mountain, what would be the rate of recession of the end of the glacier?

4. What important assumptions did you make in answering the above questions? Discuss the validity of these assumptions.

COMPUTER POWER

A Formula for Linear Systems

If there were many pairs of linear equations to be solved, it would be useful to have a formula to solve them. A program could be written for this formula, and the equations solved by computer. To find such a formula, we solve the linear system:

$$Ax + By = C \ldots \text{①}$$
$$Dx + Ey = F \ldots \text{②}$$

① × E:	$AEx + BEy = CE$
② × B:	$BDx + BEy = BF$
Subtract:	$AEx - BDx = CE - BF$
	$x(AE - BD) = CE - BF$
	$x = \dfrac{CE - BF}{AE - BD}$

① × D:	$ADx + BDy = CD$
② × A:	$ADx + AEy = AF$
Subtract:	$BDy - AEy = CD - AF$
	$y = \dfrac{CD - AF}{BD - AE}$
	$= \dfrac{AF - CD}{AE - BD}$

The solution of the above linear system is the ordered pair $\left(\dfrac{CE - BF}{AE - BD}, \dfrac{AF - CD}{AE - BD} \right)$, provided that $AE - BD \neq 0$. If $AE - BD = 0$, there may be no solution or infinitely many solutions.
A simple BASIC program for the above formula is as follows:

```
100 REM *** LINEAR SYSTEMS ***
110 INPUT "COEFFICIENTS OF EQUATION #1? ";A,B,C
120 INPUT "COEFFICIENTS OF EQUATION #2? ";D,E,F
130 Z=A*E-B*D
140 IF Z<>0 THEN PRINT "THE SOLUTION IS:";
    (C*E-B*F)/Z,(A*F-C*D)/Z
150 IF Z=0 THEN PRINT "THERE IS NO UNIQUE SOLUTION"
160 END
```

1. Use the program to solve.

   a) $3.3x - 4.2y = 12$
      $1.7x + 2.6y = 30$

   b) $86x + 49y = 97$
      $15x - 24y = -276$

   c) $9.3x + 1.6y = -8.2$
      $4.7x - 7.3y = 6.1$

   d) $26x - 34y = 105$
      $41x + 9y = 83$

   e) $243x + 155y = 528$
      $-62x + 417y = 166$

   f) $3.15x - 5.81y = 12.66$
      $8.69x + 4.07y = -19.22$

10-7 GRAPHING LINEAR INEQUALITIES

The graph shows the line defined by the equation $y = x$. The y-coordinate of every point on this line is equal to the x-coordinate.

x	y
-3	-3
0	0
4	4

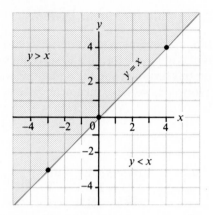

In the region *above* the line, the y-coordinate of every point is *greater* than the x-coordinate. This region is the graph of the inequality $y > x$.

In the region *below* the line, the y-coordinate of every point is *less* than the x-coordinate. This region is the graph of the inequality $y < x$.

In general, the graph of any linear equation is a straight line which divides the plane into two *half-planes*. The half-planes are the graphs of the corresponding inequalities.

To draw the graph of an inequality, follow these steps:

Step 1. Draw the graph of the corresponding equation.

Step 2. Find the coordinates of any point which satisfies the inequality.

Step 3. Plot the point on the graph. The half-plane in which the point is located is the graph of the inequality.

Example 1. Graph the inequality: $4x - 5y < 20$

Solution.   *Step 1.*
The corresponding equation is
$4x - 5y = 20$.
Make a table of values and plot the ordered pairs (x, y) on a grid.

x	y
0	-4
5	0

Step 2.
A point which satisfies the inequality is
(0, 0), since 4(0) − 5(0) = 0, which is
less than 20.

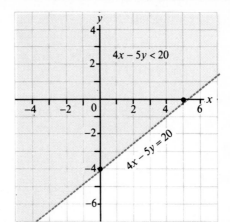

Step 3.
The point (0, 0) is the origin. Since it
lies in the region above the line, this
region is the graph of the inequality
$4x − 5y < 20$.

In *Example 1*, the line defined by $4x − 5y = 20$ is shown as a broken line because it is not part of the region defined by the inequality
$4x − 5y < 20$.

Example 2. A farmer is willing to use up to 80 acres of land to plant two crops, corn
and wheat. Draw a graph showing the area of each crop that could be
planted.

Solution. Let c acres and w acres represent respectively the area of corn and wheat
that the farmer could plant. Since *up to* 80 acres of land can be planted,
$c + w \le 80$.

Step 1.
The corresponding equation is
$c + w = 80$. The graph of this
equation is shown.

c	w
0	80
80	0

Steps 2 and 3.
A point which satisfies the
inequality is (10, 10). Since
(10, 10) lies in the region below
the line, this region is the graph
of the inequality $c + w \le 80$.

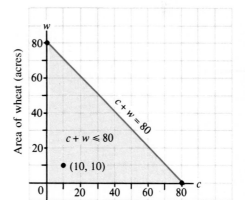

Farmer's Planting Arrangement

In *Example 2*, the line defined by $c + w = 80$ is shown as a solid
line because it is part of the region defined by the inequality $c + w \le 80$.
Only points in the first quadrant are shown, because the areas of corn
and wheat cannot be negative.

EXERCISES 10-7

Ⓐ

1. State the coordinates of any point which satisfies each inequality.
   a) $2x + y < 7$ b) $3x - 2y > 12$ c) $x - 4y \le 8$
   d) $5x + 3y > 9$ e) $2x + 3y \ge 15$ f) $3x + 4y \le 18$

2. State the coordinates of any point on the graph which satisfies the inequality and whether it lies in the region above or below the line.
   a) $x - 2y > -4$

   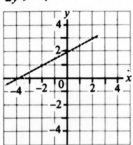

   b) $x + 2y < 4$

   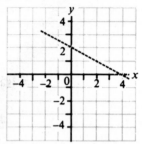

   c) $x - y < -3$

   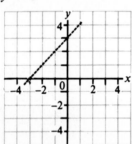

   d) $x + 3y + 3 > 0$

   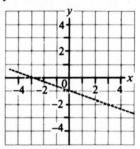

3. Write the inequality that represents the shaded region.
   a)

   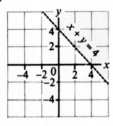

   b)

   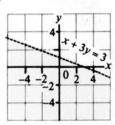

   c)

   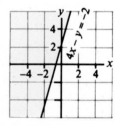

   d)

   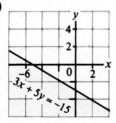

   e)

   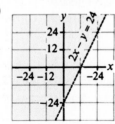

   f)

   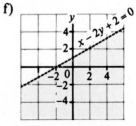

(B)

4. Graph the inequality.

a) $x + y < 5$ b) $x + y \geq 2$ c) $x - y \leq -3$

d) $x + 2y < 4$ e) $3x - 2y \geq -6$ f) $y \geq x + 8$

g) $y \leq -2x + 8$ h) $5x + 2y > -10$ i) $2x - 7y \geq 14$

5. A company makes motorcycles and bicycles. In any given week, a total of up to 400 vehicles can be made. Draw a graph showing the number of motorcycles and bicycles that could be made in one week.

6. Teri plans to spend up to 12 h reviewing Science and French in preparation for examinations. Draw a graph showing how much time she could spend studying each subject.

7. Graph the inequality.

a) $x - 2y \geq 4$ b) $3x - 2y \leq 6$ c) $4x - y < -4$
d) $2x + y > -4$ e) $y \geq 3x + 6$ f) $3x - 4y < 12$
g) $5x + 2y > 10$ h) $4x - 5y > 20$ i) $4x - 6y \geq 12$

(C)

8. Fiona plans to start a physical fitness program which requires that she jog and do calisthenics up to a maximum of 10 h each week. She must spend twice as much time jogging as she does doing calisthenics. Draw a graph showing the amount of time she can give to each activity.

9. Use the information in the news item to draw a graph showing the ages at which Chinese men and women may marry.

In China, Women Must Be 20 To Marry

Peking. A Chinese law sets minimum legal ages for marrying. The minimum legal age is 22 for men and 20 for women. In addition, couples are urged not to marry until the ages of the bride and groom total more than 52.

10-8 GRAPHING SYSTEMS OF LINEAR INEQUALITIES

In the first section of this chapter we solved systems of linear equations by graphing. If the corresponding lines intersect, the solution is given by the coordinates of their point of intersection. We can also solve systems of linear inequalities by graphing.

Example 1. Graph the solution set of this system of inequalities.

$$4x + 5y \leq 20 \quad \ldots \text{\textcircled{1}}$$
$$3x - 5y \geq 15 \quad \ldots \text{\textcircled{2}}$$

Solution. The corresponding system of *equations* is

$$4x + 5y = 20$$
$$3x - 5y = 15$$

Make a table of values for each equation.

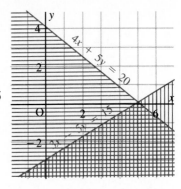

For $4x + 5y = 20$

x	y
5	0
0	4

For $3x - 5y = 15$

x	y
5	0
0	−3

Graph each equation on the same grid.

A point which satisfies inequality ① is (0,0). This point lies below the line defined by $4x + 5y = 20$. Shade the region below this line.

A point which satisfies inequality ② is (6,0). This point lies below the line defined by $3x - 5y = 15$. Shade the region below this line.

The graph of the solution set of the given system of inequalities is the region where the graphs of the two inequalities overlap, and it includes the boundaries.

Systems of linear inequalities have many applications. There are usually restrictions or limitations placed on the variables. The following example is a continuation of *Example 2* in Section 10-7.

Example 2. A farmer is willing to use up to 80 acres of land to plant two crops, corn and wheat. It costs $300/acre to plant corn and $100/acre to plant wheat. No more than $12 000 can be spent on planting the crops. Draw a graph showing the area of each crop that can be planted.

Solution. Let c and w represent respectively the areas of corn and wheat that the farmer could plant. Since up to 80 acres of land can be planted,

$$c + w \leq 80 \quad \ldots \text{\textcircled{1}}$$

The corresponding equation is
$c + w = 80$. Its graph is shown below.

c	w
0	80
80	0

A point which satisfies the inequality is (10,10). Since (10,10) lies in the region below the line, this region is the graph of inequality ①. Only points in the first quadrant are shown, because the areas of corn and wheat cannot be negative.

The cost to plant c acres of corn, in dollars, is $300c$.
The cost to plant w acres of wheat, in dollars, is $100w$.
Hence, the total cost of planting is $300c + 100w$.
Since no more than \$12 000 can be spent on planting,
$$300c + 100w \leq 12\ 000 \qquad \ldots ②$$
Divide both sides by 100.
$$3c + w \leq 120$$
The corresponding equation is $3c + w = 120$. The graph of this equation is shown on the same grid.

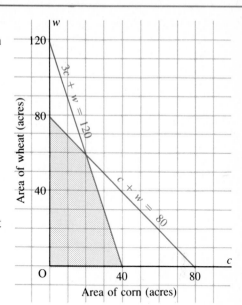

c	w
0	120
40	0

A point which satisfies the inequality is (0,0). Since (0,0) lies in the region below the line, this region is the graph of inequality ②.
The region where the graphs of the two inequalities overlap shows the area of each crop that can be planted, and it includes the boundaries.

EXERCISES 10-8

Ⓐ

1. Write the pair of inequalities that represents each shaded region.

a)

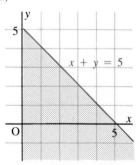

b)

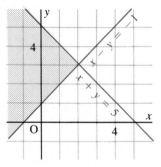

c)

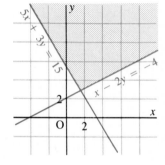

Ⓑ

2. Graph each solution set.
   a) $x + y \le 6$ b) $2x + y \le 6$ c) $x + 3y \le 3$ d) $x - 4y < 8$
       $x - 2y \ge 4$ $3x - 2y \le 6$ $4x - y < 4$ $2x + y \ge -4$

   e) $3x - y \le 6$ f) $2x + y < 4$ g) $5x + y \ge 10$ h) $4x - 5y < 20$
       $2x + y \ge -2$ $3x - 4y > 12$ $x + 3y > 6$ $3x + 2y \le -9$

3. Solve by graphing.
   a) $2x + 3y \le 8$ b) $3x - 4y \ge -9$ c) $6x + 5y < 120$ d) $5x - 3y > -10$
       $5x - 3y \le 12$ $x + 2y \ge 5$ $10x + 3y \le 100$ $2x + 3y < 9$

   e) $4x - 7y \le 140$ f) $4x + 3y < -6$ g) $12x - 5y \le 48$ h) $7x + 4y < 280$
       $2x + 5y < 60$ $3x - 4y \ge -8$ $9x + 8y \le 36$ $2x + 3y > 60$

4. A company makes motorcycles and bicycles. The physical dimensions of the work area limit the number of both kinds that can be made in one day. No more than 20 motorcycles can be made; no more than 30 bicycles can be made; and no more than 40 vehicles in all can be made. Draw a graph showing the numbers of motorcycles and bicycles that can be made in one day.

5. A unit of film-processing equipment can develop a maximum of 80 rolls of film per hour, provided there are not more than 50 rolls of color or of black-and-white. If color film is developed, there must be at least 15 rolls run at a time. Draw a graph showing the number of rolls of film of each type that can be processed in one hour.

6. Write the system of inequalities that represents each shaded region.
   a)   b)   c)

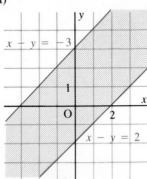
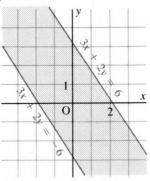
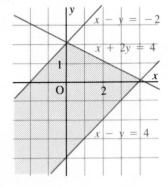

Ⓒ

7. Graph each solution set.
   a) $x - y \ge -2$ b) $5x + 2y \ge 10$ c) $x + y < 7$
          $y \le 2$ $x + 3y \ge 6$ $x + 3y < 12$
       $x + y \le 6$ $x - 2y \le -4$ $x > 0$
                                                    $y > 0$

8. Write an example of a system of inequalities that has no solution.

Choose the Strategy

1. If a 20 cm pizza serves two people, how many people should a 40 cm pizza serve?

2. A ball is dropped from a height of 2.0 m. After each bounce it rises to 75% of its previous height.
   a) What height does the ball reach after 5 bounces?
   b) After how many bounces does it reach a height of only 20 cm?

3. How many different integers satisfy the inequality $x^2 \le 1\ 000\ 000$?

4. Every prime number except 2 belongs in one of these two lists.
   > List A: 3, 7, 11, 19, 23, 31,...
   > List B: 5, 13, 17, 29, 37, 41,...

   Given any prime number, describe a simple procedure you could use to tell in which list it belongs.

5. Rectangle $OABC$ has vertices $O(0, 0)$, $A(6, 0)$, $B(6, 4)$, and $C(0, 4)$. Find the equation of the line through $D(0, 8)$ which divides the rectangle into two trapezoids with equal areas.

6. It took 3 h to drive 200 km to a summer cottage. Part of the trip was on a highway where the average speed was 100 km/h, and the rest was on a detour where the average speed was 50 km/h. Find the length of the detour.

7. A television program on gifted children began by featuring this puzzle.
   > 91 10 1
   > 87 15 ▓

   The viewers were asked to determine the number represented by ▓. At the end of the program, the "answer" as determined by the producers was announced. They had not realized that there was more than one answer. Determine a possible missing number, and explain the pattern you used to find it.

8. What number is represented by ▓ in each pattern?
   a) 3 6 1
      5 3 2
      1 2 ▓
   b) 5 3 9
      4 2 7
      1 6 ▓
   c) 1 3 5
      4 1 9
      3 1 ▓

9. Find a number which has this property. If you add 3 to it, and if you add 4 to it, the product of the two numbers obtained is the same as adding 12 to it.

Review Exercises

1. Solve by graphing.
   a) $x + y = -8$
      $x - 2y = 7$

   b) $2x + y = 8$
      $4x - 9y = 5$

   c) $x + 2y = -2$
      $-2x + y = 6$

   d) $x - 2y = -5$
      $-3x + y = 4$

2. Solve by addition or subtraction.
   a) $3x - 4y = 1$
      $3x - 2y = -1$

   b) $3a + 2b = 5$
      $9a - 2b = 15$

   c) $3x - 4y = -2$
      $4x - 3y = -5$

   d) $2s + 3t = 6$
      $5s + 10t = 20$

3. Solve by substitution.
   a) $x + 2y = 4$
      $3x + 2y = 0$

   b) $2x + y = 9$
      $x - y = 3$

   c) $2x + 3y = 9$
      $x - y = 3$

   d) $2x + 5y = -5$
      $x + y = 2$

4. Represent each of the following algebraically.
   a) Two numbers have a sum of 80.
   b) One number is 7 less than another number.
   c) The sum of three times one number and four times another number is 30.
   d) A number of nickels and dimes has a total value of $3.00.
   e) The perimeter of a rectangle with a length 5 cm greater than the width is equal to 40 cm.

5. The sum of two integers is 36. Their difference is 4. Find the integers.

6. The sum of the digits of a two-digit number is 12. The ones digit is 2 more than the tens digit. Find the number.

7. The sum of two integers is 63. The smaller is 11 more than one-third the larger. Find the integers.

8. Lynn has $3.55 in dimes and quarters. If there are 25 coins altogether, how many dimes are there?

9. From his paper route, Andy collected $5.55 in nickels and dimes. The number of nickels was 6 more than the number of dimes. How many nickels were there?

10. The sum of the digits of a two-digit number is 11. The number formed by reversing the digits is 45 more than the original number. What is the original number?

11. A 100 kg mixture of peanuts contains peanuts of two different kinds, one priced at $2/kg and the other at $2.40/kg. If the mixture is priced at $2.08/kg, how many kilograms of each kind of peanut does it contain?

12. Graph each inequality.
    a) $x + 2y \geq 4$ b) $3x - 2y \leq -6$ c) $5x - 2y > -10$

11 Statistics and Probability

A magazine company conducts a marketing survey of its readers. It determines that 74.3% of the readers are interested in sports, and 47.5% are interested in financial investment activities. Also, 6.8% are interested in neither topic. What is the probability that a randomly-selected reader is interested in both topics? (See Section 11-11 *Example 4*.)

11-1 INTERPRETING GRAPHS

In the fast-moving computer age, we encounter vast quantities of data. *Statistics* is the branch of mathematics that deals with the collection, organization, and interpretation of data. These data are usually organized into tables and/or presented as graphs. Some common types of graphs are shown below. Try to answer the question that accompanies each graph.

Pictograph

The graph shown here uses the symbol ● to represent 100 million people. A graph that uses a symbol to represent a certain amount is called a *pictograph*.
● What are the populations of North America and Europe?

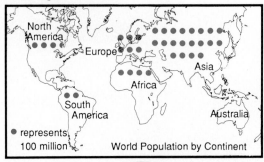

World Population by Continent

Circle Graph

In a *circle graph*, a complete set of data is presented by the circle. Various parts of the data are represented by the sectors of the circle.
● What percent of Idaho's forest fires are caused by lightning?

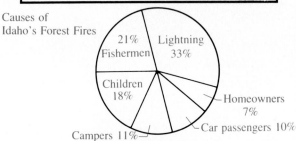

Causes of Idaho's Forest Fires

Bar Graph

The graph shown here uses a vertical bar to represent the amount of precipitation each month. Graphs of this type are called *bar graphs*. Bar graphs have horizontal or vertical bars.
● What appears to be the rainy season in Grand Forks?

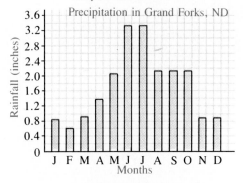

Histogram

A graph that uses bars, where each bar represents a range of values, is called a *histogram*.

The bars on a histogram do not have spaces between them because the data are continuous.

This histogram shows the number of students whose heights fall in each 5 cm interval from 140 cm to 189 cm.
● How many students are at least 170 cm tall?

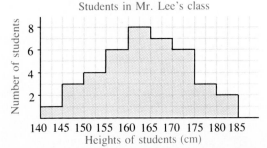

Broken-Line Graph

The graph shown here gives the population of the world at the end of each decade from 1900 to 1980. Since the exact population during each decade is not known, adjacent plotted points are joined by a line segment. Graphs like this are called *broken-line graphs*.

The only points on a broken-line graph that represent data are the endpoints of the segments.

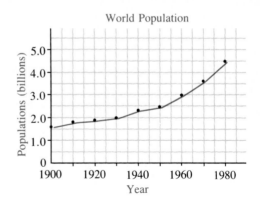

World Population

- About how many years did it take the world's population to grow from 3 billion to 4 billion?

Continuous-Line Graph

A graph that shows the value of one variable, such as speed, corresponding to the value of another variable, such as stopping distance, for all values over a given interval is called a *continuous-line graph*.

This graph shows the distance required to bring a car to rest from the moment the brakes are applied, when the car is traveling at speeds up to 100 km/h.

All the points on a continuous-line graph correspond to data.

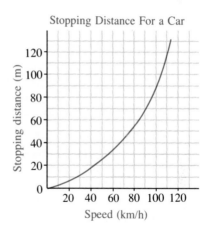

Stopping Distance For a Car

- What is the car's stopping distance when it is traveling at 60 km/h?

EXERCISES 11-1

Ⓐ

1. Name the type of graph that you think would be most appropriate for displaying each set of data. Explain why you chose that graph.
   a) Kevin's expenditures are divided as follows: 30% for entertainment, 40% for sports equipment, 22% for clothes, and 8% for school supplies.
   b) The approximate populations are given for the 5 most populous states in the U.S.
   c) The average temperature in Atlanta is given for each month of a particular year.
   d) A graph is to be drawn from which temperatures in degrees Celsius can be converted into temperatures in degrees Fahrenheit.
   e) The number of students whose final marks in mathematics were in these intervals: 0-25, 26-50, 51-75, and 76-100.

2. Explain the difference between:
   a) a pictograph and a bar graph
   b) a broken-line graph and a continuous-line graph
   c) a bar graph and a histogram.

3. What is the sum of the percents shown on a circle graph? Explain your answer.

(B)

4. The circle graph shows how an hour of radio time is spent.
   a) What percent of each hour is devoted to news?
   b) How many minutes each hour are devoted to commercials?

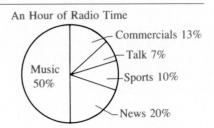

An Hour of Radio Time

Commercials 13%
Talk 7%
Sports 10%
News 20%
Music 50%

5. The bar graph shows the energy in kilojoules per minute used for different activities.
   a) Which activity burns up energy twice as fast as walking?
   b) If you cycled for 30 min, how much energy would you use?
   c) For how long would you have to run to burn up 2200 kJ of energy from a chocolate milkshake?

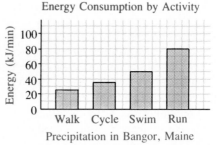

Energy Consumption by Activity

Walk   Cycle   Swim   Run

6. The histogram shows the monthly average amount of precipitation in Bangor.
   a) Which month had the most snow?
   b) Which month had the most rain?
   c) During which month did the snowfall equal the rainfall?
   d) What is the average snowfall in a year?

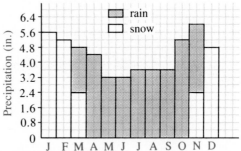

Precipitation in Bangor, Maine

rain
snow

J F M A M J J A S O N D

7. The pictograph shows the approximate distances from the sun to the four closest planets.
   a) How far, in kilometres, is each planet from the sun? Write your answers in scientific notation.
   b) About how many times as far from the sun is Mars than Mercury?
   c) Jupiter is about 780 million kilometres from the sun. Write this distance in scientific notation.
   d) What difficulty would you encounter if you tried to show the distances of all the planets from the sun using a pictograph?

Distances of the Four Closest Planets from the Sun

Each ● represents 10^8 km

Mars   Earth   Venus   Mercury

11-2 ORGANIZING AND PRESENTING DATA

The heights of the players on a school basketball team were recorded by the coach.

Art	178 cm	Jason	177 cm	Neil	175 cm
Brian	181 cm	Joe	176 cm	Paul	178 cm
Bruce	180 cm	John	175 cm	Scott	177 cm
Dick	177 cm	Kevin	178 cm	Terry	178 cm
Gordon	180 cm	Larry	179 cm		

To get a better idea of the distribution of the heights of his players, the coach made a *tally chart* or *frequency table*. The frequency of a measurement is the number of times it occurs.

Using the frequency table, the coach drew a bar graph. Each height is represented by a bar. The length of a bar corresponds to the frequency of that measurement.

Height (cm)	Number of Players	Frequency
175	II	2
176	I	1
177	III	3
178	IIII	4
179	I	1
180	II	2
181	I	1

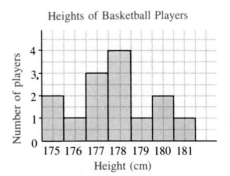

Heights of Basketball Players

Often, the number of different data is too great for each measurement to be represented by a bar. Then the information is shown on a histogram.

Example 1.   Here is a set of marks (out of 100) obtained by a class on a mathematics test.

72 53 73 59 68 83 71 67 77 78 70 67 63
65 56 86 47 78 72 79 67 74 62 84 92 88
71 74 81 70 66 64 75 65 46

a) Make a tally chart and frequency table for intervals of 10 marks.
b) Draw a histogram.
c) In which interval did most students' marks fall?
d) The pass mark was 50.
   i) How many students passed the test?
   ii) How many students failed the test?

Solution.   a) From an inspection of the marks, the lowest mark is 46 and the highest mark is 92.
Choose intervals of 10 marks from 40 to 49, 50 to 59, . . ., 90 to 99. Make a tally chart and frequency table.

Interval	Number of Students	Frequency
40-49	‖	2
50-59	‖‖	3
60-69	╫╫ ╫╫	10
70-79	╫╫ ╫╫ ‖‖‖	14
80-89	╫╫	5
90-99	‖	1

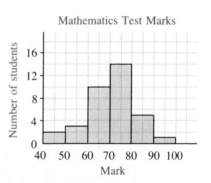

Mathematics Test Marks

b) Draw a set of axes. Label the horizontal axis with the intervals of marks. Because the intervals begin at 40, the axis between 0 and 40 is interrupted. Label the vertical axis with the numbers of students. Give the graph a title.

c) From the histogram, the interval in which most students' marks fall is the longest bar. That is, most students' marks fall between 70 and 79.

d) i) From the histogram, the number of students who passed the test is the total represented by the lengths of the bars for the interval 50 to 99.
Students who passed: 3 + 10 + 14 + 5 + 1 = 33
33 students passed the test.

   ii) From the histogram, the students who failed have marks in the interval 40-49. Two students failed the test.

In *Example 1*, suppose the chosen intervals were 45-54, . . ., 85-94. What part of the example could not have been answered from an inspection of the histogram?

Example 2. The chart shows the number of students in each grade of a high school.

Grade	9	10	11	12
Students	266	248	230	142

a) Show this information on a circle graph.
b) What percent, to the nearest whole number, of the students are in:
   i) grade 9   ii) grade 11?

Solution. a) The total student population is 266 + 248 + 230 + 142, or 886.
Each grade will be represented by a sector of the circle.
The sector angle for each grade is proportional to the number of students in that grade.
Express the student population of each grade as a fraction of the total student population, and multiply by 360°.
For grade 9 students, the angle is $\frac{266}{886}$ (360°), or 108.1°.

For grade 10 students, the angle is $\frac{248}{886}$ (360°), or 100.8°.

For grade 11 students, the angle is $\frac{230}{886}$ (360°), or 93.5°.

For grade 12 students, the angle is $\frac{142}{886}$ (360°), or 57.7°.

Write each sector angle to the nearest degree. Check to see if the angles add to 360°.
108° + 101° + 94° + 58° = 361°
Since several angles were rounded up, the total is 361°. To achieve a total of 360°, round down the angle for grade 11 students to 93°.
Draw a circle, mark the sector angles, and label each sector. Give the graph a title.

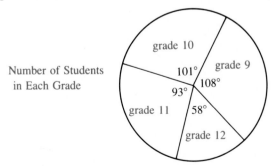

Number of Students
in Each Grade

b) i) The grade 9 students represent $\frac{266}{886}$ (100%), or about 30%.

    ii) The grade 11 students represent $\frac{230}{886}$ (100%), or about 24%.

EXERCISES 11-2

Ⓐ

1. A car dealer hired students to determine the ages of cars owned by the residents of the area. The students listed their findings in this table.

Age of car (years)	0	1	2	3	4	5	6	7
Number of cars	25	40	50	65	45	30	20	15

   Display the data on a bar graph.

2. The average daily temperature in Fairbanks, for each month, is given in this table.

Month	J	F	M	A	M	J	J	A	S	O	N	D
Temperature (°F)	− 13	− 4	9	30	48	59	62	57	45	25	4	− 10

   a) On a set of axes, plot a point for each temperature from January to December.
   b) Join adjacent points with a straight-line segment to form a broken-line graph.

3. The composition of a hot dog is given in this table.

Ingredient	Water	Fat	Protein	Other
Mass (g)	20.4	11.0	4.2	2.3

   Draw a circle graph to show this information.

Ⓑ

4. The actual mass of a 2 kg box of chocolates was checked by weighing a selection of 345 boxes. Here are the results.

Mass (kg)	1.91-1.94	1.95-1.98	1.99-2.02	2.03-2.06	2.07-2.10
Frequency	15	85	75	150	20

   a) Display this information in a histogram.
   b) Quality control dictates that any box under 2 kg must be sold as "seconds".
      i) How many of these checked boxes must be sold as seconds?
      ii) What percent of the boxes are sold as seconds?
   c) How could the intervals of mass be organized so that it is possible that fewer boxes would be sold as seconds?

5. A school's grade 9 students obtained these marks (out of 100) in an English examination.

```
55   66   64   98   56   69   68   62   52   69   65   63   51   90   69
68   32   66   72   44   80   61   84   74   66   79   61   89   78   63
66   59   75   53   69   23   92   78   73   67   38   65   67   41   75
63   71   57   77   66   56   63   73   24   56   76   71   61   51   46
84   55   63   68   86   65   69   66   60   62   68   82   73   65   76
79   88   44
```

a) Make a tally chart and frequency table, using intervals of 10 marks.
b) Draw a histogram.
c) The pass mark is 60. How many students passed?
d) What percent of students had marks:
   i) 60 or greater   ii) less than 50?

6. The table shows the amount, as a percent, that a typical family spends in each category.
   a) Draw a circle graph to illustrate this information.
   b) Suppose the family's net annual income is $30 000. How much is spent on:
      i) recreation   ii) transportation
      iii) food   iv) housing?

Item	Amount
Housing	40%
Food	24%
Transportation	15%
Clothing	9%
Savings	5%
Recreation	5%
Miscellaneous	2%

ⓒ

7. Use the information in *Example 1*.
   a) Draw a histogram with an interval of 5 marks.
   b) Compare your histogram with that on page 434. What further information could be determined from your histogram?

8. Two groups of students wrote the same mathematics test. Group A was given notice of the test and was able to prepare for it. Group B had the test sprung upon them. The groups obtained the following marks out of 20.
   A 16   17   18   20   11   18   20   19   15   20   15   15   17   12
       19   8   13   16   17   14   19   14   20   12   15
   B 12   11   15   18   12   6   9   11   5   11   11   14   11   16   17
       12   13   9   8   19   10   10   7   11   18
   a) Choose a suitable interval for the marks and draw a histogram for each set of data.
   b) What conclusions can you draw from your histograms?

9. This table shows how Americans are divided among various age groups.

Age group (years)	1-19	20-34	35-64	65 and over
U.S. population as a percent	29%	25%	33%	13%

   a) Display this information on a circle graph.
   b) Display this information on a histogram.
   c) Which graph do you think is more useful? Explain your answer.
   d) Assume a U.S. population of 247 000 000.
      i) How many Americans are under 35 years of age?
      ii) How many Americans are under 65 years of age?

11-3 MEASURES OF CENTRAL TENDENCY

Police officer
$35 000

Doctor
$90 000

Lawyer
$60 000

Pilot
$55 000

The typical salary of each of four occupations is given above. Who earns more, doctors or lawyers?

It appears from the data given that doctors have greater incomes than lawyers. This can be misleading. Many lawyers earn more than $90 000 per year, and many doctors earn less than $60 000.

We want a single number that best represents the income of all doctors or all lawyers. We are looking for an "average" income.

Three of the most commonly used averages are the mean, the median, and the mode.

> The *mean* of a set of numbers is the arithmetical average of the numbers; that is, the sum of all the numbers divided by the number of numbers.

> The *median* of a set of numbers is the middle number when the numbers are arranged in order. If there is an even number of numbers, the median is the mean of the two middle numbers.

> The *mode* of a set of numbers is the most frequently occurring number. There may be more than one mode, or there may be no mode.

The mean, the median, and the mode of a set of numbers are referred to as *measures of central tendency*.

Example 1. The recorded rainfall, in inches, for seven consecutive days in Portland, Oregon, is given.   0.25, 0.38, 0.03, 0.03, 0.03, 0.25, 0.56
Find.
a) the mean rainfall   b) the median rainfall
c) the mode for the rainfall

Solution. a) For the mean, add the numbers and divide by 7.

$$\frac{0.25 + 0.38 + 0.03 + 0.03 + 0.03 + 0.25 + 0.56}{7} = \frac{1.53}{7}$$

$$\doteq 0.22$$

The mean rainfall is 0.22 in.
b) For the median, arrange the numbers in order.
0.03, 0.03, 0.03, 0.25, 0.25, 0.38, 0.56
The middle value is the fourth value, 0.25.
The median rainfall is 0.25 in.
c) The mode is the value that occurs most often. From the list in part b), 0.03 occurs most often.
The mode for the rainfall is 0.03 in.

Example 2. The annual incomes for the people who work at the Beta Metal Works are shown below.
1 Manager: $80 000; 1 Supervisor: $45 000; 3 Mechanics: $35 000;
5 Laborers: $25 000
a) Determine the mean, the median, and the mode for the payroll.
b) Which measure could be used to make the salaries look:
   i) high   ii) low?
c) Which measure most fairly represents the average income in the company?

Solution. a) The mean salary, in dollars, is given by:

$$\frac{80\ 000 + 45\ 000 + (3 \times 35\ 000) + (5 \times 25\ 000)}{10}$$

$$= \frac{355\ 000}{10}$$

$$= 35\ 500$$

For the median, arrange the salaries in order.
80 000, 45 000, 35 000, 35 000, 35 000, 25 000, 25 000, 25 000, 25 000, 25 000
Since there is an even number of salaries, the median is the mean of the fifth and sixth values.

$$\frac{35\ 000 + 25\ 000}{2} = \frac{60\ 000}{2}$$

$$= 30\ 000$$

The mode is the salary that occurs most often, $25 000.
The mean is $35 500, the median is $30 000, and the mode is $25 000.

b) i) To make the salaries look high, the mean value of $35 500 would be chosen as being representative.
   ii) To make the salaries look low, the mode value of $25 000 would be chosen as being representative.
c) The mean value of $35 500 is earned by only 2 of the 10 employees. Therefore, it is a high representative value.
   Since every employee earns at least the mode value of $25 000, this is a low representative value.
   The median value of $30 000 probably best represents the average income.

EXERCISES 11-3

1. Find the mean, the median, and the mode of each set of data. Give the answers to 1 decimal place where necessary.
   a) 10, 12, 8, 9, 12, 14, 11, 15, 9, 12
   b) 1, 2, 2, 3, 3, 3, 4, 4, 4, 4, 4, 4, 5
   c) 2.3, 4.1, 3.7, 3.2, 2.8, 3.6
   d) 15, 18, 16, 21, 18, 14, 12, 19, 11
   e) 9, 12, 7, 5, 18, 15, 5, 11
   f) $\dfrac{1}{2}, \dfrac{1}{4}, \dfrac{2}{3}, \dfrac{5}{12}, \dfrac{3}{4}, \dfrac{2}{3}, \dfrac{1}{2}, \dfrac{7}{12}, \dfrac{1}{6}, \dfrac{1}{2}$

2. Over a period of time, some shares were purchased as follows: 10 shares at $8 per share; 20 shares at $9.50 per share; and 15 shares at $8.50 per share. What was the mean price per share?

3. For the numbers 5, 6, 7, 8, 9, find the effect on the mean:
   a) if each number is increased by 2   b) if each number is doubled.

4. If the mean of the numbers 8, 12, 13, 14, x, is 13, what is the value of x?

5. The mean of seven marks on a mathematics test is 68. However, the correction of an error in marking raises one student's mark by 14. Calculate the new mean.

6. The Cabot Manufacturing Company has the following employees at the rates of pay shown.

Position	Weekly Pay ($)	Position	Weekly Pay ($)
1 President	1730	1 Secretary	580
1 Designer	1150	1 Typist	480
1 Supervisor	770	3 Packers	385
3 Assemblers	670	3 Apprentices	290

a) Find the measures of central tendency.
b) Which measure of central tendency most fairly represents the pay structure of the company? Give reasons for your answer.

7. Two groups of students wrote the same mathematics test and obtained the following marks out of 20.

   A 16   17   18   20   11   18   20   19   15   20   15   15   17   12
   19   8   13   16   17   14   19   14   20   12   15

   B 12   11   15   18   12   6   9   11   5   11   11   14   11   16   17
   12   13   9   8   19   10   10   7   11   18

   a) Calculate the three measures of central tendency for each group.
   b) Calculate the measures of central tendency for the marks taken together.
   c) How do the results of parts a) and b) compare?

8. The number of accidents at a ski resort for five months is given.
   Which measure of central tendency best describes this data?

Dec.	Jan.	Feb.	Mar.	Apr.
25	35	40	35	5

9. Which measure of central tendency is the most suitable to describe each number?
   a) the average number of children in an American family
   b) a person's average weekly salary
   c) a class's average mark in a test
   d) the average rainfall in Buffalo
   e) the average time you spend on homework each night
   f) the average number of hours a ten-year-old child spends watching TV shows each week
   g) the average price of gasoline in a given area
   h) the average size of shoes sold by a store

   Ⓒ

10. Find five numbers that have:
    a) a mean of 9 and a median of 8
    b) a mean of 14 and a median of 8.

11. In a set of data, the smallest number is increased by 5 and the largest number is decreased by 5. What changes occur in the measures of central tendency?

12. Mary scored marks of 86, 82, 93, 97, and 78 on term tests in mathematics. What mark must she achieve on the next term test to have a mean score of 90? Explain your answer if the tests are marked out of 100.

13. Akira found that the mean of 100 numbers was exactly 26. Then he subtracted 26 from each of the 100 numbers and added the differences together. What total did he obtain?

14. Use the computer program on page xxii to help you find the mean value of the first 100 unit fractions. Is the mean value greater than or less than the median value?

COMPUTER POWER

Calculating Means and Medians

The program below can be used to determine both the mean and the median of three or more numbers. To determine the mean, the computer adds the numbers as they are entered, and then divides the sum by the number of numbers. Then, to determine the median, the computer arranges the numbers in order. If the number of numbers is odd, the computer determines the middle number, and if it is even, the computer determines the mean of the two middle numbers.

```
100 REM *** CALCULATING MEANS AND MEDIANS ***
110 INPUT "HOW MANY NUMBERS ARE THERE? (MINIMUM 3): ";N
120 DIM X(N+1)
130 M=INT((N+1)/2):SUM=0
140 INPUT "ENTER THE FIRST NUMBER: ";X(1):SUM=X(1)
150 FOR I=2 TO N-1
160     INPUT "ENTER THE NEXT NUMBER: ";X(I)
170     SUM=SUM+X(I)
180 NEXT I
190 INPUT "ENTER THE LAST NUMBER: ";X(N):SUM=SUM+X(N)
200 FOR I=1 TO M+1
210     FOR J=I+1 TO N
220         IF X(I)>=X(J) THEN Y=X(I):X(I)=X(J):X(J)=Y
230     NEXT J
240 NEXT I
250 IF N/2<>INT(N/2) THEN X(M+1)=X(M)
260 PRINT:PRINT "THE MEAN IS: ";SUM/N
270 PRINT "THE MEDIAN IS: ";X(M)/2+X(M+1)/2
280 END
```

1. Use the program to find the mean and the median of each set of numbers.

   a) 29   38   26   29   30   41   b) 238   479   506   384   726
      35   33   29   37   25   29   839   448   356   606   928
      32   33   32   28   30   31   335   668   937   46   207
      24   38   28   199   983   663   585   224
                                         669   532   496   355

2. The heights, in centimetres, of 32 students in a grade 9 class at Runnymede Collegiate were recorded as follows.

153.6	157.9	155.4	156.0	155.8	154.4	149.8	156.5	155.0
157.1	156.4	153.6	156.8	151.2	166.4	155.3	157.4	152.6
162.5	158.3	152.4	148.7	153.6	154.2	156.2	150.4	158.1
159.2	150.1	152.6	153.7	162.8

   a) What are the mean and the median heights of the students in this class?
   b) What is the height of the shortest student in the taller half of the class?

MATHEMATICS AROUND US

America's Aging Population

Modern medical science and health care are increasing the quality and lengths of our lives. Furthermore, Americans are producing fewer children per family than they were a generation ago. These two factors, increased life expectancy and decreasing family size, are raising the average age of Americans. The table below presents data from a recent census showing how many Americans are in various age groups. The age groups correspond to categories such as "pre-schoolers", "elementary school children" and "senior citizens" and are therefore unequal age intervals. Each population value has been rounded to the nearest million.

Age group (years)	0-4	5-13	14-17	18-24	25-34	35-44	45-64	65-116
Population (millions)	18	32	13	26	43	38	46	34

The histogram below presents these data graphically.

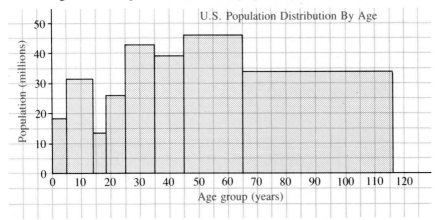

Suppose we ask, "How many Americans are not adults?"; that is, under 18 years of age. To answer this, we could add the populations of all the groups which represent people younger than 18 years of age. That is, there are $18 + 32 + 13$, or 63 million Americans below the age of 18 years. Rather than perform such computations, it is more convenient to graph the number of people between 0 and n years of age for $n = 4, 13, 17, 24, 34, 44, 64, 116$; that is, for the values of n at the upper age in each group. Such a histogram is shown below. It is

called a *cumulative frequency histogram*. The height of the bar at each
value of *n* gives the total or accumulated population over all age groups
up to the one containing *n*.

Age group (years)	0-4	0-13	0-17	0-24	0-34	0-44	0-64	0-116
Population (millions)	18	50	63	89	132	170	216	250

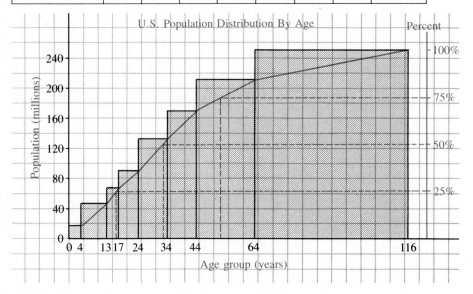

We draw a broken-line graph which joins the upper right corners of the
cumulative histogram. It can be used to answer questions such as,
"What is the median age of Americans?". Since the population of the
U.S. is about 250 million, the median age is the age, *n*, such that 50%
of the U.S. population is between 0 and *n* years of age. To approximate
the median from the broken-line graph, we find the age that corresponds
to 50% of the population.

To do this, draw a line at the right of the graph, equal to the height
of the last bar. Mark a point halfway up this line. This point represents
50% of the population. From this point, draw a horizontal line to meet
the graph. Then draw a vertical line to meet the horizontal axis at
approximately 32 years. This means that the younger half of the American
population is between 0 and 32 years of age.

We can determine the youngest quarter of the population in a similar way. From a point one-quarter, or 25%, of the way up the line, draw a horizontal then a vertical line to meet the horizontal axis at approximately 16 years of age. We say that the *lower quartile* is 16 years of age.

Similarly, beginning at a point three-quarters, or 75%, of the way up the line, we find that the upper quartile is approximately 52 years of age. This is the age such that three-quarters of the population is younger.

We say that the lower quartile, 16 years of age, is the 25th *percentile*, since 25% of the population is below 16 years of age. Similarly, 52 years of age is the 75th percentile, since 75% of the population is below 52 years of age. In general, the *n*th percentile is the age such that *n*% of the population is younger.

Percentiles provide a useful terminology for describing distributions of characteristics of a population such as age, IQ, height, weight, or examination scores. Using histograms and percentiles we have identified changes in the age distribution and observed the aging of our population as we approach the 21st century.

QUESTIONS

1. a) Why do the bars on the cumulative histogram increase in height as the age increases?
   b) Would the property described in part a) be true for all cumulative histograms? Why?

2. Use the cumulative histogram or its broken-line graph to answer each question.
   a) How many Americans are alive today?
   b) What percent of Americans are 40 years of age or younger?
   c) What percent of Americans are over 40 years of age?
   d) About 20% of all Americans are younger than Ann. How old is Ann?

3. Use the cumulative histogram or its broken-line graph to answer each question.
   a) What is the upper quartile age of Americans?
   b) Mr. Cheung is at the 86th percentile in age. About how old is Mr. Cheung?
   c) Naomi is 24 years old. At what age percentile is she?

4. Assume the births and deaths in the next decade are equal so that there is no net change in population. Estimate the median age 10 years from now. Explain any assumptions you made in obtaining your estimate.

11-4 SAMPLING A POPULATION

What television program is the most popular of those on the air at a particular time?

It is clearly impossible to poll the entire population to find out who is watching what. Instead, a representative portion of the population, called a *sample*, is polled. If the sample is carefully chosen, the viewing preferences of the sample will accurately reflect the preferences of the entire population. For example, the Nielsen ratings which rank the popularity of television shows in the United States are determined by a survey which samples less than one home in 10 000; that is, less than 0.01% of the U.S. population. Election polls assess the political preferences of the entire population by surveying fewer than 10 000 people.

If a sample is truly representative of the population from which it is drawn, then conclusions made about the population are likely to be valid. In statistics, the *population* is the whole of anything of which a sample is being taken.

A sample that is chosen in such a way that it is typical of the population it represents is called a *random sample*. It is very important that a sampling process be purely random in that all members of the population must share an equal chance of being selected.

To obtain information about a population, follow these steps.
- Decide on a sample size.
- Choose a device for selecting a random sample of that size.
- Collect the data from the sample.
- Organize and interpret the data.
- Make inferences about the characteristics of the population.

There are several ways of collecting data.
- Personal interviews — door-to-door, at shopping centers, by telephone
  For example, a roller-skate manufacturer needs to know how many roller skates of each size to make. The manufacturer would arrange to have personal interviews conducted at selected rinks.

- Questionnaires — by mail, with a purchased article, in newspapers
  For example, a politician wants to know how her or his constituents
  feel about an environmental issue. The politician would send questionnaires by mail to the constituents.

- Tests and measurements — recording instruments, quality control,
  time study
  For example, a quality-control engineer for a light bulb manufacturer
  wants to know the life of the light bulbs, and how many are defective. The engineer would conduct tests on a sample of light bulbs
  chosen at random from the production line.

Example.   A New York city company is hired by a television station to conduct
a poll to predict the outcome of a national election. To gather this
information, the company considers sampling U.S. voters in one of
the following ways.
a) Interview 100 people at random.
b) Poll a random sample of 1000 people in New York State.
c) Put an advertisement in all major newspapers asking people to tell
their political preferences.
d) Send 10 questionnaires to all major businesses to be completed by
anyone selected at random.
Describe the main weakness(es) of each method.

Solution.   a) The sample is probably too small to be reliable.
b) Political preferences are often regional in nature. A sample of voters
in New York State is not likely to be representative of the political
opinions of all U.S. voters.
c) Generally, only people with very strong political views will take the
trouble to respond to an advertisement. The sample will not be
random.
d) This sample tends to exclude such voting groups as students, farmers,
homemakers, and senior citizens, and is therefore not a random
sample.

EXERCISES 11-4

Ⓐ

1. A student visited every household within three blocks of her home and recorded
the number of persons in each household.

Number of persons in household	1	2	3	4	5	6	7
Number of households	3	7	12	21	14	8	5

a) How many households did she visit?
b) How many persons live within three blocks of the student?

2. The make of every third car in a full parking lot is noted and the number of each make is recorded.

Make of car	Ford	General Motors	Chrysler	American Motors	Foreign
Number of each make	47	64	29	25	82

   a) Which is the most popular car?
   b) How many cars were in the lot?
   c) If the parking fee is $3.50 per car, what are the total receipts for these cars?

B

3. How would you collect data to find the following information? Give reasons.
   a) The popularity of a TV program
   b) The most popular breakfast cereal
   c) The average number of children in a family

4. How would you collect data to find the following information? What kind of people or items would be in your sample?
   a) The player most likely to be voted "outstanding rookie"
   b) The top 10 movies of the year   c) The life of flashlight bulbs

5. Explain why data are collected from a sample and not a population, for each situation.
   a) The quality control in the manufacture of flash cubes
   b) The number of pets per family
   c) The purity of processed food

6. Decide what kind of a sample you need, then work singly, in pairs, or in groups to collect the following data.
   a) The age and the height of the students in your class
   b) The number of persons in cars in the rush hour
   c) The amount spent on lunch in the cafeteria

 INVESTIGATE

1. Toss a paper cup 20 times.
2. Record the number of times it lands on its top, its bottom, and its side.

3. Add the results of everyone in the class.
4. Write the number of times each outcome occurs as a fraction of the total number of tosses. This fraction is called the *relative frequency* of each outcome.
5. Discuss the results.

11-5 PREDICTING RESULTS

One of the principal uses of statistics is
in predictions.

By studying samples of voter opinions, we can forecast election outcomes.
These cannot be controlled. We cannot
say for certain what will happen. Nevertheless, sampling enables us to assess
the likelihood that a particular outcome
will occur.

Consider the previous *INVESTIGATE*, where a paper cup was tossed
20 times. Suppose the cup landed on its side 12 times. We say that
the relative frequency of the outcome ''landing on its side'' is
$\frac{12}{20}$, which simplifies to $\frac{3}{5}$, or 0.6.

Relative frequency of an outcome $= \dfrac{\text{Number of times the outcome occurs}}{\text{Total number of outcomes}}$

Example.   In an experiment, a paper cup is tossed 400 times. Here are the results.

Outcome	top	side	bottom
Frequency	106	246	48

a) Find the relative frequency of each outcome.
b) Predict how many times the cup would land on the bottom in 1000
tosses.

Solution.   a) Relative frequency of an outcome $= \dfrac{\text{Number of times the outcome occurs}}{\text{Total number of outcomes}}$

Relative frequency of landing on the top $= \dfrac{106}{400}$
$= 0.265$

Relative frequency of landing on the side $= \dfrac{246}{400}$
$= 0.615$

Relative frequency of landing on the bottom $= \dfrac{48}{400}$
$= 0.12$

b) To predict the number of times a particular outcome will occur, multiply
its relative frequency by the number of tosses.
The number of times a cup will land on the bottom in 1000 tosses is
1000(0.12), or 120.

Jane, the owner of an art shop, decided to make and sell sheets of adhesive letters used for notices and posters. She needed to know how many of each letter to put on a sheet of 500 letters.

To find the frequency with which each letter occurs in the English language, she examined a large sample of poetry. Jane chose the first three verses of *The Tiger* by William Blake.

Tiger, tiger, burning bright
In the forests of the night,
What immortal hand or eye
Could frame thy fearful symmetry?

In what distant deeps or skies
Burnt the fire of thine eyes?
On what wings dare he aspire?
What the hand dare seize the fire?

And what shoulder and what art
Could twist the sinews of thy heart?
And, when thy heart began to beat,
What dread hand and what dread feet?

Jane made a tally chart and frequency table for the letters. She counted the total number of letters in the sample. There are 301 letters. Here is the tally chart for 4 letters.

Letter	a	e	n	s
Tally	~~IIII~~ ~~IIII~~ ~~IIII~~ ~~IIII~~ ~~IIII~~ IIII	~~IIII~~ ~~IIII~~ ~~IIII~~ ~~IIII~~ ~~IIII~~ ~~IIII~~ ~~IIII~~ IIII	~~IIII~~ ~~IIII~~ ~~IIII~~ ~~IIII~~	~~IIII~~ ~~IIII~~ ~~IIII~~
Frequency	29	39	20	15

Jane found the percent of each letter by multiplying its relative frequency by 100%. For example,

Percent of letter a is $\dfrac{29}{301}(100\%)$, or about 10%.

Hence, letter a should be 10% of the sheet.
10% of 500 = 0.10(500)
$\qquad\qquad\quad$ = 50
There should be about 50 of letter a on the sheet of letters.

Jane repeated these calculations for each of the letters in the sample poetry.

Would a different poem, or a sample of prose give a different result?

Some letters of the alphabet did not appear in this sample of poetry. Should these letters be included on the sheet?

EXERCISES 11-5

1. A computer simulated the toss of a penny 319 020 times. Heads occured 160 136 times. What was the relative frequency of heads, to 3 decimal places?

2. A die has these faces.

Outcomes on 100 Tosses of a Die

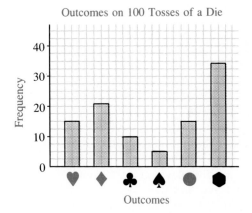

The die was rolled 100 times. The frequency of each outcome is shown on the graph.

a) Find the relative frequency of each face shown below.

   i)   ii)   iii)

b) Do you think it is a "fair" die? Explain your answer.

3. When a thumbtack is tossed, there are two possible outcomes.

             point up   point down

a) Toss 10 thumbtacks onto a desk. Record the number that land point up, and calculate the relative frequency.
b) Combine the results of everyone in the class.
c) What is the relative frequency for point up after tossing 300 thumbtacks?

4. A thumbtack is tossed 400 times and lands point up 250 times. About how many times should it land point up if it is tossed 5000 times?

5. a) Toss a coin the number of times indicated and record the frequency of heads.
     i) 10 times   ii) 20 times   iii) 30 times
b) Calculate the relative frequency of heads in each case.
c) Combine your results with those of other students to obtain the relative frequency of heads for a greater number of tosses.
d) How does the relative frequency of heads compare with 0.5 for a greater number of tosses?

6. If, in a coin-tossing experiment, you calculated the relative frequency of heads to be 0.47, what should be the relative frequency of tails?

7. Choose 200 lines from a magazine story or newspaper article. Count the number of complete sentences and the number of words in each sentence. What is the relative frequency of sentences containing:
   a) fewer than 9 words
   b) more than 12 words?

8. a) Toss two coins 30 times and record the number of times they show:
   i)   two heads
   ii) two tails
   iii) one head, one tail.
   b) Calculate the relative frequency in each case.
   c) Combine your results with those of other students to find the relative frequencies for a greater number of tosses.
   d) If two coins were tossed 5000 times, about how many times would they show:
   i)   two heads
   ii) two tails
   iii) one head, one tail?

9. By the end of the second week of the baseball season, a player has had 9 hits out of 20 official times at bat.
   a) Calculate the player's batting average.
   b) In the next game, the player gets 0 hits out of 3 times at bat. Calculate his batting average after this game.
   c) By the final month of the baseball season, the player has had 106 hits out of 425 times at bat. Calculate his batting average now.
   d) The player gets 0 hits out of his next 3 times at bat. What does this make his average?
   e) Why did a game with 0 hits out of 3 times at bat make less difference to the player's batting average at the end of the season than at the beginning?

10. When a cylinder is tossed there are two possible outcomes; it can land on an end or on its side. From a broom handle, cut cylinders 1 cm, 2 cm, 3 cm, and 4 cm long. Record the outcomes of 50 tosses for the four cylinders.

   a) What is the relative frequency of the cylinder landing on an end?
   b) What is the effect of the length to diameter ratio on the way a cylinder lands?

11. You intend to toss a coin 100 times to determine the relative frequency of heads. Investigate whether it makes a significant difference if you toss:
   a) 1 coin, 100 times
   b) 2 coins, 50 times
   c) 4 coins, 25 times
   d) 10 coins, 10 times.

COMPUTER POWER

Counting Characters

Since compiling frequencies and relative frequencies is tedious and time consuming, the computer is now used for this purpose. The following program in BASIC will do this for ten or fewer letters in any passage.

```
100 REM *** COUNTING CHARACTERS ***
110 INPUT "HOW MANY LINES IN YOUR PASSAGE OF TEXT? ";A
120 DIM Q$(10),X$(A),Y$(A,80),R(A),Q(A,10)
130 PRINT "HOW MANY DIFFERENT LETTERS DO YOU WISH"
140 INPUT "TO COUNT? ";N
150 FOR F=1 TO N
160     PRINT "ENTER LETTER NUMBER ";F;" TO BE COUNTED"
170     INPUT Q$(F)
180 NEXT F
190 FOR K=1 TO A
200     PRINT "ENTER LINE #";K
210     INPUT X$(K)
220     FOR J=1 TO LEN(X$(K))
230         Y$(K,J)=MID$(X$(K),J,1)
240         IF Y$(K,J)=" " THEN GOTO 290
250         R(K)=R(K)+1
260         FOR I=1 TO N
270             IF Y$(K,J)=Q$(I) THEN Q(K,I)=Q(K,I)+1
280         NEXT I
290     NEXT J
300     R=R+R(K)
310     FOR L=1 TO N
320         S(L)=S(L)+Q(K,L)
330     NEXT L
340 NEXT K
350 PRINT:PRINT "REL. FREQ.","FREQ.","LETTER"
360 FOR M=1 TO N
370     PRINT S(M)/R,S(M),Q$(M)
380 NEXT M
390 END
```

This program counts all characters, but not spaces. Do not enter punctuation marks or the results may be inaccurate. After entering each line of text, press [RETURN] and wait for the computer to ask for the next line.

1. Use the program to obtain the frequency and the relative frequency of each letter a, e, i, n, o, s, and t in:
   a) the three verses of "The Tiger" on page 450 (do not enter any commas)
   b) the first paragraph of this feature.
   Explain the results.

MATHEMATICS AROUND US

Counting Large Populations

Earth's population estimated to hit 5 billion today

WASHINGTON (AP) — Somewhere on Earth today, the world's five billionth person will be born, say experts at the U.S.-based Population Institute.

If true, the new milestone will come just 10 to 12 years after the four billionth person checked in. But not all experts agree today is the day.

Carl Haub, a demographer at the private Population Reference Bureau, noted United Nations estimates indicate the five billion mark won't be reached until about next March. Other statisticians have said the milestone may have already quietly passed, since many countries simply do not keep very good track of their populations.

In 1986 it was reported that the Earth's population became 5 billion. But, as this newspaper article reveals, a question such as this can never be answered accurately. It takes so long to collect the data that they will be obsolete by the time they are all collected and analysed.

QUESTIONS

1. From an almanac or some other source, obtain the most recent value of the population of the Earth. How accurately is the value given?

2. Do you think there was actually a 5 billionth person? Discuss.

3. Suppose you were counting the people in your community.
   a) Do you think you could do this correct to the nearest person?
   b) Give as many reasons as you can why you might not be able to determine the population correct to the nearest person.
   c) How accurately do you think you could determine the population?

4. Try to determine the population of your school correct to the nearest person. Include both students and staff.

11-6 EMPIRICAL PROBABILITY

The concepts of probability, chance, and likelihood play an important role in many aspects of our daily lives. However, it is surprising to observe how often these concepts are misunderstood. Study each statement below and decide whether the conclusion is justified.

In the following sections, we will study the concepts of probability and chance. Working through the exercises will decrease your probability of committing any of the errors shown in these cartoons.

When a coin is tossed there are two possible results: a head or a tail. Each of these results is called an *outcome*. If we toss a coin a large number of times, it is unlikely that both outcomes will occur the same number of times. However, we can expect that the *fraction* of times the heads outcome occurs will be approximately equal to the *fraction* of times the tails outcome occurs. We call this fraction the relative frequency of an outcome.

Definition: When an experiment is repeated *n* times, the *relative frequency* of an outcome is

$$\frac{\text{the number of times the outcome occurs}}{n}$$

Example 1. When a paper cup is tossed, there are three possible outcomes: it can land on its bottom, on its top, or on its side. The tables below show the frequencies of the three outcomes for an experiment involving 20 tosses and an experiment involving 50 tosses. Calculate the relative frequencies of all outcomes for both experiments.

a)

Frequencies for 20 Tosses		
bottom	top	side
||||	卌 |	卌 卌

b)

Frequencies for 50 Tosses		
bottom	top	side
卌 |	卌 卌 卌 |	卌 卌 卌 卌 卌 |||

Solution.   The relative frequencies are obtained by dividing the frequencies by the number of trials.

a) There are 20 trials.

Relative frequency for bottom $= \dfrac{4}{20}$, or 0.20

Relative frequency for top $= \dfrac{6}{20}$, or 0.30

Relative frequency for side $= \dfrac{10}{20}$, or 0.50

b) There are 50 trials.

Relative frequency for bottom $= \dfrac{6}{50}$, or 0.12

Relative frequency for top $= \dfrac{16}{50}$, or 0.32

Relative frequency for side $= \dfrac{28}{50}$, or 0.56

In *Example 1*, suppose you were asked to predict the number of times the cup would land on its top on 1000 tosses. If the relative frequency of the "top" outcome were 0.30 as in the 20 trials experiment, then you would predict 0.30 × 1000, or 300 occurrences of the "top" outcome. However, if you used the relative frequency obtained from the 50 trials experiment, you would predict a frequency of 0.32 × 1000, or 320 "top" outcomes. Our predictions will depend upon the number of trials used to calculate the relative frequency. When the number of trials is large, the relative frequencies are close in value. In such cases we can standardize our predictions using the concept of empirical probability.

Definition: The *empirical probability* of an outcome of an experiment is the value of the relative frequency of that outcome on a large number of repetitions of that experiment.

If the paper cup were tossed 400 times, and it landed on its top 134 times, we would predict $\frac{134}{400}$ × 1000, or 335 such occurrences on 1000 tosses. We say that the empirical probability of the "top" outcome is $\frac{134}{400}$, or 0.335.

One of the principal uses of statistics is to make predictions. For example, suppose it is necessary to know the number of Americans with type O blood. It is clearly not possible to check the blood types of all Americans. Instead, a sample is tested. From the results, the number of Americans with type O blood can be predicted.

If, in a random sample of 2000 Americans, 900 have type O blood, the relative frequency of type O blood is $\frac{900}{2000}$, or 0.45.

Since this is a large random sample, we can say the empirical probability that a randomly-selected American has type O blood is 0.45. Therefore, if all 250 000 000 Americans were tested, we would expect a "type O" outcome on 0.45, or 45% of the tests. That is, we would expect 0.45 × 250 000 000, or 112 500 000 Americans to have type O blood.

Example 2. A jar contains 3000 white, black, and red beads. The beads are thoroughly mixed and a sample of 60 taken. The sample is found to contain 17 white beads, 32 black beads, and 11 red beads. Estimate the number of beads of each color in the jar.

Solution. Relative frequency for white beads $= \frac{17}{60}$

Estimated number in jar $= \frac{17}{60} \times 3000$

$= 850$

$$\text{Relative frequency for black beads} = \frac{32}{60}$$

$$\text{Estimated number in jar} = \frac{32}{60} \times 3000$$
$$= 1600$$

$$\text{Relative frequency for red beads} = \frac{11}{60}$$

$$\text{Estimated number in jar} = \frac{11}{60} \times 3000$$
$$= 550$$

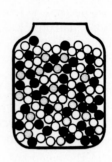

The answers in *Example 2* are only estimates of the number of beads of each color. If other samples of size 60 are taken, the results may differ. For a more reliable estimate, it would be necessary to take several samples and find the mean of the results.

EXERCISES 11-6

(A)

1. A class tossed pennies a total of 36 000 times. Heads occurred 17 563 times. What was the relative frequency of heads, to 3 decimal places?

2. A die was rolled 7200 times. The frequency of each outcome is shown in the table. What was the relative frequency of each outcome, to 3 decimal places? Do you think it was a fair die? Explain.

Outcome	⚀	⚁	⚂	⚃	⚄	⚅
Frequency	1175	1225	1142	1168	1273	1217

3. A pair of dice was rolled 5350 times. A pair of 6s occurred 140 times. What was the relative frequency of a pair of 6s, to 3 decimal places?

4. When a thumbtack is tossed, there are two possible outcomes. If the relative frequency of "point up" is found to be 0.62, what should the relative frequency of "point down" be?

point up   point down

(B)

5. a) Toss a coin 50 times and record the frequency of heads.
   b) Calculate the relative frequency of heads.
   c) Combine your results with those of other students to obtain the relative frequency of heads for a greater number of tosses.
   d) How does the relative frequency of heads compare with 0.5 as the number of tosses increases?

6. Choose 10 consecutive lines from a magazine story or newspaper article. Count the number of words and the number of syllables in each word. What is the relative frequency of words containing one syllable? more than two syllables?

7. a) Use a paper cup to shake and toss 5 coins. Record the number of heads.
   b) Repeat part a) 19 times.
   c) Calculate the relative frequency of each outcome.
   d) Combine your results with other students' to obtain more accurate values.
   e) Based on these results, if 5 coins were tossed 1280 times, about how many times would you expect to get:
      i) 1 head   ii) 3 heads   iii) 5 heads?

8. a) Roll two dice 25 times and record the results.
   b) Combine your results with those of at least three other students.
   c) Based on these results, if two dice were rolled 750 times, how many times would you expect them to show:
      i)   a sum of 7   ii)   a sum of 11   iii) a product of 12?

9. A dental survey of 360 students in Glentown High School revealed that 135 of them had two or more cavities. If the total school enrolment is 1656, about how many students would you expect to have two or more cavities?

10. The table shows the blood types of a random sample of people in the state of Alaska. Estimate the number of Alaskans with each blood type in a population of 1850.

Blood Type	O	A	B	AB
Number of Alaskans	75	59	14	8

Ⓒ

11. In a random survey, 240 homeowners in each of towns A and B were asked if they used a water softener. Eighty in town A and 66 in town B said they did. In which town should a manufacturer of water softeners concentrate his sales efforts if the populations of the towns are:
    a) 4620 in A and 5265 in B   b) 8430 in A and 7856 in B?

12. A jar contains 1250 red, blue, and yellow marbles. Ten marbles are taken out at random and their colors recorded. This is done eight times, the marbles being returned to the jar after each draw. From the following table of results, estimate the number of marbles of each color in the jar.

Draw	1st	2nd	3rd	4th	5th	6th	7th	8th
Red	5	3	3	1	3	4	2	4
Blue	2	2	3	2	3	1	2	0
Yellow	3	5	4	7	4	5	6	6

13. a) Count the number of photographs on any 20 pages in this book.
    b) Use the result of part a) to predict the number of photographs in the whole book.
    c) Combine your results with those of other students to obtain a more accurate prediction of the total number of photographs.

INVESTIGATE

A Random Walk to the Theater

A teenager lives the same distance from two theaters which are 10 blocks away but in opposite directions. She cannot decide which movie to see so she tosses a coin. If the coin comes up heads, she moves one block toward Cinema 21. If the coin turns up tails, she moves one block toward Parkway Cinema. She continues moving until she has tossed the coin 100 times. Predict how many blocks from home she will be after 100 tosses.

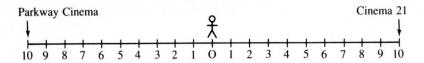

Follow these instructions to test your prediction.
 1. Work with a partner.

 2. You will need a sheet of paper, a pencil, and a coin.

 3. Have one person toss the coin 50 times and the other person record the outcomes in a tally.

 4. How many blocks from home was the teenager after 50 tosses?

 5. Toss the coin another 50 times and tally the outcomes.

 6. How many blocks from home would the teenager be after 100 tosses?

 7. Combine your tally with another pair of students in your class. How far from home would the teenager be after 200 tosses?

 8. Does the difference between the number of heads and the number of tails decrease as the number of tosses increases? Explain your answer.

 9. Calculate the relative frequencies of head and tails.

 10. Does the difference in the relative frequencies of heads and tails decrease as the number of tosses increases?

11-7 THEORETICAL PROBABILITY

Every day we encounter statements such as these:

"The probability of rain tomorrow is 20%."

This means that in the past, when weather conditions have resembled present conditions, there has been rain in 20% of the cases.

Since this probability is a relative frequency derived from observation or experience, it is an empirical probability.

"The probability of winning a prize in the draw is 1 in 50."

This means that the number of winning tickets as a fraction of the total number of tickets is $\frac{1}{50}$.

This is called a *theoretical probability* because it is computed without reference to observation or experiment.

The empirical probability of an outcome can always be found by conducting an experiment with a larger number of trials. The theoretical probability of an outcome can only be found in special cases where the outcomes are known to be *equally likely*.

When both probabilities can be found, their values are approximately equal. Therefore, from now on, we shall refer to the *probability* of an outcome. The context will indicate whether it's a theoretical or an empirical probability.

When spun, the pointer on this wheel may stop on white, black, or red. Since the three portions are the same size, we know that each outcome is equally likely.

Example 1. For each experiment
　　 i) List the outcomes.
　　 ii) State whether the outcomes are equally likely.
　　　　 a) A penny is tossed.
　　　　 b) A penny and a dime are tossed.
　　　　 c) The pointer on the wheel shown is spun.

Solution. a) i) The outcomes are head (H) and tail (T).
　　　　 ii) They are equally likely.
　　　 b) i) The outcomes are H H, H T, T H, and T T.

　　　　 ii) They are equally likely.
　　　 c) i) The outcomes are red, black, and white.
　　　　 ii) Since there are two white portions and only one black and one red, the pointer is more likely to stop on white. The outcomes are not equally likely.

For the wheel shown, since each outcome is equally likely, there is one chance in three that the pointer will stop on black.

We say that the probability that the pointer will stop on black is $\frac{1}{3}$, and we write:

$P(\text{black}) = \frac{1}{3}$.

When a die is rolled, the chances that it will show ⚁ are 1 in 6.

We say that the probability that the die will show a 2 is $\frac{1}{6}$, and we write: $P(2) = \frac{1}{6}$.

Any set of outcomes of an experiment is called an *event*.

On the roll of a die, there are 6 possible outcomes.

⚀ ⚁ ⚂ ⚃ ⚄ ⚅

Let A denote the event that we get an even number when we roll a die. Event A occurs if the outcome of a toss is ⚁ or ⚃ or ⚅.

We say that the outcomes ⚁, ⚃, and ⚅ are *favorable* to event A, because if any one of them occurs then event A occurs.

On the toss of two coins, there are 4 possible outcomes.

Let B denote the event that we obtain one head and one tail. Then, the outcomes Ⓗ Ⓣ and Ⓣ Ⓗ are favorable to event B.

The greater the number of equally-likely outcomes favorable to an event, the more likely it is that the event will occur. We define the probability of event A as follows:

> If an experiment has *n* equally-likely outcomes of which *r* are favorable to event A, then the *probability* of event A is:
>
> $P(A) = \dfrac{r}{n}$

Example 2. A lottery issued 1000 tickets, which were all sold. What is the probability of your winning if you hold:
  a) 1 ticket
  b) 17 tickets
  c) 100 tickets
  d) no ticket
  e) all the tickets?

Solution. Each ticket has an equal chance of being drawn. That is, each outcome is equally likely.

a) $P(\text{win}) = \dfrac{1}{1000}$ b) $P(\text{win}) = \dfrac{17}{1000}$ c) $P(\text{win}) = \dfrac{100}{1000}$, or $\dfrac{1}{10}$

d) $P(\text{win}) = \dfrac{0}{1000}$, or 0   e) $P(\text{win}) = \dfrac{1000}{1000}$, or 1

In *Example 2*, observe that the least probability is 0 and the greatest is 1. We can prove that this is true in general.

Since r, the number of equally-likely outcomes which are favorable to an event A, is less than or equal to n, the total number of equally-likely outcomes, we can write:

$0 \leq r \leq n$.

It follows that

$\dfrac{0}{n} \leq \dfrac{r}{n} \leq \dfrac{n}{n}$,

or $0 \leq P(A) \leq 1$

When $P(A) = 0$, we say that event A is *impossible*.

When $P(A) = 1$, we say that event A is *certain*.

For example, the probability that the toss of a coin will yield either a head or a tail is 1. The probability that it yields neither outcome is 0.

Example 3. For the wheel shown, determine the probability of each event.

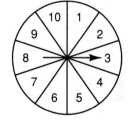

a) Event A: Wheel stops on a number equal to or less than 3.

b) Event B: Wheel stops on a number greater than 6.

c) Event C: Wheel stops on an even number.

Solution. There are ten equally likely outcomes.

a) Event A has three favorable outcomes. These are landing on 1, 2, or 3.

$$P(A) = \dfrac{3}{10}$$

b) Event B has four favorable outcomes. These are landing on 7, 8, 9, or 10.

$$P(B) = \dfrac{4}{10}$$

c) Event C has five favorable outcomes. These are landing on 2, 4, 6, 8, or 10.

$$P(C) = \dfrac{5}{10}$$

Example 4. For the wheel in *Example 3*
   a) Event D is that the wheel stops on a number from 1 to 10. What is P(D)?
   b) Event E is that the wheel stops on a number greater than 10. What is P(E)?

Solution.   a) Every possible outcome is favorable to event D.

Therefore, P(D) $= \dfrac{10}{10}$, or 1

   b) No outcome is favorable to event E.

Therefore, P(E) $= \dfrac{0}{10}$, or 0

Probability and relative frequency are closely linked. The probability of an event indicates what the relative frequency should be if the experiment is performed many times.

For the wheel shown, we know that

P(black) $= \dfrac{1}{3}$. This does not mean that in

30 spins the pointer will stop on black exactly 10 times. It means that it is more probable that it will stop on black 10 times, than any other number of times.

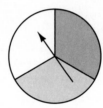

Example 5. For the wheel above, what is the probable number of times that the pointer should stop on black in 2000 spins?

Solution.   Since P(black) $= \dfrac{1}{3}$, the spinner should probably stop on black about

$\dfrac{1}{3}$(2000) times, or about 667 times.

EXERCISES 11-7

Ⓐ

1. When the pointer is spun, what is the probability that it will stop in the red sector?
   a)   b)   c)

2. What is the probability that a ball chosen at random from the jar is:

   a) black   b) striped
   c) red   d) not black
   e) either black or red   f) neither black nor red

(B)

3. Cathy and Trevor have birthdays in June. Let A denote the event that Cathy's birthday is a multiple of 5. Let B denote the event that Trevor's birthday is on Wednesday. Let C denote the event that A and B are both true and both birthdays occur on the same day.

JUNE						
Sun	Mon	Tues	Wed	Thurs	Fri	Sat
		1	2	3	4	5
6	7	8	9	10	11	12
13	14	15	16	17	18	19
20	21	22	23	24	25	26
27	28	29	30			

   a) If all days are equally likely, what outcomes are favorable to:

      i) event A   ii) event B   iii) event C?

   b) Find the probabilities of event A, event B, and event C.

4. For each experiment

   i) List the outcomes.

   ii) State whether the outcomes are equally likely.

      a) A ball is drawn from a bag containing a red ball, a white ball, and a green ball.

      b) A quarter and a nickel are tossed.

      c) A letter is picked at random from any page of a book printed in English.

      d) A ball is drawn from a bag containing 2 white balls, 3 blue balls, and 5 red balls.

      e) A wheel containing the letters A to H is spun. The letters are in equal areas.

5. A pair of opposite faces of a white die are colored red. If the die is rolled, what is the probability that the top is:

   a) white   b) red?

6. Calculate the probability of tossing a regular tetrahedron so that it lands with the 4 face down. The numbers on the faces are:

   a) 2, 4, 6, 8

   b) 1, 4, 4, 7

   c) 1, 3, 5, 7.

7. What is the probability of a regular die, when tossed, showing:

   a) 5   b) an odd number

   c) a prime number   d) a number less than 3

   e) a one-digit number   f) a two-digit number?

8. What is the probable number of times that a coin should show heads if it is tossed:

   a) 25 times   b) 100 times   c) 1000 times?

9. What is the probable number of times that a die should show 5 if it is tossed:

   a) 25 times   b) 100 times   c) 1000 times?

10. Each wheel is spun 50 times. What is the probable number of times that the wheel should come to rest with the arrow pointing to 2?

a)   b)   c)   d)

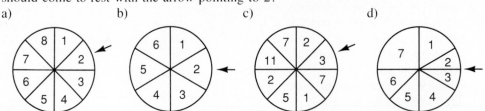

11. What is the probability that all the students in your class are older than 10 years of age?

12. You can pick one marble from any of the three bags. You win a prize if you pick a red marble. Which bag should you choose to have the best chance of winning?

Bag A contains   Bag B contains   Bag C contains
3 red and 7 white.   2 red and 3 white.   4 red and 11 white.

13. The table lists the number of cars in a parking lot by their ages.

Car's age (years)	0	1	2	3	4	5	6	7
Number	25	40	50	70	45	35	20	15

Calculate the probability that the age of a car selected at random will be:

a) 2 years   b) greater than 4 years
c) less than 3 years   d) 3 to 5 years.

Ⓒ ───────────────────────────────────

14. A die is loaded so that the outcomes have the relative frequencies shown in this table.

Outcome	1	2	3	4	5	6
Relative Frequency	0.12	0.17	0.17	0.08	0.35	0.11

What is the probability of throwing:

a) a number less than 3   b) an even number?

15. Life insurance companies use birth and death statistics in calculating the premiums for their policies. The table shows how many of 100 000 people at age 10 are still living at ages 30, 50, 70, and 90.

Age (years)	10	30	50	70	90
Number of People Living	100 000	95 144	83 443	46 774	2220

a) What is the probability that a 10-year-old child will live:
   i) to age 50   ii) to age 70   iii) to age 50 but not 70?

b) What is the probability that a 30-year-old person will live to age 90?

11-8 SAMPLE SPACES

Two 17th century mathematicians, Roberval and Fermat, considered a game between players A and B in which a coin is tossed twice. Player A wins if a head appears on at least one of the two tosses. What is the probability that player A wins?

Roberval argued as follows:
There are 3 possible outcomes.

First toss	Second toss	Result
(H)	No second toss because game ends	A wins
(T)	(H)	A wins
(T)	(T)	B wins

A wins on 2 out of 3 outcomes.

The probability that A wins is $\frac{2}{3}$.

Fermat argued as follows:
There are 4 possible outcomes.

First toss	Second toss	Result
(H)	(H)	A wins
(H)	(T)	A wins
(T)	(H)	A wins
(T)	(T)	B wins

A wins on 3 out of 4 outcomes.

The probability that A wins is $\frac{3}{4}$.

Who was correct, Roberval or Fermat?
This was a classical problem which caused much controversy among some of the early inventors of probability theory. When they tossed two coins a large number of times, they found that the empirical probability approached the value $\frac{3}{4}$ predicted by Fermat. To solve such problems, mathematicians developed the concept of a sample space.

When a coin is tossed, the outcome may be a head, denoted H, or a tail T. This set of possible outcomes {H, T} is called the sample space of the probability experiment.

In general, we define a sample space as follows:

Definition: The *sample space* of a probability experiment is the set of all possible outcomes.

When two coins are tossed, there are four possible outcomes. The sample space for this probability experiment is {HH, HT, TH, TT}.

When the outcomes can be written as ordered pairs, as in the case of tossing two coins, a dot diagram can be used to represent the sample space.

The horizontal line shows the outcomes of tossing the first coin. The vertical line shows the outcomes of tossing the second coin. Each dot represents an outcome.

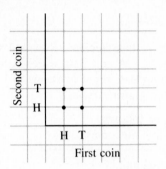

The four outcomes — HH, HT, TH, and TT — are equally likely. This means that the theoretical probability of each outcome is $\frac{1}{4}$. We denote the probability of two heads as P(two heads).

Therefore, $P(\text{two heads}) = \frac{1}{4}$

$P(\text{two tails}) = \frac{1}{4}$

$P(\text{one head and one tail}) = P(HT) + P(TH)$

$$= \frac{1}{4} + \frac{1}{4}$$

$$= \frac{2}{4}, \text{ or } \frac{1}{2}$$

Therefore, the probability that player A wins is

$P(HH) + P(HT) + P(TH) = \frac{3}{4}$

Once we know the probability of each outcome in a sample space, we can calculate the probabilities for sets of one or more outcomes, or events.

Example 1. a) Write the sample space for the roll of a die.
  b) Calculate the probability of rolling:
    i)   an odd number   ii)   a number greater than 2.

Solution.   a) The sample space is {1, 2, 3, 4, 5, 6}.
  b) The outcomes of the sample space are equally likely. Thus, the probability of each outcome is $\frac{1}{6}$.

    i) $P(\text{an odd number}) = P(1) + P(3) + P(5)$

$$= \frac{1}{6} + \frac{1}{6} + \frac{1}{6}$$

$$= \frac{3}{6}, \text{ or } \frac{1}{2}$$

ii)   P(number greater than 2) = P(3) + P(4) + P(5) + P(6)

$$= \frac{1}{6} + \frac{1}{6} + \frac{1}{6} + \frac{1}{6}$$

$$= \frac{4}{6}, \text{ or } \frac{2}{3}$$

Example 2. a) Draw a diagram to represent the sample space for the roll of 2 dice.

b) Calculate the probability of each event.
   i) a sum of 5
   ii) a pair (both dice show the same number)
   iii) anything but a pair.

Solution. a) The diagram shows each outcome of the sample space as a dot. For example, the dot with coordinates (5,3) corresponds to this outcome.

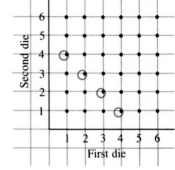

b)   i) The circled outcomes on the diagram yield a sum of 5. That is, the outcomes (1,4), (2,3), (3,2), and (4,1) are favorable.

P(sum of 5) = P(1,4) + P(2,3) + P(3,2) + P(4,1)

$$= \frac{1}{36} + \frac{1}{36} + \frac{1}{36} + \frac{1}{36}$$

$$= \frac{4}{36}$$

   ii) For a pair, the outcomes (1,1), (2,2), (3,3), (4,4), (5,5), and (6,6) are favorable.

P(a pair) = P(1,1) + P(2,2) + P(3,3) + P(4,4) + P(5,5) + P(6,6)

$$= \frac{1}{36} + \frac{1}{36} + \frac{1}{36} + \frac{1}{36} + \frac{1}{36} + \frac{1}{36}$$

$$= \frac{6}{36}$$

   iii) There are 36 equally-likely outcomes. 6 of these outcomes are pairs. Therefore, 30 outcomes are not pairs.

P(anything but a pair) $= \frac{30}{36}$

For any event E we can define the *complementary event* $\overline{E}$ (we say, "E bar") as the set of outcomes unfavorable to E. That is, $\overline{E}$ is the event that E does not occur. For example, when tossing a coin, "heads" is the complementary event to "tails". In the roll of a die, if F is the event that "number 5 is rolled", then $\overline{F}$ is the event that "number 5 is not rolled". What is the complementary event for each event in *Example 2*?

The outcomes of event E plus the outcomes of event $\overline{E}$ constitute the sample space of the experiment. Whenever the experiment is conducted, it is certain that either the event, or its complement, must occur. That is,

$P(E) + P(\overline{E}) = 1$

This equation enables us to calculate the probability of any event if we know the probability of its complement.

EXERCISES 11-8

Ⓐ

1. Write the sample space for each spinner. Are the outcomes equally likely?

   a)   b)   c)

2. Write the sample space for each probability experiment.
   a) A fair coin is tossed.   b) A standard die is rolled.
   c) A pair of standard dice is rolled.
   d) A pinwheel containing the letters A through H is spun.

3. A die is rolled. Calculate the probability of each event.
   a) an even number   b) a number that is not prime
   c) a number other than 5   d) a number more than 3

4. a) Write the sample space for the spin of the pointer.
   b) Give the theoretical probability of each outcome.
   c) Estimate the frequency of each outcome if the pointer were spun 1000 times.

   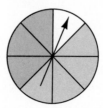

Ⓑ

5. The letters of the English alphabet are placed in a hat and one is drawn. What is the probability that it is:
   a) the letter j   b) a letter a or b or c or d
   c) a vowel   d) a consonant?

6. a) Draw a diagram to represent the sample space for the simultaneous toss of a coin and roll of a die.
   b) What is the probability of the coin showing heads and the die showing 3?

7. Toss a pair of coins 40 times. Record the relative frequency of each outcome. Compare the relative frequency of each outcome with its theoretical probability. Also compare your results with your classmates.

8. The probability of rain on a given day is 60%. What is the probability that rain will not occur?

9. Two dice are rolled. Calculate the probability of each event.
   a) a sum of 6
   b) a sum of 10 or greater
   c) snake eyes (two 1s) or box cars (two 6s)
   d) anything but snake eyes or box cars

10. When two dice are rolled the difference of the upturned faces can be determined. What is the probability of obtaining each difference?
    a) 5
    b) 3
    c) 6
    d) less than 3

11. One card is drawn from a well-shuffled deck of 52 cards. What is the probability of each event?
    a) a 9
    b) a black card
    c) a spade
    d) a red Jack
    e) a 7 or a 9
    f) a card less than 6

Ⓒ

12. In a Euchre deck, only the cards 9, 10, Jack, Queen, King, and Ace of each suit are used. What is the probability of each event in *Exercise 11* if one card is drawn?

13. The red face cards are removed from a standard deck of playing cards. What is the probability of each event in *Exercise 11* if one card is drawn?

14. If two darts are thrown at this board, what is the probability that:
    a) neither dart will land on an even number
    b) at least one dart will land on an even number
    c) at least one dart will land on a black even number?

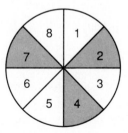

15. A jelly-beans manufacturer produces 4 different colors of jelly beans: red, yellow, orange, and black. She produces 3 times as many red beans as yellow beans and twice as many yellow beans as each of orange and black. A jelly bean is drawn at random from a bag of 60 beans. What is the probability that the selected bean is:
    a) black
    b) yellow
    c) not red
    d) either red or black?

 **PROBLEM SOLVING**

Conduct An Experiment

"Each of you", said the judge to the three prisoners before her, "will be given 5 black balls and 5 red balls. You may distribute these any way you please between two pans. Then you will be blindfolded while the 2 pans are moved around and then you must select a ball from one of the pans. If the ball you select is red you will be freed. However, if it is black you will be returned to prison."

 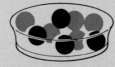 

Estimate, for each distribution shown above, the probability that a red ball will be chosen.

Understand the problem
- Is the probability that a red ball will be chosen the same for all the distributions?

Think of a strategy
- Try conducting an experiment with the balls placed as illustrated above.

Carry out the strategy
- Get 5 yellow tennis balls and 5 white tennis balls.
- Duplicate the first distribution shown above.
- Conduct the experiment described by the judge. Repeat the selection many times and estimate the probability of selecting a yellow ball. Repeat the procedure for the other two distributions shown above.
- For which distribution is it most likely that a yellow ball will be chosen?

Look back
- Is there a distribution different from those shown above for which it is more likely that a red ball will be chosen?

Solve each problem

1. Twelve pennies are placed in a row on a table top. Then every second coin is replaced with a nickel. Every third coin is then replaced with a dime. Finally every fourth coin is replaced with a quarter. What is the total value of the 12 coins on the table?

2. Divide a sheet of paper into 3 rectangles of different sizes. Color each rectangle a different color. Toss a penny many times from a distance and record the frequency of landing in each rectangle. Use these frequencies to estimate the area of each rectangle as a fraction of the area of the sheet of paper. Measure the dimensions and calculate the areas to check your answers.

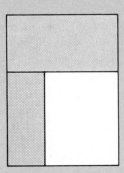

3. Estimate the probability that two cards drawn randomly from a deck of 52 playing cards will both be spades.

4. Estimate the probability that the sum of the numbers obtained on two rolls of a pair of dice exceeds 8.

5. Which of the following figures form a tesselation of the plane; that is, a covering of the plane without gaps or overlapping?
   a)   b)   c)

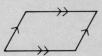

6. A wooden beam with a square cross-section is rolled along the floor. Sketch the path of one corner of the beam.

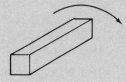

7. Seven pennies are arranged in 3 lines, with 3 pennies in each line.
   Sketch a diagram to show how 2 of these pennies can be moved so that there are 6 lines with exactly 3 pennies in each line.

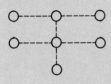

11-9 THE COUNTING PRINCIPLE

Suppose a coin is tossed and a die is rolled at the same time. How many possible outcomes are there?

We can show the sample space using a *tree diagram* such as the one below.

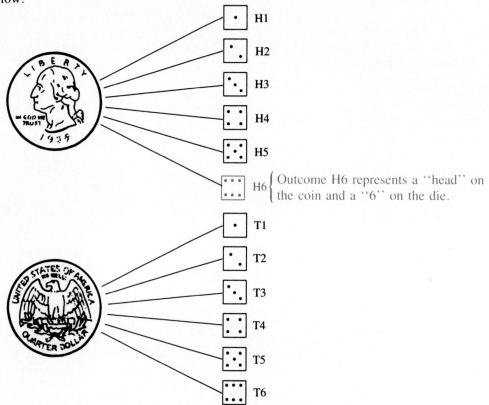

Outcome H6 represents a "head" on the coin and a "6" on the die.

A tree diagram is a convenient visual device for counting the number of possible outcomes when the sample space is small. The diagram shows that there are two possible outcomes on the coin toss. For each of these outcomes, there are six possible outcomes on the roll of the die. Therefore, there are 2 × 6, or 12 possible outcomes in all. This same counting principle is used in the following examples.

Example 1.   There are 7 roads between Hancock and Elmira. In how many ways can Ms. Brown travel from Hancock to Elmira and return by a different route?

Solution.   The road from Hancock to Elmira can be chosen in 7 ways. For each choice, the road from Elmira to Hancock can be chosen in 6 ways. (We cannot choose the road we chose from Hancock to Elmira.) Therefore, the total number of ways of travelling from Hancock to Elmira and back to Hancock by a different road is 7 × 6, or 42.

Example 2. How many even 2-digit whole numbers are there?

Solution. The first, or tens digit can be picked in 9 ways, since 0 cannot be the first digit. For each of these selections, the second, or units digit can be picked from the even digits (0, 2, 4, 6, 8) in 5 ways.

Therefore, there are 9 × 5, or 45 even 2-digit numbers.

Examples 1 and *2* apply a useful and important counting technique called the *counting principle*.

The Counting Principle
If one item can be selected in p ways, and for each of these selections a second item can be selected in q ways, then there are pq ways of selecting the two items.

The following example shows how the counting principle can be extended to count outcomes.

Example 3. At the Snack Shack, a meal consists of one sandwich, one drink, and one dessert. How many different meals can be selected from the Snack Shack menu?

SNACK SHACK MENU		
Sandwich	*Drink*	*Dessert*
egg sandwich	milk	fresh fruit
or	or	or
ham sandwich	soft drink	pie
	or	
	coffee	

Solution. The sandwich can be chosen in 2 ways.
For each of these ways, a drink can be chosen in 3 ways.
For each of these ways, a dessert can be chosen in 2 ways.
The total number of ways of choosing a meal is 2 × 3 × 2, or 12.
Therefore, 12 different meals can be selected from the Snack Shack menu.

Example 3 illustrated how the counting principle can be extended. This extension is written below.

Extension of the Counting Principle
If one item can be selected in p ways, and for each of these selections a second item can be selected in q ways, and for each of these ways a third item can be selected in r ways, then there are pqr ways of selecting the three items.

The following example shows how we can use the counting principle to calculate the probability of an event.

Example 4. A computer generates 3 personalized letters and the corresponding envelopes. They are addressed to Ms. Albert, Ms. Brown, and Ms. Carlos. The letters are placed in the envelopes at random. What is the probability that all three letters are placed in the correct envelopes?

Solution. The letters to Ms. Albert, Ms. Brown, and Ms. Carlos are denoted by A, B, and C respectively.

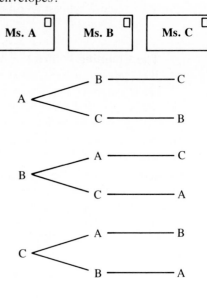

The letter inserted in the first envelope can be A, B, or C. That is, the letter can be chosen in 3 ways.
For each of these ways, the letter inserted in the second envelope can be chosen in 2 ways.
For each of these ways, the remaining letter can be inserted in the remaining envelope in 1 way.
Therefore, there are $3 \times 2 \times 1$, or 6 ways of placing the 3 letters in 3 envelopes. Only one of these 6 equally-likely choices is correct.
Therefore, the probability that all three letters are placed in the correct envelopes is $\frac{1}{6}$.

EXERCISES 11-9

1. Draw a tree diagram to illustrate the possible outcomes of each experiment.
   a) Two coins are tossed one after another
   b) Three coins are tossed one after another

2. Draw a tree diagram to illustrate the possible meals at the *Snack Shack* of *Example 3*, if one item is chosen from each category.

3. Four different books are displayed at random on a shelf. Illustrate their possible arrangements with a tree diagram. What is the probability they are arranged alphabetically by author?

4. Bill has 3 sweaters and 4 pairs of slacks. In how many ways can he select an outfit?

5. Alisha has 5 blouses, 4 skirts, and 4 sweaters in her wardrobe. In how many ways can she select an outfit, assuming she wears three items at once?

(B)

6. How many odd 2-digit numbers are there?

7. How many even 2-digit numbers can be formed using the digits 1, 2, 3, 4, 5, 6, 7, 8 if each digit is used once?

8. If each of the digits 1, 3, 5, 7, 9, is used once, how many:
   a) 3-digit numbers can be formed   b) 4-digit numbers can be formed?

9. There are 7 horses in one race and 6 in another. For a person placing a bet, in how many ways can the winners of the two races be chosen?

10. There are 8 horses in a race.
    a) In how many ways can the win, place, and show horses be selected?
    b) What is the probability in a random selection of 3 horses that the first horse selected is the winner, the second horse selected places second, and the third horse selected places third?

11. An ice-cream parlor features 64 flavors and 20 toppings, in 3 sizes. How many different sundaes can be made?

12. How many different 7-digit telephone numbers can be made using the digits from 0 to 9, if the first digit may not be 0 or 1?

13. A sports club with 30 members wishes to pick a president, vice-president, secretary, and treasurer. Assuming that no person can hold two offices, in how many ways can the selections be made?

14. Four personal letters are placed randomly in 4 addressed envelopes. What is the probability that all 4 letters are placed in the correct envelopes?

15. The final score in a soccer game is 4-3. How many different half-time scores are possible?

16. The dial on a standard 3-number combination lock contains markings to represent the numbers from 0 to 59.
    a) How many combinations are possible if no number can be used twice?
    b) What is the probability of discovering the correct combination on a random guess?

(C)

17. A ''count'' in baseball is an ordered pair indicating the numbers of balls and strikes to the batter. For example, ''2 and 1'' means 2 balls and 1 strike.
    a) How many different counts are possible?
    b) Are all counts equally-likely? Explain.

18. a) How many 3-digit numbers have digits that are all different?
    b) How many 4-digit numbers have digits that are all different?
    c) How many 5-digit numbers have digits that are all different?

19. a) Write 72 as a product of powers of prime numbers.
    b) How many factors does 72 have?

Permutations

The person on the ladder has dropped the
4 letters that spell a composer's name.
How many possible arrangements of these
four letters are there?
To answer this question, complete parts
a) and b).

a) Write an organized list showing all possible arrangements of the four letters,
$\boxed{A}$, $\boxed{B}$, $\boxed{C}$, $\boxed{H}$
You might begin listing those which
start with A:

ABCH	ABHC	ACHB
ACBH	AHBC	AHCB

b) Use a full page to draw a tree diagram showing all possible arrangements. It could
begin like this.

First letter	Second letter	Third letter	Fourth letter

```
                        C ──────── H
               B <
                        H ──────── C

                        B ──────── H
A <            C <
                        H ──────── B

       H
```

An arrangement is called a *permutation*.

c) Use the counting principle to determine the number of permutations of:
   i)   3 given letters   ii)   4 given letters   iii)   5 given letters
   iv)   6 given letters   v)   7 given letters.
   Assume all letters are different.

d) Use your answers in part c) to help you write an expression for the number of
permutations of *n* different letters.

e) Look on your scientific calculator for the key $\boxed{n!}$ called *n factorial*. Use the
n! key to calculate:
   i)   3!   ii)   4!   iii)   5!   iv)   6!   v)   7!

f) i) Compare your answers in part e) to the corresponding answers in part c).
    ii) Explain how you could calculate 10! without a calculator.
    iii) Use the factorial notation to write the number of permutations of *n* different letters.

How many 3-letter permutations can be made from the letters in the name BACH?
To answer this question, complete parts g) and h).

g) Copy and complete these statements.
    i) The number of ways of choosing the first letter from the letters in the set {B, A, C, H} is _____.
    ii) For each choice of a first letter, the number of ways of choosing a second letter from those remaining letters is _____.
    iii) For each choice of the first two letters, the number of ways of choosing a third letter from those remaining letters is _____.

h) Use your answers from part g) and the counting principle to calculate the number of 3-letter permutations which can be made from the letters in the name BACH.

i) Simplify each expression and express it in factorial notation.
    i) $1 \times 2 \times 3 \times 4 \times 5$ ii) $7 \times 6!$
    iii) $\dfrac{7!}{7}$ iv) $7 \times 6 \times 5$
    v) $1 \times 2 \times 3 \times \ldots \times n$ vi) $(n + 1)n!$
    vii) $\dfrac{n!}{n}$ viii) $n(n - 1)(n - 2)$

j) Write your answer in part h) using factorial notation.

Use the counting principle to help you complete the exercises below. You may write your answers in factorial notation.

1. How many different 3-digit numbers can be made from the digits 5, 6, and 7 if no digit is repeated?

2. How many permutations of 5 different letters can be made from the letters of the word THINK?

3. How many permutations of 3 letters can be made from the set of letters {T, H, I, N, K} if no letter is to be repeated in a permutation?

4. How many different 3-digit numbers can be formed using the digits 1, 3, 5, 7 if:
   a) repetition of digits is not allowed   b) repetition of digits is allowed.

5. The person who dropped the 4 letters A, B, C, H, picked them up and placed them in random order on the display board. What is the probability that they were placed in the proper order [B] [A] [C] [H]?

11-10 THE PROBABILITY OF SUCCESSIVE EVENTS

The following example shows how the counting principle can be used to calculate the probability of two successive events.

Example 1. A card is drawn from a standard deck, set aside and another card is drawn. What is the probability that both cards are Aces?

Solution. The probability that the two cards are Aces is

$$P(2 \text{ aces}) = \frac{\text{the number of ways 2 Aces can be chosen}}{\text{the number of possible outcomes}}$$

For the number of ways 2 Aces can be chosen:
The first Ace can be drawn in one of 4 ways.
That is, it can be a diamond, heart, club or spade.
For each of these ways, the second Ace can be drawn in 3 ways.
Applying the counting principle, the 2 Aces can be drawn from the deck in 4×3 ways.

For the number of possible outcomes:
The first card can be drawn in 52 ways.
For each draw, the second card can be chosen in 51 ways.
Therefore, the two cards can be drawn in 52×51 ways.

$$P(2 \text{ aces}) = \frac{4 \times 3}{52 \times 51}$$

$$= \frac{1}{221}$$

The probability that both cards are Aces is $\frac{1}{221}$.

In *Example 1*, the probability of drawing 2 Aces in succession:

$P(2 \text{ Aces}) = \dfrac{4 \times 3}{52 \times 51}$ could be written

$P(2 \text{ Aces}) = \dfrac{4}{52} \times \dfrac{3}{51}$ which is

$P(2 \text{ Aces}) = P(\text{Ace on 1st draw}) \times P(\text{Ace on 2nd draw following Ace on 1st draw})$

By repeating the computation in *Example 1*, for the general case in which events A and B are to occur in succession, we deduce this rule.

> The probability of two events happening in succession is the product of the probability of each event.
> $P(A \text{ and } B) = P(A) \times P(B)$

Similarly, the probability that 3 events, A, B, and C happen in 3 trials of an experiment is given by
$P(A \text{ and } B \text{ and } C) = P(A) \times P(B) \times P(C)$.

Example 2. A coin is tossed three times. What is the probability that it shows a head each time?

Solution. For each toss, $P(\text{head}) = \dfrac{1}{2}$

$$P(3 \text{ heads}) = \frac{1}{2} \times \frac{1}{2} \times \frac{1}{2}$$

$$= \frac{1}{8}$$

The rule for successive events must be used carefully, because the probability of the second event may depend on the first event.

Example 3. A bag contains 2 black balls and 2 red balls. Find the probability of drawing 2 red balls in succession if:
a) the first ball is replaced before drawing the second ball
b) the first ball is not replaced.

Solution. a) On the first draw, there are 4 balls of which 2 are red.

$$P(\text{red, on first draw}) = \frac{2}{4}$$

$$= \frac{1}{2}$$

On the second draw, there are 4 balls of which 2 are red.

$$P(\text{red, on second draw}) = \frac{1}{2}$$

$$P(2 \text{ reds in succession}) = \frac{1}{2} \times \frac{1}{2}$$

$$= \frac{1}{4}$$

Since the first ball was replaced before the second ball was drawn, the second event is independent of the first event.

b) $P(\text{red, on first draw}) = \dfrac{1}{2}$

On the second draw, there are 3 balls of which 1 is red.

$$P(\text{red, on second draw}) = \frac{1}{3}$$

$$P(2 \text{ reds in succession}) = \frac{1}{2} \times \frac{1}{3}$$

$$= \frac{1}{6}$$

Since the first ball was not replaced before the second ball was drawn, the second event is dependent upon the first event.

EXERCISES 11-10

1. A coin and a regular tetrahedron (with faces marked 1, 2, 3, 4) are tossed. Draw a tree diagram to find the probability of getting:
   a) a head and a 1
   b) a tail and an even number.

2. It is equally likely that a child be born a girl or a boy. Draw a tree diagram to find the probability that:
   a) a family of two children will be both girls
   b) a family of 5 children will be all boys.

3. a) Draw a tree diagram to show the result of tossing a coin five times.
   b) What is the probability of tossing a coin five times and getting tails each time?

4. A True-False test has 6 questions. If all the questions are attempted by guessing, what is the probability of getting all 6 right?

5. What is the probability of rolling three consecutive sixes with one die?

(B)

6. If a thumbtack is tossed, the probability that it lands with the point up is 0.6. What is the probability of tossing a thumbtack four times and having it land with the point up each time?

7. Two people are selected at random. What is the probability that they both have birthdays in September, to 4 decimal places? (Assume a year has 365 days.)

8. Assuming that the probability that a woman gives birth to a boy is $\frac{1}{2}$, what is the probability that in a family of 4 children, all of the children are the same gender?

9. Three bags contain black balls and red balls in the numbers shown.
   a)   b)   c)

   From each bag, find the probability of drawing 2 red balls in succession if:
   i) the first ball is replaced before the second ball is drawn
   ii) the first ball is not replaced.

10. Find the probability of drawing 3 red balls in succession from a bag containing 3 red balls and 3 black balls if:
    a) each ball is replaced before the next ball is drawn
    b) the balls are not replaced after drawing.

11. A box of 100 flash cubes contains 4 which are defective. What is the probability that 2 cubes selected at random from the box are defective:
    a) if one cube is selected and set aside, and then the other is selected
    b) if both cubes are selected simultaneously?

12. A card is drawn from each of two well-shuffled decks. Find the probability of drawing two cards that are both:
    a) spades
    b) red
    c) Aces
    d) the Ace of spades.

13. Find the probability of drawing 4 Aces from a deck of cards:
    a) if there is replacement and shuffling after each draw
    b) if there is no replacement of the cards drawn.

14. A die is rolled and two coins are tossed. Find the probability of getting:
    a) a 2 and two heads
    b) a head, a tail, and an odd number.

15. Suppose a die is rolled until a 6 appears. Find the probability that the throw on which it appears is:
    a) the second
    b) the third
    c) the tenth.

16. Two tetrahedrons with faces labelled 1, 2, 3, 4, are tossed. Calculate the probability that they show:
    a) two ones
    b) anything but two ones
    c) a sum of 5
    d) a sum other than 5.

17. When two dice are rolled, what is the probability that they show:
    a) anything other than two sixes
    b) a sum of 7
    c) a sum of 11
    d) a sum not equal to 7 or 11
    e) at least one 3?

18. On a certain day, the probability of precipitation was 40% in Buffalo, 70% in New York City, and 20% in Albany. What was the probability of precipitation in all three cities on that day?

11-11 THE PROBABILITY THAT EITHER OF TWO EVENTS OCCURS

The person in the cartoon counted some days twice.
We can use a diagram to help determine the fraction of the school year that students attend school.

Assume that students have 13 weeks vacation per year, and that they attend school 5 days per week. We can calculate the number of days they attend school as a fraction of a full year.

The diagram shows regions V (for vacations) and W (for weekends) as parts of the year Y.
If the area of Y is 1, then the areas of V and W are fractions of the year.
The fraction of the year when students are not required to attend school is represented by the regions labelled V, W. This is denoted V or W.

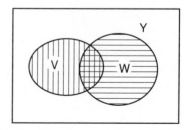

Area (V or W) = Area V + Area W − Area (V and W)

Fraction of a year consisting of non-school days

	Fraction of the year consisting of vacation days		Fraction of the year consisting of weekends		Fraction of the year consisting of weekends and vacation days
$=$	$\dfrac{13}{52}$	$+$	$\dfrac{2}{7}$	$-$	$\left(\dfrac{13}{52}\right)\left(\dfrac{2}{7}\right)$
$=$	$\dfrac{1}{4}$	$+$	$\dfrac{2}{7}$	$-$	$\dfrac{1}{14}$
$=$	$\dfrac{7}{28}$	$+$	$\dfrac{8}{28}$	$-$	$\dfrac{2}{28}$
$=$	$\dfrac{13}{28}$				

Since non-school days constitute about $\dfrac{13}{28}$ of the year, then school days constitute about $1 - \dfrac{13}{28}$, or $\dfrac{15}{28}$ of the school year; slightly more than half.

Example 1. In a class survey, 17 students like soft rock music while 12 students like heavy metal. Four students like both. How many students are in the class?

Solution. Number of students in the class = number of students who like soft rock + number who like heavy metal − number who like both
= 17 + 12 − 4
= 25
There are 25 students in the class.

The formula relating the areas on the diagram on the facing page can be applied to probabilities of events in a sample space. The corresponding formula linking the probability of the occurrence of either event A *or* event B to the probabilities of events A, B, and A and B is

$$P(A \text{ or } B) = P(A) + P(B) - P(A \text{ and } B)$$

Example 2. What is the probability of obtaining *either* a head or a 1 on the toss of a coin and a roll of a die?

Solution. If A is the occurrence of a head, then $P(A) = \dfrac{1}{2}$

If B is the occurrence of 1, then $P(B) = \dfrac{1}{6}$

Furthermore, $P(A \text{ and } B) = P(A) \times P(B)$
$$= \dfrac{1}{2} \times \dfrac{1}{6}$$
$$= \dfrac{1}{12}$$

Therefore, applying the formula above, we obtain

P(A or B) = P(A) + P(B) − P(A and B)

$$= \frac{1}{2} + \frac{1}{6} - \frac{1}{12}$$

$$= \frac{6}{12} + \frac{2}{12} - \frac{1}{12}$$

$$= \frac{7}{12}$$

The probability of either a head or a 1 is $\frac{7}{12}$.

Example 3. What is the probability that the spinner lands on either a red number or a number greater than 7?

Solution. Let A be the event that the spinner lands on a red number.
Let B be the event that the spinner lands on a number greater than 7.

Then $P(A) = \frac{5}{10}$ and $P(B) = \frac{3}{10}$

and P(A and B) = P(red number greater than 7)

$$= \frac{1}{10}$$

Therefore, P(A or B) = P(A) + P(B) − P(A and B)

$$= \frac{5}{10} + \frac{3}{10} - \frac{1}{10}$$

$$= \frac{7}{10}$$

The probability of a red number or a number greater than 7 is $\frac{7}{10}$.

In the examples above we use P(A), P(B), and P(A and B) to calculate P(A or B). The following example shows how the equation can be rearranged to calculate P(A and B) when given P(A), P(B), and P(A or B).

Example 4. A magazine company conducts a marketing survey. It determines that 74.3% of its readers are interested in sports and 47.5% of its readers are interested in financial investment activities. Also, 6.8% are interested in neither topic. What is the probability that a randomly-selected reader is interested in both topics?

Solution.   Suppose a person is selected at random.
Let S denote the event that the person has an interest in sports.
Let F denote the event that the person has an interest in financial investments.
The probability of a person being interested in sports or financial investments = 1 − probability that a person is not interested in either topic.
Change the percents to decimals.

Then
$$P(S \text{ or } F) = 1 - 0.068$$
$$= 0.932$$
$$P(S \text{ or } F) = P(S) + P(F) - P(S \text{ and } F)$$

Rearrange
$$P(S \text{ and } F) = P(S) + P(F) - P(S \text{ or } F)$$
$$= 0.743 + 0.475 - 0.932$$
$$= 0.286$$
$$= 28.6\%$$

The probability is 28.6%.

EXERCISES 11-11

Ⓐ

1. At the movies 152 patrons purchased popcorn while 118 purchased soft drinks. If 47 purchased both, how many different customers were there?

2. In a telephone sales campaign, 32 of those 100 people contacted purchased item A and 26 purchased item B. If 9 purchased both items, how many of those people contacted did not make a purchase?

3. At a summer camp 37 girls want to go canoeing and 52 girls want to go swimming. If 12 want to do both, and 15 don't want to do either, how many girls are at the camp?

4. In a club of 56 persons, 43 sold flowers and 39 sold chocolates. How many people sold both?

5. A coin is tossed and a die is rolled. What is the probability of obtaining:
   a) a head or a 3   b) a tail or a number greater than 4?

6. From a well-shuffled deck of cards, what is the probability of drawing:
   a) a King or a red card   b) an Ace or a black card?

Ⓑ

7. What is the probability of drawing a red Ace or a black Queen from a standard deck of 52 cards?

8. What is the probability of drawing a seven or a red card from a standard deck of 52 cards?

9. For each spinner, what is the probability of each event?

i)   ii)   iii)

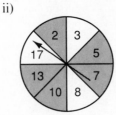
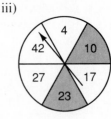

   a) an even number or a number in a white space
   b) a number in a black space or an even number
   c) a number in a white space or a number less than 3

10. In a state-wide survey, 48% of the families contacted owned their own homes, and 73% owned two cars. In addition, 32% of these families owned their own homes and two cars. What is the probability that a family selected at random will own its own home, or two cars, or both?

11. In our society, the probability of heart disease is 0.56. The probability of cancer is 0.24. If 7% of the population suffers from both, what is the probability that a person selected at random will not suffer from either?

12. The probability of an item being found defective at the first inspection station is 0.045. At the second inspection, the probability that the item is defective is 0.015. If the probability of the item being defective at both inspection stations is 0.007, what is the probability that the item is not defective?

13. A market study determines that 32% of a certain population like Mexican food while 45% like Italian food. If 37% like neither Mexican nor Italian food, what is the probability that a person selected at random will like both?

14. A student is to be selected at random from your class. The probability that the student selected: will like mathematics is 0.68; will like mathematics and science is 0.24; will not like either is 0.22. What is the probability that the student will like science?

15. A survey of symphony-goers reveals that 39% like music written by Mozart and 27% like music written by Bach. If 52% like music written by one or the other, what is the probability that a symphony-goer likes music written by both Mozart and Bach?

Ⓒ

16. A magazine publisher samples 4 different issues of its magazine for promotion purposes. The 4 issues are January, February, March, and April, denoted by J, F, M, and A respectively. There are 3 times as many Js as Fs and twice as many Fs as each of M and A. A magazine is selected at random from a stack of advertising samples. What is the probability that:
   a) it is the January issue   b) it is the February issue
   c) it is either the January or February issue
   d) it is either the March or April issue?

1. The diagram shows how heat is lost from a typical two-storey home. Draw a circle graph to show this information.

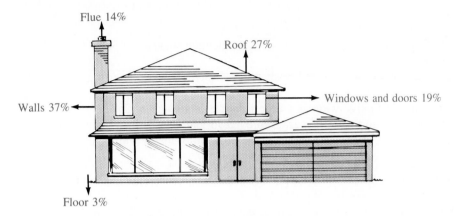

Flue 14%

Roof 27%

Windows and doors 19%

Walls 37%

Floor 3%

2. The workers in a small factory receive these salaries.

$10 000	10 000	10 400	10 800	13 200
10 800	11 200	12 000	12 000	12 400
12 400	12 400	12 400	12 800	10 800
14 000	14 000	14 400	14 800	14 800
15 200	16 000	15 600	15 200	16 000

Display the data on a histogram.

3. The table lists the defence spending of some nations of the North Atlantic Treaty Organization (NATO) as a percent of their gross national product (G.N.P.). Show this information on a suitable graph.

Country	Defence Spending as a Percent of G.N.P.
Britain	4.7
Canada	1.8
Denmark	2.4
France	3.3
Norway	3.2
U.S.A.	5.0
West Germany	3.4

4. Calculate the measures of central tendency for the salaries given in *Exercise 2*.

5. If the mean of the numbers 9, 10, 21, 27, 29, 25, 19, 13, x is 21, what is x?

6. Write nine natural numbers that have a median of 25 and a mean of 21.

7. Five hundred tickets are printed for a lottery. Carla bought 7 tickets. What is the probability of her winning if:
   a) all the tickets were sold
   b) 370 tickets were sold and the rest destroyed?

8. Shake 5 coins in a paper cup and empty them onto your desk. Record the frequency of heads. Repeat this procedure 24 times. From your results, if you did this a total of 300 times, with what frequency would you expect 5 coins to show:
   a) 3 heads   b) 4 heads   c) no heads?

9. A manufacturer of widgets has maintained a minimum standard of 95% dependability over the years.
   a) Three widgets in a batch of 75 are found to be defective. Does the batch meet the minimum standard?
   b) How many defective widgets are permissible in a batch of 250?
   c) Workmanship and materials are improved so that only 4 defective widgets are being found in every 250. What is the probability that a widget selected at random is not defective?

10. A ball is selected at random from 15 balls numbered from 1 to 15. What is the probability that the number is:
    a) even   b) prime   c) a multiple of 5   d) a 2-digit number?

11. The bar graph shows the distribution of the heights of students at Montcalm Secondary School. What is the probability that a student selected at random will be:
    a) between 150 cm and 165 cm tall
    b) taller than 175 cm
    c) shorter than 155 cm?

12. A box of coins contains 36 quarters, 45 dimes, 25 nickels, and 62 pennies. What is the probability that a coin drawn at random will be:
    a) a quarter   b) a nickel or a dime
    c) a quarter or a nickel   d) other than a penny?

13. The faces of two regular tetrahedrons are numbered 1 to 4. If they are tossed, what is the probability of getting:
    a) two numbers the same   b) a total of 5   c) a difference of 1?

14. An aviary has parakeets of four different colors. There are 10 green, 7 blue, 2 yellow, and 1 white. If two birds escape, what is the probability that they will both be:
    a) green   b) blue   c) yellow   d) white?

15. A cafeteria offers a number of choices for lunch.
    3 appetizers: soup, juice, or salad
    4 main courses: beef, chicken, pork, or fish
    2 desserts: pie or ice cream
    If a three-course meal is selected at random, calculate the probability of getting:
    a) soup   b) soup and beef   c) juice, fish, and pie.

12 Transformations

Two oil storage tanks, several kilometres apart, are on the same side of a pipeline. Where, along the pipeline, should a pumping station be located to serve both tanks so that the total length of pipe from the pipeline to the tanks is a minimum? (See Section 12-8, *Example 1.*)

12-1 INTRODUCTION TO TRANSFORMATIONS

The photographs above show some familiar transformations.

Whenever the shape, the size, the appearance or the position of an object is changed, it has undergone a *transformation*. Under a transformation, some of the characteristics of an object may be changed while others remain the same. Those characteristics that are unchanged are said to be *invariant*.

For each photograph above, identify some characteristics of the transformation that are invariant as well as some that change.

Transformation geometry is the study of transformations of geometric figures. Three transformations that do not change size or shape are *rotations*, *reflections*, and *translations*. These transformations map a figure onto its image.

A translation, whose direction and length are illustrated by the colored translation arrow, maps the black figure onto its colored image.

A reflection in the line *l* maps the black figure onto its colored image.

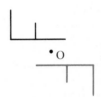

A rotation of 180° about O maps the black figure onto its colored image.

Example.   State which transformation maps each black letter onto its colored image.

a)   b)   c)

Solution.   a) Since the black G maps onto the colored G by a rotation about a point between the letters, the diagram illustrates a rotation.

b) Since the black G maps onto the colored G by a translation along a line joining the letters, the diagram illustrates a translation.

c) Since the black G maps onto the colored G by a reflection in a line between the letters, the diagram illustrates a reflection.

EXERCISES 12-1

Ⓐ

1. Name the transformation required to map each letter onto its colored image.

a)   i)   ii)   iii)

b)   i)   ii)   iii)

c)   i)   ii)   iii)

Ⓑ

2. For the figure shown, name a transformation that maps:
   a) region 4 onto region 1
   b) region 3 onto region 4
   c) region 4 onto region 2
   d) region 1 onto region 2
   e) region 3 onto region 1
   f) region 2 onto region 3.

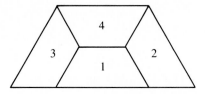

3. For the figure shown, name a transformation that maps:
   a) region C onto region A
   b) region A onto region B
   c) region D onto region C.

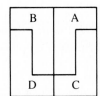

4. Copy each diagram. Divide it into two congruent parts. Name the transformation required to map one part onto the other.

a)   b)   c)

d)   e)   f)

INVESTIGATE

1. Plot the points V($-3,6$), W($1,1$), and Z($-1,-8$), and draw △VWZ.

2. Translate △VWZ as follows: move every point 7 units in the negative *x*-direction and 3 units in the positive *y*-direction.

3. Label the image points V′, W′, and Z′. Then, △V′W′Z′ is the translation image of △VWZ.

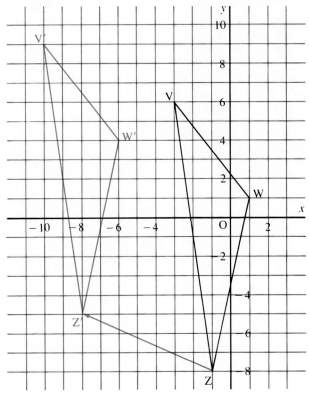

4. Measure VW, WZ, and VZ.

5. Measure V′W′, W′Z′, and V′Z′.
   - What appears to be true about the lengths of line segments under a translation?

6. Measure ∠VWZ, ∠WZV, and ∠ZVW.

7. Measure ∠V′W′Z′, ∠W′Z′V′, and ∠Z′V′W′.
   - What appears to be true about the measures of angles under a translation?
   - What appears to be true about the direction of line segments under a translation?

12-2 TRANSLATIONS

When a hockey puck moves across the ice in a straight line, it is *translated* from one position to another.

When a point or a figure is moved (or translated) in a straight line to another position in the same plane, it is said to have undergone a *translation*.

The translation illustrated here is defined by the length and the direction of the colored arrow.

$\triangle A'B'C'$ is the translation image of $\triangle ABC$.
AB = A'B'; AC = A'C'; BC = B'C'
AB ∥ A'B'; AC ∥ A'C'; BC ∥ B'C'
∠ABC = ∠A'B'C'; ∠BAC = ∠B'A'C';
∠ACB = ∠A'C'B'

Under a translation, any figure and its image are identical in all respects, except location.

You may have discovered the following properties of a translation in the previous *INVESTIGATE*.

- Under a translation, the lengths of line segments are invariant.
- Under a translation, the directions of line segments are invariant; that is, the image line segment is parallel to the original line segment.
- Under a translation, the measures of angles are invariant.

We use these properties to solve problems involving translations.

Example 1. Describe the translation that maps F onto F'.

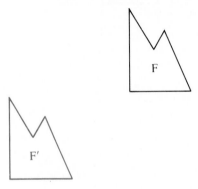

Solution. Trace the diagram. Join corresponding points Z and Z' with a straight line segment.
Draw an arrow head at Z', pointing to Z'.
The length and direction of the arrow ZZ' represent the translation that maps F onto F'.

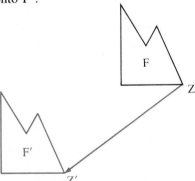

Example 2. A triangle has vertices G($-1,3$), H($4,7$), and J($3,-3$).
    a) Draw the image of △GHJ under this translation: move every point 5 units in the positive *x*-direction and 4 units in the negative *y*-direction.
    b) Write the coordinates of the vertices of the image triangle.

Solution.   a) The translation means that every point on △GHJ slides 5 units to the right and 4 units down. Thus, the *x*-coordinate of each point increases by 5 and the *y*-coordinate decreases by 4.
△G′H′J′ is the image of △GHJ under the given translation.

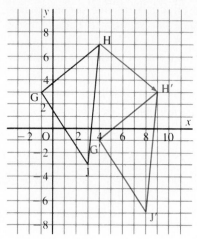

b) G(−1,3) → G′(4,−1)
H(4,7) → H′(9,3)
J(3,−3) → J′(8,−7)

EXERCISES 12-2

Ⓐ

1. Each diagram shows a figure F and its image F′ after a translation. Trace each diagram. Draw the translation arrow.

a)

b)

c)

d)

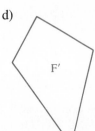

e)

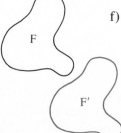

f)

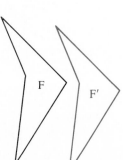

2. A translation maps the point $(1, -2)$ onto $(3,0)$.
   a) Plot the points and draw the translation arrow.
   b) Find the images of these points under this translation.
      i) A(0,2)   ii) B(5,6)   iii) C($-3, -1$)   iv) D($-4,2$)

Ⓑ

3. The graph shows points A, B, C, D, E, and a translation arrow.

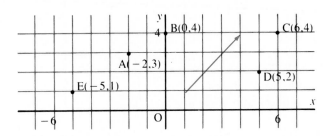

   a) Plot the points and their images under the translation. Label the images A', B', C', D', and E'.
   b) Draw line segments AA' and DD', and compare them with the translation arrow. What do you notice?
   c) Measure and compare the lengths of line segments DE and D'E'. What do you notice?
   d) Measure and compare the sizes of ∠AED and ∠A'E'D'. What do you notice?

4. A translation maps the point $(-2, -3)$ onto $(4,2)$.
   a) Plot the points and draw the translation arrow.
   b) Find the images of A($-1,1$), B(1,4), and C($2, -3$) under this translation. Label the image points A', B', and C'.
   c) Describe the effect of this translation on △ABC.

5. A parallelogram has vertices at A($-2,2$), B(2,1), C($4, -4$), and D($0, -3$). A translation maps points 4 units to the right and 1 unit down. Draw:
   a) the parallelogram
   b) the translation arrow
   c) the image of the parallelogram under this translation.

6. A translation maps the point $(2,5)$ onto $(5, -2)$.
   a) Draw the translation arrow.
   b) If P'($-3, -1$), Q'($-1,3$), and R'($-5,0$) are the images of P, Q, and R under this translation, find the coordinates of P, Q, and R.

7. What properties remain invariant under a translation?

Ⓒ

8. a) Graph this equation. $2x + y = 6$
   b) Draw the image of the graph of the line in part a) under the translation that maps the point $(3,0)$ onto $(0,0)$.

9. a) Graph this equation. $5x - 2y = 10$
   b) Draw the image of the graph of the line in part a) under the translation that maps the point $(-2,1)$ onto $(0,6)$.
   c) Explain the result.

10. Translation T_1 maps the point $(4,1)$ onto $(2,3)$. Translation T_2 maps $(-2,-3)$ onto $(3,0)$.
    a) Draw $\triangle ABC$ and its image, $\triangle A'B'C'$, under T_1.
    b) Draw the image of $\triangle A'B'C'$ under T_2. Label it $\triangle A''B''C''$.
    c) Draw a translation arrow for the single translation that maps $\triangle ABC$ onto $\triangle A''B''C''$.
    d) Investigate whether T_1 followed by T_2 gives the same result as T_2 followed by T_1.

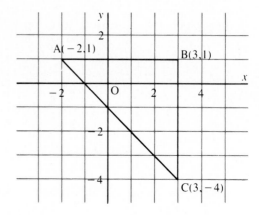

INVESTIGATE

1. Plot the points $S(-3,-5)$, $T(-1,7)$, and $U(-1,-8)$, and draw $\triangle STU$.

2. Reflect $\triangle STU$ in the y-axis. That is, fold the paper along the y-axis. With a sharp pencil or compasses point, mark the positions of S, T, and U so they appear on the other half of the folded paper.

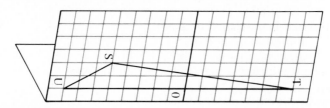

3. Open the paper and label the image points S', T', and U'. Then, $\triangle S'T'U'$ is the image of $\triangle STU$ under a reflection in the y-axis.

4. Measure ST, TU, and SU.

5. Measure $S'T'$, $T'U'$, and $S'U'$.
   ● What appears to be true about the lengths of line segments under a reflection?

6. Measure $\angle STU$, $\angle TUS$, and $\angle UST$.

7. Measure $\angle S'T'U'$, $\angle T'U'S'$, and $\angle U'S'T'$.
   ● What appears to be true about the measures of angles under a reflection?
   ● Where is the image of any point on the reflection line?

12-3 REFLECTIONS

When you look in a mirror, you see an image of yourself. The image appears to be as far behind the mirror as you are in front of it. The transformation that relates points and their images in this way is called a *reflection*.

A reflection in line l maps each point on a figure, onto its image point on the reflection of the figure.

$\triangle A'B'C'$ is the reflection image of $\triangle ABC$ in reflection line l.

$AB = A'B'$; $AC = A'C'$; $BC = B'C'$
$\angle ABC = \angle A'B'C'$; $\angle BAC = \angle B'A'C'$;
$\angle ACB = \angle A'C'B'$

The points A and A' coincide; that is, a point on the reflection line is its own image.

In the diagram, each point on $\triangle ABC$ has been joined to its image point on $\triangle A'B'C'$, with a broken line.

$BD = DB'$; $CE = EC'$
$\angle BDA = \angle B'DA = 90°$; $\angle CEA = \angle C'EA = 90°$

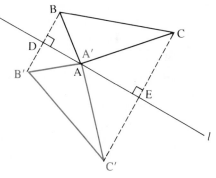

You may have discovered the following properties of a reflection in the previous *INVESTIGATE*.

- Under a reflection, the lengths of line segments and the measures of angles are invariant.
- Under a reflection, the points on the reflection line are invariant.
- The reflection line is the perpendicular bisector of the line segment joining any point to its image point.

We use these properties to solve problems involving reflections.

Example 1. Draw the reflection line that maps F onto F′.

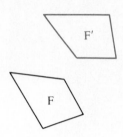

Solution. Trace the diagram.
Join corresponding points X and X′
with a straight line segment and mark
its midpoint M.
Join another pair of corresponding
points Y and Y′ with a straight line
segment and mark its midpoint N.
Join MN. This is the reflection
line that maps F onto F′.

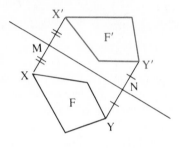

Example 2. A triangle has vertices D(4,7), E(8,3), and F(6,−2). Draw the image of
△DEF after a reflection in the *x*-axis. Write the coordinates of the
vertices of the image triangle.

Solution. Plot the points on graph paper. Draw △DEF.

Draw a line through D perpendicular to the *x*-axis (that is, parallel
to the *y*-axis). Extend this line to a point D′ such that D′ is the same
distance from the *x*-axis as D is.

Similarly, draw a line
through E perpendicular to the
x-axis and label E′ such that
E′ is the same distance from
the *x*-axis as E is.

Also, draw a line through F
perpendicular to the *x*-axis
and label F′ such that F′ is the
same distance from the *x*-axis
as F is.

△D′E′F′ is the image of
△DEF under a reflection in the
x-axis. The coordinates of the
vertices of the image triangle
are D′(4,−7), E′(8,−3), and
F′(6,2).

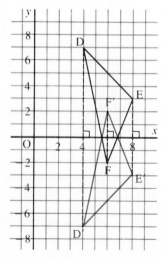

EXERCISES 12-3

(A)

1. Sketch the images of **A**, **3**, **K**, and **5** under reflections in:
   a) a vertical line
   b) a horizontal line.

2. State the time shown on the mirror image of each clock face.
   a)
   b)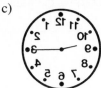
   c)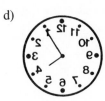
   d)

3. Each diagram shows a figure F and its image F′ under a reflection. Trace each diagram and draw the reflection line.
   a)
   b)
   c)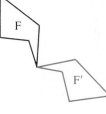

   d)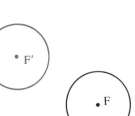
   e)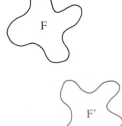
   f)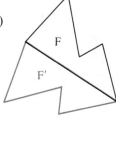

(B)

4. Triangle PQR has vertices P(2,6), Q(6,4), and R(3,2). Draw the image of △PQR under a reflection in:
   a) the *x*-axis
   b) the *y*-axis.

5. Quadrilateral ABCD has vertices A(2,5), B(6,5), C(9,1), and D(2,1). Find the coordinates of the image of quadrilateral ABCD under a reflection in:
   a) the *x*-axis
   b) the *y*-axis.

6. Triangle ABC has vertices A(4,7), B(7,2), and C(3,3). Its image under a reflection is A′(−2,7), B′(−5,2), and C′(−1,3). Graph both triangles and draw the reflection line.

7. Triangle ABC in *Exercise 6* has another image at A′(4, − 11), B′(7, − 6), C′(3, − 7). Draw the reflection line.

8. For each triangle shown below
    a) Copy the triangle.
    b) Draw its reflection image using the extended side as the reflection line.
    c) Name the figure formed by the triangle and its image.

    i) 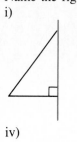   ii) 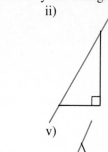   iii)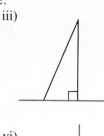

    iv)    v) 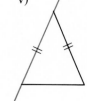   vi)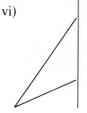

9. Each diagram shows a line OP and its reflection image OP′.
    a) Trace each diagram.
    b) Determine its reflection line.
    c) Verify that the reflection line is the bisector of ∠POP′.

    i) 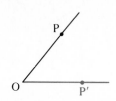   ii) 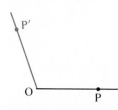   iii)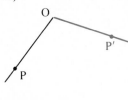

10. Triangle PQR has vertices P(−2,4), Q(4,2), and R(1, − 2). Draw the image of △PQR and write the coordinates of the vertices under a reflection in:
    a) the *x*-axis   b) the *y*-axis.

11. Quadrilateral ABCD has vertices A(−2,6), B(4,3), C(3, − 3), and D(−5, − 2). Write the coordinates of the vertices of its image under a reflection in:
    a) the *x*-axis   b) the *y*-axis.

12. What properties remain invariant under a reflection?

ⓒ

13. a) Graph this equation. $3x + 2y = 12$
    b) Draw the image of the graph of the line in part a) under a reflection in:
        i) the *x*-axis   ii) the *y*-axis.

INVESTIGATE

Rotations on a Grid

1. Plot the points P(−1,5), Q(−5,4), and R(−2,−4), and draw △PQR.

2. Trace the triangle and the axes on tracing paper. Rotate the tracing paper through 90° counterclockwise about the origin. That is, rotate the paper until the positive *y*-axis on the tracing paper coincides with the negative *x*-axis on the base paper.

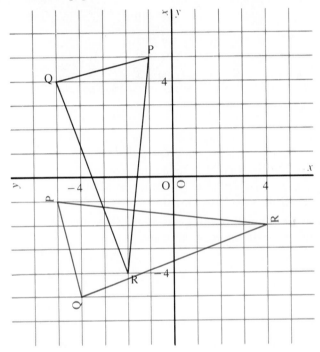

3. Mark the new positions of P, Q, and R and label them P′, Q′, and R′. △P′Q′R′ is the rotation image of △PQR after a counterclockwise rotation of 90° about O.

4. Measure PQ, QR, and PR.

5. Measure P′Q′, Q′R′, and P′R′.
- What appears to be true about the lengths of line segments under a rotation?

6. Measure ∠PQR, ∠PRQ, and ∠RPQ.

7. Measure ∠P′Q′R′, ∠P′R′Q′, and ∠R′P′Q′.
- What appears to be true about the measures of angles under a rotation?

12-4 ROTATIONS

A person on a Ferris wheel rotates about the center of the wheel. When a point or a figure is turned about a fixed point, it is said to have undergone a *rotation*. The fixed point is called the *rotation center*. A rotation in a counterclockwise direction is a positive rotation. In this chapter, all rotations will be counterclockwise.

A counterclockwise rotation of 90° about O maps each point on a figure, onto its image point on the rotation image.

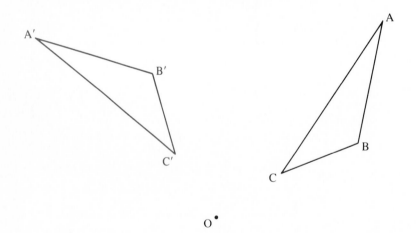

$\triangle A'B'C'$ is the rotation image of $\triangle ABC$ after a 90° rotation about O.
AB = A'B'; AC = A'C'; BC = B'C'
$\angle ABC = \angle A'B'C'$; $\angle BAC = \angle B'A'C'$; $\angle ACB = \angle A'C'B'$

You may have discovered the following properties of a rotation in the previous *INVESTIGATE*.

- Under a rotation, the lengths of line segments are invariant.
- Under a rotation, the measures of angles are invariant.

We can use these properties to solve problems involving rotations.

Example 1. Figure F′ is the image of figure F under a rotation.
a) Locate the rotation center.
b) Measure the rotation angle.

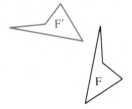

Solution. a) Trace the diagram on tracing paper.
Fold the paper so that a point X on the figure coincides with the corresponding point X′ on the image. Crease the paper.
Unfold the paper and draw a line *l* along the crease.

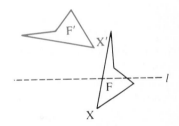

Fold the paper so another point Y on the figure coincides with its corresponding point Y′ on the image. Crease the paper, then unfold it and draw a line *m* along the crease.

The point of intersection O of *l* and *m* is the center of rotation that maps the figure onto its image.

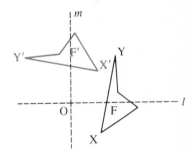

b) Draw lines from O to X and from O to X′.

∠XOX′ is the rotation angle and it is measured to be 90°.

How could you check that the rotation center and rotation angle are correct?

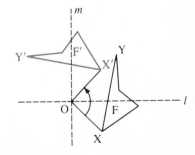

Example 2. A triangle has vertices A(3,5), B(7,1), and C(5, −2).
  a) Draw the image of △ABC under a rotation of 90° about the origin.
  b) Write the coordinates of the vertices of the image triangle.

Solution. a) Plot the points on graph paper. Draw △ABC.
  Draw OA. Place a protractor along OA, center O and mark
  90° counterclockwise. Along this line, label a point A′ such that
  OA = OA′.

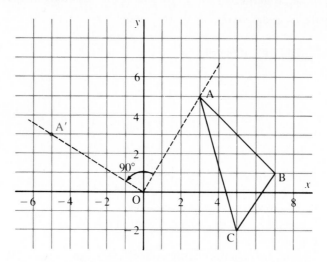

Similarly, mark B′ such that ∠BOB′ is 90° and OB = OB′.
Then mark C′ such that ∠COC′ is 90° and OC = OC′.
△A′B′C′ is the image of △ABC under a rotation of 90° about O.

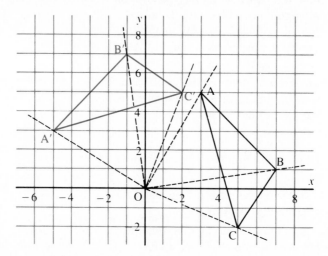

  b) The coordinates of the vertices of the image triangle are A′(−5,3),
  B′(−1,7), and C′(2,5).

EXERCISES 12-4

Ⓐ

1. Each diagram shows a figure F and its image F′ after a rotation. Trace each diagram. Locate the rotation center and measure the rotation angle.

a)

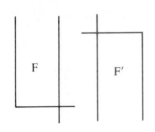

b)

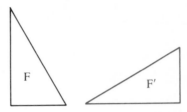

c)

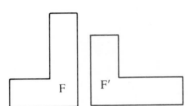

d)

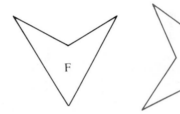

e)

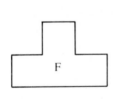

f)

Ⓑ

2. A triangle has vertices A(1,4), B(5,5), and O(0,0). Draw its image and find the coordinates of its vertices under a 180° rotation about O.

3. A quadrilateral has vertices A(1,3), B(4,7), C(6,4), and D(3,1). Draw its image and find the coordinates of its vertices under a 180° rotation about the origin.

4. A triangle has vertices P(−3,5), Q(1,−7), and R(2,1). Draw its image and find the coordinates of its vertices under a 90° rotation about the origin.

5. A quadrilateral has vertices K(−3,4), L(1,6), M(6,−1), and N(−4,−3). Draw its image and find the coordinates of its vertices under a 90° rotation about the origin.

6. a) What can be said about the line segment joining any point P on a figure to its image P′, after a 180° rotation?
   b) How do the coordinates of a point and its image under a 180° rotation about (0,0) compare?

7. For each triangle shown below
   a) Copy the triangle.
   b) Draw its image under a 180° rotation about C.
   c) Name the figure formed by the triangle and its image.

   i) 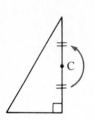   ii) 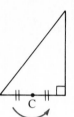   iii)

   iv)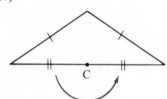

   v)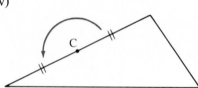

8. Sketch the image of each figure under a 90°, a 180°, a 270°, and a 360° rotation about the rotation centre O. Which image maps onto the original figure when it is rotated through 180°?

   a) 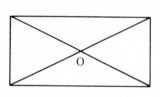   b) 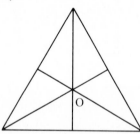   c)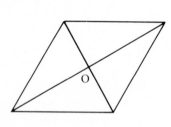

9. What properties remain invariant under a rotation?

Ⓒ

10. a) Graph this equation. $y = x + 3$
    b) Draw the image of the graph of the line in part a) under a 180° rotation about the origin.

11. a) Graph this equation. $y = 2x$
    b) Draw the image of the graph of the line in part a) under a 180° rotation about the origin.
    c) Explain the result.

Enlargements and Reductions

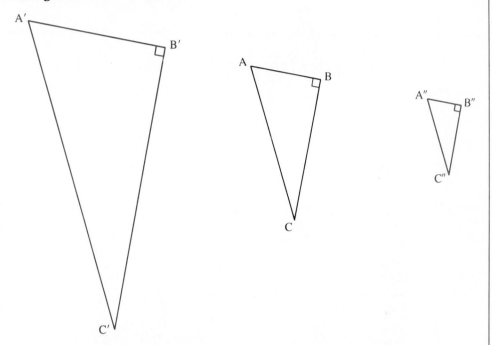

In the diagram, △A′B′C′ is an enlargement of △ABC and △A″B″C″ is a reduction of △ABC.

1. Trace the diagram.

2. Measure AB, BC, and CA.

3. Measure A′B′, B′C′, C′A′, A″B″, B″C″, and C″A″.
   - What appears to be true about the lengths of line segments under an enlargement?
   - What appears to be true about the lengths of line segments under a reduction?

4. Measure ∠ABC, ∠BCA, and ∠CAB.

5. Measure ∠A′B′C′, ∠B′C′A′, ∠C′A′B′, ∠A″B″C″, ∠B″C″A″, and ∠C″A″B″.
   - What appears to be true about the measures of angles under an enlargement?
   - What appears to be true about the measures of angles under a reduction?

6. Find the areas of △ABC, △A′B′C′, and △A″B″C″.
   - What appears to be true about the areas of figures under an enlargement?
   - What appears to be true about the areas of figures under a reduction?

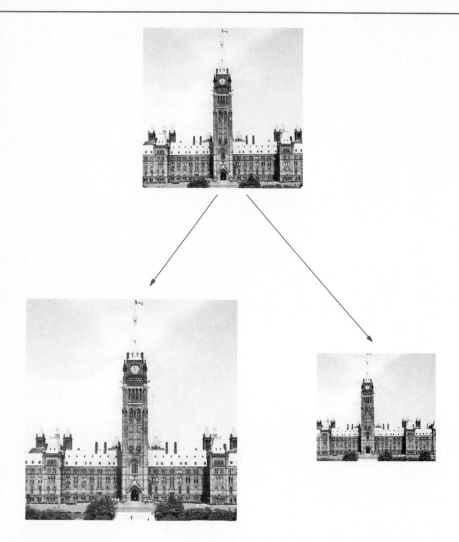

12-5 DILATIONS

When a photograph has been increased in size, it has been *enlarged*.
When a photograph is decreased in size, it has been *reduced*. In both
cases, the shapes of the objects on the photographs are invariant,
only their dimensions change.

    Enlargements and reductions are examples of a transformation called
a dilation.

> A *dilation* is a transformation that changes all dimensions by
> a factor k called the *scale factor*. For enlargements, k is greater
> than 1 and for reductions, k is between 0 and 1.

Example 1. Here are two views of the Canadian flag; F′ is the dilation image of F.

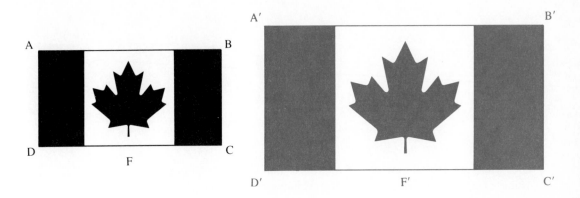

a) Find the scale factor k of the dilation.
b) Compare the length-to-width ratios of the flags.
c) Find the areas of the flags.

Solution. a) The scale factor k is the ratio of corresponding lengths.
$$k = \frac{A'B'}{AB} \left(\text{or } \frac{B'C'}{BC} \text{ or } \frac{C'D'}{CD} \text{ or } \frac{A'D'}{AD} \right)$$
By measuring, $A'B' = 7.5$ cm and $AB = 5.0$ cm
$$k = \frac{7.5}{5.0}$$
$$= 1.5$$
The scale factor k of the dilation is 1.5.

b) For flag F, $\dfrac{\text{length}}{\text{width}} = \dfrac{5.0}{2.5}$
$$= 2.0$$
For flag F′, $\dfrac{\text{length}}{\text{width}} = \dfrac{7.5}{3.8}$
$$\doteq 2.0$$
The length-to-width ratio of the flag is unchanged by the dilation.

c) For flag F, area $= (5.0 \times 2.5)$ cm²
$$= 12.5 \text{ cm}^2$$
For flag F′, area $= (7.5 \times 3.8)$ cm²
$$= 28.5 \text{ cm}^2$$

In *Example 1*, the area of F′ is *not* 1.5 times the area of F. Since each dimension of F′ is 1.5 times the corresponding dimension of F, the area of F′ is $(1.5)^2$, or 2.25 times the area of F.
Use your calculator to show that $\dfrac{28.5}{12.5} \doteq 2.25$

In *Example 1*, if we join corresponding points on the flags and extend the lines, we find that they meet at a point called the *dilation center*.

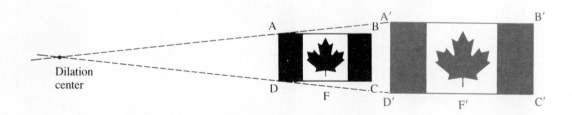

Here are some properties of dilations. You may have discovered some of these in the *INVESTIGATE* preceding this section.

Under a dilation with scale factor k

- The length of an image line segment is k times the length of the original line segment.
- The measures of angles are invariant.
- The area of an image figure is k^2 times the area of the original figure.
- Lines through corresponding points meet at the dilation center.

Example 2.   The map is a dilation of a city, with a scale of 1 : 112 000. That is, x centimetres on the map corresponds to an actual distance of 112 000x centimetres. Use the map to determine the actual distance between 43 Street and 13 Street along 5 Avenue.

Solution.   By measuring, the map distance between 43 Street and 13 Street along 5 Avenue is 2.9 cm.

Actual distance is 112 000 × 2.9 cm
$$= 324\ 800 \text{ cm}$$
$$= 3.248 \text{ km}$$

It is approximately 3.2 km from 43 Street to 13 Street along 5 Avenue.

SCALE: 1: 112000

EXERCISES 12-5

Ⓐ

1. A figure undergoes a dilation with the given scale factor. Is the image an enlargement or a reduction?

a) 3   b) 7   c) $\dfrac{1}{2}$ d) $\dfrac{3}{2}$ e) $\dfrac{1}{4}$ f) $\dfrac{5}{6}$

2. The larger photograph is a dilation image of the smaller photograph.

Measure the photographs.
a) Find the scale factor of the dilation.
b) Find the length-to-width ratios of the photograph and its enlargement.
c) Find the areas of the photograph and its enlargement.

Ⓑ

3. Triangle ABC has sides of length 5 cm, 12 cm, and 13 cm. Find the lengths of the sides of its dilation image for each scale factor.

a) 2   b) 5   c) $\dfrac{1}{2}$ d) $\dfrac{3}{4}$

4. Using O as the dilation center, draw the image of each triangle with each scale factor.

i) 2.5   ii) 0.75

a)   b)   c)

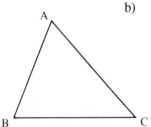

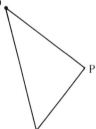
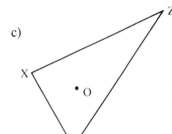

5. On a blueprint, the dimensions of a building are 640 mm by 360 mm. Determine the scale factor of the dilation if the actual building has these dimensions.
   a) 64 m by 36 m
   b) 96 m by 54 m
   c) 48 m by 27 m
   d) 80 m by 45 m

6. From the map in *Example 2*, find the actual distance between each pair of locations.
   a) 9 Ave. N. and 16 Ave. S. along 13 Street
   b) 13 Street and 28 Street along 5 Ave.
   c) the two points where the railroad tracks cross 43 Street

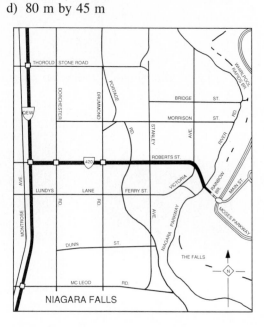

7. The scale for this map of Niagara Falls is 1 : 91 000. How far is it between each pair of locations?
   a) Dorchester Rd. to River Rd. along Morrison St.
   b) Thorold Stone Rd. to McLeod Rd. along Drummond Rd.
   c) the corner of Dorchester Rd. and Dunn St. to the corner of Bridge St. and Stanley Ave.

8. O is the dilation center for △ABC and its image △A′B′C′.
   a) Determine the scale factor *k*.
   b) Find these ratios.
   $$\frac{OA'}{OA}, \frac{OB'}{OB}, \frac{OC'}{OC}$$
   c) Copy the diagram and draw △A″B″C″, the dilation image of △ABC with scale factor 2.

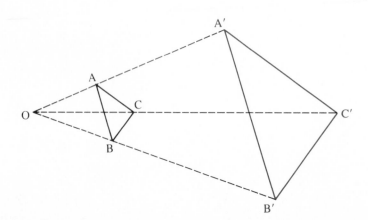

12-6 SIMILAR FIGURES

Two surveyors need to know the distance AB across a pond, which cannot be measured directly.

    The surveyors located points D and E such that DE is parallel to AB, and DE can be measured. They completed the triangle at point C.

    Triangle CAB can be considered as a dilatation image of △CDE about the dilation center C.

Hence, corresponding sides of the triangles are in the same ratio, which is the scale factor of the dilation.

The surveyors know that $\dfrac{AB}{DE} = \dfrac{AC}{DC}$.

They measured DE, AC, and DC, and these lengths are labelled on the diagram.

Hence, $\dfrac{AB}{25.7} = \dfrac{85.5}{63.0}$

$$AB = \frac{85.5}{63.0}(25.7)$$

$$\doteq 34.9$$

The distance AB across the pond is about 35 m.

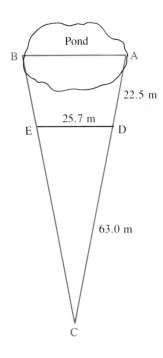

Pond

B   A

22.5 m

25.7 m

E   D

63.0 m

C

If one geometric figure is the image of another under a dilation then the figures are said to be similar.

Two triangles ABC and A′B′C′ are *similar* if the ratios of corresponding sides are equal.

$$\frac{AB}{A'B'} = \frac{AC}{A'C'} = \frac{BC}{B'C'}$$

Two triangles ABC and A′B′C′ are *similar* if pairs of corresponding angles are equal.

∠A = ∠A′; ∠B = ∠B′; ∠C = ∠C′

To indicate that △ABC is similar to △A′B′C′, we write △ABC ~ △A′B′C′.

Example 1. Given the figure with the indicated sides parallel

a) Explain why △PQT is similar to △PRS.

b) Explain why $\dfrac{QT}{RS} = \dfrac{PT}{PS}$.

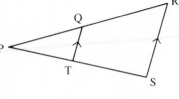

Solution. a) ∠PTQ and ∠PSR are corresponding angles.
∠PQT and ∠PRS are corresponding angles.
Since QT is parallel to RS,
∠PTQ = ∠PSR
∠PQT = ∠PRS
∠P is common to △PQT and △PRS.
Since pairs of corresponding angles are equal, △PQT ~ △PRS.

b) The ratios of corresponding sides of △PQT and △PRS are equal.

Therefore, $\dfrac{QT}{RS} = \dfrac{PT}{PS}$.

Example 2. Find the values of *x* and *y*.

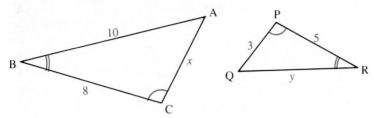

Solution. In △ABC and △PQR
∠B = ∠R
∠C = ∠P
Since two pairs of angles in the triangles are equal, the third pair of angles must be equal.
∠A = ∠Q
Since pairs of corresponding angles are equal, △ABC is similar to △QRP.
Hence, the ratios of corresponding sides of △ABC and △QRP are equal.

$$\frac{AB}{QR} = \frac{BC}{RP} = \frac{AC}{QP}$$

Substitute the given values.

$$\frac{10}{y} = \frac{8}{5} = \frac{x}{3}$$

Consider these expressions two at a time.

$$\frac{10}{y} = \frac{8}{5}$$

$$5(10) = 8y$$

$$y = \frac{50}{8}$$

$$= 6.25$$

$$\frac{8}{5} = \frac{x}{3}$$

$$\frac{8(3)}{5} = x$$

$$x = \frac{24}{5}$$

$$= 4.8$$

Example 3. The largest international standard paper size is designated by the symbol A0. The A0 size is a rectangle of length 1.19 m and width 0.84 m. The next largest size, A1, is a rectangle similar to A0 but with half the area. What are the dimensions of A1-size paper?

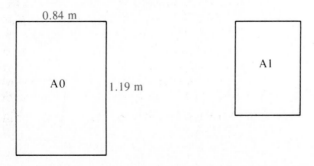

Solution. Since the two rectangles are similar, rectangle A1 is the image of rectangle A0 under a dilatation with scale factor k.

Since the area of rectangle A1 is one-half that of rectangle A0,

$$k^2 = \frac{1}{2}$$

$$k = \frac{1}{\sqrt{2}}$$

Therefore, $\dfrac{\text{length of rectangle A1}}{\text{length of rectangle A0}} = \dfrac{1}{\sqrt{2}}$

$$\text{length of rectangle A1} = \frac{1}{\sqrt{2}}(1.19)$$

$$\doteq 0.84$$

and $\dfrac{\text{width of rectangle A1}}{\text{width of rectangle A0}} = \dfrac{1}{\sqrt{2}}$

$$\text{width of rectangle A1} = \frac{1}{\sqrt{2}}(0.84)$$

$$\doteq 0.59$$

The dimensions of A1-size paper are 0.84 m by 0.59 m.

EXERCISES 12-6

Ⓐ

1. State which figures are similar.

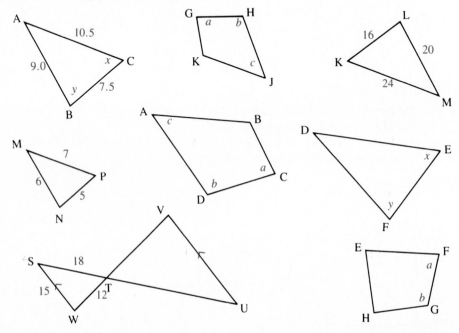

Ⓑ

2. Show that: a) $\dfrac{AB}{A'B'} = \dfrac{AC}{A'C'}$ b) $\dfrac{AB}{A'B'} = \dfrac{BC}{B'C'}$.

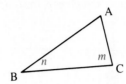
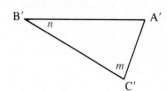

3. Show that: a) $\dfrac{DE}{DG} = \dfrac{DF}{DH}$ b) $\dfrac{DE}{DG} = \dfrac{EF}{GH}$.

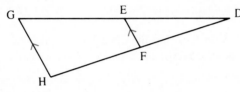

4. Find the values of *x* and *y*.

a)

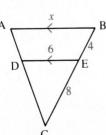

b)

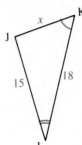

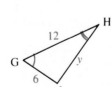

c)

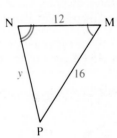

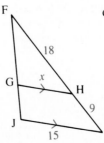

5. Find the values of *x*.

a)

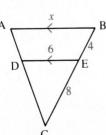

b)

c)

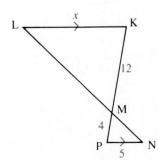

6. The shadow of a telephone relay tower is 32 m long on level ground. At the same time, a boy 1.8 m tall casts a shadow 1.5 m long. What is the height of the tower?

7. Karen is 37.5 m from a church. She finds that a pencil, 4.8 cm long, which is held with its base 60 mm from her eye, just blocks the church from her sight. How high is the church?

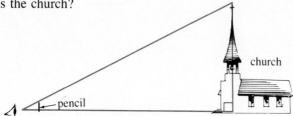

8. The shape of A2-size paper is a rectangle similar to the A1 size but with half its area.
   a) Use the data in *Example 3* to find the dimensions of the A2 size.
   b) What symbol designates paper measuring 30 cm by 21 cm?

9. Sunil has a photograph measuring 20 cm by 25 cm. He wishes to get a copy that is three-quarters the area but with the same length-to-width ratio. What will be the dimensions of the copy?

10. For the photograph in *Exercise 9*, what would be the dimensions of a copy with double the area of the original but with the same shape?

Ⓒ

11. Find the values of x and y.
   a)

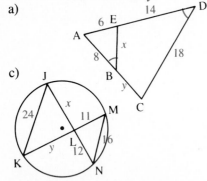

   b)

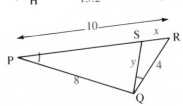

   c)

   d)

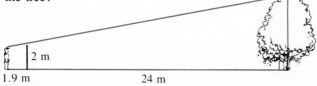

12. To determine the height of a tree, Jerry places a 2 m rod 24 m from the tree. He finds that he can just align the top of the rod with the top of the tree when he stands 1.9 m from the rod. If Jerry's eyes are 1.6 m from the ground, what is the height of the tree?

12-7 SYMMETRY

Many objects in art and nature seem to be divided, by a line we can visualize, into two matching parts. Such objects are said to have line symmetry. Perfect line symmetry rarely occurs in nature. For example, the right wing of the butterfly does not exactly match the left. In mathematics, however, we define line symmetry exactly.

> Any figure that can be mapped onto itself by a reflection is said to have *line symmetry*. The reflection line is called a *line of symmetry*.

Each of the four figures below has more than one line of symmetry. One line is shown for each; how many others can you see?

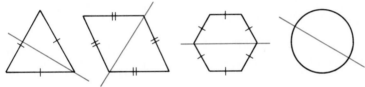

Example 1. Identify all the lines of symmetry in a regular hexagon.

Solution. There are 3 lines of symmetry joining opposite vertices and 3 joining the midpoints of the opposite sides. A regular hexagon has a total of 6 lines of symmetry.

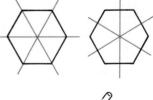

The illustration shows how, with a semi-transparent mirror, a figure having line symmetry can be drawn from any figure.

Just as reflections can be used to create figures with symmetry, so also can rotations.

> Any figure that maps onto itself when rotated less than a full turn is said to have *rotational symmetry*.

These figures have rotational symmetry because they map onto themselves when rotated the amount indicated about the turn centers shown.

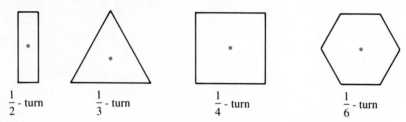

$\frac{1}{2}$ - turn $\frac{1}{3}$ - turn $\frac{1}{4}$ - turn $\frac{1}{6}$ - turn

The figures have rotational symmetry of order 2, 3, 4, and 6 respectively.

Point symmetry is a special kind of rotational symmetry.

> A figure has *point symmetry* if a $\frac{1}{2}$ turn maps the figure onto itself.

Each figure below has point symmetry about the turn center indicated.

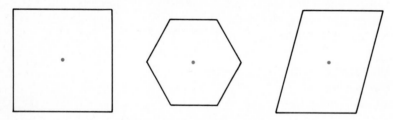

Example 2.   Under what angles of rotation will a regular pentagon map onto itself?

Solution.   Since the pentagon has rotational symmetry of order 5, five equal rotations will map it onto itself and return it to its original position. The angle of each rotation is: $\dfrac{360°}{5} = 72°$

Rotations of 72°; 2 × 72°, or 144°; 3 × 72°, or 216°; 4 × 72°, or 288°; and 5 × 72°, or 360° will map the pentagon onto itself.

EXERCISES 12-7

Ⓐ

1. Copy each figure and draw its lines of symmetry.

a) 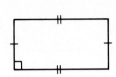   b)   c)

2. Copy each regular polygon and draw its lines of symmetry.

a)   b)   c)   d)

3. A regular decagon has ten equal sides and ten equal angles. How many lines of symmetry does it have?

4. State the order of rotational symmetry of each logo.

a)   b)   c)   d)

5. a) State the order of rotational symmetry of each regular polygon in *Exercise 2*.
   b) A regular dodecagon has twelve equal sides and twelve equal angles. What is its order of rotational symmetry?

6. For each polygon in *Exercise 2*, what is the smallest angle of rotation that maps the polygon onto itself?

Ⓑ

7. On a grid, locate and identify the quadrilateral with vertices at A(0,3), B(5, −2), C(4,5), D(−1,10). Show the lines of symmetry.

8. Draw a figure that has:
   a) only two lines of symmetry
   b) point symmetry but no line of symmetry
   c) rotational symmetry, order 6, and a line of symmetry
   d) rotational symmetry, order 6, but no line of symmetry.

 **PROBLEM SOLVING**

Consider All Possibilities

A box is designed to hold a cube marked with the letters A through F as shown. In how many different ways can the cube be placed in the box?

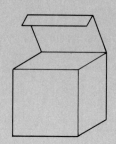

Understand the problem
- When are two ways of placing the cube in the box to be considered as "different"?
- Is there only one way to place the cube in the box so that face A is on top?
- What are we asked to find?

Think of a strategy
- Consider each letter in turn.
- Think of the number of ways the cube can be placed with that letter on top.

Carry out the strategy
- Count the number of ways of placing the cube in the box so that face A is on top.
- When A is on top, there are four different ways that A can appear, as shown in the diagram.
- Similarly, there are 4 different ways that the cube can be placed in the box when each of B, C, D, E, and F are on top.
- Therefore, the total number of ways of placing the cube in the box is 6 × 4, or 24.

Look back
- Try another method of counting the ways that the cube can be placed in the box. Do you get 24 by this method?

Solve each problem

1. How many lines of symmetry has a regular polygon of 12 sides (below left)?

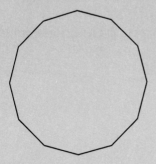 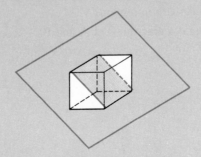

2. A plane which divides a solid into 2 parts such that each part is the reflection of the other in the plane is called a *plane of symmetry* of the solid (above right). How many planes of symmetry has a cube?

3. Place the integers from 1 to 6 inside the circles so that the sums along the sides of the triangle are equal (below left).

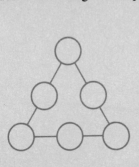 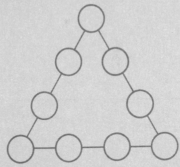

4. Place the integers from 1 to 9 inside the circles so that the sums along the sides of the triangle are equal (above right).

5. a) Choose any two prime numbers greater than 3. Find the difference of their squares. Is the difference a multiple of 24?
   b) Repeat part a) with other pairs of prime numbers.
   c) Make a conjecture about the difference of the squares of two prime numbers greater than 3.
   d) Test your conjecture using other pairs of prime numbers.
   e) Every prime number greater than 3 is either 1 more than a multiple of 4 (such as 17), or 3 more than a multiple of 4 (such as 19). Use this fact to prove your conjecture in part c).

12-8 APPLICATIONS OF TRANSFORMATIONS

We can solve certain apparently difficult problems using transformations.
Consider the problem posed at the beginning of this chapter.

Example 1. A pumping station is to be built somewhere along a pipeline to serve tanks at two points near the pipeline. Where should the pumping station be located so that the total length of the pipe from the pipeline to the tanks is a minimum?

Solution. Draw a diagram. Let A and B represent the tanks, and let *l* represent the pipeline.

Locate B′, the reflection image of B in *l*. The shortest distance between A and B′ is the line segment joining them. Let AB′ intersect *l* at P. Join PB. PB is the reflection image of PB′ in *l*.

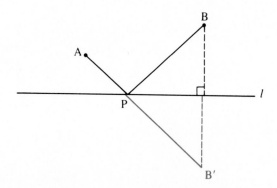

Since AP + PB′ is the shortest distance from A to B′, AP + PB is the shortest distance from A to *l* to B.
The pumping station should be built at P.

When using transformations to solve problems, we make use of the fact that reflections, rotations, and translations preserve lengths, angles, and areas. *Example 1* involved the invariance of length under a reflection.

Although dilations do not preserve length, they do preserve the ratios of lengths. This property is used in the following example.

Example 2. The image on the screen of a drive-in theatre is projected from a film 35 mm wide. The film is 150 mm in front of the light source and the screen is 14 m high. How far is the screen from the light source?

Solution. Draw a diagram.

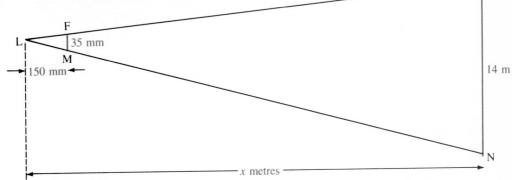

Let the distance from the light source L to the screen SN be x metres. Since the film FM maps onto the screen SN, $\triangle$LFM maps onto $\triangle$LSN under a dilation with center L.

Hence, $\triangle$LFM is similar to $\triangle$LSN.

Therefore, the ratios of corresponding lengths in the two triangles are equal.

$$\frac{150}{FM} = \frac{x}{SN}$$

$$\frac{150}{35} = \frac{x}{14}$$

$$x = \frac{150 \times 14}{35}$$

$$= 60$$

The screen is 60 m from the light source.

EXERCISES 12-8

Ⓐ

1. Show how to locate point R on line l such that PR + QR is a minimum.

2. a) Plot the points A(3,5) and B(7,2) on a grid.
   b) Locate the point M on the x-axis such that AM + MB is a minimum.
   c) Locate the point N on the y-axis such that AN + NB is a minimum.

Ⓑ

3. Using points A and B of *Exercise 2*, locate point M on the *y*-axis and point N on the *x*-axis such that AM + MN + NB is a minimum.

4. Copy this diagram.

   a) Draw the shortest path from P to l_1 to l_2 to Q.
   b) Draw the shortest path from P to l_2 to l_1 to Q.
   c) In finding the shortest path from P to Q, does it matter which line (l_1 or l_2) you go to first?

5. Two adjacent cushions of a billiard table can be represented by the *x*- and *y*-axes on a grid. Let the points B(3,6) and W(12,6) represent the positions of the brown ball and a white ball respectively.
   a) Find the coordinates of a point on the *x*-axis at which the white ball should be aimed so as to rebound and hit the brown ball.
   b) i) Find the coordinates of the point on the *x*-axis at which the white ball should be aimed so as to rebound from the *x*-axis to the *y*-axis and hit the brown ball.
      ii) What are the coordinates of the point where the ball hits the *y*-axis?

6. A fly lands at the point A(4,6) on a grid. It walks to the *y*-axis, then to the *x*-axis, and finally stops at the point B(8,3). What is the shortest distance the fly could have walked?

7. A film negative, measuring 13 mm by 17 mm, is 32 mm from a camera lens. What are the maximum dimensions of an object that can be photographed from a distance of 12.4 m?

8. To determine the distance AB across a river, a surveyor places a marker at C. She finds a point A′ in alignment with C and a prominent feature A on the far side of the river. Finally, she locates positions B and B′ so that ∠ABC = ∠A′B′C = 90°. If A′B′ = 3.8 m, B′C = 5.2 m, and BC = 14.7 m, how wide is the river at AB?

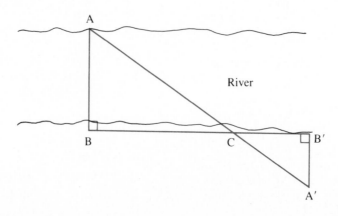

PROBLEM SOLVING

Choose the Strategy

1. A train 1 km long travels at 30 km/h through a tunnel 1 km long. How long does it take the train to clear the tunnel?

2. For which integers, n, do n and n^5 have the same ones digit?

3. a) Given 10 points on a circle, how many chords can be drawn joining them?
   b) How many chords can be drawn joining n points on a circle?

4. A sheet of 50 stamps is printed in 10 rows of 5 stamps. The edges of the stamps forming the sides of the sheet are straight. How many stamps have:
   a) 2 straight edges   b) 1 straight edge   c) no straight edge?

5. A girl is standing in line to buy a ticket. She observes that $\frac{1}{7}$ of all the people in line are in front of her while $\frac{5}{6}$ of all the people are behind her. How many people are in line?

6. a) Use the pattern suggested by the diagram to evaluate this expression.
   $$1 + 2 + 3 + \ldots + 9 + 10 + 9 + \ldots + 3 + 2 + 1$$
   b) Find a formula for this expression.
   $$1 + 2 + 3 + \ldots + (n - 1) + n + (n - 1) + \ldots + 3 + 2 + 1$$

7. Estimate the probability that a hand of 4 cards dealt from a standard deck of 52 cards contains exactly 2 black cards and 2 red cards.

8. The cost of printing greeting cards is a fixed amount, plus a fixed rate per card. The total cost of printing 8 greeting cards is $19.75 and the total cost of printing 20 greeting cards is $34.75. What is the cost of printing 15 cards?

9. What is the least number of pieces into which a circular pie can be divided by n cuts, where a cut corresponds to a chord of the circular pie?

Review Exercises

1. A translation maps $(-3,-1)$ onto $(2,-3)$.
   a) Find the images of A$(-2,4)$, B$(1,-5)$, and C$(4,1)$ under this translation.
   b) If P′$(2,-3)$, Q′$(0,4)$, and R′$(-5,1)$ are image points under this translation, find the original points.

2. Graph the points A$(2,5)$, B$(-3,1)$, and C$(1,-4)$. Find the image of each point under a reflection in:
   a) the x-axis
   b) the y-axis.

3. Graph the points L$(-2,-3)$, M$(4,-3)$, and N$(4,5)$. Find the image of each point under a 180° rotation about the origin.

4. The reflection images of A$(1,4)$, B$(3,-2)$, and C$(5,1)$ are A′$(-3,4)$, B′$(-5,-2)$, and C′$(-7,1)$. Graph both triangles and draw the reflection line.

5. Find the values of x and y.
   a)
   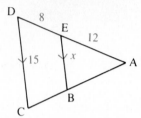
   b)
   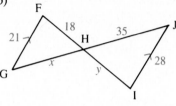

6. A building 18.2 m tall casts a shadow 7.1 m long. At the same time, how long is the shadow of a building that is 15.7 m tall?

7. A poster measures 30 cm by 45 cm. A copy is made, which has three times the area. What are its dimensions?

8. Find the values of x, y, and z.
   a)
   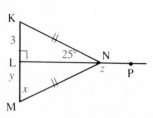
   b)
   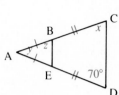
   c)
   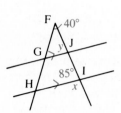

9. Copy the diagram. Draw the shortest path from P to l to m to Q.

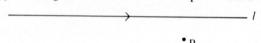

1. Solve by graphing.
   a) $x + 2y = 6$
      $2x - 3y = 5$
   b) $3x + y = 6$
      $2x + 4y = -1$
   c) $3x - 2y = -10$
      $6x + 8y = -2$

2. Solve by addition or subtraction.
   a) $2x + 3y = 7$
      $3x - 2y = 4$
   b) $x + 3y = 4$
      $3x - y = -18$
   c) $2x + 5y = -4$
      $3x + 2y = 5$

3. Solve by substitution.
   a) $y = 7 - 2x$
      $3x - 2y = 7$
   b) $2x + y = -5$
      $3x + 5y = 3$
   c) $4x - 3y = 7$
      $x - 2y = 8$

4. Sheila bought 7 baseball tickets, some at $8.50, the rest at $6.00. If she spent $49.50, how many of each did she purchase?

5. Two numbers have a sum of 26. Three times the first exceeds twice the second by 3. Find the numbers.

6. If the length of a rectangle is decreased by twice the width, the result is 8 cm. The perimeter is 40 cm. Find the dimensions.

7. The sum of the digits of a two-digit number is 10. The number formed by reversing the digits exceeds the original number by 36. Find the number.

8. Yasser invests $4500, part at 7%, the balance at $8\frac{1}{2}\%$. After one year, the interest earned on the 7% investment was $150 less than the interest earned on the $8\frac{1}{2}\%$ investment. How much was invested at each rate?

9. Triangle ABC has vertices A($-1,4$), B($-1,1$), and C($4,1$). Draw the image of △ABC under:
   a) a translation which maps P($3,5$) onto P'($6,7$)
   b) a reflection in the line $y = -1$
   c) a rotation of 90° about the origin
   d) a dilation with a scale factor of 2 and rotation center the origin.

10. A translation maps ($-2,1$) onto ($3,-1$).
    a) Find the images of P($2,4$), Q($-1,0$), and R($4,-2$) under this translation.
    b) If D'($-4,2$), E'($-2,-2$), and F'($1,3$) are image points under this translation, find the coordinates of the original points.

11. The reflection images of A($3,8$), B($1,3$), and C($6,7$) are A'($8,3$), B'($3,1$), and C'($7,6$). Graph these points and draw the reflection line.

12. The dilation image of a figure has an area of 450 cm². Find the area of the original figure for each dilation factor.
    a) 3
    b) $\frac{5}{8}$

13. The cenotaph in the town square casts a shadow of length 12.8 m. At the same time, a 1.5 m post casts a 2.1 m shadow. How tall is the cenotaph?

14. A 2.4 kg sample of nuts is found to contain 384 g of pecans, 864 g of peanuts, 768 g of hazel nuts, and the rest are cashews.
    a) What is the mass of the cashews?
    b) Draw a circle graph to display this information.
    c) What percent of the nuts are:
       i) pecans   ii) peanuts   iii) cashews?

15. Find the measures of central tendency for the following mathematics marks.

82	78	75	72	68	88	98	67	65	75
43	53	69	86	64	81	72	34	80	71
67	72	41	75	75	73	54	74	73	70

16. If each number in a set of data is increased by 3, how would each value change?
    a) the mean   b) the median   c) the mode

17. The probability of getting 4 heads on the toss of 4 coins is $\frac{1}{16}$.

    a) What is the probability of not getting 4 heads?
    b) What is the probability of getting 4 tails?

18. A pair of dice is rolled. Let A denote the event that the total number shown is even. Let B denote the event that the total number shown is less than 7.
    a) What outcomes are favorable to:
       i)   event A   ii)   event B   iii)   both events A and B?
    b) What is the probability of:
       i)   event A   ii)   event B   iii)   events A and B together?

19. In a card game known as "In Between", a player is dealt two cards. To win, the player must be dealt a third card with a value in between the first two. Calculate the probability of winning if the two cards already dealt are:
    a) a three and a seven   b) a nine and a Queen
    c) a four and a ten   d) a six and a seven.

20. What is the probability that in any year chosen at random the month of February has:
    a) exactly 28 days   b) 29 days
    c) 30 days   d) more than 27 days?

21. Kara says that the probability that a person can cross a street safely is $\frac{1}{2}$ because there are two possible outcomes, crossing safely or not crossing safely. Do you agree? Why?

Answers

The Nature of Mathematics
The Search for Pattern

Exercises, page xv

1. a) $1 + 3 + 5 + 7 = 4 \times 4$
$1 + 3 + 5 + 7 + 9 = 5 \times 5$
$1 + 3 + 5 + 7 + 9 + 11 = 6 \times 6$
b) $2 + 4 + 6 + 8 = 4 \times 5$
$2 + 4 + 6 + 8 + 10 = 5 \times 6$
$2 + 4 + 6 + 8 + 10 + 12 = 6 \times 7$

3. a) 17, 20, 23, 26, 29 **b)** Row 1

5. Answers may vary, for example,
1, 2, 3, 4, 5, 6, ...; 1, 2, 3, 1, 2, 3, 1, 2, 3, ...;
1, 2, 3, 5, 7, 10, 13, ... **7.** 16, 25, 36

The Value of Mathematical Investigation

Exercises, page xvii

1. a) 14 **b)** 24 **c)** 36
3. 35

The Power of Mathematical Reasoning

Exercises, page xix

1. a) Yes **b)** No **c)** No **d)** No

The Power of the Calculator

Exercises, page xxi

1. a) 2.283 333 3 **b)** 3.103 210 7
c) 7.071 031 7
3. Answers may vary.
5. a) 1 048 576 **b)** Answers may vary, with an
8-digit display, 2^{26} **c)** 2^{29}
7. Scientific notation 1×10^8
9. a) 9.83 08 **b)** 1.03 10 **c)** 2.345 09

The Power of the Computer

Exercises, page xxiii

1. a) 3.597 739 66 **b)** 4.499 205 34
c) 5.878 030 95 **d)** 6.792 823 42
e) 0.447 247 47 **f)** 0.914 792 47
3. a) 31 **b)** 83 **c)** 227 **d)** 616 **e)** 1674

The Utility of Mathematics

Exercises, page xxv

1. a) About 27.82 km **b)** About 464 m
3. Answers may vary.
5. a) About 1800 km **b)** About 30 km

A Famous Unsolved Problem

Exercises, page xxvi

1. 6:3,5; 5,7; 11,13; 17,19; 29,31; 41,43
3. Answers may vary. **a)** 3,7 **b)** 5,13 **c)** 11,19
d) 13,23 **e)** 17,29 **f)** 17,31 **g)** 3,19
5. 2,5; because one prime would have to be even, and
2 is the only prime that is even.
7. One number is odd, one is even, hence their
product is even.

Chapter 1

Exercises 1-1, page 4

1. a) True **b)** False **c)** Answers may vary.
d) True **e)** False **f)** True
3. a) True **b)** True **c)** False **d)** False
e) True **f)** False **g)** True **h)** False
i) False
5. a) Answers may vary. **b)** Cannot be
determined **d)** False **e)** True **f)** True
g) True **i)** False **k)** False

Exercises 1-2, page 7

1. a), c), e), h) Open sentences
b), d), f), g) Statements
3. a) {1, 2, 3, 4, 5, 6, 7} **b)** {2, 4, 6}
c) {1, 4} **d)** {2, 3, 5, 7}
5. a) {4} **b)** {16} **c)** {17} **d)** {4}
e) {1, 2, 3} **f)** {1, 2, 3}
g) {9, 10, 11, 12, 13, ...} **h)** { }
7. Answers may vary.
a) $n + 3 = 2$ **b)** $n > 0$

Exercises 1-3, page 10

1. Answers may vary.
a) Karen has not finished reading the book.
b) The radio is off.
c) The light is green.
d) The temperature is not rising.
e) Martha did go shopping.
f) The coin did not land heads.
3. a) Thanksgiving is not in November; this is false.
The statement is true.
b) February is the shortest month; this is true. The
statement is false.
c) The sun does not shine for 12 h each day; this
is true. The statement is false.
d) The Earth has two moons; this is false. The
statement is true.

e) $15 \times 8 \neq 120$; this is false. The statement is true.

f) $11 \times 29 \not> 500$; this is true. The statement is false.

5. a) False **b)** True **c)** True **d)** False

7. a) It is not true that every state has a capital city.
b) It is not true that some calculators have a square-root key.
c) It is not true that all apples are green.
d) It is not true that some boys do not like sports.

Exercises 1-4, page 14

1. a) True **b)** False **c)** True **d)** False
e) False **f)** False

3. a) Erik won a trip to Acapulco and Mina won $10 000. False
b) Erik won a trip to Acapulco and Mina did not win $10 000. True
c) Erik did not win a trip to Acapulco and Mina won $10 000. False
d) Erik did not win a trip to Acapulco and Mina did not win $10 000 cash. False

5. a) x is a perfect square less than 50. $\{1, 4, 9, 16, 25, 36, 49\}$
b) x is a multiple of 4 and of 6. $\{12, 24, 36, 48, 60, ...\}$
c) x is greater than 5 and less than 12. $\{6, 7, 8, 9, 10, 11\}$
d) n is an even prime number. $\{2\}$

7. a) My calculator does not need batteries and it does square roots. True
b) My calculator needs batteries and it does square roots. False
c) My calculator does not need batteries and it does not do square roots. False
d) My calculator needs batteries and it does not do square roots. False

9. a) It is not true that it is cold and windy today.
b) It is not true that I have a nickel and a dime in my pocket.

Exercises 1-5, page 18

1. a) True **b)** True **c)** False **d)** True
e) True **f)** False

3. a) Sharon went to the game or Barb went to the movies. True
b) Sharon went to the game or Barb did not go to the movies. True
c) Sharon did not go to the game or Barb went to the movies. False
d) Sharon did not go to the game or Barb did not go to the movies. True

5. a) x is between 3 and 10 or x is between 7 and 14.
b) One of these numbers **i)** 8, 9 **ii)** 4, 5, 6, 7 **iii)** 10, 11, 12, 13 **iv)** 1, 2, 3, 14, 15, 16, ...
c) $\{4, 5, 6, 7, 8, 9, 10, 11, 12, 13\}$

7. a) False **b)** True **c)** True **d)** False

9. a) True **b)** False **c)** True **d)** False

11. a) It is not true that John is wearing a jacket or a shirt.
b) It is not true that we will go swimming on Saturday or Sunday.

Exercises 1-6, page 23

1. a) Yesterday was Thursday. Today is Friday.
b) You get a good night's sleep. You will feel better in the morning.
c) You do your homework regularly. Your grades will improve.
d) We will stop for lunch. It rains.

3. a) $7 \times 5 = 35$; $7 \times 50 = 350$; true
b) $8 \times 3 = 26$; $3 \times 8 = 26$; true
c) $9 + 5 = 14$; $19 + 15 = 24$; false
d) $6 + 3 = 8$; $6 + 4 = 10$; true

5. a) One of these numbers
i) 4, 8, 12, 16, 20, 24, ... **ii)** No numbers exist
iii) 2, 6, 10, 14, 18, 22, ...
iv) 1, 3, 5, 7, 9, 11, 13, ...   Yes
b) One of these numbers
i) 6, 12, 18, 24, 30, ... **ii)** 3, 9, 15, 21, 27, ...
iii) No numbers exist
iv) 1, 2, 4, 5, 7, 8, 10, ...   No
c) One of these numbers
i) 1, 3 **ii)** 2, 4, 6, 12 **iii)** 5, 15
iv) 7, 8, 9, 10, 11, 13, 14, 16, ...   No
d) One of these numbers
i) 1, 3, 9 **ii)** No numbers exist **iii)** 27
iv) 2, 4, 5, 6, 7, 10, 11, 13, ...   Yes

7. a) If a natural number is a multiple of 5, then it is a multiple of 10. False
b) If two rectangles have the same length and width, then they have the same area. True
c) If an even number is a prime number, then it is 2. True
d) If a natural number is a perfect square, then it is not a prime number. True
e) If a number is a multiple of 4, then it is a multiple of 2. True

9. a) i) Yes **ii)** No **iii)** Yes **iv)** Yes; yes; if ABCD is a rectangle, then it is a parallelogram; all rectangles are parallelograms.
  b) i) Yes **ii)** No **iii)** Yes **iv)** Yes; yes; if △ABC is equilateral, then it is isosceles; all equilateral triangles are isosceles triangles.
  c) i) Yes **ii)** No **iii)** No **iv)** Yes; yes; if ∠DEF is a right angle, then it is 90°; all right angles are 90°.
  d) i) Yes **ii)** No **iii)** Yes **iv)** Yes; yes; if PQRS is a square, then it is a rhombus; all squares are rhombuses.

11. a) True **b)** False **c)** False **d)** True

Exercises 1-7, page 26

1. a) Yes **b)** Yes **c)** Yes **d)** No
3. Yes
5. No
7. a) No **b)** Yes

Exercises 1-8, page 28

1. a) True **b)** False **c)** False **d)** True
  e) True **f)** True
3. a) False **b)** True **c)** False **d)** False
  e) False **f)** False
5. a) False **b)** False **c)** False **d)** True
7. a) True **b)** False **c)** True **d)** False
  e) True **f)** True
9. a) True; true **b)** True; true **c)** False; false
  d) False; true

Problem Solving, page 31

1. Barb
3. a) White **b)** Cannot tell

Exercises 1-9, page 34

1. a) T T T T
  T F T T
  F T T F
  F F F F

b) T T T T
  T F F T
  F T F F
  F F F F

c) T T T T
  T F T T
  F T T T
  F F F T

d) T T T T
  T F F F
  F T T T
  F F T F

e) T T F T F
  T F T T F
  F T F F T
  F F T T F

f) T T F T T
  T F F F F
  F T T F T
  F F T F T

3. a) T T T T
  T F F F T
  F T T F T
  F F T F T

b) T T F F T F T
  T F F T F F F
  F T T F F F F
  F F T T F T T

5. Answers may vary.
  a) $p \rightarrow q$ **b)** $(p \rightarrow q) \wedge q$ **c)** $(p \vee q) \wedge p$

Exercises 1-10, page 37

1. a) If you live in Ohio, then you live in Cleveland; false. The conditional is true.
  b) If the ground is wet, then it rained; false. The conditional is true.
  c) If you pass the test, then you have studied; false. The conditional is false.
  d) If it is safe to cross the street, then the light is green; true. The conditional is true.
  e) If you don't win the lottery, then you didn't buy a ticket; false. The conditional is true.
3. a) If you do not live in Ohio, then you do not live in Cleveland; true. The conditional is true.
  b) If the ground is not wet, then it has not rained; true. The conditional is true.
  c) If you do not pass the test, then you have not studied; false. The conditional is false.
  d) If it is not safe to cross the street, then the light is not green; true. The conditional is true.
  e) If you win the lottery, then you bought a ticket; true. The conditional is true.
5. a) The conditional is true.
  If x is a multiple of 3, then x is a multiple of 6; false.
  If x is not a multiple of 6, then x is not a multiple of 3; false.
  If x is not a multiple of 3, then x is not a multiple of 6; true.
  b) The conditional is true.
  If $2x$ is not a prime number, then x is a prime number; false.
  If x is not a prime number, then $2x$ is a prime number; false.
  If $2x$ is a prime number, then x is not a prime number; true.
  c) The conditional is false.
  If a quadrilateral is a square, it has 4 right angles; true.
  If a quadrilateral does not have 4 right angles, it is not a square; true.
  If a quadrilateral is not a square, it does not have 4 right angles; false.

d) The conditional is true.
A parallelogram is a rectangle; false.
A figure that is not a rectangle is not a parallelogram; false.
A figure that is not a parallelogram is not a rectangle; true.

e) The conditional is true.
A multiple of 2 is a multiple of 4; false.
A number that is not a multiple of 4 is not a multiple of 2; false.
A number that is not a multiple of 2 is not a multiple of 4; true.

7. T T F F T T T T
T F F T F T T F
F T T F T F F T
F F T T T T T T

9. a) and **d)**
b) and **c)**

11. Answers may vary.
a) i) If two circles have the same area, they have the same radius.
ii) A multiple of 4 is a multiple of 2.
b) i) A parallelogram is a rectangle.
ii) If two rectangles have the same area, they have the same length.

13. Answers may vary.
a) i) If two circles have the same area, they have the same radius.
ii) Not possible
b) i) Not possible
ii) If a quadrilateral has 4 equal sides, then it is a square.

Exercises 1-11, page 44

1. a) True   **b)** True   **c)** False

3. a) If a triangle is equilateral, then it has 3 equal sides. A triangle is equilateral if and only if it has 3 equal sides; true.
b) If a polygon is a pentagon, then it has exactly 5 sides. A polygon is a pentagon if and only if it has exactly 5 sides; true.
c) If 2 circles have different areas, then they have different diameters.
Two circles have different areas if and only if they have different diameters; true.
d) If a quadrilateral is a rectangle, then it is a square. A quadrilateral is a rectangle if and only if it is a square; false.

5. a) x is an even number if and only if x is a multiple of 2.
b) Yes

7. a) $\triangle ABC$ is a right triangle if and only if the triangle contains a right angle.   **b)** Yes

9. a) True   **b)** True   **c)** False   **d)** True
e) True   **f)** False

11. a) If $x \neq 10$, then $x < 10$ or $x > 10$
$x \neq 10$ if and only if $x < 10$ or $x > 10$; true
b) If $x < z$, then $x < y$ and $y < z$
$x < z$ if and only if $x < y$ and $y < z$; false
c) If n is not a composite number, then n is a prime number.
n is a prime number if and only if n is not a composite number; false.

13. a) i) Yes   **ii)** Yes   **iii)** Yes
b) Examples may vary.

Exercises 1-12, page 48

1. a) and **e)**

3. a)

5. b)

7. a) Marlo likes brussels sprouts.
b) No conclusion
c) Marlo likes broccoli

9. a) No conclusion
b) No conclusion
c) x is a number less than 10 which is not a multiple of 3.
d) x is a multiple of 3 greater than 10.

11. Yes

13. a) x is divisible by 2.
b) No conclusion
c) x is not a multiple of 6.
d) x is not a factor of 6.

15. b), d), e) and **f)**

17. Exercise 15 f); explanations may vary.

Review Exercises, page 52

1. a), c), and **d)**

3. a) x is greater than 10 and less than 15; {11, 12, 13, 14}.
b) x is a factor of 12 and a factor of 20; {1, 2, 4}.

5. a) $37 \times 23 = 852$; $370 \times 230 = 85\,200$; true
b) ABCD is a rectangle; ABCD is a parallelogram; false

7. a) Both false   **b)** p is true; q is false
c) p is false and q is true   **d)** Both true

9. T T F F F T T T
T F F T T F T T
F T T F F T T T
F F T T F T F F

11. a) If you succeed, then you have worked hard; false.

If you have not worked hard, then you will not succeed; false.

If you do not succeed, then you have not worked hard; false.

b) If n is less than 10, then n is an even prime number; false.

If n is not an even prime number, then n is greater than or equal to 10; false.

If n is greater than or equal to 10, then n is not an even prime number; true.

Chapter 2

Exercises 2-1, page 56

1. B, -7; C, -5; F,0; H,4; I,6; K,9

3. a) a loss in altitude of 300 ft
b) a gain in altitude of 25 ft
c) a loss in altitude of 100 ft
d) a gain in altitude of 2 ft

5. a) a loss of \$10   **b)** an altitude gain of 500 ft
c) a 3 lb increase in weight
d) a temperature of $+14°C$
e) -18 **f)** $+11$ **g)** -7 **h)** 5

7. a) -2 **b)** -6 **c)** -8 **d)** -4 **e)** -9
f) -5 **g)** -10 **h)** -18 **i)** -16

9. a) $7,1,-2,-4$ **b)** $2,0,-1,-3$
c) $8,5,3,0,-2,-8$

11. a) -4 **b)** -5 **c)** 3 **d)** -7 **e)** 5 **f)** 0

Exercises 2-2, page 61

1. a) -4 **b)** 3   **c)** -3 **d)** 5   **e)** 5
f) -10 **g)** 8 **h)** 2 **i)** 2 **j)** 9 **k)** 6 **l)** 0

3. $+10°F$

5. a) $+20°F$ **b)** $+12°F$ **c)** $-54°F$
d) $+24°F$ **e)** $-8°F$ **f)** $-10°F$

7. a) -2 **b)** 5   **c)** -12 **d)** 2   **e)** 7
f) -1

9. a) i) 0   **ii)** 0   **iii)** 0   **iv)** 0   **v)** 0
vi) 0   **b)** The sum is zero.

11. a) -19 **b)** 9   **c)** 16   **d)** -4 **e)** -16
f) 8   **g)** -13 **h)** -11

13. a) -13 **b)** -8 **c)** 1   **d)** -1 **e)** 5
f) -11 **g)** -17 **h)** -21

15. a) 6   **b)** 1   **c)** -12 **d)** -15 **e)** 8
f) -2 **g)** 7   **h)** -2 **i)** -1 **j)** 0

17. $108°C$

Exercises 2-3, page 67

1. a) -30 **b)** -56 **c)** 63   **d)** 54
e) -60 **f)** 39   **g)** 72   **h)** -25 **i)** 25
j) -42 **k)** 12   **l)** 32   **m)** -42
n) -28 **o)** 27   **p)** 0

3. a) -9 **b)** -23 **c)** 2   **d)** -17 **e)** 7
f) -9 **g)** 4   **h)** -11 **i)** -11 **j)** 7

5. a) 70   **b)** -24 **c)** -120 **d)** 9   **e)** 18
f) -12 **g)** -5 **h)** 24   **i)** 120

7. a) The integers have the same sign.
b) The integers have opposite signs.
c) One of the integers is zero.

9. a) -11 **b)** -6 **c)** 0   **d)** -5 **e)** -2
f) 3   **g)** 2   **h)** 18   **i)** -3

Problem Solving, page 71

1. \$50, \$5, \$2, \$2, \$2, \$2   **3.** 13   **5.** 70¢/L

7. 2 ways: 3 @ 10, 5 @ 12, 2 @ 15;
5 @ 12, 4 @ 15

Exercises 2-4, page 76

1. A,1.7; B,1.0; C,-0.2; D,-1.6; E,-2.9; F,-3.5

3. a) $-\dfrac{1}{2}$ **b)** $-\dfrac{2}{3}$ **c)** $\dfrac{2}{5}$ **d)** $-\dfrac{2}{5}$ **e)** $\dfrac{6}{11}$ **f)** $\dfrac{1}{3}$
g) $\dfrac{2}{7}$ **h)** $-\dfrac{14}{25}$ **i)** $-\dfrac{3}{7}$ **j)** $-\dfrac{1}{3}$ **k)** $-\dfrac{3}{2}$ **l)** $\dfrac{2}{3}$

5. a) -4 **b)** -5 **c)** -7 **d)** 0 **e)** 0 **f)** -1
g) -1 **h)** 0 **i)** -8 **j)** -4 **k)** -17 **l)** -7

7. a) -2 **b)** -5 **c)** -1 **d)** -0.8
e) -2.5 **f)** -3.8 **g)** -8 **h)** -2 **i)** $-\dfrac{1}{4}$

9. a) $\dfrac{15}{4}, \dfrac{11}{4}, \dfrac{7}{4}, \dfrac{3}{4}$ **b)** $\dfrac{18}{5}, \dfrac{7}{5}, -\dfrac{9}{5}, -\dfrac{13}{5}$
c) $\dfrac{17}{9}, -\dfrac{10}{9}, -\dfrac{13}{9}, -\dfrac{20}{9}$ **d)** $-\dfrac{11}{7}, -\dfrac{15}{7}, -\dfrac{22}{7}, -\dfrac{25}{7}$

11. $-\dfrac{-18}{-9}, \dfrac{-3}{2}, \dfrac{10}{-8}, \dfrac{-12}{16}, \dfrac{5}{-10}, \dfrac{-5}{20}, \dfrac{-7}{-28}, -\dfrac{9}{-6}$

13. $\dfrac{-13}{20}, \dfrac{4}{-8}, \dfrac{-16}{40}, \dfrac{-3}{-15}, -\dfrac{19}{-60}, \dfrac{14}{30}$

15. $\dfrac{171}{188}, \dfrac{200}{201}$

Exercises 2-5, page 81

1. a) 3.232 323 23   **b)** 42.307 307 31
c) $-81.466\ 666\ 67$ **d)** 690.045 454 55
e) $-2.651\ 351\ 35$ **f)** 2.651 365 14
g) 0.069 069 07   **h)** $-0.007\ 474\ 75$

3. a) $0, 7, -17$ **b)** All are rational

5. a) $\dfrac{3}{4}$ **b)** $\dfrac{13}{4}$ **c)** $-\dfrac{5}{8}$ **d)** $\dfrac{1}{16}$ **e)** $-\dfrac{11}{4}$

f) $-\dfrac{47}{8}$ **g)** $\dfrac{82}{5}$ **h)** $-\dfrac{641}{16}$

7. 1.57, 1.14

9. $\dfrac{13}{15}, \dfrac{6}{7}, \dfrac{9}{11}, \dfrac{10}{13}, \dfrac{5}{8}$

11. a) 0.028 901 7   **b)** 0.289 017 3
c) 2.890 173 4   **d)** 28.901 734

Exercises 2-6, page 88

1. a) $\dfrac{4}{5}$ **b)** $\dfrac{4}{7}$ **c)** $-\dfrac{1}{6}$ **d)** $-\dfrac{1}{56}$ **e)** $\dfrac{1}{3}$

f) -3 **g)** $\dfrac{14}{5}$ **h)** -6

3. a) $\dfrac{1}{9}$ **b)** $-\dfrac{1}{23}$ **c)** $\dfrac{19}{16}$ **d)** $-\dfrac{13}{7}$ **e)** $-\dfrac{2}{3}$

f) 1.25   **g)** $\dfrac{4}{3}$ **h)** -0.4 **i)** -16

j) $-\dfrac{5}{3}$ **k)** $-\dfrac{1}{10}$ **l)** 100

5. a) $\dfrac{1}{4}$ **b)** $\dfrac{63}{40}$ **c)** $-\dfrac{5}{6}$ **d)** $\dfrac{3}{8}$ **e)** 3

f) $-\dfrac{8}{3}$ **g)** $-\dfrac{1}{2}$ **h)** $-\dfrac{14}{15}$ **i)** $\dfrac{22}{7}$

7. About -672.3 m

9. a) 6   **b)** $-\dfrac{1}{12}$ **c)** $-\dfrac{648}{175}$ **d)** $-\dfrac{1}{48}$

e) $-\dfrac{9}{128}$ **f)** $-\dfrac{6}{121}$ **g)** 42   **h)** $\dfrac{20}{3}$ **i)** $-\dfrac{21}{8}$

11. a) $\dfrac{13}{-14} > \dfrac{-14}{13}$ **b)** $\dfrac{-6}{7} > \dfrac{7}{-8}$

c) $\dfrac{-2387}{3592} > \dfrac{-2388}{3593}$

13. a) 1, 2, 4, 5, 8   **b)** 3, 6, 7, 9   **c)** 0

Exercises 2-7, page 92

1. a) $\dfrac{17}{12}$ **b)** $\dfrac{11}{35}$ **c)** $-\dfrac{11}{24}$ **d)** $-\dfrac{19}{24}$ **e)** $\dfrac{11}{18}$

f) $-\dfrac{22}{15}$ **g)** $-\dfrac{7}{20}$ **h)** $\dfrac{13}{8}$

3. a) $-\dfrac{11}{12}$ **b)** $\dfrac{7}{3}$ **c)** $-\dfrac{9}{8}$ **d)** $-\dfrac{11}{24}$ **e)** $\dfrac{11}{30}$

f) $\dfrac{11}{8}$ **g)** $-\dfrac{1}{12}$ **h)** 1

5. a) 2.536   **b)** 98.13   **c)** -51.2
d) -19.329 **e)** -3.49 **f)** 281.8
g) 567.37   **h)** 47.83   **i)** -0.15

7. a) $-\$161.5$ billion   **b)** $-\$92.5$ billion

9. a) 4   **b)** -8 **c)** 2   **d)** -8 **e)** -8 **f)** 18

Exercises 2-8, page 97

1. a) $-\dfrac{1}{12}$ **b)** $\dfrac{9}{8}$ **c)** $\dfrac{5}{24}$ **d)** $-\dfrac{17}{40}$ **e)** $\dfrac{37}{12}$

f) $-\dfrac{9}{5}$ **g)** $-\dfrac{4}{3}$ **h)** $-\dfrac{19}{18}$ **i)** $\dfrac{11}{4}$ **j)** $\dfrac{41}{70}$

3. a) -13.5 **b)** -6.4 **c)** -1.85 **d)** 62.6

5. a) $-\dfrac{11}{10}$ **b)** $-\dfrac{129}{98}$ **c)** $-\dfrac{18}{7}$ **d)** $-\dfrac{4}{33}$

e) $-\dfrac{31}{10}$ **f)** $\dfrac{32}{123}$

Exercises 2-9, page 101

1. a) True   **b)** True   **c)** True   **d)** True
e) False

3. a) Yes   **b)** Yes   **c)** No

5. a) Yes   **b)** Yes   **c)** Yes   **d)** Yes
e) Yes

7. a) True   **b)** True   **c)** True   **d)** True
e) True   **f)** False

9. a) -14π **b)** 1188π **c)** 1485π
d) $9x - 6$

11. 5340

Review Exercises, page 103

1. a) -6 **b)** -9 **c)** -55 **d)** 2
e) -104 **f)** -13

3. a) 3   **b)** -10 **c)** -7 **d)** 7   **e)** -5
f) 13   **g)** 9   **h)** -10

5. a) -11 **b)** 0   **c)** -13 **d)** -10
e) -3 **f)** 70   **g)** 6   **h)** -69

7. a) 120   **b)** 288   **c)** -800 **d)** 0
e) -18 **f)** 400

9. a) 1 **b)** -5 **c)** 1 **d)** 2 **e)** -13
f) 7 **g)** 21 **h)** -2
11. a) 0.375 **b)** $-0.\overline{571\ 428}$ **c)** $-0.58\overline{3}$
d) $2.\overline{2}$ **e)** -2.1875 **f)** $0.\overline{6}$
13. a) $-\dfrac{7}{12}$ **b)** $\dfrac{15}{32}$ **c)** $-\dfrac{21}{40}$ **d)** $-\dfrac{2}{3}$
e) $-\dfrac{2}{3}$ **f)** $\dfrac{192}{455}$
15. a) -5.0652 **b)** -0.6 **c)** $-29\ 717.16$
d) -32.8 **e)** 0.086 **f)** $0.967\ 73$
17. a) $-\dfrac{47}{72}$ **b)** $\dfrac{13}{60}$ **c)** $-\dfrac{91}{24}$

Chapter 3

Exercises 3-1, page 108

1. a) 15 **b)** The number of regions is 1 more than the position of the circle.
3. a) i) 20 **ii)** 380 **b)** The number of 0s is the number of Xs, multiplied by 1 less than the number of Xs. **c)** $a(a-1)$
5. a) 144 **b)** 25
c) i) The number of shaded squares is the number of the diagram multiplied by itself.
ii) The number of unshaded squares is twice the number of the diagram, plus 1.
d) $d \times d$
7. a) 22 **b)** 948
c) i) Multiply the number of the diagram by 6, then subtract 8.
ii) Cube the number of the diagram, then subtract the number of colored cubes.

Exercises 3-2, page 112

1. a) p, q; $6p$, $-2q$; $6, -2$
b) a, b, c; a, $-2b$, $9c$; $1, -2, 9$
c) C; $1.8C$, 32; $1.8, 32$ **d)** r; $2\pi r$; 2π
3. a) 352 **b)** $11d$ **c)** dr
5. a) 17 **b)** 45.5 **c)** -100 **d)** 72 **e)** 27
7. a) -1 **b)** $\dfrac{1}{4}$ **c)** $\dfrac{1}{30}$ **d)** $\dfrac{26}{55}$ **e)** $-\dfrac{59}{72}$
9. 120π cm²

Exercises 3-3, page 116

1. a) $11a$ **b)** $13m$ **c)** $-13x$ **d)** $9p$
e) $-37g$ **f)** $49b$ **g)** $52r$ **h)** $5w$ **i)** $-17p$
3. a) $m + 5$ **b)** $-c$ **c)** $10a + 3b$
d) $3x + 2y$ **e)** $8u - 8v - 7$
f) $5m + 4$ **g)** $-9x + y$ **h)** $6x - 3y + z$
i) $7p + 8q - 7$

5. a) $21a - 2b$ **b)** $-1 + 2m - 16n$
c) $-5y + 2z - 3$ **d)** $-13r + 9s + 4$
e) $25x - 4y - 3$ **f)** $-3m - 15x + 8$
g) 0 **h)** $-13c - 33d - 3$
7. a) 33 **b)** -32.5 **c)** -91 **d)** -6
e) 200 **f)** 81 **g)** -56 **h)** 14
9. a) $10x - 4y - 6z$ **b)** $2m - 4n - 12p$
c) $6a + 3b - 8c$ **d)** $-6x - 18y$
11. a) $7xy - 8yz - 5xz$ **b)** $4ab - 11bc - 6ac$
c) $5xyz + 9wxy - 11wyz$
13. a) $6x$; $2x^2$ **b)** $12z$; $6z^2$
c) $2w + 2z$; $xy + zw - zy$

Problem Solving, page 119

1. 3 g **3.** $9.75 **5.** $2.25 **7.** $31.74
9. 11 **11.** 11

Exercises 3-4, page 121

1. a) $3m - 24$ **b)** $18x + 90$ **c)** $11p + 77$
d) $-23a + 207$ **e)** $14p + 42$
f) $4a - 4b + 60$ **g)** $-56a - 8b + 8$
h) $12s + 66t - 30$
3. a) $15m + 1$ **b)** $-14c - 6d$ **c)** $8a + 4$
d) $11a + 2b + 15$
5. a) $11x + 6y$ **b)** $-18.2x - 12.6y$
c) $13x + 28.6y$ **d)** $26.2x - 11.5y$
7. a) $8ax - 8ay$ **b)** $6bc - 22ac$
c) $-5x^4 + 9x^3 - 8x^2 + 12x$ **d)** $2xy - 4x^2 + y$
e) $3x + 6y^2 - 5xy$ **f)** $4pq - 5p^2 + q^2$
g) $x^2 + 2xy - 3y^2$ **h)** $6a^2 + 3ab + 3b^2$
9. a) -27.3 **b)** 21.7 **c)** -30.9 **d)** 38.01

Exercises 3-5, page 125

Letters may vary.

1. a) $n + 5$ **b)** $m - 6$ **c)** $8x$ **d)** $\dfrac{1}{5}f$
e) $8e$ **f)** $5f + 4$ **g)** $8t - 2$ **h)** $8(b - 2)$
i) $\dfrac{1}{4}c + 3$ **j)** $\dfrac{1}{4}(s + 3)$
3. a) Six more than a number
b) Ten less than a number
c) One-quarter of a number
d) Ten times a number
e) Three-tenths of a number, and four
f) Three times a number, and two
g) Five less than four times a number
h) The product of three less than a number, and two
i) One-third of the sum of a number and five
j) The product of a number, and three less than the number.

5. a) $h, h + 1$ **b)** $a, a + 1, a + 2$
 c) $p, \dfrac{36}{p}$ **d)** $t, t + 2$

7. a) a years, $(a + 12)$ years   **b)** $f, \dfrac{1}{5}f$
 c) a years, $(21 - a)$ years   **d)** j centimetres, $(j + 15)$ centimetres   **e)** $s, 1.1s$ **f)** $p, \dfrac{76}{p}$
 g) $i, i + 1, i + 2$ **h)** $p, p + 2, p + 4$

Review Exercises, page 127

1. a) 37   **b)** The number of matchsticks is one more than three times the number of squares.
 c) $3s + 1$
3. a) $6x, 4y, 3z$ **b)** x, y, z **c)** 6, 4, 3
5. a) $12x$ **b)** $17m$ **c)** $9x$ **d)** $7a + 7b$ **e)** $8x + 2y$
 f) $25c - 2d$ **g)** m **h)** $9w + x$ **i)** $10e - 0.5f$
 j) $-1.1c - 4.8d$
7. a) $-2x - 3$ **b)** $-10a + 3b$
 c) $-3p - 7q$ **d)** $-5m - 11n$
 e) $-9e + 16f + 10g$ **f)** $-10b + 2c - 4d$
9. a) $4m + 17n - 17$ **b)** $3a - 5b + 2$
 c) $10x - 11y - z - 8$ **d)** $25d - 18e - 16$
 e) $0.9x - 1.5y + 2.4z$ **f)** $-5.1a - 3.3b$
11. a) $\dfrac{1}{10}n$ **b)** $11p$ **c)** $q + 20$ **d)** $r - 31$
 e) $5s + 14$ **f)** $\dfrac{1}{7}t + 19$

Cumulative Review, Chapters 1-3, page 129

1. a) i), iii), iv) are open sentences
 ii), v) are statements
 b) {4, 6, 8, 10, ...}; {12, 14, 16, 18, ...}
3. a) $x > 5$ and x is a factor of 24; {6, 8, 12, 24}
 b) $x > 5$ or x is a factor of 24;
 {1, 2, 3, 4, 6, 7, 8, ...}
5. Column headings are: p, q, $\sim p$, $p \wedge q$, $\sim p \vee q$,
 $\sim (p \wedge q)$, $(\sim p \vee q) \rightarrow \sim (p \wedge q)$
 T T F T T F F
 T F F F F T T
 F T T F T T T
 F F T F T T T
7. a) -37 **b)** 35   **c)** -17 **d)** -45
 e) 23   **f)** -8
9. a) 18 **b)** 39 **c)** 58 **d)** 30 **e)** -8 **f)** 12
11. a) 9.49   **b)** $-\dfrac{15}{8}$ **c)** $-\dfrac{47}{18}$ **d)** $-\dfrac{13}{30}$
 e) -3.187 **f)** $\dfrac{13}{6}$ **13.** 323 m³

15. a) -14 **b)** 36   **c)** -26.6
17. a) $-7a - 11b$ **b)** $12m - 22n$
 c) $-2x - 38y$ **d)** $-36p - 36q$

Chapter 4

Exercises 4-1, page 133

1. a) 15   **b)** 17   **c)** 34   **d)** 35   **e)** 36
 f) 0 **g)** 15 **h)** -5
3. a) 8.5   **b)** 20   **c)** 3   **d)** 16   **e)** 8.6
 f) 2 **g)** 1 **h)** 0.5
5. a) 5   **b)** 2   **c)** 4   **d)** 16   **e)** 20
 f) 11   **g)** 3   **h)** 12   **i)** -6 **j)** -7
 k) -11 **l)** -9
7. 182 chirps/min

Exercises 4-2, page 135

1. a) 6   **b)** 13   **c)** 9   **d)** 13   **e)** 36
 f) 6   **g)** 84   **h)** 28
3. a) -4 **b)** -6 **c)** 10   **d)** -6 **e)** -5
 f) -11 **g)** 3 **h)** -23
5. a) -13 **b)** -10 **c)** 8 **d)** 10 **e)** -32 **f)** 12
 g) 0 **h)** 1.5
7. a) -8 **b)** -24 **c)** 13   **d)** 75   **e)** 5
 f) -4 **g)** 4   **h)** 27   **9.** 963 km
11. a) $b - a$ **b)** $d + c$ **c)** $\dfrac{m}{3}$ **d)** $4w$
 e) $a - 3b$ **f)** $4c - 4d$ **g)** $z - 2y$
 h) $2a - b + c$ **i)** $\dfrac{b - c}{a}$ **j)** $\dfrac{m - n}{k}$
 k) $\dfrac{-b - d}{c}$ **l)** $qr - pq$

Exercises 4-3, page 138

1. a) 8 **b)** 4 **c)** -2 **d)** 5 **e)** -9 **f)** -5
 g) -2 **h)** 5 **i)** -1 **j)** 3 **k)** 3 **l)** -3
3. a) -9 **b)** 16   **c)** 16   **d)** -6 **e)** -4.4
 f) 0.5 **g)** 0.6 **h)** -30 **i)** 8
5. a) 20 **b)** -30 **c)** 8 **d)** 4.5 **e)** -1 **f)** -16.8
7. a) i) -1 **ii)** 8   **iii)** 0.5   **iv)** 6.2   **v)** 2
 b) i) $\dfrac{2}{3}$ **ii)** 1   **iii)** $-\dfrac{1}{15}$ **iv)** 7   **v)** -36
9. a) 250   **b)** 3

Problem Solving, page 141

1. $\dfrac{2}{3}$ **3.** 1 h 12 min   **5.** 1 m²   **7.** 25%
9. 7 cards, 5 cards   **11.** 72

Exercises 4-4, page 143

1. a) 2   **b)** -4 **c)** -1 **d)** -2 **e)** 2   **f)** 0   **g)** -2 **h)** 3   **i)** $\frac{2}{3}$ **j)** $\frac{1}{2}$ **k)** $\frac{1}{6}$ **l)** $\frac{7}{2}$ **m)** $\frac{11}{6}$ **n)** 2

3. a) $\frac{9}{5}$ **b)** 10   **c)** -13 **d)** $-\frac{9}{7}$ **e)** $\frac{1}{10}$ **f)** 4   **g)** -2 **h)** $\frac{2}{3}$

5. a) 0   **b)** -2 **c)** 15   **d)** 8   **e)** 3   **f)** $-\frac{1}{8}$

Exercises 4-5, page 145

1. a) 2   **b)** $-\frac{10}{3}$ **c)** $-\frac{5}{6}$ **d)** 12   **e)** -16 **f)** 14   **g)** 20   **h)** -12 **i)** $-\frac{3}{14}$

3. $\frac{2}{5}$

5. a) $\frac{65}{14}$ **b)** $\frac{9}{7}$ **c)** $-\frac{2}{5}$ **d)** -1 **e)** $\frac{1}{17}$ **f)** 1   **g)** $\frac{21}{5}$ **h)** $-\frac{5}{16}$ **i)** $\frac{186}{191}$ **j)** $\frac{119}{59}$

Exercises 4-6, page 149

1. \$21.88

3. a) $\frac{p-n}{m}$ **b)** $2c + 2d$ **c)** $\frac{b+d}{a}$ **d)** $\frac{3(k-3)}{2}$ **e)** $\frac{v-1}{w}$ **f)** $\frac{a-d}{b}$

5. a) 140.1 cm²   **b)** 4.5 cm

7. a) $\frac{V}{\pi r^2}$ **b)** $\frac{Fd}{M}$ **c)** $\frac{IP}{100}$ **d)** $\frac{2A}{a+b}$ **e)** $\frac{v}{4n}$ **f)** $3c - 3b$

9. a) $\frac{l-14.3}{0.27}$ **b) i)** 310 g   **ii)** 329 g

11. a) 16 cm   **b)** 4.5 cm

Problem Solving, page 151

1. 9 cones   **3.** 17   **5.** 7 m

7. a) Answers may vary, for example, every number can be considered as a multiple of 6 plus 1, 2, 3, 4 or 5. **b)** $6n + 1$, $6n + 5$

Exercises 4-7, page 153

1. a) x **b)** $x + 8$ **c)** $x + x + 8 = 42$

3. a) m **b)** $12 - m$ **c)** $m = \frac{1}{3}(12 - m)$

Equations may vary. **5.** $d + d - 2 = 12$

7. $2(w + w + 5) = 68$

9. $n + n + 1 + n + 2 + n + 3 = 234$

11. $x + \frac{1}{5}x = 18$

13. $g + g - 9 = 33$

15. a) $x + x + 1 = 83$ **b)** $x + x - 17 = 39$

17. a) y **b)** $65 - y$ **c)** $3y + 15 = 2(65 - y)$

19. $3x = 14 + 2(63 - x)$

21. $l - 4 + 2l - 4 = 37$

23. $x + x + 5 + 3(x + 5) = 75$

Exercises 4-8, page 156

1. 16   **3.** 64   **5.** 22, 23   **7.** 6 m, 16 m
9. 59.5 kg, 62.0 kg   **11.** 3.90 m, 3.75 m
13. 48, 49   **15.** 12 km, 6 km   **17.** 16 cm, 11 cm
19. 52, 53, 54   **21.** 112, 114   **23.** 20
25. 108, 12   **27.** 7, 29   **29.** 11, 16, 48

Exercises 4-9, page 159

1. $[5x + 10(80 - x)]$ cents

3. $2x - 1$, $2x + 1$, $2x - 4$, $2x + 3$; $x - 1$, $x + 1$, $x - 4$, $x + 3$

5. 34 years, 17 years   **7.** 6 years   **9.** 30 m
11. 136   **13.** \$16.25   **15.** 18 cm, 20 cm, 22 cm
17. 70 m

Exercises 4-10, page 164

1. a) $x < 3$ **b)** $x \leq 4$ **c)** $x > -1$
d) $x > 5$ **e)** $x \leq -2$ **f)** $x \leq 6$

3. a) $x < 2$ **b)** $x \geq 2$ **c)** $x > -\frac{9}{2}$
d) $y > 3$ **e)** $z < 2$ **f)** $y \leq 2.5$
g) $x \leq -16$ **h)** $w > 5$ **i)** $a \geq -9$

5. a) $y < -\frac{3}{4}$ **b)** $z \geq -\frac{5}{2}$ **c)** $x \leq 2$
d) $a < -2$ **e)** $b \leq -3$ **f)** $c < \frac{26}{3}$
g) $x > \frac{3}{2}$ **h)** $y \leq \frac{29}{9}$

Review Exercises, page 165

1. a) − 16   **b)** 97   **c)** 28   **d)** 10   **e)** − 34
   f) 2

3. a) 3   **b)** 3   **c)** −7   **d)** $\frac{4}{5}$ **e)** $\frac{5}{4}$ **f)** $\frac{7}{5}$

5. a) 3   **b)** 1   **c)** −7   **d)** 3   **e)** $\frac{5}{2}$
   f) $-\frac{29}{5}$

7. a) − 1   **b)** 14   **c)** 11   **d)** $\frac{49}{3}$

9. a) i) 120 cm   **ii)** 100 cm   **iii)** 80 cm
   iv) 52 cm   **b) i)** 90 cm   **ii)** 67.5 cm

11. 5   **13.** 8 km, 6 km   **15.** 5 dimes, 8 quarters

17. 49, 14

19. a) $x < -4$ **b)** $x \geq 0$ **c)** $x > -2$ **d)** $x \leq 1$

Chapter 5

Exercises 5-1, page 170

3. a) ∠ADB, ∠BDC, ∠ADC   **b)** ∠PTQ, ∠PTR,
   ∠PTS, ∠QTR, ∠QTS, ∠RTS

5. a) Infinite number, 2, 1, 0   **b)** 2, 1, 0

7. a) Infinite number, 1, 0
   b) Infinite number, 2, 1, 0

Exercises 5-2, page 174

5. d) Answers may vary, for example, ∠AOB is 180°
   hence half of it (or the sum of half of the angles
   into which it is divided) is 90°.

Exercises 5-4, page 181

1. a) ∠ABC is acute.   **b)** ∠PQR is straight.
   c) ∠XYZ is reflex.   **d)** ∠DEF is right.

3. a) 97°, 97°   **b)** 80°, 30°   **c)** 50°, 60°

5. The lines are perpendicular.   **7.** 286°

9. Supplementary angles:
   b) ∠DHE, ∠EHG or ∠DHF, ∠FHG
   c) ∠JNK, ∠KNM or ∠JNL, ∠LNM
   d) ∠DBA, ∠ABC
   e) ∠HJE, ∠EJG or ∠EJG, ∠GJF or ∠GJF, ∠FJH
   or ∠FJH, ∠HJE
   Complementary angles: **a)** ∠ABD, ∠DBC
   b) ∠EHD, ∠FHG   **f)** ∠NPL, ∠LPM

11. Answers may vary.

The Mathematical Mind, page 185

1. Yes   **3.** No   **5.** No   **7.** Several

Exercises 5-5, page 187

1. a) ∠MLS, ∠NSL; ∠KLS, ∠PSL
   b) ∠QLK, ∠LSN; ∠KLS, ∠NSR; ∠QLM,
   ∠LSP; ∠MLS, ∠PSR
   c) ∠KLS, ∠LSN; ∠MLS, ∠PSL

3. a) 120°, 60°, 60°, 60°   **b)** 55°, 115°, 55°
   c) 130°, 55°, 75°, 75°

5. No

Computer Power, page 189

1. 360°

3. The sum of the exterior angles of a triangle is 360°.

5. 540°

Exercises 5-6, page 191

1. △GHJ is right; △DEF is acute; △ABC is right,
   △KLM is obtuse.

3. a) 80°   **b)** 20°   **c)** 125°

5. a) The sum of the angles is 180°.   **b)** By folding

7. Reasons may vary. **a), b)** yes; **c), d), e), f)** no

9. a) 8   **b) i)** △ABE, △ADE
   ii) △ACB, △ECB, △DCE, △DCA
   iii) △ABD, △EBD

11. a) 125°   **b)** 145°   **c)** 48°   **d)** 36°

13. 360°

Problem Solving, page 195

1. Eagles   **3.** 37.5 cm²   **5.** 9 trains   **7.** 5 min

9. No, the sum of 2 sides of a triangle must be greater
   than the third side.

Exercises 5-7, page 198

1. a) 70°   **b)** 25°   **c)** 75°   **d)** 45°   **e)** 50°
   f) 60°   **g)** 150°   **h)** 120°   **i)** 100°

3. a) 108°, 144°   **b)** 100°, 40°   **c)** 30°, 90°
   d) 27°, 49.5°   **e)** 105°   **f)** 40°, 140°

5. a) Subtract $2x$ from 180°.
   b) i) 40°   **ii)** 130°   **iii)** 94°
   c) Subtract y from 180° and divide by 2.
   d) i) 50°   **ii)** 35°   **iii)** 81.5°
   e) $y = 180° - 2x$ **7.** 30 m

9. a) 30°, 120° or 75°, 75°
   b) 40°, 100° or 70°, 70°   **c)** 80°, 20° or 50°, 50°
   d) 45°, 45°   **e)** 35°, 35°

Exercises 5-8, page 205

1. **a)** MR = CL; RX = LP; MX = CP;
   ∠M = ∠C; ∠R = ∠L; ∠X = ∠P
   b) QP = QR; SP = SR; ∠P = ∠R;
   ∠PQS = ∠RQS; ∠PSQ = ∠RSQ
3. **a)** △ABC ≅ △DEF SAS   **b)** Not congruent
   c) △MNP ≅ △QRS AAS   **d)** Not congruent
   e) △MNL ≅ △PNL SSS
   f) △RUT ≅ △TSR SSS
5. **a)** 4 cm, 5 cm, 6 cm   **b)** 50°, 5 cm, 8 cm
   c) 131°, 6 cm, 9 cm   **d)** 4 cm, 2 cm, 3 cm
   e) 7 cm, 9 cm, 120°   **f)** 90°, 30°, 5 cm

Exercises 5-9, page 210

1. Reasons may vary.
   a) Yes; no   **b)** Yes; no   **c)** Yes; no
   d) Yes; no   **e)** No; no   **f)** Yes; no
3. Reasons may vary.
5. The properties of a parallelogram
7. **a)** 60°, 90°, 108°, 120°, 135°, 144°
   b) $\dfrac{180°(n-2)}{n}$

Exercises 5-10, page 214

1. **a)** Parallelogram, 124.2 in²
   b) Square, 4225 cm² **c)** Triangle, 3900 mm²
   d) Trapezoid, 25.41 ft²
3. $(2x^2 + 5x)$ in²   **5.** $(2x^2 + 10x)$ yd²   **7.** 20 m
9. 10 cm   **11.** 2 cm and 6 cm

Mathematics Around Us, page 217

1. As B approaches C, the sum of the angles
   decreases to 180° just before B coincides with C;
   as B moves away from C, the sum of the angles
   increases to a maximum 360° when B and C are on
   opposite sides of the globe.
3. Great-circle routes because they are shorter.
5. **a)** 187°   **b)** 266°   **c)** 443°

Exercises 5-11, page 220

1. **a)** 5 **b)** 13 **c)** 41 **d)** 8 **e)** 9 **f)** 24
3. **a)** 5.0 m, 13.0 m   **b)** 6.4 cm, 9.5 cm
   c) 5.3 cm, 4.6 cm   **d)** 1.4 units, 1.7 units,
   2.0 units   **e)** 2.1 cm   **f)** 28.0 cm
5. 8.0 m
7. No, because the greatest length in the box (the
   diagonal) is only 1.14 m long.
9. **a)** 8.5 cm   **b)** 62.5%
11. **a)** 12 cm²   **b)** Answers may vary.

Computer Power, page 223

1. **a)** 47   **b)** 126   **c)** 185   **d)** 47.2
   e) 4.79   **f)** 549   **g)** 28.7

Review Exercises, page 224

1. **a)** 37.5°, 35°   **b)** 130°, 100°   **c)** 120°, 120°
3. **a)** 10.9, 4.9   **b)** 10.0, 18.0
5. **a)** 30°   **b)** 80°   **c)** 60°

Chapter 6

Exercises 6-1, page 228

1. **a)** y^4 **b)** $(-3)^6$ **c)** $\left(\dfrac{2}{5}\right)^5$ **d)** $\left(-\dfrac{3}{8}\right)^3$
   e) $(4a)^5$ **f)** 2.9^4 **g)** m^4 **h)** $(-6x)^5$
   i) π^6 **j)** a^7
3. **a)** 64   **b)** 81   **c)** −32   **d)** 25
   e) 10 000   **f)** $\dfrac{1}{16}$ **g)** 0.008   **h)** 4.41
   i) 48   **j)** $\dfrac{9}{2}$ **k)** 1296   **l)** 162
5. **a)** 1000(2)¹   **b)** 1000(2)²   **c)** 1000(2)⁶
   d) 1000(2)¹⁰
7. **a)** 25   **b)** 10   **c)** 19   **d)** 175   **e)** 70
   f) 4   **g)** $\dfrac{56}{9}$ **h)** 5   **i)** 6.52   **j)** 19 705
9. **a)** −27   **b)** 36   **c)** 36   **d)** 144   **e)** 1
   f) 1   **g)** −1   **h)** −65 536   **i)** 1296
   j) $-\dfrac{27}{64}$ **k)** $-\dfrac{3125}{243}$ **l)** −1728
11. **a)** Multiply 1000 by 2 raised to a power equal to
   the time elapsed in hours.   **b)** 1000(2)ⁿ
   c) i) 5600 **ii)** 11 200 **iii)** 1400 **d)** 01:00
13. **a)** $0 < y < 1$ **b)** $x > 1$; $x < 0$
15. **a)** 5³   **b)** 3⁴   **c)** 10⁴   **d)** 11¹¹   **e)** 3⁶
   f) Numbers are equal.

Calculator Power, page 230

1. **a)** 180   **b)** −56   **c)** 1   **d)** 1   **e)** 74
   f) 169   **g)** 137.7   **h)** 94.09
3. **a)** 37.5   **b)** −352   **c)** −567
   d) 1 229 312   **e)** 13 122   **f)** −54 859.9688
   g) 3888   **h)** −4608

Exercises 6-2, page 233

1. a) 2.5^2 **b)** $(3a)^2$ **c)** $\left(\dfrac{2}{3}x\right)^2$ **d)** $\dfrac{1}{2}\pi r^2$

e) $\dfrac{1}{2}(5w)^2$ **f)** $36x^2$

3. a) 25 cm² **b)** 81 m² **c)** 2.25 cm²
d) 187.69 m² **e)** 0.36 cm² **f)** 6.76 m²
g) $16a^2$ square units **h)** $25x^2$ square units

5. a) 45 cm² **b)** 59 mm² **c)** 55 cm²
d) 4 cm² **e)** 85 cm² **f)** 80 mm² **g)** 229 cm²

7. \$980.18 **9.** 32.7 L **11.** 7.2 L

13. a) i) 29 cm² **ii)** 115 cm² **iii)** 461 cm²
iv) 0.2 m² **b) i)** 90 cm **ii)** 120 cm
iii) 2.5 m **iv)** 15 mm

Exercises 6-3, page 237

1. a) 3^{10} **b)** 7^{11} **c)** $(-5)^{25}$ **d)** $(2.1)^{16}$

e) $(-8)^6$ **f)** $(-1.7)^7$ **g)** $\left(\dfrac{2}{5}\right)^{22}$

h) $\left(\dfrac{3}{11}\right)^{36}$ **i)** $\left(-\dfrac{5}{4}\right)^{14}$

3. a) 3^5 **b)** 2^9 **c)** m^{15} **d)** s^{12} **e)** $-7z^8$
f) $3r^{16}$ **g)** 6^6 **h)** $(-2)^4$

5. a) m^{20} **b)** $(-t)^{15}$ **c)** a^{49} **d)** 2^{12}
e) 12^{35} **f)** 10^{12} **g)** $(-5)^{12}$ **h)** z^{27}

7. a) $5d^3$ **b)** $-9a^9$ **c)** $6z$ **d)** $3m^6$

e) $-4x^8$ **f)** $\dfrac{5a^{15}}{2}$ **g)** $3(2)^4$ **h)** $-6(3)^{12}$

i) $2n^9$ **j)** $\dfrac{3c^5}{2}$ **k)** $9m^{18}$ **l)** $-4a^8$

9. 10^{22}

Exercises 6-4, page 242

1. a) $\dfrac{1}{2}$ **b)** $\dfrac{1}{5}$ **c)** $\dfrac{1}{9}$ **d)** $\dfrac{1}{8}$ **e)** $\dfrac{1}{125}$

f) $\dfrac{1}{100}$ **g)** $\dfrac{1}{1728}$ **h)** $\dfrac{1}{10\,000}$ **i)** 1 **j)** 16

k) $\dfrac{1}{100\,000}$ **l)** 5 **m)** 32 **n)** 48 **o)** $\dfrac{16}{9}$

p) 10 **q)** 1000 **r)** 4

3. a) 5^{11} **b)** 2^6 **c)** 3^{15} **d)** 7^{-10} **e)** 11^7
f) $(-5)^{-30}$ **g)** 6^{-23} **h)** $(-9)^0$ **i)** 19^{-19}

5. a) $\dfrac{82}{9}$ **b)** $\dfrac{80}{9}$ **c)** $-\dfrac{80}{9}$ **d)** 1 **e)** 81 **f)** $\dfrac{1}{81}$

7. a) -8 **b)** $-\dfrac{1}{8}$ **c)** $\dfrac{1}{8}$ **d)** 1 **e)** -1

f) $\dfrac{1}{8}$ **g)** $-\dfrac{1}{3}$ **h)** $\dfrac{256}{9}$ **i)** $-\dfrac{9}{2}$

9. $3^{-2},\ 3^{-5},\ 3^{-4},\ 3^3,\ 3^{-6},\ 3^0;\ \dfrac{1}{729},\ \dfrac{1}{243},\ \dfrac{1}{81},\ \dfrac{1}{9},\ 1,\ 27$

11. a) 11^{-2} **b)** 13^{-2} **c)** 10^{-2} **d)** $10(10^{-2})$

e) 10^{-5} **f)** 5^{-3} **g)** $\left(\dfrac{100}{9}\right)^{-2}$ **h)** 12^{-3}

13. a) x^{-12} **b)** y^2 **c)** 3^{16} **d)** 2^{-20} **e)** 1
f) 8^{-13} **g)** w^{-2} **h)** 5^{-18} **i)** x^{-12}

15. a) $10n^{13}$ **b)** $4t^7$ **c)** $5x^{10}$ **d)** $4w^{-6}$ **e)** $-28a^{-6}$
f) $-72y^8$ **g)** $5s^{-20}$ **h)** $12m^{-9}$ **i)** $-6x^{-3}$

17. a) $-\dfrac{1}{3}$ **b)** $\dfrac{1}{3}$ **c)** $\dfrac{1}{6}$ **d)** $-\dfrac{1}{2}$ **e)** $-\dfrac{5}{6}$

f) 9 **g)** 1 **h)** $\dfrac{1}{27}$ **i)** $\dfrac{25}{81}$

19. a) i) 8 **ii)** $-\dfrac{1}{8}$ **b) i)** -8 **ii)** $\dfrac{1}{8}$

c) i) -8 **ii)** $\dfrac{1}{8}$ **d) i)** 8 **ii)** $-\dfrac{1}{8}$

e) i) $\dfrac{1}{8}$ **ii)** -8 **f) i)** $-\dfrac{1}{8}$ **ii)** 8

g) i) $-\dfrac{1}{8}$ **ii)** 8 **h) i)** $\dfrac{1}{8}$ **ii)** -8

Exercises 6-5, page 247

1. a) 1.0×10^3 **b)** 1.0×10^8 **c)** 1.0×10^2
d) 7.5×10^2 **e)** 1.1×10^3 **f)** 3.7×10^6
g) 1.0×10^{-4} **h)** 1.0×10^{-7} **i)** 1.0×10^{-6}
j) 8.5×10^{-4} **k)** 9.2×10^{-5} **l)** 8.2×10^{-9}
m) 8.5×10^1 **n)** 3.8×10^{-2} **o)** 9.9×10^3
p) $3.210\,012 \times 10^6$

3. a) 1.3×10^6°C **b)** 1.0×10^{-5} m
c) 0.000 000 000 000 000 000 000 000 92 g
d) 120 000 000 000 **e)** 4.5×10^9 years
f) 1.13×10^{-8} cm **g)** 150 000 000 km²
h) 360 000 000 km²
i) 5 900 000 000 000 000 000 000 kg
j) 8.5×10^9 F

5. a) 3 **b)** 1 **c)** -3 **d)** -1 **e)** -3
f) -5 **g)** 3 **h)** 9 **i)** 6 **j)** -7

7. a) 1.1×10^{14} **b)** 3.9×10^6 **c)** 9.9×10^7
d) 5.5×10^4 **9.** \$1 000 000 000

11. About 8.3×10^{-4} g

13. a) 3.1536 m³ **b)** 33 h 20 min

15. 1×10^{-6} mm

Mathematics Around Us, page 249

1. a) 500 **b)** 250
3. a) 1688   **b)** 844   **c)** 422

Problem Solving, page 251

1. Answers may vary.   **a)** The present time
   b) 8 h earlier than the present time
3. a) 900   **b)** 900   **c)** 27 000   **5.** 17 cm

Exercises 6-6, page 254

1. a) $9, -9$ **b)** $100, -100$ **c)** $30, -30$
   d) $0.4, -0.4$ **e)** $120, -120$ **f)** $200, -200$
   g) $0.8, -0.8$ **h)** $0.01, -0.01$ **i)** $70, -70$
   j) $0.5, -0.5$
3. a) 4 m   **b)** 100 mm   **c)** 2.5 cm   **d)** 8 m
   e) 100 m   **f)** 70 m
5. a) 10 **b)** 15 **c)** 5 **d)** 7 **e)** 6 **f)** -5
   g) 4 **h)** 8 **i)** -32 **j)** -12 **k)** 4 **l)** 10
7. a) i) 17 mm   **ii)** 68 mm   **b) i)** 2.1 cm
   ii) 8.4 cm **c) i)** 0.08 m   **ii)** 0.32 m
9. a) i) 5.02 m   **ii)** 15.05 m   **b) i)** 8.03 m
   ii) 24.08 m   **c) i)** 0.90 m   **ii)** 2.71 m
   d) i) 30.10 cm   **ii)** 90.31 cm   **e) i)** 0.10 km
   ii) 0.30 km   **f) i)** 15.05 km   **ii)** 45.16 km
11. a) $-56°C$ **b)** $-54°C$ **c)** $-39°C$ **d)** $-28°C$

Exercises 6-7, page 257

1. a) ± 7 **b)** ± 9 **c)** ± 11 **d)** ± 20
   e) ± 23 **f)** ± 25
3. a) 1.414   **b)** 1.732   **c)** 7.232   **d)** 11.336
   e) 21.703   **f)** 21.726   **g)** 21.749
   h) 21.772   **i)** 1.217   **j)** 0.016
5. a) i) 2.45   **ii)** 2.449   **b) i)** 3.32
   ii) 3.317   **c) i)** 3.61   **ii)** 3.606
   d) i) 11.14   **ii)** 11.136   **e) i)** 11.79
   ii) 11.790   **f) i)** 12.41   **ii)** 12.410
7. a) 10 cm, 100 cm²   **b)** 5 cm, 25 cm²
9. a) 3.2 m   **b)** 4.5 m
11. a) 5   **b)** 7   **c)** 6   **d)** 12   **e)** 2   **f)** 2
   g) 6   **h)** 23

Exercises 6-8, page 261

1. a) Rational   **b)** Irrational   **c)** Irrational
   d) Irrational   **e)** Irrational   **f)** Rational
3. $5\sqrt{2}, 5 + \sqrt{2}, 5 - \sqrt{2}, 7\sqrt{7} \sqrt{5} + \sqrt{2},$
   $\sqrt{7} + \sqrt{9}, 6\sqrt{21}, \sqrt{17} + 12$
5. a) Rational   **b)** Rational   **c)** Integer
   d) Natural   **e)** Irrational   **f)** Rational
   g) Irrational   **h)** natural

7. a) $\dfrac{1}{9}, \dfrac{1}{3}, \sqrt{\dfrac{1}{9}} = \dfrac{1}{3}$ **b)** Examples may vary.
9. No

Exercises 6-9, page 264

1. a) $2\sqrt{14}$ **b)** $\sqrt{154}$ **c)** -12 **d)** $6\sqrt{10}$
   e) -48 **f)** $70\sqrt{6}$
3. a) $4\sqrt{2}$ **b)** $5\sqrt{2}$ **c)** $3\sqrt{3}$ **d)** $4\sqrt{6}$
   e) $2\sqrt{2}$ **f)** $5\sqrt{3}$
5. a) $12\sqrt{3}$ **b)** $105\sqrt{2}$ **c)** $-192\sqrt{3}$
   d) $40\sqrt{15}$ **e)** $84\sqrt{2}$ **f)** $165\sqrt{2}$
7. a) $108\sqrt{2}$ **b)** 1200   **c)** 1080   **d)** $4320\sqrt{2}$
   e) 518 400   **f)** 30

Exercises 6-10, page 266

1. a) $2\sqrt{7}$ **b)** $16\sqrt{6}$ **c)** $-6\sqrt{13}$
   d) $-25\sqrt{19}$ **e)** $33\sqrt{3}$ **f)** $5\sqrt{15}$
3. a) $5\sqrt{10}$ **b)** $6\sqrt{2}$ **c)** $-3\sqrt{3}$ **d)** $-\sqrt{5}$
   e) $2\sqrt{2}$ **f)** $-2\sqrt{6}$ **g)** $-2\sqrt{5}$ **h)** $8\sqrt{6}$
5. a) $10\sqrt{3}$ **b)** $13\sqrt{3}$ **c)** $24\sqrt{2}$ **d)** $-8\sqrt{2}$
   e) $13\sqrt{6}$ **f)** $6\sqrt{5}$ **g)** $15\sqrt{2}$ **h)** $9\sqrt{7}$
   i) $10\sqrt{6} - 2\sqrt{7}$
7. a) $4\sqrt{2}$ cm **b)** $8\sqrt{2}$ cm² **c)** $(4 + 8\sqrt{2})$ cm
9. a) $2\sqrt{5}$ **b)** No   **c)** Answers may vary

Exercises 6-11, page 268

1. a) $2\sqrt{2}$ **b)** $\sqrt{7}$ **c)** $2\sqrt{3}$ **d)** $3\sqrt{5}$
   e) $3\sqrt{3}$ **f)** $\dfrac{5\sqrt{2}}{2}$ **g)** 4   **h)** 1   **i)** $\dfrac{\sqrt{2}}{7}$
   j) $\dfrac{1}{9}$

Review Exercises, page 269

1. a) 17   **b)** 72   **c)** 2.56   **d)** 13   **e)** 1
   f) 125   **g)** 32   **h)** $-\dfrac{27}{343}$
3. a) 6.3 cm²   **b)** 8.0 m²   **c)** 27.0 cm²
5. a) x^9 **b)** x^{24} **c)** x^{18} **d)** x^7 **e)** $15x^6$
   f) 2^5 **g)** $27m^6$ **h)** $(-3)^8$ **i)** $25x^2$
   j) $5x^6$ **k)** $27x^6$ **l)** $-7y^4$
7. a) 4096   **b)** 1024   **c)** 6144
9. a) w^{12} **b)** w^3 **c)** $-5x^8$
11. a) 1.0×10^4 **b)** 7.4×10^5 **c)** 1.0×10^{-5}
   d) 5.7×10^{-2}
13. a) 8 mm   **b)** 0.9 m   **c)** 7 cm   **d)** 1.5 cm
15. a) 1.6 m   **b)** 1.024 m

17. a) -2 **b)** 5 **c)** 3 **d)** 4 **e)** -2
f) 0.1

19. a) $7\sqrt{2}$ **b)** $3\sqrt{3}$ **c)** $6\sqrt{5}$ **d)** $-18\sqrt{10}$
e) $4\sqrt{15}$ **f)** $10\sqrt{3}$

21. a) $2\sqrt{3}$ **b)** 12 **c)** $2\sqrt{2}$ **d)** $\dfrac{1}{2}$ **e)** $\dfrac{3}{14}$

Cumulative Review, Chapters 4-6, page 271

1. a) -13 **b)** 22 **c)** 3 **d)** $4.\overline{8}$ **e)** -14
f) 0.6 **g)** -6 **h)** 3 **i)** 2

3. a) -2 **b)** -1 **c)** 4 **d)** 7

5. a) 8 **b)** 1125 **c)** 27

7. 8,11 **9. a)** $\triangle ABC \cong \triangle FDE$, SAS
b) $\triangle MNP \cong \triangle SRQ$, SSS;
$\triangle MNP \cong \triangle UTV$, ASA

11. a) 24 **b)** 128 **c)** -18 **d)** -8 **e)** $\dfrac{7}{3}$
f) 2 **g)** $\dfrac{1}{9}$ **h)** $\dfrac{9}{4}$

13. a) x^{10} **b)** x^6 **c)** $-21p^{-7}$ **d)** $-3m^{-14}$
e) $72x^5$ **f)** $16y^6$ **g)** $7a^{10}$ **h)** $9x$ **i)** $6s^8$

15. a) 50 **b)** -1.4 **c)** 1500 **d)** 2 **e)** 78 **f)** 13

17. a) $4\sqrt{2}$ **b)** $6\sqrt{2}$ **c)** $-15\sqrt{3}$ **d)** $60\sqrt{2}$
e) $-36\sqrt{2}$ **f)** 576

Chapter 7

Exercises 7-1, page 275

1. Answers may vary. **a)** Mrs. Adams had $\dfrac{3}{5}$ of

the profits and Mr. Singh had $\dfrac{2}{5}$ of the profits.

b) The class had $\dfrac{7}{12}$ girls and $\dfrac{5}{12}$ boys.

c) Mrs. Arbor's chain saw needs 25 parts of gasoline to 1 part of oil.

d) The scale of a map is 1 cm to 250 000 cm.

e) Brass is $\dfrac{3}{5}$ copper and $\dfrac{2}{5}$ zinc.

3. a) $\dfrac{5}{8}$ **b)** 7:8 **c)** 6:5 **d)** 8:3

5. a) $\dfrac{1}{5}$ **b)** $\dfrac{4}{5}$

7. a) 2.5:1 **b)** 4:1 **c)** 0.3:1 **d)** 5:1

9. a) 11:9 **b)** 3:55 **c)** 100:3 **11.** 159 cars

13. a) 40:14, 40:17, 40:20, 40:24, 40:28, 52:14, 52:17, 52:20, 52:24, 52:28
b) 40:28, 40:24, 52:28, 40:20, 52:24, 40:17, 52:20, 40:14, 52:17, 52:14

Exercises 7-2, page 279

1. a) 11:12 **b)** 2:3 **c)** 3:8

3. About $11 400

5. $22 400, $11 200, $16 800, $33 600

7. a) i) 104 **ii)** 97
b) i) 9 years **ii)** 9 years

9. C,264 Hz; D,297 Hz; E,330 Hz; F,352 Hz; G,396 Hz; B,495 Hz; C,528 Hz

11. a) $\dfrac{50}{77}$ **b)** 231 Gm

13. 60°, 90°, 90°, 120°

Exercises 7-3, page 283

1. a) 9 **b)** 6 **c)** 5 **d)** 3 **e)** 33 **f)** 3
g) 128 **h)** 15

3. 77 cm **5.** 138 cm **7.** 5.1 m by 9 m; 45.9 m²

9. 12 cm

Exercises 7-4, page 286

1. a) i) 30 km **ii)** 75 km **b) i)** 4 L **ii)** 18 L

3. a) About 7 gal **b)** About 768 mi

5. 96 **7.** $539.58 **9. a)** 158 d **b)** 360 d

11. $2378.00 **13.** 22 km/h **15.** 1.2 min

17. $\dfrac{z}{36}$ days

The Mathematical Mind, page 289

1. 1.618 or -0.618 **3.** 1.625

Mathematics Around Us, page 291

1. a) 60 **b)** $\dfrac{1}{60}$ **3. a)** About 1610 m
b) About 29 m/s

5. 10^6 cm³ **7.** Seconds; period

Exercises 7-5, page 295

1. a) 7% **b)** 18.5% **c)** 57% **d)** 0.8%
e) 365% **f)** 36.5% **g)** 540% **h)** 1875%

3. a) 0.24 **b)** 0.39 **c)** 0.574 **d)** 0.03
e) 0.058 **f)** 0.115 **g)** 0.016 **h)** 0.009
i) 1.37 **j)** 2.64 **k)** 3.75 **l)** 3.758
m) 0.001 **n)** 0.0203 **o)** 0.0025

5. Estimates may vary. **a)** 25% **b)** 33%
c) 25% **d)** 30%

7. a) $\dfrac{13}{50}$ **b)** $\dfrac{7}{20}$ **c)** $\dfrac{16}{25}$ **d)** $\dfrac{3}{4}$ **e)** $\dfrac{5}{8}$ **f)** $\dfrac{5}{4}$
g) $\dfrac{61}{75}$ **h)** $\dfrac{1}{6}$ **i)** $\dfrac{37}{20}$ **j)** $\dfrac{18}{5}$ **k)** $\dfrac{1}{125}$ **l)** $\dfrac{1}{800}$
9. 250%

Problem Solving, page 297

1. 37.5 km/h   **3.** 62.5%   **5.** 210 mi
7. 62.5 mph

Mathematics Around Us, page 298

1. a) About 98%   **b)** About 89%   **c)** 312 votes
3. a) 226 ballots   **b)** 215 votes

Exercises 7-6, page 302

1. a) 10   **b)** 8   **c)** 0.9   **d)** 1.75   **e)** 81.75
f) 6   **g)** 0.665   **h)** 11.7
3. a) 20%   **b)** About 11%   **c)** About 167%
d) 90%   **e)** 12.5%   **f)** About 333%
g) 0.1% **h)** 0.05%
5. $193.38 **7.** About $9383 **9.** 1280
11. $37.44   **13. a)** 7.6%   **b)** 20.0%
15. a) i) $0.85   **ii)** $0.52
b) i) $1.31   **ii)** $0.52
17. a) $197.95   **b)** $168.26

Review Exercises, page 304

1. a) 3:1   **b)** 54 g
3. a) 10.5   **b)** 6.5   **c)** 9   **d)** 63
5. $9000; $24 000, $12 000   **7.** 127.5 km
9. a) 4680   **b) i)** 12 min 49 s
ii) 8 days 21 h 40 min
11. 40%   **13.** $199.65/m³

Chapter 8

Exercises 8-1, page 307

1. a) 14   **b)** 7   **c)** 1   **d)** -1 **e)** -4
3. a), b), d), e), i), j), k), and **l)** have like terms;
c), f), g), and **h)** have unlike terms.
5. a) $14m$ **b)** $-2k$ **c)** $5x$ **d)** $-3n$
e) $-4a$ **f)** $6x^2$ **g)** $-4y^3$ **h)** $-8c$
i) $-9.4m$ **j)** 0   **k)** $\dfrac{23}{12}x$ **l)** $\dfrac{13}{18}a$

7. a) $8t$ **b)** $a + 2ab$ **c)** $-15m + 5mn$
d) $4s^2 + s^3$ **e)** $-k^3$ **f)** $2c^4 - 3c^2$ **g)** $\dfrac{5}{6}x$
h) $1.2r$ **i)** $\dfrac{7}{20}a^2$ **j)** $-3.0h$ **k)** $-\dfrac{13}{6}c^2$ **l)** $0.4n$

9. a) $1.0a$ **b)** $-0.5m$ **c)** $\dfrac{3}{4}x$ **d)** $\dfrac{5}{12}y$
e) $2c^2$ **f)** $13b^2$ **g)** $-16x^3$ **h)** $5x^2y$
i) $3abc$ **j)** $-11mnp$ **k)** $12xyz$ **l)** $-16fgh$
11. a) $7x$ **b)** $-8a$ **c)** $3p^2$ **d)** $-2y^2 - 2y$
e) $5m^2 - 5m$ **f)** $12x^3 - 4x^2$ **g)** $6a^2$
h) $-4x^2 - 2x$ **i)** $4.2c - 3.2c^2$
13. a) $6n^2 + 7n$ **b)** $3x^3 + 3x^2$ **c)** $7.3y^2 - 1.8y$
d) $-a^2 - 3a$ **e)** $\dfrac{3}{4}c^2 + \dfrac{2}{3}c$ **f)** $\dfrac{15}{8}m^3 - \dfrac{3}{4}m^2$
g) $0.7x^2 - 0.3x$ **h)** $-3y + 5y^2$ **i)** $4a^3 + a$
15. a) $-xy - 5x^2y + 7xy^2$
b) $-xy + 2x^2y - 4x^2y^2 + 3$
c) $ay^2 - 2a^2 + 4a^2y - 7ay$
d) $11w + z - 3wz - 6w^2z$
e) $9ab + 2a^2b - 4a$

The Mathematical Mind, page 310

3. Answers may vary.   **a)** 7   **b)** 17   **c)** 82

Computer Power, page 311
1. No   **3.** 161

Exercises 8-2, page 315

1. a) $9x + 6$ **b)** $7a + 4$ **c)** $5 - 6m$
d) $6x + 2$ **e)** $3 - 8t$ **f)** $4c - 5$
g) $6n^2 - 8n - 4$ **h)** $-2x^2 + 5x - 4$
i) $7 - 7c - 3c^2$ **j)** $5 - 3n + 3n^2$
3. a) $-5x + 1$ **b)** $2 + n$ **c)** $10a - 11$
d) $3 + 2t$ **e)** $-6n - 3$ **f)** $2x - 42$
g) $12x - 1$ **h)** $14a^2 - 2a - 10$
i) $x^2 - 4x - 4$ **j)** $k^2 + k - 7$
5. a) $28x + 5$ **b)** $50 - 20x$ **c)** $5n - 6$
d) $-3 - 82t$ **e)** $18n^2 + 30n - 44$
f) $0.3x - 9.2$
7. a) $6x^2 + y^2$ **b)** $x^2 + 9xy - 2y^2$
c) $-3x^2 + 10x^2y + 6y^2 - 7$
d) $3x^2 - 6x + 2y^2 - 7y + 14$
e) $5x^2 - 2x + 5$ **f)** $6y^2 + 3y - 5$
g) $9x^2y^2 - 2xy - 6$
9. a) $P = -0.1x^2 + 3.0x - 1$
b) i) $11.5 million   **ii)** $21.5 million
11. a) $-7x^2 - 10x + 25; 17$ **b)** $2x^2 - 10x - 5; 23$

Exercises 8-3, page 318

1. a) $30n^2$ **b)** $-6a^2$ **c)** $25x^2$ **d)** $-18n^2$
e) $10x^4$ **f)** $6a^2$ **g)** $10x^5$ **h)** $-56y^2$
i) $5x^4$ **j)** $\frac{1}{8}n^2$ **k)** $3.0m^3$ **l)** $1.5x^5$

3. a) x^3y^4 **b)** m^3n^4 **c)** a^3b^4 **d)** c^5d^3
e) p^3q^4 **f)** x^5y^5 **g)** $6x^3y^3$ **h)** $-12x^3y^3$
i) $6a^3b^5$ **j)** $10a^3b^3c^3$ **k)** $-12m^3n^2p^3$ **l)** $10x^3y^3z^2$

5. a) $3x^2 + 2x$ **b)** $5a^2 - a$ **c)** $3n - 7n^2$
d) $-x^2 + 2x$ **e)** $-3c^2 - 5c$ **f)** $3x^3 - x^2$
g) $y^4 - 5y^3$ **h)** $2r^2 - 7r^3$
i) $3n^4 - 5n^3 + n^2$ **j)** $-5x^5 + x^4$
k) $3a^4 - 2a^3 + a^2$ **l)** $-7s + 2s^2 - s^3$

7. a) $3x^3y - 3x^2y^2$ **b)** $-2a^3b^2 + 2a^2b$
c) $4m^2n - 4mn^2$ **d)** $-3p^2q^2 + 3p^2q$
e) $5a^2b^2 - 5a^3$ **f)** $-4x^3y + 4xy^3$
g) $-2m^3n^2 + 6m^2n^3$ **h)** $14a^3b^2 - 21a^2b^3$
i) $-6p^2q^2r + 12pq^2r^2$ **j)** $1.25m^2n^3 - 2.5m^3n^2$

9. a) 1140 **b)** 1360 **c)** 1563

11. a) $8x^2 + 10xy$ **b)** $4m^2 + 5mn$ **13.** 112π cm^2

15. a) **i)** $12x^3 + 24x^2$
  ii) $26x^2 + 28x$
  iii) $12x^2$
 b) **i)** \$959.52 **ii)** \$374.85

Exercises 8-4, page 322

1. a) $x^2 + 8x + 15$ **b)** $a^2 + 6a + 8$
c) $n^2 + 8n + 7$

3. a) $a^2 - a - 2$ **b)** $n^2 - 5n + 6$
c) $y^2 + y - 20$ **d)** $b^2 - 3b - 18$
e) $a^2 - 16a + 60$ **f)** $n^2 + 22n + 120$

5. a) $-a^2 + 4a - 3$ **b)** $-x^2 + 2x - 1$
c) $2y^2 + 9y - 5$ **d)** $2z^2 - 2z - 4$
e) $-\frac{1}{8}x^2 + \frac{3}{4}x + 9$ **f)** $15x^2 - 4x - 4$

7. a) $x^2 + 7xy + 10y^2$ **b)** $a^2 - ab - 6b^2$
c) $6m^2 - 5mn + n^2$ **d)** $20x^2 + 7xy - 3y^2$
e) $6r^2 - 17rs - 3s^2$ **f)** $56a^2 + 113ab + 56b^2$

9. i) a) $63x^2 - 108x + 45$ **b)** $32x - 28$
c) 5265 square units; 292 units **ii) a)** $15x^2 + 6x$
b) $16x + 4$ **c)** 1560 square units; 164 units

Exercises 8-5, page 326

1. a) $x^2 + 10x + 25$ **b)** $x^2 + 2x + 1$
c) $x^2 - 6x + 9$ **d)** $n^2 - 14n + 49$
e) $c^2 + 8c + 16$ **f)** $x^2 - 2x + 1$
g) $a^2 + 4a + 4$ **h)** $a^2 - 12a + 36$
i) $4 + 4a + a^2$ **j)** $25 - 10x + x^2$
k) $t^2 + 18t + 81$ **l)** $100 - 20m + m^2$

3. a) $9a^2 - 6a + 1$ **b)** $4a^2 + 12a + 9$
c) $49x^2 - 70x + 25$ **d)** $36a^2 + 48a + 16$
e) $9n^2 - 48n + 64$ **f)** $25 - 90x + 81x^2$
g) $100 - 60c + 9c^2$ **h)** $144x^2 + 120x + 25$

5. a) $x^2 + 14x + 49$ **b)** $a^2 - 4a + 4$
c) $n^2 + 8n + 16$ **d)** $4x^2 - 4x + 1$
e) $25c^2 + 30c + 9$ **f)** $4 - 12m + 9m^2$
g) $16 + 40x + 25x^2$ **h)** $64 - 48x + 9x^2$

7. a), b), c), d) $x^2 - 6x + 9$

9. a) 961 **b)** 169 **c)** 841 **d)** $10\ 609$
e) 3721 **f)** 8464

11. a) $1\ 999\ 999$ **b)** $249\ 999$

Exercises 8-6, page 328

1. a) 3 **b)** 4 **c)** $2x$ **d)** $7x$ **e)** y^2 **f)** $4z^2$

3. a) $7(2x^2 + 5x - 1)$ **b)** $-5(2 + 5a - 6a^2)$
c) $10(2n^2 - 3n + 4)$ **d)** $5x(1 + 2x + 3x^2)$
e) $3c(3c^2 + 5)$ **f)** $x^2(-x + 1)$
g) $4x(1 - 2x + 3x^2)$ **h)** $-3y^2(2 + y + 4y^2)$
i) $4m(3 + 4m - m^2)$

5. a) xy **b)** $3xy$ **c)** ab **d)** 4 **e)** $-5xy$
f) $6pq$ **g)** $2mn$ **h)** $3x^2y$

7. a) $b^3(b - 3)$ **b)** $3b^4(1 - 2b)$
c) $-a^2(a^2 - 3a + 2)$ **d)** $21x(1 + 2x + 3x^2)$
e) $-d^4(1 - 5d)$ **f)** $6m(4m^2 + m - 2)$
g) $-3x(4 + 3x + x^2 + 2x^3)$
h) $x^3(2 + 3x - 4x^2 + 5x^3)$

9. a) $6a(3 - b^2)$ **b)** $4xy(3x + 4)$
c) $-4abc(2b + 3ac)$ **d)** $5(m^2 + 3mn + 5n^2)$
e) $4xy^2z(x - 4z)$ **f)** $3x(x + 2y^2 - 4xy^2)$
g) $-y(5x - 6 - 3xy)$ **h)** $a^2b^2(9a + 7 + 18b)$
i) $-7a^2b^2(a - 2b + 3)$
j) $-4p^2q^3(3 + 5p - 2q)$

11. a) $2a^2b(a - 8b^2 + 2ab + 3b - 4ab^2 + 6)$
b) $5x^2y^2(3x^2y - 5xy^2 + 2y - x + 6x^2y^2 - 7)$

13. a) $3(3t - 1)(2t + 3)$ **b)** $a(a + 2)(a - 1)$
c) $5x(x + 7)(x - 2)$ **d)** $-(2n + 3)(n + 4)$
e) $2(r - 3)(r + 4)$ **f)** $x^2(x + 4)(x - 1)$
g) $3a^2(a - 1)(a - 2)$ **h)** $4a(2a - 5)(3a + 4)$

Problem Solving, page 331

1. a) $\dfrac{3}{4}, \dfrac{7}{8}$ **b)** $4x + 7y, 5x + 9y$ **c)** 11, 16

   d) 29, 35

3. A-hexagon in circle, B-hexagon in hexagon,
C-circle in square, D-square in triangle

5. $\dfrac{n(n + 1)}{2}$

Exercises 8-7, page 334

1. a) $(x + 2)(x + 5)$ **b)** $(x + 2)(x + 3)$
   c) $(m + 6)(m + 4)$ **d)** $(a + 1)(a + 7)$
   e) $(x + 3)^2$ **f)** $(n + 7)^2$ **g)** $(t + 8)(t + 5)$
   h) $(x - 6)^2$ **i)** $(x + 4)(x + 5)$

3. a) $(x - 4)^2$ **b)** $(x + 6)^2$ **c)** $(a + 2)^2$
   d) $(p - 1)^2$ **e)** $(x - 3)^2$ **f)** $(t - 5)^2$
   g) $(x + 7)^2$ **h)** $(b - 8)^2$ **i)** $(x + 10)^2$

5. a) $(x - 4)(x - 2)$ **b)** $(x + 3)(x + 6)$
   c) $(a - 2)(a - 9)$ **d)** $(m + 4)(m + 7)$
   e) $(n - 5)^2$ **f)** $(3 - n)(10 - n)$
   g) $(p + 8)^2$ **h)** $(y - 7)(y - 6)$
   i) $(x + 8)(x + 7)$

7. a) $(x - 8)(x + 3)$ **b)** $(x + 10)(x - 5)$
   c) $(a + 9)(a - 8)$ **d)** $(n - 8)(n + 5)$
   e) $(m + 7)(m - 6)$ **f)** $(8 + x)(1 - x)$
   g) $(y + 4)(y - 1)$ **h)** $(s - 9)(s + 2)$
   i) $(2 - t)(1 + t)$

9. a) 240   **b)** $(x - 5)(x + 3)$ **c)** 240

11. a) $(x + 9)(x + 7)$ **b)** No factors
   c) No factors   **d)** $(t + 3)(t + 8)$
   e) $(n - 5)(n - 7)$ **f)** No factors
   g) $(x + 12)(x - 5)$ **h)** No factors
   i) No factors   **j)** No factors
   k) $(7 + t)(8 - t)$ **l)** No factors

13. a) $R = (7 - x)(5 + x)$
   b) i) $36\ 000$ **ii)** $35\ 000$ **iii)** $32\ 000$

15. a) $(x + 5y)(x + 3y)$ **b)** $(x - 7y)(x - 2y)$
   c) $(x - 5y)(x + y)$ **d)** $(x + 9y)(x - 2y)$
   e) $(c - 7d)(c + 3d)$ **f)** $(m + 9n)(m + 5n)$
   g) $(3x - y)(2x + y)$ **h)** $(4a + b)(2a - b)$
   i) $(7a - b)(4a + b)$ **j)** $(2x + y)(6x + y)$
   k) $(5x - 1)^2$ **l)** $(4a - b)(5a - b)$

17. a) $y = (x + 1)(x + 11)$
   b) 24, 39, 56, 75, 96, 119, 144, 171, 200, 231
   c) 7, -19

Exercises 8-8, page 337

1. a) 5,1   **b)** 9, -1 **c)** $-2, -3$ **d)** $-6, 2$
   e) $-3, -5$ **f)** 4, -2

3. a) $(x - 2)(5x + 1)$ **b)** $(d - 3)(2d - 1)$
   c) $(3x + 4)(x - 1)$ **d)** $(2f - 5)(f + 1)$
   e) $(2x + 1)^2$ **f)** $(h - 2)(3h - 2)$

5. a) $(2n + 3)(n + 2)$ **b)** $(5x - 3)(x - 2)$
   c) $(x - 2)(3x + 4)$ **d)** $(3k + 2)^2$
   e) $(x + 2)(2x - 3)$ **f)** $(5m - 4)(m - 2)$

7. a) $(u - 8)(5u + 1)$ **b)** $(6q - 7)(2q - 1)$
   c) $(2x - 3)(3x + 1)$ **d)** $(4m + 1)(3m + 4)$
   e) $(2x - 5)(7x - 1)$ **f)** $(5x + 6)(2x - 1)$

9. a) $(2y + 3)(3y + 4)$ **b)** $2(4q + 3)(3q - 1)$
   c) $(9z + 4)(2z + 3)$ **d)** $2(5b + 7)(4b + 1)$
   e) $(3a + 4)(7a - 5)$ **f)** $(4a - 1)(2a - 3)$

11. a) $(2c + 5)^2$ **b)** $(4x - 5)(7x - 3)$
   c) $6(d - 2)(2d - 1)$ **d)** $(7z - 2)(5z - 8)$
   e) $(4e + 3)(6e + 5)$ **f)** $(4y - 3)(2y - 5)$

13. a) $-25, 10$ **b)** $-5, -32$ **c)** 7,16
   d) $-8, -14$ **e)** 12, -18 **f)** 9, -13

15. a) $2a(3c - 2)^2$ **b)** $6x(2y - x)(3y + x)$
   c) $2p(4q + 5p)(7q - p)$ **d)** $n(7m - 3)(5m - 4)$
   e) $2c^2(3d + 5)(3d + 2)$ **f)** $y(7x - 5)(3x + 2)$

Calculator Power, page 339

1. a) $83\ 200, 85\ 000, 86\ 400, 87\ 400, 88\ 000$
   b) $88\ 000, 88\ 200, 88\ 000, 87\ 400, 86\ 400$
   c) Answers may vary.

3. a) $(5,45), (6,32), (7,21), (8,10), (9,5), (10,0),$
   $(11, -3), (12, -4), (13, -3), (14,0), (15,5)$
   b) 12

Exercises 8-9, page 341

1. a) $(x + 5)(x - 5)$ **b)** $(a + 7)(a - 7)$
   c) $(x + 6)(x - 6)$ **d)** $(y + 10)(y - 10)$
   e) $(x + 1)(x - 1)$ **f)** $(x + 2)(x - 2)$
   g) $(m + 8)(m - 8)$ **h)** $(n + 12)(n - 12)$

3. a) $(3a + 2)(3a - 2)$ **b)** $(5x + 3)(5x - 3)$
   c) $(4s + 1)(4s - 1)$ **d)** $4(3 + 5n)(3 - 5n)$
   e) $(10x + 11)(10x - 11)$ **f)** $(12p + 7)(12p - 7)$
   g) $\left(\dfrac{1}{2}x + \dfrac{2}{3}\right)\left(\dfrac{1}{2}x - \dfrac{2}{3}\right)$ **h)** $(2.5 + n)(2.5 - n)$

5. a) $2(x - 3)(x + 3)$ **b)** $5(x - 1)(x + 1)$
   c) $3(a + 4)(a - 4)$ **d)** $3(n^2 + 10)$
   e) $7(1 - 2y)(1 + 2y)$ **f)** $2(a^2 + 6)$
   g) $x(x - 5)(x + 5)$ **h)** $a(a + 7)(a - 7)$

7. a) $(x^2 + 1)(x - 1)(x + 1)$
   b) $(a^2 + 4)(a - 2)(a + 2)$
   c) $(4c^2 + 1)(2c + 1)(2c - 1)$
   d) $2(1 + x^2)(1 + x)(1 - x)$

Exercises 8-10, page 343

1. a) ± 3 **b)** ± 5 **c)** ± 2 **d)** ± 2 **e)** ± 1
f) $\pm \sqrt{6}$ **g)** ± 7 **h)** $\pm \sqrt{7}$

3. a) ± 3 **b)** $\frac{1}{3}, 2$ **c)** $\frac{1}{2}, -2$ **d)** $-\frac{1}{2}, -\frac{1}{3}$
e) ± 2 **f)** $\frac{2}{3}, -1$ **g)** $-\frac{1}{4}, 1$ **h)** ± 8 **i)** $-\frac{3}{2}$

5. 1 s, 5 s

7. a) 12 cm by 16 cm **b)** 14 cm by 14 cm
c) 8 cm by 20 cm **9.** 17 cm

11. a) -180 **b)** 4 or 7 **c)** Answers may vary.

13. a) About 1.4 s **b)** About 2.0 s
c) About 2.9 s

15. About 2.5 m **17.** 9 in. **19.** $-6, 18$ or 4,8
21. 5 m

Exercises 8-11, page 347

1. a) $4x^3$ **b)** $2y^4$ **c)** $9y^3$ **d)** $-3m^2$
e) $9y^2$ **f)** $\frac{3n^2}{5}$ **g)** -5 **h)** $\frac{3c^3}{2}$ **i)** $6x^3$
j) $-4y$ **k)** $-\frac{9a^2}{4}$ **l)** $\frac{3}{2}x$

3. a) $4x^3y$ **b)** $-6a^2$ **c)** 7 **d)** $-3b^2$
e) $-3x^2y^2$ **f)** $5abc$

5. a) $3x^2 - x + 5$ **b)** $1 + 3c - 2c^2$
c) $x^2 - 3x + 2$ **d)** $4 + a - a^2$
e) $3x^2 - 6x + 1$ **f)** $-3a^2 - a + 2$

7. a) $1 - 3x^2y^2 + 6xy^3$ **b)** $b(4a^2b^2 - 3ab + 2)$
c) $n(-n^2 + 2mn - 3m^2)$ **d)** $\frac{3x^4y^2 - 2x^3y + 1}{x^2}$
e) $3a^2 - 2ab + b^2$ **f)** $yz^2(3 - 2xyz + x^2y^2z^2)$

9. $\frac{R}{3}$

Exercises 8-12, page 350

1. $\frac{3a^2b}{2}; \frac{4m^2n^2}{3mn}; \frac{3}{5}; \frac{x-6}{5}; \frac{3-4y}{2y}; -\frac{4}{3}; 3x^2 + 1;$
$\frac{4 + 3m^2}{2m^3}$

3. a) $\frac{2x^4}{y}$ **b)** $\frac{5x^3y}{9}$ **c)** $\frac{m}{6}$ **d)** $\frac{3ab^2}{2}$
e) $-2x^3$ **f)** $\frac{5c^2d}{2}$ **g)** $\frac{-9y}{8}$ **h)** $\frac{3a}{4}$
i) $\frac{xy^3}{6}$ **j)** $\frac{-4p^3q^2}{5}$ **k)** $\frac{-12b^3}{a^3}$ **l)** $\frac{4n^6}{35m}$

5. a) $\frac{2}{x}$ **b)** $\frac{a-11}{3a^2}$ **c)** $\frac{1-2m}{m}$ **d)** $\frac{5y+1}{3y^3}$
e) $\frac{3x-7}{x^4}$ **f)** $\frac{2+n}{2n^2}$ **g)** $\frac{6x+2}{3x^2}$
h) $-\frac{y+1}{y^3}$ **i)** $\frac{6a-3}{5a}$

7. a) $\frac{x+5}{2x^2}$ **b)** $\frac{-2y+10}{3y^3}$ **c)** $\frac{-2+m}{2m}$
d) $\frac{13+a}{a^3}$ **e)** $\frac{2x-14}{3x^2}$ **f)** $\frac{-2a+11}{4a^3}$

9. $\frac{xy}{x+y}$

Review Exercises, page 352

1. a) $-x + 7$; first degree
b) $6y^3 + 13y^2 + 4y$; third degree
c) $3a^4 - a^3 + 2a^2 + 9a$; fourth degree

3. a) $35a^2$ **b)** $-15b^2$ **c)** $16y^2$ **d)** $-63x^5$
e) $-8y^3$

5. a) $6y(1 + 3y)$ **b)** $-3a(1 - 4a^3)$
c) $5a^2(1 - 5a)$ **d)** $a(3a^2 + 4a + 7)$
e) $3xy(2x - 1 + 3y)$ **f)** $2ab(4 - 2ab + 3b)$

7. a) $x^2 + 6x + 9$ **b)** $y^2 - 10y + 25$
c) $25 - 10q + q^2$ **d)** $36 - 60y + 25y^2$

9. a) $a^2 - 16$ **b)** $x^2 - 64$ **c)** $4 - y^2$

11. a) $7, -3$ **b)** $-8, 7$ **c)** $\frac{3}{2}$

13. a) $\frac{-5b^3}{8c}$ **b)** $6x$ **c)** $\frac{-2}{m^2}$ **d)** $\frac{3x+8}{2}$
e) $\frac{-m-11}{3}$

Chapter 9

Exercises 9-1, page 356

1. A($-2,5$), B($-4,3$), C($-3,1$), D($-5,-2$),
E($-2,-3$), F(1,-5), G(3,-3), H(5,-2),
I(5,3), J(3,5)

3. a) On the *y*-axis **b)** On a line parallel to the *x*-axis,
and 4 units below **c)** On the left of the *y*-axis
d) To the left of the *y*-axis, and above the *x*-axis
e) Along a line through the origin, that is the same
distance from both axes, passing through the
quadrants where *x* and *y* are both positive, and
x and *y* are both negative.

5. c) Parallelogram **7. a)** $(3, -2)$
b) $(-3, -2)$ **c)** $(-1, 4)$ **d)** $(0, 3)$

9. a) $(9,0)$, $(3,6)$, or $(-3,0)$
  b) $(5,-3)$, $(5,9)$, or $(-1,5)$
  c) $(-3,-4)$, $(9,6)$, or $(-7,6)$
  d) $(2,6)$, $(-2,0)$, or $(2,-6)$

Exercises 9-2, page 359

1. a) 20 square units   **b)** 21 square units
  c) 7.5 square units
3. a) Parallelogram   **b)** 6 square units
5. a) 32 square units; $4\sqrt{2}$ units
  b) 34 square units; $\sqrt{34}$ units
  c) 50 square units; $5\sqrt{2}$ units
7. a) 16 square units, 18 square units   **b)** $\dfrac{8}{9}$
9. 88 square units

Exercises 9-3, page 364

1. a) $\{(1,0.50), (2,0.95), (3,1.35), (4,1.70), (5,2.00)\}$
  b) $\{(-5,-2), (-4,3), (3,5), (7,2), (5,-1), (2,-3)\}$
5. a) i) 30, 40   **ii)** 5, 15   **iii)** 15, 20   **iv)** 25
  b) i) 6, 10   **ii)** 13   **iii)** 2, 16   **iv)** 2
  c) $\{(2,40), (2,30), (6,5), (6,15), (10,15), (10,20),$
  $(13,25), (16,30)\}$
7. $\{(1,0), (2,0), (3,0), (4,0.32), (5,0.64), (6,0.96),$
  $(7,1.28), (8,1.60)\}$
9. a) $\{(4,0.75), (5,1.50), (6,2.25), (7,3.00), (8,3.75),$
  $(9,4.50), (10,5.25), (11,6.00), (12,6.75),$
  $(13,7.50), (14,8.25), (15,9.00), (16,9.75)\}$
  c) Allowance: y; age: x; $y = 0.75x - 2.25$

Problem Solving, page 367

1. About 9:53   **3.** About 145 m   **5.** 96 m by 48 m

Exercises 9-4, page 371

1. a), c) Linear   **3. a)** $(0,4)$, $(3,0)$
  b) $(0,-3)$, $(6,0)$ **c)** $(-2,0)$
  d) $(0,4)$, $(-2,0)$ **e)** $(0,3)$
  f) $(0,-1)$, $(-4,0)$
5. a) About 6.5 h   **b)** About 4.5 h   **c)** About 8.5 h

7. a)

x	y
0	2
5	-2
10	-6

b)

x	y
2	0
6	3
10	6

c)

x	y
1	-2
4	0
7	2

d)

x	y
0	0
7	5
-7	-5

e)

x	y
0	-7
7	0
3	-4

f)

x	y
0	3
2	3
4	3

9. b) i) About 195°F   **ii)** About 250°F
  iii) About 390°F   **c) i)** About 30°C
  ii) About 50°C   **iii)** About 95°C
  d) i) About -5°C   **ii)** About -20°C
  iii) About -25°C   **iv)** About -30°C

Exercises 9-5, page 375

1. $\dfrac{1}{3}$
3. a) $\dfrac{4}{7}$ **b)** $\dfrac{1}{8}$ **c)** 0   **d)** $\dfrac{7}{9}$ **e)** $-\dfrac{10}{11}$
  f) $-\dfrac{8}{7}$ **g)** $\dfrac{12}{7}$ **h)** -1 **7.** $\dfrac{1}{40}$
9. The lines appear to be parallel.
11. b) AB and CD have the same slope; BC and AD
  have the same slope   **c)** Parallelogram

Exercises 9-6, page 379

3. a) $y = \dfrac{5}{2}x - 2$ **b)** $y = -\dfrac{1}{3}x + 2$
  c) $y = \dfrac{3}{2}x - 2$
5. b) Answers may vary.
7. a) $y = 2x + 3$ **b)** $y = -x + 4$ **c)** $y = \dfrac{2}{3}x - 1$
  d) $y = -\dfrac{4}{5}x + 8$
11. $-\dfrac{A}{B}$; $-\dfrac{C}{B}$ **13.** $y = 2x + 8$

Exercises 9-7, page 383

1. i) a) 0, 7, 14, 28   **b)** $y = 7x$
  ii) a) -3, -9, -12, -15 **b)** $y = -3x$
  iii) a) 1, 2, 3, 4   **b** $y = \dfrac{1}{4}x$
  iv) a) 2, 4, 8, 10   **b)** $y = \dfrac{2}{3}x$
3. a) $y = \dfrac{2}{3}x$ **b)** 14   **c)** 22.5
5. a) $V = \dfrac{3}{88}W$ **b)** 4.5 L
7. a) i) 2.14 L   **ii)** 1.93 L   **b) i)** 293°C
  ii) -131.5°C
9. Mercury 89, Venus 225, Earth 365, Mars 691,
  Jupiter 4355, Saturn 10 739, Uranus 31 017,
  Neptune 60 985, Pluto 91 642

Problem Solving, page 385

1. a) Odd **b)** Even **c) i)** $-\dfrac{1}{2}n$ **ii)** $\dfrac{1}{2}(n + 1)$

3. a) 64 **b)** n^2 **5.** 11 units

7. All orders give the same result.

Review Exercises, page 390

1. c) A rectangle

3. a) $\{(-2,-1),(-1,0),(0,1),(1,2),(2,3),(3,4)\}$
   b) $\{(5,4),(5,-4),(3,3),(3,-3),(1,1),(1,-1),(0,0)\}$

9. a) $y = -\dfrac{1}{2}x - 4$ **b)** $y = \dfrac{4}{3}x - 6$

Cumulative Review, Chapters 7-9, page 391

1. a) 1.6 **b)** 75 **c)** 4 **d)** 14

3. 150 km **5. a)** 75 **b)** 40% **7.** $408

9. a) $9m - 12n$ **b)** $-6a + 3b$ **c)** $-3x - 11$
   d) $4y^2 - 12y - 7$

11. a) $x^2 + 7x - 44$ **b)** $2x^2 - 13x + 21$
   c) $20 + 51a + 27a^2$ **d)** $9m^2 - 25$
   e) $8x^3 + 10x^2 - 3x$
   f) $-84a^3 + 200a^2 + 64a$

13. a) $2x - 7$ **b)** $2x^2 - 3x + 5$ **c)** $\dfrac{5x^2}{12y^3}$
   d) $-\dfrac{5m^2n^2}{9}$ **e)** $\dfrac{3x^3y}{2}$ **f)** $-\dfrac{16}{9c}$

15. Trapezoid **17. a)** -1 **b)** $-\dfrac{1}{2}$

19. a) $y = -\dfrac{2}{3}x + 4$ **b)** $y = \dfrac{6}{5}x + 3$

Chapter 10

Exercises 10-1, page 396

1. a) $(2,3)$ **b)** $(2,4)$ **c)** $(4,3)$ **d)** $(-3,-5)$
   e) $(0,-4)$ **f)** $(4,5)$ **g)** $(-3,1)$
   h) $(-4,2)$

3. a) $(30,-20)$ **b)** $(0,30)$ **c)** $(25,-30)$
   d) $(-14,4)$

5. a) $(2,3)$
   b) $4x + y = 11$. Line passes through $(2,3)$.
   c) $2x - 3y = -5$. Line passes through $(2,3)$.

Exercises 10-2, page 400

1. a) $6x + 3y = 14$; $4x + y = 6$
   b) $5x + 2y = 27$; $x + 8y = 3$
   c) $4x + 3y = 2$; $2x - 7y = -16$
   d) $2x + 2y = 20$; $16x - 6y = 4$

3. a) $(1,3)$ **b)** Answers may vary.
   $3x - 2y = -3$; $x + 4y = 13$
   c) Lines pass through $(1,3)$.

5. a) i) $6x - 2y = -14$ **ii)** $3x + 6y = 24$
   $\quad\quad 3x + 12y = 6$ $\quad\quad 10x - 6y = 2$
   b) i) $9x + 10y = -8$ **ii)** $13x = 26$
   c) i) $3x - 14y = -20$ **ii)** $7x - 12y = -22$

Exercises 10-3, page 403

1. b)

3. a) $(4,-2)$ **b)** $(3,5)$ **c)** $\left(\dfrac{1}{2},\dfrac{1}{3}\right)$ **d)** $(2,3)$
   e) $\left(\dfrac{25}{11},\dfrac{20}{11}\right)$ **f)** $(-3,5)$ **g)** $(2,-1)$
   h) $(4,-6)$

5. a) $(2,3)$ **b)** $(11,3)$ **c)** $(3,2)$ **d)** $(10,4)$
   e) $(3,8)$ **f)** $\left(4,\dfrac{1}{2}\right)$ **g)** $(8,2)$
   h) $\left(\dfrac{116}{13},\dfrac{106}{13}\right)$

Exercises 10-4, page 405

1. c), d)

3. a) $(-1,3)$ **b)** $(2,-2)$ **c)** $(2,1)$ **d)** $(3,1)$
   e) $(-2,-3)$ **f)** $(4,-3)$ **g)** $(20,-6)$
   h) $(4,-3)$

5. a) $(5,-1)$ **b)** $(-1,1)$ **c)** $(3,2)$
   d) $(-2,1)$

Investigate, page 406

1. The lines intersect at $(1,5)$.

3. The lines coincide.

5. Answers may vary. **i)** If the equations, in their
   simplest form, have the same y- and x-coefficients,
   but different constant terms
   ii) If the equations, in their simplest form, are
   identical

Exercises 10-5, page 408

1. 16, 9 **3.** 115, 67 **5.** 8 – $2, 3 – $5

7. 20 quarters, 12 dimes **9.** $0.75, $2.00

11. 15, 10 **13.** $1.20, $1.30

15. 12 cm by 20 cm **17.** 6, 9 **19.** $\dfrac{3}{2}$

Exercises 10-6, page 412

1. 59   **3.** 61   **5.** $150, $6   **7.** 71   **9.** 40 g, 15 g
11. $550, $250   **13.** $555.55, $444.45
15. 61, 39   **17.** 7   **19.** 51   **21.** 150, 300
23. $15/d; $0.10/km   **25.** $175, $325   **27.** 331

Problem Solving, page 417

1. 9 h, 13 h   **3.** 30 min
5. About 5 h 42 min, about 34.2 km
7. About 34.4 mph, about 309.4 mph
9. 3 min 45 s   **11.** 44.1 kg, 5.9 kg

Mathematics Around Us, page 418

1. a) About 145 years   **b)** Answers may vary
   c) Answers may vary   **3.** 48.5 m/year

Computer Power, page 419

1. a) $(10,5)$ **b)** $(-4,9)$ **c)** $(-0.66, -1.3)$
   d) $2.3, -1.3)$ **e)** $(1.75, 0.659)$
   f) $(-0.950, -2.69)$

Exercises 10-7, page 422

1. Answers may vary.
   a) $(1,1)$ **b)** $(10,0)$ **c)** $(0,-2)$ **d)** $(2,1)$
   e) $(0,5)$ **f)** $(1,1)$
3. a) $x + y > 4$ **b)** $x + 3y < 3$
   c) $4x - y \leq -2$ **d)** $3x + 5y \leq -15$
   e) $2x - y < 24$ **f)** $x - 2y + 2 > 0$
5. Equation is $x + y \leq 400$

Exercises 10-8, page 425

1. a) $x + y \leq 5, x \geq 0$
   b) $x - y \leq -1, x + y \leq 5$
   c) $5x + 3y \geq 15, x - 2y \leq -4$

Problem Solving, page 427

1. 8   **3.** 2001   **5.** $2x + y - 8 = 0$
7. 6 or 7   **9.** 0 or -6

Review Exercises, page 428

1. a) $(-3, -5)$ **b)** $\left(\dfrac{7}{2}, 1\right)$ **c)** $\left(-\dfrac{14}{5}, \dfrac{2}{5}\right)$
   d) $\left(-\dfrac{3}{5}, \dfrac{11}{5}\right)$

3. a) $(-2, 3)$ **b)** $(4, 1)$ **c)** $\left(\dfrac{18}{5}, \dfrac{3}{5}\right)$
   d) $(5, -3)$

5. 20, 16   **7.** 24, 39   **9.** 41   **11.** 80 kg, 20 kg

Chapter 11

Exercises 11-1, page 431

1. Answers and reasons may vary.   **a)** Circle graph
   b) Pictograph   **c)** Broken-line graph
   d) Continuous-line graph   **e)** Histogram
3. 100%
5. a) Swimming   **b)** 1050 kJ   **c)** About 28 min
7. a) 2.25×10^8 km; 1.5×10^8 km, 1.0×10^8 km, 5.0×10^7 km
   b) About 4.5 times   **c)** 7.8×10^8 km
   d) The pictograph would need a large number of symbols for the farthest planets.

Exercises 11-2, page 433

5. Answers may vary.
   a) 20 to 29,2; 30-39,2; 40-49,4; 50-59,11; 60-69,33; 70-79,16; 80-89, 7; 90-99,3
   c) 59   **d) i)** 76%   **ii)** 10%
9. d) i) 133 380 000   **ii)** 214 890 000

Exercises 11-3, page 440

1. a) 11.2, 11.5, 12   **b)** 3.3, 4, 4
   c) 3.3, 3.4, no mode   **d)** 16, 16, 18
   e) 10.3, 10, 5   **f)** $\dfrac{1}{2}, \dfrac{1}{2}, \dfrac{1}{2}$
3. a) Mean is increased by 2.
   b) Mean is doubled.   **5.** 70
7. a) A: mean 16; median 16; mode 15, 20;
      B: mean 11.84; median 11; mode 11
   b) Mean 13.92; median 14; mode 11
   c) Answers may vary.
9. Answers may vary.
   a) Mode   **b)** Mean   **c)** Mean   **d)** Mean
   e) Mean   **f)** Mean   **g)** Mean   **h)** Mode
11. a) No change in the mean; median and mode may or may not change.
13. 0

Computer Power, page 442

1. a) 31.285 714 3, 30   **b)** 517.041 667, 501

Mathematics Around Us, page 445

1. a) Reasons may vary.
   b) Yes, reasons may vary.
3. a) 52 years   **b)** 63 years   **c)** 38th

Exercises 11-4, page 447

1. a) 70   **b)** 290

Exercises 11-5, page 451

1. 0.502   **3.** Answers may vary.

5. Answers may vary.   **d)** The greater the number of tosses, the closer the relative frequency gets to 0.5.

7. Answers may vary.

9. a) 0.450   **b)** 0.391   **c)** 0.249   **d)** 0.248
e) Because the total number of times at bat was greater.

11. Answers may vary.

Computer Power, page 453

1. a) a, 29, 0.059 304 703 5; e, 63, 0.128 834 356;
i, 47, 0.096 114 519 4; n, 39, 0.079 754 601 2;
o, 31, 0.063 394 683; s, 33, 0.067 484 662 6;
t, 35, 0.071 574 642 1
b) a, 8, 0.045 977 011 5; e, 22, 0.126 436 782;
i, 18, 0.103 448 276; n, 14, 0.080 459 770 1;
o, 13, 0.074 712 643 7; s, 15, 0.086 206 896 6;
t, 11, 0.063 218 390 8

Exercises 11-6, page 458

1. 0.488   **3.** 0.026   **5.** Answers may vary.
7. Answers may vary.   **9.** 621
11. a) Town A   **b)** Town A
13. Answers may vary.

Exercises 11-7, page 464

1. a) $\frac{1}{2}$ **b)** $\frac{1}{4}$ **c)** $\frac{1}{3}$

3. a) i) June 5, 10, 15, 20, 25, 30
  ii) June 2, 9, 16, 23, 30   **iii)** June 30
b) $\frac{1}{5}, \frac{1}{6}, \frac{1}{30}$

5. a) $\frac{2}{3}$ **b)** $\frac{1}{3}$

7. a) $\frac{1}{6}$ **b)** $\frac{1}{2}$ **c)** $\frac{1}{2}$ **d)** $\frac{1}{3}$ **e)** 1   **f)** 0

9. a) 4 **b)** 17 **c)** 167 **11.** 1

13. a) $\frac{1}{6}$ **b)** $\frac{7}{30}$ **c)** $\frac{23}{60}$ **d)** $\frac{1}{2}$

15. a) i) 0.834 43   **ii)** 0.467 74   **iii)** 0.366 69
b) 0.023 33

Exercises 11-8, page 470

1. a) {red, white}, yes   **b)** {red, white}, no
c) {red, white}, no

3. a) $\frac{1}{2}$ **b)** $\frac{1}{2}$ **c)** $\frac{5}{6}$ **d)** $\frac{1}{2}$

5. a) $\frac{1}{26}$ **b)** $\frac{2}{13}$ **c)** $\frac{5}{26}$ **d)** $\frac{21}{26}$

7. Answers may vary.

9. a) $\frac{5}{36}$ **b)** $\frac{1}{6}$ **c)** $\frac{1}{18}$ **d)** $\frac{17}{18}$

11. a) $\frac{1}{13}$ **b)** $\frac{1}{2}$ **c)** $\frac{1}{4}$ **d)** $\frac{1}{26}$ **e)** $\frac{2}{13}$
f) $\frac{4}{13}$

13. a) $\frac{2}{23}$ **b)** $\frac{13}{23}$ **c)** $\frac{13}{46}$ **d)** 0 **e)** $\frac{4}{23}$
f) $\frac{8}{23}$

15. a) $\frac{1}{10}$ **b)** $\frac{1}{5}$ **c)** $\frac{2}{5}$ **d)** $\frac{7}{10}$

Problem Solving, page 473

1. $1.19   **3.** $\frac{1}{17}$

5. a) Yes   **b)** Yes   **c)** No

Exercises 11-9, page 476

3. $\frac{1}{24}$ **5.** 80   **7.** 28   **9.** 42   **11.** 3840
13. 24 360   **15.** 20   **17. a)** 19   **b)** No
19. a) $2^3 \times 3^2$ **b)** 12

Investigate, page 478

c) i) 6   **ii)** 24   **iii)** 120   **iv)** 720   **v)** 5040
e) i) 6   **ii)** 24   **iii)** 120   **iv)** 720   **v)** 5040
g) i) 4   **ii)** 3   **iii)** 2   **i) i)** 5!   **ii)** 7!
iii) 6!   **iv)** $\frac{7!}{4!}$ **v)** $n!$ **vi)** $(n + 1)!$
vii) $(n - 1)!$ **viii)** $\frac{n!}{(n - 3)!}$

1. 3!   **3.** $\frac{5!}{2!}$ **5.** $\frac{1}{24}$

Exercises 11-10, page 482

1. a) $\frac{1}{8}$ **b)** $\frac{1}{4}$ **3. b)** $\frac{1}{32}$

5. $\frac{1}{216}$ **7.** $\frac{36}{5329}$

9. a) i) $\frac{1}{4}$ **ii)** $\frac{1}{5}$ **b) i)** $\frac{4}{9}$ **ii)** $\frac{1}{3}$

c) i) $\frac{9}{16}$ **ii)** $\frac{1}{2}$ **11. a)** $\frac{1}{825}$ **b)** $\frac{1}{825}$

13. a) $\frac{1}{28\ 561}$ **b)** $\frac{1}{270\ 725}$

15. a) $\frac{5}{36}$ **b)** $\frac{25}{216}$ **c)** $\frac{1\ 953\ 125}{60\ 466\ 176}$

17. a) $\frac{35}{36}$ **b)** $\frac{1}{6}$ **c)** $\frac{1}{18}$ **d)** $\frac{7}{9}$ **e)** $\frac{11}{36}$

Exercises 11-11, page 487

1. 223 **3.** 92 **5. a)** $\frac{7}{12}$ **b)** $\frac{3}{4}$ **7.** $\frac{1}{13}$

9. i) a) $\frac{5}{8}$ **b)** $\frac{7}{8}$ **c)** $\frac{6}{8}$ **ii) a)** $\frac{5}{8}$ **b)** $\frac{6}{8}$

c) $\frac{4}{8}$ **iii) a)** $\frac{5}{6}$ **b)** $\frac{4}{6}$ **c)** $\frac{4}{6}$ **11.** 27%

13. 14% **15.** 14%

Review Exercises, page 489

5. 36 **7. a)** $\frac{7}{500}$ **b)** $\frac{7}{370}$

9. a) Yes **b)** 12 **c)** 0.984

11. a) $\frac{22}{65}$ **b)** $\frac{17}{65}$ **c)** $\frac{2}{13}$

13. a) $\frac{1}{4}$ **b)** $\frac{1}{4}$ **c)** $\frac{3}{8}$

15. a) $\frac{1}{3}$ **b)** $\frac{1}{12}$ **c)** $\frac{1}{24}$

Chapter 12

Exercises 12-1, page 494

1. a) i) Reflection **ii)** Translation **iii)** Rotation
b) i) Translation **ii)** Rotation **iii)** Reflection
c) i) Rotation **ii)** Translation **iii)** Reflection
3. a) Rotation **b)** Reflection **c)** Reflection

Exercises 12-2, page 498

3. a) A′(1,6), B′(3,7), C′(9,7), D′(8,5), E′(−2,4)
b) They are the same length.
c) They are the same length.
d) They have the same measure.
5. A′(2,1), B′(6,0), C′(8,−5), D′(4,−4)
7. Lengths and directions of line segments, measures of angles, areas of figures
9. c) The line maps onto itself, because the translation arrow is parallel to the line.

Exercises 12-3, page 503

5. a) A′(2,−5), B′(6,−5), C′(9,−1), D′(2,−1)
b) A′(−2,5), B′(−6,5), C′(−9,1), D′(−2,1)
7. $y = -2$
11. a) A′(−2,−6), B′(4,−3), C′(3,3), D′(−5,2)
b) A′(2,6), B′(−4,3), C′(−3,−3), D′(5,−2)

Exercises 12-4, page 509

3. A′(−1,−3), B′(−4,−7), C′(−6,−4), D′(−3,−1)
5. K′(−4,−3), L′(−6,1), M′(1,6), N′(3,−4)
7. c) i) Parallelogram **ii)** Parallelogram
iii) Square **iv)** Rhombus **v)** Parallelogram
9. Lengths of line segments, measures of angles, areas of figures
11. c) The image and the original line coincide because the rotation center lies on the line.

Exercises 12-5, page 515

1. a), b), d) Enlargements **c), e), f)** Reductions
3. a) 10 cm, 24 cm, 26 cm
b) 25 cm, 60 cm, 65 cm
c) 2.5 cm, 6 cm, 6.5 cm
d) 3.75 cm, 9 cm, 9.75 cm
5. a) 100 **b)** 150 **c)** 75 **d)** 125
7. a) About 4.4 km **b)** About 5.3 km
c) About 4.3 km

Exercises 12-6, page 520

1. △ABC ~ △MNP ~ △DFE;
Quad GHKJ ~ quad CDAB;
△KLM ~ △TWS ~ △TVU
5. a) 9 **b)** 10 **c)** 15
7. 30 m **9.** 17 cm by 22 cm
11. a) 7.2, 7 **b)** 7.04, 3.8 **c)** 16.5, 18
d) 1.6, 3.2

Exercises 12-7, page 525

3. 10   **5. a)** 3, 4, 5, 8   **b)** 12

Problem Solving, page 527

1. 12   **3.**   6
                      1 2
                    5 3 4

5. a) Yes   **c)** The difference of the squares of two prime numbers greater than 3 is always a multiple of 24.

Exercises 12-8, page 529

5. a) (7.5,0)   **b) i)** (4.5,0)   **ii)** (0,3.5)
7. 5.0 m by 6.6 m

Problem Solving, page 531

1. 4 min   **3. a)** 45   **b)** $\dfrac{n(n-1)}{2}$ **5.** 42

7. Answers may vary. $\dfrac{3}{8}$ **9.** $n+1$

Review Exercises, page 532

1. a) A$'$(3,2), B$'$(6,$-$7), C$'$(9,$-$1)
   b) P($-$3,$-$1), Q($-$5,6), R($-$10,3)
3. L$'$(2,3), M$'$($-$4,3), N$'$($-$4,$-$5)
5. a) 9   **b)** 26.25, 24   **7.** 52 cm by 78 cm

Cumulative Review, Chapters 10-12, page 533

1. a) (4,1)   **b)** (2.5,$-$1.5)
   c) Approximately ($-$2.3,1.5)
3. a) (3,1)   **b)** ($-$4,3)   **c)** ($-$2,$-$5)
5. 11,15   **7.** 37
9. a) A$'$(2,6), B$'$(2,3), C$'$(7,3)
   b) A$'$($-$1,$-$6), B$'$($-$1,$-$3), C$'$(4,$-$3)
   c) A$'$($-$4,$-$1), B$'$($-$1,$-$1), C$'$($-$1,4)
   d) A$'$($-$2,8), B$'$($-$2,2), C$'$(8,2)
11. The reflection line is $y=x$.
13. About 9.1 m
15. Mean, about 70; median 72; mode 75
17. a) $\dfrac{15}{16}$ **b)** $\dfrac{1}{16}$
19. a) $\dfrac{6}{25}$ **b)** $\dfrac{4}{25}$ **c)** $\dfrac{2}{5}$ **d)** 0
21. Answers may vary – both outcomes are not equally likely.

Photographic Credits

The publisher wishes to thank the following sources for photographs and other illustrative materials used in this book. We will gladly receive information enabling us to rectify any errors or references in credits.

Cover, Robert Simpson; Fred Phipps, xxii; Bettmann Newsphotos, xviii, xxiv; NASA, xxv; Al Harvey/Masterfile, 1; © Jeffery Sylvester/FPG International, 2; UPI/Bettmann Newsphotos, 5; AP/Wide World Photos, 8; Carmine Fantasia, 12; Carmine Fantasia, 16; Miller/J. Jacquemain, 20; UPI/Bettmann Newsphotos, 30; Phil Huber/Black Star, 40; AP/Wide World Photos, 40; AP/ Wide World Photos, 41; AP/Wide World Photos, 41; Al Harvey/Masterfile, 42; Addison-Wesley photo library, 46; The Bettmann Archive, 51; The Bettman Archive, 51; CP Photos, 53; SSC-Photocentre, 54; Addison-Wesley photo library, 68; Alan Harvey/Masterfile, 70; Lisa Guthro, 71; By Chris Johns © 1987 National Geographic Society, 72; Miller Services Ltd., 78; Department of Fisheries and Ocean Communications, 86; Miller Services Ltd., 90; Canadian Government Travel Bureau, 94; Miller Services Ltd., 105; Jeremy Jones, 106; Addison-Wesley photo library, 110; Ian Crysler, 114; Fraser Day Photography, 120; Ian Crysler, 123; Addison-Wesley photo library, 131; Miller Services Ltd., 132; Joseph Nettis/Masterfile, 140; Ian Crysler, 147; Fraser Day Photography, 158, 162; Ministry of Industry and Tourism, 167; Bob Alexander, 168; Michael King, 168; Addison-Wesley photo library, 168; Government of the Yukon Territory, 168; Miller Services Ltd., 169; Lee Valley Tools Ltd., 172, 176; Mike Dobel/Masterfile, 194; Bob Alexander, 201; Warren Morgan/Masterfile, 218; Lisa Guthro, 225; Photograph Reproduced with the permission of the Michener Institute, Toronto, Canada, 226; Addison-Wesley photo library, 245; Photograph Reproduced with the permission of the Michener Institute, Toronto, Canada, 249; Metropolitan Toronto Hockey League, 250; Miller Services Ltd., 252; Canapress Photo Service, 256; MacMillan Bloedel Limited, 273; Greg Stott/Masterfile, 277; Lynne Gulliver, 281; Addison-Wesley photo library, 285; Jaguar Canada, 285; NASA, 289; ROM, Department of Invertebrate Palaeontology, 289; Addison-Wesley photo library, 292; Lisa Guthro, 292; De Havilland Aircraft, 296; Miller Services Ltd., 297; National Baseball Library, 298; Lynne Gulliver, 299; Miller Services Ltd., 305; Lisa Guthro, 312; Addison-Wesley photo library, 317; Miller/Mario Madau, 353; Ontario Ministry of Agriculture and Food, 357; Miller Services Ltd., 361, 368; Augustin Estrada, 386; Prince Edward Island Tourist Office, 389; Canadian Ladies' Golf Association, 393; Al Harvey/Masterfile, 394; All-Sport Photography, USA/Tony Duffy/Masterfile, 410; Outboard Marine Corporation of Canada Ltd., 414; David Alexander, 418; Addison-Wesley photo library, 429; Fraser Day Photography, 433; Hot Shots, 438; Miller Services Ltd., 438; Roy Nicholls Photography, 438; Western Airlines, 438; Miller Services Ltd., 446; SSC-Photocentre, 449; James Guthro, 454; SSC-Photocentre, 491; Addison-Wesley photo library, 492; Miller Services Ltd., 492; Benjamin Rondel/Masterfile, 492; Miller Services Ltd., 496; Lisa Guthro, 501; CNE, 506; SSC-Photocentre, 512; Miller Services Ltd., 515; Addison-Wesley photo library, 517; Royal Ontario Museum, Toronto, Canada, 523; CP Rail, 531